George C. Marshall at home in Leesburg, Virginia
August 1944
Thomas D. McAvoy, The LIFE Picture Collection, Getty Images

To

my son, Shannon Patrick Strange, in my heart and soul from his beginning;

and

my husband, Kennard Arthur Thompson, who gave us his love, and the gift of Kathy, Kristy, and David

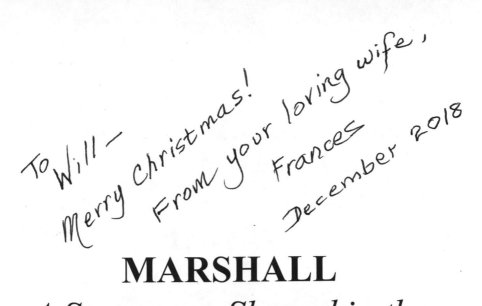

To Will —
Merry Christmas!
From your loving wife,
Frances
December 2018

MARSHALL
A Statesman Shaped in the Crucible of War

Rachel Yarnell Thompson

THE GEORGE C. MARSHALL
INTERNATIONAL CENTER

Published by the
GEORGE C. MARSHALL INTERNATIONAL CENTER, INC.

George C. Marshall International Center, Inc., corporate offices:
312 East Market Street, Suite C, Leesburg, VA 20176

Includes bibliographic references and index
ISBN 978-0-615-92903-3

Book Designed by Ryan Jenkins

Cover Design by Kathleen Dyson

Cover Photo: Harris and Ewing, the George C. Marshall Research Library

Printed in the United States of America by

Books International, Inc.
22883 Quicksilver Drive
Dulles, VA 20166

Third Printing of First Edition, 2017

Reprinted to commemorate the 70th Anniversary of Marshall's
June 1947 speech launching the Marshall Plan.

10 9 8 7 6 5 4 3

Contents

Foreword

Marshall: A Statesman Shaped in the Crucible of War is an impressive piece of work by a dedicated Marshall scholar. Mrs. Thompson has masterfully interwoven the fabric of George Catlett Marshall's prodigious professional career with glimpses into his personal life, enabling the reader to better know this great man.

Marshall led a life of many challenges and achievements, beginning with his education at the Virginia Military Institute in the late 19th and early 20th centuries. Marshall always acknowledged a lasting debt to VMI for developing in him his discipline and leadership skills. Through the years, he was an interested and much involved alumnus of the institute. True, he had wanted to attend the U.S. Military Academy at West Point, but local politics and other factors denied him that opportunity.

Marshall admired West Pointers and never felt discrimination because he did not attend the academy. On the contrary, senior officers with academy backgrounds were his foremost advocates. General John J. Pershing, head of the American Expeditionary Forces in World War I, provides one such example. Marshall's close relationship with him continued until Pershing's death in 1948.

Pershing was a constant sponsor of Marshall, never missing a chance to urge his advancement to senior commands. He never forgot the superb service the young officer performed in planning the key World War I Meuse-Argonne offensive in 1918. Marshall's extraordinary performance hastened the surrender of the German army and brought him to the attention of the U.S. Army and Allied leaders. When Pershing became U.S. Army chief of staff in 1919, he selected Marshall as a key assistant. In 1930 when Marshall the widower married Katherine Tupper Brown, Pershing served as his best man.

Marshall began his army career shortly after graduating from VMI. The commission had not been easy to achieve, but Marshall's determination prevailed, and in 1902 he became a second lieutenant. Shortly thereafter, he was assigned to the Philippines, where once again he excelled and was identified as an officer of great promise.

The U.S. Army is an institution that of necessity becomes one of conformity, but Marshall was an officer of creativity. Within the bounds of military protocol, he was able to use this hallmark of talent to bring about change in the organization. In examining his career, we see that Marshall was an officer of enormous growth, possessed of people skills, work habits, and leadership traits that gave others the confidence to follow his direction. For example, during the Great Depression when the Civilian Conservation Corps was established, Marshall was an able and highly successful backer. Although the CCC was not a military training program, the army played an administrative role in establishing and running the camps. This project afforded Marshall an opportunity to learn more about the young American male of military age and his potential as a soldier. These were invaluable insights on the eve of the great war only a few years away.

Winston Churchill referred to Marshall as the "Organizer of Victory." This epithet related not only to the buildup of American defense capabilities but also to the plans for Overlord, the Allied invasion of Normandy, which bore the Marshall stamp and would set the stage for bringing the war in Europe to an end. He was originally to be the commander of the forces, but he stepped aside at the request of President Roosevelt, who felt it was essential that he remain in Washington as chief of staff.

Both of Marshall's stepsons joined the army. The youngest, Allen Tupper Brown, was commissioned through the Armored Officer Candidate School and commanded an armored tank unit in General Mark Clark's Fifth Army moving up the boot of Italy toward Rome in 1944. He was killed by a German sniper only eight days before the Normandy landings in France. Mrs. Marshall was devastated, but it was also a grievous loss for the general, who had forged a special bond with Allen. Nevertheless, Marshall had to bear the death with silent sorrow as he looked to the demands of D-Day in the coming week.

The close of World War II was not the end of Marshall's service to the nation, but the beginning of a new era that made him one of the greatest men of the 20th century. The European Recovery Program that bore his name—the Marshall Plan—and brought about the rehabilitation of a devastated Europe also led to his being awarded the Nobel Peace Prize in December 1953. Perhaps the greatest spontaneous recognition of General Marshall occurred earlier in the year at the coronation of Queen Elizabeth II. President Eisenhower had chosen Marshall to be part of the official U.S delegation to the coronation. When the great wartime leader and former secretary of state entered Westminster Abbey unannounced, the congregation of over a thousand rose to honor him.

Many historians who study George Washington use one word to describe him—"character." It is a trait that the self-effacing George Catlett Marshall shares with the Father of Our Country. Indeed, examples of Marshall's character permeate Mrs. Thompson's exceptional biography.

John Ortho Marsh Jr.
Secretary of the Army, 1981–1989
U.S. House of Representatives, 1963–1971

Preface

To know the story of George C. Marshall is to take a journey through the major events of 20th-century American history. He was a man not given to self-aggrandizement, and many of Marshall's accomplishments are credited to others—presidents, prime ministers, generals. One purpose for writing this new biography is to help the reader appreciate the energy, commitment, and dogged determination that it took for him to accomplish all that he did during 50 years of service to his country. I wanted to get specific about the complex tasks that he tackled, shedding light upon the significance of *his* leadership to the whole military-diplomatic scene. While placing him squarely in the stream of these mega-events, I also sought to set him apart from other key players whose names appear before his in the history books.

Although reared in a small Pennsylvania town, Marshall began his military life as a cadet at the Virginia Military Institute. As a relatively young officer in World War I, he was crucial in the planning of the St. Miheil-Meuse-Argonne offensives that finally brought victory in that brutal war. Afterward, he served as General John J. Pershing's top aide, learning the delicate art of balancing the relationship between the military and an elected civilian government. In the heart of the Great Depression, Marshall commanded a district of the Civilian Conservation Corps, President Franklin Roosevelt's favorite New Deal program, which combined rebuilding the nation's infrastructure with providing food, clothing, and training for out-of-work young men. That experience offered Marshall a rich tutorial on how to lead the nation's future citizen soldiers.

Rising through the ranks, he served as U.S. Army chief of staff in World War II. Marshall was a vital figure in twelve wartime Allied conferences and, while working in the top echelons of power, helped shape strategic outcomes of global importance. Shortly after the war, he was tapped by President Harry Truman to be a special emissary to China, navigating a complex political and military environment to mediate the forces of democracy and communism vying for control of that government. While secretary of state, Marshall developed a unique and enlightened approach to the reconstruction of Europe, the European Recovery Program—the Marshall Plan. Finally, as secretary of defense during the Korean War, he helped rebuild an alarmingly small army, which had been demobilized during the postwar flush of victory. Although by training and inclination Marshall was a professional soldier, he used those experiences to evolve as diplomat and internationalist. Indeed, Marshall was shaped by the grueling and unique challenges of two world wars into a remarkable postwar statesman.

While this biography covers the broad scope of Marshall's service, I have told it from a unique perspective. I first learned about George C. Marshall, the five-star general and Nobel Peace Prize winner, by spending a great deal of time at Dodona Manor, his home in Leesburg, Virginia. When the Marshalls bought the house during World War II, only 1,700 residents lived in that town. Now, it is a bustling place, an extension of suburban sprawl west of Washington, D.C. Thanks to the efforts of the George C. Marshall International Center, his private retreat remains as it was in the 1950s when he was finally able to retire. As a researcher and educator at the Center for 16 years, I have spent many hours there. In the early days, long before the velvet ropes were in place, I would take a break from a current project to enjoy a cool drink while seated on the glider on the white-columned front porch. At other times in warm weather, I savored a simple lunch on the low wall of the "Stone Court," a back patio where the Marshalls often took a noontime rest from their yard work, dressed in gardening attire unsuited in those days for the front yard. They no doubt had many conversations during these breaks—the grandchildren might come, a pressing upcoming travel schedule required special packing, old friends would be in town on Saturday, last night's rain would help the corn crop. Marshall relished these quiet interludes with Katherine far from the pressures of workaday Washington.

On winter days, when fewer visitors requested a tour, I have perused Marshall's library. It was to this inviting room off the main hall that he and Katherine decamped when the weather outdoors drove them inside. On the shelves, interspersed among his wife's favorite titles, are Marshall's choices. Some are serious tomes, including John J. Pershing's *My Experiences in the World War;* Douglas Southall Freeman's *Lee's Lieutenants,* Clella Reeves Collins's *When Your Son Goes to War;* Mark Clark's *From the Danube to the Yalu*—all reflecting his interest in the military arts and the work of a professional soldier.

One day I noticed, sixth row down on the left, a beautiful leather-bound volume titled *Austria,* so elegant, so lovely that I donned white gloves to look inside. On the flyleaf I found a poignant inscription:

> To Mr. George C. Marshall, the Great American of the Great American people, the Creator of the World's Greatest Work of Civilization, The Marshall Plan. . . . In Admiration and Respect from one of the millions of Austrians. Vienna, June 5, 1952.

I held in my hands this uniquely special memento of Marshall's monumental efforts in advancing a progressive program that helped restore Europe after a ruinous war.

Sharing space with these solemn names were plenty of less serious books, including Western novels like *Six-Shooter Showdown* and *The Savage Gentleman.* There were mysteries, too—*The Adventures of Sherlock Holmes, The Room with the Iron Shutters*—all offerings that could make a rainy afternoon in front of the fire fly by.

During the restoration of the Marshalls' home, the book conservator came for days at a time to examine those treasures, eventually taking them away temporarily for cleaning and repair. Most likely he didn't realize the significance of a thin volume, *Woodberry Forest, A Venture in Faith*, which told the story of the private Virginia high school where Marshall's stepson, Allen Tupper Brown, had graduated. In 1944 he was a casualty of war, killed in the fierce fighting around Anzio in Italy. The conservator also found books with the name "Elizabeth C. Coles" written neatly inside their front covers. Had we heard of her? he asked. Indeed, we had, came the quick answer. She was Marshall's first wife—he called her Lily—who had died suddenly at only 53.

So it was that as I spent time in the home of this well-known man, I sensed the interplay of his private and professional life. When I imagined the Marshalls on their cool Stone Court or ensconced comfortably in that study—Katherine sitting cozily in a buttercup-yellow chair and her husband with feet up on a favorite well-worn red recliner—I discovered key elements of this public figure. He was for certain the soldier-statesman, but also loving husband, stepfather, and friend. Perhaps the reader is accustomed to stories of Marshall's unimpeachable good character and his position in the sweep of mid-20th-century American history, but he is sometimes seen as austere and unknowable—one writer described him as having "a strong personal reserve." I wanted to write a book that revealed both sides of Marshall's personality. By doing so, I hope the reader will learn abundantly about his impressive accomplishments, yes, but also see that behind the uniform or three-piece suit was a kind, thoughtful, and caring man who experienced two great loves, suffered deep personal losses, and knew well both the joys and challenges of family. Finally, here was a man who, after 50 years of public service, was "at ease" in a small town called Leesburg.

Rachel Yarnell Thompson, March 17, 2014

Chapter 1

Uniontown Boyhood

A Simple Life

1880-1897

When George Catlett Marshall was 77 years old, he sat down with his biographer, Forrest Pogue, to share with him some memories of his childhood in Uniontown, Pennsylvania. Roaming freely through the mental snapshots of his youth, his first recollection was of climbing a ladder to reach the hayloft of the big barn in his backyard.

> I was being very cautious and a little frightened, and I came to a windowless opening from which I could look out between the rungs. It seemed to me . . . that this was my first look at the world. A creek ran through our place, and my line of vision went down the line of the creek. I saw . . . highly colored ducks swimming about, there was a dog or two along the bank, [and] chickens wandering about. All of it fascinated me and it seemed a whole world exposed in an instant to my eye.[1]

Beyond that barn, as Marshall said later, "The country was beautiful, very rich in surface farming and in the coal which underlay the region and which eventually destroyed a great deal of its beauty." He added wistfully, "The life was very simple."

It was in this town south of Pittsburgh that George Marshall was born on a cold New Year's Eve in 1880. His mother, Laura Bradford Marshall, had already borne three children, Stuart Bradford, Marie Louise, and another son who had died before he was six months old. The sadness of the past loss was tempered by the birth of this boy, named for his father.

Throughout Marshall's growing-up years, the family rented a two-story brick house at the end of West Main Street, which was part of the famous National Road. Begun around 1810 and completed in 1838, the thoroughfare had carried settlers to the Ohio Valley in an earlier time, and now it provided

George C. Marshall Sr., Born: 1845

Laura Bradford Marshall, born: 1846

(L-R) Marie Louise, born: 1876; Stuart Bradford, born: 1875;
George Catlett, born: 1880

the east-west connection for the railroads and ports of eastern Pennsylvania and Maryland. Across the street from the Marshall house was the White Swan Tavern, which in the past had offered shelter to many a traveler by stagecoach or Conestoga wagon. Surely the tales of the famous men who came and went along this road provided excitement for a naturally curious boy.

Marshall's boyhood home on the National Road, Uniontown, circa 1890
George C. Marshall Research Library

With its 3,000 or more citizens, Uniontown itself was a dynamic place during Marshall's boyhood. The enterprising and ambitious were being swept into the great boom created by America's industrialization, cranking out goods and services to feed the mighty steel mills of nearby Pittsburgh. It was this boom that had brought Marshall's father to the town in 1872. In partnership with his friend, A. W. Bliss, the elder Marshall had formed a company that would eventually be the primary producer of a new and improved beehive coke, or soft coal, oven.

By the time Marshall was born, his father's company had expanded its investments, and the Marshalls enjoyed a comfortable lifestyle. However, in 1889, Marshall Sr. sold his company and most of his property to steel magnate Henry Frick for more than $100,000 (its value would be 10 times as great in today's dollars). Investing almost all of those profits in what

Main Street, Uniontown, 1889

4

seemed like a never-ending land boom, Marshall purchased a company that controlled Luray, an area in Virginia's Shenandoah Valley whose centerpiece was a large and dramatic cavern. He and his partner imagined building a recreational mecca in that beautiful mountain landscape. Unfortunately, the boom became a bust, and the Marshall family suffered a severe reversal of fortune.[2] Despite these strained circumstances, the family would always be considered among the town's respected middle class.

An outgoing man who took his position in the community seriously, the senior Marshall was active in the Masons, served as a vestryman in the Episcopal Church, and was passionately committed to the Democratic Party. Marshall would later remember the excitement of marching with his father in torchlight parades supporting the campaign of William Jennings Bryan as a "Free Silver" candidate for the presidency, and for other Democrats.

During his boyhood, the passions of his father were of little interest to Marshall, since he was much too busy with his own youthful enterprises. When school wasn't in session, he had a thousand plans for his free time, almost always to be carried out in league with his best friend, Andy Thompson, who lived across the street. Some of those schemes involved small businesses, which the boys opened not only for pocket change—they charged only pennies for their valuable wares—but for the fun of it as well. They set up a restaurant operation in a lean-to that they built against the springhouse in Marshall's backyard. Having installed an amateurishly constructed counter, they used an old stove, discarded from the Marshalls' home, to bake sweet potatoes and apples. As Marshall would say later, "Everything was anointed with sugar," and apparently that worked, since the neighborhood kids came with their pennies.

One year Marshall's father, who liked to try out new products, ordered the recipe and supplies to make bottled root beer at home. When it was finished, everyone in the family agreed that it was undrinkable. Over time, however, the two boys discovered quite by accident that the root beer had fermented and, according to Marshall, "tasted great." That led the two of them to open a "bar" in the lean-to. This brisk business was short-lived, as Marshall's father shut them down as soon as he found out about it.

One rather serious business venture for the team of Marshall and Thompson came about after they went with their mothers to visit a greenhouse on the edge of Uniontown. The boys became excited when they considered the money they could make just by sticking a few seeds in the soil. Soon they had painted the lean-to green, thinking the color had something to do with making it an authentic operation, and filled some old tin cans with a manure-based soil from an old stable that his father had torn down. With $1.50 each in start-up capital from their parents, they purchased some seedlings and soon had their counter lined with a surprisingly large array of healthy greenery.

One day, while reading through a seed magazine, Marshall and Thompson saw an advertisement that immediately captured their entrepreneurial interest. It seemed that the Peter Henderson Company had developed a new tomato hybrid and was having a contest to select the best name for it. Whoever grew the tomato and sent in the winning entry would win $50. That was more money than the boys could imagine. They sent off an order for the seeds, and when they came in the mail, they promptly planted them in the rich soil where the stable had been. The green shoots soon poked through, and seemingly overnight the two of them had grown huge red tomatoes. The local grocer couldn't believe the beauty of this produce and began to purchase for a pittance all that the boys could supply.

After great consideration, the friends decided on a name for this tomato. With his brand new "Dollar Kodak" camera, Marshall took a picture of their plumpest offering with a silver dollar leaning against it to show scale. The boys mailed the photograph, along with a short letter typed on Marshall's toy typewriter. Pretty soon a reply came back from the seed company: Another name had been chosen for the new tomato, it read, but would the boys ask one of their parents to write back and explain how they grew those big tomatoes? It was Marshall's father who responded, explaining the rich base the boys had used for their seeds. He ended by saying that the problem was that you couldn't always tear down a stable to grow a tomato plant.

Another Marshall and Thompson enterprise, the ferryboat business, brought the boys nothing but trouble. The boat was homemade and flat-bottomed with a plug in it for draining unwanted water. Marshall and Thompson used their ferry for crossing Coal Lick Run, the small creek that ran near the Marshall home. Thompson was the navigator and wielded the pole to push the boat. Marshall, the conductor, put his cap on backwards and sold tickets, which he had made on his toy typewriter. The neighborhood girls were the customers. They paid pennies for tickets to ride the ferry as a shortcut along their way to school.

One day the girls refused to give up their tickets to the conductor. Thompson laughed at Marshall's discomfort, and the girls began to giggle. It was embarrassing to be made fun of by his best friend, not to mention the girls. Marshall looked down at the floor of the craft, and an idea came to him. He pulled the cork, up shot the water, and down went the boat. The creek wasn't very deep, so no one was hurt; nevertheless, everybody's clothes and shoes were soaked and covered with mud. The girls blamed Marshall for what happened, and ran to tell their parents. Of course, Marshall's father heard about it, so the "conductor" took the punishment, and the ferry business went under. Despite the consequences, Marshall remembered later that the situation demanded quick thinking, and sinking the boat had made him "the temporary master of the situation."

From other youthful encounters Marshall learned that impulsiveness did not always pay off. He and his friends enjoyed playing pool, but there were only two pool tables in town. One was in the home of a prominent judge, whose nephew was a good friend of Marshall's. During a game in the judge's home, Marshall noticed on the nearby wall a painting of Christ with a crown of thorns on his head. He blurted out rather bluntly to his friend that the painting of Christ positioned so close to the pool table was quite an odd combination. As Marshall later recalled, "This was repeated to the old judge, who was a very severe character, and he forbade me [to come to] the house from then on; so my pool education ceased right there while all my friends could go and play." Marshall added, "I learned early in the game the lesson of keeping your mouth shut unless you've thought very particularly of what you were going to talk about."

These boyhood experiences did not foretell Marshall's future as a highly successful adult, nor did his school days. During the first years of his education, he attended a private school that was academically undemanding. However, when Marshall was about nine, the downturn in his father's financial status made private school tuition unaffordable, so the boy was sent to a public school. To determine Marshall's grade placement, the school superintendent interviewing him asked a number of simple questions that he could not answer. His father, who was ambitious and watchful of his son's development, was humiliated at this poor showing. Deficient in oral reading, arithmetic, spelling, and handwriting at the time, Marshall recalled: "I had a very painful time in public school, and I was ashamed to admit my ignorance." As he said later, "If the subject was history, that was all right; I could star in history." Although Marshall would later call his time in public school a "necessary and democratizing experience," the fact is that as soon as the family's financial situation improved, by 1893 he was enrolled in the

Uniontown Academy, a private school.[3] Despite his weaknesses in many typical elementary school subjects, there was one area of strength.

The Father's Influence

Perhaps it was the influence of his father that gave Marshall an appreciation of things past. The Pennsylvania countryside surrounding Uniontown boasted sites rich with American history, including the ruins of Fort Necessity, where, as a colonial officer in the French and Indian War, George Washington had surrendered his troops. Mr. Marshall combined many a fishing and hunting trip with history lessons for his son, each time explaining the connection of a particular site to the development of America. A favorite spot of Marshall's was at the grave of General Edward Braddock, since the story of this English officer and his demise was quite dramatic.

In 1755, Braddock and his British troops were assisting George Washington and the colonial army in fighting the French and their Indian allies. Braddock was killed in battle not far from present-day Uniontown. His soldiers buried him in the middle of the trail and rode over his grave to tamp down the dirt so their enemies would not disturb the body. Later, Braddock's remains were found and reburied in a proper grave enclosed by a fence. Marshall's father related other tales of the Revolutionary War and local history as he and his son walked the fields and woods while hunting birds or fishing in the streams. Marshall remembered vividly these special one-on-one trips with his father. It isn't surprising that in addition to his lifelong interest in history, two of his favorite sports were hunting and fishing.

Despite Marshall's slow start in school, Uniontown citizens who knew him remembered him as a boy with a quick, facile, and subtle mind. Perhaps this was strengthened by Marshall's love of reading, a passion that may have been inspired by his father. Some evenings, especially in long Pennsylvania winters, Marshall Sr. read aloud to the whole family, often for several hours at a time. Even as an elderly man, Marshall could recall in great detail some of these novels, including one of his favorites, James Fenimore Cooper's *The Last of the Mohicans*. This habit encouraged Marshall to delve into similar volumes. He devoured popular, fast-paced adventure stories, as well as mysteries. As an adult, he continued to enjoy fiction, especially C. S. Forester's Horatio Hornblower series. The bookshelves in his study were also lined with well-read biographies, many about military figures, including his heroes, Robert E. Lee and George Washington.

Marshall's father was constantly working to shape and teach his son, including acquainting him with the proud ancestry of the family. The Marshall and Bradford lines, rooted in Virginia and Kentucky, included doctors, judges, ministers, and ambassadors. Marshall's dad was thrilled about his family's connection to John Marshall, the famous chief justice who served on the Supreme Court from 1801 to 1835. On the other hand, young Marshall was often annoyed by his father's boasting about his grandfather's first cousin. Many years later, Marshall related to his biographer, "I thought the continued harping on the name of John Marshall was kind of a poor business. It was about time for someone else to swim for the family."

As a young, playful boy Marshall was not as impressed as his parents with the family genealogy until one day, while reading the family history book, he discovered a short but intriguing entry. Although not proven, it appeared that a female ancestor had married Blackbeard the pirate. Marshall was delighted. As he said later, "I had [all my friends] beaten because I had a pirate who had a very bloody, cruel history, with a long beard to help out." Marshall took the book and showed it to all of his friends. His father, who was quite sensitive about his family, was not delighted when a friend's father poked fun at him over the supposed connection. Marshall remembered that his father was embarrassed and "perfectly furious." The story of Blackbeard the pirate was squashed, and quickly.

For a boy as curious, lively, and mischievous as George Marshall, staying on good terms with his demanding father was one of his most difficult tasks. If Marshall got into trouble, which he often did, he had to take his punishment. The father was quite strict with his youngest son and must have believed in the parental axiom, paraphrased from a biblical reference, "Spare the rod and spoil the child," because he sometimes used corporal punishment— "lickings"—to correct perceived misbehaviors. Describing his father as "rather high-tempered," Marshall later defended his actions, saying that his father never punished him for something unless it was deserved.

Marshall remembered the last time his father gave him a "licking." The boy had been given the task of hosing down the paved part of the street that ran in the front of their house. One morning while completing this daily chore, he saw the door open and, thinking his sister was coming out, turned the hose in that direction, hitting the victim square in the face. As he said later, "She screamed and I continued to play the hose on her. She couldn't call [out] much because the water would go in her mouth." Moments later, Marshall realized to his horror that he wasn't hosing down his sister but rather his mother! After Mrs. Marshall recovered her glasses, which the force of the water had knocked off, she collected herself and started laughing, although not for long. Marshall's older brother, Stuart, told his father, who came out to punish the boy on the spot.

His mother was patient, and not as strict as his father. Of her Marshall would say, "She had a very powerful influence on my youth." In later years Marshall assessed their relationship in some detail: "I was always close to her, as her youngest child and because for some years my brother and my sister were away at school while I was at home with her. She was both gentle and firm, very understanding, and had a keen but quiet sense of humor, which made her my confidante in practically all my boyish escapades and difficulties." Marshall described her as "not only a woman of character and great determination, but [also] of great understanding." According to him, his mother enjoyed listening to accounts of Marshall's adventures, seeming to recognize that his antics did not foreshadow a failed future. As Marshall recalled to his official biographer, Forrest Pogue, "I told her everything I did, and she never corrected me. Because if I told her [something I had done], I realized it was wrong and there was no use telling me again it was wrong."[4] Moreover, Marshall told Pogue, sometimes when he got into a scrape, Mrs. Marshall kept his misdeed from the harsh judgments of her husband.

Despite differences in parenting styles, it seems clear that both his mother and father loved their son deeply, providing a supportive home life that shaped a powerful, emotionally balanced man. Marshall biographer William Frye described the influence of both:

> For all his bearing his father's name, young George was Laura Marshall's son in looks and temperament. As the years passed it became increasingly evident that he had his mother's reserve, her great dignity, her steadiness, the same profound moral integrity, tempered perhaps by some of his father's easy manner and that indefinable quality which gentlefolk call presence.[5]

Sledding with his father on the hill of the town's main street; waking on Christmas morning to a candle-lit tree with longed-for presents beneath; the sounds of his mother playing familiar tunes on the piano in their living room; the fragrance of her hickory nut cake—Marshall treasured the memories of boyhood late in life, long after he had traveled the world and become a famous man. Of his youth in Uniontown, Marshall said, "I saw what you might call the end of an era, because it was a very simple life and a very charming life, and it had a long history behind it."

As Marshall grew into his teenage years, he saw Uniontown begin to change. A switchboard in town provided telephone connections as far away as Chicago. Streetcars clanked by his house, power lines went up on Main Street, and he could easily go 10 miles away to the next town on his "newfangled" bicycle. Beyond the protected world of these Pennsylvania hills, much bigger changes were coming. The Industrial Revolution was bringing new jobs, machines, and products at a rapid pace. Americans everywhere anticipated a new century, with its promise of new markets, influence, and power. It was the beginning of a new era, and time for young George Marshall to move along.

Corporal Marshall in Uniontown, 1898
George C. Marshall Research Library

Marshall at about age 20
Virginia Historical Society

Chapter 2

VMI Years

Brother Rat to First Captain

1897–1901

When it was time for George Marshall to go to college, he told his parents he wanted to attend Virginia Military Institute in Lexington, Virginia. It was a conversation between Stuart, his older brother, and his mother that would set Marshall's course for VMI. Marshall was only nine years old when Stuart had begun his four years there. The older brother had done well academically, majoring in chemistry and returning to Pennsylvania upon graduation to ply his profession in private industry. Stuart had been concerned when he later heard Marshall talking about attending his alma mater.

Marshall related the story to Pogue this way: "When I was begging to go to VMI, I overheard Stuart talking to my mother; he was trying to persuade her not to let me go because he thought I would disgrace the family name. Well, that made more impression on me than all instructors, parental pressure, or anything else. I decided right then and there that I was going to 'wipe his eye.'" Marshall later noted that his determination to go to VMI came from Stuart's challenge: "The urging came from overhearing this conversation, and it had quite a psychological effect on my career."[1]

The U.S. Military Academy offered a free education, but this fine institution was not a possibility for Marshall. Among other factors, young men were chosen based on a competitive examination, and Marshall's academic performance had been less than stellar. Second, as a youngster he had injured his right elbow, and since it had never healed properly, he could not completely straighten his arm. That condition most likely would have kept him from passing the West Point physical fitness test. Finally, admission to the Academy was by political appointment. Marshall's father was a staunch Democrat in a state dominated by the Republican Party, making it more unlikely that his son would be appointed.

Although it cost almost $400 a year to attend VMI, a far cry from a free West Point education, apparently Marshall persuaded his mother. The family was still financially strapped, so Mrs. Marshall sold some property in Pittsburgh to pay for his education. Marshall would begin his advanced schooling among an august group, since at that time less than four percent of all college-age youth were enrolled in higher education.

An entrance exam was not required at VMI—the school was more concerned with "character and acceptable antecedents."[2] Marshall passed those tests with flying colors. He had a built-in Virginia heritage through John Marshall. His father was a solid citizen, his brother was an alumnus, and there were seven other Marshalls on the campus during his four years. Marshall was in.

On September 11, 1897, George Marshall went alone by train to Lexington, Virginia. From the window as the train pulled into the station, he got his first view of Virginia Military Institute, fortress-like on the sweeping high ground of the town. Arriving in the late afternoon, he made his way across town, past the imposing colonnades of Washington and Lee University, to VMI. Marshall's first impressions were quite strong, even years later: "I will never forget walking down the long approach avenue to the barracks and hearing the bugle sound the assembly for dress parade and seeing the adjutant and the sergeant major strut out to form the line on which the battalion would form. I thought they were very wonderful looking figures." In his pocket, the young Marshall carried an envelope bearing the letterhead of his father's company, for the school's superintendent. It included a short message: "I send you my youngest and last. He is bright and full of life, and I believe he will get along very well." As Marshall scholar Larry Bland described it, "Presenting himself and his letter and check to the very martial-looking General Scott Shipp . . . he converted himself from free man to Rat."[3]

The total VMI enrollment for the 1897–98 school year was 222. Marshall was the last of the 122 freshmen to register. Having been stricken with typhoid fever during that past summer, a disease he most likely got from swimming in polluted pond water, he arrived 10 days after school started, still physically weakened by the illness. From the first, he was behind. His "Yankee" accent with a Pittsburgh twang did not go unnoticed among these Southern cadets. After all, it was only 32 years after the Civil War in a town where Stonewall Jackson was buried and where Robert E. Lee had been president of neighboring Washington and Lee University. According to historian Mark Stoler, "He was academically ill prepared, tall, awkward, and shy. According to one story, 'He could not drill. He could not march. All he could do was sweat, look uncomfortable and be embarrassed whenever spoken to.'"[4]

In the background, the VMI barracks as it looked at about
the time Marshall arrived in 1897

George C. Marshall Research Library

These traits brought George Marshall more than the usual amount of hazing from the upperclassmen, who used this extreme kind of teasing or harassment to initiate the freshmen. Although a long tradition at VMI, the administration discouraged unusual or overly severe treatment. Traditionally, to separate the classes, the seniors were known as Firsts, juniors Seconds, sophomores Thirds, and the freshmen Fourths, also called Rats as they were considered "the lowest form of life on earth." Rats were fully initiated mostly by the Thirds, and the class had to earn its way out of the Rat Line before the freshmen could be considered *real* cadets. Having arrived later than the others, and with space tight on post, Marshall was assigned a room on the same floor as the Thirds. This made him not only more noticeable than other Rats to the Thirds but also handier for continued harassment.

An often told story about Marshall and VMI hazing goes like this: Not long after he arrived, several Thirds came to Room 88, where he resided with his roommates. Wedging a bare bayonet firmly between the floorboards, point up, they ordered the newest cadet to squat over it. Marshall complied, and managed to hold that position for about 20 minutes until he slipped to the floor. His injury wasn't serious, but it could have been. He had a good-sized gash in his buttock that kept him from marching for four days. He went to the VMI doctor for treatment of the cut but did not name the cadets who had caused the accident. Had he told, the participating Thirds would have been severely punished.

One wonders why Marshall refused to tell, since some Rats might quickly have pointed a finger at the guilty ones. Perhaps it had something to do with Marshall's sense of the so-called "VMI Spirit"—being part of the group, keeping the trust, and therefore not giving in even when the treatment was harsh and degrading. According to historian William Frye, "The victimized Rat won the regard of the Corps for his silence. There was a more tangible result, as well: a chastened collection of upper classmen declared an armistice which exempted the occupants of No. 88 from any hazing for the remainder of their Fourth Class year."[5]

When asked about his first year at VMI, General Marshall explained, "The routine of cadet life I became accustomed to and accepted. I think I was a little bit more philosophical about this thing than a good many boys. It was part of the business, and the only thing to do was accept it as best you could and as easily as you could."[6]

Living conditions at VMI Marshall later described as "rather severe."

16

According to the "Old Grads" of the Institute, though, the amenities had improved. The cadets were allowed to sleep on mattress cots rather than on the floor. By the time Marshall arrived, there was electricity, water piped by a spigot to each corner of the barracks, and inside toilets. The walls of the building had been stuccoed so the wind didn't whip through large gaps around the windows. That made for warmer rooms, although it helped little, since cadets were required to sleep with the windows open. Despite these modernizations, it was, Marshall recalled, "a pretty stern affair."[7]

Adjustment to college academic life was difficult as well. Marshall told his biographer, "My first year away at school was very poorly done." Records show that it was not quite as grim as Marshall remembered. He stood 18th among 82 classmates the first year; 25th among 69 the second; 19th of 42 classmates in the third; and almost in the middle—15th of 33— in his final year. Although during his senior year Marshall stood fifth in his major, engineering, his academic performance overall was average.

Despite his unimpressive academic performance, Marshall's authority as a cadet officer was sterling. He excelled in military tactics, taking to its routines like a duck to water. Each year at VMI he was the top military student in his class. In his second year, he was first corporal; the third year brought him to first sergeant; and for his senior year, he was named first captain, the highest cadet honor at VMI. He wore the stripes of his rank on his coat sleeve with pride, especially when he went home to Uniontown.

By fall of 1900, Marshall was beginning his senior (First) year. One of his main responsibilities was monitoring the cadet corps through their meals, which he said was "the principal time that you had to exercise some talent at leadership." As first captain, he recalled, "I was responsible for the entire corps every meal all through the year. And if I do say it, with hardly a loud laugh." Mealtime was a serious affair at VMI. A cadet did not have time to spare when it came to eating, but the young men were usually allowed to socialize quietly during the meal. Only once that year did Marshall face a situation that called for a quick and firm decision. The cadets had just started to enjoy a rare dessert treat of fresh strawberries when they decided to challenge Marshall's authority.

There had been a recent case at West Point that had become serious enough that it led to a congressional investigation. The academy corps had given complete silence to a tactical officer, which was considered *worse* than being too loud and boisterous, since it was a means of ridiculing or mocking the official authority—the one in charge. In trying the same type of behavior at VMI, the corps was putting its leader to the test. As Marshall recounted: "There was a complete silence while they were eating and that attracted some fellow's attention, so he shushed the rest and they all settled down to a complete silence to see what I was going to do. . . . I merely got up, and called them to attention, and marched them out of the mess hall when the strawberries were only about a third eaten."

Without losing his temper, George Marshall regained control, punished the guilty, and ended the incident without any further reproaches. He exhibited that same decisiveness time and again throughout his later career as an officer. Of his experiences at VMI, Marshall would say:

> What I learned at VMI was self-control and discipline, so that it was ground in, and the problems of managing men which fell to the . . . cadet officer. He was very seriously judged by his classmates if he was slack. If I had been a first class private . . . I would have been very different about matters and made it a practice . . . to be as slack as I could be. . . . But I, in my job of first captain, had to exercise authority all the time, and I had to do it in such a way that it didn't create resentment.[8]

Marshall was admired by other cadets because he was fair and honest in his dealings with others. Marshall historian Mark Stoler noted that this was indeed a tribute to that self-control and discipline, but also to his leadership and ability to manage men. Although Marshall credited VMI for developing these traits, Stoler made the point that the school perhaps simply nurtured what were natural strengths within this young man:

> Driven to excel by Stuart's insults . . . he transformed his childhood traits so he could succeed by VMI's norms and developed additional strengths as needed. Shyness, for example, became austerity and coolness, and stoicism and hard work translated into perfection on the drill field. [His leadership] was marked by austerity, discipline, and distance from his peers, and it gave Marshall what he wanted most from them and from his superiors at VMI: not love but respect.[9]

One measurable mark of Marshall's self-control was that at the end of his time at VMI he, along with only five other cadets, had no recorded demerits. This was quite an achievement, since the class mean was well over 100 demerits each year.[10]

There was not much leisure time at VMI. The young men were allowed to go downtown only on Saturday afternoon. Marshall might go with friends, but with an allowance of only $5 per month, he could do little but window shop. On Sunday mornings, the entire corps was required to attend church— they could go with their own companies, which attended the town's four churches in rotation, or they could make their own choice. In the afternoon, cadets had approximately two hours to wander the countryside around the campus, but they were not permitted downtown, and had to be back for evening dress parade.

Vacations were reserved strictly for summer, with only four holidays during the school year—thus no time for traveling to see family on Christmas or Thanksgiving. On these rare days, though, the cadets did what they could to get away from post and enjoy the leisure. Always interested in the outdoors and exercise, some of Marshall's ideas were not everyone's definition of fun. He once talked his roommates into hiking to the top of a nearby 3,600-foot mountain at a "regulation infantry step and marching cadence without a single stop until the round trip was complete." Undeterred by loud and bitter protests, he led the way, and all three completed the course. It took weeks for the blisters to heal.[11]

In his junior year, Marshall tried out for football. He had promised his mother that because of his elbow injury and the typhoid fever, he wouldn't play for two years. His third-year glory days were short-lived, since a typhoid fever epidemic that resulted in the death of one cadet closed down the football season. Cadet Marshall tried out again the next year, and made it, playing left tackle. VMI won Southern Conference honors that year in football, so Marshall enjoyed a fine season, even getting his name in the newspaper sports column a time or two. Lexington's local newspaper described the reception the team received when it arrived back in town after defeating its archrival, Virginia Polytechnic Institute, thereby nailing down VMI's spot as seven-state champions: "Hundreds of sky rockets and roman candles brightened the heavens and torches of white flares lighted up the surroundings. At the train station, a procession was formed with the band leading, followed by members of the team in carriages and Cadets behind. It was a triumphant march from the station to the Institute. Even ladies cheered and waved along the route."[12]

An Auburn-Haired Beauty

It was one special lady who would gain Marshall's interest in his senior year. One day while walking near VMI's Limit Gates, he heard beautiful piano music emanating from a small house. He soon learned that the pianist was Elizabeth Carter "Lily" Coles, an auburn-haired beauty who lived with her widowed mother, a descendant of one of Virginia's most revered first families. Marshall walked by the house several times before he worked up the nerve to stop and introduce himself to the vivacious young woman. It was love at first sight, and mutual. As Marshall described it, they were soon "steadies." It was said in Lexington that when Lily first met the tall, handsome first captain, she said, "I'm going to marry him."

Marshall took certain risks to see Lily. In the evening after "lights out," he would often "run the block" (illegally leaving the barracks), a dismissal offense. As a cadet known for following the rules, this was quite a departure, but as Marshall explained to his biographer, "With the assistance of my two roommates . . . there was no general suspicion that I was offending in this way. I was very much in love and willing to take the chance."[13] By June 1901, Marshall and Lily were informally engaged to be married, despite some misgivings of her mother. A woman with deep roots in the South, she was a bit suspicious of a young man from Uniontown, Pennsylvania. Marshall later related that Mrs. Coles thought his place of birth sounded like a rather "recent affair." She soon learned that in fact the industrial city of his youth was founded before his future mother-in-law's beloved Lexington.

After graduation, Marshall wanted to join the U.S. Army as a commissioned officer. That was easier said than done. Since only West Point graduates were automatically commissioned in those days, Marshall's only hope as a civilian was to take an examination, and to do that he would need authorization from the War Department. Although a recent expansion of the military, prompted by the United States' broadened position as a world power following the Spanish-American War, opened more officer slots than usual, his chances were slim.

Moreover, Marshall's parents weren't pleased that their son wanted to join the army, which was small and offered limited opportunities for advancement, low pay, and little prestige. Yet seeing that Marshall was set on this course, his father wrote to VMI Superintendent Scott Shipp and asked him if he thought his son would make a good soldier, and, if so, could he recommend him for the exam. The letter written by Shipp to President William McKinley on January 13, 1901, surely gave Mr. Marshall his answer: "I assert with absolute confidence that if commissioned in the army, young Marshall will, in all respects, soon take his stand much above

VMI football team, 1900: George Marshall is in the second row, second from the right.

George C. Marshall Research Library

the average West Point graduate."[14]

With new confidence in his son's future, Marshall's father wrote to some of his influential political and business friends in Washington, D.C., asking them to write letters of introduction for his son. To strengthen his potential for selection, George Marshall alone had to visit the capital city, and time was of the essence. By April 1901 there were only 147 vacancies left, and 10,000 applications.

Young Marshall took the train through Virginia's Shenandoah Valley almost 200 miles to the nation's capital to make his case. Armed with his father's business card, along with some letters of introduction, the once awkward boy, by now an emboldened young man, made the rounds of powerful Washington figures, including the House Military Affairs chairman and the U.S. attorney general.

To make certain he had taken his cause to the highest office, Marshall paid a visit to the White House, which in 1901 was open and accessible to the public. Having no appointment of any kind, Marshall walked into President McKinley's office anteroom and sat waiting patiently. When a family of three was escorted by an attendant to see the president, as Marshall told it, "I simply attached myself to the tail of a procession." The attendant glared at him, but Marshall kept moving. After the family's short visit, Marshall stayed behind. Recounting the bold move to his biographer, he remembered: "Mr. McKinley, in a very nice manner, said what did I want. I stated my case to him. I don't recall exactly what I said, but from that I think flowed . . . my authority to appear for examination."[15] Whether it was this visit, or the two letters of recommendation that Marshall's father persuaded the Republican senator from Pennsylvania to write to the War Department, on September 23, 1901, Marshall reported to Governor's Island, New York, to begin the four-day test.

Finally, in December 1901, Marshall received the longed-for news—he had passed the examination. Since he had to be 21 before he could accept the commission, and his next birthday wasn't until New Year's Eve, it would be January 4, 1902, when it was finally confirmed by Congress. The young officer called it "a very acceptable Christmas present." By law, an applicant for a U.S. Army commission had to be single, so the long process of acquiring it had delayed his marriage to Lily Coles. With his commission in hand, he was free to say, "I do." The wedding took place on February 11, 1902, at the very house where he had first heard his beautiful bride play the piano.

"He is of fine physique and soldierlike appearance...with natural powers of command and control." Superintendent Shipp, 1901

George C. Marshall Research Library

The honeymoon to Washington, D.C., would be short-lived. Lieutenant Marshall was assigned to the 30th Infantry Regiment in the Philippine Islands. Wives of junior officers were not allowed to accompany their husbands to this posting. The trip for Lily would have been too difficult anyway, since she suffered from a weak heart—a chronic condition that might have worsened in a tropical environment. The Marshalls did get one small break: Although he was to have reported to his new assignment on February 13th, just *two days* after the wedding, a sympathetic officer bent the rules to provide a little extra time for the newlyweds. By February 18th Marshall had to say good-bye to his young wife and report for duty. Lily would stay in Lexington with her mother for the two-year assignment. For Marshall, a 43-year career in the U.S. military was about to begin.

The Wedding Party on February 11, 1902

Left to right: Marie, Lily, George, Stuart, Mrs. Marshall, Mr. Marshall, and Mrs. Coles (Lily's mother)

George C. Marshall Research Library

Chapter 3

A Young Lieutenant

Philippines to the Great War

1902–1916

Marshall's first assignment as a fresh-faced, raw second lieutenant took him to the steamy, dank jungles of the Philippine Islands. His duty would be with the United States' army of occupation in the aftermath of the Spanish-American War. The young officer had witnessed the 1899 victorious return of Company C of the 10th Pennsylvania Regiment to Uniontown after their service in that brief war. It had been the summer after his sophomore year at VMI, and long afterward he remembered it well. "The bricks of Main Street were painted red, white, and blue, and triumphal arches erected in every block." Marshall described the elaborate treatment afforded the hometown heroes: a medal for each, a sword for every officer. As he said, "No man in Company C could make a purchase in the community. The town was his." Recalling a final jubilation at the fairgrounds, he noted, "It was a grand American small town demonstration of pride. . ." but he also added: "Years later most of us realized that it was much more than that. It reflected the introduction of America into the affairs of the world beyond the seas."[1]

Indeed, the United States was spreading its wings. The Industrial Revolution that brought better machinery and consequently higher productivity had created a need for new consumers. The nation was in an expansionist mood. Senator Alfred Beveridge of Indiana cried in 1899, "Today we are raising more than we can consume. Today, we are making more than we can use. Therefore, we must find new markets for our produce, new occupation for our capital, new work for our labor."[2] Even technological advances in the implements of war led some Americans to believe that the country could forsake its traditional strict adherence to isolationism; perhaps it could join the "imperialist fever" that was raging throughout Europe. Further, the era saw the revival and expansion of the 1840s' emphasis on "manifest destiny," the idea that Americans were divinely compelled to spread their institutions over the earth, to bring Christianity and democracy to the "less fortunate" of the world.

In light of such expansionist motivations, by 1901 the United States military was significantly increased in size. At the time Marshall was seeking his commission, the regular army was enlarged from its Spanish-American War size of 65,000 to 100,000. This was what had created the need for more officers and opened the door for Marshall to enter the military. It represented a huge policy shift, since typically the United States dismantled its fighting force as soon as peacetime came. Now, a developing overseas empire that included the Philippines, Cuba, Guam, Puerto Rico, and Hawaii would require military supervision.

After a month-long ship's voyage, Marshall arrived on May 13, 1902, in Manila, the Philippines' capital of this newly acquired American outpost. Most likely his attentions were more focused on local matters, not the specifics of U.S. government policy toward its new possessions. He had landed in the midst of a virulent cholera epidemic that before it ran its cycle would kill more than 100,000 in the Philippine Islands. Marshall knew that cholera was a disease spread through unsafe water, raw or unclean food, and dirty hands or utensils. It dehydrated the body and, in that primitive island setting, was usually fatal. Moreover, he needed to find transport to his new assignment—Manila was an expensive city, and he had very little money.

Getting to the island of Mindoro, where Marshall was to join G Company, a detached force of the 30th Infantry Regiment now occupying the island, proved harder than he could have imagined. He managed to get aboard the *Isla de Negros,* which was the last boat to his destination for three months. Describing the boat as "greasy and dirty," with virtually no deck room, Marshall soon found out he would be on it for a while. Because the 250-ton ship chartered by the army was placed in cholera quarantine for five days, its passengers and cargo could not get to Calapan, the capital city of the island and Marshall's destination. He and the others languished in the 100-degree heat, the vessel quiet in the water. Desperate to cool off, Marshall and another young officer decided to swim. A padre who was onboard suddenly let out a piercing scream, followed by the dreaded word "shark." Marshall said he looked around and spotted two of them, their fins sticking up and headed straight toward him. In seconds, he and his officer friend were in a race to the rope hanging over the boat's railing. Later Marshall recalled, "I never showed such strength and agility in my life as going up the side of that boat. So we laid there, stewing in the heat."[3]

Even that experience did not top the typhoon that hit the next day. "I am not exaggerating at all when I state that the boat would tilt over until the lifeboats on the upper deck would go in the water. Then it would just poise there for a little bit, and it would seem like it was never going back again. Then it would go up and go to the other side, these huge waves," Marshall later recalled. The captain was so frightened or sick he just left the bridge. The Filipino who took the wheel had his ribs mashed in and was gone. Marshall and his colleague had to take over. As he said, "We just battled the thing all night long." The Filipino deckhands, keeping the fires going in the engine room, panicked when water started pouring through the open ventilated space and abandoned their efforts. Marshall and the young officer forced them back at gunpoint to continue their work. It was a harrowing experience, but the next morning all was calm.[4] When the quarantine lifted, Marshall was able to get to his duty station at Calapan. It was an inauspicious beginning for what would be a brilliant military career.

Although the Spanish-American War had officially ended four years earlier, rebels who opposed the U.S. takeover of the islands had continued to fight. But the guerrilla leader, Emilio Aguinaldo, had been captured, and by spring of 1902 most of the fighting was over. As a token symbol of empire, and to handle incidents arising from sporadic attacks by a few remaining pockets of "insurrectos" and *ladrones* (bandits), 34,000 American troops were still in the Philippine Islands. Marshall would command a Company G detachment of 50 soldiers. Calapan, a town of 5,600, was composed of hardly more than a group of native huts surrounded by jungle. The young officer's greatest challenge would not be the rebels, although there were periodic flare-ups; rather, the stultifying heat and humidity, isolation, and disease would sorely test his leadership.

The Scourge of Cholera

Indeed, Marshall had hardly begun his duties when cholera struck Mindoro. By way of explaining how quickly this dreaded disease could take hold, Marshall related to his biographer that just after he arrived, two of the officers had introduced him to three Filipino sisters. The young officers would while away afternoon free time on the front porch of their thatched-roof home. Marshall described the ladies as quite cultured, with beautiful singing voices—one of them played the harp. "I mention these sisters in particular," Marshall noted, "because suddenly the cholera broke out . . . almost in a day. We had no warning of it there. We thought we were safe. It broke out [that morning] and the three sisters—I helped bury them all by three o'clock that afternoon."[5]

It was Marshall's duty to protect his company, and he acted quickly. A strict quarantine forbade the men from contact with the people of the island and established stringent rules of sanitation. The soldiers were confined to quarters; everything they ate or drank was boiled; hands were scrubbed; mess

U.S. patrol, Philippine Islands, 1902

George C. Marshall Research Library

kits were scoured and rinsed, and no shortcuts in sanitation were allowed. "You had to enforce these things very carefully or they would skimp them. A very little skimping would cost you your life," Marshall said. More than 500 died on Mindoro before the epidemic ended, but except for the death of one soldier, the company remained in good health, no doubt partly because of Marshall's strict methods. Although the men had survived a vital threat, they were bored from a long confinement in close quarters, the tedium of constant cleaning, and the monotony of routine. By the time the quarantine lifted that late June, the soldiers were ready for a break.

Morale Building

In early July 1902, it was the officers of Company G who decided that an Independence Day celebration would boost morale. Marshall was placed in charge and, as he later wrote, was "given the chore of organizing the celebration of the day in a rather gloomy, depressed command." The garrison adjutant had declared that the activity du jour would be a Field Day, and named the events that were to be included. The men of the garrison were not in a celebrating mood; not only was morale low, but most of the older officers complained that strenuous activity in the tropical heat would do little to raise spirits. Further, the young men were resentful and bruised, the effects of an arbitrary and tyrannical previous commander of the post. Nevertheless, everyone was under orders to attend the festivities whether they wanted to or not. The day before, Marshall went from officer to officer collecting money to offer as prizes in the athletic events. They had few places to spend their money, so it wasn't difficult to get more than $30 in half-grudging contributions from each of them. At first, the soldiers did not know about the prize money, and they bridled at being forced to "celebrate." When July 4 dawned steamy and hot, this young junior officer was faced with "men all sore and outraged and standing around in sullen silence."

Marshall called for the first race, and after what seemed like an interminable silence, three men stepped up and got in line for the 100-yard dash. Marshall proceeded to give the runner who came in first $20; the number two man received $15, and the number three man $10. As he later explained, "As a soldier's pay was only $13 a month, those were huge prizes." When the second race was announced, there were so many runners they could not all compete. Their interest aroused, the soldiers finally embraced the possibility of fun and recreation, and spirits soared. Marshall's success in improving the command's morale demonstrated this young officer's leadership ability, but, further, it was early evidence of his concern for the welfare of the citizen soldier, whose needs he never forsook.

Only days after the July 4th Field Day, Marshall turned over his detachment to another officer and left Calapan to take command of the entire company at its Mangarin headquarters, a post that biographer William Frye described as "inhabited by . . . a handful of malarial natives, and what seemed to be half of all the world's mosquitoes."[6] As a young officer stuck in this forbidding, isolated environment, Marshall continued to sharpen his ability to command, often in situations that were not "from the book."

One day while on patrol just outside of Mangarin, he led the men through a barrio [small village] to avoid a swamp. The soldiers saw some of the people trying to help a pony whose hip had been half-bitten off by a crocodile. As he later said, "They were just sewing him up without any regard to the pony's feelings, and that horrified the men." Just after they passed by the pony, Marshall took the men through a deep stream. As he told it, "We went into this stream single file. I had seven men. They were behind me and holding their rifles and the ammunition belts up, to keep them clear of the water. When we got about two-thirds of the way across, there was a splash upstream and some fellow yelled 'crocodile.' In about a second they all plunged ahead. They ran over me. I was ground right down to the bottom. Their feet went up my back and over me and up the other side. I finally came to the surface pretty well done up."[7]

Marshall did some fast thinking. The men had not intended to run over him or to hurt him, but they had panicked, a dangerous reaction for men who might one day face battle. "I got to the surface . . . went up the steep bank where the seven men were standing . . . looking very guilty and very unsure of themselves," Marshall recalled. "I took my position in front of them, wet and covered with mud, and fell them in [called them to attention] very formally. I then gave them 'right shoulder arms,' faced them to the right, and marched them down into the stream and clear to the other side. As they reached the other bank, I gave them 'to the rear, march.' They came back up out of the crocodile stream. Then I halted them, faced them toward me, inspected their guns, and . . . gave them 'fall out.' Then we started our excursion up into the mountains. . . . They never referred to it. I never referred to it. . . . I had done what I think was just about right."[8] As Marshall said, "It wasn't a time for cussing around." Indeed, he had acted decisively, applied discipline, restored his right of command, and boosted the confidence of his men.

Biographer Mark Stoler described the young officer's growth during his time in the Philippines:

> The twenty-one-year-old Marshall quickly established friendships with key local civilians and exerted his authority over the company by a combination of qualities that would mark his later military career. He relied heavily on subordinates . . . maintained discipline, and exhibited a rare resourcefulness for a person of his age and experience.[9]

By Christmas 1902, Marshall was back in Manila, a city of 245,000, for a pleasant change of scene from the dank forests of Mindoro. Garrison duty didn't prove difficult—he was free most days by lunchtime. Marshall took up riding and enjoyed the city's variety theaters, as well as camaraderie with other officers at the Army and Navy Club on post. By November 1903, a more seasoned second lieutenant was headed back to the states. The *Sherman* steamed out of Manila and, with stops at Nagasaki and Honolulu, traveled homeward.

Once back in the States, in late 1903, and after a short leave to visit Lily in Lexington, Marshall's next assignment was at Fort Reno, an army post in the remote and primitive Oklahoma Territory. Eventually his wife joined him, but in the beginning he stayed in bachelor officers' quarters. As in the Philippines, Marshall's role was in policing a conquered territory, in this case the nearby reservations of the Cheyenne and Arapaho tribes, although this duty required little attention. The climate was forbidding, and there wasn't much to inspire a young officer who wanted to advance his career. The emphasis at Fort Reno was "Old Army" and its traditions. Most days were spent in drills and inspections that were based on the importance of spit and polish, a preoccupation with the look of a soldier, and the precise ordering of the military society by the rules of rank and discipline. It was all about "the immaculate uniform, the varnished wheel spokes," or the "correct alignment of a row of tent pegs," and had little to do with realities that might be faced in a time of war.[10] Indeed, Marshall's life was dictated by garrison routine and little action beyond the post walls. Yet one four-month stint in detached service proved anything but routine.

It was from Fort Reno in 1905 that Marshall set out for Fort Clark, Texas. His task: to oversee the mapping of 2,000 square miles of the southwestern Texas desert on the Pecos River bottom. With a small detail of soldiers, a four-line mule team, and an escort wagon, plus 20 pack mules driven by a 58-year-old "packer," he covered 10 or 15 miles a day, sketching topographical features. Marshall called it "an endurance contest of the first class," and described conditions where the temperature climbed daily to 130. He recalled that "at one period the old packer and I were without water for eighteen hours and had to travel pretty nearly fifty miles."

When Marshall returned to Fort Clark, mission accomplished, he had lost 35 pounds and was "burnt almost black" from the scorching sun. Marshall related reporting with "an old sergeant" to Malin Craig, the captain of the company and later U.S. Army chief of staff. Marshall was wearing what he described as a "heterogeneous costume," which included "an old Panama hat that a mule had bitten the top out of." Of the meeting, Marshall recalled, "He [Craig] didn't think I could be an officer and talked entirely to the old sergeant." Despite the outfit, Marshall had done excellent work. The chief engineer officer of that region told him his map "was the best one received and the only complete one" of the seven drawn by teams sent out that summer.[11]

The mapping expedition complete, Marshall took a long extended leave saved from his many months on duty in the Philippines and, with Lily, looked forward to visiting Uniontown, the place of his birth. Although it had been only four years since he had been home, when he arrived, he hardly recognized it. Marshall's parents no longer lived in the old home place; in fact, the sturdy brick structure on the vital National Road had been torn down, the lot leveled and filled. The creek of his early exploits had been reduced to a trickle, clogged with the debris of a growing town. Mr. and Mrs. Marshall had moved to a modern, 11-story apartment building. His father was ailing, stouter, slower, no longer the powerful man of affairs that had so characterized Marshall's memory of him. Marie was preparing for her wedding; Stuart had already married and had moved away. Most of Marshall's friends had left the town as well; some of their parents had died. Even his best friend's dog, Trip, who had once followed them everywhere, had barely looked up when Marshall called to him as he sprawled in the sun beside a water pump.

Marshall would return to Uniontown several times, including for a parade in his honor in September 1939. While he no longer considered this Pennsylvania town his home, in his mind it remained a place of warm childhood memories. After leaving Pennsylvania, Marshall spent the remainder of his leave with Lily and her Coles relatives in Albemarle County, Virginia. By late January 1906, he was back in Fort Reno with his wife, and her mother. He was restless. After four years he was still a second lieutenant in a western outpost requiring little that was challenging.

Twice since his arrival at Fort Reno, Marshall had taken the test for the U.S. Infantry and Cavalry School in Fort Leavenworth, Kansas, but both times higher-ranking officers had garnered the spots. Marshall even applied to become a professor of military science and tactics at his alma mater, VMI, an assignment that Lily would have liked for her husband, but Superintendent Scott Shipp noted that "an officer of higher rank, an older man" would be best. Nevertheless, on his third attempt for admission to Leavenworth, he was accepted. As Marshall was to say later, "I was the only one who put down, 'yes,' I wanted to go, and therefore I got the detail."[12]

With an efficiency report from his Fort Reno commander describing Marshall as "a first class, all-around officer," the second lieutenant arrived at Fort Leavenworth, Kansas, in August 1906. Marshall's time at Fort Leavenworth would coincide with ongoing changes in the military brought about in part because of America's industrialization after the Civil War. While the United States had emerged victorious in the Spanish-American War, Elihu Root, secretary of war between 1899 and 1904, understood that the outcome reflected the weakness of Spain's fading empire rather than the military capability of the United States. He and other military reformers after him set about to change the face of the U.S. Army.

In the past, the nation's approach to the military was to maintain a small professional army controlled by an unwieldy system of bureaucratic organizations that in wartime drew on state militias to build a hastily trained fighting force. While this local method satisfied traditional fears that a large standing army was dangerous to the republic, it was never fully successful. In the modern industrial world where weaponry, food, clothing, medical supplies, and transport vehicles could be mass-produced, and where quick decisions were required under fast-moving circumstances, the old ways of preparing were simply inadequate.

Army leadership was also being influenced by the rise of the Progressive movement. Fearing the chaotic results of industrialization, turn-of-the-century reformers imagined ways to bring order and rationality to these changes. Progressives were optimistic that society could be improved, and while they believed that growth and advancement were part of the nation's destiny, in their view these changes must be guided by expertise, efficiency, and a "good dose of middle-class morality."[13] In the political and economic realm, this meant expanding the federal government to control corruption by regulating the "robber barons," as well as being more responsive to the needs of the people through child labor laws and similar reform legislation.

In the military, reform would involve a similar centralization of power. Thus, beginning with Root's guidance, the army would be reorganized.

Rather than the old fractured chain of leadership, it would be controlled from the top by a general staff accountable to the secretary of war, who served at the president's pleasure. Led by a U.S. Army chief of staff, along with 44 highly trained officers, the army's emphasis would be on education, training, efficiency, and military preparedness.

These significant changes would certainly influence what this young lieutenant would learn as he began his studies at Fort Leavenworth. Although trained in the traditional spit-and-shine military of the 19th century, Marshall stood on the threshold of the reforms shaping the 20th-century professional army that by 1939 he would lead. In 1906, when Marshall arrived at Fort Leavenworth, his concerns were considerably more local. He was dismayed to find that some of the other 53 students, especially those from the cavalry, had been coached on what to expect, and some had even been given copies of the previous years' exams. He later admitted his fear: "I wondered what was going to become of me without preparation of any kind." Not only did he have no background, but also he was the only second lieutenant in the class; all the other students outranked him.

Marshall realized that the work would be difficult. He knew the drill. Only the top half of the class would be allowed to return for the second-year General Staff School, a stepping-stone to the Army War College established by Elihu Root. In the newly reformed military, with its emphasis on professionalism, this post-graduate training was the path to promotion for a career officer. The competitive Marshall was also spurred on in part because of a conversation he overheard in the first few days after his arrival. Some senior officers were listing those students that they thought would be in the top half of the class—"the fortunate 24"—and therefore go on to the second year. Marshall's name was not among them. That seemed to motivate him in the same way that Stuart's "Don't let him ruin the family reputation at VMI" remark had fueled his ambition when he entered college. Marshall was to later say that "it was the hardest work I ever did in my life."

All of these students had to work. The courses were difficult, the standards exacting, and the competition for class standing intense and constant. Each student's marks were ranked to hundredths of a percentage point. Differences could be small but vital. For example, one day Marshall scored 100 on a map problem, but his friend, whose mark was what seemed like a respectable 95.17, was ranked 47th among the 54 students for this exercise. According to William Frye, it was not unusual for a student to suffer a physical or nervous collapse from the pressure. The school finally agreed to give each student his grades confidentially instead of posting them for all to see.[14] Nevertheless, Marshall later spoke about what he considered the benefits of this pressure for perfection at Fort Leavenworth:

> It was invaluable to me as a matter of training because I learnt a thoroughness which stood me in good stead through all the clamor and push and excitement, lack of time, and also during the war, particularly in the preparation for the Meuse-Argonne battle [World War I], where it was thrown in my lap (the concentration for it) all in a moment, without any previous warning of any kind. . . . My habits of thought were being trained. While you might say . . . [that] I learnt little I could use, I learnt how to learn. Right away I began to develop along more stable lines.[15]

Indeed Marshall rose to the Leavenworth challenge. "I finally got into the habit of study, which I never really had before. I revived what little I had carried with me out of college and I became pretty automatic at the business," Marshall told his biographer. Once Lily arrived at Fort Leavenworth, he used his wife's frail health as a reason for not socializing in the evening, leaving more time for study. At the end of the first year, after all grades and rankings were averaged, Marshall was first in the class—number one. His hard work and perseverance had paid off—he would continue for the second year at the General Staff School. Furthermore, in March of that first year he took his examination for promotion to first lieutenant. Amidst all of his other studies, he passed with flying colors, and at last claimed the next rank.

That second year at Fort Leavenworth (1907–1908) was much easier for Marshall, less of a grind, more enjoyable. Students at that level were not officially ranked, but that did not keep him from working hard. Once again he finished at the top of his class, and once and for all gained the discipline of a life-long learner.

Marshall's comment that what he had learned was of little use most likely stemmed from the fact that much of the class work was still based on traditional rote memorization. Yet one instructor, Major John F. Morrison, was introducing ideas that would eventually shape a modern army. In his tactics class, for example, Morrison would use an "applicatory" style by having the officers solve operational problems rather than simply memorize formulas.[16] Instead of constantly reviewing drill regulations and other petty matters, the students were studying logistics, how armies moved, military hygiene, and weapons.

The Marshalls at Fort Leavenworth, about 1908
George C. Marshall Research Library

At Fort Leavenworth: "My habits of thought were being trained."
George C. Marshall Research Library

That second year there was even more emphasis on exercises geared to mold future staff officers capable of advising senior commanders. The classes focused on broader aspects of their duties: strategic issues, field fortifications, the problems of fortress warfare, map maneuvers, and a host of other practical applications. Fort Leavenworth was the "intellectual center" of this new, reformed army. As Marshall would later comment, "We were in the midst of a transformation and we knew it."

In the summers between sessions, the post's chief of staff, General Franklin

Bell, assigned the five best students at Fort Leavenworth to teach at National Guard camps as a way of extending the modernizing influences of the school. Marshall saw this as an opportunity to work in the field with citizen soldiers. He enjoyed a high level of command as he trained these young men. It allowed him to use and even expand the new concepts and techniques that he was learning at Leavenworth.

The National Guard had evolved from the colonial militias that were organized in the days before the American Revolution. Since the early 1800s, every state in the Union had organized state militias under the control of their respective governors. State executives called them into service from time to time to maintain law and order in case of floods, labor disputes, danger to the public's health, riots, or other emergencies. In 1903, as a part of a military reform impetus, important national defense legislation gave federal status to the militias. These state units were given five years to conform to certain standards outlined by the regular army. Each unit was required to attend 24 drills and take part in five days of annual training per year, and was subject to inspection by regular army officers.

The regular army had the duty of training these men in summer camps across the states, introducing the guardsmen to new techniques, weapons, and procedures that prepared them as a reserve force for the national army. This strengthening of the National Guard made it more likely that the United States could hold onto one of its fundamental principles of government: to keep the permanent standing army small while maintaining national preparedness. Marshall's determination to treat these training experiences as serious preparation for future military action can be inferred from the emphases of his report to Captain Charles D. Rhodes after a week of National Guard training at Mt. Gretna, Pennsylvania:

> Every officer . . . seemed anxious to acquire all the practical knowledge possible of Military Art . . . and appeared to realize the futility of spending all the valuable hours of the encampment in normal "parade ground" drills and ceremonies, and endeavored to utilize all the time practicable in advance and rear guard, outpost and attack formations adapted to . . . actual conditions as closely as possible. The drills were seldom held on the parade ground.

Even though Marshall's approach favored the practical, his observations during the Mt. Gretna experience led him to believe that the camp was not organized toward that goal:

> . . . the method adopted is one that discourages progressive practical work . . . and fosters a system [that] spends itself in encouraging a natty appearance . . . in the execution of few practical field formations, and then, in cut and dried fashion, following the diagrams of the text books . . . regardless of actual conditions.

Marshall continued:

> Men can be taught to salute, squads right and left, in the armories [back home] . . . but a correct handling of troops in the advance to the attack and on the defensive can only be secured by movements on varied ground with as close an approximation to war conditions as possible.[17]

Following the two years of study at Fort Leavenworth, Marshall was appointed to stay on for two more years as an instructor in the Army Service Schools and Staff College, teaching engineering and military arts. Of his time there, one historian noted that it fostered what became the Marshall legend. While at VMI he had struggled as a student; as an instructor he was gifted. The young officer was on the cutting edge of the reforms that were professionalizing the U.S. Army, and he zealously embraced those changes.

It was while Marshall was at Fort Leavenworth in September 1909 that he received word of his father's death from a stroke. As he and his sister and brother returned home to Uniontown for the funeral and to make arrangements for their mother's move to Pittsburgh, Marshall realized that once and for all, he was saying good-bye to the town of his boyhood and youth.

In the summer of 1910, Marshall was off once again to a series of National Guard camps in New York and Massachusetts. After departing Leavenworth that fall, he took a four-month leave to vacation with Lily, completed a few brief assignments, and then settled in for a year of instruction with the Massachusetts National Guard. During that stay, he commanded a large joint regular army and National Guard maneuver that involved 17,000 officers and men. The activity included troop movements that crossed state lines and involved multi-state forces. It was strenuous work, and Marshall took it seriously. Even a *New York Times* reporter covering the scene described the sleepless Marshall as "the busiest man in the field." Secretary of War Henry Stimson was among those who were present to observe this massive maneuver. Marshall's superior, Brigadier General Tasker Bliss, also present, credited Marshall with much of the field exercise's success. As biographer

Ed Cray noted, "The young lieutenant was now recognized as a surpassing staff officer by the loftiest of the Army's aristocracy."[18] This was a seminal time for Marshall—he would later use what he learned here to prepare troops for military operations in World Wars I and II, when massive forces of men and matériel were moved across combat zones covering hundreds of square miles.

The Philippines—Again

Despite Marshall's successes in these detached assignments, the fact remained that it had been nine years since he had completed foreign service. He was at the top of the list for this required duty. In May 1913, he received orders to report for service with the 13th Infantry near Manila. This time Lily would accompany him, although she would spend the hot summer months in Japan.

The "insurrecto" cleanup from Aguinaldo's rebellion was no longer the task. Rather, the army there was on guard against the possibility of an invasion by the Japanese, an island nation 2,000 miles away that was becoming increasingly aggressive. The country's victory in the Russo-Japanese War in 1905 and the annexation of Korea five years later signaled Japan's rise as the preeminent naval power in the Pacific. American relations with Japan were tense. The Japanese were excluding American trade from many of the areas they controlled. In California, anti-Japanese labor laws, along with inflammatory stories from Hearst newspapers about the "Yellow Peril," fueled differences.

The American-fortified Philippines stood directly in Japan's path, a potent and threatening reminder to Asian powers of America's outward expansion. "Although the cloud over the Pacific was not very dark, it was sufficient to prompt the Philippine garrison to hold maneuvers designed frankly to test island defenses," noted Forrest Pogue. The situation for Marshall could not have been better. As Pogue observed, "It was one of those [maneuvers] that was soon to provide Marshall's career with a myth of the kind familiar in the lives of heroes—the moment when suddenly his native genius was supposed to stand revealed and [no one] could doubt that he was marked for the highest success."[19]

Thus it was that Lieutenant Marshall had barely arrived in the Philippines when General Bell, one of the commanding generals of the Philippine Department, detailed him as adjutant on the staff of a unit of 4,800 men that would soon take part in this elaborate mock invasion of Luzon and the capital, Manila. Marshall's group was part of the invading "White Force," which would stage an amphibious attack against the defenders of the capital, the "Brown Force." The mission: to test the army's defense systems against attack from the sea. General Bell had been impressed with Marshall's performance when he was at Fort Leavenworth, and he was keeping an eye on this promising officer.

Little did Bell know how quickly Marshall's skills would be put to the test. As it turned out, the commander of the White Force proved to be so incompetent that Bell's staff wanted to remove him, lest the maneuvers fall apart before they began. Marshall, the lowly lieutenant, made the case for keeping the colonel in command for the sake of morale but giving him (Marshall) a free hand. Bell agreed. Still more authority came to the young lieutenant only one day later when the chief of staff became so ill from a malarial attack that he had to return to Manila. Stuck, the umpires of the maneuvers suggested that Marshall step up to chief of staff; thus, a mere lieutenant would be both planner and commander of an invasion of 4,800 men.[20] Not everyone liked the idea. One senior officer was finally told by Bell to accept direction from Marshall or go before the retirement board.

By the time the maneuvers were over, the respect for Marshall was genuine and widespread. Lieutenant Henry H. "Hap" Arnold, who would later lead the U.S. Army Air Forces in World War II, provided a compelling snapshot of Marshall at work. He described seeing him with unit commanders gathered around, sprawled on the ground with his back against a fence under the shade of a bamboo clump, staring at a map spread on a board and fastened to a tree. After studying the map for some time, Marshall dictated his field orders to the active participants. It was long and involved, but without looking at his notes, he laid out an elaborate plan of attack. Every component had its orders, not one factor had been overlooked. The result was the complete routing of the defending detachment and a march straight into Manila. As Arnold remembered, "When I returned from the maneuvers, I told my wife I had met a man who was going to be chief of staff of the army some day."[21] Perhaps General Bell would have agreed. Having watched Marshall develop as an officer at Leavenworth, and now in the Philippines, he described him as having the greatest potential of any wartime leader in the army.[22]

Although Marshall was never given to public self-aggrandizement, perhaps he could not resist providing an unabashedly proud account of his role in the maneuvers' success for his brother Stuart. Writing in March 1914, he gave a detailed portrayal of the action, even including a map of the "invasion" sites and explaining the magnitude of the operation by listing quantities:

125,000 rations; 20 days' forage for 1,050 animals; 100 army wagons; a field hospital; a rolling bakery that provided 6,500 loaves of bread per day. Remarking on the challenges, he left no doubt about his role:

> You can imagine the difficulty of landing on the beach all the animals and impediments concerned, particularly when the boats could not stand in closer than ¾ miles from shore to dock. I had practically the entire burden of the thing, coupled with the difficulties connected with a first lieutenant ordering colonels . . . in the regular army.

As if to emphasize the real-life nature of the action, he explained that there were no restrictions, except as to "real bullets." He relished the victory: "Det. No 1 [the Whites] chewed the other side up, captured two of their six cavalry squadrons, and smashed up their infantry." He asks Stuart to tear up the letter and to "disabuse your mind that I am rather a remarkable braggart. I don't tell you things about . . . my successes, but this one was rather unique."[23]

Indeed, Marshall had performed his duties brilliantly. In June 1914, his company commander wrote Marshall's year-end efficiency report: "This officer for his years of service, age and rank, is one of the most completely equipped for military service it has been my lot to observe." He concludes by saying, "Should the exigencies of active service place him in exalted command I would be glad to serve under him."[24] The effort Marshall had expended to bring about these successes, however, had taken its toll. His body was suffering from the stress of his work in the Philippines. He described his condition as "a tight, dry feeling," and an inability to relax. Doctors called it neurasthenia, a general term that could cover conditions ranging from physical exhaustion to a nervous breakdown.

To recapture his good health, he took a four-month combination sick leave and regular leave, traveling with Lily to Japan and then to Korea and Manchuria, where he studied the battlefields of the Russo-Japanese War, and later sent a detailed report to his commander. Despite the tension in Japanese-American relations, Marshall remarked that the Japanese officers treated him royally and talked freely about their training methods. He recalled that he had "dozens of opportunities to watch Japanese troops at work," and that the officers talked candidly about new training systems, the skillful use of the bayonet, methods of throwing hand grenades, and the value of night attacks. Despite what seemed a "busman's holiday," he found time to rest, but also to get more exercise. He rode horseback, walked long distances, played tennis—tried to relax more. Altogether, he called it a "tonic, for muscles, nerves, and spirit."

After the rejuvenating leave, Marshall returned with Lily to the Philippines and settled down to pleasant garrison life—light duty, evening dances, quiet dinners with other officers. The new military department commander of the Philippines, Brigadier General Hunter Liggett, had made Marshall his aide-de-camp. Although in better shape physically, in terms of his professional life Marshall was not a happy man. At 36, and still only a first lieutenant, his career seemed on hold. Despite his stellar performances, in the small army of that period there were too many officers ahead of him. Further, because he was more capable than his rank, generals like Bell and Liggett had tapped him as personal aides. That meant he was in a staff position, rather than commanding troops in the field, making promotions all the more difficult.[25]

The year before, in a moment of deep frustration, he had written to VMI Superintendent General E. W. Nichols, bemoaning the "absolute stagnation in promotion in the infantry," and explaining his intention to resign from the army "as soon as business conditions improve." The reply barely concealed a sense of alarm that such a promising man would leave the military: "Now my dear fellow, I would think twice and think long before I gave up my commission were I in your place. You are an eminent success in your present line of endeavor, highly esteemed by everyone who knows you and with a standing in the service of the very highest bar none." Mentioning some proposed federal legislation that would increase the size of the army and put Marshall in line for promotion to captain, he warmly encouraged him to "stick to it."[26] As biographer Mark Stoler noted, Nichols turned out to be correct on all counts. The next year, Marshall became captain, and in the following year, the involvement of the United States in the European war already raging would create plenty of opportunities for Marshall's ambitions and talents.

The powder keg of European tension that would bring world conflict had already been ignited in 1914. On June 28 of that year, Archduke Francis Ferdinand, heir to the Austro-Hungarian throne, was assassinated by a Serbian nationalist in Sarajevo, Bosnia. What was to become the Great War began that August with Austria-Hungary's invasion of the tiny Balkan nation of Serbia. Soon it had grown into a worldwide armed conflict, engaging the armies of the major nations of Europe. The war crushed forever the delicate balance of power that had held Europe together since the early 1800s.

Though many Americans were horrified at events across the Atlantic, most thought it had little to do with them. Biographer Forrest Pogue commented

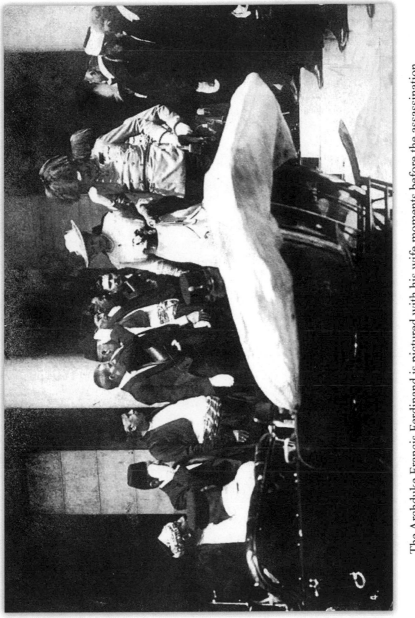

The Archduke Francis Ferdinand is pictured with his wife moments before the assassination.
Creative Commons, Europeana 1914-1918 Collection

that even in the exchanges between Marshall and Nichols on the subject of the young officer's future in the army, neither mentioned "the outstandingly relevant fact of the time: the great war in Europe, with its threat to draw America in and provide Army officers with opportunities for promotion to overmatch their most extravagant dreams. Neither man, like the overwhelming bulk of his fellow citizens, had any notion that the quarrels of the Central Powers and the Allies would involve the United States in war."[27] They would be proven wrong.

Chapter 4

"Over There" and Back

Duty with Pershing

1916–1924

On July 1, 1916, George Marshall reported to the Presidio at San Francisco as a captain, nine years after he had been promoted to first lieutenant, although his new rank wouldn't be official until that August. Back home now from the Philippines, Captain Marshall found the newspapers replete with stories of U.S. military action on the Mexican border. South of the Rio Grande, trouble had been brewing for some time: the resignation of one leader, the struggle for power of another, and developing factions vying for control. The tumult and bloodshed had threatened to spill over the border into the United States. That March, the troops of Brigadier General John J. Pershing had begun tracking the rebel army of Pancho Villa, who, in the wake of the political chaos, was seeking to destabilize President Venustiano Carranza's fragile relationship with President Woodrow Wilson's administration. Earlier that year, Villa had taken 16 Americans from a train in Northern Mexico and killed them; in March, he led a raid across the border into New Mexico, and 19 more U.S. citizens died. When Pershing's troops began a 300-mile pursuit expedition into Mexico to find Villa, the Carranza government, still holding tenuous power, saw the foray as an invasion and resisted the army in two major skirmishes.[1]

Having taken Superintendent Nichols's advice, Marshall had decided to remain in the army, and he fully expected to draw active duty with Pershing as his forces crisscrossed Mexico in search of this rebel bandit. It was not to be. Once again, Marshall's skills as a staff officer prevailed. He would serve as aide-de-camp to General J. Franklin Bell, his old friend and mentor. While it would not be action on the Mexican border, it would be a busy summer.

Perhaps in part it was the war raging in Europe that came to bear on that busy summer. The previous May, the Germans had sunk the British passenger liner *Lusitania*, killing 128 Americans and more than 1,000 others. This attack and other violations of neutrality by Germany created tense conditions that, although temporarily settled, gave notice to Americans that the country might be drawn into this war. With storm clouds darkening over Europe, and Pershing pursuing rebels in Mexico, the attitude of the American people toward military preparedness began to shift. According to Stoler, "Marshall and his superiors . . . discovered new and substantial support among the civilian populace for expansion and reform of the armed forces."[2] In fact, despite President Woodrow Wilson's campaign slogan, "He kept us out of war," it became increasingly likely that his claim might not last the summer. So it was that in early June, as Nichols had predicted, Congress passed the National Defense Act, which expanded the regular army to 175,000 and the National Guard to 400,000. It allowed National Guardsmen to be drafted into active service in case of war and added an organized army reserve corps.

The new law also provided for increased training camps for the Officer Reserve Corps so that civilians who were potential officers of a wartime army would receive updated and more rigorous military training. (The need for better training was so very apparent: When 100,000 poorly trained National Guardsmen had been called to the Mexican border after the Carranzo skirmishes, their confused and chaotic performance said it all.)[3] These reserve volunteers would go for a month's training, without compensation, to earn army commissions. They signed up in droves.

So it was that experienced instructors like Marshall were needed to assist in providing this training. General Bell first tasked him to look into and recommend changes in the summer training of civilian volunteers at Monterey, California. Twelve hundred trainees age 18 to 53, many of them professionals—doctors, lawyers, brokers—showed up for the course.[4] Since they were paying for the privilege, the expectation was that they would be treated gently, but General Bell wanted the training harder, more rigorous. Marshall was the man for the job. He saw the need for discipline and a more rigorous schedule. Observing the training agenda, he found that nothing much was happening. The maneuver exercises were undemanding, unfocused, and often ended at lunch. Then from the surrounding cities came the wives and girlfriends, some of them driving Rolls-Royces, bringing out picnic baskets that contained rich fare and champagne. After one such lunch, Marshall had the troops in a close-order drill exercise, and found that they were so sluggish they could barely participate. Commenting on the light morning activity and the lunch they'd had with their "sweeties" under the shade trees, Marshall told them drily, "Now, you are so exhausted from this 'war service' that you can't do a damn thing. I'm going to go out there and drill you again, and if you can't drill, I am going to march you in and report you as wholly ineffective." Yet as demanding as Marshall was, the men soon came to respect him and began to shape up. Marshall said later that although

48

they called him "Dynamite Marshall" for the dramatic changes he brought to the training, he continued friendships with them for many years.[5]

After the Monterey experience, Marshall reported to Fort Douglas, Utah, to become a prime mover in a training camp under the command of Colonel Johnson Hagood. The colonel found a way to turn the program over to the talents of this capable junior officer. Marshall's methods focused on the practical—target practice, long marches, scouting expeditions, camping in the open no matter the weather, and the solving of tactical problems. These rigorous activities were not what the trainees had expected—a mildly structured adventure away from their usual jobs. Rather, it was challenging duty. Nevertheless, Marshall's tact and self-effacement counterbalanced his seriousness and inspired the volunteers to accept his rigorous demands. Morale remained high. When the training was over and Marshall returned to California, Hagood was required to submit an efficiency report on the captain's work at Fort Douglas. When asked the question: "Would you desire to have him under immediate command in peace or in war?" Hagood wrote:

> Yes, but I would prefer to serve under his command. In my judgment there are not five officers in the Army as well qualified as he to command a division in the field. [He is] the best officer in the Army below the grade of major, and there are not six better in any grade. . . . He is of the proper age, has had the training and experience, and possesses the ability to command large bodies of troops in the field. . . . The Army and the nation sorely need such men.[6]

Meanwhile, since July 1914, the war in Europe occupied more and more of President Woodrow Wilson's attention. The Central Powers—Germany, Austria-Hungary, and later Bulgaria and Turkey—were battling it out with the Allied Powers, including nations of the British Empire, France, Russia, Serbia, and Belgium, as well as other associated powers such as Japan, Greece, Romania, and Portugal.

At first, the president had declared the United States "neutral" and asked Americans to remain so, "in fact as well as name." American farmers and industry owners gained early benefits from this neutrality, selling food and materials to both sides. Yet, most people strongly sympathized with the Allied forces, with the exception of Irish-Americans (traditionally anti-British) and some German-Americans. Even after the German sinking of the *Lusitania*, the United States was not willing to get involved in the European war. In the presidential campaign of 1916, Wilson steadfastly promoted the continued neutrality of the United States. At the 1916 Democratic Convention, the keynote speaker remarked on Wilson's diplomatic achievements, and, responding to the chant of delegates, "What did we do? What did we do?" he intoned over and over again, "We didn't go to war. We didn't go to war."[7]

Yet five months after Wilson's reelection, the United States, in April 1917, entered the war on the side of the Allies. The factors that led to America's involvement were many. Perhaps the strongest was Germany's decision to use unrestricted submarine warfare to cut off vital matériel to the British. Germany made it clear: if the United States continued to supply the Allies, her ships would be sunk. When American merchant ships were threatened by this activity, the United States, as it had been in 1812, insisted that our right to "freedom of the seas" had been violated. Despite our efforts to negotiate with the Germans, the possibility that the United States would continue in its neutral role diminished. Hostile feelings against the autocratic German government of Kaiser Wilhelm increased, along with a more sympathetic view of Great Britain, with whom the United States shared a common language, culture, and belief in democratic government.

Then in February 1917, the British turned over to Wilson an intercepted inflammatory telegram from the German foreign minister, Arthur Zimmermann, to the government of Mexico. The message proposed that in the event of war between Germany and the United States, the Mexicans should join the struggle against the Americans, and, in exchange, they would regain their "lost provinces" to the north.[8] Citizens "to the north" were outraged. Further, that March a revolution in Russia toppled the czarist regime, and a new provisional government was declared. Now the United States would be spared the embarrassment of an alliance with a despotic monarchy. The war for a "progressive world order" could proceed.

When German submarines sank three American ships in mid-March 1917, more of the citizenry began clamoring for war. The next month, President Woodrow Wilson called for a special session of Congress, petitioning it to participate as a "concert of free peoples [to] bring peace and safety to all nations and make the world itself at last free."[9] Congress agreed, and on April 6, 1917, the United States declared war against Germany. Despite the improvements made by the National Defense Act, the United States had committed to war but had virtually no army. When Wilson decided to send General John J. Pershing and a U.S. Army division to Europe, the reality was that there was none to be had. Pershing would go to Europe to "show our flag" while the army scrambled to put together a single division to be shipped to Europe. Most of them would be hastily trained draftees. (The regular army was only 130,000 strong at that point.) Wilson had asked for and gotten from Congress a Selective Service Act that mid-May. While 2 million volunteers would eventually join the various branches of the armed services, and the draft would bring in 3 million more, in the early summer of 1917 that army had by no means materialized.

When the war broke out that April, General Bell had been transferred to Governors Island in New York to head up the Eastern Department of the army. Due to a serious case of the influenza, he was soon hospitalized. Marshall, who had come east with him, acted on his behalf and, as was so often the case, had duties way above his grade. As Marshall later said, "So he went off and left me with a staff of about fifteen old colonels at the head of all the various departments, and I was the [captain] and all the pressure of the war was coming on."[10] His task was helping to set up training camps, as well as organizing and supplying the massive force being drafted for service in Europe. This included the Officers Training Camps at Plattsburg, New York. It was a challenge. For one thing, the crush of manpower arriving daily was not well supplied. Marshall learned this quickly as calls came in complaining about the "lack of this" and the "lack of that." One severe problem: not enough blankets or mattresses. When Marshall could not find adequate stocks, he ordered them from as far away as Chicago and had them shipped express. The quartermaster complained about the costs and told Marshall he wanted him to know what he was "letting the government in for." Marshall responded that he wanted to make clear to him what the government was in for if it didn't properly supply these men, whom he described as "freezing" in the crisp late spring nights of New York State. He then presented the quartermaster with a carefully organized list of the deficits within each camp, which had been scrupulously documented by another of Bell's aides. It included every need from pencils to rifles to kitchen stoves, and enumerated the shortages relative to the demands of the incoming troops. The old colonel was impressed—he'd never seen anything like that—and his eyes were opened. After that there were no more arguments about requests coming from Marshall's desk.[11]

The supply problem wasn't the only one Marshall faced. He felt pressure from people who wanted to use their influence to get themselves or someone they knew promoted or into the officers' training camps that were being formed across the Eastern Department. Marshall complained that every day "the Governors Island ferryboat would be jammed with fellows coming

Captain Marshall with Major General J. Franklin Bell
Governors Island, New York, spring 1917
George C. Marshall Research Library

over" and seeking admittance. As Marshall pointed out, they "all seemed to think they could get what they wanted right away just by the stating of their desire."[12] He said he even found himself up against ex-president Taft, who wanted to get his son in, and the likes of the mega-financier, J. P. Morgan. Marshall continued to make the selections on merit. When complaints came and the supplicants couldn't get at General Bell—the fact that he was in the hospital with this serious flu was kept a secret—Marshall stood them off. As he said, "I didn't know them, and they didn't know me and I could go right ahead." It was a difficult time, though. He later admitted, "I was using three phones at one time, and I was being seen by everybody that came to the island; so it was exceedingly hectic, and I had to learn how to do business very quickly."[13]

General William L. Sibert was the man chosen to head the First Division that would head to France that early June. As he prepared to go, he remembered Marshall's excellent work in Monterey that previous year. By then it was clear that General Bell was too weak from his illness to accept an overseas assignment. Sibert asked Bell by telegram if he would consent to Marshall's becoming his general staff officer, noting that the request was for "immediate service abroad." Bell's answer, to Marshall's delight, read, "Detail suggested agreeable to me."[14]

Marshall's assignment from General Sibert was as chief of staff for Operations. Among other duties he assisted in supervising new officers, getting them ready to leave for France. Early on, Marshall was to meet young second lieutenants—the best of the lot from the numerous training camps that had been set up across the country—and prepare them to go with the First Division to Europe. Years later, he vividly remembered the first nine who came in. Every one of them had gotten married as soon as they had received duty orders. Their wives had come to New York with their husbands to spend as much time as possible with them. Marshall remembered his own entrance into the army as a second lieutenant and his brief honeymoon in Washington, D.C., before leaving for the Philippines. Realizing that their ship would not sail for three days, Marshall gave the young men liberty so they could be with their brides a bit longer. He told biographer Forrest Pogue, "I lost track of two. The other seven, every one of them was [later] killed in the First Division."[15] As for Marshall, he had quickly made arrangements for Lily to travel to her brother's home in Charlotte, North Carolina, where her mother was visiting. From there mother and daughter would return to Lexington for the duration of the war. It would be two years before Marshall would see them again.

A soldier says good-bye to his sweetheart, 1917.
U.S. National Archives 165-WW-476(21)

Ill-Equipped and Poorly Trained

It was June 14, 1917, when the *Tenadores,* formerly a United Fruit Company banana boat, headed out of New York Harbor. During the trip over, Marshall got a good look at just how ill-equipped the United States was as it sent its young men "over there." He was astonished that on the first day at sea the officers (including him) were poring over the organization charts of the

British and French armies, since, as he said, "None of us understood the method in which the staffs of the Allied armies functioned. . . . Today it is inconceivable that we should have found ourselves committed to a war while yet in such a complete state of unpreparedness."[16] Speaking before a group in 1938, Marshall recalled the First Division's predicament as it sailed to France: "We found that the organization of the troops was entirely new to us, that there were four regiments of infantry in the division instead of the nine of our previous experience; that there were units of which we had never before heard, armed with weapons of which we knew nothing." Worse yet, Marshall noted, it wasn't until they arrived in France that they made another alarming discovery: many of the weapons listed as having been issued to the new troops "were non-existent, and . . . the troops which on paper were charged with operating those weapons had never seen even a model of one. We found that eighty percent of the men in ranks were [new] recruits, [whose] rifles had been issued on the trains between the Mexican Border and Hoboken [New Jersey]. They were all good men, they were all splendid Americans—but they were not soldiers."[17]

The First Infantry Division of the American Expeditionary Forces (AEF) landed in France on June 26, 1917. General Sibert was the first man off the ship, and, as Marshall noted, "by fortunate coincidence" he was the second man ashore. The Americans had arrived. Despite their lack of training, they were optimistic, confident the war would be over soon, and excited at the prospect of visiting a foreign country, especially France. They were in for a terrible surprise. Wendy Lubetkin, writing in her biography, *Marshall*, explained, "The eager young American troops could not have imagined the horrors that awaited them on the front stretching from the English Channel to the Swiss frontier: the foggy battlefields strewn with mines and barbed wire; the muddy, corpse-filled trenches: the clouds of poisonous gas."[18]

The French were in for a surprise as well. They had cheered wildly when Pershing arrived with his staff of 50, and they cheered again on July 4th when one battalion of the 16th Infantry paraded in Paris. One writer described the frenzy of flowers and kisses: "Men and women even dropped to their knees, tears streaming down their faces, as the Yanks went by." What the people *and* the French and British armies expected was a miracle, or at the very least a seasoned division of regular soldiers, as had been promised. Marshall commented that you would have to go around with a microscope to find a regular soldier. He described the day shortly after the division's arrival when the French commanding general turned up at headquarters to extend a welcome to the first American soldiers, thinking he was calling on an organization of the regular army. The sentry at the gate did the best he could to salute. The Frenchman was in full dress uniform, but this Tennessee soldier had an unbuttoned blouse and a watch chain stretched across his stomach. When the French officer asked the sentry about his rifle, he handed it over and proceeded to sit down on a nearby post to roll a cigarette. Marshall personally walked over, got him up, and buttoned his blouse. As Forrest Pogue noted, "That incident and others like it created an impression of bumbling amateurism in the minds of many in the French command which for a long time they insisted on believing was typical of the American Army."[19]

Unprepared or not, the French and British desperately needed the Americans. The situation could hardly have been more grim. After three years of trench warfare, the Allied troops had been virtually gutted. The Russians, now led by a provisional government, were threatening to withdraw. The Allies had launched offensives in 1917 that had met with failure, calculated in more than a million casualties, which they no longer had the manpower to replace. At the very least, the First Division would provide a psychological lift, a morale boost for the beleaguered armies holding out against the Central Powers.[20]

Considering the American army's lack of training, and the Allies' greatly reduced ranks, it's not surprising that both the French and British generals wanted to integrate American troops with their own. They would train the young men, but also get them into the lines. It set the French officers on edge to wait in desperation while Pershing's army—sent from America but assembled in France—got ready for action. Nevertheless, backed by President Wilson, Pershing insisted that the American army would act as an independent force, not cannon fodder for their exhausted British and French counterparts. He well understood that the people of the United States would not tolerate the horrendous death tolls that the French and British generals seemed to accept as a given of modern warfare. Further, as Marshall biographer Ed Cray noted, "To put Americans under the command of French and English generals would be to submerge the United States' contribution to the war. National pride, if not international politics, would not allow this."[21]

The training ground for U.S. troops would be in Lorraine, an area of the Allied line that was relatively quiet—it had not seen action since a German drive in 1914. Pershing's plan was to bring four more divisions in as rapidly as possible. By mid-July the First Division's headquarters had been established at Gondrecourt. Marshall's task had been to find at least minimal billets—something as simple as haylofts, for example—for the troops in six or seven nearby villages. For himself and several other American officers, quarters would be in the small home of Monsieur and Madame Jouatte near headquarters.

Through the winter of 1917–1918 Madame Jouatte would do much to make the officers' grim challenges more bearable. She prepared delicious meals, even learning to make American-style biscuits, and generally created, as Marshall said, a "très gentille" atmosphere for the men as they returned from the harsh duties of war.[22]

Marshall stands with other officers at Gondrecourt, 1917; Madame Jouatte (left), a French refugee, and her daughter are seated in front.
George C. Marshall Research Library

That August of 1917, Marshall received word that he would be promoted to major, a temporary rank. Advancements came faster in time of war, and this was especially important for a captain holding down a position usually held by a lieutenant colonel. By now, with billeting and other organizational tasks complete, Major Marshall was deeply involved in the planning and training of the First Division.

The French were especially adamant that the Americans should be trained in trench warfare, the sooner to get them into the battle. But Marshall believed something much more basic was needed to turn this "collection of men" into soldiers. General Sibert agreed. His training order stated that "all possible means will be employed with the utmost vigor to improve the appearance, military bearing, and the spirit of the officers and soldiers of this command."[23] It was after a month of such drilling that the men were minimally ready to receive combat training. General Pershing took an avid interest in this, since despite his resolve to use the U.S. troops as an independent force, he was under considerable pressure to get them combat ready, and quickly. That pressure filtered down the command. Although training manuals and clear procedural orders had not been made available to the divisions, they were expected to train the men in elaborate "combat demonstrations."

On October 3, Pershing and some of his staff paid a short-notice visit to watch a demonstration in trench warfare using short-range bombs. The French had dug the trench lines, and the exercise, developed by Major Theodore Roosevelt Jr., was to instruct these soldiers in methods of attacking and defending from these unfamiliar static positions. Marshall, acting as chief of staff for the division, had overseen the development of the exercise. General Sibert had been away and was thus observing the exercise at the same time as Pershing and his staff. When the AEF commander asked Sibert for an assessment of the maneuver of which he had little knowledge, Pershing found his critique lacking. He then asked another officer to respond, and that wasn't satisfactory either. As Marshall said, Pershing went into this long tirade and just began to "give everybody hell," but especially General Sibert. Marshall saw this as an injustice to his commanding officer, whom he respected. As Marshall explained it, "He [Pershing] was very severe with General Sibert . . . in front of all the officers . . . and generally he just scarified us. He didn't give General Sibert a chance to talk at all." As Marshall listened to Pershing's tongue-lashing, he grew more and more angry, and stepped up to explain what had happened. He felt responsible because he had been involved in planning the maneuver. General Pershing shrugged his shoulders, turned, and started to walk away.

For a moment, Marshall did not seem to consider the outcome of a junior officer boldly taking issue with a field commander's action. He put his hand on the arm of the highest-ranking military officer of the American forces and insisted on talking to him, or rather at him. "We have never received anything from your headquarters," Marshall began. "When I was down there two months ago, I was told about this Platoon Chiefs' Manual that was coming up. It's never come out yet," Marshall intoned, blue eyes flashing.

Pershing turned to one of the other officers, saying something like: "What about that, So and So?" And "So and So" said, "Well, we've had trouble with the French printers." Pershing continued walking, but told Marshall, "You know we have our troubles." Marshall shot back, "Yes, I know you do, General, but ours are immediate and every day and have to be solved before night." Marshall hadn't finished, but by now Pershing was listening: "We've had a very hard time. We've worked very, very hard. The men have had no advantages of any kind and they don't expect any. But they ought to get a fair deal at any rate."[24] As biographer Ed Cray noted, "Facts came tumbling out. The inadequate supplies; men were walking around with gunnysacks on their feet because the quartermaster did not have enough large shoe sizes. The inadequate quarters: troops were sleeping in barns for a penny a night; the lack of motor transport that slowed down training in the field."[25] Marshall himself would later admit, "I was just mad all over. I thought I had gotten in it up to my neck—I might as well not try to float but to splash a little bit."

After Pershing and his staff stalked off, as Marshall later related, "My bosom friends bade me farewell. I had to be relieved." Even General Sibert was regretful that Marshall had made this "sacrifice play," in part on his behalf. Marshall himself had no regrets. To those showing concern, he said, "All I can see is that I might get field duty instead of staff duty, and certainly that would be a great success."

To everyone's surprise, there were no repercussions from Marshall's outburst. General Pershing did not mention the incident again, but from then on, when he revisited the First Division, he often sought Marshall's opinions. Marshall was awed by this trait of Pershing's; that is, his ability to accept and even encourage straight, constructive criticism from subordinates. As Marshall later noted, "I've never seen a man who could listen to as much criticism . . . [and] would not hold it against you for an instant." Marshall would learn to do the same.[26]

By October, battalions of First Division's artillery and infantry went into training in a so-called "quiet" sector on the front line. Thirty days were allotted for this training, one battalion from each regiment going into the line for 10 days, alongside French units. Surprisingly, since this was supposedly a dormant sector, a company of the men one foggy morning found themselves heavily bombarded by the Germans. Three soldiers died, the first of more than 116,000 American battle deaths of the war. It was Major Marshall who wrote an immediate and detailed report of the action. By late winter 1917,

General John J. "Black Jack" Pershing at Chaumont, France, October 1918
George C. Marshall Research Library

the First Division's training had included maneuvers that required overnight marches, sleeping on the ground, standing in the open during hours of waiting in drenching cold rain and biting winds. Nothing could interfere with the most rigorous training. By now, they had been welded into a battle team that could act as an impressive and independent unit.[27]

Even as training continued, another change was on its way. That December Pershing had Sibert replaced as the commander of the First Division. Pershing had found him too conservative; that is, too willing to accept the pessimistic view of the French that nothing could be done to break out of the trench warfare mode. Pershing was pushing for warfare of maneuver, a means of replacing this stagnant method that so far had led to unimaginable losses on both sides with little ground gained. Sibert's replacement was General Robert Bullard, who knew Marshall's work and wanted to make him his chief of staff. It was not to be. Although Marshall respected Bullard, he thought Sibert had been treated badly, and he didn't hold back his criticism of headquarters. As Marshall said, "I demonstrated to General Bullard I had no business being made chief of staff in that state of mind." He remained in the subordinate role of chief of operations. It was a lesson for Marshall. He understood that he needed to control his temper. As he was to later say, "I never made the mistake—I don't think—again. I think it delayed [me] a great deal. I think I would have been chief of staff . . . and I would very quickly have been made brigadier general."[28]

As Marshall continued his work in training the division, the fortunes of the Allies continued to fall. That previous November, the provisional government in Russia was overthrown by the Bolsheviks (Reds), who immediately made plans to withdraw from the war. By March 1918 they had signed the treaty of Brest-Litovsk with the Central Powers. With the Russians out, that meant the Germans could transfer huge numbers of men from the Eastern to the Western Front. Bent on breaking the French and British before the Americans were ready for the fight, by mid-March the enemy had launched a series of offensives in France, covering 25 miles in five days. By early June 1918 they were threatening Paris.

As the crisis deepened, the Allies made Marshal Ferdinand Foch the commander-in-chief of all forces. Although his powers were limited, it was the beginning of a coordinated unified command. As Mark Stoler noted, Marshall would remember and build upon that concept in World War II. To help stem the tide, and to improve the morale of the Allied forces, Pershing offered newly trained First Division troops. In late May, those forces began a successful attack, which Marshall had helped plan, against an exposed German position at the town of Cantigny, and managed to stop seven counterattacks in three days.[29] Marshall, who had broken his ankle in a fall from his horse only days before, refused evacuation, and hobbled around making adjustments related to battle logistics on a pair of too-short crutches. Marshall described the demands of the operation in his memoirs, "For a week I did not have my clothes off and worked sixteen to eighteen hour days. The ankle ached so severely that I could not rest comfortably [but] there was plenty of work to do for anyone who was awake." Although the taking of Cantigny was a relatively small operation, and cost high casualties for the ground gained, Pershing thought its success was very important: it demonstrated that American tactics could break the stalemate on the Western Front. For Marshall, it was significant for that reason and another as well. It would be the last time he would see combat as an infantryman.

Not long after the Cantigny campaign, Marshall had written a formal request to be relieved of his staff position for troop duty. Not that he was a typical desk officer. As historian Alan Saunders commented, "One of the many factors that made him a superb staff officer was his unwillingness to accept hearsay as fact. Often, on his own initiative, he would venture to the front to see for himself. He was even cited for bravery under fire." As the officer in command, Marshall believed that to fully understand what the troops were experiencing, he had to personally observe those situations. "More relevant, though," Saunders noted, "was his willingness to learn, to listen to the comments and experience of line officers, to fit orders to field conditions."[30] Further, he stood no chance of being promoted to the permanent rank of colonel, since that position was reserved for those commanding combat troops. Once again, it was not to be. General Robert L. Bullard refused the request. In justifying his position, he offered his rationale: "Because I know that Lieut. Col. Marshall's special fitness is for staff work and because I doubt that in this, whether it be teaching or practice, he has an equal in the Army to-day." Despite requests from two division commanders to have him serve as brigade or regimental commander, he would stay on staff duty.

Meanwhile, the American army was continuing to make its mark. In early June, the Second and Third Divisions, 45,000 strong, took the brunt of the brutal fighting at Belleau Wood and Chateau-Thierry, halting the German advance on Paris. At the headquarters of the French general, Marshal Petain, one staff officer became emotional, exclaiming of the American effort: "Life arrived in floods to reanimate the mangled body of a France bled white by the innumerable wounds of four years."[31]

Saint-Mihiel and the Meuse-Argonne

By July 1918, U.S. combat strength was at 600,000 with 250,000 troops coming in each month.[32] Finally that midsummer Pershing declared the U.S. First Army, comprised of a half million men, operational. At about the same time, he transferred Marshall to his headquarters near Chaumont. The previous month, when General Bullard had turned down Marshall's request for troop duty, he had mentioned that Marshall's "experience and merit should find a wider field than the detailed labors of [this] Division Staff." Apparently Pershing agreed. Marshall reported to Colonel Fox Conner, the chief of the Operations Section of General Headquarters (GHQ), a friend and respected professional colleague. It was an exciting time. Spearheaded by American troops, that midsummer the Germans' last offensive was reversed at the Second Battle of the Marne. It was the beginning of a series of Allied offensive drives that would eventually halt Germany's power to resist. Marshall and Conner would be deeply involved in these operations. Mark Stoler summed it up: "Together they would form the core of the group that planned the two great U.S. offensives of the war—Saint Mihiel and Meuse-Argonne."[33]

At Saint-Mihiel there was a bulge, or salient, in the German defensive line that Pershing had planned to attack for more than a year. If that bulge was reduced or eliminated, then railroad communications to Paris would be free all along the front. That July 1918, Pershing had received a tentative agreement from Foch that the Americans, acting as a separate entity, would in fact attack the salient. Exactly how this blow would be delivered seemed still unclear, so much so that Marshall had drawn up four different operational plans. Now, on August 30, with the Germans on the defensive, Foch wanted Pershing to abandon the Saint-Mihiel plan and release two divisions to take part in a joint attack with the French north of the Marne River. Pershing said absolutely not, since in his view it would have the effect of placing his best divisions under French supervision and leave him to tend the rest in a quiet sector of the front. American participation would not become invisible, he protested! Foch was furious, exclaiming: "Voulez-vous aller à la bataille? (Do you want to go into battle?)"[34]

Seeing that he would not get agreement from Pershing, Marshal Foch compromised. The attack on the Saint-Mihiel salient would take place, but with limited objectives. After a two-day assault, the bulk of the American divisions would be transferred to the region between the Argonne Forest and the Meuse River. Supported by the French army, they would fight a second battle, but as a distinct American army. The Saint-Mihiel action would begin on September 12, but by September 26 the troops would be shifted to the Meuse-Argonne. It was this circumstance that brought Marshall his final chance to lead combat troops. The Second Division commander, Marine Corps General John A. Lejeune, asked Conner if Marshall could be transferred to take over one of the division's regiments for the Saint-Mihiel action. That would not happen: Marshall would report to First Army headquarters and, under orders from Colonel Hugh Drum, would plan the transfer of American soldiers from Saint-Mihiel to the Meuse-Argonne.[35] It was one of the most significant tasks he would ever complete, and he did it brilliantly.

It would not be easy; in fact, Marshall later described it "the hardest nut I had to crack in France." With his colleague, Colonel Walter S. Grant, Marshall set about to prepare this plan. It was an unusual task, to say the least. As Marshall said several years later, "I could not recall an incident in history where the fighting of one battle had been preceded by the plans for a later battle to be fought by the same army on a different front, and involving the issuing of orders for the movement of troops already destined to participate in the first battle, directing their transfer to the new field of action. There seemed no precedent for such a course, and, therefore, no established method for carrying it out."[36]

The attack was going to take place in an area so central to the Germans that they had fortified that part of the line to a depth of 13 miles. Mark Stoler noted that to accomplish this unprecedented transfer, Marshall had "to withdraw eleven French and Italian divisions with two corps headquarters from the front and replace them with fifteen U.S. divisions . . . a movement of 220,000 men out of the line and 600,000 into it." Of those, 400,000 would be from Saint-Mihiel.[37] With them came 4,000 artillery pieces, 40,000 tons of ammunition, field kitchens, hospitals (34 in total to be set up along the line), the headquarters operation, and much more. The operation would include 3,500 trucks and more than 90,000 horses and mules—with mechanized and hoof-drawn advancing at different speeds. All of this would be transported 60 miles along only three main roads and three rail lines. Movements took place at night, under cover of darkness, to maintain secrecy.[38]

Marshall once noted that "war is a ruthless taskmaster, demanding success regardless of confusion, shortness of time, and paucity of tools." By now a temporary lieutenant colonel, this young officer understood his responsibility all too well. He stewed about it for several days. Finally, having pored over maps and other information, and after taking the time to sit on a river bank next to an old French fisherman and contemplate, Marshall set about writing the order for this complex action. As he said, "I started with the proposition that the only way to begin is to commence. In less than an hour I had evolved a method for the procedure, and had completed the order."[39] When he turned in the order for "Release and readjustment of units following reduction of the Saint-Mihiel Salient," he was far from confident of its efficacy. The next morning, Marshall was called to General Pershing's office by Drum, a solemn man short on words, to review the plans. To Marshall's amazement, Drum turned to him and stated matter-of-factly, "That order for the Meuse-Argonne concentration . . . is a dandy. The General thought it was a fine piece of work." Others thought so as well; in fact, word of Marshall's brilliant plan for a brief time earned him a nickname, "The Wizard." That fall Marshall was promoted once more, this time to the temporary rank of full colonel. General Fox Conner certainly took note of this officer's talents. He told another young officer named Dwight Eisenhower to get an assignment with Marshall if at all possible, for, as he said, "in the future we will have to fight beside allies and George Marshall knows more about the techniques of arranging allied commands than any man I know. He is nothing short of a genius."[40]

On September 26, 1918, this great offensive began and did not end until the armistice in November. In six weeks the losses: 26,277 killed and 95,786 wounded. Involving most of the ground forces that Pershing had brought to Europe, the fighting raged over a 200-mile span of rough, hilly terrain that the German army had been fortifying for four years. The objective: capture the railroad hub at the city of Sedan to break the train net supporting the German army in France and Flanders, and force the enemy's withdrawal. The contribution of the Americans to this final thrust was momentous. American units in that action used more ammunition than the entire Union army had in the four years of the Civil War. By the end of October 1918 they had helped push the Germans to their own border and had cut the enemy's line of supply to the front. Furthermore, American soldiers occupied almost 25 percent of the Allied line. A weary German army was outmaneuvered, in retreat, and facing fresh forces. Over 1 million U.S. troops were involved in the Meuse-Argonne operation. Allied troops maintained this series of relentless battles against the German lines, finally forcing the surrender of the Central Powers. The armistice was signed at the 11th hour on the 11th day of the 11th month of the year 1918, bringing the Great War to an end.

After the armistice was signed, the Allies prepared to make the peace

Build up for the Meuse-Argonne offensive, fall 1918

George C. Marshall Research Library

American soldiers are testing telephone lines left by
retreating Germans, Saint-Mihiel, September 1918.

www.history.army.mil

official. The negotiations would take place in the Palace of Versailles's
great Hall of Mirrors, a beautiful setting not far from Paris. President
Woodrow Wilson, head of the American delegation, was intent on creating
a "new world order." Wilson had justified his country's participation in a
"foreign war" by emphasizing the opportunity to bring more democratic
governments to Europe. His idealism was in sharp contrast to that of French

and British leaders, who, having borne the brunt of the war in terms of both lost lives and property, wanted to see Germany thoroughly punished. Over the months of negotiation, however, Wilson fought hard for what he called his "14 Points," which really narrowed to three key concepts: the readjustment of the enemy's border to include new nations, and the principle of self-determination would be applied; changes in international conduct would be forthcoming, emphasizing freedom of the seas, no secret treaties, free trade, and a reduction in armaments. Finally, there would be a "league of nations" that would help implement these principles.

In the end, the president compromised away some of his cherished points to meet the roadblocks of the European Allies. The French premier, Georges Clemençeau, had said, "Peace is the continuation of war by other means." He intended to make Germany pay. Marshall read of the negotiations with the same disillusionment as other Americans. The United States had 116,708 deaths from that war; in addition, it had cost the country $23 billion. For this bickering, vindictive European fight? Despite the distaste on the American side of the Atlantic, in that compromised version of the treaty Germany was forced to admit guilt for the war, stripped of its overseas colonies, and made to pay harsh reparations.[41]

Included in the Treaty of Versailles, however, was Wilson's treasured League of Nations. Although he wasn't satisfied with other aspects of the treaty, he believed that the League would provide a forum for discussing the treatment of member nations, including Germany. He reasoned that some of the harshness of the treaty might be softened in postwar League sessions. Though he recommended that the United States accept the treaty (imperfect as it was), the Senate refused to ratify it. That meant the United States would not be part of this collective organization. Without the leadership and support of the very country that had advanced the idea, the League was like a table with one leg missing. Not strong enough to bear the weight of power struggles that arose in the unstable postwar world, the organization proved weak and useless.[42] The severity of the treaty, and the failure of the League of Nations, helped create social and political conditions in Europe that would set the stage for another war. Marshall would not forget the harsh effects this "peace" had on the defeated countries of World War I.

While the treaty negotiations continued in Paris, Marshall was busy with wrap-up duties that followed the armistice—training troops for occupation duty, lecturing to other officers and visiting dignitaries about the wartime challenges and accomplishments of the AEF. Marshall had emerged from the war as an impressive officer with a sterling reputation. General Pershing had recommended him as brigadier general the previous year, during Meuse-Argonne. The promotion didn't go through until after the armistice, though, and Congress froze the advancement list. Nevertheless, Pershing recognized his excellent service and, by April 1919, had asked him to be one of his postwar aides.

Until September 1919, Marshall would be with Pershing as he toured European capitals, basking in the admiration of victors who staged dozens of victory parades and demonstrations, including elaborate military extravaganzas in Paris and London. In the British capital, Marshall met the king and queen of England, the Prince of Wales, other "assorted princes and princesses," and Winston Churchill, who at that time was the British secretary of state for war. In his memoirs Marshall mentioned that after his group inspected the guard of honor, they were driven to their hotel—all accommodations compliments of the British government—in three of the royal carriages. Marshall soon realized that Pershing was a heroic figure to be honored and, tangentially, all who traveled with him. Sometimes the fame heaped upon Pershing could create challenges. Describing an occurrence during a ball that followed an elegant celebratory dinner at the House of Commons, Marshall noted that when Pershing appeared, a mob scene erupted. The "girls started for him to get his autograph," and the crowd became so unmanageable that Marshall and two other aides had to get him up on a platform so the throng could not. Although Marshall wrote to his wife that the tiaras on the royal women "were so massive that they did not much appeal to me as they looked like glass," it must have been a heady experience.[43] As Alan Saunders said in *George C. Marshall, General for Peace*, "Marshall was a dashing 38, a colonel in a triumphant army and at the right hand of its leader. What polish he might have lacked he quickly acquired. He was also to see how power worked at the highest circles. The men he met and the views they expressed would prove useful to him, for 20 years later he would face the same men or their successors either as enemies or allies."[44]

Home—Lily and a Victory Tour

By the fall of 1919, after a return to Paris and another spate of ceremonies in Italy, the glamour of these celebrations had begun to pale. Marshall's duties were no more demanding than separating the various medals that would be given to military and royal dignitaries along the way. He was ready to return to a more "normal" life; further, he longed to see Lily and home. On September 1, Pershing, his staff, and selected members of the First Division sailed from France aboard the *Leviathan,* arriving in New York City on the 8th. Lily was there to greet him. Once more there were celebrations, welcoming committees of city fathers, the governor of New York, selected national officials, even the vice president of the United States. In addition to an impressive ticker-tape parade, cheering multitudes, and elaborate banquets, however, as Forrest Pogue said, "New York had what every returning hero wanted most, wives and families—home." Pershing and his party, including the Marshalls, continued on to Philadelphia, where they were wined and dined, before traveling to Washington, D.C. Twenty-five thousand combat veterans, led by General Pershing, paraded down Pennsylvania Avenue to the White House, while thousands of cheering citizens provided a tumultuous welcome.

Victory parade to honor General Pershing, New York City
September 10, 1919
www.photographyblog.dallasnews.com2012

After a month with Lily, Marshall once more said good-bye as he began months of travel with Pershing aboard a special train. That fall they visited army camps in Georgia, Alabama, Kentucky, Ohio, and a half dozen other states. After Christmas, the journey resumed, with tours of Texas and the

Far West. The hurrahing crowds rushed the train in dozens of cities, anxious to catch a glimpse of Pershing. By June, the entourage was at West Point, where the famous American Expeditionary Forces commander gave the speech for the graduating class. At Marshall's urging, Pershing also visited VMI in Lexington, Virginia, although he created a bit of a controversy in the national press when he visited the grave of the *Confederate* general, Stonewall Jackson, in the town's cemetery.

Back in Washington, Marshall worked closely with Pershing as he prepared the final report of the First Army, AEF, to Congress. Marshall also wrote the wrap-up operational reports, including a section entitled "Military Lessons of the War." A key point: "The unprepared nation is helpless in a great war unless it can depend upon other nations to shield it while it prepares." In his view, this problem of unpreparedness had been brought home so clearly in that war. In one report, Marshall had written: "Everywhere on the battlefield individuals were paying the price of long years of national unpreparedness. They paid with their lives and their limbs for the bullheaded obstinacy with which our people had opposed any rational system of training in time of peace."[45]

This issue was front and center in the immediate postwar period. General Pershing vehemently opposed his predecessor General Peyton March's proposal for a large standing army of 500,000 as a counter to the inadequacies of the military during the opening months of World War I. With the country's traditional fears of large standing armies, Pershing believed Congress would never approve such a plan, especially in a time of postwar military budget tightening. Rather, the chief of staff, and Marshall, supported a plan advanced by Colonel John M. Palmer, also on Pershing's staff. Palmer proposed instead expanding the army to 300,000 to act as a "core and mentor" to the militias, and called for an 11-month universal training program that would ready them for expedient service in time of war. Those trained under the Universal Military Training (UMT) program would have a four-year reserve obligation. In the end, neither proposal won support. The army's size was reduced as Congress clamored for budget cuts, and training programs remained weak. Throughout his military career, Marshall would fight for and support programs that countered this minimalist approach to peacetime preparedness.

Even before they had arrived in the United States from Paris, Pershing had been informed that he had been given the permanent rank of general of the armies, along with four stars. Marshall knew he was lucky to be working with this great leader at the very pinnacle of his power, but he was still unhappy with his own status. His promotions to major, lieutenant colonel, and colonel during the war had been only temporary. Once the war was over, the size of the army was reduced, and fewer officers were needed. Yet, it seemed his impressive work as a staff officer would be rewarded, because on July 1, 1920, he was promoted to the *permanent* rank of major, *regular army*; by 1923 he would be a lieutenant colonel. Other advancements would have to wait.

In July 1921, General John J. Pershing was appointed by President Warren G. Harding as army chief of staff. During the next three years, as assistant to the army's top man, Marshall learned the ropes in all areas of general staff work. He sat in on meetings between Pershing and President Harding, wrote and sometimes gave speeches for the chief of staff, and prepared Pershing for testifying before Congress on military issues. Over time, Pershing trusted Marshall to take on more and more of his responsibilities, especially since he traveled frequently. When the chief of staff vacationed in France, once being away for six months, Major Marshall filled in for him. This often put him in contact with the highest-ranking members of Congress, cabinet-level officials, and important figures in the civilian world, including Wall Street financier Bernard Baruch. All of these associations would prepare him well for his duties when he became U.S. Army chief of staff during World War II. It helped him develop a keen understanding of the relationship between the military and civilian government at the highest levels—an understanding that would be essential to the challenges of war.

About Rose

One positive aspect of being in charge of Pershing's office was that it allowed the Marshalls to reside in Washington, a city still essentially Southern that Lily, with her Lexington, Virginia, roots, especially enjoyed. By late 1919, after Marshall came back from his U.S. victory tour with Pershing, he and Lily had settled down in a residential hotel at 2400 16th Street, near Pershing's office. The residents there were senators, high government officials, a few diplomats, professional men, and a fair number of colonels and generals. They all knew each other well, since almost all of them ate in the communal dining room, where each tenant family had its own special table. It was there that the Marshalls met Thomas and Celeste Page and the couple's three children. They would become very close to Rose, the Pages' youngest, and only eight years old when the Marshalls moved into the building. Lily's health had always been frail, which perhaps accounted for the fact that the couple remained childless. Nevertheless, they both loved interacting with the few young children who lived in the complex, and especially Rose, whom they treated like a daughter. It was a relationship that would last throughout the remainder of Lily and George Marshall's lives.

Much later, in 1968, Rose Page Wilson wrote *General Marshall Remembered*, recalling charming stories about her experiences with the Marshalls. She spoke of elaborate, carefully planned picnics in Washington's famous Rock Creek Park, walks on Sunday afternoon, horseback riding lessons, trips by car into the beautiful Virginia countryside, camping, sleepovers, even a trip into the Shenandoah Valley to pick up Lily from a visit with her mother. Rose loved Lily, describing her as delicately beautiful with thick auburn hair, and as feminine, gracious, and kind.

To the young girl, Marshall was a heroic figure, even more so than General Pershing, who came for a visit one evening. Rose Wilson later wrote that Marshall exhibited the same qualities in his private life that he did in his professional life—integrity, patience, tolerance, and understanding. She credited him with teaching her fairness, impartiality, and compassion. She also simply loved his company, finding him full of good humor, and attentive, in contrast to her own father, who loved her but was rather remote. Marshall played pranks on her, and, as she said, sometimes "lapsed into foolishness," even writing light and trivial poems for her amusement. Rose was a spirited child, sometimes full of mischief, and more than once Marshall took it upon himself to teach her a lesson.

One such lesson came when she was in the fourth grade and was selected as a member of a committee assigned to organize a "fruit shower" for the teacher as a gift. This was a tradition at the school—a beautiful basket was provided, and every child brought one perfect piece of fruit to fill it. One problem: Rose hated the teacher, Mrs. Swift. She talked the group into agreeing to literally shower Swift with the fruit. Pelting might be a better description. On the day of the "fruit shower," the principal heard the ruckus and entered the classroom just as Rose was poised to hurl an apple.[46] At the end of that disastrous week, report cards were handed out. Boldly marked on Rose's were two Fs, one in arithmetic, which she struggled with, and another in conduct. Also neatly folded in the envelope was a long "vituperative" letter from the teacher. After hours of weeping, and following harsh reprimands and threats of punishment from her parents, her mother delivered the biggest blow of all. Rose was to take her report card and show it to Major Marshall. When he opened the door, Rose's sobs began. Marshall took her onto his lap and tried to console her while she whimpered out her transgressions. As Marshall said, "Whew, you've really made an awful bust." After he'd heard the whole story, he told her that there was nothing more to be done about her past behavior, but from then on, she had to be scrupulous in her conduct at school: work ably, cut out even the smallest offenses, absolutely no tricks. Then he walked Rose to the door and with a hug told her, "Good-bye for a while, Rose. I shall have to deny myself the pleasure of speaking to you until you receive your next report card."[47]

Rose then went through what she described as the most miserable month of her young life. Lily was not bound by the "shut-out," but Marshall kept his word. Even in the elevator with Rose present, he talked only to her sister, who felt the need to tell him, "Rose is getting to be a positive genius in arithmetic." "I'm delighted to hear that, Celeste," Marshall responded, not once making eye contact with the wayward younger sister. How happy Rose was on the day she knocked on the Marshalls' door to show them a report card with an A in conduct, and a B in arithmetic. She was back in the major's good graces, and he would never mention it again.

There was still one more lesson to learn when she was 10, and that had to do with the hazards of gossip. One day Rose asked Colonel Marshall about a rumor she had heard. The story was that a young and flashy woman who lived in their apartment building was having a romance with a well-known married general who was a resident there as well. Marshall's reaction to her questions surprised her. As she said, "To my dismay, Colonel Marshall exploded, saying, 'Don't you ever repeat talk like that again!' He said he didn't know if the slander. . . was true, and neither did anybody else. He curbed his anger immediately and replied gently that perhaps he hadn't made it clear to me why he disapproved of gossip. It was wrong, he explained, because whether it's flattering or unkind, it has a numerator of personal opinion, a denominator of doubtful facts, and is multiplied by exaggeration. 'So, you see, Rosie, the answer is bound to be wrong.'"[48]

Rose's first sign of a coming change in her relationship with the Marshalls occurred when they moved to Quarters #3 at Fort Myer, across the Potomac River in Virginia. After all, General Pershing had become the U.S. Army chief of staff—he lived on the post at Quarters #1, the so-called "White House" of the army—and Marshall was still his aide. Lily fixed Rose a room in the charming small house, and the young girl visited for many fun-filled weekends; nevertheless, she missed the daily close contact with her favorite adults. An even harder adjustment came when Marshall informed Rose in the early summer of 1924 that he and Lily would be leaving for China. In her sadness, Rose would have been uninterested in the details of Marshall's motivations. The fact was that Pershing's term as chief of staff was ending; if Marshall wanted further advancement in his career, he needed and very much wanted duty with troops. The requested assignment was granted: he would report for duty in Tientsin, China, where he would be the acting commander of the 15th Infantry Regiment.

The Marshalls pictured at about the time they met Rose.

George C. Marshall Research Library

When Lily and George Marshall came to say good-bye to Rose, she was inconsolable, tears streaming down her face. Marshall told her, "I wish I could spare you this hard time, Rosie." After she gave and received many hugs and kisses, inevitably her beloved friends had to go. Trying her best to gather a bit of control, Rose called to them, "So long for now. I'll see you when I'm 16."[49]

75

Colonel Marshall poses with Rose Page the Sunday
before he and Lily left for China, June 1924.
From General Marshall Remembered – Rose Page Wilson

Chapter 5

Adventure, Loss, Renewal

Tientsin to Vancouver Barracks

1924–1938

Lieutenant Colonel Marshall was ready for his new assignment; nevertheless, his service with General Pershing had been enormously important in his growth as a professional soldier. Not only did Marshall deeply respect Pershing, he genuinely liked him, and the feeling was mutual. Marshall would later write to his former boss, "My five years with you will always remain the unique experience of my career. I knew I would treasure the recollection of that service, but not until I actually landed here [in China] . . . did I realize how much my long association with you was going to mean to me, and how deeply I will miss it."[1] Marshall had taken leave of General Pershing at a farewell luncheon the chief of staff had held in his honor at the Shoreham Hotel in Washington in early June 1924. By the 12th, Marshall, Lily, and her mother had arrived in New York to board the *St. Mihiel* for San Francisco and thence to the Orient.

It was an easy crossing, with stops in Panama and Hawaii. On Oahu, the Marshalls had a chance to visit military friends residing there and to take a long driving tour of the lush tropical island. Arriving in China on September 7, the party made its way to Tientsin, a river port city of nearly a million people 90 miles from Peking, and second only to Shanghai as China's greatest commercial metropolis. Marshall would take up his duties there as the executive officer of the 15th Infantry.

Since the mid-19th century, the Europeans had been in China, importing and exporting goods to meet market demands within and without that vast country. For the outsiders, Tientsin was of great interest not only because of its strength as a flourishing commercial area, but also because of its path along the international railway that connected Peking (Beijing) 90 miles away to Mukden in Manchuria 185 miles to the north. Despite the thriving business opportunities, foreign traders, entrepreneurs, and diplomats found that they had little protection from the violence generated by disputes among warlords and by anti-foreign sentiments. The Europeans demanded safe zones for their respective countries, where free-wheeling enterprises could flourish. The Chinese imperial government, in response to protocols imposed by the European powers at the end of the Boxer Rebellion, had

77

allowed outsiders "concessions," areas of influence and control that their own military forces could protect against the ever increasing political turbulence of China. These concessions were contained in a five-square-mile area within the city.

The Americans also had certain business interests in this region. Yet, since the United States had declared an "open door" policy in China that would supposedly recognize and respect the territorial integrity of the Chinese, it at first did not seek a concession. However, after Dr. Sun Yat-sen overthrew the imperial dynasty in 1912, but could not consolidate his power against the warlords, the United States saw the need to join Europeans on the edge of the protected concession zone of Tientsin, establishing its own "safety area" in a space vacated by the Germans during World War I. They scrupulously paid rent to the Chinese government for the privilege. It was here that the almost 1,000-man 15th Infantry was stationed, and the place where Marshall would take up troop duty. Like the nearby European forces, the goal of the Americans was to protect the interests of its citizens from the surrounding civil chaos, making sure none of the disturbances spilled over into the other concessions.[2]

Marshall had barely arrived when, as he told Pershing in a letter, he found himself "in the midst of a Chinese civil war." That September three warlord armies whose alliances had shifted were in battle around Peking. As was typical in these situations, when one army was defeated, it created a whole horde of armed stragglers, along with a rambunctious array of victors. In this case, more than 100,000 troops fit one or the other of these categories. Chinese troops were forbidden to enter the concessions, but the trick was to actually keep them out without getting involved in the fight. Regarding this complicated situation, Forrest Pogue noted, "While the deployments were military, the weapons . . . were psychological—bluff and persuasion." In this case, Marshall had ordered that five outposts be established outside the city where fleeing Chinese soldiers were offered cabbage and tea in exchange for their arms, or were talked into taking the long way around the city. Because of the work of the 15th during this alliance-shifting dust-up, no armed Chinese got loose in the city. The people of Tientsin were so grateful that they presented the Americans with a marble memorial gate, which remained with the regiment until 1938. Afterward, it was set up at Fort Benning, Georgia, in honor of the 15th.[3] Marshall handled these off-and-on battles among competing Chinese forces, especially as each tried to gain control of the crucial railroad, with what was later described as "unusual tact, patience, and foresight." A part of his ability to negotiate these turbulent waters was his ability to speak Chinese, which he taught himself within months of his arrival.

Despite these successes, the garrison was far from adequate to deal with the kind of shifting alliances that, as Pogue acknowledged, "revealed the absence of a nation but did nothing to create one." Throughout Marshall's three years in China, there were "repeated alarms and excursions, repeated anti-foreign demonstrations, and student strikes."[4] By 1926, the commanding general at Tientsin asked either for additional forces or that the garrison be withdrawn. Neither happened. The regiment remained exposed in the city and continued to try to defend it with a totally inadequate force.

Despite the potential for trouble outside the protected areas of the city—as Marshall said, "Out here we blow hot and cold with little pause between currents"—often his duty was light and pleasant. In a letter to Pershing, he wrote, "I am relearning much about the practical side of handling men." His task was to keep the men out of the clutches of "cheap liquor and cheaper women," in part by keeping them occupied in athletic and recreational facilities on the mission's compound or beyond.[5] About 175 miles north of the city, the regiment had built a firing range camp where the soldiers went periodically for training. Marshall made sure the purpose of the camp was expanded to include the opportunity for families to come for camping, swimming, and sightseeing. In the winter season, Marshall managed to get an ice rink built at the compound, complete with electric lights and warm dressing rooms. These low-key efforts seemed inconsequential when compared to what he had done in World War I, or contrasted with the continuing "swirling chaos" of China, but he relished it. After all, it was duty with troops, and that was always his preference.

In Tientsen, Marshall enjoyed more time for exercise and socializing than he had in years. He trained a Mongolian pony, which he rode for more than an hour each morning, and played tennis as weather permitted almost nightly. In one letter home he described the compound's newly built country club with its impressive facilities—ballroom, pavilions, swimming pool, permanent orchestra, large dining room—and commented that "the charges [for services] were ridiculously small."[6] Marshall also had more time than ever to be with Lily, whose health remained stable throughout the tour of duty. Their social life couldn't have been more pleasant, as Marshall described it: "frequent teas and dinner dances, skating parties, riding breakfasts, numerous home parties, amateur theatricals—there is something to do every day if one is so disposed."[7] The couple had very desirable quarters in the American enclave, with servants to care for their every need. Lily had her

79

mother with her, so they shopped for the treasures of the Orient: Chinese rugs, lacquered furnishings, brocades, and other items that could not be acquired at such low prices stateside.

Marshall on one of the Mongolian ponies during his time in Tientsin
George C. Marshall Research Library

As the months of Marshall's service began to wind down, he still found it difficult to define the political and military situation in China. In August 1926 he had explained to Pershing in a letter, "Conditions in China are too confused to admit of a reasonably accurate estimate as to what it is all about. Fighting is continuous." Late that December his assessment was not very encouraging either:

How the Powers should deal with China is a question almost impossible to answer. There has been so much of wrong doing on both sides, so much of shady transaction between a single power and a single party; there is so much of bitter hatred in the hearts of these people and so much of important business interests involved, that a normal solution can never be found. It will be some form of an evolution, and we can only hope that sufficient tact and wisdom will be displayed by foreigners to avoid violent phases during the trying period that is approaching.[8]

Marshall would soon leave these concerns behind, not to take them up again until 22 years later, when the outcome of these complex struggles would be his to broker.

Even before the Marshalls returned to the United States, he knew what his new assignment would be. As he confided to a colleague in a letter: "Administrative desk jobs have always been my pet abominations, but with so few regiments and so many lieutenant colonels, one has little choice." Despite these limited options, Marshall had been asked to lecture at the War College in Washington, D.C. While it was still desk duty of sorts, he was honored, since he himself had not gone to this institution, founded in 1903 to train officers and develop war plans.

Lily, at the railroad station in Tientsin, fall 1926

George C. Marshall Research Library

Back in the United States, the Marshalls began a leisurely trip from San Francisco to Lexington, Virginia, to Lily's mother's home. As they traveled, it was clear to Marshall that Lily was not well. Always frail with a serious heart condition, she had begun a rather alarming decline. Plenty of rest at her mother's home did little to help. In late July, they moved into an apartment in Washington that a colleague had lent them so they could more slowly organize their airy new brick house on the grounds at Washington Barracks. Marshall tried to prepare for his lectures, but found it difficult as Lily's health deteriorated. She was finally admitted to the army's Walter Reed Hospital for tests. Doctors determined that Lily had an enlarged thyroid—a goiter—that was aggravating the heart problem, and required surgery. Since she was too weak to sustain the anesthesia and rigors of the procedure at that time, Marshall was told to take Lily home so she could get strong enough to handle the operation. Although not fully unpacked, by now their belongings had been moved into these white-columned quarters. Lily improved, gaining nine pounds over several weeks, although with the goiter pressing against her windpipe, she found it hard to breathe. Finally, by August 21, the surgeon agreed that she could have the operation, and Marshall drove her back to Walter Reed. The surgery the next day was long and very serious, since the goiter had grown deep within her chest. Rather than a 20-minute procedure, it took two hours. She began what was an anticipated long convalescence. Marshall, who by then was lecturing at the War College, spent every spare minute by her side, watching her progress. He saw her go from a state of near coma—she had been under morphine for five days and nights afterward—to that of a recovering patient looking forward to arranging furnishings in a beautiful new home.

The news came a little after nine in the morning on September 15, 1927, as Marshall lectured at the War College. A guard who came to summon him to a telephone call later recounted that when Colonel Marshall answered, he talked for a minute and then put his head on his desk in deep grief. The guard asked if there was anything he could do. "No," Marshall said, "I just had word [that] my wife has just died." All had seemed so hopeful. The doctor had told Lily she could go home the next day. That morning she had taken out writing paper to tell her mother the good news. When a nurse entered the room a bit later, she found Lily slumped over the letter, with a pen in her hand.[9]

Lily's death plunged Marshall into a deep, soul-aching, and painful time. As Marshall biographer William Frye noted, "Her death was a shattering blow. To an extraordinary degree, his wife had satisfied every need of his mind and spirit, and absorbed every interest he had outside his profession and shared his burden in that. Now, suddenly and brutally, he was alone and adrift."[10] Marshall soon resumed his duties as lecturer, but in the evenings he wandered numbly about the house, the house that Lily had planned to decorate with their Chinese treasures.

Marshall immediately received a telegram of condolence from his friend and mentor General Pershing, who perhaps was able to provide him some comfort because of a unique and profoundly tragic event that he had experienced. In the early morning hours of August 27, 1915, Pershing had lost his wife and three daughters in a fire that swept his quarters at the Presidio in San Francisco. Only his son had survived. As Pershing said in his letter to Marshall on October 6, "No one knows better than I what such bereavement means, and my heart goes out to you very fully at this crisis in your life. It is at such moments that we realize that our reliance must be placed in the Father who rules over us all." Marshall acknowledged this in a reply to Pershing on the 14th: "The truth is the thought of all you had endured gave me heart and hope. But twenty six years of most intimate companionship . . . leaves me lost in my best efforts to adjust myself to future prospects in life. . . . However, I will find a way."[11]

That way out would be hard work, but not at the War College. In his state of grief, the scope of his duties in Washington was not great enough to absorb his energy. As he would say later, "At the War College desk, I thought I would explode." The answer came from Fort Benning, Georgia. The assistant commandant there was completing a tour at the prestigious Infantry School. Army Chief of Staff Charles Summerall, with whom Marshall had served at the end of the war, gave him options: would he like to take that position, go to Governors Island as chief of staff of that corps area, or stay at the War College? Marshall's choice was clear: "I thought it best professionally and in my present frame of mind to go to Benning."[12] The orders came in October, and by November 1927 he was at his post, situated not far from Columbus, Georgia.

Marshall came to Benning as the assistant commandant. However, in effect, he was in charge of the school, since the title of commandant belonged to the commanding general of the post. The Infantry School, with 300–500 students and a staff of 60–80 instructors, was designed for training company-level infantry officers in small-unit tactics. It also offered refresher courses for senior officers of the Reserves and the National Guard. Marshall had very strong opinions about training in all of these areas; in fact, this job tapped an ongoing and deep professional interest. Further, it required a level of energy that might distract him from his grief. General Marshall later recalled, "The change to Benning was magical . . . caught me at my most restless moment and gave me hundreds of interests, an unlimited field of activity, delightful associates, and all outdoors to play in."[13]

As the head of the Academic Department at Benning, Marshall set about putting in place the changes he thought were needed to prepare officers for leadership. According to Forrest Pogue, "It was a happy circumstance that at his 'most restless moment' he was given a teaching job . . . with . . . the authority and scope to make a mark not only on the Infantry School but on the United States Army." Fresh in his memory were the tough lessons of World War I. Marshall thought that training methods for infantry officers at Fort Benning had been based on the American experience in that war, and it had not given them a true understanding of modern warfare. After all, the United States had entered late and had participated in "a very special form of fighting, one of static or siege warfare." In one lecture Marshall noted, in describing the enemy in World War I: "We had photographs of his principal emplacements. We usually knew his strength, the location of most of his cannon and machine guns . . . the history of his organizations as [they] confronted us." Marshall went on to say that "green" troops had a chance of saving themselves from the full penalty of their errors because of this experiential knowledge. In contrast, in the *opening* of a war, there is no such static circumstance, no well-mapped trenches or elaborate telephone networks, as the First Division had found when it first arrived in France in 1917.

Marshall provided a vivid description of the scene: "Picture the opening campaign of a war. It is a cloud of uncertainties, haste, rapid movements, congestion on the roads, strange terrain, lack of ammunition and supplies at the right place and the right moment, failures of communications, terrific tests of endurance." He continued: "Add to this a minimum of preliminary information of the enemy . . . poor maps, and a speed of movement . . . resulting from fast flying planes, fast moving tanks, armored cars, and motor transportation in general." Making his final point, he warned, "There you have warfare of movement such as swept over Belgium or Northern France in 1914, but at far greater speed. That, gentlemen, is what you are supposed to be preparing for."[14]

Marshall updated the methods of military tactics at the Infantry School, concentrating on three main ideas. First, orders and plans given to officers had to be kept simple: "brief, concise, oral orders, based on the ground you can see or on maps with very little detail." In fact, Marshall emphasized,

"We must develop . . . methods so simple . . . that the citizen officer of good common sense can readily grasp the idea." Second, officers had to be offered the freedom to innovate and deal with the unexpected in combat situations. Speed of thought and speed of action would be crucial in battle, requiring a kind of free-wheeling flexibility. At Benning, he banned written lectures, insisting that the trainees be placed in field situations and given "hands-on experience," forcing them to do quick and original thinking. When he set up maneuvers for his students, he often excluded maps, or gave them maps with missing sections, to encourage problem-solving. He pointed out, "The art of war has no traffic with rules, for the . . . circumstances and conditions of combat never produce the same situation twice." Finally, he understood and emphasized that the next war would be one of movement, in which the fields of battle would be greatly enlarged by modern war machinery, especially airplanes, tanks, and trucks. Marshall taught his officers that the best army would be a highly mobile army. He believed this approach was especially suited to the American character and a citizen-soldier army.[15]

The traditional army methods of fighting a war were being changed, and some of the regular staff and student officers at first had difficulty in making the adjustment. Marshall's leadership skills helped the instructors understand and accept the changes, so they could gradually work them into their teaching routines. "We bored from within," Marshall would later say. He wanted the instructors to use the new methods because they considered them better, rather than simply following his orders. Marshall's leadership techniques and his efforts to upgrade the efficiency of the instruction given to army officers became known as the "Benning Revolution." Marshall biographer Ed Cray wrote: "In just short of five years, Marshall managed to thoroughly revamp both the instructional style and the technical concepts taught the 150 lieutenants and captains in each year's class."[16] More than 200 of "Marshall's Men," as they called themselves, served as generals in World War II, 150 of whom had been students, and 50 of whom had been instructors.[17] Some became famous, including Omar Bradley, an important general in both World War II and the Korean Conflict, and Joseph Stilwell, who would command the China Theater during the war.

While the work of the Benning Revolution kept Marshall busy, he was still a man in deep bereavement. As he had told Rose Page shortly after Lily's death, in a moment of unmasked sadness, "Rosie, I'm so lonely, *so lonely*." His health had suffered in the wake of the loss. He had lost weight, which made his already lean face border on gaunt. A thyroid problem that caused an irregular pulse had flared. A post doctor and friend, Lieutenant Colonel

General Marshall and instructors, Fort Benning, Georgia, 1930-31. Joseph Stilwell is seated to the left of Marshall on the front row; Omar Bradley is second from the left on the back row.

George C. Marshall Research Library

Morrison Stayer, ordered Marshall to give up cigarettes and scotch, and recommended more exercise, which he had always enjoyed. That helped, but still didn't fill the ache that was so very apparent. When Marie Singer, Marshall's sister, came for long visits to help him set up his house and to provide company from time to time, it bothered her that her brother had every room filled with photographs of Lily, so that he never for a moment forgot his grief. One by one, other links to his past were broken: less than a year after Lily's passing, in 1927, his mother died, and the year after that, Lily's mother.

Never one to succumb to depression, Marshall's answer was to keep almost frenetically busy, playing tennis, swimming, hunting, riding horseback, even cross-country "treasure" hunts and amateur theatricals. He said yes to an endless round of social invitations, and hosted dinner parties, sometimes for young officers, at his home. In the summer of 1928, less than a year after Lily's death, Rose Page had visited Marshall at Fort Benning, taking the train from Washington, D.C. Marshall was delighted to see her, and with the help of his sister, Marie, pulled out all the stops, entertaining her in every way possible for the two weeks she was there. Rose sensed Marshall's loneliness, despite his enthusiastic cheerful demeanor. She recounted that near the end of the trip she worked up the nerve to tell him, "Colonel Marshall, I've been thinking. You should have a wife, you really should, and the best thing for you to do is keep your eyes open and find yourself a nice lady." Rose said he smiled and patted her hand, but made no reply.[18] It would be a while before a "nice lady" would come along.

Katherine Tupper Brown

Indeed, a dinner invitation from friends in the summer of 1929 brought a new and different kind of woman into Marshall's life. It so happened that Katherine Brown, a Baltimore widow who was visiting in nearby Columbus, was also invited for this occasion, along with her daughter, Molly. Katherine had demurred, explaining that she was "not going out," but agreed to come when her former college mate said it would be a very small gathering, just her husband, herself, and "a very interesting officer from Fort Benning." When she arrived at her friend's house, Marshall was already there, standing in the living room by the fireplace. In her book, *Together,* Katherine Marshall wrote, "My first impression was of a tall, slender man with sandy hair and deep-set eyes. He refused the cocktails when they were served and this attracted my interest." It was, after all, still during the time of Prohibition. She said to him, "You are a rather unusual army officer. I've never known one to refuse a cocktail before." Marshall asked her how many army officers she knew, and she replied, "Not many." In describing him later, she said, "I will never forget. George had a way of looking right through you. He had such keen blue eyes and he was straight and very military."

When it was time to leave the dinner party, Colonel Marshall asked if he might drive her to the home of Mrs. Blanchard, where she was staying. Since her daughter had left earlier in the evening, Katherine agreed. They drove around and around the streets of Columbus for about an hour. Finally, Katherine Brown asked the colonel how long he had been at Fort Benning, and he told her two years. "After two years," she said, "haven't you learned your way around Columbus?" Marshall replied, "Extremely well, or I could not have stayed off the block where Mrs. Blanchard lives."[19] The next day, Marshall invited her to a huge reception on post, where because he totally monopolized her time, she met few of the other guests. Marshall's friends let him know about it, since it was apparent that the assistant commandant had brought a pretty lady to the event, and they couldn't have been more curious! Katherine soon returned to Baltimore, and thus began a courtship that continued with letter writing; escalated when she agreed to a return visit

Katherine Tupper Brown with her children: Allen, Molly, and Clifton, 1922
George C. Marshall Research Library

to Columbus, during which time Marshall cleared his evenings to spend every free moment with her; and was sealed during a five-week vacation for Marshall at Katherine's Fire Island, New York, summer cottage in the summer of 1930. During that long visit, he won the enthusiastic support of his future bride's children, especially the youngest, Allen, who at that time was in his mid-teens.

At 47, Katherine was attractive, stylishly dressed, poised, and gracious. She was born in Harrodsburg, Kentucky, in 1882 to Henry Allen Tupper, a Baptist minister—like his father before him—and Marie Louise Pender, who had been born in North Carolina but after her parents' death was reared in Virginia by a relative—also a Baptist minister. Given this background, it must have been surprising to her parents that after she graduated from Hollins College (a women's school for higher education near Roanoke, Virginia), Katherine wanted to study the theater. Even more surprising, her parents supported her, allowing her to attend the Academy of Dramatic Arts in New York City for two years. As an extension of her interest, Katherine received permission to study the theater in England. She and her sister, Allene, arrived in London in 1904 and took up residence in a boarding house, with expenses covered by their father. However, Katherine had firmly decided that she must act in public theater productions rather than simply study it as an entertainment discipline. She signed on with a highly respected Shakespearean company headed by Sir Frank Benson. After lessons in diction to rid her of a soft Southern accent, she began to get small but respectable speaking roles in a series of plays.

As professional acting was not thought to be a reputable profession for a refined young woman, Henry Tupper refused further support. Nevertheless, since Allene still received financial help from their father, the two sisters lived modestly, and traveled with the company for almost three seasons. Katherine eventually garnered bigger roles in five Shakespearean plays, including *Romeo and Juliet* and *As You Like It*. In her third season, though, she became ill, perhaps in part because of exhaustion brought on by a grueling travel and performance schedule, and came back to the United States for treatment. Having secured a release from her contract with Benson in England, she tried acting again, this time in Chicago, but soon the painful illness returned. While resting and recuperating at a resort in the Adirondack Mountains, she became reacquainted with a friend from Baltimore, Clifton Stevenson Brown, a Baltimore attorney, and soon they fell in love.

Although Katherine struggled with the decision to give up a promising stage career, a choice that she must confront if she planned to make a conventional marriage, she was wed in 1911. From that point on, her life seemed to proceed happily as she managed a beautiful home and bore three children, Molly, Clifton, and Allen. She soon embraced the rich social life typical of wives married to prominent lawyers. That all ended in 1928. One June morning she called her husband's office to say that a real estate agent had closed the deal on a summer property the couple had purchased on Fire Island, in New York. When no one answered the phone in this bustling law office, she was puzzled. Soon two policemen arrived at her door to deliver stunning news: her husband had been shot and killed in the hallway of his office building by a deranged client. Dazed from shock, Katherine went to live with her sister in Connecticut for eight months, traveled to Hawaii with her daughter for a two-month stay in Waikiki, and had stopped in Columbus, Georgia, on her way home to visit the family of her college roommate, Etta Blanchard.[20] It had been this set of circumstances that more than a year after her husband's death brought Katherine to that dinner party, and changed the course of her life forever.

On October 15, 1930, Marshall and Katherine Tupper Brown exchanged wedding vows at Emmanuel Episcopal Church in Baltimore, Maryland. They had planned a small wedding with just family and close friends. But when word got out that General John J. Pershing would be Marshall's best man, a crowd formed outside the church to greet the famous general, along with the wedding party. The Marshalls left the ceremony and, following a brief reception, went directly to the train, where an even larger crowd had gathered. So much for a quiet wedding. By the next afternoon, the newlyweds were back at Fort Benning, where Katherine barely had time to change her clothes before they were to attend the "commandant's reception," organized specifically to honor the bride. Being a former stage actress who was constantly before the public, Katherine was a "quick study" for her role as an officer's wife. The newlyweds would join the commandant in the receiving line, where Katherine would be introduced to Marshall's colleagues from his stint in China and young officers who were taking classes on the post, along with Infantry School instructors—all with their wives. She remembered well this first in a series of many such protocol events that would become a staple of her future. She described it as a beautiful stage setting, recalling a warm Georgia evening, an illuminated dance floor, orchestra music, fragrant flowers, the officers "spick and span" in their dress uniforms. Katherine did her best to be gracious and charming, but as she noted wryly, "I believe I did well for the first five hundred [guests] or so, but after that the smile began to freeze on my face."[21]

Katherine Tupper Marshall, 1939

George C. Marshall Research Library

Colonel Marshall had a new role as well—that of stepfather. He fit into this new position comfortably and easily. Though he did not adopt them, Molly, Clifton, and Allen became the family he'd never been able to have in his first marriage. Molly and Clifton called him "The Colonel." Allen, the youngest and closest to Marshall, liked to say he was one of the few people, along with his mother, ever to call him "George."

Marshall's last two years at Fort Benning could hardly have been more contented or productive. At a personal level, having healed from the deep grief of Lily's death, he had met the new love of his life and remarried. His "Benning Revolution" had only added to his already sterling reputation. Under regulations, in 1931 his tour as assistant commandant was to have ended. But he had been so successful in strengthening the school's programs that the War Department arranged to attach him to the 24th Infantry, which was part of the garrison on the post, and effectively gave him another year as assistant commandant.[22] Nevertheless, by the spring of 1932 it was time for him to get a new assignment, and it would be one he would relish. Marshall would command a battalion of the Eighth Infantry at Fort Screven, Georgia, a short distance from Savannah.

The military post had fewer than 400 men, but Marshall wrote to General Pershing that even if the post was small, it kept him "out of doing just office work." Katherine Marshall had described the new post as "rather dilapidated after Benning," but Marshall set about to improve not only the camp, but the morale of the men as well. In the beginning, he had found the post in a state of confusion, since the officers there were getting several hundred new inductees settled. Taking his time, though, he tackled perceived problems in a low-key manner that proved nonthreatening to junior officers who knew his Benning reputation for no-nonsense hard work. Before long, under his careful inspections, the post was spotless, with barracks repaired, lawns weeded. He even personally oversaw the layout of gardens and chicken yards that the enlisted men could use to save on food costs. Marshall applied crisp discipline to training and inspections, but to compensate he also renovated the post gymnasium and had constructed a recreation area complete with barbecue pits, pavilions, and a life-guarded "swimming hole" achieved by damming a small creek.

With Marshall's prewar National Guard experiences, and the importance he attached to the training of citizen soldiers, he understood the need to strengthen ties between the military and civilian societies at every place he went. In this case the city of Savannah was only 17 miles from the fort. The Marshalls' friends at Fort Benning had told them that people in Savannah wanted little involvement with the army post. Undaunted, the first Sunday after arriving, they visited the Episcopal church in that old southern city. During the year the Marshalls were at Screven, they made friends with Savannah's mayor and many members of the business and professional community. Marshall made a point of inviting all of these "dignitaries" to Screven for special inspections and reviews, including a patriotic July 4th parade, which had the added effect of giving the immaculately uniformed troops a sense of pride. Marshall was so respected and well liked that when he left that post in June 1933, a large civic dinner was held in his honor, and he was presented with a ceremonial engraved military baton inscribed with the words: "To the Marshal of Savannah."[23]

By July 1933, Marshall was transferred to Fort Moultrie, South Carolina, not far from Charleston, where he would command the entire Eighth Infantry Regiment. With the transfer came word of a promotion to the permanent rank of colonel, although it wouldn't become official until that September. When the Marshalls arrived at Moultrie, the United States was already in the throes of the Great Depression. Unemployment was as high as 25 percent. Crop failures forced farmers into bankruptcy and pushed many of them to the cities in search of work. Breadlines stretched for blocks in major cities, and people were desperate. The troops stationed at Fort Moultrie were better off than many civilians, but they suffered as well when Congress cut back on funds for the armed services. Though the cuts affected military officers—second lieutenants, for example, saw their pay lowered to one-fifth what it would have been 25 years previously—the lower ranks were hardest hit. A private's pay was reduced by as much as 44 percent, sergeants by 25 percent, and both groups got fewer "perks" associated with housing and medical costs.[24] Knowing that the men were having a hard time feeding their families, Marshall introduced a unique "lunch pail" system. The mess officer was ordered to prepare larger portions of the midday meal, and was allowed to sell at cost the extra hot meals for the men to take home in their lunch pails for their wives and children. A soldier was able to feed his entire family for 15 cents a day. "We ate this midday dinner ourselves until the custom was well-established, so that we might know what the men were getting," recalled Katherine Marshall. She noticed that Marshall put as much thought into the welfare of his men as he did their military training.

When Franklin D. Roosevelt became president in March 1933, he resolved to do something about the depression that gripped the nation, promising a "new deal" for the American people. By the time Marshall got to Fort Moultrie, one aspect of this "new deal," the creation of the Civilian Conservation Corps, had already come to bear quite specifically on his work. Only weeks after his inauguration, Roosevelt had sent a proposal to Congress asking for the creation of this organization, which in its overall design would serve to get unemployed males into productive service, thus reducing the possibility that such idle and desperate young men could create serious unrest in the population. The specific mission of the CCC was twofold: it would give jobs and training to young, unmarried, physically healthy, out-of-work men who were 18 to 25 years old. Along with room, board, and medical care, each young man would earn $30 a month but would send $22 of those earnings home to dependent members of his immediate family. Its second mission: providing for the restoration of the country's depleted natural resources and infastructure.[25] Examples of these restoration projects included the planting of 200 million trees in a vast soil conservation effort; cleaning streams and cutting firebreaks; building bridges, visitor centers, campgrounds, and trails in national parks, and more than 97,000 miles of roads. The program, which was in place only 37 days after Roosevelt's inauguration, was run by civilian departments—Labor, Agriculture, and Interior—but would be overseen by the U.S. Army. That July of 1933 the army had created 1,468 work camps of about 200 men each across the nation, and had settled 275,000 young men into them. That's where Marshall came in.[26]

Even while he was still at Screven, Marshall had begun his work with the "Cs." At the end of May 1933 he commanded two companies of 406 men. By the time he left, he had supervised the creation of 10 camps housing 1,879 young men, and, as he wrote to his replacement for that duty with some pride, "All this [has been] running on a little post headquarters without the addition of a single extra army clerk from outside." To another colleague he explained the impact of this new duty: "Here I am busy with several thousand Forestry boys. . . . Between satisfying the Auditor for the War Department and meeting the pressure to proceed at top speed, it has been an interesting and illuminating experience."[27]

When Marshall arrived in Moultrie he commanded even more CCC inductees, eventually overseeing the building of 19 camps, spread throughout Florida, southeastern Georgia, and South Carolina. The goal was to house, feed, clothe, and provide work for these rough-hewn arrivals. According to one of his assistants at Screven, Marshall "ate, breathed, and digested the many CCC problems." He enthusiastically supported the CCC concept, believing that these young civilian men needed discipline, education, health, and career guidance. Marshall regularly visited and inspected the camps under his control, making sure they were clean and orderly. From one visit to the next, he was pleased to see the changes and improvements made in the young men. "From the first," Katherine Marshall said, "he was fascinated with the opportunities the CCC afforded to build up the minds and bodies of the youth of this country and also to lessen the hardship of the Depression."

Marshall's work with the CCCs was straightforward and practical. Leonard Mosely, in *Marshall, Hero of Our Times,* wrote: "He brought in dentists and cleaned up the appalling condition of their teeth. He gave them food and taught them to eat it for the best physical results. He gave the illiterate lessons in reading and writing. He had the boys build a seawall in South Carolina and then showed them how to fish from it. . . . He went down to South Florida, where the great beach hotels were lying empty, and parlayed the managers into renting him rooms for next to nothing, then moved in his boys for courses in sailing and swimming."[28]

Marshall was very proud of the camps that he commanded, and he found

A typical CCC camp, this one on the West Coast, in the 1930s.

U.S. National Archives

opportunities to show them off. Katherine recalled one example when her husband "made a diplomatic agency of the CCC." A French cruiser was on a goodwill tour and had put in at Charleston harbor. Marshall invited the skipper and crew to a dinner, reception, and dance at Fort Moultrie. The skipper reciprocated, inviting the garrison to a dinner and dance aboard the ship. Marshall mentioned to him that a new CCC camp was opening up nearby, and it just so happened that it was at the spot where the Marquis de Lafayette had made his first landing in America. To the Frenchman's delight, Marshall said he wanted to name the newly developed site *Camp Lafayette* in honor of the man who had lent his support to our Revolutionary cause, and he invited the captain to raise the flag, with his crew present.

The captain was most honored, and asked the French consul to come down from Philadelphia, which he did. "Much saluting and ceremony accompanied the raising of the French flag by the Consul and the American flag by the Captain," Katherine remembered. "All of the surrounding CCC camps had been given a holiday, so as far as you could see lines of young American boys and French sailors stood at attention. It was a thrilling site." The French ship, decorated from stem to stern and well lit, lay anchored in the waters, providing a sharp contrast to the modest and rustic camp that had just been dedicated. After a picnic of standard CCC fare for the members of the crew and the camps, Marshall talked to the captain long into the night, explaining the value of this CCC program for these young men so deeply affected by the nation's economic downturn. But as Katherine would later write, "There was no depression at Camp Lafayette that day; for one afternoon at least we were all joyously happy."[29]

That fall of 1933 Marshall had settled into his role as regimental commander at Fort Moultrie and expected to stay there for two years. Katherine was busy fixing up their quarters, including purchasing 325 yards of curtaining for the 43 French doors on two floors that opened onto a sea-view veranda. As it turned out, it was the very week when all of these curtains were being hung that word came: U.S. Army Chief of Staff Douglas MacArthur recommended that Marshall be transferred to Chicago.[30] He would be assigned as the chief of staff (senior instructor) for the 33rd Division of the Illinois National Guard, a 10,000-man operation. This was a blow. It meant that once again Marshall was to be removed from troop command. Detached service with the National Guard was considered a professional backwater—a dumping ground—for career officers who were seen as ineffective. Besides his disappointment that he would not complete the work he had enthusiastically begun at Screven, this staff assignment with "once a week" warriors was, in his view, a roadblock to further promotion. Marshall was so upset with the change that he wrote to MacArthur asking that he be allowed to remain with his regiment. It did no good.

Perhaps, in fact, the Illinois National Guard did need a reputable officer who, as MacArthur put it, "had no superior among Infantry colonels." The 33rd's commander, Major General Roy Keehn, a man with considerable influence in Washington, was being criticized in Chicago for leading a National Guard division incapable of coping with threatened disturbances in that area. After all, Americans were in the deepest depression of their history. In this Midwestern industrial region, half of the wage earners were unemployed. Violent labor unrest, strikes, and massive hunger marches were anticipated for the coming winter. In Keehn's view, the 33rd needed a robust training program, and that required an officer of proven substance.[31] "[Marshall] appreciated the War Department's view that the Chicago post was important because of the danger of riots that the National Guard might have to deal with," Forrest Pogue noted. "Nevertheless, he was not reconciled to going." That November the Marshalls arrived in the gritty, wintry city, moving into an apartment near his office on the North Side of the Loop.[32] Katherine later recalled, "Those first months in Chicago I shall never forget. George had a gray drawn look which I had never seen before and have seldom seen since."

Though Marshall was depressed at first with his new assignment, by Christmastime he had regained his spirit. His task was to supervise approximately 35 regular army officers and noncommissioned officers who were the 33rd's instructors, as well as to take over the planning and oversight of training programs. It didn't take long for Marshall to see changes in the division. Since he set a standard both by order and example, the men soon understood that military correctness and discipline would prevail. Forrest Pogue described well the "usual flurry of alarm at the arrival of the new colonel. [He] was meticulously turned out in well-tailored uniform and shiny boots, a lean, tall, straight figure whose cold blue and seldom smiling eyes could make a man feel singularly silly and superfluous—a self-possessed officer who asked hard questions in his soft voice. The colonel was a taskmaster who in drill demanded smartness, promptness, and precision." Further, noted Pogue, Marshall's toughness derived not from a power trip, but from a firm belief that the men wanted to belong "to a highly disciplined, hard-working businesslike organization" about which they could feel proud. "The stricter the better," Marshall had said, "within the prescribed hours." By the following summer the federal inspectors found every unit of the division at least satisfactory. It was the first time in years that they all had passed muster.[33]

Over time, Marshall settled in comfortably to his life with the guard. By his third year, he and Katherine, who felt confined by city living, moved to a pleasant cottage 40 miles from Chicago, where they could breathe country air, and he could ride. He had some time with his stepchildren: Clifton was in the real estate business in the area and came often; Molly, who had studied abroad during the second winter, now lived with them at home; Allen, a student at the University of Virginia, visited during summer vacation.

From a professional perspective, Marshall was focusing his training programs toward huge Second Army maneuvers scheduled for August 1936. The 33rd would participate as a part of a 26,000-member team in an exercise that would last two weeks. Afterward, Marshall felt that his reserve officers "did a beautiful job," but the maneuvers confirmed the impracticality of current techniques and theories used for training. He couldn't believe the deluge of detailed orders and reports that were foisted on these units, taking up incredible amounts of time and slowing down the "war games." Marshall said he had "never learned more in my life in a similar period of time" about the need for teaching methods that translated to a field of battle, whether simulated or real.[34]

Throughout his time in Chicago, Marshall had a nagging worry in the back of his mind: timely promotion to the rank of one-star general. For some time he had hoped that one day he would be appointed as the army chief of staff, the highest position possible for an army officer. To achieve this goal, he had to be at least a two-star general. Not only that, but the unwritten rule was that the officer appointed army chief of staff had to be young enough to serve in that post for four years before reaching the mandatory retirement age of 64. Now in his mid-50s, Marshall needed to jump-start his stalled career if he was to have a chance. As he told his mentor and friend General Pershing in a letter, "I have possessed myself with patience, but I'm fast getting too old to have any future of importance in the Army." Marshall took the unusual step of asking Pershing to write a letter to the secretary of war, simply encouraging this cabinet-level official to read his (Marshall's) efficiency reports, going back to 1915. He believed he could stand on his record—that the reports would reveal an officer worthy of promotion. It is clear that Pershing did as Marshall requested, but he also spoke to President Roosevelt, who wrote the secretary of war in a brief note sometime in May 1935: "General Pershing asks very strongly that Colonel George C. Marshall (Infantry) be promoted to general. Can you put him on the list of next promotions?"[35] Despite the convolutions of seniority, and a shifting of major military roles among General MacArthur and others, Marshall finally received word on October 1, 1936 that he was to be a brigadier general. Virtually every professional colleague writing to congratulate him made note in some way or another that this rank was long overdue. As biographer William Frye wrote, "After almost thirty years, the star had come out of his pocket to rest on his shoulder."[36]

With the new rank came a transfer. The Marshalls would be moving to Vancouver Barracks, Washington, a post just north of Portland, Oregon. Here he would command the Fifth Infantry Brigade of the Third Division and, much to his pleasure, supervise CCC camps in the district that covered Oregon and part of Washington. The Marshalls could hardly have been happier. He surprised Katherine by trading in their beat-up old Ford for a shiny new 1936 Packard, and with Molly they enjoyed a slow, three-week sightseeing trip across the country. As they took in the tourist sites along the way, Marshall seemed almost euphoric. Katherine would later say of the trip that her husband was their travel guide, since "he knew Indian Wars and frontier history by heart." All was well: he would be commanding troops; he was back on the right path for his career; he would be working with the CCCs, which he found very satisfying duty. Even his dog, Pontiac, could not curb his enthusiasm. Before reaching Vancouver Barracks, General Marshall telegraphed ahead saying he wanted to enter the post quietly, with no ceremonies. That was not to be, however, because when they arrived at the gate on October 27, 1936, a guard of honor and a band were waiting for them. Pontiac was there, too—an orderly held him on a leash during the review of troops. However, when his master got out of the car, Pontiac began yelping and straining against the leash. It soon broke, and he came bounding. He was so excited he ran all around the line of officers who were waiting to greet the new general, and completely broke up the formality of the review. Marshall kept his military bearing, and no one would have guessed that, as Katherine said, "Such a welcome from his dog meant more than any formal reception that could have been given him."[37]

Marshall had barely completed his first review of troops when he suffered a reoccurrence of his irregular pulse problem. It had flared up before he left Chicago and had earlier been diagnosed as a malfunctioning thyroid gland. After extensive testing, a surgical thyroidectomy seemed the only option. Doctors successfully removed the diseased lobe at a San Francisco hospital in early 1937. Since Marshall wanted to quell rumors that he had health issues—one had circulated that the moment he received his general's star, he had collapsed and been carted off to the hospital—very little information

The infantry barracks as they would have looked during the time the Marshalls were there.

George C. Marshall Research Library

was released about his surgery.[38] Supposedly, he was recuperating from the flu. After he returned to the post, Marshall was pronounced fit by military doctors, and he quickly plunged right back into vigorous and high-profile activity. That May he spent a month with troops on maneuvers, although he was careful not to overdo it. He got more exercise—tennis and riding— more sleep, and overall seemed healthier both in mind and spirit than he had been in years.

At some point in his first year at Vancouver Barracks, Marshall wrote to his friend and colleague, General Keehn, in Chicago about his new assignment at the post, and explained that his most pressing duty was the command of 35 CCC companies. He assured Keehn that the camps were beautifully organized and run quite capably by a staff of reserve officers. Marshall was impressed with these young men, remarking to his friend that "they are a fine lot, hard working, studious in following the educational courses we provide, and seeming to develop considerable ambition." Marshall mentioned that the camps were situated in beautiful settings—on the coast, the mountains, and the lakes.[39] Sometimes he combined inspection trips with fishing or hiking in this magnificent countryside, often taking Katherine with him.

For the most part, then, Marshall was enjoying a relaxing and predictable command. However, on June 20, 1937, Vancouver Barracks, and General Marshall as its commanding officer, would experience quite an exciting episode that would gain national attention. The Soviets had for some time planned what they hoped would be the first successful nonstop transpolar flight from Europe to the United States. The itinerary called for three Soviet airmen to fly from Moscow to San Francisco via the North Pole. Having begun the adventure three days earlier, the plane ran low on fuel, and the pilots had to make an emergency landing 600 miles short of their destination at the nearest airfield, which happened to be on post. Marshall was notified immediately. He ordered a guard around the plane and took the three men to his own quarters. Katherine was in for a shock when she opened the door on a quiet Sunday morning and saw these three "polar bears" walk in. As she said, "they wore huge parkas of fur, and their faces were so streaked with oil and dirt, so haggard and covered with beards, the men hardly looked human." She and her husband set about to make the three disoriented Russians comfortable, providing them with a hearty breakfast, a bath, and sleep. Meanwhile, as Katherine noted, "the circus began." Soon more than 75 reporters, along with more than a dozen newsreel cameramen, had arrived on the scene. Marshall turned over the library to one group, and the front porch to the other. Katherine did her part by providing ham sandwiches and hot coffee as they waited restlessly for the foreign visitors to emerge.[40]

Meanwhile, although it was Sunday, Marshall called a local department store owner in Portland at his home and explained the unusual situation. He asked if he would have someone load a truck with 20 suits in assorted sizes, along with shirts, shoes, and underwear from his men's department, and get these items to the post as quickly as possible. The owner immediately agreed, and within a couple of hours sent not only the clothing, but two tailors as well. When the fliers awoke, all was ready, and they soon appeared downstairs clean-shaven and appropriately attired to meet the press. The store owner would accept no payment for the suits—he just requested that he be able to display one of the pilot's flight suits for two weeks in his show window. By early evening the Russian ambassador had arrived from San Francisco, and he became a guest of the Marshalls as well. By then Marshall had found a reserve officer on post who spoke Russian and could act as an interpreter. The next day Marshall organized a reception and parade to honor the pilots and the ambassador, so the whole garrison could get in on the excitement. Afterward, he accompanied the entourage to a Portland Chamber of Commerce luncheon. By late Monday afternoon the pilots left for Washington to be greeted as heroes across the country.[41]

General Marshall with his wife, Katherine, and stepdaughter, Molly, pose during the reception with the Russian airmen and the Soviet ambassador, June 1937.
Courtesy of The Oregonian, Portland, Oregon

As commander of an important army post, Marshall was a highly visible member of the Portland community, and the cooperation of both entities in the "Russian Fliers" incident was an indication of that cordial relationship. Just as he had in Chicago, Marshall developed friendly ties, personally and officially, with these political and business leaders. He staged military displays at the post for the pleasure of the local citizens and made the military band and units of soldiers available for civic celebrations or parades. Marshall was often a popular speaker for various civic and community organizations, often promoting the value of the program he loved, the Civilian Conservation Corps. Once, he asked the chamber of commerce if he could invite some outstanding young men from area CCC camps to speak at one of their luncheons. After all, as he had told Keehn, "The boys all seem to like this country, and I imagine that this peaceful invasion will have a marked effect on the future development of the region, as many of these young men remain out here to marry and settle down."[42] The Portland businessmen did not immediately see what these boys had to offer the community. But after hearing the stories of their lives, especially how the corps had helped them, the chamber of commerce members were very touched, some of them teary-eyed. Also, through the example of these young men, it was evident how powerful this New Deal agency had been in improving their lives. Once again, Marshall strengthened the bond between his work and that of the community.

Marshall did everything possible to improve morale in the camps. For example, if a young man had driven a truck for a certain distance without an accident, perhaps 5,000 miles, then he received a personal letter of congratulations from Marshall, which he could later use when he sought employment. Marshall started a Vancouver District CCC newspaper, *The Review,* which was a big success. It was a sharp-looking publication, packed with local news, along with poetry, photographs, and letters to the editor. It made the men feel important and helped them with their reading and writing skills.[43]

Marshall tried several other innovative programs. One rather unusual project was a dental survey. As participants in the CCC, these young men got dental care, often for the first time in their lives. Katherine Marshall noted that "if a boy's teeth were in bad condition, woe befell the CCC dentist who extracted when he could have filled." Because the boys were sent to Oregon and Washington from all over the country, Marshall decided that to raise awareness about dental health, he would use the 10,000 CCCs to conduct a national survey. Its purpose: to see which areas of the country had the best, and the worst, preserved teeth. One of the U.S. Army dentists agreed to complete this project. Results were published in the *Oregon* Journal, some dental journals, and eventually *Time* magazine.[44]

As he had at Forts Screven and Moultrie, Marshall would try anything to publicize the positive accomplishments of the CCC. Commenting on the agency's work, he would later say, "It was the most instructive service I have ever had, and the most interesting." Long after he left the Vancouver area, he said he wished he could have been the CCC's national director. Had that been so, he would have added more military training and discipline, which he thought would better prepare the next generation for citizenship. Forrest Pogue made the point that Marshall, especially after his return from China in 1927, was often thrown in with civilians—the National Guard, the organized reserves, and the CCCs—and that he welcomed the contact. In fact, Pogue said, "from long, varied, and sustained experience with citizen soldiers he drew his faith in the value and effectiveness of a citizen army. A member of his staff commented that 'he had a feeling for civilians that few Army officers . . . have had. . . . He didn't have to adjust to civilians—they were a natural part of his environment.'"[45]

What Katherine Marshall would later remember as "two of the happiest years of our lives" were about to come to an end. In May 1938, Brigadier General Marshall received orders that he was to report to Washington, D.C. His role: assistant chief of staff of the War Plans Division. Katherine called it a "distinct blow." Once again Marshall would have staff duty, not troop duty. As he wrote General Pershing in late May, "I loathe a desk. I would not mind much, except that I have so few years left for active service that I hate to lose them to desk instead of command work."[46] Equally important, though, was Marshall's belief that only through troop duty would he stand a chance of becoming a major general (two stars), which would make it more likely that he might reach his highest ambition: appointment as army chief of staff when General Malin Craig retired from that post in 1939.[47] But, once again, orders were orders.

That beautiful June in Washington State—dramatic land of giant firs and cool rushing waterfalls—Marshall relished his last month, resting, fishing, hiking, and, with Katherine, saying farewell to friends and professional associates. Civil and social groups from both Portland and Vancouver arranged parties and ceremonies in the couple's honor. On their last night on post, the Vancouver High School and Seventh Infantry bands serenaded them at their quarters. Marshall would say 14 years later:

Altogether, we experienced one of our most delightful periods of Army service and one that we look back on with additional warmth because there followed from the very month we left the Northwest long fearful strain and struggle with a work turmoil that has not yet subsided. Those days along the rivers of the Northwest, among its magnificent mountains, and its picturesque seashore appeared to us a pleasant dream in comparison with the troubled days that followed.[48]

By June the Marshalls were en route to the nation's capital via train, stopping along the way to visit friends in Chicago. Not long after their arrival, Katherine and Molly headed for Fire Island, while Marshall settled down for War Department duty in the humid, oppressive heat of a Washington summer.

Chapter 6

Vancouver to Washington

Distant Fires

1938–1941

Memories of the rather idyllic life he had enjoyed in Washington State must have faded fast as Marshall reported that July 7 in 1938 for duty as assistant chief of staff of the War Plans Division. It was the beginning of the most remarkable, eventful years of Marshall's life. In Europe and Asia the dark scudding clouds of a coming war were already gathering. Its fury would spread to all parts of the world and pull George C. Marshall directly into its center. The heat lightning had been visible for a long time, since the early 1920s. Whether Marshall read newspaper accounts of these rather alarming events or reviewed their details during heightened discussions in the War Plans Division, a storm was clearly gaining strength. The first warning had come from Europe's boot.

Brigadier General Marshall, assistant chief of staff, 1938
George C. Marshall Research Library

The Rise of the Dictators

As early as the 1920s, clouds darkened Italy's usually sunny skies. Although victors in World War I, its leaders resented the settlements of the Treaty of Versailles, believing that they had been cheated by their Allies—Britain, France, and the United States—of their rightful territorial gains. Further, Italy was seeing an upsurge of working-class militancy—strikes, bread riots, even violence, which they blamed on "bolshevist" influences.[1] In the parliament, a number of unwieldy and unstable political coalitions gained temporary power, but none seemed able to solve postwar economic and social problems.

In 1919, Benito Mussolini, once a socialist journalist but by then an anticommunist nationalist, had formed the Fascist Party, galvanizing the support of many unemployed war veterans. Organized into armed squads of "Black Shirts," these discontented men terrorized their political opponents. In 1922, with the country slipping into chaos, Mussolini and his followers marched on Rome, where he presented himself as the only hope of restoring order. Seeing the need for more focused leadership, the king invited Mussolini to form a government, making him prime minister in October 1922. Once he was head of state, Mussolini systematically dismantled Italy's institutions of democratic government, and by 1925 he had completed his transformation into dictator.[2] Expanding the nation's boundaries, in his view, was an absolute necessity. In his description of fascism in a 1932 Italian encyclopedia, Mussolini declared that "the growth of empire is an essential manifestation of vitality, and its opposite a sign of decadence."[3] Not surprising, then, was his invasion of the East African country of Ethiopia in 1935, using bombers and tanks against spears and ancient firearms. When the League of Nations protested this action, Italy simply withdrew from the organization and formed an alliance with Nazi Germany. Then there was Nazi Germany; Marshall had his eyes on that developing storm.

At the end of World War I, Germany was a defeated nation, humiliated by the terms of the Treaty of Versailles and the losses of territory and economic stability that followed. Not only that, in 1919 the nation underwent a huge political change, from an autocratic monarchy to a full-fledged representative democracy. But this Weimar Republic proved too young and weak to tackle the enormous problems of the postwar years. The German people were starving, in part because of the continued blockade by the Allies into early 1919. Reparations obligations contributed to hyper-inflation, driving prices to ridiculous

107

levels and dramatically devaluing the mark relative to other currencies. As a possible socialist counterweight, the threat of communism loomed large.[4]

Into this threatening brew came Adolf Hitler. Born in Austria in 1889, as a young man he fought in World War I and received several medals for bravery, including the Iron Cross. Adrift after the war, he finally found work as a political official for the army in Munich. In this capacity he attended a meeting of the so-called German Workers' Party—later the National Socialist German Workers' Party (Nazis)—and soon found a match for his own extremist beliefs. This organization was vehemently anti-Marxist and it was opposed to the Weimar Republic along with the democratic concepts that spawned it. Believing that the Treaty of Versailles had been a scourge, the party urged that its terms be rejected. The Nazis also advocated extreme nationalism, and militaristic expansion to allow living space (*Lebensraum*) for the so-called "racially superior" German-Aryan race. With a Pan-Germanic outlook, Nazis saw it as their right to annex predominantly Aryan populations such as Austria. Perhaps the umbrella of all their beliefs was a fanatical hatred of Jews, a group they called "racially inferior" and for whom they blamed virtually all of Germany's woes.[5]

Hitler soon became the party's "young, forceful, and hypnotic leader," whose speeches wooed converts to the party with "masterful demagoguery."[6] Although he and his party faithful attempted to gain enough support for the eventual overthrow of the Weimar Republic in the Beer Hall Putsch of 1923, that effort failed. While in prison for the crime of treason, Hitler wrote *Mein Kampf (My Struggle)*, laying out a plan for the achievement of both his goals and those of the Nazi Party. Once released, he used the tools of propaganda and intrigue to propel himself to power, with his cause gaining steam as the worldwide depression of the 1930s deepened. In 1932, German president Paul von Hindenburg reluctantly appointed Hitler chancellor, asking him to form a coalition government.[7]

With important Nazis in key positions, and given legal sanction by the Reichstag through the Enabling Act of March 1933, Hitler and his cabinet gained full control of the government. Ruthlessly determined, and with the help of brown-shirted, street-brawling storm troopers (SA)—the party's own army—he crushed opponents. In 1934, though, when the SA's violent behavior stood in the way of Hitler's gaining control of the old-guard German army, which saw the group as thuggish and threatening, he eliminated its leaders in one long murderous night. After von Hindenburg's death the next year, Hitler abolished the position of "president," sealing his dictatorship with the title "Fuhrer and the Reich Chancellor." Now the regular German army was reluctantly in his camp. With a tight-knit and fiercely loyal set of bodyguards—the famed SS, or Secret Police—willing instruments of mass murder and terror, he held absolute power.[8] By the time George Marshall arrived in Washington in July 1938, Hitler had rearmed Germany, marched troops into the so-called demilitarized Rhineland—both moves violating the Treaty of Versailles—and, in the spirit of Pan-Germanism, annexed Austria.

The Allies raised only weak diplomatic protests in the face of Hitler's defiance, but Marshall already saw the looming danger. A friend of his, a military attaché in Warsaw, had written him the previous year that the problem "that agitates every foreign office is simply when and where Hitler will embark on an inevitable military adventure."[9]

On the other side of the world in imperial Japan, the winds of an impending war were gaining speed. This crowded island nation of 80 million was packed into an area the size of Montana, with only one-sixth of its land usable for agriculture and its population growing by a million a year. The only way to accelerate Japan's industrial potential was through trade, but that route was blocked by tariff barriers put in place after World War I. The raw materials that Japan needed—rubber, tin, tungsten, oil—belonged to nearby colonies of Great Britain, France, and Holland. The worldwide depression of the 1930s only made the situation worse.

Within Japan, the increasingly powerful armed forces, which blamed the nation's problems on corrupt politicians, became more aggressive and further drawn to the idea of expansion. In early 1931, military leaders hatched a plot whereby they would arm a mob that would then use some 300 bombs to destroy the Japanese parliament (Diet), along with the headquarters of the major political parties. The army then intended to step in and declare a military dictatorship. At the last minute the military's most influential general thought better of it, and the planned coup was called off. Meanwhile, the Japanese Kwantung Army, which had been guarding Japanese business interests in the Chinese province of Manchuria since 1905, used the blowing up of Japanese-owned railroad tracks near Mukden in September 1931 as a justification for invading and occupying Manchuria. They had absolutely no authorization from the government in Tokyo for this action; nevertheless, after a bit of "sputtering," the government accepted the takeover. Unrest driven by cabals of young army officers continued, resulting in harassment and even assassination at the highest levels, especially of moderates who were critical of this increased military activity.[10]

Even within the cabinet itself, the military perspective was gaining power. The war and naval ministers were appointed, not elected, and could be recalled at any time by the military services' top officers. Only those ministers who promoted these expansionist and militaristic views remained for long, and soon they became the voice of the cabinet's policy. As U.S. Ambassador Joseph Grew put it: "Whatever way it falls out, one thing is certain and that is that the military are distinctly running the Government and no step can be taken without their approval."[11]

By 1937, a skirmish between a small Chinese unit and Japanese troops who were "protecting Japanese businesses" near Peking provided Japan with an entrée into a full-scale war. One by one, major cities fell to the Japanese—Peking, Tientsin, where Marshall had served for three years in the '20s, Shanghai. China's leader, Chiang Kai-shek, withdrew a battered army to the interior, leaving the coastal city of Nanking virtually defenseless. Twenty thousand young Chinese men were marched out of the city and used for bayonet practice; others were machine-gunned or, after being covered with gasoline, set on fire. Conservatively, at least 20,000 women were raped or killed. Before it was over, more than 200,000 Chinese had been butchered. That city's fate would forever be remembered as "The Rape of Nanking." Chiang joined forces temporarily with the Communist guerilla leader, Mao Tse-tung, to hold out against the Japanese.[12]

In the United States, President Roosevelt condemned this aggression, prompting a leading Japanese, Yosuke Matsuoka, to lash back: "Japan is expanding and what country in its expansion era has ever failed to be trying [demanding] to its neighbors? Ask the American Indian or the Mexican how excruciatingly trying the young United States used to be." In terms of action, Roosevelt maintained a neutral position, for while the United States had its internationalists, in fact, most Americans were overwhelmingly isolationist. They didn't want to be involved in the events, however disturbing, in far-off Asia.[13]

The Shift

This, then, was the world situation as Marshall arrived in Washington that summer of 1938. As Marshall biographer Ed Cray notes, "He was to spend three months in the War Plans Division familiarizing himself with the plans and budgets of a skeletal army battling [a] cautious president and niggardly Congress for appropriations to ready itself for war."[14] The troublesome happenings in Europe and Asia were not isolated; already, Rome, Berlin, and Tokyo had allied in pacts that would eventually tighten into the fearsome and aggressive tripartite Axis powers.

While all of this was brewing, behind the scenes at the War Department, plans were already well under way to clear the path for Marshall to become U.S. Army chief of staff. Despite Marshall's concerns that his desk job, rather than the command of troops, would ruin his chances of a second star and advancement to the prized post, he needn't have worried. In October 1938, he moved closer to the coveted spot when the assistant secretary of war made him the army's deputy chief of staff. What he didn't realize at the time was that he was entering a political minefield.[15] Secretary of War Harry Woodring and Assistant Secretary Louis Johnson were so at odds with each other that a "virtual state of war" existed between them. It had to do with personal ambition, but also a much broader conflict: differing views on how to respond to the expansionist moves of Italy, Germany, and Japan. Woodring was the isolationist and Johnson the interventionist. As Mark Stoler put it, they "mirrored the split in American society and further paralyzed the department." Although both supported Marshall as the future chief of staff, he refused to be drawn into the fray but walked a frustrating political tightrope.[16]

During this same year, President Roosevelt, now serving his second term, increasingly recognized the menacing posture of the Axis powers and saw that they could eventually threaten American security. However, the president was walking his own tightrope. He was still trying to get his New Deal agenda through Congress and did not want to alienate the more conservative isolationists. As a means of controlling the danger of being drawn into these external crises, he had supported neutrality acts passed by Congress in both 1935 and 1937. The laws prohibited the sale or shipment of U.S. arms to *any* foreign nations engaged in war. American citizens were not allowed to travel on ships owned by any nation at war. Trade would be limited to nonmilitary items and must be paid for in cash and transported by the warring country ("cash and carry").[17] By fall of 1938, though, the possibility of war in Europe loomed larger, and something more proactive seemed required.

That September, Hitler and Mussolini had invited French and British leaders to a conference in Munich, Germany. It was a region of Czechoslovakia, the Sudetenland—hugging Germany's border—that was the subject of the meeting. Both of the invited countries had alliances of one kind or the other with Czechoslovakia. Claiming that the area, occupied by ethnic Germans, had been wrongfully taken from the "Fatherland" by the Treaty of Versailles, Hitler insisted that Germany should be able to annex it. The Czechs said they would fight rather than to yield to that pressure. At a meeting several months earlier, Hitler had not gotten his way, and he warned that if the Czech government didn't agree to his demands, the Reich army would invade. The French and British, who still had the horrors of world war fresh in their memories, wanted badly to preserve peace. Negotiating on behalf of the Czechs, they agreed to Hitler's terms in return for his pledge

At the signing of the Munich Agreement: from left to right, Neville Chamberlain; French Prime Minister Edouard Dalidier; Adolph Hitler, and Benito Mussolini
German Federal Archive: Bundesarchiv,Bild 183-R69173 / CC-BY-SA

that he would expand no further. The Fuhrer agreed, promising, "This is the last territorial claim I have to make in Europe."[18] Signing the Munich Agreement on September 28, 1938, the leaders allowed Hitler to annex the Sudetenland, but supposedly with conditions: there was to be oversight by a "commission," and a plebiscite held for mixed-race areas.

In the end, the Germans took much more land, and no plebiscites were forthcoming. Most people realized that the European democracies had only bought some time. Nevertheless, the British prime minister, Neville Chamberlain, who had represented his country in the negotiations, held up the agreement at the airport when he returned and assured the people that the paper signaled "peace for our time."[19] Some called it peace, but others called it appeasement. While respectful of Chamberlain, Winston Churchill told the parliament on October 5, "We have sustained a total and unmitigated defeat," and warned that what he found "unendurable" was his sense of their country "falling into the . . . orbit and influence of Nazi Germany."[20] Throughout the crisis, the U.S. president and the War Department waited it out. When the agreement was reached, Roosevelt wired Chamberlain, "Good man," but in private he noted that Britain and France "would wash the blood from their Judas Iscariot hands."[21]

The Munich affair set off a flurry of rearmament activity in the United States. To keep the isolationists at bay, Roosevelt's approach in 1938 was to make the case to the American people that rearming the country was a means of *defending* U.S. neutrality should war break out. Perhaps in part based on that logic, in October Congress appropriated $300 million for national defense. But exactly how was this money to be spent? As deputy chief of staff, Marshall was about to be drawn into the crosshairs of the debate raging within the executive branch regarding the answer to this question.

Since World War I, proponents of air power, including persuasive figures like Colonel William "Billy" Mitchell, had taken the position that strategic bombing of enemy cities could do so much industrial and psychological damage that it could actually win wars. They called for a large air force independent of the U.S. Army Air Corps that could come close to replacing traditional army and naval services. Many disagreed with this assessment, including Marshall, who, although a strong advocate for enlarging American air power, was much too aware of the overall weakness of the military. He wanted a more balanced approach for all of the services and saw the primary function of technically advanced airplanes as support for the army and navy.[22] The president's view was different. Not only was he impressed with the air power arguments, but as Forrest Pogue put it, he had other motivations as well: "Almost certainly Roosevelt at this time was thinking in terms of helping Britain and France to build air strength that might be sufficient to hold Hitler in check or, if war came, to defeat him without United States participation."[23]

As deputy chief of staff, General Marshall was called to a high-level White House meeting, along with top officials from the departments of war and treasury, on November 14, 1938, to hear Roosevelt outline this plan. The Germans, according to the president, had a vastly superior air force. The United States needed to create a large air force so that the country would not need a huge army. He pointed out that, politically speaking, he could not send troops, so this powerful air force was essential to back up his foreign policy. He made a case for the United States needing 10,000 airplanes, and the capability to build 24,000 more each year.[24] Marshall recalled that the president "wasn't much for getting the men to man the airships or for munitions and things that they required," noting that "he was principally thinking of getting airships for England and France."[25] Marshall was unhappy with the president's reasoning, worrying that this concentration on aircraft would leave little for soldiers, ammunition, and military equipment. After all, the army had only nine under-strength field divisions as compared to 90 fully trained German divisions, Japan's 50, and Italy's 45.[26]

After Roosevelt laid out the plan, he asked the military chiefs present for their thoughts. Marshall disagreed with this unbalanced approach and believed his opinion was shared by the other officers. To his amazement, they all agreed with Roosevelt. As Marshall later said, "He finally came around to me. . . . I remember he called me 'George.' (I don't think he ever did it again. . . . I wasn't very enthusiastic over such a misrepresentation of our intimacy.) So he turned to me . . . and said, 'Don't you think so, George?' I replied, 'I am sorry, Mr. President, but I don't agree with that at all.'" That ended the conference, with the president giving the newcomer "a startled look."[27] Marshall said the generals were telling him good-bye as they left the meeting, believing his tour in Washington was over. Yet Marshall related to his biographer years later: "I want to say in compliment to the President that that didn't antagonize him at all. Maybe he thought I would tell him the truth so far as I personally was concerned, which I certainly tried to do in all our conversations."[28]

Toward the end of 1938 and into the spring of 1939, Marshall as deputy chief of staff was tasked with writing drafts of bills for emergency appropriations. This was a stressful job—apportioning funds among the competing branches, building up airplane production while planning for those balanced forces, testifying before opposing legislative camps within congressional committees. Marshall described those grueling weeks and months well: "[I] had to work like lightning, compromise endless disagreements, sit in on difficult scenes." He recalled one meeting as "a tumultuous morning with much emphatic argument."[29] However, in terms of working with the president, Marshall soon found an important liaison in Harry Hopkins, a brilliant Iowan and Roosevelt New Dealer. He had run the Works Progress Administration in the early 1930s and later, as head of the Federal Emergency Relief Administration, had overseen the distribution of $8.5 billion in relief projects. In late 1938 the president had made him secretary of commerce; moreover, Hopkins was Roosevelt's most trusted adviser. "He all but lives in the White House," said one cabinet member, and, in fact, later on, he did. Hopkins also sat in on many official meetings with the president.

Marshall and Hopkins arranged to meet each other in late December 1938. Hopkins listened intently as Marshall described the terrible state of the army and its defenses, and to his arguments that developing a balanced military force rather than air power as the "be all–end all" was the way to prepare for the possibility of war. In subsequent meetings a few days later, it was Hopkins, along with Marshall, the secretary of war, and the army chief of staff, who made the argument that airplanes without trained pilots, crews, and ground support were useless. The president yielded—he would ask Congress for a $552 million emergency appropriation, but only $180 million would go for "3,000 of the airplanes Roosevelt wanted 'to impress Germany.'"[30]

In 1939, as winter inched toward spring, the situation in Europe and Asia continued to deteriorate. Hitler was now spending 60 percent of Germany's budget on the military; that March his army invaded Czechoslovakia—so much for "his last territorial claim." Mussolini's troops marched into tiny Albania. In Japan, the Foreign Ministry was calling for "a new order" that would bind together Japan, China, and Manchuria "economically" and would make "Southeast Asia, Indonesia, and the Philippines colonies."[31] In his State of the Union Address, Roosevelt warned that "our neutrality laws may give aid to an aggressor and deny it to the victim." That spring, he even made a

Deputy Chief of Staff Marshall gives defense budget
testimony before a House Committee, January 19, 1939.

Associated Press

worldwide appeal to Hilter and Mussolini, asking them to ensure peace
by respecting the borders and territories of 31 nations for 10 years.[32]
Hitler mocked the plea in a speech to the Reischstag to the derisive
laughter of its members.

It was against the backdrop of these turbulent international circumstances
that Roosevelt had to consider who would succeed Army Chief of
Staff Malin Craig, whose term was about to end. Marshall, of course,
was in the running. Although 33 generals outranked him in seniority,
according to an army tradition, none would be considered unless they
were young enough to serve the four-year term as chief before reaching
the age of 64. Based on that factor, there were only four who would
be seriously considered. One of those was General Hugh Drum, who
was campaigning vigorously for the post. As Cray noted, "He curried
newsmen, prompting fulsome articles in national magazines. He asked

influential visitors to write the president . . . lined up politicians, and solicited other endorsements."[33] Marshall, on the other hand, wanted no publicity; in fact, he saw it as a negative. In November 1938 he had written Leo Farrell, who was the political editor of the *Atlanta Constitution,* "Reference any publicity regarding me . . . I am now, in my particular position with low rank, on the spot in army circles. The fact of my appointment as Deputy while a brigadier general, junior to other generals of the general staff, makes me conspicuous in the army. Too conspicuous, as a matter of fact. My strength with the army has rested on the well known fact that I attended strictly to business and enlisted no influence of any sort at anytime."[34] In the end, Drum's politicking worked against him. Cray noted that Roosevelt was a canny politician himself and recognized an orchestrated campaign when he saw one. Further, Drum, although the most senior officer and with an impeccable record, was also pompous, vain, and hindered by the zeal of his own ambition. Marshall, bent on *not* campaigning, still had powerful backers as well, especially General Pershing and, by then, Harry Hopkins, who through his meetings with the deputy chief of staff had come to respect him immensely.

So it was that George C. Marshall, and not Drum, was summoned to the White House on April 23, 1939. Apparently telling no one, not even the secretary of war, of his decision, President Roosevelt conveyed to Marshall that he would be the next U.S. Army chief of staff. General Craig would take leave at the end of June, and he would retire officially on August 31. Marshall would take office the next day. Although this was the position that Marshall had wanted for a very long time, he had no intention of sacrificing honesty to hold it. He told the president in the 40-minute meeting that he must be able to speak his mind, and asked him if that would be all right. The president said, "Yes." Then Marshall said to Roosevelt. "You say 'yes' pleasantly, but it may be unpleasant." Roosevelt nodded and smiled. That guideline established, Marshall said, "I feel deeply honored, sir, and I will give you the best I have."[35] So often in Marshall's earlier military career, he had been disappointed with the slowness of his promotions. Now he gained ground with extraordinary speed. As Mark Stoler said, "Chief of staff was the highest rank in the army, a rank that carried with it the four stars of a full general. Just prior to the appointment, Marshall had had only one star. Three years earlier, he had had no stars. Finally, however, all the praise and predictions, all the positive assessments by his superiors, had had their impact. At age 59, Marshall had satisfied his ambition and reached the top of his profession."[36]

While Marshall had been the acting chief of staff since July, he was to officially assume his duties on September 1, 1939. A formal ceremony was planned, but as it turned out, his swearing in and promotion to four-star rank was a quick affair. At 3:00 that morning, Marshall had received word that Germany had invaded Poland. As one writer put it, Hitler had unleashed "the full fury of his Stuka dive-bombers and his rumbling Panzer tanks into that hapless country."[37] Just one week before, Germany had signed a cynical nonaggression pact with the Soviet Union. The parties pledged that they would not attack each other for a period of 10 years, they would settle any disputes amicably, and, as part of a secret protocol, they would divide Poland. The way was clear, then, for Hitler to strike westward without fear of a two-front war. The British and French would not tolerate it. Despite their fears of another war, fears that had rendered them virtually impotent up to that point, this was the final straw. Although they had done nothing but weakly protest the Fuhrer's "rape of Czechoslovakia," now the two countries made it clear: no further appeasement—they would defend Poland's territorial integrity against attack. As Marshall headed back to his new quarters on post at Fort Myer, Virginia, that evening, after a day of emergency meetings, he understood the situation perfectly. As he told a colleague in a letter a few days later, "My day of induction into office was momentous, with the starting of what appears to be a World War."[38] By the time he wrote the letter, Britain and France had been at war against Germany and Italy for three days.

As Marshall made his way to the Munitions Building on Constitution Avenue in the nation's capital, he surely contemplated the myriad of problems that faced the nation's military in the wake of Germany's aggression. Speed and firepower defined new tactics that the Wehrmacht had introduced in the Polish campaign. Blitzkrieg, or "lightning war," had as its central aim the crushing of the enemy's forces before they had time to rally their defenses. It was backed by high levels of organization, disciplined soldiers, and awesome supply and support lines. The Poles, although highly skilled and tenacious, could not hold out for long against this modern army. They were beaten within 26 days of the invasion; soon the Soviets entered Poland from the east, and the carving up of the land began. Marshall was deeply concerned—the American army that might one day face such a foe was a force of less than 175,000 ranked only 19th in the world behind countries such as Bulgaria and Portugal.[39]

General Marshall being sworn in as U.S. Army chief of staff, September 1, 1939. Left to right: Secretary of War Harry H. Woodring, Marshall, and Adjutant General Major Emory S. Adams

George C. Marshall Research Library

The new chief of staff knew that his first priority was to impress upon both the president and Congress the need for an expansion of that army.

Only a few days after the invasion, Roosevelt's rhetoric suggested a shift. In one of his famous "Fireside Chats" on September 3, 1939, he reiterated that the country would remain neutral, but he couldn't ask the American people "to remain neutral in thought." By September 13, the president had called a special session of Congress to consider revising the Neutrality Acts. While previously forbidding any sale of war matériel to belligerents, the new legislation permitted them to purchase military equipment from the United States on a "cash and carry" basis. Buyers, then, had to send their own ships for the purchases, and U.S. vessels were forbidden to enter combat zones. The revisions at least allowed some "wiggle" room for selling needed supplies to the French and British. Roosevelt also authorized a slight increase in the army and the National Guard, but when Marshall asked Congress to fund the equipping of the additional troops, he met with resistance. He told a House committee in February 1940, "We have to put our house in order before the sparks reach the Western Hemisphere." The plea fell on deaf ears: the committee cut the president's proposed $850 million armed forces budget by 10 percent that April, including funds for an important defensive air base in Alaska. Just six days later Hitler's Wehrmacht invaded Norway and Denmark.[40]

Increasingly alarmed at the fierceness of Hitler's storm, Marshall tapped powerful resources. Bernard Baruch was a wealthy and shrewd New York businessman. He had a great interest in government, but no desire to run for political office, a circumstance that allowed him certain flexibility in influencing both Congress and the president. As a sage and global thinker, he had become a valuable link between the civilian industrial/commercial world and official Washington. For nearly a year Baruch had pressed the president and Congress for defense preparations. Marshall understood Baruch's unique capacities and, well aware of his point of view, asked for his help directly. Providing him with a report he had sent to the president outlining the importance of getting Congress to restore funding for the Anchorage base and other military matériel, Marshall suggested that Baruch personally mention this to Roosevelt. Rather, the financier decided to take the matter up with a powerful South Carolina senator, James Byrnes. Together they arranged a meeting with a dozen or more key senators so Marshall could make his case in a more informal setting. The evening session lasted until the wee hours of the morning.

At first Baruch made the arguments, but before long Marshall told him, "Let me take over," and proceeded to eloquently and with passion lay out the situation. He even told the group, "My job as Chief of Staff is to convince you of our needs and I have utterly failed. I don't know what to do." The sincerity and logic of his arguments seemed to do the trick. Colorado Senator Alva Adams, one of the attendees that Marshall most wanted to convince, sat silent after Marshall's cataloguing of needs. Finally, he nodded toward the chief of staff: "You came before the committee without even a piece of paper and you get every damned thing you want." Well, not everything, but Baruch wrote later that the meeting was a turning point in convincing key congressional leaders that it was time to rebuild the military's defenses.[41]

Having made his case before this cadre of powerful legislators, Marshall still had concerns about the president's reluctance to accept a more balanced approach to military preparedness. He turned to Secretary of the Treasury Henry Morgenthau, a Hudson Valley native who had worked with Roosevelt since his days as governor of New York and was one of the most influential men in the president's inner circle. Morgenthau was sympathetic to the army's budget problems, and he believed the president wasn't moving as effectively as he could because he didn't have the "big picture." In his view, the War Department had been feeding information to Roosevelt in too many "bits and pieces." Morgenthau told Marshall to give him the whole story of a balanced defense proposal that he could take to the president. The presentation to Morgenthau took place on May 11, 1940, just one day after Luxembourg, Belgium, and the Netherlands upped Hitler's conquests to eight since his annexation of Austria. Marshall biographer, Forrest Pogue, described Marshall's litany of needs:

> In addition to increases in the Regular Army, enough planes to build a modern air force, and plants for the manufacture of ammunition, he wanted reserve equipment and munitions for a Protective Mobilization Plan force, including Regular Army and National Guard troops that would ultimately total nearly one and one-quarter million men. Additional troops required pay, shelter, rations, clothing, and maintenance; the Air Corps must have planes of all descriptions, trainers, fighters, and bombers. The regular army and forces later to be called would need rifles, field artillery, anti-aircraft guns . . . ammunition."[42]

The cost: $650 million. Morgenthau said, perhaps with a gulp, "I don't scare easily. I am not scared yet." Marshall replied, "It makes me dizzy." Morgenthau answered back, "It makes me dizzy if we don't get it."[43]

Both Marshall and Morgenthau realized that the president had to be persuaded—it was important to do something other than just build more planes, a whole range of other needs had to be addressed. On May 13, 1940, General Marshall and Morgenthau, along with the secretary and assistant secretary of war, went to see Roosevelt to get approval for this $657 million funding request for broad-based military needs. Morgenthau actually made the presentation of Marshall's proposal to Roosevelt. It was received, Marshall later said, with a sort of "smile and sneer." The president joked and teased and rambled on to distract from the secretary's appeal. Morgenthau pressed on. When he suggested that Marshall should be the one to present the proposal to Congress, the president demurred, "I'm going to have a message. Don't go up and tell them anything."[44] Back and forth it went, with Roosevelt doing most of the talking. Finally Roosevelt said no, undeterred from his plan to ask Congress to build an outrageous 50,000 planes per year.

At length, after what seemed the end of an unproductive session, Morgenthau turned and asked the president to hear what General Marshall had to say. Breezily, Roosevelt said, "I know exactly what he's going to say. There's no need for me to hear him at all." The president's response greatly angered Marshall, but, repressing his fury, the new chief of staff asked for just three minutes to state his view. Completely changing his rather flippant demeanor, the president said, "Of course, General Marshall." In an impressive explanation that lasted fifteen minutes rather than three, Marshall described the military situation in Europe and Asia, outlining in detail how disastrous it would be if the army, in its present pathetic state, was asked to fight the enemies now facing Britain and France. He filled in the facts and figures. Didn't the president understand that the U.S. Army couldn't possibly throw more than 15,000 men into combat at a time, while the Germans had 2 million men massed in 140 divisions in Europe? What good would our five divisions, now compressed from the under-strength nine of 1938, do against such a force? Didn't the president realize, he asked, that only American preparedness was the answer? Finally, standing tall over Roosevelt, who was seated at his desk, he said with an astonishing intensity: "If you don't do something, and do it right away, *I don't know what is going to happen to this country!*"[45]

Roosevelt's reply was cold and clipped, without the usual friendliness.

"Thank you, General. And thank you, Henry," was all he said. Morgenthau and Marshall gathered their belongings and turned to exit the room. As they reached the door, Roosevelt called, "Oh, General, come back and see me tomorrow. And bring me a list in detail of your requirements." The next day Marshall was discussing with the president a more than $650 million supplemental army appropriation amount that would provide a more balanced force. Morganthau estimated that he would get at least three-fourths of what he requested.[46] By late May, Roosevelt asked Congress for defense funding of $1 billion in line with the chief of staff's requests. Marshall saw this as a second breakthrough in his fight for preparedness. From that time until America's entry into the war, he had an easier time convincing the president, who in turn sought to convince Congress of the need for preparedness.

"The whole fury and might of the enemy"

Part of the shift in the attitude of the president, Congress, and the American people had much to do with escalating events in Europe as Hitler's army continued its European rampage. No matter their point of view regarding American involvement, most citizens took notice when the Wehrmacht panzers rumbled over the *neutral* Netherlands in only 7 days, and Belgium in 18. They were further alarmed when they heard the news in late May 1940 that German armed forces had bypassed the so-called impregnable French defensive wall, the Maginot Line, and rolled through the semi-mountainous "tank-impassable" Ardennes Forest toward the channel ports. The panzer divisions, stopping just short of the coast, perhaps to await infantry support, provided the British with just enough time to make a hasty and almost "miraculous" evacuation of 338,000 British and French soldiers from the seaside resort town of Dunkirk. It was an armada of 693 vessels, everything from destroyers and minesweepers to yachts and fishing trawlers, whose crews plucked the imperiled men from the beaches and got them back across the choppy channel to England. Although it seemed like a grim defeat, especially since all kinds of British heavy equipment was left on the French beaches, the fact is that in addition to the rescued French soldiers, fully 85 percent of the British Expeditionary Force had eluded the German trap and would live to fight another day.[47] Winston Churchill, who had built a new coalition government that replaced Neville Chamberlain's, was now prime minister. If Hitler thought the British would be easily discouraged by their retreat, he was mistaken. Churchill's words before the House of Commons on June 18 set the tone for the future struggle:

123

The whole fury and might of the enemy must very soon be turned on us. Hitler knows that he will have to break us in this Island or lose the war. If we can stand up to him, all Europe may be free and the life of the world may move forward into broad, sunlit uplands. But if we fail, then the whole world, including the United States, including all that we have known and cared for, will sink into the abyss of a new Dark Age made more sinister, and perhaps more protracted, by the lights of perverted science. Let us therefore brace ourselves to our duties, and so bear ourselves that if the British Empire and its Commonwealth last for a thousand years, men will still say, "This was their finest hour."[48]

Standing up to Hitler would indeed be difficult. On June 22, at a railroad car in Compiegne, the site of Germany's surrender in World War I, the French capitulated, signing an armistice that divided the country in two: three-fourths would be occupied; the other part would be free. That "free" government, established at Vichy and led by Marshal Henri P. Petain, fully collaborated with Germany, appointed all officials, controlled the press, and practiced arbitrary arrests. Legally both the unoccupied and the occupied portions of France remained under Petain's seemingly dictatorial control, but it was Germany that was in overall command. Further, to the sorrow of Parisians living within the occupied zone, by June 1940 German soldiers were strolling on the broad avenues or enjoying their cafés au

Hitler in Paris, June 1940
German Federal Archive: Bundesarchiv, Bild 183-H28708 / CC-BY-SA

lait in the charming "City of Light" bistros. Now Britain stood alone.

That summer of 1940, as the news from Europe turned ever darker, Marshall was conflicted. He saw as top priority the buildup of a trained American army, but he also realized how desperate the British were for support. One worry plagued him: what if Britain did not survive? What if it was the *United States* standing alone, having drained its military resources to a lost cause? Congress was concerned as well. That June it forbade the sale of war matériel outside the country unless both Marshall and his naval counterpart, Admiral Harold Stark, certified that it was nonessential to the American military. In the fall of 1940, Marshall did agree to release World War I arms as "surplus" for sale to American firms, which in turn would sell them to the British on a "cash and carry" basis.

Nevertheless, when President Roosevelt once more made his case for planes so badly needed to face the Nazi menace, Marshall told him sternly that the United States itself had only 49 bombers fit for duty, except for those in its island possessions. Eventually, though, when he saw that the British were determined to hold out, Marshall allowed some of the new bombers coming off the assembly line to be battle "tested" in England. Marshall admitted, "I was a little ashamed of this because I felt that I was straining at the subject in order to get around the resolution of Congress" regarding neutrality laws. However, he later said that in fact the British found difficulties with the planes, so it had been legitimately useful for the United States that they were tried out in those circumstances. Roosevelt also worked with the navy to shape a "destroyer for bases" program, couched as strengthening the country's western hemispheric defenses—the British would receive 50 desperately needed destroyers in return for leases on military installations in their Caribbean possessions.[49]

One thing seemed clear: the alarming events in Europe were making it easier to get military funding. By mid-1940, Congress had appropriated more than $17 billion, nine times as much as the 1939 budget. While it was finding the means to manufacture the weapons of war, the question of expanding the army loomed large. Purchasing arms was a far cry from the possibility of sending American men into war. Roosevelt, running for reelection in the fall of 1940, didn't want to endorse a conscription bill, since isolationists would see it as moving the country closer to armed involvement in Europe. As the head of the U.S. Army, Marshall did not want to initiate such a proposal either, since it also would be viewed suspiciously. Better if the impetus came not from the president or the head of the armed forces. Indeed, it came from Greenville Clark, an influential lawyer from New York, the head of the Military Training Camps Association, and an advocate of preparedness since World War I. At Clark's recommendation the first peacetime draft bill in American history was introduced by Congressman James Wadsworth of New York and Senator Edward Burke of Nebraska.[50]

Although Marshall wanted an increase in the size of the army, initially he did not support the draft bill. He preferred that the expansion come from 120,000 new recruits who would fill out the nine planned infantry divisions to the full strength of 375,000. He saw it as a better option, since it allowed for gradual training of this sudden influx of untried soldiers. In the end, he became convinced that only the draft would build the needed army, and he testified in favor of the bill before both houses of Congress. If passed, it would create an army of 1.5–2 million men by mid-1942.[51] He also requested enormous sums to arm and equip this expanded army, and advocated the immediate call-up of all National Guard units to assist with training. That August, with the draft bill still pending, Marshall boldly asked for a supplemental appropriation of $4 billion to outfit a much larger army not yet approved! Acknowledging the tragedy of a country that found itself spending enormous amounts of money for nonproductive war-making purposes, he also emphasized that "we must meet the situation that is facing us," and noted that he saw no way of doing that "except by preparing." When one isolationist senator opined that maybe an improvement in the situation abroad would allow the army to abandon part of this proposed program, Marshall said frankly, "Senator, I am sorry that I cannot entertain any such hope at present."[52] That September 14 Congress agreed to Marshall's requested appropriations, along with calling up the National Guard and Reserves for a 12-month stint. This would build an army of 800,000 by year's end.

During this time period, Marshall's influence with Congress grew enormously. Senators and congressmen from both parties came to respect him. Able to persuade legislators through straightforward, well-prepared, detailed testimony, he also respected that in a democracy, lawfully elected leaders make the decisions and American taxpayers foot the bills. He never lost sight of this. Moreover, he had a reputation for honesty. When Marshall came to the Capitol to testify, he gave the impression of a self-disciplined, frank, and knowledgeable leader. He remained nonpartisan, despite often speaking for President Roosevelt, whose views tapped deeply held political feelings. Speaker of the House Sam Rayburn recalled, "He would tell the truth even if it hurt his cause. Congress always respected him and would give him things they would give no one else." When reading from a text, he wasn't a great speaker, but Marshall was absolutely spellbinding when asking Congress for something he passionately believed in.[53]

As Marshall strove for preparedness, the situation in Europe worsened. Britain valiantly fought to fend off the Germans. Beginning in August 1940, an air war between the Royal Air Force and the German Luftwaffe, soon to be called "The Battle of Britain," raged over England's coastal areas and the channel. Hitler's air force commander, Reichsmarschall Hermann Goering, knew that air superiority over that 20-mile expanse would be necessary for German success in a planned invasion of the British Isles, code-named "Operation Sea Lion" and scheduled for the late summer or fall. With the benefit of radar and intrepid British pilots, that goal was not achieved, and eventually the invasion was called off.

However, in an attempt to demoralize the British people into a peace settlement, the Germans began nighttime bombing raids against English cities, especially London. Beginning on September 7 and continuing nightly until November 3 (57 consecutive days), the "London Blitz" brought an average of 200 German bombers over the capital city each night, with the industrial areas and docks the heaviest hit. Many London parents sent their children to live with relatives in the country, beyond the range of the bombers. Each evening, those who were left listened for the warning sirens, then headed for the air raid shelters or retreated into the subway undergrounds while bombs fell night after night. The resilience of the Londoners became legend. Winston Churchill wrote proudly that the city "was like some huge prehistoric animal, capable of enduring terrible injuries, mangled and bleeding . . . and yet preserving its life and movement." Still, the city paid its price: 48,381 killed; 50,856 seriously injured. The London raids became intermittent after mid-November, as the German air force switched its focus to knocking out industrial centers such as Coventry, Plymouth, and Liverpool.[54] In the autumn of 1940, the English people, still clinging to life, desperately needed American aircraft if they were to survive. While the United States had for a long time been willing to sell war matériel to the British, there was one enormous problem: the beleaguered English simply could no longer pay for these goods. The country's resources, including the gold supply, had been demolished by its valiant defense of the islands.

Knowing that Britain could not stand alone, Roosevelt proposed the Lend-Lease bill in December 1940. The president urged that "lending" or "leasing" war matériel to those fighting the Nazis was a way to defeat Germany without direct U.S. military involvement. He made the case that Americans had the capability to turn the country into a powerful "arsenal of democracy," supplying Great Britain so that the great island nation would not fall to the Nazis. If the Nazis prevailed, he warned, the Axis powers would be in a position to bring enormous military and naval resources against this hemisphere. In a December 17 press conference, he laid out the logic of lend-lease in terms that American citizens could readily grasp:

> Suppose my neighbor's home catches fire, and I have a . . . garden hose four or five hundred feet away. If he can take my hose and connect it up with his hydrant, I may help him to put out his fire. . . . I don't say to him before that operation, "Neighbor, my garden hose cost me $15; you have to pay me $15 for it." I don't want $15—I want my garden hose back after the fire is over.[55]

Although isolationists railed against the plan, Congress passed the Lend-Lease Act in March 1941. The law enabled the British to buy war goods on credit with a promise to pay either in cash, goods, or services after the crisis was passed. Congress funded the building of more shipyards and factories to offset the drain on war materials. General Marshall supported the plan. At a news conference he made the point that with lend-lease aid, Britain could withstand a German invasion; without it, it could not. Further, remarking on Germany's prodigious air power, he noted that the U.S. Army Air Corps was sufficient to resist an enemy "under present conditions," but *not* if Britain surrendered. Marshall also realized that lend-lease represented a clear shift from a neutral position and opened up the possibility of new defense plants that would hasten the supplying of both nations for the coming struggle.[56]

Just as America's production levels were rising to meet Britain's needs while helping the U.S. Army rebuild its forces, another player entered the war. On June 22, 1941, Hitler invaded Russia. Ed Cray described the beginning of Operation Barbarossa: "Three million troops, led by over 3,500 tanks, surged across the Polish border in a three-pronged attack aimed at Leningrad, Moscow, and Kiev. . . . The greatest military assault in history came as a bolt of lightning in the summer sky. . . .

President Roosevelt signs the Lend-Lease bill into law, March 1941
U.S. Library of Congress LC-USZ62-128765

It stunned Marshal Joseph Stalin, who had chosen to ignore repeated
. . . warnings that Hitler intended to violate their non-aggression pact."
Within the first two weeks, the German army overran surprised Soviet
defenders along a front that extended from the Baltic to the Black Sea.[57]
Soviet losses were staggering. Stalin turned to the United States for
help. Swallowing their distaste for communism, Americans agreed to
rearm the Soviet Union by extending the lend-lease program to them. At
first Marshall opposed such aid, doubting the USSR's capacity to hold
out for long against the Nazis. By September 1941, though, he testified
before the House of Representatives that "what little we can do to keep
the Russian army in the field aggressively resisting the Germans is to
our great advantage."

As for the British, Winston Churchill was unambivalent in his support
of the Soviets. Although fiercely anticommunist, he declared that "any
man or state that fights on against Nazidom will have our aid." To his
private secretary he remarked, "If Hitler invaded Hell I would make at
least a favourable reference to the Devil in the House of Commons."[58]
Indeed, the British were overjoyed at Russia's entry into the war—at

last the prodigious energies of the German Reich were turned toward the East. For Marshall, though, aid for the Soviets meant that once again supply priorities had to be shifted, leaving his preparedness plans for the U.S. Army in line behind the frantic demands of Great Britain and, now, Russia.

By the time Germany invaded the Soviet Union in the summer of 1941, and as America's involvement deepened, Marshall already understood that the Selective Service Act of October 1940 that had expanded the army for a 12-month period would need to be extended; otherwise, his hard-won army of National Guardsmen and selectees would be demobilized by fall. Rumors soon flew among the ranks that soldiers would not be sent home in October 1941 as expected, and it stirred a firestorm of controversy. That June, for example, Marshall had received a letter from Rose Lumetta, whose son was in the army: "If you do that you will have the hatred of every mother, wife and sweetheart and also the boys themselves," she wrote. Despite how busy he was, Marshall replied: "The War Department does not wish to keep your boy or any of the others in the service for one day longer than is necessary for the safety of the country, but it is impossible to tell at this time what that necessity is."[59] Draftees found their own way to protest, in some cases painting O.H.I.O. on their barrack walls, threatening to go "Over the Hill in October" if their service was extended.

According to Katherine Marshall, it occurred to her husband while he was on a horseback ride that he could use the chief of staff's biennial report, usually submitted to the secretary of war by July 1, not only as a statement about the army's accomplishments, but also as an argument for the extension of the Selective Service Act. The press would get these findings out to the public and raise awareness regarding the dangers of dissolving the army so recently created. Working feverishly with his staff, Marshall met the deadline. It was a powerful, well-organized description of how a military force, now able to offer the nation an adequate defense, was about to be dissolved. Marshall emphasized three points that he hoped would be heard not only by the secretary of war, but also by Americans and, more specifically, their representatives in Congress: the provision that draftees could serve only in the Western Hemisphere should be dropped; the National Guard should remain on active duty; and there should be an unlimited extension of the draftees' terms of service.[60]

Despite the clarity of this report, Congress was deeply worried about the extension bill. Marshall realized that some of their opposition was related to politics, especially a deep dislike of President Roosevelt's New Deal principles, and fear of what some conservatives thought was his willingness to pull the U.S. deeper into foreign war. Marshall made it clear that this recommendation was based on military imperatives and not political considerations. One night Marshall arranged for a meeting with 40 Republican congressmen—all of them opponents of the bill— and made his case from 7:00 p.m. until midnight. One isolationist in attendance told him brusquely at the end of the evening, "You put the case very well, but I will be damned if I am going along with Mr. Roosevelt." This angered Marshall, who shot back: "You are going to let plain hatred of the personality dictate to you to do something that you realize is very harmful to the interest of the country!"[61] Of the assembled congressmen, Marshall had only a few who said they would support the bill. Several more began to get on board, but each let him know in one way or the other that it would cost them the 1942 midterm election. Marshall told these courageous legislators that he would personally go to their districts and vouch for their patriotism when the time came. But as Marshall noted, "The war came along and then there was no necessity for that."[62]

Homing in on the provision of the previous bill that allowed extended service for the guardsmen and selectees when Congress declared that the national interest was imperiled, Marshall made the case. That peril was real, he emphasized, "whether or not the Congress declares it." His intensity obvious, he added, "I am asking you to recognize the fact. I am not asking you to manufacture a fact."[63] Despite vicious attacks, including personal abuse and threats—he told a friend, "I am being called a Benedict Arnold, a skunk, Hitler, a stooge, Traitor, and am getting knocks from every side"—in the end Congress passed it.[64] The tally: in the Senate, 45–30; in the U.S. House of Representatives, 203– 202, *a one-vote margin.* Later Marshall told his biographer, "People have forgotten entirely the hostility of that time," but added, "I have no regrets. I think that I did what was right . . . even more right when I look at it from the longer distance of the present time."[65]

"The general has left his office"

Marshall could handle the criticism that came with the myriad of decisions that he was called upon to make during this intense and complex prewar period; yet, it was up to Katherine Marshall to provide him with a safe haven from that hustle and bustle. Although highly educated and accomplished in her own right, it was apparent that during this period she saw her role as support for her husband. The couple lived at the "White House of the Army," Quarters 1, Fort Myer in Arlington, Virginia, near Washington. As Katherine wrote in her memoir, *Together: Annals of an Army Wife,* "From Christmas 1940 it became apparent to me that my one great objective must be to keep Quarters Number 1 at Fort Myer a place of peace and quiet, a sanctuary for my husband where he could rest and relax and gather strength from the time he entered his home in the evening until he had to face the demands of the next day."

Everything at Marshall's home was geared to meet his schedule. When he left his office in the Munitions Building in Washington around noontime, Marshall's secretary would call to say he was in his car—the drive would take 15 minutes. Katherine described it as if "an electric switch had made contact through the house." The secretary might also mention that two or four or even six guests would be coming as well, all involved in "war business." The staff quickly adjusted for the "extras." As soon as Marshall arrived, he went straight to the dining room; afterward, if circumstances permitted, he took a 15-minute nap on the chaise lounge in the sunroom before his driver took him back to work.[66] Sometimes word came that "General Marshall has been detained at the White House," other days there was no time for lunch at Fort Myer. During 1941, for example, Marshall was on Capitol Hill, testifying for 21 days in 15 separate hearings.[67]

Katherine understood the pressure her husband was under and, as she said, made sure that "no confusion, no household irritations" concerned him. After work, Marshall would try to fit in a ride on a favorite mount from the stables at Fort Myer. Evenings, he and Katherine would take a walk, or go to the post theater for a movie, arriving after the feature started so as to not attract attention. When the weather got too hot for riding, the two would sometimes take a canoe trip on the Potomac, stopping for a picnic along a bank, finding some peace and quiet in the early evening—that is, until the newspapers discovered this. In one 1940 Sunday supplement a cartoon of the Marshalls, featuring the general lying back in the canoe, appeared. The caption: "General Marshall and His Sweetie."[68] No wonder Marshall was later to say, "I think what I value most is privacy." With his high-profile responsibilities, it wasn't easy.

Marshall out for a ride at Fort Myer, with the family's exuberant
Dalmatian, Fleet, not far behind, 1941
George C. Marshall Research Library

Despite his schedule, Marshall managed to communicate often by phone or letters, often handwritten, with his stepchildren, Molly, Allen, and Clifton Brown. The year before, in June 1940, he had been scheduled to fly to Alaska for an inspection, but the situation in Europe, with the fall of France, was so bad that it seemed unwise to leave Washington. That allowed him two days from the "fire and plunder" of the European war to attend Allen's wedding to Margaret Goodman Shedden in Westchester County, New York. A bit later, Marshall took time to answer the first happy letters from the couple, remarking with fatherly pride, "I gather that so far there have been none of the preliminary battles over toothpaste in the bathroom, the shirt on the floor, and other casual gestures common to men, about the house."[69] At Fort Myer on Christmas Day 1940, it was he who had given Molly in marriage to Captain James Winn Jr., a field artillery officer in the U.S. Army.

Meeting at Sea

In early August 1941, as the Selective Service extension debate was drawing to a close, Marshall prepared for a trip with the president. He had been called to the White House on July 30 and told to prepare in "utmost secrecy" for a meeting at sea with Prime Minister Winston Churchill and his advisers. Although Marshall didn't know the location of the rendezvous, he was advised that he would be away for about 10 days, and, as he relayed to Katherine, he needed to pack cool-weather uniforms.[70] Knowing that any news of such a high-level conference with the British would raise alarms among the isolationists that the president was leading the U.S. into war, Roosevelt left Washington on his pleasure craft, the *Potomac*, telling inquiring newsmen that he was off on a weekend fishing trip to the north. Marshall and the other service chiefs, traveling on other vessels, eventually met up with the president aboard Admiral Ernest King's flagship, *Augusta,* in Newfoundland's Placentia Bay. (The *Potomac* was still cruising New England's coastline, with a Roosevelt look-alike waving from its deck.)[71] Roosevelt had suggested to his top adviser, Harry Hopkins, as early as December 1940 that a lot of questions of interest to the United States and Britain "could be settled if Churchill and I could just sit down for a while." Now, according to Forrest Pogue, after the German invasion of the Soviet Union, Roosevelt agreed that indeed it was time for a face-to-face exchange with Churchill and his military staff. The prime minister was delighted. He desperately needed the president's help in maximizing the contributions of the United States to his nation's brave effort to survive German aggression. Now he had a chance to plead his case in person.

With so much at stake, it was certain that Churchill's team would come well prepared. By contrast, the American military heads—Marshall, U.S. Army Air Forces General Henry "Hap" Arnold, and Chief of Naval Operations Admiral Stark—had only two days to get ready for their British counterparts. Marshall later explained that the nature of the conference came as a complete surprise: "We had no knowledge of it until we were well up the coast on the cruiser *Augusta*. . . . To me the meeting was largely a get-together for the first time, an opportunity to meet the British Chiefs of Staff, and to come to some understanding with them as to how they worked and what their problems were. We were in no position at that time to lay very heavy matters before them."[72] Marshall noted that the British were looking for much more from the Americans. "They were at this business every day, all day, on a very definite war-making basis. We were in the position of mobilizing and equipping an army." He also pointed out that this Newfoundland meeting was occurring at the same time the U.S. House of Representatives was moving toward the final vote on the Selective Service extension. Would Marshall come home to an army, or no army? Although the law had passed by the time he returned to Washington, Marshall remembered that during the time he was in Newfoundland, "We were in a struggle for our survival against the misunderstandings of our public."[73]

The meeting between the principal parties, Roosevelt and Churchill, began quite cordially. That August 9, 1941, the prime minister arrived on the brand new battleship HMS *Prince of Wales,* its band playing "The Star Spangled Banner," with the Americans responding with "God Save the King." It was the British who first boarded the *Augusta* for the initial introductions. The two leaders quickly fell into easy conversation, talking comfortably as the service chiefs and other officers mingled on the quarterdeck. The following day the American contingent made their way to the *Prince of Wales*, the president making a herculean effort to stand, despite heavy, locked leg braces, the permanent fallout from polio. It was Sunday morning, so all personnel were present for a church service on board, with the British and American sailors sharing the hymnals. When in full volume they sang "Onward Christian Soldiers," tears ran down Churchill's face.[74]

So it was that over the three days, through formal and informal meetings, the two sides discussed, explained, and debated both political and military questions. The British point of view, delivered in various and detailed reports, not only asked for specifics—150,000 rifles, for example—but also strongly suggested that the United States enter the war as a belligerent. As much as the British presented evidence that it would take the United States to stop the Nazi menace, Roosevelt's position was still clear: Americans would provide maximum aid "short of war." Beyond that, Roosevelt made few specific military commitments.

Both men, however, seemed to want some statement of "general

Aboard the Prince of Wales, Sunday, August 10, 1941. Marshall stands behind
Roosevelt; next to him are Admiral Ernest King and Admiral Harold Stark.

George C. Marshall Research Library

agreement" between the two governments. The result, after the editing
of a succession of versions, was the Atlantic Charter, which set forth
certain principles "on which to base a better future for the world."[75]
It included lofty ideals: self-government for all people, no territorial
changes except those approved by the people involved, the people's
right to choose their own form of government. The document did have
the effect of binding together these two principals—Great Britain,
already the belligerent, and the United States, the neutral power—since
it specifically noted the desire for peace and safety after "the final
destruction of Nazi tyranny."[76]

When Marshall returned from Newfoundland, he still had an army,
but he was concerned about what he saw as a continuing drift toward
war. During the summer U.S. naval ships had begun to convoy British
ships as far as Iceland—Roosevelt called it "hemispheric defense" and
had declared the western Atlantic a neutral zone. That fall Nazi subs
began a campaign against American shipping, sinking the destroyer

Greer in September. The president retaliated, declaring that in those waters American ships could fire "on sight" at German U-boats. The next month the American destroyer *Reuben James* was sunk, killing 115 U.S. sailors. In essence, the president had launched a naval war against Germany in the Atlantic.[77]

In October 1941, when Winston Churchill requested that a U.S. naval squadron be sent to Singapore to keep the Japanese at bay, Marshall was alarmed. The relationship between Japan and the United States had continued to deteriorate, and he urged caution. Speaking of what he called "our bare cupboard," he noted that "We are not now prepared and will not be prepared for several years to come" for any military effort in the Far East. Marshall called Churchill's request about "as unfavorable a moment as you could choose" for stirring up trouble with the Japanese.[78] The chief of staff desperately needed time to gear up his army to meet the two-front tempest bearing down hard on the nation. He would not get it.

Chapter 7

War Duty in Washington

"Air Raid on Pearl Harbor. This is not a drill."

1941

Marshall expressed quite clearly in a letter to his stepdaughter, Molly, on October 20 that the summer and fall of 1941 had been a trying time:

> Each day I think I have reached the peak of difficulties and pressures, but last week was the worst of all, a combination of Russian affairs, the Japanese situation, supplies to England, the political pressures, developments in relation to National Guard and some Regular officers over relief from command, the development of the next period of training for the Army, the approaching hearings on the Lease-Loan, etc., etc. do not give me many peaceful hours.[1]

Marshall had told a colleague that June, "If I lose this job perhaps I can get a six ball juggling act, if there are any vaudeville shows left."[2]

Katherine had done her part to find a way to ease the pressure. The previous fall she had seen a beautiful old Virginia home set on almost four acres in the charming small town of Leesburg, some 35 miles from Washington. Although the dwelling's original structure dated to the early 1800s, the 16-room house, with additional wings and columned porch, had been modernized. With plenty of space for gardening, and tall oaks for summer shade, Katherine saw its possibilities as a weekend getaway for her husband, and perhaps later as a permanent residence. By spring of 1941 the final negotiations for the property were well under way. In an April letter, Marshall commented that he had gotten his first look at it. However, that May 7, he was so busy that a proxy acted on his behalf at the deed signing. Marshall, writing to his daughter-in-law, Madge, made no mention of the house, but told her that a scheduled trip to the West Coast—California, Washington State, and then Alaska—had been postponed because he "had to go to the White House" instead.[3] Indeed, by this time, Marshall's schedule was dynamic, based on ever-changing circumstances, and he had few opportunities for leisure. For the rest of that year he would rarely see their new "country" home. Even at Fort Myer, walks or trips to the movies were few and far between. In the evening, Marshall came home with maps, papers, and books that he would

Dodona Manor in Leesburg, Virginia, at the time the
Marshalls purchased it in 1941.

George C. Marshall Research Library

spread across the dining-room table, poring over them until bedtime.

Despite the problems abroad, one on the home front had been particularly thorny; that is, Marshall's view on officer promotion policies. As he began to build the expanded army, he was determined that its commanders would be the best and brightest. In Marshall's view, those were not necessarily the officers who, because of seniority, were automatically in line to lead these newly formed units. The previous summer he had appeared before the House Military Affairs Committee to make the case for authority to bring younger officers into positions of command by retiring "in line" officers considered no longer fit for combat. Marshall explained that when these senior officers got toward retirement age, very few still retained the physical stamina or other characteristics of control that were sorely needed. In the time since World War I these officers had not been challenged, he remarked, so there was bound to be "deterioration when there is no active responsibility." Marshall told Pogue that he was accused right away of "getting rid of all of the brains of the army," but as he noted, "I couldn't reply that I was eliminating considerable arteriosclerosis."[4]

With permission to level the automatic promotion chain, granted via an amendment to a military appropriations law, Marshall began the process of evaluating the senior officers by creating a "plucking committee" of six retired officers. The group would make recommendations after examining records and recommendations as to performance. In a "six month period," noted Ed Cray, "the committee removed 195 captains, majors, lieutenant colonels, and colonels; in the five years it would ticket 500 colonels for retirement."[5] Marshall made the point that not everyone of that age was ineffective, naming George Patton as an example of a general who was still competent and vigorous.

This shake-up among senior officers was one of the most controversial moves Marshall made as chief of staff. He had known some of these men since World War I, and many of them were friends, so this was very difficult. As Marshall remarked, "No man would agree to himself that he was not quite up to the punch." However, the chief of staff's priority was to organize "the spine for the new army," one that could defeat a looming enemy or enemies, and in his view, vigor was a key requirement. "Leadership in the field depends to an important extent on one's legs, and stomach, and nervous system, and on one's ability to withstand hardships, and lack of sleep, and still be disposed energetically and aggressively to command men on the battlefield," Marshall explained."[6]

Recognizing the morale issue inherent in the policy, he decided that to be fair, he, too, should resign. After all, he was approaching 60 when the process began. In February 1941, Marshall met with the president, along with Harry Hopkins, to explain that he wished to submit his resignation, and why. He promised that he would help find the right man for the job and would stay long enough to train a replacement. Roosevelt reacted by thanking him and then quickly shifting the conversation to something else. Hopkins told him later, "The president just laughs at you—he says no one resigns, it was just talk." Marshall disagreed: "I told him that wasn't the case at all, that really I was dedicated to try to do this thing, and I had this serious situation in the army and that I didn't think it could be cured without terrible damage to morale if it was done by an old man—like I was in years." Nevertheless, after another visit to the Oval Office, where he made his plea once again, Marshall gave up. "I never got any action from the president, so my efforts to resign were defeated."[7]

Despite these internal military matters, Marshall's attention more and more was focused on Japan. Troubling news: in September 1940 it had formalized a relationship with Germany and Italy by signing the Tripartite Pact, thus creating the Rome-Berlin-Tokyo Axis. In 1939, as punishment for Japan's continued aggression in China, the United States had already terminated a 1911 commercial treaty with the country, limiting access to certain badly needed industrial and military resources.[8] Now, with Tripartite negotiations in progress, the president stopped foreign shipment of iron and steel scrap except to Great Britain and Latin America.[9]

That summer of 1941 there were other disturbing signs that Japan was in a militaristic, expansionist mode. In July a new cabinet under Prince Fumimaro Konoye had formed. While he himself was not an extreme militarist, his new war minister was Hideki Tojo, a chief proponent of increased military power. As foreign minister, Konoye named Yosuke Matsuoka, an American-educated "firebrand" who had led the move to get Japan out of the League of Nations in 1933.[10] It was Matsuoka who, in a troubling interview on August 1, 1940, had formalized Japan's aggressive posture by announcing the Greater Asia Co-Prosperity Sphere, a pan-Asian/Japan-centered concept for economic expansion and prosperity that became the cornerstone of imperial aggression in Asia. The foreign minister called it "a natural step that people who are closely related with each other geographically, racially, culturally, and economically should first form a sphere of their own."[11] While rooted in late 19th-century ideas of Japanese cultural superiority, its 1940s version was based on the business and political realities of an island nation. With raw materials more and more limited, the Japanese cabinet increasingly supported expansion that might hasten the ousting of the Western powers, and which would make these resources more readily available. Now, with Great Britain distracted by its death-grip fight with the Nazi war machine, and considering that the Netherlands and France had surrendered to the Germans, the Japanese cabinet saw opportunities in French Indochina and the Dutch East Indies favorable to these pan-Asian goals. It was more than just an idea, too. In early 1941, Matsuoka had proclaimed that Japan would take steps to "surmount all obstacles for the purpose of establishing this sphere throughout greater Asia."[12]

Toward that end, on July 24, 1941, Imperial troops moved into Indochina and, with the "approval" of Vichy France, gained permission to use its airfields and harbors for launching military actions. Marshall and other key members of the military knew this was coming. In August 1940, U.S. cryptologists had cracked Japan's most secret diplomatic code, Purple; the Americans called it Magic. So it was that a limited number of high-level officers had access to a July 14, 1941, message that Japanese officials had

141

radioed to Tokyo: "We will endeavor to the last to occupy French Indo-China peacefully but, if resistance is offered, we will crush it by force, occupy the country and set up martial law."[13] Equally disturbing, the same message outlined plans to send an ultimatum to the Netherland Indies and to seize the British possession of Singapore. This could not go unnoticed, but President Roosevelt was in a quandary: if he imposed a complete oil embargo, it would force a showdown that could lead to war. "It is terribly important for the control of the Atlantic for us to help to keep peace in the Pacific. I simply have not enough Navy to go around," he reasoned, "and every little episode in the Pacific means fewer ships in the Atlantic." Marshall and his navy counterpart, Admiral Stark, advised Roosevelt not to impose the embargo, since they so badly needed more time to beef up their defenses.[14] Still, as the president had told Japanese Ambassador Nomuro, "Americans could not sit idly by while Japan used American oil to further its aggressive goals on the Asian continent." So it was that on July 25, Roosevelt sent a message to his overseas commanders to take "appropriate precautionary measures" because the United States was imposing economic sanctions against Japan, embargoing almost all trade exports, and freezing Japanese assets and funds.[15] Britain and the Netherlands soon followed suit.

Worried about the situation in the Philippines, on July 26, 1941, Marshall called Douglas MacArthur from retirement to active duty to command the U.S. Army forces in the Far East, activated the Philippine armed forces, and authorized $10 million for strengthening the island's defenses.[16] In May 1940 Roosevelt had already moved the U.S. Pacific Fleet into its naval base at Pearl Harbor, and in the spring of 1941 he had decided to keep it there indefinitely instead of sending it to the North Atlantic. That February Rear Admiral Husband E. Kimmel had become the naval commander of the Pacific Fleet, and army Lieutenant General Walter Short had taken over the protection of the base and the fleet. Marshall had strengthened it the previous year with an additional antiaircraft artillery regiment and 81 additional pursuit planes.[17] Nevertheless, not long after Short arrived in Hawaii, Marshall had written him that Kimmel had complained to his superior about the deficiencies of the army's support at Pearl Harbor. Marshall told Short that "what Kimmel does not realize is that we are tragically lacking in this matériel throughout the Army, and that Hawaii is on a far better basis than any other command in the army."[18]

Whether Marshall's army was ready or not, relations between Japan and the United States were now on a collision course to war. The de facto result of Roosevelt's freezing of Japanese assets was that virtually all of its needed resources were now unavailable, including 80 percent of its oil supply. Tokyo could either repair relations with the United States or look elsewhere for the flow of supplies—perhaps by invasion of the British and Dutch possessions in the Pacific. Under Konoye's leadership, though, there was a slight glimmer of hope. He replaced the hotheaded Matsuoka with the more levelheaded Admiral Teijiro Toyoda. Upon his suggestion, on August 27, Konoye requested a personal meeting with President Roosevelt to consider solutions between the two countries. U.S. Secretary of State Cordell Hull, reading the Magic diplomatic messages daily and thus seeing Japan's planned aggression in Southeast Asia, nixed the idea. In his view, Konoye did not have firm enough control over his cabinet to tamp down the militaristic spirit. Although Marshall and Stark reiterated that the United States needed more time, Roosevelt, after discussions with Hull and other high-level cabinet secretaries—all urging a strong line—agreed to meet with Konoye but only if he would guarantee beforehand that Japan would respect the territorial integrity of China.[19] This Konoye could not promise, so while envoys were exchanged, no meeting took place. There seemed little alternative to war.

As if to validate Hull's point about the Japanese government's leadership, in October the militants in Tokyo forced Konoye and his cabinet to resign and soon replaced him with the leader of the war party, General Hideki Tojo, who also retained his position as minister of war. Imperial Japan's foreign policy was now formally controlled by the military. Marshall said later that his response was to do all in his power to delay the break with Japan because of the army's "unpreparedness" and "our involvement in other parts of the world."[20] For a few weeks, Tojo, dreading the possibility of a military showdown with the United States but committed to an expansionist agenda, made moves toward negotiating through the government's ambassadors Nomura and Kurusu in Washington. Offering a kind of modus vivendi—a temporary or provisional agreement—their proposal proved unacceptable. It mentioned no change in Japan's occupation of China, although it did tender a promise to withdraw from French Indochina in exchange for the resumption of full trade, including oil, and the unfreezing of assets.[21]

For starters, Secretary of State Hull and the president saw allowing Japan to continue in China as appeasement, a giving in as the British and French had done with Hitler and the Sudetenland. In the spirit of negotiation, and to buy desperately needed time, Roosevelt was preparing his own modus vivendi. But as Secretary Hull was reviewing it on the evening of November 25, word came through U.S. Army Intelligence that a huge Japanese convoy

The Japanese ambassadors, Nomura and Kurusu, flank
Secretary of State Cordell Hull, November 14, 1941.

National Archives of Japan

of warships and troop transport was steaming south toward the Dutch
East Indies. Not only that, Hull was reading Japanese intercepts that set a
November 25 deadline for the ambassadors "finishing their conversations
with the Americans," with any signings to be "completed by the 29th."[22]
"After that," according to the message, "things are automatically going to
happen." With this information at his disposal, Hull was convinced that the
Japanese proposals were insincere, that an attack was inevitable in days. He
dropped Roosevelt's more conciliatory draft and, writing a stiff reply, sent
it out on November 26. Later referred to as the "Ten Points," it outlined
stern requirements for the Japanese, including the conditions under which
they could once again have access to resources. The document demanded
that they withdraw from not only Indochina but China as well, including
Manchuria, and that they accept the legitimacy of the Nationalist Chinese
government at Chungking.[23] The Japanese were not about to yield on China,

so the "die was cast." The Japanese intended no further talks. A planned attack on the American naval base at Pearl Harbor, masterminded for almost a year by the brilliant Admiral Isoroku Yamamoto, was already in its staging phase, with a December date set for its execution. In fact, on the morning that Hull's Ten Points went to the Japanese Embassy—November 26, 1941—the Japanese strike fleet, under radio silence, was sliding into the North Pacific, headed south.[24]

As November ground to a close, the diplomatic intercepts made it plain that the Japanese government planned an attack. Just two days previous, on the 25th, Roosevelt had told his war cabinet—Secretary of War Henry Stimson, Secretary of the Navy Knox, and his army and navy service chiefs—"We are likely to be attacked perhaps next Monday [December 1] for the Japanese are notorious for making an attack without warning."[25] Hull was pessimistic as well. Looking directly at Marshall and Stark, he drove home his point, "These fellows mean to fight; you will have to be prepared."[26] When Marshall left to observe maneuvers in North Carolina on the 27th, he had already approved a communiqué, written by army and navy staff, that could be sent through the War Department to American forces in Southeast Asia if conditions warranted it. As messages continued to come in indicating that a large Japanese expeditionary force was continuing its journey south, closer and closer to British territory, or even the Philippines, Stimson got permission from the president to send a final warning to General MacArthur to be on the alert. After further meetings with the secretaries of the army and navy, along with the secretary of state, Stimson decided a broader warning was in order. Although intended for MacArthur, it was to be sent, *with an amendment*, to Hawaii, the Canal Zone, and San Francisco. Using Marshall's preordered draft, the message went out under his name late on the 27th:

> Negotiations with Japan appear to be terminated to all practical purposes, with only the barest possibilities that the Japanese Government might come back and offer to continue. Japanese future action unpredictable but hostile action possible at any moment. If hostilities cannot, repeat cannot, be avoided, the United States desires that Japan commit the first overt act. This policy should not, repeat should not, be construed as restricting you to a course of action that might jeopardize your defense.[27]

Forrest Pogue noted that this part of the message "was straightforward and left no chance for confusion." Further, all the "wires" that went out contained the statement Marshall had stressed in the meeting the day before: "Prior to hostile Japanese action you are directed to take such reconnaissance and other measures as you deem necessary. Report measures taken."[28]

This was left in its original form in MacArthur's message, but in the communications that went to Hawaii, the Canal Zone, and San Francisco, someone added: "but these measures should be carried out so as not, repeat not, to alarm civil populations or disclose intent." General Short at Pearl Harbor later called this the "do-don't" message, and claimed that it deterred him from taking stronger action in Hawaii. Apparently Stimson added this sentence because he had not wanted the large Japanese civilian population in Hawaii to say that our military moves provoked a Japanese attack. Nevertheless, following this message, Short soon saw another, this one given to him by his navy counterpart, Admiral Kimmel, and sent from the navy department in Washington: "This dispatch is to be considered a war warning."[29] That seemed like a very clear message, but according to Pogue, Stark weakened it by saying the strike would likely be against the Philippines, Borneo, or the Thai Peninsula. After all, even though intelligence officers were tracking Magic intercepts, the Japanese Foreign Office from whence the messages derived did not concern itself with the movement of armed forces. They were receiving diplomatic communications that were related

Pictured at left is Lieutenant General Walter C. Short, U.S. Army commander, Hawaii Department; right: Admiral Husband E. Kimmel, commander of the United States Fleet at the time of the attack on Pearl Harbor.

www.ibiblio.org
U.S. Naval Historical Center: NH 50266

to planned military movements, but not the specifics of those operations. Therefore, despite all the work of the decoders, a certain "intelligence haze swathed Japanese intentions."[30]

Convinced that Hawaii, so much farther from the Asian coast, would not be the target for the anticipated aggression, and worried about subversive activities by Japanese living on Oahu, Short put the base on "Alert Number One," the defense against sabotage, rather than the highest Alert Three, which would have meant 24-hour air reconnaissance, and a "man your battle stations" all-out defense of the island.[31] So it was that when the attack came, the U.S. Army planes were wingtip to wingtip on the tarmac, to be more easily and closely guarded. Nevertheless, Marshall later minced no words in describing his belief that Short failed in carrying out his instructions: "I feel that General Short was given a command instruction to put his command on the alert against a possible hostile attack by the Japanese. The command was not so alerted." At another time he spelled out a whole list of steps that should have been taken:

> His own planes, high fighter and interceptor planes in particular, should have been ready for action. . . . They should have been armed. Pilots sufficient for the first flight should have been ready; planes, presumably, might have been in the air in the early morning; the radar [which was used only three hours a day] should have run 24 hours a day as they did in Panama.[32]

After the war, the Army Board investigating the surprise attack on Pearl Harbor agreed that there was "command failure" in Hawaii, but it also censured Marshall and the head of the War Plans Division, General Leonard Gerow, for failing to see that Short had not responded properly to their warning by not putting the base on full alert. While Gerow was willing to take the responsibility, Marshall shifted the blame to himself. He told the committee that he could not definitely recall having read Short's reply to the warning, saying, "That was my opportunity to intervene and I did not do it." Nevertheless, he also made the point during the testimony that "I am not a bookkeeping machine and it is extremely difficult for me to take each thing in its turn and give it exactly the attention that it had merited."[33] The fact was that during that time Marshall's attention was on the Philippines, not Hawaii. Having received General MacArthur's report that all was in readiness for any eventual attack challenge, Marshall wrote back positively, obviously pleased by what he read. However, he ended his response with: "There is no, repeat no, improvement in the international situation."[34]

By early December, Tojo had told his council that Hull's Ten Points would "deprive Japan of her authority, and jeopardize her very existence." He noted that Japan would back down if the United States offered "just terms," but otherwise to "preserve her empire," Japan must go to war. That this would be the outcome was telegraphed to Admiral Yamamoto aboard his flagship, *Nagato,* on December 2. The date of the attack would be December 8 Tokyo time; December 7 in Honolulu. The Japanese ambassador in Berlin was advised to tell Hitler that negotiations "now stand ruptured, broken."[35] U.S. code breakers by December 3 discovered that Japanese embassies in Hong Kong, Singapore, Batavia [Indonesia], Manila, Washington, and London had been ordered to destroy their code machines and ciphers, a sure indication that Japan intended to break diplomatic relations, an almost certain prelude to war.[36]

Still seeking to avert hostilities, President Roosevelt on Saturday, December 6, decided that he would make a last appeal for peace directly to Emperor Hirohito. Whether the president was aware of it or not, the emperor had steadfastly conveyed to his government that he wanted diplomacy over war, insisting that Japan would "seek a peaceful settlement up to the last." That September, with Konoye still in the lead, Hirohito had met with both his cabinet and the Supreme Military Command to hear their case for war preparations. As he recognized the group's collective intention—not "Will we go to war?" but "When?"—Hirohito took the unprecedented step of speaking to them directly rather than through his advisers. To their amazement, he pulled from his pocket a poem entitled "The Four Sides of the Sea," written by his grandfather, the emperor Meiji. Telling his listeners that he was striving to introduce his grandfather's "ideal of international peace," he read:

> Methinks all the people of the world are brethren, then
> Why are waves and winds so unsettled nowadays.

"Everyone present was struck with awe," Konoye remembered, and hastened to assure Hirohito that "they would resort to arms only when there seemed no other way out."[37]

Now, on the very eve of hostilities, the president of the United States sent his appeal to Japan's highest authority: "Developments are occurring in the Pacific area which threaten to deprive each of our nations and all humanity of the beneficial influence of the long peace between our two countries. These developments contain tragic possibilities." He appealed to the emperor to find "ways to dispel the dark clouds."[38] Greeting guests at the White

House that evening, he told them, "This son of man has just sent his final message to the Son of God."[39] Roosevelt's appeal went by telegram to U.S. Ambassador Drew in Tokyo. It was destined to be delayed for 10 hours, as Pogue notes, either by design or bureaucratic interference. It reached Tojo, who was to have arranged for Drew to present it personally to the emperor, just as planes from the Japanese carrier force were taking off to attack Pearl Harbor.[40]

At the war and navy departments, intelligence experts did not have Saturday, December 6, off. They were hard at work interpreting Magic intercepts. Before evening, a message from the Foreign Office in Tokyo indicated that a 14-point reply to Hull's severe Ten Points program would soon follow. By early evening, the first 13 parts had been decoded, the task made easier because it was in English and thus did not have to be translated from the Japanese. Oddly, part 14 would not be wired to Ambassador Nomuro until the following morning. By evening, the navy's intelligence officer, Lieutenant Commander Alwin Kramer, delivered the 15-page first part in a locked pouch to Roosevelt at the White House. The president read intently for 10 minutes, taking in the argumentative, sharp, and unusually hostile tone of the message. The U.S. demands regarding China ignored Japan's sacrifices, it read, and menaced the existence of the empire; "therefore, viewed in its entirety [the Ten Points], the Japanese Government regrets that it cannot accept the proposal as a basis of negotiations."[41] As he finished his review of the document, the president said to Harry Hopkins, who was pacing the floor as he read, "This means war."

The president called Admiral Stark, the navy chief, before midnight. While he would later testify that the president had telephoned, and they must have discussed the message, Stark did not see it as "anything requiring action," since he had already concluded that Japan was "likely to attack at any time." The message, according to him, was simply "confirmation, if anything."[42] Meanwhile, Kramer had also delivered a copy to the secretary of the navy, who told him he would be meeting the following morning with Secretary of State Hull, at which time the document would be discussed. As for the army's intelligence officer, Colonel Rufus Bratton, he made certain that the State Department received the intercept that night, but decided to wait until part 14 came in—perhaps its contents would be crucial—before sending it to Marshall. Apparently that Saturday evening, Marshall and Katherine had spent a quiet night at home, since she was still recovering from injuries suffered in a fall that previous October.[43]

In the wee hours of the morning, more messages came into the intelligence offices, including part 14, essentially severing diplomatic relations—"The Japanese Government regrets to have to notify hereby the American Government that in view of the attitude of the American Government it cannot but consider that it is impossible to reach an agreement through further negotiations." Two other lines of the message praised the embassy staff for their work in difficult times. The fourth instructed Nomura: "Will the ambassador please submit to the United States government (if possible to the secretary of state) our reply to the United States at 1:00 p.m. on the 7th, your time." The fifth message ordered that the remaining cipher machines, the codes that had been used, and all secret documents should be destroyed. Bratton, who by now was back at work, recognized the importance of the specific Sunday hour—1:00 p.m.—and surmised correctly that the Japanese were going to attack somewhere in the Pacific at that time or shortly thereafter. Believing that a warning should go out to all commanders in the Pacific, he immediately hurried off to find someone who could take action. Neither Marshall nor Gerow were in their offices, so Bratton put in a call to Fort Myer.[44]

After a long and demanding week, the chief of staff had his breakfast an hour later than usual, and then called the stable for his mount. He made his 55-minute trip along the Potomac, riding at what he described as a lively gait, first at a trot, then a canter, and finally at a full run. While he was gone, Bratton's call came through. He told the orderly of this "vitally important message" that Marshall should receive at once. Somehow Bratton didn't fully convey the urgency because the orderly didn't go to find him, although perhaps that would have taken as much time as was needed for Marshall to return on his own. As soon as the chief of staff walked in the door, he picked up the phone to call Bratton, who said he would bring this urgent message directly to him. Marshall replied that it wouldn't be necessary—he would be coming into his office soon, and would read it then. Marshall showered quickly, dressed, and arrived at the War Department by 11:00 a.m.[45] Bratton handed him the 14-point communiqué at once, and Marshall, in his usual deliberate and methodical way, read it from start to finish. The last intercept, regarding the 1:00 p.m. time reference, Bratton held in his hand. Finally, after what seemed an eternity, Marshall finished the lengthy document and accepted the "trigger dispatch."[46] As soon as he read it, he understood its significance. After some discussion with Gerow, who by then had arrived, Marshall pulled out a piece of scratch paper and wrote out a longhand message:

> The Japanese are presenting at 1 p.m. Eastern Standard Time, today, what amounts to an ultimatum. Also, they are under orders to destroy their code machine immediately. Just what significance the hour set may have we do not know, but be on the alert accordingly. Inform naval authorities of this communication. Marshall.[47]

Before the message went out, Marshall talked with Stark, who agreed that the communication should be sent and asked that the dispatch include an instruction for his people to inform their "naval opposites." Marshall asked that Bratton get it out "at once by the fastest safe means." As Bratton left, General Gerow called out, "If there is any question of priority, give the Philippines first priority." Hawaii was still not considered under threat of this clearly imminent attack. The message was transmitted by telegraph to Panama, then to MacArthur in the Philippines, and by 12:11 to the Fourth Army in San Francisco. The message for General Short in Hawaii, though, could not go by military telegraph because of "atmospheric conditions," although Marshall was not informed that this was the case. Some later wondered why Marshall did not just send this crucial message by telephone. In fact, he did not consider that option. Believing that the Japanese might crack the "dubious scrambler" of telephone messages and discover that the diplomatic code had been broken—a risk that he could not take—he would not use that access.

In the end the message was sent commercially, Western Union. Japanese pilots were beginning their flight to the naval base at Pearl Harbor when Marshall's message reached the telegraph station in Honolulu. Not marked "priority," it was sent by a Japanese messenger boy, who ran into roadblocks and suspicious soldiers along the way. Before the communication ever reached General Short, the Empire of Japan had done its work, and Pearl Harbor lay in ruins. As for Marshall, assured that his message had gone out posthaste, he went back to Fort Myer for a quick lunch before returning for a meeting with the president already scheduled for three o'clock. As Pogue noted, "While at his quarters he received the announcement that was soon blaring forth from radios across the land: "Air raid on Pearl Harbor. This is not a drill.""[48]

The president was having lunch with Harry Hopkins in the Oval Office when the call came in at about 1:40. After verifying the "not a drill" message, he called Hull, who was scheduled to receive Nomura and Kurusu, the Japanese ambassadors. They had a reply to his Ten Point message, they explained, but had called with apologies to postpone a one o'clock appointment until a bit later. Roosevelt told the secretary of state "to receive their reply formally and coolly and bow them out." Of course, Hull knew exactly what the Japanese response was—he had read the 14-point message—diplomatic relations were to be broken so that a state of war could exist. The gentlemen were to have brought the document to Hull as instructed at the designated hour so that the severing of relations would have preceded the attack, albeit by minutes, but due to deciphering and typing difficulties at the embassy, they had not been as efficient as the Magic team. Thus, the timing of the visit to Hull was off by more than an hour—a disastrous difference. Indeed, as they arrived, neither diplomat realized that at that moment Oahu's tropical skies were blackened by the billowing smoke of torpedoed U.S. battleships, and American sailors and airmen were fighting for their lives against the raining bombs of the Empire of Japan. Hull could hardly control his fury. After taking a look at the document being formally presented to him, he "transfixed" Nomura with a chilly eye, and said:

> In all my fifty years of public service I have never seen a document that was more crowded with infamous falsehoods and distortions . . . on a scale so huge that I never imagined until today that any Government on this planet was capable of uttering them.[49]

Nomura, a kindly man whose efforts at diplomacy had been sincere, walked out beneath Hull's icy stare "under great emotional strain." He later wrote in his diary that "the report of our surprise attack against Hawaii reached my ears when I returned home from the state department."[50] Diplomacy had been sacrificed for war.

By three o'clock the president had assembled what would turn out to be his war cabinet—Marshall, Stark, Stimson, Gerow, and Knox. As they gathered, they mostly waited for fragmentary damage reports coming in from Hawaii: battleship row was aflame—the *Arizona* was burning, consumed by an explosion, its demise shielded by a roiling cloud of slate black smoke; the *Tennessee* next to her could catch fire any minute; the *California* was down at the stern—the captain had called "abandon ship"; the *West Virginia* was sinking, her captain dead—on and on it went. Three hangars were destroyed, several hundred aircraft were burning, casualties were heavy. Soon word came in that a second wave of Japanese bombers was coming over the island. Marshall began to act—he reviewed troop placements with the president, assured him that he had contacted both Panama and the Philippines, told him he would immediately mount guards around defense plants and increase security at the White House.[51] Finally,

Pearl Harbor, December 7, 1941   U.S. National Archives 80-G-19930

anxious to get to the War Department, he headed out with Secretary of War Stimson. Once at the Munitions Building, more bad news streamed in: Hong Kong, Bangkok, and Singapore had been bombed; British Malaya had been invaded. Marshall soon learned that the Japanese carrier force had struck the Philippines, and, to his astonishment, he discovered that apparently four hours after the alert, most of MacArthur's airplanes were on the ground and in the open as perfect targets. Marshall would later say, "I sweated blood to get planes to the Philippines. It is inexplicable."[52]

By evening all of the statistics weren't in from Pearl Harbor, but it was clear that the damage was terrific. In less than two hours the Japanese had destroyed 188 planes and damaged 159 more, while they had sustained a total loss of only 29 aircraft. Eighteen ships had been sunk or badly damaged, including eight battleships. The *Arizona* and the *Oklahoma* were a total loss, although the other five ships would eventually return to service. The human loss was great: 2,403 died, including U.S. sailors, marines, and soldiers, almost half of them trapped inside the sunken *Arizona*, and 68 civilians; 1,178 were wounded.[53] Fortunately, all three of the Pacific fleet's aircraft carriers and seven of its heavy cruisers were out to sea and spared. The oil storage tanks and maintenance facilities were also unharmed. These resources would be used by the surviving ships of the fleet. On that ghastly day, though, what might have been saved took back seat to all that had been lost. As Katherine later wrote, her husband came home late that night "grim and gray."[54]

In the fading winter light of December 7, after his war cabinet had dispersed, President Roosevelt called his secretary, Grace Tully, to the Oval Office— he wanted to dictate a message to Congress. In the tightly phrased 500-word address, delivered in six minutes before a somber legislative body at 12:30 p.m. on the next day, the president stated the situation with total clarity: "Yesterday, December 7, 1941—a date that will live in infamy—the United States of America was suddenly and deliberately attacked by naval and air forces of the Empire of Japan."[55] He listed the magnitude of Japan's aggression:

> Last night, Japanese forces attacked Hong Kong.
>
> Last night, Japanese forces attacked Guam.
>
> Last night, Japanese forces attacked the Philippine Islands.
>
> Last night, the Japanese attacked Wake Island.
>
> And this morning, the Japanese attacked Midway Island.

President Franklin D. Roosevelt asks for a declaration of war
from the U.S. Congress, December 8, 1941.
Franklin D. Roosevelt Presidential Library

"Hostilities exist," he continued, and then asked that Congress declare war against the Empire of Japan for this "unprovoked and dastardly attack."[56]

War was declared unanimously, with the exception of one lone vote in the House of Representatives, that of Jeanette Rankin, the first woman elected to the House of Representatives and an ardent pacifist. Nevertheless, Montana Senator Burton Wheeler, who had been one of the most vocal isolationists, had changed his tune: "The only thing to do now," he intoned, "is to lick the hell out of them."[57] On December 11, Germany and Italy, as members of the Axis supporting their partner, Japan, declared war on the United States. The debate was over. This was "not a drill."

Chapter 8

Pearl Harbor to the Shores of Tripoli

"We are all in the same boat now."

December 1941–November 1942

On the evening of December 7, Winston Churchill was having dinner with American envoy Averell Harriman and John Winant, the U.S. ambassador to Britain. The wireless radio crackled the evening news in the background as they conversed over the meal. They had missed the opening lead story as they talked, but mid-report the announcer came back to it, adding more detail. Suddenly the three men sat up in their chairs at full attention: did the commentator say Hawaii had been attacked by the Japanese? At about the same moment, Churchill's butler entered the room. "It's quite true," he said. "We heard it ourselves outside." The prime minister sprang into action, saying as he left the dining room, "We shall declare war on Japan." Winant followed him out the door: "Good God, you can't declare war on a radio announcement!" Immediately, the two of them put in a call to the president. When Roosevelt came on the line, Churchill asked point-blank, "What's this about Japan?" "It's quite true," he answered. "They have attacked us at Pearl Harbor. We are all in the same boat now." "That certainly simplifies things," Churchill told him, and then, with a voice full of emotion, added, "God be with you."[1]

By the next day, Churchill was making plans to cross the Atlantic to convene with Roosevelt, suggesting to the president in a telegram on the 9th, "Now that we are, as you say, 'in the same boat,' would it not be wise for us to have another conference?" Churchill recalled later that working out a complete understanding between Britain and the United States regarding war aims outweighed all else. Getting to Washington with the strongest team of expert advisers possible became his priority. Indeed, Churchill looked forward to joining forces with the Americans, tapping their prodigious resources and the fresh, strapping strength of their young men. Here was an ally to defeat an enemy against which his beleaguered nation had stood alone these many months. After the war Churchill remembered his jubilation when he realized that at last Great Britain would have help:

> No American will think it wrong of me if I proclaim that to have the United States at our side was to me the greatest joy. I could not foretell the course of events. I do not pretend to have measured accurately the martial might of Japan, but now at this very moment I knew the United

States was in the war, up to its neck and in to the death. So we had won after all! Yes, after Dunkirk, after the fall of France; after the deadly struggle of the U-Boat war . . . after seventeen months of lonely fighting and nineteen months of my responsibility in dire stress. We had won the war. England would live; Britain would live, the Commonwealth of nations and the Empire would live. . . . Once again in our long Island history we should emerge, however mauled or mutilated, safe and victorious.[2]

Well, perhaps, but even with the anticipated full commitment of the United States, things did not look promising. Although Americans could barely comprehend the magnitude of what had happened that Sunday, as they huddled around their radios to glean details from hourly news broadcasts, they understood that the facts were bleak. That Monday the president had already listed the initial Japanese targets: Guam, the Philippines, Wake Island, Midway, Hong Kong. Now came word that Malaya was under attack . . . Burma, Borneo, Thailand, Singapore.[3]

The news coming from the British would soon get worse. On the evening of December 9, 1941, Churchill was meeting with the admiralty to see how the "pride of the line," the battleships *Prince of Wales* and *Repulse*, might best be used in the Pacific to shore up the American fleet damaged in the Pearl Harbor attack. At that point both vessels had been sent to Singapore, where they might "exercise some vague menace . . . upon all hostile naval calculations."[4] Various ideas were discussed, but no decision made. It was a shock, then, on the next morning when a telephone call from the First Sea Lord announced to Churchill with a "cough and a gulp" that both of these magnificent vessels had been sunk by the Japanese. Churchill remembered the British sailors who had shared hymnals with the Americans aboard the *Prince of Wales* that Sunday morning of the Atlantic Conference. Half of them had died along with the captain, as shore-based torpedo aircraft rained down their deadly payloads. Churchill recognized the impact immediately: "There were no British or American capital ships in the Indian Ocean or the Pacific except the American survivors of Pearl Harbor, who were hastening back to California. Over all this vast expanse of waters Japan was supreme, and we everywhere were weak and naked."[5]

Meanwhile in Washington, Marshall was wrestling with this exact Pacific reality. Perhaps at any moment Hawaii would be invaded; most of the air force that might have been effective against the Japanese was now in smoking ruins; angry charges against the military leadership at Pearl Harbor fueled fearsome questions—how could this have happened in the United

States of America? The West Coast of the United States was in a state of panic driven by rampant rumor. As Marshall scrambled to find planes, men, and supplies to aid MacArthur in the Philippines, word came that the British were on their way, ready to "review the whole war plan in the light of reality and new facts."[6] Marshall would have preferred that this meeting come after the New Year. After all, it would be his responsibility to make the military case for the Americans.

Nevertheless, by December 14, the prime minister and his party were headed for the United States. As the *Duke of York* zigzagged to avoid U-boats, racing westward through heavy gales and rough seas, the captain insisted that his human cargo remain safely below deck. This was not a problem: the prime minister was energized, focused, and extraordinarily productive. During the trip over, he produced three papers on the future course of the war, his service chiefs and aides whipping them into print so that the president and his military advisers could receive them upon his arrival. Churchill wired the Americans from sea that the British hoped to reach agreements on certain key points, number one being a "fundamental basis for joint strategy." Churchill worried that after Pearl Harbor "the whole fury of the nation would be turned upon Japan."[7] Yes, he took a certain comfort from the position that the president had taken in 1939 and '40: If the United States entered a war that involved both Germany and Japan, the United States would take a defensive posture against the relatively weak Japan and concentrate with Britain on the Atlantic European Theater. But what about the anger, fear, and outrage against Japan that had catapulted the American people out of their prewar ambivalence? Would they understand a "Europe first" approach?

British fears proved ungrounded. Roosevelt and his military advisers, including Marshall, were still committed to the defeat of Germany. In fact, the firm resolution that Hitler must be defeated first was in line with the view of American army and navy war planners, refined in the light of developing events and articulated by the chief of naval operations, Admiral Stark. Identified as Plan Dog in exploratory talks with the British in early 1941, the proposal stated that, faced with a two-front war, the main effort would be made in the Atlantic and European area and would involve a large-scale ground offensive. In the Pacific and Far East, U.S. strategy would be defensive, with the largest area of focus the Alaska-Hawaii-Panama triangle.[8] Stark's view was that the defeat of Germany would make the defeat of Japan a matter of time, whereas the defeat of Japan would not materially weaken Germany.[9] Although Marshall would constantly adjust troops and matériel to meet the demands of the Pacific Theater commanders, who continuously felt the brunt of this approach and complained about it bitterly, neither he nor military planners veered too far from this key point of view until Germany was defeated.

That part was writ large and not in question, but accomplishing it? That would be the problem, and it was not an easy one. Despite the "common cause" of the two nations, the American military leaders were not willing to be used to carry out a strictly British strategy. Later, Marshall conceded that he could see why Churchill and his staff thought that, given "our state of shock" over the Pearl Harbor attack, we wouldn't be able to act in a cohesive way on our own. Thus, perhaps they could "draw on United States manpower and weapons as if these had been swept into a common pool for campaigns tailored to suit the interests of the British."[10] In fact, Marshall understood the country's military deficits all too well. Although he had worked hard to develop collaboration among the president, the cabinet, and the service chiefs, in reality no integrated system of defense control existed. British Field Commander John Dill, who would later become not only a colleague but a friend of Marshall's, was to say of the American military in this phase, "The country has not—repeat not—the slightest conception of what the war means, and their armed forces are more unready for war than it is possible to imagine."[11] So it was that the American military heads came warily to the table of these skilled professionals.

Churchill and his team were to stay more than three weeks in what came to be known as the Arcadia Conference. The players, many of whom would dominate these conferences throughout the war, soon arrived: for the Americans, Marshall represented the army; General Henry "Hap" Arnold, the army air forces. Two naval chiefs completed the delegation: Admiral Stark as chief of naval operations and Admiral Ernest King, who was at that time commander of the U.S. Navy Fleet but would take over both tasks the following March. On the British side the staff, well-seasoned by 18 months of war under Churchill's leadership, had agreed on basic issues and were extremely well prepared. In fact, although prime minister, Churchill had been directly involved in military operations, since he had created for himself the new post of minister of defense in 1940. His most senior representatives at Arcadia were Admiral Dudley Pound, the First Sea Lord, and Air Chief Marshal Charles Portal, chief of the Royal Air Force. Lord Beaverbrooke, chief of war production, was also on board. Marshall's army counterpart, Field Marshal Alan Brooke, the chief of the Imperial General Staff (CIGS), was left behind to manage the War Cabinet as word came in "about the terrifyingly rapid Japanese advance across south-east Asia."[12]

Arcadia was the first Anglo-American conference post-Pearl Harbor, and for Marshall it was a delicate situation. Churchill was literally in the White House—he had set up his office, map room, and command center very near the president's bedroom, thus making it possible for this very persuasive Brit to confer with Roosevelt late at night. While Churchill as minister of defense briefed his military leaders often, Roosevelt tended not to do the same. At the White House on the very first evening, Churchill outlined his strategy. Roosevelt, without his military advisers nearby, was in an expansive mood and seemed to agree with most of the prime minister's proposals. This was exactly the kind of situation that Marshall and his colleagues dreaded.[13]

President Roosevelt and Prime Minister Churchill hold a press conference
at the White House, December 23, 1941.

Franklin D. Roosevelt Library

One such incident concerned the Philippines. Although involved in the Arcadia conference, Marshall continued his efforts to get desperately needed reinforcements to that besieged island, but he was having difficulty due to the Japanese blockade. In one of these evening meetings, Roosevelt agreed to consider sending those reinforcements for the defense of Singapore if they could not get through to MacArthur. Marshall and the other service chiefs were appalled that Roosevelt would take it upon himself to make such an offer. Secretary of War Henry Stimson threatened to resign over the matter, and Roosevelt soon reneged on his offer.[14]

Help for staving off what Marshall would later call the "sideshows" of Churchill and Roosevelt came from a surprising source. Field Marshal Sir John Dill, formerly the British chief of the Imperial General Staff, came with the British delegation to Arcadia as the head of the British Joint Staff Mission, a post that he would hold until his untimely death in November 1944. At the close of the Arcadia Conference, he was to be based in Washington, and worked closely with Marshall throughout the war. Their professional association, begun at the Atlantic Conference, soon turned to a deep friendship. On Christmas Day 1941 the Marshalls had Dill and his wife to dinner at Quarters #1. It was Dill's birthday, and Katherine managed, despite bakeries closed for the holidays, to get him a cake embellished with tiny British and American flags. The table guests shared a good laugh when they realized that both flags were made in Japan. In some ways, both Marshall and Dill had similar personalities: both were committed to duty above personal preference, and neither sought publicity. They trusted each other explicitly, and that intimate relationship proved pivotal.

Field Marshal Sir John Dill and Marshall, Arlington, Virginia, April 1942
George C. Marshall Research Library

Both Marshall and Dill soon realized that in terms of communication with their respective military staffs, Churchill and Roosevelt took two very different approaches. Churchill's method was to keep his chiefs fully informed. For example, as Marshall explained it, when a message from Roosevelt came to Churchill, everybody who should know got a copy of it immediately. Roosevelt, on the other hand, was "always sensitive about the reports on his own conduct of affairs." He didn't want a record of cabinet meetings, and often Marshall never saw messages that the president sent to Churchill, even though, as he said, "It directly affected the affairs of the army and the air and maybe the navy."[15] As Dill and Marshall came to recognize this pattern, Dill began to share the information that he received. Marshall described it to biographer Forrest Pogue this way:

> When a message would go from the president to Churchill, Dill would get a copy of it. Then Dill would come over to my office, and I would get Mr. Roosevelt's message. . . . I had to be very careful that nobody knew this . . . because Dill would be destroyed in a minute if this was discovered. . . . [Further] when the prime minister sent a message to Mr. Roosevelt, Dill would bring me a copy, and I never disclosed that fact to any of the chiefs of staff, and certainly not to the president. But it kept me au courant with what was going on.[16]

Marshall noted that sometimes Churchill would ask Dill to ascertain Marshall's views on certain matters. The two of them—Marshall and Dill—would discuss it and make up a reply. If Marshall disagreed strongly, he could make his case to Dill in a way that never would have been acceptable directly to Churchill. As Marshall noted, "It was rather a curious set up, but a very effectual one in this business, because these were all strong men—Mr. Roosevelt and Mr. Churchill—and the coordination of these matters was of vital importance."

For Marshall, this December 1941 Arcadia Conference marked the beginning of 13 wartime meetings whose task it would be to seek and seal the strategy of the Anglo-American alliance. Marshall was pivotal in overcoming the difficulties inherent in such a huge endeavor. According to Mark Stoler, he was "primarily responsible for the establishment and smooth functioning of the alliance's coordinating machinery." Further, in the end it would be the acceptance of Marshall's key strategic concept for Allied victory that would win the day—the Normandy Invasion into the heart of Nazi-held Europe.[17]

One situation Marshall had tried to correct within his own military circle was the fierce competition between the services. He would later say that the rivalry between these commands was its own "vicious little war." Even Roosevelt, who had once been undersecretary of the navy, seemed to favor that branch of the armed forces over the other. Marshall once complained that he wished the president would quit using the terms "my navy" and "your army" in discussing these military matters. Marshall also believed that the lack of communication between the army and navy in the lead-up to Pearl Harbor had contributed to the success of the surprise attack by the Japanese. Since becoming army chief of staff, Marshall had insisted on the importance of the two branches cooperating rather than competing.

The Joint Chiefs of Staff are pictured at a luncheon in the fall of 1942. From left to right are Admiral Ernest J. King, Marshall, Admiral William D. Leahy, and General Henry "Hap" Arnold.

George C. Marshall Research Library

Early in February 1942 Marshall suggested a new command structure for the Joint Chiefs of Staff. By that time it was clear that Admiral Stark would be transferred to London as a naval liaison and that King would remain as the head of naval forces on the Joint Chiefs. Marshall immediately recognized the problem inherent in this arrangement: two army heads—himself and army air forces chief Henry "Hap" Arnold, and one navy chief—King. Marshall suggested that retired Admiral William Leahy be made the president's personal chief of staff. With that title he would also serve as the chairman of the Joint Chiefs, and thus the balance would be struck: two army, two navy. Roosevelt was none too happy about this arrangement, telling Marshall, "But you are the chief of staff." No, Marshall had replied, "There is no chief of staff of all of the military services." The president still wasn't convinced: "Well, I'm the chief of staff; [since] I'm the commander-in-chief." Marshall made the case that Leahy would be useful to him, would relieve him somewhat of a "Superman" burden. Eventually, Marshall convinced Roosevelt.[18] According to Ed Cray, Marshall was "creatively bending the rules to suit his needs. The Joint Chiefs, created without legislative authority, were to have an equally extralegal chairman."

"Unity of command"

Even before this firming up of the Joint Chiefs, Marshall had realized that another issue was the fundamental organizational challenge in the combined efforts of the British and American leadership. If there was a "vicious little war" to be fought within the U.S. command, he could only imagine the task of putting these two allied forces together in some cohesive way. As the Arcadia meetings continued that late December, he decided to tackle this problem by introducing a concept with the rather bland title "unity of command." Marshall proposed that the ground, naval, and air forces of all the Allied powers in a particular theater of war be placed under a single commander. He could see what a problem effective communication and interconnected chain of command were going to be in these far-flung arenas. Marshall made his case: the issue could not be managed just by cooperation, citing human frailties that would make an officer in the field unwilling to place his troops under the command of another service.[19] No, he insisted, it had to be established as a policy.

Marshall sprang his idea in a meeting focused on the question of Allied dispositions in the Pacific, where the Philippines and Singapore were threatened. Initially, neither the American nor British chiefs saw this idea as viable; in fact, they seemed stunned at such an approach. Each raised their respective concerns. Stark was noncommittal; Portal stalled for time, hoping for a postponement. Since it was Christmas Eve, and not the time to take on such an unprecedented proposal, they ended the discussion and left for their respective holiday celebrations. Marshall realized that he hadn't been adequately prepared to explain his position, and that the chiefs, focused on the realities of the Pacific Theater where the enemy was running rampant, couldn't imagine how this might work.

To better describe his proposal, Marshall directed Brigadier General Dwight D. Eisenhower, whom he had only recently brought to the War Plans Division, to "draft immediately a letter of instruction for the supreme commander of the Pacific area, outlining the mission," and addressing national sovereignty concerns.[20] (During a tour in Panama, Eisenhower had impressed General Fox Conner, Marshall's respected colleague and friend. Eisenhower had also served as MacArthur's chief of staff in the Philippines—an area of obvious strategic interest—and had distinguished himself in Third Army maneuvers that Marshall observed in Louisiana before the war. All of these factors landed Eisenhower in War Plans at this crucial time.)

By the time Marshall visited Roosevelt with the proposal, he had in hand Eisenhower's details of how it might work in a real-time situation. The president approved. Now Marshall took the idea back to the American navy commanders, and after plenty of back and forth, some of it strident (especially when Marshall suggested that the first united commander would be General Wavell, a Britisher), he finally got their okay. Armed with the approval of one side, he tackled the British contingent. As Secretary of War Stimson later said, "They kicked like Bay steers." Marshall systematically addressed their fears, arguing that this united commander didn't have to know everything about technical issues, but rather needed to possess the qualities of good judgment and the ability to avoid exploiting one area of his theater at the expense of another. Finally, the British shifted their position, so much so that at the end of the meeting, to Marshall's astonishment, a couple of the British navy officers and Dill came up and hugged him![21] Now, only Churchill had to be convinced.

The showdown with the prime minister came in Churchill's White House bedroom on the morning of December 28. Marshall found him propped in bed, papers and memoranda spread around him, and ready for action. When Churchill protested the concept, asking what an army officer could know about handling a ship—a very special thing, he said—Marshall answered: "What the devil does a naval officer know about handling a tank?" Marshall told him that he wasn't interested in "Frobisher or Drake," but in having "a unified front against Japan, an enemy which was fighting furiously." Churchill continued the debate, once leaving the bedroom for a bath and coming out clad only in a towel but still arguing vehemently as he paced. If they used this idea, he said, Marshall would "have to take the best with the worst." Marshall's forcefulness in presenting a position he firmly believed in came through, though, because Churchill finally agreed. By the end of the day, Churchill had telegraphed the Cabinet that the president had "urged" this unity of command concept, and that Marshall had "pleaded [the] case with great conviction." Back in London "minding the store," General Alan

Brooke called the whole idea "wild and half-baked." Nevertheless, once both the president and Churchill had agreed, it was a fait accompli.[22]

In addition, during the remainder of the Arcadia Conference, Marshall got approval for a unified war council, the Combined Chiefs of Staff, composed of the American and British chiefs who met continuously throughout the war in Washington and that would give orders to theater commanders. Churchill appointed representatives of his military branches who acted on their behalf during these sessions except during actual strategic conferences when the British chiefs could be there in person. Fortunately for Marshall, it was Dill who headed up the British delegation in Washington; on the American side it included all of the joint chiefs, but most often Marshall was the key leader. This Anglo-American unit directed the strategy of the war and allowed the Allies to work closely on military matters. It didn't always work perfectly, arguments were often heated, sometimes the system broke down completely, but in the end it led to the development of a unified strategy that would result in victory.

The Philippine Conundrum

As Marshall worked his way through these organizational issues and discussions of overall strategy, he was also scrambling to get help to MacArthur and his troops in the Philippines. As early as December 10, the Joint Chiefs had ordered the eight-ship *Pensacola* convoy to those islands, with bomber and fighter planes, air force personnel—including pilots—and supplies. However, because the Philippines were in such an uncertain state, the convoy was diverted to Australia in the hopes it could be sent later. General Marshall desperately sought anything by air or sea that could break a daunting Japanese blockade, but it proved difficult. As Secretary of War Stimson noted, "The Navy had been rather shaken and panic-stricken after the catastrophe of Hawaii." Marshall biographer Forrest Pogue wrote that one could hardly question the navy's reluctance to send most of its fighting strength 5,000 miles away into Japanese-dominated waters to an area where the enemy had air superiority at a time when the Hawaiian Islands were still considered vulnerable.[23] Stimson and Marshall continued to seek a way to get relief to MacArthur, keeping hope alive into February.

It was only one week after Pearl Harbor that Marshall's new War Plans deputy, General Eisenhower, had arrived at Union Station to begin his duties. A couple of hours later, even before taking his luggage to his brother Milton's home in the Virginia suburbs, Eisenhower, at Marshall's request, was called to the chief of staff's Munitions Building office along Constitution

Avenue. The question at hand: what to do about the crisis in the Philippines. Indeed, this would be task one, even preceding what Eisenhower would later describe as the "talk, talk, talk" sessions of Arcadia.

Marshall explained the situation in the Pacific: the battleship fleet wouldn't be available for months; Hawaii needed reinforcement, the Philippine Air Force was hard-hit, and the Japanese were invading Luzon. Putting Eisenhower to the test, he asked him, "What should be our general line of action?" Perhaps a bit nonplussed but undaunted, Eisenhower responded, "Give me a few hours." By evening he came back with his report, concluding that major reinforcements couldn't be sent to the Philippines for a long time, too long for the garrison to hold out with dribs and drabs of assistance, especially if the Japanese applied major forces to their reduction. Eisenhower recommended that America's base be Australia and said that "great risks" and "any amount of money" would be required to "secure our communications to it." Still, Eisenhower insisted, everything humanly possible should be done to help "our Philippine wards and American troops" there. Marshall agreed, telling him, "Do your best to save them."[24]

Marshall himself set about to do that. He discussed with Roosevelt the possibility of asking Russia to launch an attack on Japan to relieve the pressure, using Lend-Lease allotments as an inducement. Still hard-pressed by the Germans now deep in Russia, Stalin stalled. Further, and not surprisingly, the British opposed such a plan, since that would invite the full ferocity of Hitler's army onto the British Isles. MacArthur continued his pressure for reinforcements, even suggesting that commercial ships be chartered to run supplies through enemy waters and insisting that planes could be flown in from British or Dutch bases. Marshall and Eisenhower were considering these options as they sought to build up supply depots in Australia.

Sometimes when things seem bad, they get worse. With the outbreak of war, new planes had been diverted from their intended destination, the Philippines, to Australia; perhaps they could be ferried to MacArthur by Christmas. Unfortunately, a piece of equipment essential to the plane's firing mechanism was thrown away with the crates to which they were attached. Although later used when the mistake was corrected, the chance to transport the planes to MacArthur had passed. Marshall did manage to get 15 B-24 bombers on the way, but with the Japanese noose tightening, the opportunity of getting them onto the island dimmed. Marshall's cables to MacArthur that a million dollars worth of supplies were being amassed in Australia for delivery to the Philippines seemed to offer slight hope, but in fact getting them there proved next to impossible. Finally, Marshall authorized funds for the purpose of hiring commercial ships as blockade runners, but there were few takers, although at least three made it through to unload 10,000 tons of food, ammunition, and medical supplies. Former secretary of war Patrick Hurley, who had been sent to Australia to oversee this effort, could accomplish little. As he was to later say, "We were out-shipped, out-planned, out-manned and out-gunned by the Japanese."[25] For all practical purposes, at this early stage of the war, MacArthur was on his own.

Without air support, and hindered by untrained and poorly equipped Filipino reserves, MacArthur had decided by Christmas Eve to pull back all of his forces on Luzon into Bataan, a 30-mile peninsula separating Manila Bay from the South China Sea. As the army retreated in good order, but with many supplies left behind, he prepared to move his headquarters to Corregidor, a small rocky island in the bay. With Manila now an open city, on January 1 the Japanese entered the capital without resistance. The American and Filipino troops dug in on Bataan, but they were woefully short of food, ammunition, and medicine—especially quinine for relief against malaria so needed in the steaming, mosquito-infested jungles. From the relative safety of Corregidor, MacArthur kept promising help for the troops on Bataan, whose morale dipped low from hunger, disease, and incessant Japanese air raids. As historian Mark Perry described it, "MacArthur retreated to his headquarters, bored deeply inside a railroad tunnel . . . and peeked out only for highly photogenic inspection trips of the positions of his soldiers on Bataan."[26] From the suffering troops on that beleaguered outpost MacArthur soon gained a nickname—"Dougout Doug." Nevertheless, he publicly vowed that he would stay until the end to be taken prisoner or die on Corregidor, and most historians opine that he would have done so. With the Japanese breaking through each line of defense, MacArthur reiterated to Marshall in late January that "I intend to fight it out to complete destruction." Quite dramatically, he named a successor in case of his death.[27]

With MacArthur by now being lionized within the United States as the general "bravely, cannily fighting off superior hordes of Japanese invaders," neither Roosevelt nor Marshall was going to have "the hero of Bataan" taken prisoner or killed. The impact on the nation's morale, profoundly discouraged from continued defeats in the Pacific, would be disastrous. Further, MacArthur was a brilliant general, whose contribution to future military operations was vital. The president ordered that he escape to Australia, where he could lay the groundwork for a future battle as commander of all forces in the southwest Pacific. MacArthur, finally convinced that he could best launch an attack on the Japanese in the Philippines by overseeing the buildup of troops and supplies from the safety of Australia, agreed. On the evening of March 11, 1942, the general, along with his wife and son plus 17 staff members—including his publicist—slipped away from Corregidor on PT-boats, traveling for two days in radio silence without lights to Mindanao, thence by B-17 for a dangerous 10-hour flight to Darwin, and finally via train to Melbourne. To make certain that the press did not paint this as a general abandoning his troops, Marshall saw to it that MacArthur received the Medal of Honor, writing the official acknowledgment himself, citing "gallantry and intrepidity above and beyond the call of duty." Marshall explained to Stimson that it was a necessary step because not only did he believe MacArthur deserved it but also it would "offset any propaganda by the enemy directed against his leaving his command," and, further, would have a "constructive morale value."[28]

General Douglas MacArthur and General Jonathan Wainwright, October 10, 1941
Center of Military History: United States Army

General Jonathan Wainwright, left in command of all American and Filipino troops on the island, was now directing the defense from his Corregidor headquarters. He was in constant contact with Bataan and knew full well that the situation was becoming untenable. By the end of March, only one-fourth of Bataan's defenders were combat-effective, with malaria rampant and food rations reduced to 10 ounces of rice a day and an ounce or two of canned fish. In early April the Japanese launched a huge offensive, and by the 7th, Major General Edward King, who had been in charge at Bataan since Wainwright's command appointment, surrendered 76,000 soldiers. On Corregidor, with Wainwright leading a valiant defense, 13,000 soldiers, including 2,000 who had escaped from Bataan, held out until May 6, 1942, when fatigue, hunger, endless bombardment, and death did their grim work. Wainwright cabled the president, "With broken heart, and head bowed in sadness but not in shame . . . I must arrange the surrender of the fortified islands of Manila Bay."[29] The Japanese paraded these Corregidor survivors through the streets of Manila before shipping them to their destination. The sick and starving Bataan prisoners had it worse. They were marched 65 miles to the railroad that took them to a prisoner-of-war camp, a journey later recalled as the "Bataan Death March." Seven thousand died along the way, in part from weakness brought on by near starvation or the complications of wounds; in part from the cruel treatment of the Japanese guards, which included systematic bayoneting, shooting, and even beheading. The rest, said one doctor who survived the experience, made it to imprisonment "by the marrow of their bones."[30] MacArthur had said from his new headquarters location in Australia, "I came through, and I shall return." Indeed, but it would take a while.

The news from the Pacific that spring of 1942 had been nothing if not grim. The unified command of the Australian, British, Dutch, and American (ABDA) forces under General Wavell had disintegrated as the Japanese claimed victories in a vast and thinly defended ocean that now seemed their own. Guam had fallen to the Japanese just after Pearl Harbor; then Wake Island and Hong Kong. British Malaya, with its all-important rubber and tin supply, was gone, and with it the so-called impregnable fortress of Singapore. The Dutch East Indies came under Japanese control in March. The loss of Burma in April was an enormous blow, since the Japanese then controlled the Burma Road, the route of crucial supplies to the Chinese.[31]

The "Battling Bastards of Bataan" had put up a fierce fight in the Philippines for five months, but now the "rising sun" flew over Manila. Despite a virtual typhoon of defeat, a plan to overcome these losses had to be put into place.

The northern Philippine Islands

George C. Marshall Research Library

171

Under Marshall's guidance, the Pacific commands were reorganized: MacArthur would officially have unified control over the South West Pacific Theater, which included the Philippines, the Dutch East Indies, Australia, Borneo, and New Guinea; Admiral Chester Nimitz would have authority over the Pacific Ocean Areas (POA). With the strategic accent still on "Germany First," and despite the incessant demands of these commanders, the emphasis at the moment would be to contain rather than reduce Japanese aggression. In due time, when the weight of men and matériel could be placed on those theaters, MacArthur would move from Australia through New Guinea and eventually back to the Philippines; Nimitz would press from Hawaii toward major Japanese island outposts in the central Pacific. Eventually, the two missions would come together to invade Japan itself.[32]

Such an orderly plan for reversing Japanese aggression in the Pacific must have seemed like a pipe dream to Marshall in the early days of 1942. As Forrest Pogue noted, "Every ounce of his stamina and every particle of his logic was needed to cope with the monstrous difficulties that followed in the train of Pearl Harbor." Every new disaster resulted in frantic appeals for help that threatened Marshall's effort for a cohesive strategy. Stimson described these crises as the stopping up of "urgent rat holes." Marshall saw them as a "dangerous dispersion of resources." Eisenhower agreed: "We've got to go to Europe and fight—and we've got to quit wasting resources all over the world."[33]

On the home front Marshall tried to get the army organized to meet such a challenge. He had already told his military heads that "the time was long past when matters could be debated and discussed . . . ad infinitum." He instructed them to "get action where action was needed."[34]

With the ground and air force rapidly growing post–Pearl Harbor, Marshall put Lieutenant General Joseph McNarney in charge of a massive reorganization of a bureaucratic, red tape–laden War Department. As historian Mark Perry wrote, "Known for his candor (he had once responded to one of Marshall's suggestions by blurting out 'Jesus, man, you can't do that,' a frankness that his boss appreciated), McNarney was thick-skinned and uninterested in the inevitable power politics among Marshall's staff."[35] Indeed, under his leadership, said Pogue, "The word went out that efficiency, tighter control, reduction in the number of General Staff officers, and the number of individuals having direct access to the Chief of Staff [would be reduced] from some sixty to about six who were essential to a successful war effort."[36] In the new streamlined arrangement, there were three "super commands"—Army Ground Forces (General Lesley McNair),

Army Air Forces (Arnold), and Services of Supply (Lt. General Brehon Somervell). General Headquarters and War Plans were incorporated into a fresh organization titled the Operations Division—Eisenhower would be promoted as its head.

Marshall's correspondence during the three-month period after Pearl Harbor reveals the width and depth of the chief of staff's responsibilities, as paraphrased from his letters below:

Quick action is needed for building 1,000 bombers a month.

We have 35 divisions, 10% are fully equipped, but the rest will [only] be 50% equipped by year's end if production levels are met.

Theater commanders will decide if over age officers will be allowed combat duty.

Are we overdoing the number of troop installations for protecting Washington, D.C.?

Yes, lend-lease shipment of tanks, jeeps, and trucks to the Brazilian army is needed.

Regarding the radio comments of Yellow Cab's owner, calling himself an expert and saying he could improve the army's motor transport operations—military and civil operations are two different things.

No, there will be no sleeping car accommodations for the transport of military personnel. Getting uniforms for a 2-million-man army is costly, so the ideal of smart, well-fitting uniforms may be sacrificed.

Yes, we do need pilot training at West Point.

Yes, ample mosquito netting must be supplied to troops on the west coast of Africa.

Question: The president wishes to know what the air route to China will be with the loss of Burma to the Japanese.

The president states that, yes, all of the Queen Mary should be refitted and utilized for troop accommodations.

(To MacArthur) Yes, naval weakness due to Pearl Harbor is being corrected, but very heavy convoy duties have limited aggressive operations.

No, since protecting all key installations on the Pacific Coast—thousands—would immobilize the army, the local military commander will decide, but will be forced to take risks.

It's the undersecretary of war who will have to respond to Congressman McCormack, who doesn't want a rabid critic of the president to get an assembly plant in his district.

Yes, blackouts should be required along the coast to thwart U-boat activity. Yes, Red Cross kits need to be redesigned—too heavy for a soldier to bother with.[37]

Although outwardly in control—"George Marshall was the most self-confident man who ever wore pants," one newsman had said—the fact is, he felt the strain. Every evening, after arriving home at Fort Myer, he and Katherine would walk along the streets of Arlington, Virginia. Katherine remembers that her husband would talk, talk, and talk. She said little on the walks back through darkened neighborhoods to Quarters #1, for as she later wrote, "I was listening to a man steeling himself to carry a burden so tremendous in magnitude and so diverse in its demands that it was difficult to comprehend how one man could carry it alone. I had the feeling he was talking to himself. It was as though George Marshall was someone he was constantly appraising, advising and training to meet a situation." He confided to her, "I cannot afford the luxury of sentiment, mine must be cold logic." Though in public his decisions were firm, he once told his wife, "I get so tired of saying 'No,' it takes it out of me. I am really thankful when I can say 'Yes.' It is not easy to tell men where they failed. My days seem to be filled with situations and problems where I must do the difficult, the hard thing."[38] Certainly Katherine worried about her husband's well-being, but Marshall worried for his wife's health as well. On March 23, 1942, he wrote to his stepson, Allen Brown, regarding his mother: "The battle over her health is a most difficult one. The trouble is, I cannot persuade her to lighten her own burdens: telephone, mail, and committees." He goes on to say that in addition to her war duties, she had unremitting concern for her own family. Resigned, he concludes, "It is idle to expect her to change her ways at this time, we just have to make the best of it," and closes, "I am very busy, so this can be but a hasty note."[39]

Bolero, Sledgehammer, and Roundup

Indeed he was busy. Axis successes that early winter of 1942 in both the Atlantic and the Pacific put intensifying pressures on him to disperse troops and provide matériel for a range of desperate needs. Despite the talks of Arcadia, there was still no unified strategy for global war. Further, even though Marshall had acquitted himself well at the conference, the better organized and prepared British had dominated the strategic discussions. Churchill's view of how to win the war did find its way into deliberations. According to historian Mark Stoler,

> It was a strategy of attrition centering on the use of Allied sea and air instead of land power to bring about a German collapse with minimal cost to Western lives. Blockade, strategic bombing, commando raids, and support of resistance movements were all emphasized in this strategy as a means of weakening Germany but not suffering heavy losses. Here Hitler's Italian and Balkan allies could be defeated and knocked out of the war, thereby weakening the German empire and perhaps triggering a chain reaction similar to the one that had precipitated German surrender in 1918.[40]

Specific to that approach, Churchill had already proposed "Gymnast," the invasion of French North Africa as a backdoor effort to aid his British troops already fighting in Egypt and to draw off forces from the German thrust into the Soviet Union, still very much in progress. Churchill thought he had the president's approval of this idea. Marshall worried that might be the case as well—he knew that during Arcadia the prime minister had made his case to Roosevelt late at night when the president did not have his own advisers as counterweights. (The fact was that by mid-March 1942, because of Allied defeats in the Pacific, the Gymnast operation was on hold.) American military advisers, including Marshall, did not like Churchill's strategic view. In the past, the United States had relied on a direct approach, not the kind of peripheral opportunistic strategy that perhaps suited a seafaring nation such as Great Britain. Indeed, within the U.S. War Plans Division, the favored line of attack was to concentrate a superior force and strike at the heart of the most powerful enemy army, to some degree a natural extension of the long-ago agreed-upon Germany first strategy. To do otherwise, in their view, would result in a long and indecisive war.

Marshall directed Eisenhower to draw up the details of this approach. Often referred to as the Marshall Memorandum (or sometimes the Eisenhower Doctrine), it became the prime planning instrument for the United States and Great Britain during the war. The document called for "an immediate concentration of Anglo-American forces in Britain (Bolero) for a massive cross-channel attack of 48 divisions into occupied France in the spring of 1943 (Roundup).[41] A modified plan, code-named Sledgehammer, was advanced as an emergency proposal for the late summer of 1942 in case Germany showed unusual vulnerability, or if the Red Army was near collapse. Marshall called such an attack "a sacrifice for the common good." Roundup was the main focus, and according to the report, only Western Europe offered the right circumstances: the buildup could take place in England just across the channel from the enemy-occupied coast of France; the airfields in Great Britain offered the best air cover; the North Atlantic supply lines were already being protected by American and British naval forces; even the staging-in-England part of the plan (Bolero) would make the German army less focused on the east and thus provide indirect relief to the Soviets.[42]

On March 25, 1942, the War Cabinet met with the president, along with Harry Hopkins, to present the strategic plan. At first it did not go well. Marshall described how Roosevelt had a habit of tossing out new operations in what the chief of staff later called "his cigarette holder gesture." The president was toying with possible offensives in the Middle East and the Mediterranean. Eventually, the army leaders steered him back. Marshall's presentation was very strong, and soon he won Roosevelt's support for the cross-channel plan. At the end of the meeting, Hopkins, who wanted to see the proposal quickly put into action, recommended that the formal report outlining the approach be taken directly to Churchill, bypassing the Combined Chiefs in Washington, whose British members would tear it apart before either Churchill or Brooke even saw it.[43]

By April 4, 1942, Marshall was on his way with Hopkins to London for a series of meetings, code-named Modicum, with Churchill and his chiefs. During the early part of the flight, one of the plane's engines failed, and the pilot had to prolong his first stop in Bermuda for repairs. Thus it was that General Marshall was on the island for Easter Sunday. When the governor-general asked that Marshall read from the Bible as part of the service at a local church, the chief of staff agreed. Having read the verses ahead of time, Marshall felt prepared; however, once he arrived he noticed that several more had been added. He had no time to practice the names of the seven churches of Asia Minor—Ephesus, Smyrna, Pergamum, Thyatira, Sardis, Philadelphia, and Laodicea. Marshall said that the only one that he recognized was "Philadelphia," so he "intoned" that one "in an impressive manner."

Later, in London, he would be teased a bit about the "unpronounceable" list. Nevertheless, while still at the church that morning, an elderly man who was native to Pennsylvania came up to tell him, "I'm from Philadelphia, too."[44] The Easter morning Bible reader and his colleagues continued their flight the next day, traveling under aliases—Marshall was Mr. C.G. Mell—and wearing civilian clothes.

After a stopover in Ireland, Marshall and his party arrived in London and soon got a glimpse of war up close—grimy streets, bombed-out buildings, rubble, air-raid shelters, and screaming sirens. That very afternoon, Marshall and Hopkins met with Churchill in his austere underground Cabinet War Rooms deep under the government buildings of Whitehall, not far from 10 Downing Street. In the two-hour session, the chief of staff laid out the American proposal. Marshall noted later that Churchill already seemed familiar with the proposition—quite true, since a British liaison officer in the United States had gotten information about the basic concepts to be presented and had forewarned the prime minister. At dinner that evening was the first time Marshall met his opposite number, General Alan Brooke, chief of the Imperial General Staff (CIGS), described by historian Thomas Parrish as "swarthy, eagle-faced, stoop-shouldered, and immaculately turned out."[45] Brooke had excellent military credentials, including impressive service in World War I, skillful handling of British forces in the Dunkirk evacuation, and broad experience in key posts within the British army. Throughout the London meetings, each man would take the measure of the other; neither was impressed. Marshall compared Brooke to Dill and noted that while the CIGS "may be a good fighting man, he hasn't got Dill's brains." Brooke had his opinion of Marshall as well: "The American might be a good general at raising armies" and at bridging the deep between the military and political worlds, "but his strategical [sic] ability does not impress me at all."[46] As Pogue notes, both men later revised their estimates upward.

During the meetings in London, the strategic battle lines were drawn with the Americans favoring an almost immediate cross-channel attack and the British taking the position that Germany had to be weakened through opportunistic engagements before the risk of returning to the continent could be considered. American naval historian Samuel Eliot Morison described the difference between the two strategies to "the massive thrusts at the enemy's heart" versus "successive stabs around the periphery to bleed him to death, like jackals worrying a lion before springing at his throat." Marshall and Brooke would become the standard-bearers for these two differing points of view.[47]

Marshall, third from right, observing maneuvers on the Salisbury Plain in England, during his first wartime meeting with the British, April 1942.

George C. Marshall Research Library

The British particularly had problems with Sledgehammer—a "sacrifice play" in '42 should the Russians be beaten down to the point of surrender. Mark Stoler pointed out that although the plan seemed courageous and noble, the fact was that American troops could not be amassed in England before 1943; thus, courage and nobility for the "sacrifice" would fall primarily to the British. Even Marshall later admitted, "Our embarrassment was that we didn't have many troops in England to help with the operation."[48] Despite British reservations, two days before the Modicum meetings ended, Churchill gave guarded consent to "offensive action in 1942, perhaps, and in 1943 for certain." In one dinner meeting he had lifted a glass in toast, stating rather grandly that he had no hesitation in accepting the plan, and that Briton and American would henceforth march together in a "noble brotherhood of arms." The prime minister's chief of staff, General Hastings Ismay, wrote shortly after the conference, "Our American friends went happily homewards under the mistaken impression that we have committed ourselves to both Roundup and Sledgehammer" and recalled afterward that when the British rejected Sledgehammer, the Americans felt that "we had broken faith with them." Ismay admitted that the British should have come clean, much cleaner than they did, and should have said, "We are frankly horrified [regarding an invasion of the continent] because of what we have

178

been through in our lifetime—60,000 in one day, the 1st of July 1916 [Battle of the Somme in World War I] . . . 60,000. We, who had survived, had got that into our minds, never again, you see. We are not going into this until it is a cast-iron certainty."[49] There was also a more immediate reason that Churchill and Brooke did not come totally clean. According to historian Andrew Roberts:

> If Roosevelt and Marshall came to believe that they [the British high command] opposed a cross-Channel operation outright, the Americans would switch their attention to the Pacific, adopting a Japan First policy instead. This would leave Britain in renewed and possible mortal peril, a return to the cold winds of strategic isolation she had experienced in the twelve months between the evacuation of Dunkirk and Operation Barbarossa [invasion of the Soviet Union].[50]

Marshall's April 28, 1942, letter to Churchill thanking him for his hospitality during the London trip seemed clear: he had taken the prime minister's word that he supported Sledgehammer and wrote of its preparations as if it were a done deal. Marshall referred to the meeting as having established a "firm foundation," noting that the American and British military leadership had experienced a "full measure of cooperation." It would take a while for him to realize that the British were in no way ready to accept the plan he had delivered in London.

Despite the gloom that had gripped the country with news of MacArthur's retreat from the Philippines, when Marshall returned to the United States the capital city was flushed with a moment of victory. That April 18, 16 B-25 bombers had left their carrier base 800 miles from Japan to bomb Tokyo, Yokohama, Kobe, and Nagota before landing safely in China. The name of the raid's leader, Lieutenant Colonel James Doolittle, was on everyone's lips. While the sortie had not done a lot of damage, the boost to morale was palpable. At a personal level, Marshall was about to get a morale boost as well.

During the general's two-week absence in London, Katherine planned a surprise for her husband, perhaps one that would ease the strain he had been under in the first months of America's entry into the war. The previous year, the Marshalls had bought a home in Leesburg, Virginia, about 35 miles from Washington, D.C. The residence, named by its previous owners Dodona Manor, had been built before the Civil War and remodeled in the 1930s. Since Marshall had been thrust into the crisis of war, he and Katherine had rarely been able to go there—perhaps a weekend visit now and then. Just as soon as her husband left for Europe, Katherine went to work. She hired building contractors, bricklayers, and yardmen to transform an overgrown property into a beautiful place. Workmen built a two-car garage, a tool shed, and brick walkways to accent a newly groomed lawn. Katherine looked forward to showing her husband all that she had accomplished during his absence.

When Marshall returned to Washington after two weeks, Katharine greeted him at the airport with the request that they head into the country at once. He told her he had to go directly to his office, but as soon as he had finished, they would drive out to Leesburg. In the late afternoon of a beautiful spring evening, they began their trip. It was sunset by the time they pulled into the circular driveway in front of the house. The recently manicured grounds looked lovely, with spring flowers in bloom and the grass a vibrant green. Katherine gave her husband a tour, pointing out each improvement as she went. Marshall was delighted. He had lived on army posts all of his adult life, and this was the first home he had ever owned. In a voice husky with emotion, he told his wife, "This is home after 41 years of wandering."[51] Throughout the war, when he could, he stole away from Washington for a few hours or a day to work in the vegetable garden he would plant there each summer.

As much as the news of Wainwright's surrender in the Philippines had cast a pall over the War Department, when summer arrived, so did a glimmer of good news from the Pacific Theater. That May, in what would later be called the Battle of the Coral Sea, the Allies had thwarted an effort by the Japanese to take Port Moresby in New Guinea, which would have allowed them to cut supply lines between the United States and Australia/New Zealand. Further, after marauding over the Pacific for more than five months, this was the first time a Japanese invasion force had been turned back without achieving its objective. This battle was unique in naval history, since it was the first time such an action was fought only to and from the air, with none of the ships on either side seeing the others. Although the Japanese forces withdrew, they believed that they had won. Nevertheless, as one writer put it, "It was a tactical victory for the Imperial forces. However, the encounter was a strategic victory for the Americans. The Coral Sea battle meant the end of Japanese expansion southward. They would never again threaten Australia and New Zealand."[52]

"The Closest Squeak"

Another boost came in June 1942. Following the Battle of the Coral Sea, the commander of the Japanese Combined Fleet, Admiral Yamamoto, devised a plan to draw the U.S. Pacific Fleet into a battle where it could be destroyed. He was especially determined to sink carriers, since torpedo planes and dive bombers launched from these flattops, which could remain out of range of battleship fire, were proving a primary menace during battles at sea. His island of choice: Midway, the outpost of Hawaii and key to its defense. Fortunately for the Americans, Admiral Chester Nimitz, who commanded the naval forces in that area, knew that an attack of enormous proportions was coming, thanks to the work of cryptologists who had broken the enemy's naval code. "We are actively preparing to greet our expected visitors with the kind of reception they deserve," Nimitz had written to Admiral King in late May. During the Battle of Midway (June 4–5, 1942), the American navy's three carriers—*Enterprise, Hornet*, and *Yorktown*—managed to sink four Japanese carriers—*Kaga, Akagi, Soryu*, and *Hiryu*—and in the process many of its best air crews and pilots. Although the *Hiryu* inflicted mortal damage on the *Yorktown* before it was sunk, the impact of this four-carrier loss to the Japanese would prove irreparable. "These were super-critical moments," Marshall would later recall. "The closest squeak and the greatest victory [in the Pacific] was at Midway. The Navy performance there was magnificent and self-sacrificing to the last degree. There, by a very fortunate series of events, and by very superb action by the Navy and its air [force] . . . the dominance of the Pacific was recaptured."[53] Though the war was far from won—some would say it would be the later fighting on Guadalcanal and in the Solomon Islands that would turn the tide—the fact is, the Japanese would score no more knockout blows in the Pacific.

A Losing Battle

MacArthur and King saw the Midway victory as an opportunity to launch a major attack against the Japanese; it had never seemed easier to set aside that "Europe First" concept. On the other hand, Marshall and Stimson both viewed the outcome as a chance to once again focus on a European offensive in 1942. Marshall soon found out that the military option he had in mind—Operation Sledgehammer, an invasion into France that fall—was not what Churchill wanted, although he had so clearly indicated support of it that spring in London. Even as early as May, Churchill had begun to work on Roosevelt, hoping to steer him away from any invasion of the continent in the near future. Late in that month the prime minister had sent Roosevelt two telegrams setting out his doubts about any cross-channel effort in 1942. Churchill listed the major reasons for his concerns about an invasion onto the continent: the strength of the Luftwaffe at paratrooper landing sites; the lack of enough landing craft, and, most importantly, the fact that American troop strength for such an operation wouldn't be ready until 1943.

Churchill raised the possibilities of his favorite alternatives: an attack on Norway (Jupiter) or, better yet, the North African endeavor—"We must never let Gymnast [the proposed invasion of North Africa] pass from our minds," he had told the president. When Soviet Foreign Minister Molotov visited London that month to negotiate a long-term treaty of alliance, Churchill had made the case to him that the British and Americans would be unlikely to make any move that would relieve the eastern front in 1942, and he warned of the problems inherent in an amphibious invasion.[54]

At the invitation of the president to visit Washington as a guest at the White House, Molotov arrived in late May, directly from his London meetings with Churchill. (Oddly, a valet unpacking his bag was surprised to discover that along with clothing and personal items, the guest had brought a hunk of black bread, a roll of sausage, and a pistol.) Roosevelt prided himself on his personal diplomacy talents, but the first evening of meetings proved strained, with Molotov stone-faced and impenetrable despite the president's best efforts to find common ground. The next morning Marshall and King met with him. The foreign minister noted that while he had been received politely in London, he had gotten no commitment for a second front. What he wanted was an Allied invasion into Western Europe in 1942 big enough to draw off 40 German divisions before the enemy could deliver a crushing blow.[55]

The president turned to Marshall to ask if preparations were being made for such a front, and he answered yes to this general question, especially given the agreement he thought he had with the British during the Modicum meetings. Roosevelt then turned back to Molotov and promised that a front would be on its way "this year." Marshall hedged, saying that given shipping shortages, it would depend on how many troops the Allies could transport to France. In a meeting the next day, though, Roosevelt informed Marshall that the situation on the eastern front was so severe that he proposed to inform Churchill that the United States wanted to commit to a second front by August.

Marshall wanted the invasion in 1942, that was certain, but such a specific date was troubling. For one thing, the chief of staff knew the British would bridle at being tied down in that way.[56] Yet believing that assurances had to be given the beleaguered Russians, Roosevelt persisted. The statement released to the press on June 11 read: "Full understanding was reached with regard to the urgent task of creating a Second Front in Europe in 1942." Molotov flew back to London, where Churchill did the hedging. In a meeting in front of his colleagues in the Cabinet Room, he explained to the foreign minister that indeed the Allies were making preparations for a landing in August or September, [but] the shortage of landing craft meant that "We can therefore give no promise in the matter."[57] Never mind, Molotov had the official public statement of the Americans—that was the important commitment that he would take back to the Kremlin.

Early in June, Churchill had sent his Combined Operations commander, Admiral Mountbatten, to Washington, supposedly to check on landing craft production, but with the added task of meeting with the president to point out the many drawbacks of Sledgehammer. Marshall and King heard about these meetings only via Dill, since Roosevelt did not invite them to sit in on these discussions. When Marshall read the summary of the conversation, which, again, he got by way of Washington-based British sources, he was appalled at how much Roosevelt had shifted his views. The president had even suggested that an invasion of Libya or Morocco might be a good alternative to Sledgehammer. Apparently, Churchill got the message loud and clear—the president's resolve on a cross-channel operation "was losing ground."[58] Time for another trip to the White House.

Late on the evening of June 17, 1942, the prime minister's "flying boat" touched down on the Potomac, and General Marshall was there to welcome him and his military staff. Already well aware that the president was showing signs of "jumping the traces" earlier that day in a meeting with him and his advisers, Marshall was prepared with arguments in favor of the Bolero-Sledgehammer-Roundup concept. Further, before the president left for his estate along the Hudson for a weekend with Churchill, the American chiefs gave Roosevelt a strong written restatement of the strategy that they had previously agreed upon so he could read it before he met with the prime minister.

On June 19, Churchill arrived by plane at Hyde Park—the "roughest bump landing I've ever experienced," he said—and was greeted by Roosevelt in his blue Ford. With the hand-controlled levers, which allowed the president, a polio survivor, to operate the car himself, he took the prime minister for a drive through the beautiful local countryside. As Churchill would later say, "All the time we talked business, and . . . we made more progress than we might have done in formal conference." That was certainly true for the prime minister, who saw an excellent opportunity to deliver a full frontal attack on Sledgehammer: Did they, the American military, have a plan?

What troops could be used? Where would they land? What shipping and landing craft were available? Who would command the operation? What British aid was required? The Germans had five or six times as many men as the Allies could put ashore, Churchill insisted. Maybe they could launch an amphibious landing, he argued, but the cost would be huge, it would not be enough to help the Russians, and the effort would have to be primarily British. Churchill reiterated that no responsible British military authority believed that any plan for attack on the Continent in 1942 had a chance to succeed unless the Germans were in a state of collapse, "of which there was no likelihood." Further, even if there was no Sledgehammer—clearly that was out of the question in Churchill's mind—a buildup in London throughout 1942 with no military action until 1943 was unacceptable. "Can we afford to stand idle in the Atlantic theater for the whole of 1942? Ought we not to be preparing within the general structure of Bolero some other operation . . . and also directly or indirectly to take some of the weight off Russia?"[59] Well, then, it followed logically, according to Churchill, that if Sledgehammer was not practicable in 1942, then the answer had to be North Africa in 1942.

While Roosevelt and Churchill were at Hyde Park, Marshall worked on Brooke, the chief of the Imperial General Staff. He found that despite Brooke's concerns about cross-channel invasions, he was against Gymnast, Churchill's proposal to invade North Africa to relieve British troops in that region. The British were fighting fiercely in the theater of the Middle East (North Africa); Brooke feared that any Northwest African operation would take troops and materials away from that region. Although not in favor of Sledgehammer, Brooke encouraged the Allies to continue planning for the 1943 invasion of the Continent (Roundup). Marshall invited him for lunch at Fort Myer, in part to get away from what the Brit called "stinking hot" Washington. The shade and cool drinks at Quarters #1 Fort Myer provided little comfort as the two shared visions of what their chiefs "were brewing up together at Hyde Park." As Marshall would later say, "The president was always ready to do any sideshow and Churchill was always prodding him. My job was to hold the president down to what we were doing."[60] As they suspected, the two leaders, meeting in the stifling hot study off the mansion's porch, had indeed discussed Marshall's plans, and under Churchill's barrage of argument, Roosevelt was having some doubts.

Even before leaving Hyde Park, the president sent a telegram to Marshall and King: an effort on the part of the Russians to recapture the city of Kharkov had gone badly, and now the German summer offensive was beginning—

perhaps the Soviets could be virtually at the point of collapse. Given this situation, and worried about the cold facts of Churchill's assault on Sledgehammer, he had a question for them. Where could American ground forces, "prior to September 15, 1942," launch an attack on German forces or in German-controlled areas that could compel the Germans to withdraw from Russia?[61] Roosevelt had instructed Marshall and King to meet him and the prime minister at the White House the next morning with some answers.

All of that would be put on hold for a moment because of a chilling piece of information that Roosevelt received from an aide that Sunday morning, June 21, 1942. The news had to do with the British battle against Field Marshal Erwin Rommel's Afrika Korps in North Africa. (That fight had begun for the British in 1940 against the Italians, who hoped to use their Libyan colony as a base from which to capture Egypt and the Suez Canal. Initially the British had thwarted that effort, but when Rommel and his seasoned soldiers entered the fray, the tide turned. Because the canal as well as oil resources was so strategically vital, it was paramount that the British hold on in that region.) The president gathered with Hopkins, Churchill, his chief of staff Ismay, and Brooke in the White House study before he read the pink slip of a message. Glancing at the short sentence, Roosevelt hesitated for only a moment before handing it to the prime minister. "Tobruk [in Libya] has surrendered with 25,000 men taken prisoner," he read aloud. Clearly shaken, Churchill paled and then bowed his head. Briefly unwilling to accept the news, he sent Ismay to check on it. "True," said Ismay. It was a blow. "Defeat is one thing, disgrace is another," Churchill would later write. He recalled that "Impregnable Singapore had already fallen, with 85,000 men surrendering to inferior numbers of Japanese. Now in Tobruk, a garrison of 25,000 [actually 33,000] seasoned soldiers had laid down their arms to perhaps one-half of their number. I did not attempt to hide from the President the shock I had received. It was a bitter moment."[62] Now the British fleet base in Alexandria, Egypt, the all-important Suez Canal, and the oil fields of the Near East stood vulnerable. Roosevelt's reaction to this grim news was a succinct six words, "What can we do to help?" Brooke would later say that he was impressed by the president's heartfelt sympathy—"not one word too much or too little."[63]

Churchill, trying to think fast, asked for Sherman tanks, as many as could be spared. At that point Roosevelt called Marshall in and asked him what could be done. Although the Shermans were just coming into production and were being issued to American armored divisions that had been using obsolete equipment, and thus sorely needed them, he quickly shifted his view. "It's a terrible thing," he said, "to take weapons out of a soldier's hands," but added, "If the British need is so great, they must have them." His offer was generous: he would provide an armored division to go to North Africa fully equipped and trained. Within a short time afterward, Marshall realized that it would take into November to get an armored unit there; instead he sent 300 tanks and 100 105-mm guns by fast convoy to North Africa. Later, Brooke, whose opinions of American leadership, both civilian and military, had been less than complimentary, would tell his biographer: "I always feel that the Tobruk episode in the president's study did a great deal toward laying the foundations of the friendship and understanding built up during the war between the president and Marshall on the one hand and Churchill and myself on the other."[64]

In that long day of meetings on June 21, what Churchill had wanted for months—Gymnast, an invasion via Morocco and Algeria that would relieve his nation's beleaguered troops on the African continent—could now be brought front and center. He put all of his argumentative skills to work making the case. Finally, toward midnight, Ismay laid it out in a semantically careful statement: yes, operations in France or the Low Countries would yield the best strategic gains. "Plans and preparations . . . in this theater are to be pressed forward with all possible speed. . . . If a sound and sensible plan can be contrived, we should not hesitate to give effect to it. If on the other hand detailed examination shows that despite all efforts, success is improbable, we must be ready with an alternative." As Pogue noted, the last line was the stinger, since everyone understood that Churchill had already made the case over and over again that a successful cross-channel operation was highly "improbable." Everyone also understood the alternative: Northwest Africa. After all, Tobruk had fallen—the British were particularly vulnerable in that region. As Andrew Roberts noted, the British had effectively used this as their trump card, "somehow trading on their very weakness . . . to get what they wanted."[65]

Not to be outdone by Churchill's barrage, for the next three days Marshall argued against Gymnast—the North African offensive—finally extracting from the British and the president an agreement to at least "study" the feasibility of the operation again. With that decision then on hold, Marshall took the British contingent to a field demonstration by three divisions (60,000) of American soldiers training in the blistering heat of Fort Jackson, South Carolina. It even included a parachute drop of 600 paratroopers. Churchill delighted in the whole event. Brooke was less than impressed, commenting that "they had a lot to learn against the Hun." Churchill

Churchill observing the parachute demonstration at Fort Jackson, South Carolina, June 1942. From far left to right: Marshall; Dill; Churchill; Stimson; Major General Robert Eichelberger, and General Sir Alan Brooke

George C. Marshall Research Library

realized the troops were green, but he told Brooke, "You're wrong. They are wonderful material and will learn very quickly." As it turned out, both men would be proven right in due time.[66]

Soon after their trip to the South, Churchill and his staff returned to England to stave off a "no confidence" motion in Parliament. He faced a tough and boisterous battle in the House of Commons, whose members were loudly demanding an explanation for British reverses, especially Tobruk. This strengthened Churchill's resolve not to risk an operation onto the Continent that could meet with disaster he could not risk. His life as prime minister could be saved "only by a victory in the field."

In the meantime, Marshall had selected General Eisenhower as the European Theater commander, presumably to begin preparations in London for the Bolero portion of the cross-channel attack. Eisenhower, with one of his corps commanders, General Mark Clark, had arrived in the capital city on June 23, 1942. It didn't take long for the two of them to understand that the

British had no such operation in mind. On July 8, Churchill made it official in a telegram to Roosevelt: Sledgehammer was definitely out for 1942, and concentration should be placed on Gymnast. Marshall received the news directly from Dill. In the communiqué, the prime minister presented a long list of objections, all of which Marshall had heard numerous times before. The decision seemed final, and Marshall was "very stirred up and emphatic over it," Stimson later said, noting that the chief of staff was weary of "those constant decisions that do not stay made."[67]

In the Joint Chiefs meeting on the 10th, Marshall raised vital questions: Should the Americans agree to Gymnast, and did the British really intend to invade the continent in 1943, thus keeping their support of Roundup, the larger and more important operation? In the discussions that followed, Marshall seemed to take the position that an invasion of North Africa would delay the buildup in England and thus postpone Roundup until 1944. With this conviction, he advanced his "showdown" strategy—if there was going to be no attack against the Germans on the continent, then American troop strength should be diverted to the Pacific, a move that Marshall said would "concentrate rather than scatter U.S. forces." Admiral King, who struggled constantly with getting needed men and matériel to the Pacific, thought this sounded like a fine approach—after all, with the victory at Midway fresh in his mind, he longed for a counterstrike against the weakened Japanese. Stimson agreed. That day the three of them signed a memorandum to send to the president suggesting that "we should turn to the Pacific and strike decisively against Japan." Years later, Marshall would concede to his biographer that in his case, "it was a bluff, but King wanted the Pacific alternative."[68]

Meanwhile, Dill was alerting his colleagues in London as to the hornet's nest that was being stirred on the American side. Having talked with Marshall at length about his "veiled threat," Dill conveyed to Churchill and his staff that they had to give every impression that they still supported Bolero (the buildup in England) and Roundup (the 1943 cross-channel invasion), and thus were only rejecting Sledgehammer. "Just because the Americans can't have a massacre in France this year, they want to sulk and bathe in the Pacific," Churchill groused. Meanwhile, Roosevelt, having read the memorandum, and perhaps detecting the element of bluff, called Marshall from Hyde Park on July 12, telling him that he wanted a full report on this Pacific alternative from the service chiefs: estimated times of landings; number of ships, planes, men; how resources would be shifted from the defense of the Atlantic; and the effect of the change on the Soviet Union and the Middle East. In fact, the service chiefs had no detailed plan and had to admit that the alternative would not improve the strategic situation. On the 15th, Roosevelt returned to Washington and met with Marshall that morning. He reiterated what Marshall had already heard from him the day before by phone—he was rejecting the Pacific alternative. The written draft that Marshall had presented came back with "Not approved" written across the upper-right-hand corner, and underneath, "See substitute." The alternative was that Marshall, King, and Hopkins were to fly to London and meet with Churchill. Marshall could make his case one more time regarding Sledgehammer, but if it was impossible to carry out, then the chiefs had to determine with the British another place to fight in 1942. He wanted an answer within a week. "There would be no American threats to the British," Roosevelt said. "That would be like taking up your dishes and going away."[69]

When Marshall arrived in London, he met immediately with American planners who were already there, especially General Eisenhower. Armed with as much information as he could glean from this source, Marshall argued Sledgehammer for three days with the British chiefs. Although he knew by then that this portion was dead, he kept the debate going in an effort not to lose Bolero or Roundup in 1943. Finally, on July 23, 1942, after the British flatly rejected Sledgehammer, Marshall admitted defeat and wired the White House for instructions. Roosevelt sent a list of five possibilities, with Gymnast listed as number one. The next day Marshall finally accepted the situation. As he would later relate:

> So we were at a complete stalemate. Churchill was rabid for Africa. Roosevelt was for Africa. Both men were aware of political necessities. It is something that we [in the military] fail to take into consideration. . . . One morning at Claridge's [Hotel in London] I sat down in my room and began to write. I recognized we couldn't do Sledgehammer and that there was no immediate prospect of Roundup. What was the least harmful diversion? I always had to bear in mind that we didn't have much and that much of what we had was in an amateurish stage— particularly Air. I started writing a proposal [on which we might agree]. It called for an expedition into North Africa with operations, limits, nature, and the like. Just as I was finishing, King came in. It is remarkable, but he accepted without a quibble. Usually we argued over all plans.[70]

On July 30, Roosevelt made the word official to the military chiefs in Washington: Sledgehammer, the proposed 1942 invasion into France, was no more. What lay ahead was a move into Northwest Africa—Gymnast, now optimistically rebaptized as Torch.

Marshall learned a lesson from this fierce fight for a cross-channel invasion in 1942. As historian Thomas Parrish had written: "He [Marshall] had not appreciated the calculus of military need, political pressure, and psychological understanding that guided the president in making the decisions of grand strategy. It was now clear that future strategic decisions must be reached in cooperation with Roosevelt. As Marshall later conceded in an oddly worded phrase that nevertheless left his meaning clear, 'I did not realize how in a democracy the public has to be kept entertained.'" Indeed, the American public wanted to see their military forces striking back—they wanted action.

With mid-term elections looming, Roosevelt naturally hoped this invasion, with a preliminary date set for October 30, 1942, would in fact be launched before voters went to the polls. One day during a meeting with Marshall as plans were shaped for the offensive into North Africa, the president put his hands together as if in prayer, entreating the chief of staff to "Please make it before election day." It didn't work out that way, but as Marshall commented, "When he found we had to have more time, the president never said a word. He was very courageous." Marshall deeply respected that.[71]

Marshall was not convinced that anything could be gained for the Americans by following Churchill's approach. As far as he was concerned, this peripheral action in North Africa, if successful, would be a victory for the British Empire, yet it wouldn't speed the final victory in Europe. This line of attack, he believed, would result in a "long tortuous approach that would leave his forces in the Pacific beleaguered and neglected for months and perhaps years." Marshall would continue in every way he could to tie the British to a major offensive on the European continent against the Germans. In the meantime, all energy was focused on Morocco and Algeria, and the young Americans who would soon do battle upon those coasts.[72]

"We interrupt this game . . ."

Katherine Marshall was worried about her husband. The demands on him over the spring, summer, and early fall of 1942 had been tremendous. She was pleased when he told her that he planned to go duck hunting on the season's opening day in late October. However, on the evening before the hunt, an 11:00 p.m. call coming in on his scrambled phone line at Quarters #1 put an end to that. When he told Katherine that he was headed to his office, she begged him not to cancel the recreational trip with a friend, reiterating how badly he needed some relaxation. Exasperated, she asked him, "Why can't you go?" "Because the matter is very important," came the reply. "Every little thing is important but you," she said as she left the room, shutting the door "rather firmly" behind her. In fact, the matter had to do with a crucial aspect of the North African invasion, particularly the Allied armada that was concentrating 600 miles west of Gibraltar.

Then came November 8, 1942. The Marshalls had been given box seats for a Washington Redskins football game, and Katherine once again urged her husband to attend. This time Marshall simply told her that he could not be out of touch with his office. Resigned, she went with friends, all of the time thinking that it was a shame her husband couldn't be there to hear the cheers of 25,000 fans as the home team advanced against the scoreless Chicago Cardinals. Suddenly, midway through the evening, came a voice from the loudspeaker: "Stop the game; important announcement." The crowd was suddenly silent as the public address system amplified the news: "The President of the United States of America announces the successful landing on the African Coast of an American Expeditionary Forces. This is our Second Front." As Katherine later described the scene, "Like waves of the ocean, the cheers of the people rose and fell, then rose again in a long-sustained cry . . . the crowd simply went wild."[73] Finally, action!

American troops prepare to land at Oran in Algeria during
Operation "Torch," November 8, 1942.

British Imperial War Museum

Chapter 9

Casablanca to Quebec

"The global struggle to free the world"

Late summer 1942 – August 1943

El Alamein and Torch—"End of the beginning"

The stultifying heat of a Washington summer had given way to crisp autumn relief, and now a hint of winter, as each morning Marshall continued to drive himself from Fort Myer to his Munitions Building office. His mind almost certainly shifted from the changing seasons of the capital city to the desert climes of North Africa. The invasion plan agreed upon that late August 1942 was shaping up, but as D-Day for Operation Torch approached, Marshall felt the weight of the unknowns involved in such an operation. It would be the most ambitious amphibious landing in history—more than 500 vessels from four convoys, all breaking through U-boat-infested waters, with the three spearheads of the landings covering 650 air miles and stretching from Morocco on the Atlantic to Algiers on the Mediterranean.[1]

The "unity of command" concept would be put to work, with Eisenhower giving orders to British officers who, although respectful, generally saw themselves and the men they led as superior to him and his "green" troops—after all, they said knowingly among themselves, just wait until these Americans have to fight the Germans as we have. As much as Marshall had stressed and pushed for extensive training, and despite the pride he showed when he brought Churchill to Fort Jackson, South Carolina, in early 1942 to see American armor and infantry units, the fact was that not one of these young men had seen a day of combat; further, most of them had never been in the military until two years before. Although troops would not be facing Germans in the initial landings, they would encounter units under Vichy control—French soldiers, along with colonial and legionary forces, whose fighting abilities and loyalties were unknowns.

Marshall was reconciled to the invasion, and, having left it in what he considered the capable hands of Eisenhower, of necessity he had to shift his energies to other matters: Roosevelt's figures to the Bureau of the Budget fell far short of expectations, in Marshall's view, and would mean disbanding 14 army divisions that might be needed in case of heavy losses in North Africa. The grinding work of ensuring needed manpower and matériel was never-ending. He also persisted in laying the groundwork for the cross-channel invasion, although he realized it might not come until 1944. Making his way to his office in his usual methodical way, Marshall must have longed for some piece of good news.[2]

Perhaps it had been the work of Winston Churchill some two months before that had set in motion changes in the Middle Eastern Theater that would eventually bring that good news. The British general Sir Claude Auchinleck had been in command of that area since mid-1941. By early August 1942, disappointed with the military reverses in Egypt, the prime minister was desperate for some sort of victory before those Torch landings, and he constantly badgered Auchinleck for an offensive. On August 4, Churchill had flown to Cairo to look over the front for himself and supposedly to consult with the Middle East commander regarding strategy. The fact is his plan was to relieve Auchinleck. The prime minister believed the troops had lost confidence in the general's leadership; further, according to some, the problem was that Auchinleck had steadfastly refused to be bullied into launching a major offensive before his troops were ready. Churchill replaced him, later describing it as like "killing a magnificent stag"; by the time Churchill headed back to England, General Sir Harold Alexander had taken Auchinleck's command.[3]

But perhaps an even more key change was this: to take over the supremely important Eighth Army within the theater command, Churchill named Lieutenant General Bernard Law Montgomery. Described as "lean, tough, conceited, [and] insolent," this stern disciplinarian, who neither smoked nor drank, nevertheless soon injected into the thoroughly dispirited British and Canadian army a surge of confidence.[4]

Montgomery's mission that early autumn was clear-cut—Churchill's orders had spelled it out: "Your prime and main duty will be to take or destroy at the earliest opportunity the German-Italian Army commanded by Field Marshal Rommel, together with all of its supplies and establishments in Egypt and Libya."[5] Montgomery knew that the brilliant and feared Erwin Rommel was then preparing a final push toward Alexandria, Egypt, and the Nile, with its strategic jewel, the Suez Canal. With supreme confidence, Montgomery propped a photograph of the general in his headquarters, declaring, "Give me a month and I can chase him out of Africa." It would take longer. Nevertheless, the British strengthened their lines against an anticipated attack around El Alamein, an arid town 60 miles west of Cairo, at a point where the potential battleground narrowed between the Mediterranean Sea and an impassable rock canyon. Although Hitler ordered medals struck to honor the anticipated victory of the Afrika Korps, it was premature; the

British line held. Rommel himself flew to Germany to meet with Hitler complaining that the RAF bombers were destroying his panzers with 40 mm American-supplied shells. Hitler's air chief, Reich Marshal Hermann Göring, scoffed at the idea: "All the Americans can make are razor blades and refrigerators." Rommel's reply: "I only wish, Herr Reichmarschall, that we were issued similar razor blades!"[6]

General Bernard Montgomery watches his tanks move up during the North African campaign, November 1942.

British Imperial War Museum E18980

The medals would not be used. The British overwhelmed the advance German positions and began to clear their own minefields to make way for the offensive. In the end the Axis enemy was "outnumbered, out-weaponed, and overwhelmed."[7] Ironically, the great Rommel was away in Austria at the time of the battle; his replacement, General Georg von Stumme, fell dead of a heart attack in the midst of the action. Two days later Rommel was back. Although Hitler ordered him to "never retreat, to hurl every gun and every man into the fray," the field commander refused, calling it "unsurpassed madness," and began a disciplined retreat.[8]

So it was that on November 4, 1942, just on the edge of the North African landings, Marshall heard of the victory. The British forces had finally turned back the Germans at El Alamein. He must have recalled that gloomy exchange months earlier at the White House when Churchill had received the grim news of defeat from North Africa. In his telegram of congratulations to the prime minister after this triumph, Marshall wrote: "Having been privileged to witness your courage and resolution on the day of the fall of Tobruk I am unable to express to the full my delight over the news from the Middle East and my admiration for the British Army." In his reply, Churchill remembered "at the time of Tobruk, the delicacy and kindness that all of you showed."[9] A few days later, speaking at the lord mayor's luncheon in London, Churchill himself summed up the meaning of the battle in his own inimitable style: "Now this is not the end, it is not even the beginning of the end. But it is, perhaps, the end of the beginning."[10] It was indeed, because just two days earlier, the promised Allied invasion of North Africa had begun. Rommel, his army driven out of Egypt and Libya to the French-controlled nation of Tunisia, now faced the dreaded war on two fronts—British Eighth Army troops pursuing him from the east, and Americans and British forces breathing down his neck from the west.

In late October, three task forces had stood poised to proceed to their pre-designated locations. From England 39,000 Americans embarked for Oran in western Algeria, and 23,000 Brits set sail for Algiers. In addition, 35,000 Americans under General George S. Patton headed for western French Morocco near Casablanca. All were transported and protected by the U.S. and Royal navies.[11] Patton had provided a dramatic send-off to his officers and senior navy commanders as they gathered at their debarkation point in Norfolk, Virginia: "I'm under no illusion that the god-damn Navy will get us within a hundred miles of the beach. . . . It doesn't matter. Put us in Africa. We'll walk."[12] With full understanding that the "die was cast," Eisenhower expressed his thoughts regarding the invasion with less bombast, telling Marshall in a letter, "We are standing, of course, on the brink and must take the jump—whether the bottom contains a nice feather bed or a pile of brickbats."

Apparently the navy commanders did their work well, for in the early morning hours of November 8 a series of war vessels and transports began to assemble from Morocco's Atlantic coast to Algeria along the Mediterranean. The Vichy French resisted, enough that it upset invasion timetables; nevertheless, Oran was seized by the 10th, and Algiers was taken soon afterward. The resistance at Casablanca in Morocco proved fierce, but by the 11th Patton had control of that area.[13] From the unoccupied French capital Vichy, Marshal Petain sent the order to the head of the North African

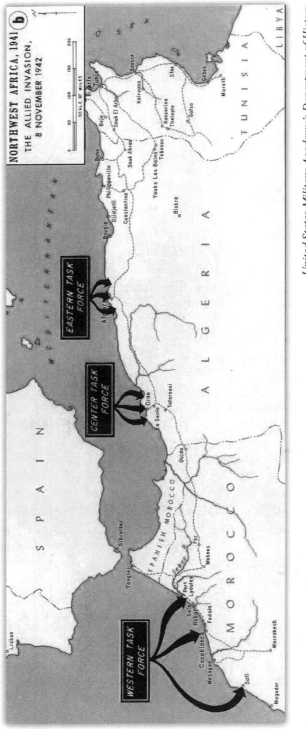

United States Military Academy's Department of History

forces: continue the fight. If the Allies had nurtured the hope that the French military would welcome the Americans as occupation liberators, they were mistaken.

North Africa posed a dicey political situation for the Allies. This was "Overseas France," far from Vichy, the portion of France unoccupied by the Germans because its government had decided to collaborate with the invader. While most of North Africa was indeed under the control of Vichy, portions of it were occupied by the Germans, and some of it was in colonial limbo interspersed with Free French. Both the Americans and British knew they would have to address this complicated state of affairs. In fact, they had already tried to find a French military figure around whom most of the French North Africans would rally.[14] Perhaps a logical choice would have been the Free French leader, anti-Nazi patriot General Charles de Gaulle, who, after having refused in 1940 to be a part of the "Vichy" deal with the Germans, had set up a government in exile in London. Perhaps not. That August, in a letter Marshall wrote to the president, he expressed concern that the de Gaulle forces couldn't keep a secret, explaining, "The principal trouble in this matter is that General de Gaulle's headquarters is very 'leaky.' Matters discussed with them quickly become rumored about. . . . All of which is dangerous to our purpose."[15] De Gaulle was also dour-faced, icily self-confident, and arrogant, traits that did not inspire immediate allegiance.

If not de Gaulle, then whom? Eisenhower had begun negotiations with representatives of the French general Henri Honoré Giraud, a hero of World War I. He had a dramatic story to match his rather impressive military bearing. Having been taken prisoner by the Germans, he had escaped that previous April and was fired up to fight the Nazis. Although he lived in Vichy, he was covertly forming his own Free French movement. In a secret rendezvous at Eisenhower's Gibraltar headquarters that lasted for hours, it was suggested that after the landings Giraud would call for a cease-fire among all French forces and would then become their commander. Giraud proved difficult, saying that unless he was made Allied commander-in-chief over the *whole* Torch operation, he wouldn't "play." Brickbats were beginning to fly.[16] Although not promising to meet Giraud's demand—Eisenhower's negotiators had been vague—the French officer did agree to fly to North Africa, arriving in Algiers on November 9.

In the meantime, the Allies, not putting their political eggs in one basket, had approached another Frenchman of note. It so happened that the commander of all French forces, the opportunistic fascist collaborator, Admiral Jean Darlan, was in Algiers. Tightly associated with Marshal

Petain's government—he had been its deputy premier and was considered a possible successor to the aging leader—Darlan had no use for the British. This feeling dated back to the time in 1940 when the French government surrendered to the Germans. Darlan, as head of the fourth-largest naval force in the world, swore that he would not turn the French fleet over to the Nazis. Churchill, however, was not at all certain that the French commander had the power to prevent it and, in his view, could not take the risk of the fleet's falling into the hands of the enemy.

The prime minister had proposed several ways to make sure the French fleet remained safe, including the suggestion that the ships be sailed to British ports, or to French possessions in the Caribbean, where they could be escorted into English waters. Darlan refused, believing that his fleet was not threatened, based on the language of the agreement with the Germans; thus, in a highly controversial operation code-named Catapult, Churchill ordered the navy to accost these vessels and neutralize them. In early July, several of the most powerful French battleships were in port in French Algeria. When their captains resisted British orders to board and rejected four conditions under which the vessels could be neutralized, they were fired upon. In the ensuing action one battleship was sunk and several damaged, but the human toll was greatest—1,297 French sailors, who only 10 days earlier had been fighting *with* the British as allies, perished.[17] With such memories fresh, Darlan was not going to negotiate with the British, only the Americans.

It was for personal rather than professional reasons that Darlan was in Algiers that early November—he was there on the day of the invasion to see his son, who was hospitalized in the city after having been diagnosed with polio. Placed under house arrest that morning, Darlan met with Eisenhower's deputy, General Mark Clark, and after hours of talk finally agreed to a cessation of hostilities in Algiers. He fell short of calling for a complete cease-fire over the whole area. The political imbroglio deepened on the 9th when Giraud arrived. His efforts that day to assume command of the French forces were rebuffed; in fact, his radio broadcast directing French troops to stand down and join the Allies was ignored. This made negotiations with Darlan all the more important, especially because he also controlled what remained of the French fleet. The next day, Clark continued to meet with the French naval admiral, pressing him to make a deal.

Finally, on November 12, it was agreed. In return for a general cease-fire of all forces under his control, Darlan would continue as the high commissioner in North Africa—head of its Vichy civil government—and Giraud would be commander-in-chief of the French military forces in those areas.[18] All of the

French North African territories (except Tunisia) aligned themselves with the Allies, which included the French naval base at Dakar on the Atlantic coast of West Africa and the powerful French naval squadron stationed there.

Following the Allied landings in French North Africa, Hitler could not risk an exposed flank on the French Mediterranean. By November 11, 1942, German troops were advancing from central France toward Vichy and Toulon, where the French fleet was anchored. The Vichy government limited its active resistance to radio broadcasts objecting to the violation of its armistice agreement. On the 27th, Hitler sent troops to the Toulon navy base to seize the ships. French sailors resisted long enough to scuttle some 70 ships.[19] Admiral Darlan had always said that the French fleet would not fall into German hands, and most of it did not.

In the United States, the political fallout from the Darlan deal ignited a firestorm of controversy. The press denounced the arrangement, calling it expediency over principle. After all, as Mark Perry noted, "The agreement . . . put aside any Allied intention to prosecute Darlan or any of his senior officers for collaborating with the Nazis and left the French administration of the region intact." [20] Roosevelt acknowledged that it was an expedient, but only a "temporary" one, "justified solely by the stress of battle." This was a statement for the public, but in a private message to Eisenhower, he wrote frankly, "We do not trust Darlan," and "It is impossible to keep a collaborator of Hitler and one whom we believe to be a fascist in civil power any longer than is absolutely necessary."[21] Churchill called it "disgusting." Nevertheless, he and Roosevelt had both given Eisenhower permission to make an agreement, any agreement, that would end French resistance. As Churchill later confessed, "If I could meet Darlan, much as I hate him, I would cheerfully crawl on my hands and knees for a mile if by doing so I could get him to bring that fleet of his into the circle of Allied forces."[22] The president justified the decision with an old Bulgarian proverb, "My children, you are permitted in time of great danger to walk with the Devil until you have crossed the bridge."[23]

When word came back to Eisenhower describing the vehemence of the attacks on him because of this arrangement, he defended his actions, pointing out that only Darlan had the power to control the loyalty of the French forces. Days later he wrote his chief of staff that "many messages from London indicate great concern and anxiety of our governments because we had to deal here with a skunk." He reassured Marshall that "we are not committing ourselves and certainly are not, repeat, not, attempting to commit our governments as to future political action." He went on to add that he "had tried to force Giraud on them [the French in North Africa] but they wouldn't take him." Eisenhower defended his rationale: "As a result of the agreements . . . we have [been able to] press our concentration toward the east for battle in Tunisia without worrying about our rear."[24] Understanding his role in Washington's political arena, Marshall wrote back: "I am doing my utmost to support you by meetings with the press, with members of Congress, with State Department and with the President," and reiterated to him, "Do not worry about this, leave the worries to us and go ahead with your campaign."[25]

Still concerned about the criticism of the Darlan affair, which continued unabated, Marshall wrote Eisenhower on November 22, requesting his permission to release casualty figures for the North African campaign, telling him, "The notice of these casualties would prove the seriousness of the situation and the tremendous advantage we gained toward Tunisia and North Africa in general by Darlan's orders which stopped the fighting."[26] Eisenhower agreed, and the figures were released on the 23rd; the *New York Times* cited the data the following day. On Christmas Eve, the whole Darlan association ended when he was assassinated by a member of an Algiers French family, Bonnier de la Chapelle, an anti-Nazi, anti-Vichy royalist. Churchill noted that the "youthful assassin had under much persuasion worked himself into an exalted state of mind as the savior of France from wicked leadership." French military authorities executed Chapelle by firing squad two days later. [27]

Upon Darlan's death Marshall sent Eisenhower word that he had authority to appoint General Giraud as high commissioner. Now that the perfidious Darlan was out of the equation, the path was cleared for de Gaulle to make overtures to his Free French rival, General Giraud in North Africa, but it would take a while. De Gaulle asked for talks with the new French leader. Although Churchill characterized the hatred between these rivals as "a basket of snakes," perhaps a future meeting would make possible the "end of the beginning." Despite the thorny road ahead between these two contentious would-be leaders, the United States was no longer backing an arch-collaborationist of the Vichy régime. According to historian Ed Cray, Marshall learned a lesson from the public outrage over the Darlan deal. As he noted, "The government leaders and diplomats might trim their sails to the political winds; soldiers could not. Thereafter Marshall the soldier would circle wide around political issues."[28]

Although by mid-November resistance had ended in French Morocco and Algeria, and American troops with their British allies were on the ground,

Eisenhower could by no means claim victory in North Africa. In the east, Montgomery's Eighth Army was in pursuit of the Afrika Korps, now retreating into Tunisia. Despite Rommel's entreaty to Hitler that the Germans leave Tunisia and Libya to save the troops to fight another day, the Furher reinforced the Korps, shipping experienced soldiers into the region from Sicily and Italy and ordering reinforced air wings of German dive-bombers. By mid-December "hard bitten veterans of the 5th Panzer Army" were in place, probing Allied lines, then falling back until more support arrived to launch an offensive.[29] Eisenhower was confident that despite German reinforcements he could overrun Tunisia, telling Marshall that he was "well satisfied with all my people." He mentioned the professional ability of his commanding officers, noting that "Long hours and incessant work roll off their backs like water off a duck." By mid-December, he was less optimistic. Allied troops were bogged down in Tunisia's winter rains as much as by the strong unbroken line of German defenses. Meeting with his generals the last week of the year, Eisenhower called off a Christmas offensive because of the "absolute impossibility" of moving vehicles through the mud.[30]

Some Good News

Despite the drawbacks of weather for the Allies in North Africa, the fact is that there was good news from other fronts. In Stalingrad by mid-November, already hindered by the bitter icy snows of a Russian winter, the German Sixth Army under Field Marshal Friedrich Paulus was in trouble. Soviet Field Marshal Georgi Zhukov had brought up reinforcements and launched counterattacks against the invaders. As the Germans tried to make headway into the city, they found virtually every building mined, and they suffered the enfilading wrath of dozens of sniper nests. One Nazi lieutenant described it well: "By day it is an enormous cloud of burning, blinding smoke; it is a vast furnace. . . . And when night arrives, one of those scorching, howling, bleeding nights, the dogs plunge into the Volga and swim desperately to gain the other bank. The nights of Stalingrad are terror for them. Animals flee this hell; the hardest stones cannot bear it for long; only men endure." It would take another month for General Paulus to surrender his Sixth Army to the Russians, but by Christmas the tide of war was beginning to turn.[31]

These Soviet successes meant that victory in Europe was still possible, and the need for the cross-channel invasion to open a second front still valid. Further, although Marshall had struggled with the burden of a two-front war throughout 1942, continuing to balance the demands of Europe with those of MacArthur and Nimitz in the Pacific, there was good news from that part of the world as well. In the summer of '42 the Japanese had attempted to build an air base on Guadalcanal in the Solomons from which to strike American convoys headed for Australia. If they were successful, Allied supply lines would be cut. That August, 10,000 marines had landed to oust the enemy. Offshore intense sea battles raged, with both sides seeking to bring in and/or stop reinforcements. The see-saw nature of those encounters turned toward the Allies in November, but not before the damage or loss of three carriers, *Enterprise, Wasp,* and *Hornet.* Nevertheless, the marines, bolstered by the Army and air cover, began to make headway on the island. It could hardly have been more brutal, pure hell. As historian David McCullough described it:

> The heat was terrible; there were drenching rains, rats, and bugs of every description; men were struck down by malaria and dysentery and their skin broke out with jungle rot. But worst of all was the enemy. He came screaming out of the jungle at night in wild suicide charges.[32]

Still, the American troops fought on, and by the end of the year victory was near. It would be February before the evacuation of the last Japanese soldiers from Guadalcanal, the first land defeat for them since the beginning of the war. While all of these operations suffered from lack of enough men and matériel, more of both was on the way. Marshall's army now numbered 5.4 million (37 divisions and 67 air combat groups), up from 1.6 million in late 1941, with 20 percent of that number deployed abroad, and the ranks were growing daily. Moreover, American industry was cranking out the supplies and tools of war in prodigious amounts.[33]

That Christmas of 1942, on behalf of the U.S. Army, Marshall presented both President Roosevelt and the prime minister with 50-inch 750-pound globes. In a December 12 letter to Churchill that predated the delivery of his globe, Marshall optimistically opined the future of the Allies.

> In order that the great leaders of this crusade may better follow the road to victory, the War Department has had two . . . globes specially made for presentation on Christmas Day to the Prime Minister and the President of the United States. I hope that you will find a place at 10 Downing Street for this globe, so that you may accurately chart the progress of the global struggle of 1943 to free the world of terror and bondage.[34]

President Roosevelt admires the new addition to his office, December 1942.
Franklin D. Roosevelt Library

Casablanca—"The whole global picture"

For the Allies, then, in early 1943 there was a bit of light on the horizon, but as of yet not full force. The Germans were by no means out of North Africa. Nevertheless, both Churchill and Roosevelt were convinced that their combined armies would succeed in closing the pincers around Rommel's legions, and that it wouldn't be long. After that, then what? Somehow throughout this last year, the Allies had succeeded, but, as Ed Cray noted, more through improvisation than strategic vision. Now that the Allies were on the offensive, the two leaders agreed that it was time to get all of the key players together to shape a cohesive strategy. The proposal for a meeting as a follow-up to the invasion was primarily Churchill's. Although Soviet Premier Joseph Stalin had been invited to attend, he declined, saying that because the Russians were ready to launch a major counteroffensive against the Germans, he could not leave the country. Nevertheless, in his "regrets" reply he reminded the two leaders rather pointedly that he hoped they had not changed their minds about opening a second front in Europe in early 1943.[35]

There was a good bit of discussion back and forth between Roosevelt and Churchill regarding a setting for the meeting. Public opinion in the United

States might not support the idea of the president being away from Washington on what would be considered a dangerous trip. Roosevelt's thinking was that if Africa was the site of the meeting, he could justify the trip, since he could also meet with the military commanders of the Torch operation and inspect American troops. In the suburbs of Casablanca, Morocco, a large hotel built oddly like the structure of an ocean liner, with well-appointed surrounding villas, would provide the place for the conference. Eisenhower assured Marshall by letter that General Patton, who had secured that area during the Torch landings, would make certain that the president and his party would be well provisioned and protected.[36]

Indeed, the hotel complex, bordered by bougainvillea and orange groves, was surrounded with barbed wire, infantrymen, and Secret Service; fighter squadrons patrolled overhead. Roosevelt's departure and his destination had been kept a carefully guarded secret; in fact, no press knew about the conference until it neared its end, just before the president departed Morocco to return to the United States. The chief executive was setting new precedents—he was the first president to leave the country during wartime; the first to do so by plane rather than ship; and the first to visit a theater of military action since Lincoln.[37] The meetings, code-named Symbol, were scheduled to begin on January 14, 1943, but the American and British military chiefs would get there a couple of days earlier to hold preliminary discussions before Churchill and Roosevelt arrived.

The key American military representatives traveling to Africa—Marshall, King, Arnold, and Lieutenant General Brehon B. Somervell, head of the U.S. Army's Services of Supply—were by no means unified regarding a strategic plan. This had already been made clear when on January 7, just two days before their departure, Roosevelt had called a meeting to discuss this very thing. Were they all "agreed that we should meet the British united in advocating a cross-channel strategy?" The answer was equivocal: yes, the Joint Chiefs favored operations in the north rather than in the Mediterranean, but beyond that the question was not settled.[38] (Marshall stuck to his belief in a cross-channel operation; King wanted to apply more military pressure in the Pacific to follow up on recent victories, insisting that the Japanese would exploit any lull in the offensives thus far launched. In both cases the competition for men and supplies informed the arguments.) Roosevelt no doubt understood that the British would be pushing for further action in the Mediterranean, and he tried for a compromise: couldn't they make the case for the continued buildup in England (Bolero) in preparation for an invasion of Europe, but hold off on the final decision regarding where and when for a month or two? The president had made the point that after Tunisia was secured, at least a half million men would be available for immediate military action. Where would they be used while preparations continued for the invasion of Europe?[39]

Sensing that Roosevelt was aiming for the option of further action in the Mediterranean and, based on conversations with General Dill, realizing that most likely the British would push for action in Sardinia—a move that he thought would only deepen the war in that region—Marshall took the position that if that idea was advanced, he would oppose it. He suggested that if the British insisted on following up the momentum of North Africa, Sicily would be preferable, since it would at least put the Allies closer to Occupied France and would result in fewer losses in shipping. (Despite the amazing military production output of the United States, the shortage in shipping continued. After all, the Germans had sunk 7.8 million tons of Allied shipping in 1942; even with the extraordinary efforts of American shipyards, planners anticipated a deficit for 1943 of 1.3 million tons.)[40] Although Admiral King agreed with the Sicily option, nothing was settled, and the discussion ended in indecision. This lack of unanimity would hinder the Americans when they faced the thoroughly organized British, who had settled any internal differences before they left for Morocco and thus would speak as one when outlining a strategic plan.

Elaborate arrangements were made for General Marshall's trip to Casablanca, also organized in great secrecy. His aide, Lieutenant Colonel Frank McCarthy, had planned thoroughly for every eventuality. Leaving National Airport in Washington on January 9, the plane carrying Marshall and his party was loaded with life rafts, portable radios, survival kits—all of that standard for these long flights into war zones. In addition, though, McCarthy packed things that might be needed in the event of a crash landing in the desert, including tents, cooking equipment, even trinkets for the Arabs in case they proved hostile. Before landing at Bathurst, British Gambia, on the fifth leg of the 18-hour trip, McCarthy explained quite solemnly that mosquitoes, which brought the inherent danger of malaria, were rampant in North Africa. He provided the group with mosquito gloves and headgear, the latter "resembling a bee-keeper's hat, with a net veil that came down in front." Somehow the aide convinced Marshall that he should don this garb, including the gloves and hat, for the landing. The chief of staff, almost unrecognizable in his protective gear, was chagrined to see the welcoming party all dressed in cool shorts. With what McCarthy later described as a "disgusted look," Marshall swept off the hat and gloves immediately and, handing them to his aide, brusquely ordered, "Here, you take these."[41]

Although Roosevelt, in setting up the conference with Churchill, had suggested "a very small staff" (the political leaders and the "three top [military] men" from each side), the British had arrived at Casablanca with a huge delegation, and even had a special communications ship anchored offshore that allowed full exchanges of information between Casablanca and London and housed an impressive library of reports and maps.[42] Churchill fully understood that his military advisers had to present their plan, which would focus more on the Mediterranean than France, to the Americans in such a way that their Allied partners did not feel pressured. The possibility loomed of a major shift to the Pacific on the part of the United States. No, Churchill told his chiefs, there had to be "full discussion and no impatience," it had to be like "the dripping of water on a stone."[43]

When the Americans arrived with their small staff and no cohesive strategic narrative, their British counterparts were ready. General Brooke laid out the possibilities: the Allies should ride the wave of success once North Africa was secure by attacking targets in the Mediterranean such as Sicily and Sardinia that would open the path for knocking Italy out of the war, a move that would force Germany to disperse her forces in response. Churchill had described the approach as a "Strike at the under-belly of the Axis in effective strength and in the shortest time."[44] Brooke continued to argue that the Allies could not land on the Continent in force until Germany was weakened through these peripheral engagements, thus reiterating the old "war of attrition" approach that the British had always supported. Sure, it was important to continue building up troops and resources in England, Brooke explained, and if somehow the German military forces showed clear signs of deteriorating because of Russian pressure, then the Allies *could* attack the Continent in '43. But otherwise it was out of the question—not enough landing craft; not enough divisions to overwhelm and stay once a beachhead was established. Holding out a carrot to Marshall, he insisted that every American should be able to count on an invasion of the Continent in 1944.[45]

It was then Marshall's turn. He would lead the American chiefs in making a "last stand" for a cross-channel operation in 1943. After two days of argument—Brooke described it as the "slow and tiring business" of gradually getting the Americans to "assimilate our . . . policy"—Marshall realized that he was bargaining from a weak position. Those troops released from North Africa had to fight somewhere, and the British, who still had most of the men and ships in the European Theater, were not going to go for it. Even Eisenhower had told him the invasion would take twice as many divisions as he had originally thought, and amphibious landing training was far from complete. Further, if the arguments continued, it seemed likely that Roosevelt, already ambivalent, might himself move to the Mediterranean option. Marshall was prepared to accept Sicily as a target, but he wanted to know if that would be the end of it. Would the next step be Italy, another digression, "a suction pump" as he called it, from the "main plot"?[46] In the end, Marshall had to yield. Even King was impressed that opening up the Mediterranean would help save Allied shipping in those waters; and Arnold liked the possibility of new air bases in Sicily to strike at Germany from the south.

General Marshall, seated beside General Arnold, at a Joint Chiefs
meeting, Casablanca, January 1943

George C. Marshall Research Library

Marshall also had to make the case for increased action in the Pacific—definitely a part of the "main plot." He proposed that the apportioning of resources between the Atlantic and the Pacific be defined: 70 percent for

Europe; 30 percent for the Pacific. King agreed, especially since at that time the Pacific distribution of military assets was more like 15 percent. The British did not like the percentages approach and began to argue that the United States was abandoning its "Germany first" agreements. Marshall vigorously countered that notion but still argued that the Japanese could not be allowed to consolidate their gains. The Japanese had repeatedly shown their military prowess and could not be permitted to regain the initiative— "We must not allow any pause," Marshall warned. To make this happen, Marshall argued, Burma had to be recaptured (Operation Anakim) so that a supply route to China could be reestablished. If that didn't happen, a situation might arise that would "regretfully" result in a withdrawal from the European Theater. "The United States could not stand for another Bataan," he cautioned.[47]

The British realized that they would have to offer something to the Americans in terms of increased activity in the Pacific. Finally, it was agreed: Burma was to be recaptured—a move that would secure a supply line to China, and, *if* it did not jeopardize the military operations that could defeat Germany in 1943, offensive actions against the Gilbert, Marshall, and Caroline Islands would be allowed following the capture of the Japanese base in Rabaul, New Guinea. Further, Churchill pledged that as soon as Germany was defeated, the British would make available all resources for the defeat of Japan—he even agreed to sign a treaty to that effect, which Roosevelt declined.

In the final report of the conference, then, it was decided that in addition to maximizing naval support to weaken dreaded German U-boat attacks that threatened shipping to any theater, and a commitment to provide the Soviets with maximum supplies, the main line of offensive action in 1943 would be in the Mediterranean. It would include the occupation of Sicily as a means of making lines of communications more secure, diverting German forces from the Russian front, and intensifying pressure on Italy. Germany would be bombed around the clock from bases in Great Britain, and the buildup of troops and landing craft would continue in England. The Allies would make every effort to bring neutral Turkey into the Allied fold so as to secure bases for launching air attacks; the U.S. Air Force in China would be increased, and in the Pacific, pressure would continue *as long as it didn't hinder* the Germany–first emphasis.[48]

In addition to firming up the strategic plan for 1943, there was another matter: the rivalry between Charles de Gaulle, the leader of the London-based Free French government in exile, and General Giraud, who, after Darlan's assassination, had become the high commissioner of North Africa, based in Algiers. That sticky situation had to be stabilized, so both men were invited to Casablanca for talks. Giraud accepted immediately, but de Gaulle obstinately declined—he considered the "big powers" overseeing what he considered an internal French matter like parents settling a dispute among siblings. He found it insulting. De Gaulle refused three invitations until Churchill threatened to withdraw British support for his government, or name another Free French leader, and that did the trick.[49] He arrived, as Harry Hopkins noted, "cold and austere."

The two French generals did meet, even sharing brief moments of cordiality. Roosevelt and Churchill worked on a proposal for a "representative French committee under joint control," and Giraud said he would sign it; de Gaulle would not, since the committee would include certain "traitorous" Vichy officers. Frustrated, Churchill intoned, "Mon General, il ne faut pas obstacler la guerre." Finally, Roosevelt, ever persuasive, talked de Gaulle into releasing a joint declaration. It said little: "We have met. We have talked. We have registered our entire agreement on the end to be achieved, which is the liberation of France and the triumph of human liberties by the total defeat of the enemy. The end will be attained by a union in war of all Frenchmen."[50]

French Generals Henri Giraud and Charles de Gaulle
shake hands, January 24, 1943.

Franklin D. Roosevelt Library

On the last day of the conference, January 24, 1943, as the meeting of the French leaders with the president and Churchill broke up, 50 photographers, flown in from Algiers and unaware of what news event they were covering, gathered. Soon they would flash images of these leaders around the world, with articles describing this momentous 10-day secret meeting. Seizing an opportunity, Roosevelt asked Giraud and de Gaulle to shake hands for a photograph. Giraud stepped up, taking it in stride, while the Free French leader looked bewildered and reluctant. The awkward handclasp was so quick that the photographers had to ask that they do it one more time. Irritated but compliant, De Gaulle approached the general again.[51]

After the two French leaders departed, Roosevelt and Churchill gathered the newsmen around them. Roosevelt described the purpose of the conference—the need to define "the whole global picture." Then he delivered a zinger: "The elimination of German, Japanese, and Italian war power means the *unconditional surrender* of Germany, Italy, and Japan." While his statement seemed spontaneous, at some time previously Roosevelt had at least mentioned this idea to his Joint Chiefs, and the term was included in the notes he used to make his remarks. Nevertheless, in the previous references to the term, it seemed to have been mentioned in a broader sense, not as the rigid condition for peace that it later became. Having used the term at the close of the conference, though, Roosevelt explained, "It does not mean the destruction of the population of Germany, Italy, or Japan, but it does mean the *destruction of the philosophies* in those countries which are based on conquest and the subjugation of the people." There would be no negotiated settlements with Hitler. Marshall apparently agreed. As Pogue noted, "When the outcome of the Allied endeavor was far from certain, when the Russians were still unhappy over the failure to open a second front, and when there was no possibility of holding out prospects of quick liberation to the French and other conquered peoples, it was useful to make clear that the Allies remained set on the defeat of the Axis powers."[52]

At Casablanca, the British had "come in droves," as Marshall's aide, Lieutenant General Albert Wedemeyer, had pointed out, and every one of them had written a paper about some military aspect. By the end of the conference Brooke gloated that "we got practically all we hoped to get when we came here."[53] Indeed, the British chiefs had the full and determined backing of Churchill, while Roosevelt seemed often in a waffling gray middle between the two strategic views. The Americans realized that they had not been unified or as well prepared as their British associates. The results were obvious. One of Marshall's planners complained, "We came, we listened, they conquered."[54] Never mind, the lesson was learned and duly noted—it would not happen again. Despite outcomes, though, for both sides these strategic sessions had been infinitely complicated, with serious and legitimate positions argued. It was in fact a world war, with the availability of men, matériel, and ships stretched thin. As army historian Maurice Matloff explained, Casablanca represented "the last real fling of the 'either-or' school of thought in American strategic thinking." *Combined* offensives would be the substance of future offensives. It would not be *either* the Mediterranean *or* a cross-channel operation, but rather an examination of various alternatives that, in concert and simultaneously, would compose the military operations of the Allies. "The problem," he said, "would no longer simply be either this *or* that undertaking, but rather this *and* that."[55] It was a reality that would be faced by both the British and the Americans in the days ahead.

Tunisia: Facing Rommel

As soon as Marshall left Casablanca, he headed to Eisenhower's headquarters in Algiers. The chief of staff was worried about his North African commander: he had a cold and high blood pressure, was smoking

Generals Eisenhower and Marshall at Allied Headquarters, Algiers, June 3, 1943
George C. Marshall Research Library

three packs of cigarettes a day, and seemed—to put it mildly—frazzled. Marshall thought Eisenhower was doing too much, going too often to the front, meeting with too many of his commanders, getting involved in the political tug-of-war among the French. To ease the stress, Marshall suggested that Eisenhower needed "a roving deputy," someone high-ranking and respected who could go out into the respective headquarters and bring back information. That person was General Omar Bradley, a West Point graduate and someone considered "solid and stable." Meanwhile, Marshall, like a father to a son, outlined Eisenhower's schedule telling him: "Get up at ten, conduct business of importance only, leave at noon, exercise at lunch, work, get a rubdown, return to the office, work, get dinner, and then relax."

Marshall was also concerned about the performance of the troops. He understood perfectly that the British lacked confidence in the ability of these American fighters, and apparently their behavior since the landings had done nothing to dispel that notion. The British had already managed to get General Sir Harold Alexander appointed to Eisenhower's command staff as deputy, even though he outranked the American general. Described as the quintessential British officer, tidy but rakish, smiling but tough-minded, and a fastidious example of military spit and polish, Alexander's appointment pleased Eisenhower.[56] However, the motivation of the British, by Brooke's own admission, was to push Eisenhower "up into the stratosphere and rarefied atmosphere of a Supreme Command." By kicking the "Kansas farm boy" into a coordinating role, the day-to-day military authority would devolve to Alexander, who would "restore the necessary drive and coordination," which in his view "had been so seriously lacking."[57]

Although expressing full confidence in Eisenhower, Marshall himself was disappointed with this second tier of American commanders responsible for these men, believing they had been too cautious, moved too slowly, and had not exacted a high degree of military discipline from the troops. It was as if they were waiting for Montgomery to meet up with the German army, now in a defensive position on the borders of Tunisia, and take care of the problem for them. Just the day before this meeting, Montgomery had captured Tripoli, the capital of Libya, and was within six days of crossing the border into eastern Tunis. Marshall believed that if Eisenhower's divisions could press vigorously eastward, they could do their part and demonstrate their capability for future action in a cross-channel invasion.

The next weeks of the battle for Tunisia did nothing to suggest that this would happen; indeed, it did not go well for the Allies. Although they had made their way east of the Atlas Mountains, the Germans did not intend for

213

them to stay there. General Rommel launched a fierce offensive in February 1943 in an effort to push the Allies back through the passes, and beyond. On the 14th in the area around Kasserine Pass, Rommel personally led an assault of two battle-hardened divisions against the inexperienced American II Corps troops. It was a humiliating study in ineffectual command and outright panic—two units actually broke and ran. The Germans swept up tanks, mounted guns, and a huge haul of trucks, along with 2,400 dazed prisoners. According to Ed Cray, it would take three weeks before the Allied front could be reorganized, and another three weeks before they could take back what they had lost. A tremendous number of supplies had been captured or destroyed, and army units were re-outfitted only through the unusual cooperation of Admiral King. Alexander wrote to Brooke in London, expressing his view of the Americans' performance: "They have little hatred for the Germans and Italians, and show no eagerness to get in and kill them." He was preaching to the choir: Brooke had called them "soft, green, and quite untrained," and lacking the "willingness to fight."[58] Even for Eisenhower, the trouncing that American troops took at Kasserine Pass was sobering, although the men had recovered to once again go on the attack.

Perhaps neither Eisenhower nor Marshall was able to admit it, but this debacle cast doubt on their strategic vision and supported the British view that the Americans weren't ready to face the full brunt of the German army on the European continent. Surely if these troops had landed in France and fought as they had at Kasserine Pass, it would have been a disaster.[59] Admitting it or not, Eisenhower swallowed national pride and asked that experienced British officers act as liaisons with American divisions to sharpen training.[60] With the previously slow-moving II Corps now under the command of General Patton, who reorganized it, applied a stricter discipline, and gave them "a shot in the arm," the Germans were pushed back through the mountains, while Montgomery pressed from the east. When Patton was sent to train troops for the upcoming Sicily campaign, Eisenhower shifted General Omar Bradley from "roving" deputy to command of the II Corps, writing to Marshall that his having suggested this highly competent general for the North African operation had been a "godsend in every way."[61] It would take until May 13, 1943, but the Wehrmacht would finally be cleared from North Africa.

In a confidential letter to Major General Withers Burress, commander of the 100th Infantry Division at Fort Jackson, South Carolina, dated February 27, 1943, Marshall declared his determination that stateside officers, tasked with getting troops ready for battle, read what Eisenhower had written regarding military operations in North Africa only two days after the brutal mauling at Kasserine Pass. Making the best of his troops' efforts, Eisenhower noted that "after the initial shock of open battle," they recovered quickly, and he even mentioned that in the last phases of the German advance, the enemy encountered "stout defensive action and some sharp counterattacks on our part." Then Eisenhower made two points that he considered important to American forces. The first: a considerable quantity of equipment must be made available. Second, he explained, "All our people from the very highest to the very lowest have learned that this is not a child's game, and are ready and eager to get down to the fundamental business of profiting by the lessons they have learned." He told Marshall that he was going to make it a "fixed rule" that no unit in theater would ever stop training. Marshall then explained to Burress that he was taking the unusual step of sharing this top secret communication in hopes that the division would profit by a better understanding of field difficulties. The chief of staff closed by noting that he thought this was a better method than "mimeographed training orders" that make "a very limited impression."[62]

Tunisia had dried up any possibility of a cross-channel invasion in 1943; Marshall understood that. Still, he was encouraged by what had happened in the last weeks of the North African encounter, even though the whole Torch operation had been costly. (Empire, French, and American units' casualties had numbered 71,810, including almost 11,000 deaths; U.S. units had suffered 12,618 killed, wounded, or missing.) Still, the troops had done better toward the end. They were "bloodied," and they were fast learners. Marshall wrote Eisenhower that he wanted to express his "deep satisfaction" in the "progress of affairs" under his direction.[63] Perhaps the chief of staff paused for a moment to take heart. Sicily beckoned, though—Patton was already working on an invasion plan. No rest for the weary: Churchill and his staff were making their way to Washington, which, in addition to details of the Sicily operation, included one huge query: what about the problem of Mussolini's fascist Italy?

Trying to Catch a Break

That early March 1943, the weary Marshall, sick with a cold, had tried to get some rest—he and Katherine headed to Miami Beach, with the arrangements for an oceanfront house made in the greatest secrecy. Dressed in casual civilian clothes, the first evening there the two of them were enjoying the cool air on beach chairs in front of their cottage. Soon a coast guardsman appeared and explained to the Marshalls that they could not be there after

7:00 p.m.—there was a curfew, a "time of war" regulation. "I think it will be all right," Marshall explained. Soon, to her astonishment, Katherine saw coming at them a military formation, led by an officer in naval dress, who stopped at their chairs, yelling a loud "Halt!" to his men. With deep-voiced authority, he began a violent tirade, threatening to arrest this offending pair, finishing his diatribe with a stern, "Didn't they know there was a war going on?" Without comment, Marshall took pillows, chairs, and his wife and began to head toward their rented house. The naval contingent followed close on as if ready to pounce at the least wrong move. Finally, Marshall had had enough. "What is the reason for this ridiculous display?" he demanded. The leader of the group then recognized the U.S. Army chief of staff and quickly "stood down." Marshall opened the door and went inside. For the rest of the trip, he and Katherine enjoyed evening breezes and sunsets from their balcony.[64]

In mid-March Marshall had returned to Washington slightly rested, but just in time for the Pacific military commanders' conference, with the highest-level officers present, representing both MacArthur and Nimitz, the dual chiefs of the Pacific. Although not involved in the day-to-day meetings, Marshall heard plenty about it from Admirals King and Leahy. Throughout 1942 in the Pacific, the inter-service fights between army and navy for resources and personnel were often carried out with prickly letters and telegrams sent over the vast distances of the world's largest ocean. Now, they met face-to-face to hammer out issues related to shipping, planes, equipment, and troops. The major question for them: how could they use their respective commands to apply maximum pressure against the Japanese within the context of that Casablanca ruling, which granted increased support in the Pacific but *only* as long as it did not impede the planned military actions against Germany. The second issue: the building of strategic partnerships that allowed dynamic flexibility between the authority of Admiral Nimitz, who commanded the Pacific Ocean Area, and the egotistical and demanding General MacArthur, who tenaciously pushed for more of everything in his Southwestern Pacific Theater.

After several days of meetings, with the back-and-forth of bitter argument bringing no real results, the Joint Chiefs got involved, and some compromises were worked out. Among them, MacArthur would have specific naval support for his army operations, and that support *could not be withdrawn* by Nimitz for other actions—a situation that had occurred before. Beyond that, the admiral still controlled the Pacific Ocean Area.[65] The army and navy offensives on the other side of the world from European strategic concerns would continue against Japanese dispositions in heavily fortified bases. Both offensives had one goal: steady progress toward the home islands of Japan.

Trident—A Bit Closer to the Goal

Churchill was on his way to Washington—his party of almost 100 had left London on May 5 aboard the *Queen Mary*. The prime minister could see some of the results of the recent action in North Africa, since traveling with them was a large clutch of German prisoners from that campaign. Churchill's mission was, as he described it years later: "What should we do with our victory [in North Africa]? Were our fruits to be gathered only on the Tunisian tip, or should we drive Italy out of the war and bring Turkey in on our side? These were fateful questions, which could only be answered by a personal conference with the President." By Churchill's admission, he and the staff worked "ceaselessly" on the trip over to hone their response to the arguments that they knew would come. Arriving in New York on the 11th, the British party entrained for Washington—Roosevelt awaited them on the platform at Union Station and, as Churchill noted, "whisked me off to my old rooms at the White House."[66]

For 14 days, May 12–25, 1943, during what would be called the Trident Conference, the president and the prime minister met six times with the Combined Chiefs of Staff at the White House. The CCS held additional sessions almost every day in the hot, smoke-filled Board of Governors room in the stately Federal Reserve Building on Constitution Avenue not far away.[67] The fateful questions for General Marshall, the Americans' chief spokesperson for this conference, were related to Churchill's, but with a very different view. Marshall understood that shutting down operations in the Mediterranean altogether would not work—the British would not agree to it; yet the U.S. Navy, the American people, and the nation's Asian allies would not permit any reduction in the Pacific Theater, and, in fact, they wanted more and were pressing hard for it. If these two sets of needs had to exist simultaneously, how could they be limited sufficiently to allow for a buildup in England for the 1944 cross-channel attack? These were the ongoing questions—an extenuation, expansion, and refinement of the endless arguments of Casablanca. Heated debates ensued, so much so that a couple of times Marshall cleared the junior officers from the room so that "frank and forthright" talks could be "limited to the principals."[68]

In the opening meetings Churchill reaffirmed his loyalty to the cross-channel attacks but, as expected, pressed for further action in the Mediterranean. He was convinced that a "collapse of Italy would cause a chill of loneliness [to settle] over the German people, and might be the beginning of their doom."[69] Aware that Roosevelt and Marshall were constantly emphasizing the need to open a second front for the Russians, the prime minister made the argument that if the Italians capitulated, it would force Hitler to move German troops into Italy to hold it. As Brooke noted, to attack Italy would "achieve the maximum diversion of German forces from Russia." Further, when successful, it would free the "boot" as a launch site for aerial bombardment of Germany. He argued that the Americans had to understand that in other wars, "our side" had counted on the support of 80 French divisions, none of which were now available. Brooke warned of long lines of communications once troops advanced toward the Ruhr, argued that the RAF wasn't ready to operate tactically with the armies and that British manpower was weak— on and on it went. Brooke concluded that, given those circumstances, "no major operation would be possible until 1945 or 1946."[70]

Just hearing 1945 and '46 in the same sentence with "major operations" struck Marshall like a body blow. The same old song was playing again— the delaying arguments of the British. He understood that neither British nor American troops could stay unoccupied for long, but he feared that the proposed Mediterranean operations up the boot of Italy would ultimately far exceed estimates for needed resources. He reminded his colleagues of what had happened in the Tunisian campaign, which had sucked more and more troops into the fray and had extended from November 8, 1942, to quite literally the first May day of these meetings. Marshall conceded that once such operations were undertaken, they had to be backed to the limit, so the only time to control the situation was before launch, not afterward. As he saw it, to invade Italy would stall the cross-channel landings, stringing out the war in Europe and delaying the defeat in Japan, a situation that Americans would not tolerate.[71]

The meetings continued, with the Americans more and more frustrated by this stretched-out timetable and the interminable discussions of the Mediterranean. Both naval chiefs, Leahy and King, were in full agreement with Marshall and took the position that if the British would not make a "firm commitment" about Roundup (the cross-channel invasion), then "we ought to convert our forces into the Pacific."[72] Without question, this was America's trump card, and it was more than an idle threat; after all, the civilian sector—congressmen, senators, and the press—were questioning why this had not already happened. Wasn't it Japan that had struck the United States of America? Further, British motives were coming under sharp criticism: was this European war about protecting colonial interests in the Mediterranean region, or was it to vanquish Hitler so that the bulk of military operations could be concentrated to defeat Japan? As Marshall floor-managed the American position, he was also dealing with this clamoring political firestorm outside those stately rooms.

Marshall was not without a spirit of compromise, conceding that perhaps this cross-channel attack would have been suicidal in 1942. However, he continued his argument for the invasion, insisting that intense bombardment of Germany to obtain air superiority would greatly reduce risk for 1944. Further strengthening the American side of the debate, the U.S. Army was now bigger, stronger, more confident, and better trained—in fact, they would be the dominant force for such an invasion. Marshall also had another high card up his sleeve. This time the president was fully committed to the cross-channel operation. One British staff member recognized the change: "The Americans had done some very hard thinking, and Marshall was at the president's elbow to keep in his mind the high urgency of a second front."[73] Indeed, Roosevelt did not waver from his insistence that the cross-channel attack had to come in '44—two years was long enough to put off the decision, he said.

Before the arguments of the Trident Conference were settled, the president and the Joint Chiefs arranged a weekend for the British delegation in Williamsburg, Virginia. It had only recently been restored to its pristine 17th-century beauty by John D. Rockefeller Jr. The Americans pulled out all the stops to entertain their guests. Marshall's aide, Frank McCarthy, arranged wonderful dinners featuring traditional colonial fare: terrapin, crab meat, fried chicken, Virginia ham, and fine bourbon, all served by Rockefeller's personal butler in the elegant dining room of the Williamsburg Inn. Brandy, coffee, and a tour of the colonial governor's mansion followed. Churchill's chief of staff, Ismay, described the May weekend as "a memorable interlude in a fortnight of hard slogging, and enabled us to get to know each other much better. The war was never mentioned until we returned to our offices in Washington."[74] Marshall made the trip to Williamsburg and planned on that Sunday morning to take General Brooke, an avid birdwatcher, to look for the orioles native to the region. But at 10:50 a.m., Marshall and British Air Marshal Sir Charles Portal were called off to see the president and the prime minister at Roosevelt's getaway near Washington, "Shangri La" (now Camp David) in the Maryland mountains, where the two heads of state had been meeting in a casual deep-woods setting.[75] Apparently, unlike Ismay, they did discuss strategic issues before returning to Washington that Monday. In a May 24th letter to his stepson, Allen Brown, Marshall wrote,

Roosevelt and Churchill are shown with the Combined Chiefs at the White House during the Trident Conference, May 24, 1943. Standing from left to right: Field Marshal Sir John Dill; Lieutenant General Sir Hastings L. "Pug" Ismay, Churchill's chief of staff; Air Chief Marshal Sir Charles F.A. Portal; General Sir Alan Brooke, chief of the Imperial General Staff; Admiral Sir Dudley Pound, the British First Sea Lord; Admiral William D. Leahy, Roosevelt's chief military adviser; General Marshall; Admiral King; Lieutenant General Joseph T. McNarney, of the U.S. Army Air Forces, and Marshall's deputy chief of staff. General Henry "Hap" Arnold was not present.

Franklin D. Roosevelt Library

220

"I have seen very little of your mother . . . during the presence of the British Chiefs of Staff."[76]

The social atmosphere notwithstanding, the complexity of global war did not yield immediate harmony between the two Allied camps. Brooke understood the situation, writing in his diary: "The Americans are now taking up the attitude that we led them down the garden path taking them to attack North Africa," and that "at Casablanca we again misled them by inducing them to attack Sicily!! And now they are not going to be led astray again."[77] Nevertheless, slowly, some agreements were reached. The British would support a four-phase bombing attack to be launched from England against Germany in preparation for the buildup for the invasion of the Continent. Further, at last, a date for the cross-channel attack was decided upon: May 1, 1944, with 29 divisions to be involved. To placate the British, Marshall had agreed that the massive invasion would be pared down a bit— bigger than Sledgehammer, less than Roundup. The Trident version would soon be code-named Overlord. However, Marshall coupled this compromise with a refusal to send any more resources to the Mediterranean. Further, he insisted that after the invasion of Sicily (Operation Husky) was complete, seven of those freed-up divisions (four American and three British) would be shipped to England for the buildup in England (Bolero). Marshall and the Joint Chiefs agreed with the British that there would be some expansion of operations in the Mediterranean that would have the effect of eliminating Italy from the war, but the specifics would be decided by Eisenhower after the launch of Husky, based on the military conditions revealed by the extent of German resistance. The final outline for the invasion of Sicily was agreed upon, and while the conference was still in session, Eisenhower confirmed that July 10, 1943, would be D-Day for the Sicily operation.[78]

On the next to the last day of the conference, May 24, 1943, the Combined Chiefs were at the White House presenting their final report, when to their astonishment, after a short discussion of Sardinia, Churchill launched into an hour-long monologue trying to extend the whole Mediterranean Theater into Yugoslavia and Greece, ending by asking that the final agreement be put off until the next day. Brooke was horrified, knowing that this absolutely would not fly with the Americans. Even Roosevelt had already congratulated the Combined Chiefs and accepted the report. As Brooke protested, "Now, in the eleventh hour Churchill wanted to repudiate half of it." Further, it went against hard-fought, mind-numbing, detailed negotiations that he had gone through with Marshall and the others. Brooke wrote later that Churchill just "crashed in where angels fear to tread."[79]

Neither the Combined Chiefs nor the president took Churchill's bait, and the next day he accepted the report as previously written. Nevertheless, perhaps as a consolation prize from the president, Churchill was told that Marshall would join him and Brooke on a trip to Algiers to meet with Eisenhower. The prime minister was traveling there no doubt with a view of using personal argument to win Eisenhower over to his position of what should follow success in Sicily. With Marshall aboard, perhaps he could whip up support from him about the advantages of an extensive Italian campaign. Further, as he wrote later, he didn't want to be accused of exerting undue influence on Eisenhower. Marshall had six hours' notice of this journey, and immediately had to cancel a trip to the Pacific Theater, which had been planned for some time. He was irritated with the change, telling Secretary of War Stimson that he "rather hated to be traded like a piece of baggage."[80]

A Message to Stalin

In the early part of the 17-hour flight to Algiers, Churchill struggled with a full folder of drafts that he and Roosevelt had worked over before he left the States. The task was to write a communiqué to Stalin informing him that the promised second front of 1943 had now been postponed until 1944, and framing it with the plans that had been agreed upon during Trident. Finally, after wrestling with the material awhile, Churchill turned the papers over to Marshall. The chief of staff thumbed through the varied drafts and finally decided to start afresh. He finished it in two hours, turning over a clean typed version to the prime minister. Churchill was impressed, remarking on its "clarity and comprehension" in matters both military and political. Up until then, Churchill later wrote, "I had thought of Marshall as a rugged soldier and a magnificent organizer and builder of armies. But now I saw he was a statesman with a penetrating and commanding view of the whole scene."[81]

With that work finished, Marshall set about to distract Churchill on a variety of subjects, since he was not about to discuss any unfinished business of the Washington Conference (Trident), especially the post-Sicily part, before he had met with and gotten Eisenhower's views. He and Churchill talked about the difference between impeachment in the United States and bills of attainder in Great Britain; they covered Rudolph Hess's abortive mission to Scotland in 1941; and Marshall even impolitically inquired, after he ran out of topics, about Churchill's role in the abdication crisis of Edward VIII when he renounced the throne to marry Wallis Simpson. The prime minister had been among the few who had supported the king. Marshall later described it as "a marvelous lecture, just marvelous."[82]

Algiers—The Italian Question, Again

Once arrived, Churchill and his accompanying staff, especially Brooke, began their effort to persuade Eisenhower of the advantages to knocking Italy out of the war. The prime minister correctly inferred that the general was wavering. Still, both he and Brooke kept open how far the British wanted to go up the Italian boot, not wanting such specifics to alarm Eisenhower. Nevertheless, their very vagueness worried Eisenhower, who was fearful of a "bottomless Mediterranean pit." When Churchill's foreign minister, Anthony Eden, talked in one of the meetings of "our troops reaching the Balkans," the prime minister immediately "scrambled to shove the cat back into the bag," denying that he intended to send an army into that region.[83]

In the end, no commitment was forthcoming, and would not be until the Sicilian campaign yielded its results. Further, Marshall was not convinced of any extended action in Italy; in fact, he wanted just enough to tie up German troops and knock Italy out of the war, and there would be no compromise on the seven divisions that were to be released for the Normandy buildup in England. In the last meeting there, General Montgomery, who would be the commander of the Sicily campaign, gave a briefing regarding a plan for its capture. Marshall decided to hold his peace regarding the extension of the Mediterranean campaign, so all ended cordially. Churchill interpreted that hopefully—perhaps he had gained ground with the chief of staff. Not so. When Marshall returned to Washington on June 7, 1943, he told Stimson with some pride that he had kept all the gains of Trident without jeopardizing his cordial relations with the prime minister.[84]

Before leaving to return to the United States, Marshall had agreed to brief the British and American correspondents assigned to Eisenhower's headquarters at the St. Georges Hotel in Algiers. As Ed Cray noted, "It was a press conference remembered as 'an incredible performance' by one reporter . . . and 'the most brilliant interview I ever attended in my life' by another." Marshall sat at a large mahogany table, with 30 correspondents and photographers around him. He requested that each of them ask their questions one by one, and after all had asked, then he would answer. Each one spoke in turn, with Marshall acknowledging the question and then nodding to the next person. Some of the questions were technical, some strictly military, some global in scale. After all had spoken, he amazed the group by taking up each query in order and addressing his reply to the man who asked the question. In a remarkable 40-minute narrative, Marshall fit each comment into a larger global picture. The photographers were so mesmerized, they did not take up their cameras until Marshall was leaving

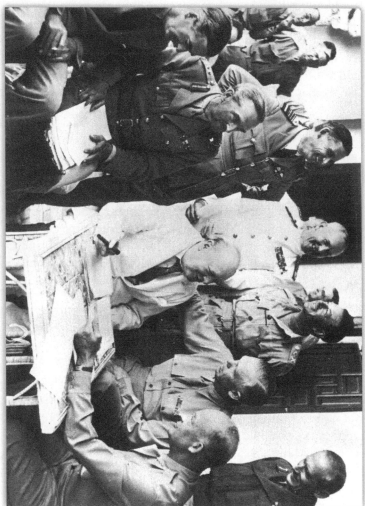

The Allied Chiefs at Algiers, June 3, 1943. Left to right seated: British Foreign Secretary Anthony Eden; General Sir Alan Brooke; Prime Minister Winston Churchill; Generals George C. Marshall and Dwight D. Eisenhower. Standing behind Churchill are Air Chief Marshal Sir Arthur Tedder, Admiral of the Fleet Sir Andrew Cunningham, and General Sir Harold Alexander. General Sir Bernard Montgomery is standing on the far right.

George C. Marshall Research Library

224

the room.[85] Much later, when asked how he did this, Marshall downplayed it, saying that, after all, he was deeply immersed in these matters and thus it was no trick to remember. Besides, he said, "I'd been doing this with Congress all the time without any notes, because I found that the minute you began to read, you lost your audience."[86]

Brush Fires, Speeches, and a Summer Evening at Dodona

Marshall returned from Africa on June 7, 1943. The following morning he headed for his Pentagon office just across the Potomac River from the capital city. He had moved that previous November from his Munitions Building suite to the third floor of this new massive army headquarters building, which covered 35 acres and had been completed in record time. Without even a day's rest, he set about to answer an avalanche of correspondence on various matters. One letter had to do with his stepson, Allen Brown, who had just completed Officer Candidate School, Armored Force, Fort Knox, Kentucky, and was set to graduate as a second lieutenant. The commanding general at Fort Knox, Major General Alan Gillem Jr., had written the chief of staff to ask that he address the graduating class of his "stepson." Responding rather succinctly, Marshall noted that although he appreciated the courtesy, he could not accept. Further, he continued, he had hoped that Allen could get through the school without his identity being disclosed, and asked that "his graduation bear no comment on his connection with me." The chief of staff explained: "The fact that it is known that he is my stepson denies him a good bit of the credit for earning his own way and I am distressed that it has become public."[87] While both Allen and Marshall's older stepson, Clifton Stevenson Brown Jr., as well as his son-in-law, Major James Winn, were all serving in the military, Marshall's sense of fairness did not permit him to give them a "favored status" that would advance them beyond their capabilities. Neither would they be spared the dangers inherent in military service. Whatever they achieved and in whatever theater they faced the enemy, it would not be because of family connections.

Back at his desk, Marshall was also disturbed to read of a scurrilous "slander campaign" against the personnel of the Women's Army Auxiliary Corps, the WAACs. From early 1941 the chief of staff had supported the efforts of Congresswoman Edith Nourse Rogers to establish a Women's Army Corps separate and distinct from the Army Nurse Corps. The recommendation that women be inducted into the regular army with full benefits caused an uproar of criticism. As one newspaper editorial inquired, "Who will then do the cooking, the washing, the mending, the humble homey tasks to which every woman had devoted herself, who will nurture the children?"

Nevertheless, in early 1942, after much debate, Congress did approve the WAAC organization as *auxiliary* to the United States Army.[88] The day the law passed, Secretary of War Stimson made Oveta Culp Hobby its director. On June 15, Marshall wrote a letter of apology to Hobby after newspaper articles claimed that because of the "immoral conduct of the women," the army was issuing contraceptives to all WAAC personnel. "I wish to assure your subordinates," he wrote, "of the confidence and high respect in which they are held by the army."[89]

Only six days later Marshall still had this on his mind as he delivered a speech before the Governors' Conference in Columbus, Ohio: "I returned from Africa two weeks ago to find the most atrocious, if not subversive, attack being directed against an organization of the Army, one of the finest we have ever created. I refer to the Women's Army Auxiliary Corps. There was no foundation for the vicious slander, though it was given wide publicity. Some seem to be intent on the suicide of our own war effort, not to mention the defamation of as fine an organization of women as I have ever seen assembled."[90] The next month Congress would enact legislation, fully supported by Marshall, that established the Women's Army Corps—a regular army designation. The women who served in this organization—99,000 at peak strength—received the full benefits allowed to other service members— overseas pay, insurance, medical coverage and death benefits. Marshall's promotion of the WACs and its predecessor was based primarily on wartime needs rather than civil rights. The recruiting slogan "Free a man for combat" would have been embraced by Marshall. In the chief of staff's view, there were thousands of jobs—telephone switchboard operators, clerks, typists, secretaries, motor pool drivers—that a woman could accomplish so that another young man could go to the front lines. Mark Stoler pointed out that "at no time did the conservative Marshall seek to use the military to advance social causes." Although he fully supported the Tuskegee Airmen program, he continued the army's traditional racial segregation policies. Marshall firmly believed that the army "should not conduct 'experiments' in wartime 'which would inevitably have a highly destructive effect on morale'—meaning military efficiency." While his focus was on the war rather than civil rights, Marshall's formidable standard of fairness led him to believe that qualified women who wanted to serve should be allowed to do so. Later, in 1950, Marshall would cause quite a public stir when as secretary of defense he made a liberal Jewish woman, Anna M. Rosenberg, the assistant secretary of defense for manpower.[91]

Oveta Culp Hobby is shown taking the oath of office as a colonel in the Army of the United States, July 5, 1943, as commander of the Women's Army Corps.
George C. Marshall Research Library

In this same speech, Marshall laid bare the complexities of world war. The recent grueling work with the British was surely on his mind. He began with a positive, saying that the most potent factor in the war thus far had been that "we have secured a method of arriving at unity of operations among the Allies." Then in the spirit of "Let me tell you what we're up against," he went into the details:

> I might give you some idea of the intricacies of these problems if I tell you how one of these conferences that you read about, like Casablanca, or the recent one in Washington . . . go about it. It generally takes us about a week, sometimes a day or two less, to arrive at a tentative idea of what we think we might do, which we all agree about. But that's only a tentative affair and it takes about a week to arrive at that because it covers the entire world. Then it takes us almost a week longer, having arrived at a tentative agreement on that, to calculate whether that can be done. You are now involved in ships, cargo, dry cargo, wet cargo, troop lift. You're involved in escort vessels because for every movement you require so many escorts. There are just so many and no

more. The security of these convoys depends on that. You're involved in most operations in landing affairs, that means landing crafts, special landing crafts, that means so many engines, so many this, so many that. That means the transportation of these awkward crafts to this place or that place. You can't ship them around, change your mind at any minute—that thing has to be calculated far in advance. You get all the compromises, you figure the turn around in the boats.[92]

Marshall must have realized that his days of conferencing with the British over the next moves in Europe would soon be on the horizon. From his headquarters in Algiers, Eisenhower was ready to launch Husky, the invasion of Sicily, July 10, 1943, since the tides were favorable at that time. After that, the "what next" question regarding Italy would come up again. The fight for Overlord would continue. It wouldn't be long before the intricacies of alliances would once more be revealed in another meeting—this time it would be at the beautiful Chateau Frontenac in Quebec, overlooking the St. Lawrence River.

In early August, during a weekend at Dodona Manor, the Marshalls' home in Leesburg, Virginia, a rare opportunity presented itself. The whole Marshall family was at home: Allen, on leave before departing to join the First Armored Division in Rabat, Morocco, arrived from Katherine's Fire Island summer home, with his wife, Madge, and their young son, Tupper, now almost two. Molly and her husband, Major Jim Winn, were there, with the two babies, Jimmy and Kitty. Clifton came as well up from duty at Antiaircraft Artillery Headquarters in Richmond, Virginia. As Katherine and her husband went outside on that summer day, the three young men were stretched out on the cool grass, engaged in a friendly discussion regarding the relative merits of tanks (Allen), antiaircraft fire (Clifton), and field artillery (Jim) in battle. Madge and Molly were coming to the support of their husbands as the debate continued. General Marshall weighed in, too, concluding that "when the fighting is the fiercest, it is invariably the Infantry that carries the ball over for the touchdown." No one really wanted to dispute that, so they gathered on the stone patio in the back of the house for a picnic.

For such a special day, Katherine had prepared all of their favorite foods. After the meal, "they had quite a ceremony." It seems she had found an old horseshoe in the lower yard. It was Allen who got out the ladder to hang it on the front of the garage, and everyone drank a champagne toast to the good luck of the men as they continued their respective military duties. A protest went up when someone suddenly realized that Allen had hung the

228

horseshoe with the points down. No, they said, it had to be the other way, so the luck couldn't run out. The mistake was quickly corrected. The couples stayed on the lawn until it was too dark to see. The next day, Allen left for his assignment.[93]

At an earlier family gathering on Fire Island in New York State, August 1939, Marshall is shown with his adult stepchildren: Allen Brown is on the left, Molly Winn is seated, and Clifton Brown is on the right.

Thomas D. McAvoy, The LIFE Picture Collection, Getty Images

President Roosevelt— "Clear and definite"

Marshall barely had a day to savor the time with his family. On August 9, he met with the president at the White House to discuss "the line of action" for Quadrant, as the Quebec meeting, scheduled to begin on August 14, 1943, would be called. The invasion of Sicily had not been seamless—British Field Marshal Bernard Montgomery and the American commander, Patton, seemed at times to be competing with each other rather than the enemy.

As Ed Cray noted, "The Allies were improvising their strategy, British and American generals scrambling for personal honors."[94] Eisenhower, operating from his headquarters in Algiers, struggled to keep the battlefield leaders under control. Nevertheless, by the time of Marshall's meeting with the president, it was clear that the German forces on that island were close to defeat. Now the chief of staff's worry was all too familiar. Once the Germans were out of Sicily, Churchill would be encouraged to make the case for expanding action in the Mediterranean. Already directing a limited war in the Pacific, Marshall wondered if he could keep military commitments restricted in Italy as well. He wasn't the only worrier—army planners were concerned that the Mediterranean trend had gone too far, perhaps almost irreversibly.[95]

Roosevelt didn't do a lot to allay fears. During the meeting the president pointed out that these army and navy planners were "always conservative and saw all the difficulties." Yes, he was definitely committed to Overlord, but he thought more could be done post-Husky in the Mediterranean, an operation now dubbed "Priceless." Roosevelt told Marshall that after the seven promised divisions were sent to England, he would like to dispatch seven fresh divisions from the United States to the Italian front. No, he assured Marshall, he didn't want any expansion into the Balkans. He was simply in favor of securing a position north of Rome and taking Sardinia and Corsica—that way southern France would be threatened. He promised Marshall that he wouldn't agree to a British expedition that would draw off ships and landing craft intended for Overlord. Nevertheless, Marshall reminded the president that the United States "had strained resources well to the limit" in the agreements already made for Overlord and Priceless.[96]

The army planners that same day presented a report on the implications of the "seven fresh divisions" proposal, and concluded that while those troops could in fact be spared for Priceless, the transport ships required to get them there could best be used in moving military units to England. Furthermore, Eisenhower himself had reported to them that with the forces currently available in Sicily, he could meet the goals of occupying Italy north of Rome and taking Sardinia and Corsica. In the Joint Chiefs of Staff meeting the next day, just before the whole group conferred with the president, Marshall made a key point: Roosevelt should be apprised that even if those seven divisions were sent to Italy, they wouldn't arrive before June 1944, and most likely they would be considered by the British as available for expanded operations in the Balkans—again, distracting from the goals of Overlord on the Continent. Admiral King supported him on this, since he was worried that provision for shipping those divisions to the Mediterranean would curtail Pacific operations.[97]

While the Joint Chiefs were meeting, Secretary of War Stimson, having only a few days earlier returned from the United Kingdom where he had met with the British chiefs, was greeting the president in the White House. He held a long letter in his hand, one that he would ask Roosevelt to read. So serious were the recommendations he had outlined earlier in the day that he had asked Marshall to read the document so he could get his reactions beforehand. The chief of staff, who since 1940 had worked so closely and harmoniously with Stimson, quickly perused the report and said he had no objections. However, as Marshall later told his biographer, he merely told [Stimson] that he didn't want it to appear that Stimson had consulted him about the contents.[98] Stimson was ready for that, telling the chief of staff that for that very reason, he had already signed the paper before he showed it to him or anyone else.

Arriving at the White House at noon, Stimson exchanged pleasantries with the always ebullient president and then handed him the letter. What followed, the secretary of war would later say, "was one of the most satisfactory conferences I have ever had with the President."[99] Seventy-six years old, Stimson was serving his second president as secretary of war after a distinguished career in the law and public service. So it was, then, that he brought plenty of gravitas to the recommendations of the letter. "We cannot rationally hope to be able to cross the Channel and come to grips with our German enemy under a British commander," the report read. It must be given to an American, for the "shadows of Dunkerque [sic] still hang too heavily over the imagination of his [Churchill's] government." Stimson defined the basic problem between the British and Americans as "a vital difference in faith." He outlined the American war planners' position, and that of Marshall, perfectly: Victory could be accomplished "only by massing the great vigor and might of the two countries under overwhelming mastery of the air." The British, he said, held to the notion of "a series of attritions in the Mediterranean and the Balkans."[100]

Then Stimson gave a warning to the president. Both Britain and the United States had committed to opening a second front to relieve pressure from the herculean military efforts of the USSR, and its leaders would not be fooled by this whole "pinprick warfare" concept. That, he wrote, presented a special danger in light of the Soviets' rising power potential in the postwar. He then put the onus directly on the president of the United States: "I believe therefore that the time has come for you to decide that your government must assume the responsibility of leadership in this great final movement of the European war which is now confronting us. We cannot afford to confer again and close with a lip tribute to Bolero which we have tried twice and failed to carry out." Finally, regarding who should be the American commander, he expressed to Roosevelt how fortunate he was. While Lincoln had fumbled by "trial and error" to find the right man, the president had General Marshall, [who] already "has a towering eminence of reputation as a tried soldier and as a broadminded and skillful administrator." Stimson closed his letter by reminding the president that no one knew better than he what a loss Marshall would be for the organization and worldwide strategy centered in Washington, but as he said, "I see no other alternative."[101]

President Roosevelt read the letter, approving each recommendation step after step, and, as Stimson wrote in his diary, "saying finally that I had announced the conclusions which he had just come to himself."[102] The next day when the Joint Chiefs met with the secretary and the president to discuss the conference, it was clear that the president was behind their plans for Europe. Stimson recorded his delight in his diary, noting the "clear and definite" stand of the president on the conduct of the war. When the American military chiefs left for Quebec, they were a different lot than had faced the British at Casablanca. They were now a match.[103]

Early on at Quebec, the word was already getting out: Overlord would be commanded by an American, and while by no means official, it was speculated that it would be Marshall. What a change in the power differential: during early 1943 discussions of Overlord, it had been projected that approximately the same number of British and American troops would take part in the invasion. Churchill had made the case that since the North African operation had been led by Eisenhower, overall "unity of command" for Overlord should be given to a British general, Field Marshal Sir Alan Brooke. After all, the whole buildup would be based in Great Britain, and Brooke had commanded a decisive battle at Dunkirk at the beginning of the war. The prime minister had told Brooke at least three times that he would lead the invasion. By the summer of 1943, however, it was increasingly obvious that with British manpower and resources strained to the limit, and with the American effort "just beginning to boil," by the projected launch date the "preponderance of troops" would be American.[104] Still, as Churchill and the president traveled together by train from Hyde Park, where they had held preconference meetings, toward "cold and bleak Quebec City," the prime minister had plenty of time to talk, and one last chance to persuade Roosevelt to accept Brooke. Nevertheless, even before the formal meetings began, Churchill had conceded that this time Roosevelt would not be moved—the command would be given to an American.[105]

It was the second day of the meetings that Churchill sent for Brooke to give him the news. The prime minister and the president were staying at the picturesque Citadel, not far from the Chateau Frontenac, the scene of the meetings. The military stronghold stood 200 feet above the St. Lawrence River, with magnificent views. Brooke later wrote in his diary, "As far as I can gather Winston gave in, in spite of having previously promised me the job!!"[106] In his memoirs Churchill stated that before his discussion with Brooke, he had actually taken the initiative in proposing that the commander should be an American. Whatever the case, Brooke was given the official word and, according to Churchill, "bore the disappointment with soldierly dignity."[107] In fact, historian Andrew Roberts wrote, "It was a shattering blow to his [Brooke's] hopes, which had been so assiduously stoked by Churchill for so long. 'I remember it as if it was yesterday as we walked up and down on the terrace outside the drawing room of the Citadel,' Brooke recalled. 'Looking down on that wonderful view, as Winston spoke all that scenery was swamped in a dark cloud of despair.'" What made it worse for Brooke was that "'for not one moment did he [Churchill] realize what this meant to me . . . He offered no sympathy, no regrets at having had to change his mind.'"[108] As the British and American staffs went about their daily meetings at the Frontenac, surely Marshall understood that all around him expected the president to name him as the chief officer of this long-anticipated invasion. Marshall's reaction would be entirely different from Brooke's when in due time President Roosevelt "had to change his mind" about the American who would become the supreme allied commander of Overlord.

As Roosevelt, Churchill, and their respective staffs, including the devastated Brooke, settled in on August 14, 1943, for the 11-day session, the news from the European battlefronts was encouraging. Reports that the Italians were making serious peace moves continued. It was only days before the Germans evacuated Sicily. Meanwhile, the Russians were beginning to turn the Germans back toward their own borders. The Combined Bomber Offensive over France and Germany, approved at Trident, was finally ramping up. In the devastating U-boat war against Allied shipping, the tide was also turning. There was good news on the Pacific front as well—the Japanese were out of the Aleutians; MacArthur was on the offensive in New Guinea. Only the China-Burma-India Theater seemed static.[109] Nevertheless, while plenty of fierce fighting was ahead in all theaters, the Allies were on the move.

Chapter 10

Quebec to Cairo

"Who will command Overlord?"

August–December 1943

Quadrant—Overlord Must Not "Suffer Unduly"

In contrast to the stifling heavy heat of a Washington summer, it was cool and damp as Marshall arrived in Quebec on August 13, 1943, for the third major Anglo-American conference in seven months. The accommodations at the Hotel Frontenac were first-rate. Oranges were flown in from New York for the delegates' juice, and an appetizing "running buffet" was in the foyer near the conference room for occasions when intense meetings made trips to the dining room difficult.[1] Despite the setting, according to Chiefs of Staff historians Marshal Lord Bramall and General Sir William Jackson, "both sides approached Quadrant in an exasperated mood, verging on outright mistrust of each other."[2]

For Marshall, his task was well defined. He would continue putting pressure on the British to launch Overlord. Sure, it made sense that with victory in Sicily the Allies should occupy as much of the Italian peninsula as possible, as well as Sardinia and Corsica, since it was a means of drawing off German divisions from the continent and establishing air bases for strikes against Nazi-held territories. There was a caveat, though. None of these operations must threaten the accumulation of men and matériel in Britain. A briefing paper from Field Marshal Dill to his compatriots before the meetings began defined the mood of the American chiefs precisely: "[There is] a feeling that the British are not standing firm enough to [the] considered decision of 'Trident,' and are tending too readily to depart from decisions and to set aside the operations agreed upon. They realize [the] importance [to] put Italy out of the war, but are not prepared to see . . . the Pacific or 'Overlord' suffer unduly in consequence [of] new commitments in the Mediterranean."[3]

As the sessions began, the British had a counterargument to the American position, one that the chief of the Imperial British Staff, Sir Alan Brooke, had advanced in various scenarios at previous conferences: continued successes in Italy were necessary to draw off German forces, which then would not be available to effectively repulse the invasion, even if it meant *keeping* some of those seven divisions promised at Trident for transport to England on the peninsula. Brooke presented this approach as an integral part of the Overlord operation—weaken the enemy so he can't respond in force. In a way, it was an application of the "nibbling away" strategy that the British had always promoted as a prelude to the cross-channel invasion. So the showdown began. The Combined Chiefs met on the 15th, just after Brooke had been given the "crushing blow" that an American would lead the invasion. His mood was dark as he recorded his view of the day's discussions in his diary: "I entirely failed to get Marshall to realize the relation between cross-Channel and Italian operations and the repercussions which the one exercises on the others. It is quite impossible to argue with him as he does not begin to understand a strategic problem."[4] The talks were, as Brooke later said, "pretty frank," and some, as in the Trident Conference, were "off the record" closed sessions with aides dismissed.

One such gathering literally got explosive. Admiral Lord Louis Mountbatten of British Combined Operations had been impressed by an invention of Geoffrey Pyke, which showed that a mixture of water and sawdust could be frozen into a compound six times stronger than ice. He proposed shaping this substance—Pykrete—into 2,000-foot-long vessels that would act as aircraft carriers. During one of these closed meetings, Mountbatten, to make his point about the strength of the material, first shot his service revolver into a block of ice, which splintered as expected into dozens of sharp slivers that went flying. Next, he fired into the Pykrete. As promised, it was indeed impenetrable, so the bullet ricocheted between the U.S. naval chief Admiral King and the British air chief Portal; both scrambled for cover. The junior officers in the hallway were not only startled but alarmed when they heard the blast. "Good heavens," one said, "they've started shooting now!"[5]

Despite the drama of these closed sessions, the Combined Chiefs of Staff wanted compromise, since all feared "sideshows" and "eccentric operations" if the final decisions were left in the hands of Roosevelt and Churchill. By August 17, the CCS was firming up its recommendations for the European Theater to its respective leaders. Overlord was to be "the primary U.S.-British ground and air effort against the Axis in Europe," with a launch date of May 1, 1944. If resources were limited, support for Overlord would be the "main objective"—Marshall had wanted a stronger "overriding priority" phrase, but in the end he had accepted the less muscular wording. The Americans agreed to extended operations in the Mediterranean north of Rome, which would allow for an Italian-based air offensive against the continent. However, all would be carried out with resources defined at Trident, less the seven divisions, *unless* the Combined Chiefs of Staff decided otherwise as the situation on the ground warranted. Marshall realized this

In the foreground Roosevelt and Churchill sit with the Canadian prime minister, Mackenzie King, during the Quadrant Conference, August 18, 1943. On the back row, to the right of General Arnold are Air Chief Marshal Sir Charles Portal; General Sir Alan Brooke; Admiral King; Field Marshall Sir John Dill; General Marshall; Admiral of the Fleet Sir Dudley Pound, and Admiral William D. Leahy.

Franklin D. Roosevelt Library

"unless" provided wiggle room for the British, preferring a statement with "no strings attached." Nevertheless, in the spirit of cooperation, he agreed.[6] Finally, there would be a landing on the south coast of France (code-named Anvil, later Dragoon), with both American and newly armed French troops providing the invasion forces, to coincide with Overlord.

In the midst of these meetings, good news arrived from Sicily. That morning, General Patton had accepted the surrender of the port city of Messina, within firing range of the Italian mainland.[7] More good news: while the invasion of Sicily had already brought down the Mussolini government—he had fled to German protective custody that July 25—since then negotiations for an armistice agreement with the Italians had continued.[8] In part, it had been this development that precipitated the Quebec meeting in the first place. Now word came that Marshal Pietro Badoglio, Mussolini's replacement, was working through emissaries to sign a separate peace with the Allies.[9] Coupled with the navy staff's report that the tide had finally turned in the Battle of the Atlantic—the U-Boat War—and accounts detailing the increased effectiveness of the unrelenting air war over Nazi-held territory, including France and Germany, the CCS had reasons for optimism about the future.

China, Burma, India (CBI)

Still, the future included the war in the China-Burma-India/Pacific Theaters, and more "heated, clear the room" meetings were to follow as the talks moved to operations in these complicated far-flung arenas. As early as August 14, Marshall had made the case for the Americans, urging a stronger and more deliberate strategic link between Europe and the other two mega-theaters. He especially emphasized the importance of China as a key player in the defeat of Japan, a point that seemed lost on the British, who tended to see that region as a military backwater. The theater had proven complicated for the Americans as well. The United States had supported the Kuomintang (Nationalist) Party of Chiang Kai-shek since the war's beginning, and many in the country viewed him as a "loyal, valiant, and democratic ally" in the struggle against Japan.[10] A Chinese insurgency under the Communist revolutionary Mao Tse-tung, which had gained traction in the 1930s, was complicating the internal politics of the nation.

In February 1942 General Marshall had sent Lieutenant General Joseph Stilwell, one of his most valued officers, to China as Chiang's chief of staff and as commander of the China-Burma-India Theater. By the time Stilwell arrived, the Japanese were already overrunning Burma, a British colonial

237

possession that provided the only major supply lines to China from India and other Allied locales, and had cut off all land and sea routes back to China. By April the British and Indian troops had made a tactical retreat.

That May of 1942, only three months into his mission, Stilwell realized that despite a valiant defense by Chinese troops on loan from Chiang, the jig was up—those soldiers would need to be evacuated from Burma to India. When a C-47 transport aircraft arrived to take Stilwell to safety, he refused to go—it would be an abandonment of his staff, plus several divisions of Chinese troops under his command. Instead, he loaded the plane with as many officers and headquarters personnel as possible and informed the pilots that he "preferred to walk."[11] Left with some 114 staff members, including advisers, and cut off by the daily encroachment of the Japanese, he led the group through a frightening 140-mile, two-week retreat on foot out of the jungle. CBI historian Donovan Webster described the conditions this group faced: "impenetrable bamboo thickets, demoralizing switchbacks, steep and jungled mountainsides, biting ants, blood thirsty bugs and leeches, dehydration, hunger . . . muddy bivouacs, withering sun, wild elephants, blistered heels, devastating bouts of food poisoning, and several cases of malaria."[12] Stilwell was determined to eventually get back to that theater, even though, as Webster noted, "he dangled last on the Allies' list of tactical or supply importance."[13]

As demanding as this command role was, it was by no means Stilwell's only task in China. He was to oversee Lend-Lease supply shipments and provide "Allied style training" for 2 million Chinese troops with a view toward eventually meshing them with the larger Allied fight. In reality, Chiang, who on paper had control of the Chinese forces, proved to be an "authoritarian warlord" who showed little interest in helping the Allied cause. The generalissimo seemed to think that it was the task of the American armed forces, not China's, to defeat Japan; in fact, according to Mark Stoler, Chiang's goal appeared less focused on the current crisis and more on a desire to "build up his forces with Lend-Lease aid so that they could destroy Mao after Japan was defeated."[14] It was because Marshall had recognized the difficulty of this complex set of circumstances that he had appointed Stilwell, a fiercely competitive West Point graduate who had served in China for three stints before the war, spoke the language fluently, including several dialects, and knew the Chinese culture inside and out. Further, the chief of staff, having witnessed Stilwell's gifts during the Fort Benning years, considered him an exemplary general and warrior. Marshall had once described him as having "a genius for instruction" and "qualified

General Stilwell stands with the Generalissimo and Madame Chiang Kai-shek in Burma, early April 1942. Captured in a light moment, the scene did not accurately portray a complicated relationship between the Chinese leader and the American.

U.S. National Archives 531135

for any command in peace or war."

Stilwell soon developed contempt for the corrupt government of Chiang, telling Roosevelt that the Nationalists were "playing the USA for a sucker."[15] Although Stilwell deeply respected the Chinese people, his criticism of what he called Chiang's "gang of fascists" was up front and in the open. As for their leader, he was, according to Stilwell, a "vacillating, tricky, undependable old scoundrel."[16] Stilwell not only had scarcely hidden disdain for Chiang, he also clashed with certain American colleagues, especially Major General Claire L. Chennault. Webster described him as "a hard-faced, tenaciously charming Louisiana Cajun with a solid jaw and sun-scarred face." In China and the United States, he was something of a heroic figure.[17] Having acted as an adviser to Chiang's air force since 1937, he had also led a group of volunteer U.S. fighter pilots, the famous Flying Tigers, as they aided the beleaguered Chinese against the empire of Japan.[18] Chennault, recalled to active duty after Pearl Harbor, was a big believer in air power, which ran counter to Stilwell's emphasis on building up China's ground forces. Indeed it was Stilwell's view that without a strong Chinese army, the air fields would soon be in the control of the Japanese and thus could staunch the work of the air force. Given the fact that resources for this so-called "forgotten theater" were always scarce, and would continue to be lacking until the European war was won, Roosevelt backed Chennault, who not only believed he could do the job from the air, as long as he continued to get needed supplies, but who also was more diplomatic and supportive of Chiang.

Despite this tricky political-military situation, getting supplies for Chiang's army was nevertheless crucial, in Marshall's view, since he thought that without it China might actually be forced out of the war altogether. At Quadrant, Marshall wanted follow-through on the liberation of Burma, including opening up supply routes on the Burma Road by using not only the air force but ground operations as well. Brooke took issue with this, since it was his belief that China would stay in the war come what may, and thus the resources for a Burma campaign could be best used elsewhere until after the defeat of Germany.[19] In the end, the air route to China was to be strengthened with "vigorous steps taken to defend it through operations in the northern part of Burma."[20]

As a means of establishing unity of control for the area, and with the urging of Churchill, at Quadrant the Southeast Asia Command (SEAC) was created, which included India, Burma, Ceylon, Malaya, and Sumatra. Admiral Sir Louis Mountbatten would be at its head, with General Stilwell as his deputy supreme commander. It was an odd circumstance, since Stilwell would also continue as chief of staff to Chiang and commander of U.S. and Chinese forces in that area. As Marshall explained to Stilwell, "Your status will be dual and on an ordinary organizational basis is illogical, but there appears to be no other way to meet the complexities of the situation." He also tried to reassure Stilwell regarding the benefits of the change, telling him that the prime minister was "endeavoring to vitalize the effort as regards Burma." He described Mountbatten as "full of energy, drive and imagination to a point that irritates staid British high officials. You will find him a breath of fresh air."[21] Stilwell understood that his main role would be to see to it that Chinese forces and the U.S. 14th Air Force under Chennault played their parts in Burma operations. In Quebec, just after confirmation of the new Mountbatten-Stilwell roles, Marshall excused himself from the meeting to confer with T.V. Soong, who was at Quadrant in his capacity as the Chinese ambassador to the United States; he also happened to be the brother of the generalissimo's powerful wife, Soong Mei-ling—Madame Chiang. The chief of staff informed Soong in no uncertain terms that China would be expected to put troops in combat under this new command structure "instead of confining themselves to lip service and letting someone else do the fighting."[22]

Admiral Sir Louis Mountbatten, February 1942
George C. Marshall Research Library

A 12-Month Timetable—The War in the Pacific

The respective Allied delegations continued to chip away at the issues, their negotiations characterized, according to Brooke, by "differences of opinion, stubbornness, stupidity, and pig-headedness," a gloomy point of view that arose most often when he had to yield to the Americans. That was more frequent now than it had been in past conferences.[23] The British faced the united front of Marshall and Roosevelt, and increasingly it was apparent that power had shifted to the American contingent. Moreover, Admiral King, as the sentinel of the navy war in the Pacific, put the British on notice: his theater of emphasis had to have more material resources to accelerate military advances in the region. Despite the Europe First strategy, the Pacific commanders—Nimitz and MacArthur—constantly complained that the needs of their commands got short shrift, and both chomped at the bit for more action. The U.S. chiefs wanted a two-pronged offensive in the next 16 months—General MacArthur was to continue driving up the north coast of New Guinea, a part of his return to the Philippines; Nimitz would lead an attack from Hawaii through the Gilbert and Marshall Island groups to Palau in the Central Pacific. In the end, the Allies came up with no

General Douglas MacArthur and Admiral Chester W. Nimitz

www.*ibiblio.org/hyperwar*

cohesive long-range strategy for the Pacific, kicking it toward some future conference, but the British did agree that the Americans would have a free hand to launch their drive through the Central Pacific, thus moving the war into higher gear.[24]

The Allies set a particular course on the subject of Rabaul, a port in Australian New Guinea within MacArthur's command that the Japanese had held and fiercely defended since 1942. It was strategically important because of its proximity to the Japanese Caroline Islands, which included Truk Atoll, home anchorage for Japan's South Pacific fleet; moreover, it was the hub of the region that threatened Australia. Although an assault on Rabaul had been authorized during the conference at Casablanca, at Quadrant the Allies agreed that instead of capturing that port, which would take a prohibitively costly naval and army effort, the American and British forces would "neutralize it," bypassing it by establishing a ring of airfields and naval bases on the islands around it. Cut off from resupply and under continual air attacks, the base would eventually become useless. Perhaps, according to Marshall historian Larry Bland, this was the "first official pronouncement of what was to become the island-hopping strategy" of the Pacific War.[25] Another worry: the timetable for ending the war after the defeat of Germany. Marshall feared that with "mission accomplished" in Europe, Britain, which had been at war since 1939, might feel disinclined to hurry the end of the struggle on the other side of the world. One of Churchill's cabinet memos might have confirmed Marshall's concern had he read it. The prime minister had written that subduing Japan might take "several years, and might cause 'heart burnings' among the British public."[26] Marshall and the American delegation pressed hard for a tightened timetable, and got it; the British reluctantly agreed to the goal of defeating Japan within a year of Germany's surrender.[27] And so the conference ended, after 12 grueling, grinding days.

Rumors Abound

When Marshall returned from Quebec, he must have enjoyed a moment of satisfaction: the date was set for his hard-fought cross-channel invasion, and, although by no means official, everything pointed toward his being named the supreme allied commander of Overlord. Early in September Roosevelt had announced that Marshall's term as chief of staff would be extended indefinitely beyond the September 1 end to his four-year term because of the "outstanding service he had contributed to the nation."[28] The word among the CCS was that an "acting chief of staff," presumably General Eisenhower, would be appointed to replace Marshall during his time in Europe, and that he would return to his Washington position when Germany was defeated. Even in the public arena, by the first week in September the word of Marshall's likely appointment had been leaked, and not by accident, to the press. Both Admiral King and General Hap Arnold were vehemently against Marshall being taken from his position as their trusted colleague and as the acknowledged leader of the Joint Chiefs. Admiral Leahy agreed as well and told the president so, but King made his opinion more broadly known. "We have a winning combination," he declared. "Why break it up?"

His arguments seemed valid. As presidential aide Harry Hopkins's biographer Robert Sherwood noted, neither Eisenhower nor anyone else "could possibly have Marshall's extraordinary sense of the requirements of global war, his knowledge of land, sea and air logistics, his balanced judgment as to the importance of one theater or one ally or one arm of the service as opposed to the other." Further, "if Eisenhower were to become Acting Chief of Staff the regrettable but real lack of cordiality which characterized the relationship between him and MacArthur could become a source of major embarrassments."[29] Earlier, when he was in the Philippines before the war, Eisenhower had been the general's subordinate assistant, and was once quoted as saying, "I learned dramatics under MacArthur." The Pacific general, on the other hand, damned with faint praise, calling Eisenhower "the best clerk I ever had." According to historian Stanley Weintraub, "Privately, they detested each other. Publicly, they remained businesslike and mutually admiring."[30] It wasn't difficult to be businesslike and admiring thousands of miles apart in independent commands, but if Eisenhower had to tread the thorny terrain of the Euro-Pacific tug of war, the chief of naval operations was convinced it would be disastrous. King was in contact with two journalists to whom he sometimes provided off-the-record briefings, and he asked them to "help us out with articles and editorials saying how much Marshall is needed right here, and emphasizing what a good job he is doing."[31]

By mid-September, even Marshall's mentor and friend, the aging and unwell General John J. Pershing, weighed in on the subject, apparently dictating his letter of concern to the president from his hospital suite at Walter Reed Hospital. He was disturbed, he told Roosevelt, regarding newspaper articles that Marshall was to be transferred to a tactical command in Europe. "We are engaged in a global war of which the end is still far distant, and for the wise strategical guidance of which we need our most accomplished officer as Chief of Staff," he wrote. Naming Marshall as "that officer," Pershing made the case that the Overlord command would be in a "limited area, no matter how seemingly important." Finally, he said, "I know of no one at all comparable to replace him as Chief of Staff."[32] In classic Rooseveltian style, the president responded: "You are absolutely right about George Marshall—and yet, I think, you are wrong too!" He explained that Overlord was to be the biggest operation of the war, and, further, rather than a limiting theater command, he planned to expand Marshall's role to the whole European Theater. Besides, he told Pershing, "The British want to have him sit with their own Joint Staff in all matters that do not pertain to purely British island affairs." Finally, the pièce de résistance: "I think it's only fair to give George a chance in the field. . . . The best way I can express it is to tell you that I want George to be the Pershing of the second World War."[33]

It didn't take long for the story of the proposed change to gain a momentum all its own. The well respected *Army and Navy Journal* made the editorial claim that "powerful influences" wanted to get rid of the reliable and capable Marshall by kicking him into the European Theater. The public outcry that followed seemed to revolve around Lieutenant General Brehon Somervell, who served as the head of the important Army Service Forces, formally Service of Supply, which had come into existence when Marshall reorganized the service commands in 1942. Somervell, at about the time the story broke, was seeking to reorganize this important element of the army. Its changes, if supported by the Congress, would affect the War Department general staff, the office of the undersecretary of war, and at least six supply arms and services. Although Marshall fully favored the project and Somervell, he was much too involved in the day-to-day grind of the war to get involved directly. Secretary of War Stimson, however, wasn't keen on the idea, questioning the wisdom of such a dramatic change at mid-war, and worried about the political and military implications.[34]

Somehow, though, in this brewing storm of controversy, Somervell's reorganization plan became linked with Roosevelt's resolve to appoint Marshall and send him to Europe. It was rather a remote connection, but the fact was that at one time Somervell, an army engineer, had been associated with Harry Hopkins in New Deal WPA projects. During the war, the media often painted Hopkins as an unofficial "behind the scenes" Rasputin-like figure in the White House, always suspected of wielding too much influence. Perhaps, the newspaper articles speculated, Roosevelt would make Somervell the chief of staff, since he was more amenable to the president's political agenda, shaped by this backstage liberal.[35] In fact, the charge was loudly proclaimed as part of a New Deal plot to use the war emergency as a means of communizing America.[36] Although totally untrue, the worst stories claimed that in his reorganization scheme, Somervell was recommending replacing a total of 16 generals with political appointees, presumably New Dealers.[37] It got even more ridiculous, with one newspaper asserting that Somervell might become "an Army running mate of Mr. Roosevelt on a fourth-term ticket to offset the possible Republican nomination of Gen. Douglas MacArthur."[38]

Somervell was thoroughly embarrassed at these false accusations, writing to Marshall in a private letter, "How such swine can exist is beyond me. I am . . . distressed that my name was mixed up in it in any way, that you had this stupid thing to contend with in addition to your other burdens. [39] Marshall, who was such a private man, was horrified at this "hullabaloo" so focused on him personally, and declined to remark on his own transfer. He did, however, vigorously defend Somervell during a breakfast meeting of the House Military Affairs Committee, and allayed their fears by assuring them that the promotion of army officers was done completely without political interference.[40] Many members of Congress were still worried, and opposed sending Marshall to the field. Three ranking Republicans came to see Stimson to express their concerns; the secretary of war recorded how the meeting went in his diary:

> They told me how much they relied on him [Marshall] not only individually but how they were able to carry controversial matters through with their colleagues if they could say that the measure in question had the approval of Marshall. They had even had the fear that the proposed movement was aided and abetted by enemies who wanted to get Marshall out of his present position where his influence was so great in the Joint and Combined Chiefs of Staff. I told them that the proposal didn't come from Marshall's enemies but his close friends. . . . I told them most confidentially that I happened to know that instead of the assignment being repugnant to Marshall, it would fill one of his deepest hopes of his heart.[41]

After a while newspapers across the country called for a halt to these attacks, condemning the "mixture of unauthenticated 'news,' rumor, guesswork and innuendo which has exploded a teapot tempest around the figure of General Marshall."[42] As much as Marshall was embarrassed by all of this attention, he did find a bit of humor in one news source. A Nazi broadcast from Paris had announced that "General George C. Marshall, the U.S. Chief of Staff, had been dismissed. President Roosevelt has taken over his command." Someone who was monitoring the communiqués sent a copy to Marshall, who passed it on to Harry Hopkins, with a note: "Dear Harry: Are you

President Roosevelt with Harry Hopkins, his closest adviser
during the White House years

U.S. Library of Congress, ID# ftp0003

responsible for pulling this fast one on me? G.C.M." Hopkins gave it to the
president, who wrote in pencil on the same note: "Dear George—Only true
in part—I am now Chief of Staff but you are President. F.D.R."[43]

A Pleasant Side Trip

By mid-September, in the middle of the whole Overlord command public
controversy, General Marshall and Katherine got a change of scenery.
Marshall had been asked more than a month before to be a guest of the
Mexican government during the yearly fiesta celebrating that nation's
independence. Despite the fact that Marshall usually tried to avoid these
types of extravaganzas, it must have seemed a relief to get out of town.
Beginning on September 14, it was a fabulous three-day respite, far from
the tumult of Washington. The Marshalls went by plane with an overnight
layover in New Orleans. It had been arranged for them to dine at the famous
Antoine's Restaurant in the historic section of the city. Katherine reported
that when they arrived, the owner himself greeted them "literally with open
arms" and oversaw a sumptuous feast for the special guests. Served with
great drama, the dessert was "topped by two [sugary] white doves. On the

ribbon caught in their beaks was printed in gold letters, 'General and Mrs. Marshall.'" It was a lovely beginning to their trip.

When the Marshalls arrived in Mexico City, they were met by four official delegations, all of which presented Katherine with orchid corsages. Shrieking sirens cleared the way for the special guests from the north as they were escorted to their hotel. The city was beautifully decorated with flags, bunting, and flowers; thousands gathered in picturesque costumes to take in the events. Katherine wrote several years later, "It was like coming from darkness into bright sunshine. Did people really laugh and play and celebrate like this; was this the same world in which we had lived for the past three years?" Marshall was, of course, the honored public figure at the luncheons and dinners that filled the weekend.[44] Returning to the reality of the capital, General Marshall wrote a report to President Roosevelt describing the visit. It is a measure of his concentration on the cross-channel invasion and other military matters that, to his chagrin, he realized that he had not mentioned to either the president or the secretary of war that he was going. He wrote follow-up letters to both. Marshall ends his missive to the president by saying, "I am sorry I became involved in such an affair without due and formal reference of the matter. The truth is, I was so deeply occupied in other matters that I must plead that as an excuse." Roosevelt answered him cordially, "Dear George, I am delighted that you had such a successful trip in Mexico."[45]

Doubts

Roosevelt seemed unperturbed by the firestorm arising out of the Somervell reorganization issue; moreover, the president hardly took the time to answer what he considered bogus charges that he was motivated to get rid of Marshall's influence at top-level conferences because of their differences regarding strategy. Roosevelt cabled Churchill that all of the loud beating of press drums was dying down, and he minimized the fallout. He observed that, after all, if decisions were influenced by such campaigns, "We will find ourselves with the newspapers running the war."[46] Nevertheless, perhaps he did take to heart some of the more valid concerns raised by balanced voices that weighed in on the brouhaha.

That letter from Pershing, the venerated hero of World War I and close friend of Marshall? Perhaps the old general's arguments resonated. Further, did the president read the editorial of newspaper columnist Ernest Lindley, who laid out so clearly the loss that would ensue were Marshall to leave the capital city? Indeed, Lindley noted the dread of Marshall's colleagues that the Joint Chiefs would be deprived of his counsel as well as of his prestige in Congress, "now almost without precedent." "It is a staggering tribute to one man," he continued, "that he is regarded by so many diverse but competent judges as, if not indispensable, at least the best equipped to administer the American Army, to represent it before Congress, and the public, to represent it on the highest Allied strategy-making body, and to command not only it but all the Allied forces in what may well prove to be the most intricate and hazardous but most powerful offensive campaign in the history of warfare."[47] Did the president see the piece written by reporter Richard Strout in the *New Republic,* who described watching Marshall deliver congressional testimony: "He is one of the most effective witnesses I ever followed. His testimony killed the bill. There were no false notes in his testimony, no mugging and gagging, nor the mawkish kind of deference and deprecation that so frequently go with a congressional hearing. Because he set a forthright tone, the members of the committee followed along on the same level too." Strout went on to say, "He is not the military glamour type, like General MacArthur, and he is somewhat more articulate and practiced than General Eisenhower, able though the latter is."[48]

Roosevelt had another concern: how would he answer the argument that going from U.S. Army chief of staff to the commander of Overlord, no matter how important the operation, was a demotion? Sure, he had said that he had plans to expand Marshall's overall responsibilities, to make it broader than a theater command, but how exactly would that work? In his reply to Pershing's letter, he had tried to allay the general's concern about the limited perimeters of Overlord by telling him that he intended to make Marshall the commander of the whole European Theater. Through Hopkins, Stimson had suggested that for Roosevelt to make the appointment large enough, Marshall should command not only northwest Europe but the Italian/Mediterranean Theater as well, and the president liked the idea.[49] Perhaps Churchill did not: he cabled Hopkins on September 26 that he was concerned about all of the newspaper talk to the effect that Marshall was to become supreme commander in chief of all the forces in Western Europe. The prime minister reminded Hopkins of the Quebec decisions: the Allies had agreed that while Marshall would advise the British chiefs and the Combined Chiefs from time to time, he would not be empowered to make decisions outside the sphere of Overlord.[50] In fact, it was unlikely that Churchill would yield all-inclusive authority to Marshall; he was still determined to lengthen the Allied strategic hand in the eastern Mediterranean along the Aegean Sea, and this he already knew Marshall would vehemently oppose.[51]

Roosevelt was ambivalent all right; that seemed clear. He wrestled with his desire to keep Marshall in Washington, taking heed of the long list of reasons supporting that option and weighing it against his sense of fairness. Marshall had fought "tooth and nail" for three years, starting with Roundup, and had finally secured an invasion date; he deserved his chance to lead it to a dramatic finish, no matter how demanding. The president struggled with these two sides of the coin, especially since the whole idea of an expanded command for Overlord had not been settled. Thus, as September cooled into October, he declined to announce the commander. Nevertheless, the indications were that the prize would be Marshall's, so the chief of staff proceeded to shape a team that would help him in London if he were in fact given the role.

At Casablanca, the Combined Chiefs had already appointed British General Frederick E. Morgan to begin work on the invasion plan. He was to be the chief of staff to the supreme allied commander (COSSAC), who would be appointed at some later time—much later, apparently. Morgan had already presented a tentative plan at Quebec: an attack on the Normandy coast— firm and wide beaches for armor, predictable tides, good exit routes, lateral roads, access to the port at Cherbourg, suitable for air support.[52] Yes, it would require a sea voyage of more than 100 miles as compared to only 26 miles between Dover and the Pas de Calais, the shortest route. However, with the Germans convinced that Pas de Calais was a likely target, it was most heavily reinforced, and thus not recommended. With these basic premises in mind, Morgan came to Washington to develop details of the invasion with the president, Marshall, and the other chiefs.

Supposedly, Morgan's visit was to have been short, but Marshall encouraged him to stay for six weeks. The chief of staff had heard that the COSSAC leader had "taken no rest whatsoever for a long time," which he found troublesome, since he believed that overstressed, overworked generals were less effective. Marshall proceeded to arrange leave for the general so that he could take a tour of the beautiful Shenandoah Valley in nearby Virginia, to learn more about the Civil War and temporarily take his mind off the one in progress.[53] Morgan enjoyed the tour enormously and made plenty of friends, especially Southerners who seemed impressed with his knowledge of the finer points of "good bourbon and branch water."[54] Marshall also took the British general to observe infantry, artillery, and airborne training sites, as well as the port of embarkation in New York Harbor. Morgan was astounded at the "profusion on an unlimited scale" as Liberty ships were fully loaded for the trans-Atlantic trip.[55] Once back in Washington, Morgan gave the JCS the firm sense that he supported the invasion wholeheartedly; thus many of the concerns over Churchill's efforts to divert the "main show" were diminished. Marshall liked Morgan, trusted him, found him frank and likable. Marshall let him know that there was some doubt about who would lead Overlord; nevertheless, he told him, the plans needed to be advanced, so they would proceed as if he [Marshall] were supreme commander.

When Morgan visited the White House, Roosevelt asked him what he needed as he moved forward. The Brit told him, "Your Army, your General Marshall, and your Ambassador Biddle [diplomat to the European governments in exile]." The president's reply was full of foreshadowing. He told Morgan that under proper conditions he could have the army, but he couldn't promise the other two. In fact, he hinted, for political reasons he might not be able to spare Marshall for the invasion.[56] Nevertheless, Marshall began to shape a list of key commanders: definitely Omar Bradley, Mark Clark, Patton, and Eisenhower, who had made it clear that he hoped to remain as an army group commander under Marshall. Although the word was that it would be Eisenhower as chief of staff, or acting chief of staff, the current European Theater commander fervently hoped that he would not be "stuck with a desk job in Washington."

British General Frederick E. Morgan, appointed at Casablanca to serve as chief of staff to the supreme allied commander of the Normandy Invasion

www.ibiblio.org/hyperwar

Presidential Boomlets

As Marshall worked to get his command staff in place, to his absolute distaste he found out in early November that Senator Edwin Johnson, a Colorado Democrat opposed to a fourth term for Roosevelt, proposed General Marshall as a Democratic candidate for president in 1944. No, he wasn't a candidate, said Johnson, but "This is a time to draft men. . . . He is not a candidate and will emphatically say so, but no patriotic American from George Washington down can refuse such a call. George Marshall is not only a very great soldier . . . he is a fine Christian gentleman and a statesman in the highest concept of that much abused term."[57] The press, of course, jumped on the idea, with one columnist opining: "On the basis of personal merits, can you think of a more desirable successor to President Roosevelt?" Marshall could certainly name a few, and he proceeded to squelch this astonishing surge of unwanted attention.

Knowing that Stimson had a press conference scheduled a few days hence from this flurry, in a memo on November 8 he enclosed some of the "Marshall for President" clippings and laid out exactly what Stimson should say regarding the matter, literally putting words in the mouth of the secretary of war: "I can speak with authority in stating that there has been no discussion of this nature with General Marshall by anyone. Further, that he will never permit himself to be considered as a possible Presidential candidate. His training and ambitions are not political."[58] In addition to presidential boomlets, others wanted to capitalize on Marshall's celebrity. An important publishing house of the day had written to Marshall's aide, Frank McCarthy, to inquire about the chief of staff writing a book. McCarthy was as no-nonsense as Marshall himself in his response. "He has made up his mind quite firmly that he can give no thought at this time to writing a book, and, in fact, he has no intention of writing a book after the war. I don't like to be so categorical on this, but I know the General well enough to say that, in view of this statement, any further effort on our part would be fruitless. He keeps no diary of any kind . . . and I am perfectly sure no amount of persuasion would cause him to do any further thinking about the matter at present, and I do not believe he will ever change his mind about writing a book in later life. While I realize this letter is somewhat blunt, I am sure you would want me to give out the straight story. That is it."[59]

"Be prepared for a stiff fight"

As far as Katherine Marshall knew, she and her husband would soon be vacating the chief of staff's residence at Fort Myer, since all indications were that he would soon be making his way to London to be "on the ground" for planning the invasion. In fact, since Marshall had returned from Quebec, Katherine had been moving furniture, rugs, and other items for everyday living in small batches, using a little trailer "covered by a green canvas to conceal its contents" to Dodona Manor, in Leesburg, Virginia. Having made it quite comfortable, she noted to a friend that "We are all but moved out of Quarters Number One." While the Marshalls were in Mexico, Katherine had hired two Mexican women to come as nursemaids for Molly's children, since they would be staying through the winter with her in Leesburg as well. Writing after the war, she recalled that her husband had been relieved, "for he had hated to leave for Europe with our domestic affairs unsettled."[60]

Since midsummer the president had been working to arrange diplomatic meetings with Soviet Premier Joseph Stalin and Generalissimo Chiang Kai-shek, each one separately. Stalin refused to meet with Chiang, since the Soviets had signed a five-year neutrality pact with Japan dating to 1941. Although the Soviets would later break this agreement to enter the war on the side of the Allies, at this point Stalin stood by it. Finally, in early November it was agreed that there would be talks with Chiang in Cairo, code-named Sextant, and soon after with Stalin in Tehran, code-named Eureka. So it was that Marshall left his Pentagon office on November 11 ready to begin his travels, not to Europe, but once again to the Middle East, first stop Egypt's capital city. He was joining the president's large party of 60-plus officers of air, logistics, and joint committees that would soon board the sparkling new ship, *Iowa*. The vessel, one of a dying breed of battleships, was specially equipped with a bed one foot longer than usual, an elevator, and a large square bathtub with metal handles, all intended to accommodate the president's disability. The ship left port from the Chesapeake Bay at six minutes after midnight on Saturday, the 13th, even though all had been ready to depart since midday on the 12th. Apparently, former navy man President Roosevelt believed it was bad luck to go to sea on a Friday. Precautions had been taken to reduce any possibility of bad luck—the ship was protected by an antisubmarine screen of three destroyers, and two escort carriers provided air cover along the way. Despite such safety measures, one of those destroyers accidentally, due to "spectacular carelessness," unloosed a torpedo, which whizzed astern the *Iowa* 600 yards out as it made its way across the Atlantic. "Torpedo defense, this is NO drill," droned the loudspeaker. Imagine the consternation of the destroyer's captain when he took in the fact that his crew had almost sunk a ship carrying the president of the United States; perhaps it was even worse for this seafarer when he realized that also on board was the navy's chief officer, Admiral Ernest King.[61]

It was a crossing characterized by hard work, as the various branches were determined that they would be ready for any effort on the part of the British to backtrack on Quadrant—indeed, the Americans would insist that their allies either "fish or cut bait." Further, according to army historian Ray S. Cline, embodied in the upcoming conferences would be the whole strategy of the global war: the "beat Germany first" concept; the roles of the United States, Great Britain, the USSR, and China in the coalition effort—all were in "balance." General Morgan was wise to have warned Winston Churchill and the British chiefs that they had to be well aware of the "temper of American representation" and "be prepared for a stiff fight, in comparison with which Quadrant might be 'child's play.'"[62]

In daily meetings during the crossing, the Joint Chiefs all agreed that one such tough fight would be over the concept of the unity of command— one general over the entire strategic bombing forces operating against the Germans in Europe, and the same for the Mediterranean/Middle East Theater. However, they and the president thought that the latter should be a subset of the supreme allied commander, who was to be Marshall. All understood that the British would not want this arrangement, preferring an independent Mediterranean command under a British general. All were in agreement that they would fight hard against any further operations in the Balkans or the eastern Mediterranean, or any other move that would weaken the May 1, 1944, deadline.

Interlude

By November 20, the president and the Joint Chiefs had arrived in Oran, Algeria, now in Allied hands. They were met by General Eisenhower, along with Roosevelt's two sons, who, when the small launch that carried him from the ship arrived at the dock, helped their father stand to receive the welcome. The European Theater commander had made careful and extensive arrangements for the visit of such an august group of civilian and military leaders. Soon the entire contingent was aboard C-54s making the three-hour flight to Tunis. For an overnight visit, the president would stay at Eisenhower's villa, Marshall and King at a cottage nearby. The next day, Roosevelt toured the Carthage battlefields with Eisenhower, and while indeed they did talk of Romans and Carthaginians and recalled the heavy fighting of more recent days, it was also clear that Roosevelt was still wrestling with the Overlord command decision. After all, if the president made Marshall the supreme allied commander, it would be Eisenhower who would head to Washington as the chief of staff. At one point Roosevelt told the general how he dreaded taking Marshall out of the capital city where he had been so effective, but then he laid out his dilemma: "Ike, you and I know who was the chief of staff during the last years of the Civil War, but practically no one else knows, although the names of the field generals—Grant, of course, and Lee, and Jackson, Sherman, Sheridan, and the others—every schoolboy knows them." Then he got to the punch line—his concern: "Fifty years from now practically nobody will know who George Marshall was. That is one of the reasons why I want George to have the big command—he is entitled to establish his place in history as a great general." Eisenhower wanted very badly to be a commander under Marshall, and not back in Washington, so, as he would write later regarding this possibility, he "was sweating it out in big drops." Nevertheless, Eisenhower responded blandly, with as much sincerity as he could muster, that he was a soldier and would go wherever the government sent him.[63] As the president said good-bye the next evening, ready to fly on to Cairo, he surely understood that the window for making this crucial decision was narrowing—he would have to figure it out, and soon.

Eisenhower with President Roosevelt aboard his plane on a
flight from Oran to Tunis, November 20, 1943
Franklin D. Roosevelt Library, Map Room Papers

Sextant—"The Chiangs have arrived"

Marshall and his party deplaned in Cairo by the late afternoon of November 21; en route the pilot had flown low over the recent battlefields of Libya

255

and Egypt—shifting sands could not fully cover burned-out tanks, trucks, and planes, darkened reminders of war's carnage. Spirits lifted as they saw the verdant, emerald strips of the Nile Valley and gazed with awe when the Great Sphinx came into sight. The U.S. ambassador's residence would be the temporary home of the president; the Australian ambassador's would host the prime minister. Marshall shared a small, crowded villa with Arnold and six others. The conference itself was held at the luxurious Mena House Hotel, whose windows and terraces offered dramatic views of the pyramids. Generalissimo and Madame Chiang Kai-shek had arrived two days before, a fact that irritated Churchill. That would mean the China question would take center stage first in the negotiations, and European operations would be put on the back burner. The prime minister viewed Chiang as a peripheral figure and couldn't see that the Chinese were going to contribute much to the war effort.[64] Roosevelt, on the other hand, was convinced that China's status could be elevated, if not by actual contribution to the war, to that of a great power. To strengthen that possibility was one of the purposes of bringing Chiang in person to Cairo. As Ed Cray noted, "Doing so would enlist one quarter of the world's population in his gestating concept of a United Nations to keep the postwar peace."[65] Working through the U.S. ambassador to the USSR, Roosevelt had already gotten agreement from the Russians to include China as a part of what would soon be dubbed "The Big Four," along with the United States, Great Britain, and the Soviets. Marshall wanted to aid China, but he, like General Stilwell, did not have confidence in the Nationalist leader.

The Chiangs, along with five Chinese generals and Stilwell, were invited to attend the first plenary meeting on Tuesday, November 23, 1943, and they made quite a dramatic entrance. Historian Forrest Pogue described the exotic Chinese couple as they took their places, composed among these Westerners:

> Impassive, his skin stretched tautly over prominent facial bones, giving him an almost ascetic look, [he] appeared . . . more like a traditional Chinese scholar than a powerful, ruthless military and political leader, controlling the destinies of millions of his countrymen. At first sight he seemed unobtrusive and colorless in contrast to his beautiful, American-educated wife, who spoke excellent English and seemed to be the more decisive of the two. Stunningly dressed, with charm compounded of femininity and forcefulness, she kept a watchful eye on the proceedings, correcting her interpreter from time to time and adding clarifications that some of her hearers suspected were an

improvement on the original.[66]

Even Alan Brooke noticed Madame Chiang's beauty, and the fact that her black satin dress had "a slit that . . . exposed one of her shapely legs," mentioning in his diary entry how he thought that among some of his young staff men "he heard a suppressed 'neigh.'"[67]

Winston Churchill and Roosevelt are seated between the Generalissimo and Madame Chiang Kai-shek, November 1943, Cairo.
Franklin D. Roosevelt Library

With the Chinese contingent seated, it would be the Quadrant-appointed SEAC commander, Lord Mountbatten, who would make the case that morning for an operation to take the former British possession, Burma. Troops from India would move eastward; Chinese forces would move west, creating a pincer that would close near the China-Burma border. Meanwhile, according to the proposal, the British would stage an amphibious attack, code-named Buccaneer, against the Andaman Islands 300 miles southwest of Rangoon, Burma, to keep the Japanese fleet distracted from the main event.[68] Marshall and King argued in support of the plan, believing it would open China and thus make staging the Pacific War much easier; Brooke was against it. The discussions, centering on the availability of shipping and air operations for this plan, got steamy. General Arnold described it rather blandly, recalling that it "became quite an open talk, with everyone throwing his cards on the table, face up." At the Combined Chiefs meeting later in the day, Brooke requested that discussion of the Andaman invasion be postponed. His motivations seemed clear when he asked if it would be possible to divert the landing craft set aside for the Andamans for more action in the eastern Mediterranean/Aegean, the same eastern theater that Churchill constantly sought to expand. Fur began to fly.

Stilwell's description was much more vivid than the dry official minutes' version: "Brooke got nasty, and King got good and sore. King almost climbed over the table at Brooke. God he was mad. I wish he had socked him." Later in the week, when Brooke, in the midst of a meeting that was moving toward compromise on a variety of Euro-CBI matters, suggested a postponement of Buccaneer altogether, Marshall expressed his opinion in no uncertain terms as well. British Air Marshal Sholto Douglas called the exchange "the father and mother of a row." After bitter arguments, though, the U.S. chiefs would not accept the abandonment of Buccaneer and finally said that any decision to "throw in the towel" would have to come from the president himself.[69]

"Muskets must flame"

On the evening of November 23, 1943, as the president entertained the Chiangs, Marshall was invited to dine alone with the prime minister. Marshall later told Forrest Pogue that Churchill almost always asked him to dinner—just the two of them—on the first night of a conference, adding that "he could talk to me very frankly and very persuasively, and then when he finally couldn't turn me, he might [later] turn someone else."[70] There in Cairo, at the Australian ambassador's home, as the conversation took twists and turns until 2:00 a.m., Churchill opined that it would take two and one-half American divisions to face a single German division. Marshall, weary with the British view that U.S. soldiers were inferior to their Allied counterparts, let his temper momentarily flare: "I never want to hear this again," he snapped. Churchill backed off and would not make that argument at any other time.[71] Later on, the prime minister pressed for his eastern Mediterranean gambit, an assault on the German-held island of Rhodes. To strengthen his view, he had all of the British chiefs in, and they all supported Churchill's outlook against Marshall's, who firmly believed it would drain resources from Overlord. The chief of staff later described the scene to Pogue, "It got hotter and hotter. Finally, Churchill grabbed his lapels and said, 'His Majesty's Government cannot stand idle. Muskets must flame,' and other fine English like that. I said, 'God forbid, if I should try to dictate, but not one American soldier is going to die on [that] goddamned beach.' The others were horrified, but they didn't want the operation and were willing for me to say it. Churchill never held it against me, but Ismay [his chief of staff] had to stay up with him all night."[72]

"Now, let me get this straight"

The next afternoon the Combined Chiefs were in discussion once more with the Chinese generals, seeking a commitment of Nationalist troops for the Burma campaign. The Chinese pressed harder for the Andaman assault but hedged on their part in opening the Burma Road. They called the whole plan inadequate and arrogantly listed what they needed to enter into the agreement. They demanded additional supplies, including that 10,000 tons a month be flown into China no matter what the circumstances. They also demanded beefed-up air coverage far beyond the capacity of available transport aircraft and refused to go along with the plan unless they had "explicit guarantees" that land operations would be supported by major coordinated air, naval, and amphibious attacks.[73] When Marshall explained that there were no transports for the shipment of these additional supplies, one of the generals said China had been promised supplies by air; they had "rights" in the matter. Marshall glared in anger as he admonished the generals: "Now let me get this straight. You [Chinese] are talking about your 'rights' in this matter. I thought these were *American* planes, and *American* personnel, and *American* matériel. I don't understand what you mean by saying we can or can't do thus or so." Later, Brooke took on the Chinese generals with a barrage of questions that they wouldn't answer, since by that time Chiang himself was not at the meeting. "A ghastly waste of time," Brooke told Marshall, who retorted, "You're telling me!"[74]

The next day, Chiang was present and waffled again on the Burma campaign, pleading not enough support from the Americans. Despite the testiness of these exchanges, though, certain agreements were reached. The president promised to arm and equip a Chinese army of 90 divisions and agreed that some kind of amphibious operation across the Bay of Bengal (the Andaman Islands option) would be carried out within a few months. This was something that Chiang held out for, and Roosevelt seemed to think that he had to show substantive support for that relatively neglected theater. Even though the Andaman operation (Buccaneer) would require LSTs (landing craft—landing ship, tank) that were in short supply and needed for Overlord, Marshall had to reinforce his president. The chief of staff also agreed to the arming of a Chinese army, but he didn't want any commitment of American combat troops to the China-Burma-India Theater. His hope was that very soon the Allies would be transferring power to the Pacific—in other words, the Germans would have been defeated—and he wanted the Pacific to be the theater of emphasis. Further, despite the amphibious operation that Roosevelt had promised, the when and where was still up in the air, with the British lukewarm on the topic. If it didn't happen, Marshall sought Roosevelt's backing to move the resources that would be needed for that mission either to Overlord or to the Pacific, *not* for the expansion to the east in the Mediterranean.[75]

A "Thankful" Break

It so happened that Thanksgiving fell during the Allied conference in Cairo. To the amazement of the British, President Roosevelt had brought along a supply of turkeys. A delectable traditional meal prepared for 20 guests, including Marshall, King, Arnold, and their British counterparts, was brought into the dining room with great ceremony at the ambassador's stately villa. Churchill described it as "a pleasant and peaceful feast." The president, "propped high in his chair," carved "two enormous turkeys for all with masterly, indefatigable skill." Formally dressed in a dinner jacket, Roosevelt gave a toast after explaining the Lincoln-based origin of the holiday, and remarked "how our American soldiers are spreading that custom all over the world." Afterward, an army band provided the entertainment. Churchill asked for "Carry Me Back to Old Virginny," and "Ol' Man River"; Roosevelt returned the compliment by requesting "The White Cliffs of Dover." When the band struck up the "The Marines' Hymn," Churchill was on his feet, flashing the "V for Victory" sign as the president sang along.[76] As Roosevelt later wrote, "For a couple of hours we cast care aside." Indeed, only for a few hours. It was the very next day that Brooke and Marshall had their "father and mother of a row."

Overlord vs. the Mediterranean—Tipping Scales

Amidst the China discussions, Churchill did get the chance to raise the issues of the theater that interested him most—European operations—although at the end of the Cairo Conference these talks would reach an unsatisfying and indecisive conclusion, perhaps for a reason. According to historian Maurice Matloff, "Each side was holding its full fire and only rehearsing its arguments for the meetings soon to take place with the Russians." Even Roosevelt noted that the final resolution would depend on the outcome of the conference with Stalin. The central question remained, though, as to "whether Overlord could be retained 'in all its integrity' and, at the same time, the Mediterranean be kept 'ablaze,'" Matloff noted. [77]

The "Prime" Argument

At Cairo Churchill painted a gloomy picture of the Allies' progress in Italy. Having landed that September, the American and British troops had made 300 miles of progress up the boot. Nevertheless, the Germans put up fierce resistance, and by mid-November Allied armies had been stopped cold in a wintry, mountainous region 87 miles south of Rome.[78] Churchill linked this halt not to German reinforcements, but to his having agreed "with heavy heart" to transfer seven divisions from the Mediterranean to the United Kingdom to meet the terms of Trident. Further, in his opinion, the Allies hadn't taken advantage of an open Adriatic coast to cause "chaos in the Balkans." If only Eisenhower had sent a few troops to help in the taking of the Dodecanese Islands in the Aegean, which included Rhodes, the prime minister argued, they could have had "cheap prizes" and opened the way to other countries in the region—Crete and Greece, for example.[79] Sure, he understood that the goal was to liberate Rome and the airfields to the north for support of Overlord, since, as he said, "whoever holds Rome holds the title deeds of Italy." Further, Churchill declared, "Overlord remained top of the bill," but then came the caveat: it "should not be such a tyrant as to rule out every other activity in the Mediterranean." There should be a "degree of elasticity" in the use of landing craft that had to go for Overlord—it might result in just a short delay, he said: Rome in January; Rhodes in February— with Rhodes the Aegean would be dominated by the Allied Air Force; supplies to the Yugoslavs—the hard-fighting partisans there just needed material assistance; a settlement of the command arrangements. This would put pressure on neutral Turkey to enter the war on the side of the Allies. If that happened, according to Churchill, the Allies could dominate the Black Sea with submarines and light naval forces and give a "right hand" to the Russians. All of the plans for Overlord should go "full steam" ahead, but within the Mediterranean framework. Even if only one-tenth of Allied troops not currently in action were made available for the eastern Mediterranean, Churchill avowed, significant gains could be made.[80]

Unsettled Business

All of this discussion of moving to the right (east into the Balkans) from north Italy, for seizing opportunities and necessities in the Mediterranean, and for postponing the target date for Overlord confirmed Marshall's worst fears and that of his chiefs. He saw it as "dangerous," and would involve military operations in a region of "inhospitable terrain, primitive communications, and turbulent peoples." No, Marshall was against it, and stuck to his belief that maximum pressure should be applied to the Germans in Italy until Rome was free, and then the focus should shift to England and intense preparation for Overlord.[81] If there was one thing that both the British and Americans understood with great clarity as a result of Sextant, it was that the issue of the availability of landing craft, especially the LSTs, would be important in framing the larger strategic questions regarding amphibious assaults, whether along the coasts of Italy, Greece, or Burma. At the end of the Cairo conference, Roosevelt sent out a request for increased production of landing craft during the next six months; that production would be given precedence over all other munitions of war. Even so, shortages would remain, and choices would have to be made.[82]

While many issues had been debated at Cairo, much was left unsettled. The conference with Stalin in Tehran awaited. Roosevelt understood perfectly, as did most of the military chiefs, that based on the Soviets' impressive counteroffensive against the Germans, they would need to be reckoned with as a power when the war was over. The American delegation also knew that the Anglo-British alliance had to produce a promised second front to the Russians. Stalin was losing patience with what had turned into delayed military operations. Marshall was worried about how this conference would come out as well. Suppose the Russians simply grew weary waiting for the Allied front and decided to sign a separate peace with the Germans? After all, they had done that in World War I; moreover, it wasn't the Russians who had agreed to "unconditional surrender" terms. Thus, this upcoming meeting was crucial. According to Marshall-Roosevelt historian Thomas Parrish, Roosevelt "was determined to involve the Soviet Union as a willing partner in postwar settlements, basing his betting on the belief that Russians needed peace and in exchange would cooperate with the West. He would strive to promote the process of bringing the aloof, suspicious Russians back into the family of nations they had left in 1917. . . . The face-to-face talks with Stalin would merely begin the process."[83]

The Stalin Factor

On November 27, the British and American delegations departed Cairo for the Eureka conference with a flight to the Iranian capital, Tehran. Historian Maurice Matloff described the city as "lying within a vast horseshoe of snow-capped mountains . . . surrounded by earthen ramparts and a moat," where ancient "bazaars and modern shops, plodding burros and lend-lease trucks" offered a sharp contrast.[84] While Churchill would stay at the British

Legation within those ramparts, and Roosevelt initially at the American compound outside the walls, the Joint Chiefs settled into the headquarters of the Persian Gulf Command, made up of American troops who had been there since 1942 transporting lend-lease war material to Russia. The military quarters, six miles from the city, were cramped, and very uncomfortable in the chill of the desert night. The next morning the president met with the chiefs to go over their positions on certain matters that might arise based on the dynamics of Soviet military movements. For example, the Soviets would soon be in Romania, headed from the east into the Balkan region. What if they needed immediate help? That was likely to devolve into the eastern Mediterranean debate. Did this Soviet progress into the Balkans mean that Stalin would press for more action there and be less concerned about his long-sought second front in France? Marshall recognized that some course correction might be necessary, but he thrummed away at the main idea: Allied troops could not operate in too many places simultaneously—it diluted the mega-mission. Still, he offered some possibilities, including opening up small ports on the Adriatic to aid partisans in Yugoslavia. Perhaps after Eisenhower was in Northern Italy, troops could push toward Austria—such moves might contain a couple of German divisions. That said, Marshall primed the president to beware—Churchill would try to "suck him in" for the Rhodes operation and other efforts in the Aegean and would suggest that those forays into the eastern Mediterranean should be in lieu of the Bay of Bengal Andaman action to relieve Burma. He must hold the line against such designs.[85]

Since, according to Roosevelt, the chiefs were not needed during the rest of that first day, Marshall and Hap Arnold left to visit the Soviet military zone. Meanwhile, Stalin sent a message to Roosevelt: their intelligence sources warned that Axis agents (some dressed in U.S. military uniforms) were in the city to assassinate the president. The Soviet premier proposed that his American colleague stay at the thick-walled, heavily guarded Russian compound, and Roosevelt agreed. That afternoon at three, the two leaders met for the first time. Stalin arrived to call on the president dressed "in a khaki tunic with the star of the Order of Lenin on his chest." Roosevelt commented that he had tried for quite a while to meet the Soviet leader. Stalin replied that it had not happened strictly because of "his preoccupation with military matters," a clear reference that the Russians had been in battle against the Germans for 30 months.[86] Churchill was not there to comment that the British had been in the war almost two years before the Soviets, at a time when Stalin's nation was still in a nonaggression pact with Hitler's Nazi régime. Nevertheless, the president understood the importance of getting off

263

on the right footing with the Russians. Implying a reiteration of the second-front promise, he made it clear to Stalin that he wanted to bring about the removal of 30 or 40 German divisions from the eastern front, and that this conference was an opportunity to discuss that very thing. And, knowing Churchill as he did, the president wasted no time in telling the Soviet leader that he and the prime minister sometimes disagreed on military actions in France.[87]

"The greatest concentration of worldly power"

After a short time of such conversation, Stalin suggested that they call Churchill over and get right to work. So it was that Marshall, much to his chagrin, missed the first, and perhaps one of the most crucial, of three plenary sessions. King and Leahy were close by and could be located, but not Marshall and Arnold; thus it was the navy contingent that represented the JCS for the rest of the day; all of them would attend the remaining meetings of the conference. Soon Churchill arrived, but not in the best form—he was suffering from a terrible cold, had almost lost his voice, and, as Brooke later wrote in his diary, "was not in the best of moods." Churchill recalled that he had gotten through the conference only with the help of his doctor, Lord Moran, who traveled with him throughout the war, and who in this case "applied sprays" and "ceaseless care."[88] The fact that the president was in the Russian compound did not please the prime minister, since he immediately got the sense that he was something of an outsider. Further, in addition to the limits imposed by his ailment, it immediately became apparent that his usual long and complex discussions would not gain currency in this situation. Every word had to be translated, so quick conversational exchanges that Roosevelt favored would work best. In this setting, when Churchill waxed eloquent, he soon lost his audience as translators struggled to keep up. Still, even as the meetings began, the prime minister in a hoarse voice struck a historical note, remarking about how all three were witnessing "the greatest concentration of worldly power," and that the "future of mankind" was in their hands. Stalin responded briefly, but soon cut such exchanges short with a quick, "Now let us get down to business."[89]

Roosevelt began the meeting by talking about the Pacific Theater. Beyond the geopolitical aspects, General Marshall and the war planners had already apprised the president regarding the military importance of Russia coming into that war after Hitler was stopped. Without it, the planners said, Americans would find the cost and casualties of efforts against Japan "immeasurably increased." Those present liked how Stalin responded to the discussion: he quickly said how appreciative he was of the Allied effort there and indicated that it had only been his army's concentration against the Germans that had kept them from participating. When Germany capitulated, though, he explained, "then by our common front we shall win."[90] That was encouraging to Roosevelt, since it seemed a clear indication that Stalin intended to help defeat the Japanese once victory in Europe was complete, an option that was sure to be a part of the week's discussion.

About That "Disagreeable body of water"

It didn't take long for the topic of Overlord to come up. Roosevelt assured Stalin that the invasion date, pushed into May of 1944, was determined, not because they were putting off a second front, but because the English Channel "was such a disagreeable body of water," and that it was unsafe for military operations prior to the month of May. Churchill chimed in to note that every Brit was thankful it was such a "disagreeable body of water," an indication that his nation had been fending off Germans across that channel much longer than the other two. Roosevelt asked Stalin what he thought about extended operations in the Mediterranean, dreading the answer. The recently appointed U.S. ambassador to the Soviet Union, Averell Harriman, present at this meeting, recalled that to the president's surprise, Stalin replied that "it seemed unwise to scatter the Allied effort, and argued for treating Overlord as the main operation." That did not stop Churchill from taking up his cause: "The spring and summer of 1944 were still six months away however," he later recalled saying, "and the President and I have been asking ourselves what could be done during these six months with the resources available in the Mediterranean that could best take the weight off Russia, without postponing Overlord for more than perhaps a month or two."[91] Roosevelt immediately responded that it could be "worth it" to have their respective staffs look at Mediterranean options, even mentioning an Adriatic operation to link them with partisans in Yugoslavia, but he wanted *no* delay of Overlord. Churchill pressed on, saying that "he favored some flexibility in the exact date of Overlord."

Stalin was unimpressed and adamant. He didn't support scattering the Allied forces in the Mediterranean. The Allies should remain on the defensive in Italy, since from Russian military experience, Stalin explained, he considered the Alps an almost "insuperable barrier" to an invasion of Germany.[92] Overlord should be the main thrust, he insisted, with a supporting invasion of southern France to occur before or at the same time, thus providing a pincer into which the German army could be trapped. Any actions besides those would be "diversionary." Sensing that he wasn't getting far with his point of view, Churchill put the best face on their differences by saying, "Although we are all great friends, it would be idle for us to delude ourselves that we saw eye to eye on all matters."[93] With that the first session ended, and the leaders adjourned for dinner. It was Roosevelt's mess crew from his yacht *Potomac*, fresh from roasting Thanksgiving turkeys, who prepared the meal, although they had just moved into a hastily supplied kitchen four hours before. This time it was American fare—grilled steaks. When Marshall and Arnold arrived back at their quarters in the evening, King and Leahy conveyed the news, and there was plenty of it. The chief of staff could not have dreamed that the first plenary session would go so much in his favor.

The "Four Policemen"

The next morning Churchill reached out to Roosevelt, asking to meet and compare notes regarding the previous day's plenary session. To his surprise, the president, with whom he had forged such a strong relationship, rebuffed him, saying that he thought it would not look good if Stalin knew they were meeting privately and made the point that he didn't even think they should be conferring together during these meetings in a language they understood but Stalin didn't. Despite such reasoning, Roosevelt did meet with Stalin privately. That afternoon he shared his developing vision with the Soviet leader, an idea that had percolated since the very first meeting between the president and Churchill at the Atlantic Conference back in 1941. Roosevelt explained his dream for a postwar organization to keep the peace. What he had in mind was a United Nations organization led by what he called "The Four Policemen" (the United States, Britain, the Soviet Union, and China) that could deal immediately with any international threats or emergencies; a general assembly to discuss world problems and make recommendations; and, finally, an "executive committee" to handle issues that were nonmilitary—world health or economic matters, for example.

Stalin said he didn't think China would be a big player after the war, but Roosevelt countered that the nation of 400 million had to be a part of it. The Russian leader asked other questions having to do with the dynamics of power, especially the possibility that American troops might end up in Europe. The president made the point that in case of European trouble, he could see sending only U.S. aircraft and ships, but no troops. Stalin wasn't sure about the whole concept, questioning in what ways Japan and Germany would be controlled postwar and whether the decisions of such an organization would be binding.[94] However, by the end of Eureka he had agreed to the idea of an international, although not a regional, organization. Following this meeting of the duo, they went next door where Churchill presented a specially commissioned ceremonial saber, the Sword of Stalingrad, to honor the Soviet resistance in that city. It was acid-etched with the words, "To the steel-hearted citizens of Stalingrad, the gift of King George VI, in token of homage of the British people." This inscription was translated into Russian on the reverse of the 36-inch double-edged blade. It was very solemn and touching moment, each of these powerful leaders taking note of the mighty struggle that united them. Nevertheless, as the three sat down to business, that sense of unity quickly dissipated.[95]

Soviet Marshal Kliment Voroshilov holds the Sword of Stalingrad that had just been presented to Joseph Stalin, who stands behind him.

British Imperial War Museum

A Military Trio

That morning while the president convened privately with Stalin, making his case for the United Nations and other matters, Brooke and Marshall met Stalin's military representative, Marshal Kliment Voroshilov. Brooke, who had been in the meeting the day before, outlined for the Russian general the British plan: end runs around the German right flank in Italy to capture Rome; help for the Yugoslav partisans; capture of Rhodes; and the assertion that to do all of that, Overlord would have to be postponed. Further, he explained, they couldn't possibly launch a two-pronged attack onto the continent, as Stalin had proposed and that had been talked about at Quebec—not enough landing craft. Then Voroshilov, perhaps thinking that Brooke was stalling, got direct. He understood from Marshall's remarks that the Americans considered Overlord of "the first importance," but "he was interested to know whether General Brooke, as chief of the Imperial General Staff, considered Overlord as important as General Marshall had indicated that he did." Brooke, backed into a corner, said, yes, he saw the invasion as vital, but equivocated: "He knew the defenses of Northern France and did not wish to see the operation fail." In his opinion, "under certain circumstances it was bound to fail." Voroshilov minimized Brooke's arguments and came down firmly on the side of Overlord and against "auxiliary" Mediterranean operations that would delay or hinder it in any way.[96] Further, he said, Marshal Stalin wanted Overlord executed on the date already planned.

When Marshall spoke, he made the case for Overlord once more, stating that once the invasion secured a French port, the United States had 50 divisions training stateside who could land directly on the continent, and then acknowledged that it wasn't manpower that was the problem, but rather the shortage of landing craft.[97] The Soviet marshal didn't seem to understand the issue of landing craft, telling Marshall that, after all, in recent action against the Germans, the Red Army had been forced to cross several large rivers. The fact that they did it, he told the chiefs, was "the results of the efforts of all of their people. They had the will to do it." "The difference between a river crossing, however wide, and a landing from the ocean," Marshall pointed out, "is that the failure of a river crossing is a reverse while the failure of a landing operation from the sea . . . means the almost utter destruction of the landing craft and personnel involved." He went on to explain to the general that in the last two years he was learning a lot about the ocean, whereas "prior to the present war he had never heard of any landing craft except a rubber boat. Now," he said, "he thought of little else."[98] Voroshilov, who clearly seemed to respect Marshall, told him, "If you think about it, you will do it." "That is a very good reply," Marshall responded. "I understand thoroughly."

Crisis Point

At four o'clock, as the Combined Chiefs and Soviet Marshal Voroshilov arrived for the second plenary session, the discussions between their respective top leaders were about to reach a crisis point. As Roosevelt-

Churchill historian Jon Meacham pointed out, "More than two years of Allied debate, changing minds, tactical feints, and evasive cables were coming to a head around the green-covered [conference] table." Marshall, having missed the meeting the day before, was getting his first view of Marshal Stalin. After listening to reports from Brooke and Marshall in the morning meeting with Voroshilov, Stalin cut to the chase: "Who will command Overlord?" Roosevelt replied that he had not yet decided. According to Churchill, Stalin then spoke bluntly, saying that "the operation would come to naught unless one man was placed in charge of all preparation for it." Churchill raised the name of General Morgan and how he was laying out the plan for whoever would be appointed at a future date. Roosevelt made the point that the command structure—whether it would be expanded to include other theaters—was still not settled, intimating that this was why the decision had not been made. Seemingly unimpressed with either of these rationales, "Stalin made it plain that until the supreme commander was appointed he could not take seriously the promise of a cross-Channel invasion." Roosevelt whispered to Admiral Leahy that "the Old Bolshevik is trying to force me to give him the name of our supreme commander. I just can't tell him yet because I have not made up my mind."[99] Perhaps Roosevelt was tempted to name a commander right then and there, but as Meacham pointed out, the president could see that indeed Overlord was going to be the next great commitment, so "he took the blow and let the conversation roll on." Before the meeting was over, Stalin pushed for a firm invasion date in May. "I don't care if it is the 1st, 15th, or 20th," he said bluntly, "but a definite date is important."[100]

A Poor English Donkey

Churchill was still not yet ready to give up on his strategic view. Harriman remembered that he "talked of keeping the enemy busy capturing Rhodes, then starving out the other Greek islands." He argued for using 68 landing craft designated for Normandy for that purpose, potentially postponing the invasion by two months. Since that was the case, he explained to Stalin, he didn't want to make a firm commitment on dates. The Soviet premier went then to the heart of the matter and made the query that echoed Voroshilov's to Brooke that morning: "I wish to pose a very direct question to the Prime Minister about 'Overlord.' Do the Prime Minister and the British Staff really believe in 'Overlord'?" Churchill replied, with the eloquence seemingly always at his command: "Provided the conditions previously stated for 'Overlord' are established when the time comes, it will be our stern duty to hurl across the Channel against the Germans every sinew of our strength."[101]

Back and forth it went, but Churchill must have realized that it was two against one—Roosevelt was somewhat passive, but it seemed clear he was in Stalin's camp on this. Indeed, throughout these contentious interactions, Roosevelt was either silent or took Stalin's side. Hopkins historian Robert Sherwood, reading the conference documents years later, observed the remarkable interchange among the three: "Churchill employed all the debater's arts, the brilliant locutions and circumlocutions, of which he was a master, and Stalin wielded his bludgeon with relentless indifference to all the dodges and feints of his practiced adversary; while Roosevelt sat in the middle, by common consent the moderator, arbitrator, and final authority."[102]

That evening, on the second night of the meetings, it was Stalin's turn to entertain at a classic Russian dinner, with "rivers of vodka and wine." Roosevelt and Stalin teased the prime minister throughout the evening, including an exchange where the Soviet premier said seemingly quite seriously that after the war the entire General Staff of the Nazi army would be liquidated—"Fifty thousand should be rounded up and shot," he said in solemn tone. As Churchill "began to rumble an objection," Roosevelt got into the act, saying that, no, it should apply only to 49,000 officers. The prime minister, still not feeling well, and not happy with how this conference was shaping up, didn't notice Stalin's sardonic smile. Sharply, indignantly, Churchill rebutted such a statement with an assertion that "the British Parliament would never tolerate mass executions!" He was so furious he stalked out of the room. When Stalin went after him, declaring "they were only playing," and that nothing of such a serious character "had entered their heads," Churchill simmered down, and all went pleasantly the rest of the evening. Nevertheless, the prime minister, who had endured this war since 1939, understood that power had shifted. Even Marshall noticed the change. "He [Stalin] was turning the hose on Churchill all the time, and Mr. Roosevelt, in a sense, was helping him."[103] Later the prime minister would write, "I realized at Tehran for the first time what a small nation we are. There I sat with the great Russian bear on one side of me, with paws out stretched, and on the other side sat the great American buffalo, and between the two sat the poor little English donkey who was the only one . . . who knew the way home."[104]

Wrap-Up and Farewell

The next morning, the Allied delegations met to draft a brief statement of their military plan in Europe for 1944. Once more the British argued for delay of the cross-channel attack until June, offering a means of extending the date at least a little without alarming Stalin regarding their will to proceed. Marshall was still opposed to the Rhodes option, and Brooke to the Andaman proposal. In the interest of getting out a statement, they referred both issues to the president and prime minister for a decision. At lunch, Roosevelt presented the three major points arrived at by the CCS: the Italian campaign would press north of Rome, the cross-channel invasion would take place "sometime" in May, with an operation in the south of France to correspond with Overlord. Stalin and the Russian delegation were pleased and pledged a Red Army offensive simultaneous with the two-pronged invasion into France.[105] Roosevelt in turn promised that the commander of Overlord would be chosen within three or four days. Stalin had been told unofficially that it would be Marshall, calling that "a reassuring choice," he noted.

The plenary session that afternoon was short but important. Churchill proclaimed that the Allies would deliver Overlord with "smashing force," and the Russians repeated their earlier pledge to declare war on Japan after victory in Europe. In the official report of the conference, the three powers approved a further effort to get neutral Turkey into the war, and they would support the anti-Fascist partisans of Yugoslavia—who, led by Josip Brov Tito, had fought the German occupation—with supplies and equipment.

The wary allies, Stalin, Roosevelt, and Churchill, pose for
official photos at Tehran, November 1943.

U.S. Army

Stalin tentatively agreed, as he had told Roosevelt, to support the United Nations Organization.

It was the last dinner of the conference—this time, Churchill's turn to entertain, and why not? It was his 69th birthday. His two powerful colleagues and their staffs would come to his turf—the British Legation. Sarah Churchill, traveling with her father's entourage, remembered a "never-to-be-forgotten party," a table set with "British elegance," and "the crystal and silver sparkling in the candlelight."[106] After this intense conference, there was an air of celebration; the prime minister could feel the possibility of victory within his grasp:

> This was a memorable occasion in my life. On my right sat the President of the United States, on my left the master of Russia. Together we controlled practically all the naval and three-quarters of all the air forces in the world, and could direct armies of nearly twenty millions of men, engaged in the most terrible of wars that had yet occurred in human history. I could not help rejoicing at the long way we had come on the road to victory since the summer of 1940, when we had been alone, and, apart from the Navy and the Air, practically unarmed, against the triumphant and unbroken might of Germany and Italy, with almost all Europe and its resources in their grasp.[107]

Toward the end of the evening, after enough champagne to "float a battleship" was consumed with toast after toast, Stalin asked his host if he could speak. "I want to tell you from the Russian point of view what the President and the United States have done to win the war. The most important things in this war are machines. The United States has proven that it can turn out from 8,000 to 10,000 airplanes per month. Russia can only turn out, at most, 3,000 airplanes a month. England turns out 3,000 . . . which are principally heavy bombers. The United States, therefore, is a country of machines. Without the use of those machines, through Lend Lease, we would lose this war." Ah, the power had shifted. Stalin had taken the focus from the long-suffering British and put it squarely on the potent capabilities of the United States. Churchill was gracious, but would write later for posterity, "I might have added, but did not, that we had been the longest in the war."[108]

General Marshall and his military colleagues left Tehran early on December 1 for a side trip to Jerusalem, which included a tour of that ancient city and its holy sites. By the afternoon, he was headed by plane back to Cairo, where there were more loose ends to tie up. Surely, as he looked down on the desert landscape, he must have thought with some satisfaction that finally there would be that long-sought invasion, perhaps recalling the arduous evolution of Bolero, Roundup, and now Overlord. At last his plan would see the full light of day. As Mark Stoler noted,

> The long debate was finally over. After two full years of controversy and more than ninety days of meetings, the Allies had adopted a unified, coordinated strategy for the defeat of the Axis. Much of the credit belonged to Marshall. It was he who had championed the concept of inter-service and inter-allied planning as well as unity of command in the field. . . . He was also the individual who had first proposed formally the cross-channel concept in early 1942, and had fought doggedly for it against repeated opposition from the British, the navy, and his own president. He had survived early defeats, learned his lessons from them, and returned to the battle with a deeper understanding of all the complex factors involved in creating a coalition strategy.[109]

Cairo Again: Unfinished Business

Roosevelt and Churchill, having said their farewells to Stalin at Tehran, once back in Cairo took as their first task meetings with the Turkish president and foreign minister. The goal: to induce Turkey, with its strategic location on Russia's border, to enter the war on the Allied side. It opened up the prospect of airfields and strengthened Churchill's view that military gains could be made in the eastern Mediterranean if they could set up air bases and supply lines in that "bridge land" country. Despite the persuasiveness of Roosevelt, and especially Churchill, the Turks were disinclined to do so, fearing they would be destroyed by the German army. Could the Allies ensure that they could strengthen them to such a degree that they would not be decimated? The Allies could not, so the meetings ended as they had begun, "undecided," although Churchill had not given up on the possibility.[110]

Another order of business at the second Cairo Conference was the question of whether to carry out the proposed amphibious assault on Burma by way of the Bay of Bengal and the Andaman Sea (Buccaneer), or to shift the landing craft from there to the Mediterranean, where they could be used for the southern France invasion (Anvil) or for other possible uses in the Aegean if Turkey entered the war. Based on the arguments presented by the Chinese in the first Cairo Conference, Marshall believed Chiang would not participate in North Burma operations if he was denied Buccaneer. Churchill had been against it all along, and cleverly argued that since the Soviets had agreed to come into the war as soon as victory in Europe was achieved, the importance of the entire operation was considerably diminished. After all, the

Allies could have air bases in Eastern Siberia rather than China. Finally, on December 5, Roosevelt notified Churchill that he had called off Buccaneer, and shortly thereafter he sent a message to Chiang, citing the problem of landing craft required for the upcoming European invasions (Overlord/ Anvil). As army historian Maurice Matloff noted, "The Presidential decision was the turning point for China and its importance to the Allies in the war. The promise of China was now to be replaced by the promise of the Soviet Union as the valuable ally in the Far East."[111]

"I didn't feel that I could sleep at ease"

For the president, one nagging but crucial decision lingered before leaving Cairo. It was time to name the commander of Overlord. One fact remained clear: the British would not agree to an expanded role for the supreme allied commander—the Mediterranean would stay under a British officer. With that reality on his mind, Roosevelt surely knew that the September arguments that Marshall could not be spared in Washington would arise again from every public sector. Then there was the recent crystal-clear evidence of the chief of staff's capability: his excellence in treading the rough terrain of these thorny Tehran-Cairo meetings, effectively battling Brooke and, often, Churchill; the obvious respect that Stalin had for his broad strategic view; his potential for taking on the big personalities of the Pacific as the focus shifted in that direction. The president's worry that Marshall would not be remembered in history had to be weighed against all of these factors.[112]

Still conflicted, Roosevelt had Harry Hopkins invite Marshall to lunch to sound him out. No help there. The chief of staff made it clear that he would go along "wholeheartedly with whatever decision the president made. He need have no fears regarding my personal reaction."[113] The next day, December 5, Roosevelt had Marshall come directly to his villa. "As I recall, he asked me, after a great deal of beating around the bush, just what I wanted to do. Evidently it was left up to me," Marshall later told Pogue. The president asked almost exactly the same thing that Hopkins did, and "I just repeated again, in as convincing language as I could, that I wanted him to feel free to act in whatever way he felt was in the best interest of the country . . . and not in any way to consider my feelings." That concluded "the affair and that I would not command in Europe—because he said, 'Well, I didn't feel that I could sleep at ease if you were out of Washington.'"[114] The commander would be Eisenhower.

That was that. One chore was left. Marshall needed to draft a telegram to Stalin: "The appointment of General Eisenhower to command of Overlord operation has been decided upon," he wrote. The president picked up a pencil and added the word "immediate." Later that evening Marshall recovered the draft from the message center, and wrote across the bottom: "Dear Eisenhower: I thought you might like to have this as a memento. It was written very hurriedly by me as the final meeting broke up yesterday, the President signing it immediately, G.C.M."[115] Hopkins recalled that the next day Roosevelt flew from Cairo to Tunis, where he was met by Eisenhower. He told him straightaway: "Well, Ike—you'd better start packing."[116] The trip would not be to dreaded Washington, but to London, where he would dive into the preparation for the greatest amphibious landing in history.

Chapter 11

Tehran to Omaha Beach

"You are to enter the heart of Europe"

December 1943–June 1944

Marshall would not make the return trip with the president aboard the *Iowa*—he was headed for the Pacific. Even before the Tehran Conference had begun, Marshall had this trip on his mind. From Cairo he had written to an aide, "I am giving superficial consideration to the possibility of continuing on around the world instead of returning by the Atlantic. . . . Have the returning courier bring me a summer cap and my khaki kepi, also a waist belt—none were included in my baggage." At least twice before, during 1943, General Marshall had made plans to visit the Southwest Pacific Theater commanded by Douglas MacArthur. Both trips were diverted by either the president or the prime minister. Now that Marshall knew he would continue as chief of staff, it seemed all the more important that he convene with the "prickly" general who perhaps was feeling neglected.[1] His change of schedule had one outcome that he later regretted. Had he not made the trip to the Pacific, he would have stopped off to see his stepsons, Clifton and Allen, both in the Italian Theater. That plan had to be scrubbed. He would never see the younger man again.[2]

So it was that by midday on December 8, 1943, Marshall was aboard a C-54 transport for a 20,000-mile journey, with nearly 100 hours of flying time.[3] The chief of staff's aide, Lieutenant Colonel Frank McCarthy, who was with him during the entire long trip, saw no sign from Marshall that he was the least bit disappointed in the decision that the president had just made. As Ed Cray noted, "No word. No facial expressions suggested he had just lost the one posting he most coveted, command of the field armies he had created for the invasion of France." McCarthy would later comment, "He was really a stolid man. He was really a duty-bound man."[4]

The first stop was still in Egypt at Luxor for a brief respite that included a moonlit look at the Egyptian Temple at Karnak. The next leg took them to Karachi, Pakistan, thence to Australia by way of Ceylon (now Sri Lanka). Then came the most dangerous part of the flight, since the only emergency landing fields during that 17-hour portion of the trip were in Japanese hands. By the 13th, the party landed in Darwin; by the 14th, Port Moresby, New Guinea. At every stopover along the arduous journey, Marshall made an effort to inspect camps, talk with troops, and visit hospitals.[5]

While Marshall might have expected to meet the Southwest Pacific commander at his offices in the heart of Brisbane, that did not occur. Even when he arrived in Port Moresby, MacArthur was not there—the chief of staff was met by a Fifth Air Force officer, who entertained him for a portion of the day with shelling along the beach and even chasing kangaroos by jeep. Finally, on the 15th, he flew Marshall to Goodenough Island some 200 miles to the east, where MacArthur just happened to be closer to the action than he would have been at his office building headquarters. By either design or coincidence, Lieutenant General Walter Kreuger's Alamo Force was that very day launching from the island the first phase of an amphibious operation in western New Britain in an effort to outflank the huge Japanese base near Rabaul.[6]

The two generals had not seen each other since MacArthur retired as chief of staff in 1935 at a time when Marshall was a colonel training the Illinois National Guard. Oh, how things had changed. Now the "colonel" was the chief, and his former superior one of six theater commanders. It must have been awkward for the prideful MacArthur. After luncheon, Marshall gave a briefing on the dual theater situation of the Pacific. Lieutenant General George C. Kenny, present at the meeting, remembered that Marshall had a "long and frank discussion." As Ed Cray described it, the chief of staff told MacArthur:

> China no longer figured heavily in their plans; . . . the assault on the Japanese homeland would come from the west. . . . The Americans were to continue the two-pronged advance of Admiral Chester Nimitz in the Central Pacific and MacArthur in the Southwest Pacific. Nimitz was to have first call on men and supplies for successive campaigns that would take the Marshall Islands in January, the Carolines in July, and the Marianas in October. Meanwhile, MacArthur was to clear New Guinea and the Solomons; they had not reached a decision about the Philippines attack MacArthur so ardently urged as a follow-on.[7]

In the discussion that followed, MacArthur complained bitterly about the "paucity of men and matériel" that he was getting compared to the other theaters. Marshall replied that he realized the imbalance and regretted it, but there was little he could do to "alter the low priority accorded the area."[8] Interservice rivalry reared its head as MacArthur carped about the navy's "inside track" with Roosevelt and Leahy under the influence of Admiral King. Even Marshall admitted later to Pogue regarding this tension that it was "so bitter, the prejudice so great, the main thing was to get in agreement. Whichever side you could get agreement [from], that is the one you would take, because you were in a war of personalities—a very vicious war."[9] Marshall was well aware that MacArthur was "supersensitive about everything" and that he thought "everybody had ulterior motives." Although careful of MacArthur's ego, Marshall's temper flared momentarily during the discussion that afternoon. One too many times MacArthur began a sentence with "My staff," only to have Marshall sharply interrupt him with "You don't have a staff, General. You have a court."[10]

Generals Marshall and MacArthur, December 15, 1943. The other officers are, from left to right: Lieutenant General George C. Kenney, commander of the Allied Air Forces in the Southwest Pacific; Major General Stephen J. Chamberlin, MacArthur's operations officer; and on Marshall's right, Sixth Army commander, Lieutenant General Walter Krueger.

George C. Marshall Research Library

Despite MacArthur's accusations that all of the Joint Chiefs and the president were arrayed against him, Marshall had fought hard in Washington and at Cairo for that theater, working to give the army a clearly defined role in the Pacific as a part of the final assault on Japan. He had stood up to his U.S. Army Air Forces colleague, General Hap Arnold, who made the case that Japan could be bombed into submission with the new long-range B-29 bomber. Even at a personal level, Marshall sometimes ran interference for MacArthur. Once when King was viciously maligning the general during a Joint Chiefs meeting, the chief of staff had pounded the table, shouting, "I will not have any meetings carried on with this hatred."[11] As Cray wrote, "Marshall had not entirely prevailed" in these meetings, "but he had saved MacArthur's theater from becoming a forsaken backwater of the Pacific War," and added, "MacArthur was not especially appreciative."[12] Nevertheless, the "prickly general" did write in his memoirs that Washington became "more generous" after Marshall's visit, and he specifically mentioned the 50 P-38 fighters added to the aircraft complement already ordered for his theater.[13]

Marshall stayed overnight at Goodenough Island, flying to the New Guinea mainland the next day. He visited exhausted courageous troops who were still trying to pry the Japanese from key points along the island's northern coast. Unlike MacArthur, who seemed to avoid such visits, he toured the military hospital with its 600 patients suffering from wounds, dysentery, and gruesome skin infections labeled "crud." A dietitian who met Marshall on this stop remembered 40 years later that "He had sparkle, a presence, very military," and showed a sincere interest in the hospital and "that little segment of the army." She recalled that he teased her, complaining that "A dietician will ruin the mess sergeants."[14]

Marshall left New Guinea that afternoon but made stops on Guadalcanal, from which he was flown over the northern Solomons to review military action in progress there. He made a stop at a service hospital in New Hebrides, and then on to Fiji, where he watched troops embarking and visited still more hospitals. On Oahu he observed jungle-fighting maneuvers and encouraged the troops afterward in a short off-the-cuff talk. Finally, it was time to head home—he would arrive three days before Christmas. None too soon. Knowing that Roosevelt would agree to nothing without consulting with Marshall, Churchill cabled the chief of staff in Honolulu telling him, "Do hasten back to the Capital as much necessary structure hangs in mid-air pending your arrival."[15]

Even after arriving back in Washington, Marshall had plenty of follow-up—contacting the wife of an officer who commanded troops in Fiji to provide a reassuring assessment of his situation; writing Christmas letters to both of his stepsons; drafting a memorandum for the president on their acceptance of Field Marshal Montgomery to command Overlord's ground forces; composing a communication to Eisenhower recommending that he keep Sir Frederick Morgan, "a very capable officer," in charge of Overlord planning.[16] It was Christmas Eve before Marshall could finally make his way to Dodona in Leesburg, where, despite the circumstances of war, Katherine and Molly were preparing the best Christmas possible for little James "Jimmy" Winn, and his baby sister, Kitty. When Marshall swung open the front door, festively bedecked with a sleigh-belled Oregon holly wreath, he was immediately in the embrace of his wife. As Katherine would later write, "When there is lead in your heart and it suddenly disappears, joy rushes in with such force that it is almost unbearable. So I felt that Christmas Eve. Inside the house lights were all blazing, the fires crackling. Now it was to be a real Christmas."[17]

Man of the Year

When Marshall received his issue of *Time* magazine for January 3, 1944, it was a familiar face that graced the cover—his own. With the caption, "He armed the republic," the chief of staff's uniformed image announced *Time*'s "Man of the Year." The article inside offered high praise:

> The American people do not, as a general rule, like or trust the military. But they like and trust George Marshall. This is no more paradoxical than the fact that General Marshall hates war. The secret is that American democracy is the stuff Marshall is made of.

> Hired by the U.S. people to do a job, he will be as good, as ruthless, as tough, as this job requires. There's where his ambitions stop. "He has only one interest," said one of his intimates, "to win this damned war as quick as he can, with the fewest lives lost and money expended, and get the hell down to Leesburg, Va., and enjoy life."

Echoing the sentiments that characterized the command-of-Overlord debate that fall, *Time* noted:

> The link between the biggest military establishment in U.S. history and the U.S. people, George C. Marshall was at year's end the closest thing to "the indispensable man." Had he taken over the command of the European invasion, the U.S. Army would have remained without the one and only U.S. citizen who . . . could at any time get a unanimous

vote of confidence from Congress. The U.S. needed General Marshall at home.[18]

Olympian Fury

If "to win this war" was Marshall's paramount interest, the news coming into his office the week after Christmas was both discouraging and infuriating. Secretary of War Stimson explained: the president had reason to believe that the Railway Brotherhoods would probably strike on December 30, 1943. Roosevelt had notified Stimson that if no agreement was forthcoming, he wanted the War Department to take over the railroads. When the railroad unions were informed, they yielded temporarily but refused to withdraw the strike order. Thus, on the 27th, Roosevelt granted the War Department power over 233,670 miles of railroad track in the United States.[19] It would be January 18, 1944, before the railroads were returned to private control. To Marshall, who was fighting tooth and nail to get needed supplies and equipment to troops in the field and had just returned from the fighting-front realities of the Mediterranean and Pacific theaters, this move by the union was simply outrageous.

Normally, Marshall would have steered clear of any labor disputes, but now he was angry. Stimson sent him to talk with James Byrnes, the head of the Office of War Mobilization, at which time Marshall told him he was so worried about this situation that he had not been able to sleep. The chief of staff could not fathom how disputes over wages would trigger workers to withhold needed resources and services in wartime from those who were making the sacrifices abroad. Further, he was especially concerned that the German propaganda machine would pick up signs of divisions within the United States and, by picturing it on the "brink of chaos," spread that propaganda to the Balkan region, where partisans were showing promising signs of defecting from their Nazi occupiers.[20] As if to drive home his point, Marshall would later write to Byrnes that an analysis of the intercepts from the Nazi propaganda campaign showed that the enemy's objectives included stressing Axis unity in comparison to U.S. disunity and presenting the United States as a place of social unrest and insecurity, with the four freedoms meaningless.[21]

On the 31st, coincidentally Marshall's 63rd birthday, Byrnes gathered a group of 20 newsmen for a "not for attribution" conference. Pogue described Marshall's generally tightly controlled moments of rage as having two temperatures—freezing or blazing. In this case it was blazing. Marshall historian Thomas Parrish noted that "*Time*'s apolitical, Olympian 'trustee of the nation'" was not in a birthday mood. What the reporters got was more like the hot-tempered young major who had taken on Black Jack Pershing in World War I. A *Time* article recorded the blast: "He banged his white-knuckled fist on the desk, and although not a blasphemous man, he swore bitterly," the reporter wrote in awe. Marshall added that a strike "could literally cost hundreds of thousands of American lives."[22]

Even though these remarks were "not for attribution," it didn't take long for the speaker to be identified, and labor salvoed back. Soon, Marshall found himself in a rare public controversy. Perhaps an underlying worry, too, according to Pogue, was that Marshall saw "that at all levels Americans were slipping into the comfortable belief that the war was nearing an end and that there could be a shift to business as usual."[23] Moreover, the chief of staff was weary—the endless meetings in Cairo and Tehran; the fierce back-and-forth arguments with Churchill and the British command regarding Overlord; the effects of Stalin in the power equation—it had taken its toll.

Most news outlets reacted favorably to Marshall, saying that, after all, he hadn't attacked labor, but had just pointed out the results of strike threats. The *Christian Science Monitor* avowed, "The fact is that labor disputes, whatever the provocation, do weaken the war effort." Others opined that "Marshall had only recently returned from the battlefronts and was speaking strictly as a soldier."[24]

On February 3, as Marshall spoke at an American Legion event in Washington, he still had the welfare of ordinary soldiers on his mind, telling his audience that the nation hadn't faced the realities of war, the "savage, desperate conditions of the battle fronts." Marshall reemphasized the importance of homeland support: "Our soldiers must be keenly conscious that the full strength of the nation is behind them; they must not go into battle puzzled or embittered over disputes at home. . . . Our small sacrifices should be personal rather than financial. They should be proof positive that we never forget for a moment that the soldier had been compelled to leave his family, to give up his business, and to hazard his life in our service."[25] Marshall also knew that high productivity was crucial in Americans' industrial plants if the Allies were to defeat a fearsome enemy.

One way to accomplish that: provide an incentive to workers by showing them strong images of the battle theaters. In an early-January letter to Lieutenant General Millard Harmon, a commander in the South Pacific area, he asked for more warfare film footage and outlined specifics—actual combat scenes; scenes showing casualties during and immediately after the action without

Using a flamethrower, a marine clears a path through
the jungle during the Battle of Tarawa, November 1943.

U.S. Marine Corps

"the usual effort to eliminate the tragic aspects of battle or campaign"; and also results obtained by American artillery, bombs, grenades, and mortars.[26]

"We had a fine rest"

In early January 1944, Marshall must have recognized that he needed a rest. He wrote a friend that "Prior to my return from abroad I was deeply involved for a week or ten days in catching up with affairs. Tired both from the trip and from the heavy pressures. . . I took Katherine and slipped off to Miami Beach where we had a cottage and a private bathing beach, and were completely cut off from outside contacts. We had a fine rest without our presence being known."[27] Perhaps the chief of staff was taking some of his own advice, since he had just finished three days of intense meetings with General Eisenhower, insisting that he come home for "R and R." Poised to head to London to immerse himself in plans for the Normandy invasion, the supreme allied commander was under a great deal of stress and needed a change of scene. He had protested vehemently that he couldn't possibly leave Europe, but Marshall thought differently, telling him, "I am interested . . . that you are fully prepared to bear the strain and I am not interested in the usual rejoinder that you can take it"; he further noted that it was important

283

for Eisenhower to be "mentally fresh." Perhaps Marshall was also concerned that Winston Churchill hadn't given up on further Mediterranean operations, with the possibility of postponement of Overlord; it might be good to have Eisenhower review "Washington thinking" before heading to London for head-to-head meetings with the Brits.[28] Still another underlying motive might have been an effort on Marshall's part to reintroduce Eisenhower to his wife, Mamie. Since the North African campaign, rumors had abounded that his relationship with Kay Summersby, his svelte and attractive British driver, was in addition to professional also personal.[29] "Now come on home and see your wife and trust somebody else for twenty minutes in England," Marshall had written.[30]

Eisenhower was in Washington by January 2. In a "secret" letter to the president on January 4, Marshall informed him that he had brought Eisenhower home "over his strenuous objections, to force him to take a brief rest before he undertakes his heavy obligations in England." The chief of staff requested that the president, who was ill with the flu and thus confined to bed, meet with Eisenhower toward the end of the visit, since the supreme allied commander's appearance at the White House would surely stir publicity, and Marshall wanted to get him out of town as quickly as possible to avoid the throngs of newspaper reporters pressing for answers too militarily delicate to discuss.

Eisenhower was to stay in the United States two weeks, part of that time in the capital, making his rounds in an unmarked limousine, his general's stars covered by an overcoat, to brief Stimson and top congressional leaders regarding operations in North Africa and Italy. He also traveled with his wife to West Point to see their son, and flew by private plane to Kansas to see his elderly mother—Mamie did not go since she had a fear of flying. He rejoined her for a few days at a luxurious resort cottage in White Sulphur Springs, West Virginia, for some private relaxation before his return to D.C. for his time with the president, and thence to London.[31]

Not surprisingly, when Marshall met with Eisenhower at the Pentagon, they talked about manpower, weaponry, especially proposals for an innovation that had to do with rockets that could be attached to tanks, and a myriad of other D-Day–related matters, including commanders. General Bernard Montgomery had already been confirmed as the leader of all of the invasion's "troops on the ground." As various names were raised, Marshall left the decisions to Eisenhower, offering only "cautionary" comments. Nevertheless, the chief of staff surely influenced some of the choices; after all, he had already discussed a "commander's list" with General Morgan that previous summer when it was assumed he would lead Overlord. General Omar Bradley, who had earned Marshall's regard as an instructor at the Fort Benning Infantry School, would lead the U.S. Army ground forces on D-Day. Eisenhower had said of Bradley, "He has brains, a fine capacity for leadership and a thorough understanding of the requirements of modern battle. He has never caused me one moment of worry. He is perfectly capable of commanding an Army."[32] Marshall couldn't have agreed more. J. Lawton Collins, also a "Benning Revolution" instructor who had been deeply respected as a division commander in the Pacific, would direct the Seventh Army onto Utah Beach on Day 1 of the invasion. Ed Cray noted that in fact "most of the senior commanders were identified as 'Marshall's Men,' by inclination or training."[33] But then there was the difficult question of General George S. Patton Jr.

The Matter of General Patton—"Lions tremble"

Patton had acquitted himself well as the commander of the Western task force landing in North Africa during Operation Torch, securing a coastline that included French Morocco. After the Kasserine Pass debacle of February 1943, Eisenhower had summoned Patton to reorganize and strengthen the demoralized II Corps to "fighting pitch." He arrived to do just that on March 7, 1943, in a speeding convoy of armored vehicles, sirens shrieking, outriders on motorcycles racing ahead. As Omar Bradley later described it, "In the lead car Patton stood like a charioteer . . . scowling into the wind." Already this general had a reputation for flamboyance, with his gleaming helmet, rigid bearing, and ivory-handled pistol.[34] Shortly after the Torch landings, one Moroccan sultan gave him his kingdom's highest decoration, with the citation, *"Les lions dans leurs tanieres tremblent en le voyant approacher"* (The lions in their dens tremble at his approach.)[35] Not surprising, then, that Eisenhower warned him about forgoing "personal recklessness," reminding him that the British general Alexander controlled that theater under the principle of unity of command.

Patton immediately recognized that within the II Corps, military regulations were being ignored, including casual disregard for uniforms, which he viewed as a sign of slovenliness, a sure weakness among soldiers. Marshall almost certainly would have agreed with this aspect, once explaining to Pogue that even in combat conditions there couldn't be too much "spit and polish." In fact, he said, "the deeper the mud, the more important it was to spruce them [the troops] up as quickly as you could thereafter."[36] Soon Patton whipped the II Corps into shape, restoring discipline and a fighting spirit. As historian Mark Perry remarked, "He stormed his way through. . . .

He cajoled and punished, he was profane and sympathetic, he listened and screamed—but mostly he imposed discipline."[37]

After a month of nearly constant battle, these units were turned over to Omar Bradley, and Patton returned to Morocco to plan the invasion of Sicily. Even though his leadership style was decidedly controversial, the troops had fought hard for him, many almost to a point of collapse, because although they may not have loved this general, they respected him. Patton later was proud of the fact that when the 10th Panzers attacked, one of his platoons "died to a man." He described it as "a fine thing," adding that the last thing he heard from his soldiers was their yelling, "Come on, you Hun bastards."[38]

Lieutenant General George S. Patton in North Africa, March 20, 1943
U.S. Library of Congress: LC US262-25122

In their Pentagon briefings, surely Marshall and Eisenhower discussed Patton's role in the Sicilian invasion (Operation Husky) that previous July. It had been the Allies' first foray into Hitler's "Fortress Europe." The Allies had brought 500,000 men to the fight against the 200,000 soldiers of the Axis, more than half of them disheartened Italians ready to give in.[39]

Despite mistakes during the landings, a doomed paratrooper drop, and other evidence of inexperience and muddled leadership, the British and American troops did force the evacuation of the enemy. The Allied victory spurred the collapse of Mussolini's government and opened up airfields for future operations up the boot of Italy. Nevertheless, as an example of the unity-of-command concept that Marshall saw as so crucial to the Anglo-American partnership, it was virtually disastrous, and Eisenhower, as theater commander, knew it. The British general Harold Alexander had authority over all ground troops in Sicily but had trouble controlling the power issues that arose between Patton, who at that time commanded the Seventh Army, and his British counterpart, Field Commander Bernard Montgomery, head of the Eighth Army of recent El Alamein fame. As they fought tenacious Axis forces, both jockeyed for dominance on the island.

Lieutenant General Patton stands with General Montgomery at Palermo. Patton's deputy is to Montgomery's right; summer 1943.

U.S. Army Signal Corps, www.liberationtrilogy.com

Patton and his deputy commander, Omar Bradley, believed that because the British lacked faith in the fighting ability of the Seventh Army, their troops had been relegated to a back-up flanking position in the fight—after all, Alexander and Montgomery were in cahoots to "steal the whole show," complained Patton. Further, in his view, Eisenhower was doing little to change that. In the end, Patton took it upon himself to operate rather independently, making bold moves to take Palermo and Messina ahead of the British, finding ways to explain his shifts away from the instructions of his superior. Eisenhower was frustrated with everyone's performance,

287

including Alexander's, since he seemed to have allowed his subordinates to "pull and push levers of command . . . to compete for glory—to allow the battle to run itself."[40]

But despite Patton's showy victories and the accolades for him from home, including the president's, Eisenhower was also upset with the feisty and bold Seventh Army commander and told him so. Always prideful, and stung by the cold water thrown on the flush of victory, Patton chaffed, angry with Eisenhower, Alexander, and Montgomery, as well as the limiting conditions of allied warfare.

It was just days after Patton's army had rolled into Messina that Eisenhower got a report from the chief surgeon at Allied Headquarters in Algiers that set him on edge. Apparently Patton had visited an evacuation hospital on that August 4 and, after placing medals on severely wounded soldiers, stopped at the bed of First Division soldier Charles H. Kuhl, who appeared uninjured. Inquiring as to his problem, the young man put head in hands saying, "I just can't take it, sir." Patton flew into a red-faced fury, called him a coward—"a gutless bastard," kicked him, and literally dragged him out of the tent.[41] That was not the only occasion. On August 10, Patton visited yet another "in theater" hospital where he also found a seemingly uninjured patient. "It's my nerves," he explained to the visiting general. "Your nerves, hell," Patton scoffed, "you're just a goddamn coward, you yellow son of a bitch," telling the soldier he was "going back to the fight." If not, he raged, "You ought to be lined up against a wall and shot." As if to do that himself, Patton reached for his pistol, waved it in front of the young man's face, and slapped him hard. The attendant doctors and nurses rushed to restrain him, as he yelled, "I want you to get this man out of here right away. I won't have these other brave boys seeing such a bastard babied."[42]

When the story broke, Eisenhower was already greatly stressed, and news of this did nothing to lower his blood pressure. He ordered the reporting head surgeon to investigate the charges, and fired off a letter to Patton: "Firm measures are sometimes required," he told him, but "this does not excuse brutality, abuse of the sick, nor exhibitions of uncontrollable temper in front of subordinates."[43] He outlined concerns about Patton's judgment, and his "future usefulness." Eisenhower ordered Patton to apologize to the hospital and headquarters staff and, later, to every division of the Seventh Army. The chastened general was frightened as he considered the effects the whole incident might have on his career, and expressed his "chagrin and grief" at Eisenhower's displeasure.

Amazingly, despite the fact that newsmen covering the Sicily invasion heard all about "the slapping incidents," they agreed not to report it. Eisenhower was still anxious about how to describe this to Marshall—after all, the chief of staff might say he wanted Patton relieved, or even suggest a court martial, which was warranted given the circumstances. By August 24, Eisenhower did write to Marshall about Patton, but most of the letter focused on "effusive praise" for his capabilities, and only *hinted* at the negatives: "His habit of impulsive bawling out of subordinates, extending even to personal abuse of individuals, was noted in at least two specific cases. I have had to take drastic steps, and if he is not cured now there is no hope for him," Eisenhower wrote, but also added, "Personally, I believe he is cured."[44] Stopping short of the "slapping" details, though, he made the case that one had to look at Patton's virtues as a commander, to see his "good qualities without being blinded by his love of showmanship and histrionics."[45]

Perhaps the journalists had agreed to keep the story mute, but in November the Washington columnist Drew Pearson had broken it, and the furor over the incident flared.[46] By the time of Eisenhower's visit to the United States in January 1944, many letters had poured into Marshall's Pentagon offices. "Since when do we use Nazi tactics in our Army? Patton should be dishonorably discharged," wrote an Ohio woman. A Washington State citizen suggested that Patton should get the same punishment he dished out—a hard slap. The powerful Louisiana Senator Russell Long expressed shock that "a man, long notorious . . . for his erratic and inhuman conduct, should be continued in command of any army of American boys." Others took up for Patton. As one Virginia man declared, "Let those who never did anything in high temper 'throw the first stone'. . . . Hurrah for Patton, cussin,' kickin'—and all the rest." A Miami businessman opined that it was whoever tipped off Drew Pearson that should be punished.[47] When Pearson's story broke, Marshall wanted all of the details, the better to head off a congressional investigation that could follow and derail Patton's military career. At Marshall's request, Stimson did damage control with the chair of the Military Affairs Committee, Senator Robert Reynolds, explaining that appropriate punishments had been given, and that he hoped Patton would not be recalled out of "national security necessity."[48] During the Pentagon talks, Eisenhower had told Marshall he wanted Patton, "hot temper and all," and reminded the chief of staff that "the volatile, offensive-minded Patton would always serve under the even-handed Bradley."[49]

With Eisenhower back in London, on January 19, 1944, Marshall sent Eisenhower a secret radiogram. Patton was still without a specific command—still in the Mediterranean Theater, now under the command of the British general Sir Maitland Wilson, and his deputy, General Jacob Devers. Devers wanted orders as to where Patton was to serve, since Patton had been relieved of Seventh Army command. Marshall told Eisenhower that he had thought of bringing Patton back to the United States for a while, but in view of the recent publicity, he said, it "might result in reopening the entire matter with vituperative discussions . . . as to his future." Eisenhower in his reply agreed, and asked that Patton be sent to the United Kingdom.[50] It was on January 26 that the supreme allied commander informed the general that he would command the Third Army, most of which at that time was still in the United States.

As Omar Bradley noted, until the next August, Patton would be in the English Midlands, far from the traffic of the invasion force. In his diary on the 26th, Patton complained, "All are novices and in support of Bradley's First Army—not such a good job, but better than nothing. Well, I have an Army and it is up to me."[51] Soon he would also be the commander of the First United States Army Group (FUSAG), a fictitious army built to deceive the Germans regarding the point of entry for the Normandy Invasion.

A 200,000-Man Shortfall

"If a man . . . can catch a fast ball"

Returning to Washington from his rest with Katherine in Miami, Marshall tackled the long list of concerns that fell to the chief of staff. One of them had to do with manpower. He had built a huge army—by the end of 1944 it would number 7.5 million. Ed Cray described its distribution across the planet: "Almost 4 million were overseas, half of those arrayed against Germany, half against Japan. Six divisions were fighting in Italy, eleven training for Overlord in Britain, and thirteen scattered on as many islands in the Southwest Pacific. Sixty more were in training or were authorized."[52] Despite this display of strength, draft deferments for "occupational, medical, and family reasons—some 5 million of them—had left the army short by 200,000 men by the end of 1943. In the wake of these deficits, Marshall wanted a reassessment of such deferments—were they absolutely necessary?[53] For example, why were prominent athletes being turned down by army medical officers, in one case because a professional baseball catcher had been placed on limited service as he had two broken fingers. Marshall thought it ridiculous that a man who could catch a fast ball with such a "disability" was not doing his duty. The chief of staff wanted the Inspector General to look into the matter, and he told the colonel to whom he raised the issue the previous November, "If an army officer on active duty is a participant [in allowing these deferments], then we are responsible, and I don't want any damn serious complaints."[54]

Another aspect of medical deferments was weighing on Marshall at the end of 1943. He wrote the surgeon general a rather long rough draft of a memorandum that he wanted distributed. It concerned the number of rejections or discharges for psychological and "neuro-psychiatric" reasons. The chief of staff was disturbed that since the previous June, 200,000 of the medical rejections and discharges, 25 percent and 35 percent respectively, were for psychiatric reasons. While Marshall acknowledged the difficulty of accurately diagnosing these kinds of disorders—some professionals were either "over-enthusiastic or over-cautious"—he also admitted that "functional nervous diseases are recognized as entities by neuro-psychiatrists but these disorders cannot as a rule be definitely measured nor confirmed by . . . objective findings. For this reason there is a greater divergence of opinion regarding these cases than in any others." Nevertheless, Marshall was clearly bothered by the possibility that some of these patients were "malingerers" who were taking up the services of cooks, nurses, and doctors, all of whom were already in short supply on the battlefield.

To some degree, Marshall placed the blame at the feet of local officers by suggesting that perhaps "the primary reason for these men being in hospitals is not because doctors made patients of them but because line officers were unable to make soldiers out of them." He recognized that in such a large army there was no way to allow some inductees a longer period of time to adjust to the realities of military life. Was it possible that the necessity for a "one size must fit all" training approach led some officers to use "sick bay" as a solution for some slow-to-adapt inductees? Finally, Marshall opined that unlike "our enemies," who had been taught to endure hardships and prepare for war, "our young people were led to expect luxuries . . . and to look upon soldiers and war as unnecessary and hateful." Marshall concluded his draft by once again acknowledging the difficulty of making fair assessments, while noting that "A determined effort is being made throughout the Army to better this situation."[55]

For those "suffering the hardships"

Marshall was acutely aware that the cruel grind of war was very hard on young men far from home. He supported a variety of programs that he saw as beneficial to the mental health of soldiers. In early 1944 he made the case to President Roosevelt that members of the air force receive the Air

Medal for valiant and praiseworthy service, but there was no corresponding award for infantrymen. Recently, Marshall had made the initial proposal to the secretaries of war and navy, as well as the Joint Chiefs, to create a new medal, the Bronze Star, for "heroic or meritorious" service.

Regarding this request, in early February he responded to a complaint by President Roosevelt that perhaps too many medals were being given out to servicemen, and thus this Bronze Star addition was not needed. The chief executive spoke of "coats loaded down with service medals" and described the case of one soldier who had been in the army only six months but had so many medals he "looked like a Christmas tree."[56] Marshall disagreed that these types of awards "cheapened" their value, saying that decorations and ribbons were very important, especially when they were presented *on the battlefield.* "Permit these young men, who are suffering the hardships and casualties, to enjoy their ribbons . . . while in uniform. . . . The fact that the ground troops, infantry in particular, lead miserable lives of extreme discomfort and are the ones who must close in personal combat with the enemy, makes the maintenance of their morale of great importance." So it was that on February 4, 1944, the president issued Executive Order 9319 establishing the Bronze Star award for distinguished service for military or naval personnel "not involved in aerial flight."[57]

"Whiz kids" over there

As Marshall worried over replacement shortfalls during that early winter of 1944, he made the decision to eliminate the Army Specialized Training Program (ASTP). A pet project of Secretary of War Stimson, the idea had been to take 150,000 of the brightest draftees and offer them college educations. They were inducted into the army as privates, which paid their room, board, and tuition, plus $50 a month, while they studied subjects of anticipated military importance—math, engineering, foreign languages, dentistry, and medicine. ASTP had potential benefit not only for the military, but also for colleges, which in wartime stood to face financial ruin. Some not chosen resented these young scholars, mockingly referring to the program as All Safe Till Peace.[58] By February 10 Marshall had informed Secretary of War Stimson that he had to reduce the program to 30,000, that number "being required largely for the supply of doctors and dentists and such other highly trained technicians as the Army may be unable to procure from other sources." Although he knew both Stimson and Roosevelt would oppose the reduction of the program, Marshall made the point that "it represents the only source from which we can obtain the required personnel, especially with a certain degree of intelligence and training, except by *disbanding already organized combat units*" [Marshall's emphasis]. Historian Stephen Ambrose noted, "What an asset—at a time when every other combatant was taking conscripts too old, too young, too ill to fight, the U.S. Army was feeding into its fighting forces its best young men." It was quite a change, though. As an officer in Fort McCoy, Wisconsin, told a young ex-ASTPer, "With your ability and background you are something special, and we are therefore going to give you a choice," and then added, "What will it be, rifle, machine gun, or mortar?"[59]

"Who is handling this business?"

With his mind on increasing the number of troops in the field, in late January Marshall was bothered by numerous comments he had received regarding publicity deficits in the recruitment for the Women's Army Corps (WACs). He wanted to see those recruitment numbers go up, since every woman who filled a suitable noncombatant position freed a young man for the front lines. In a memorandum to the Bureau of Public Relations, he wrote of these criticisms, which indicated that the "WACs were not given sufficiently important work to attract the best type of women and to hold the interest of others." Marshall provided several examples within his own office of women holding highly responsible jobs, including Lieutenant F.T. Newsome, who, the chief of staff noted, "under certain periods . . . performs the duty of Acting Secretary, General Staff." He wanted to know, "Who is handling this business?" Out of this complaint, WAC director Colonel Oveta Culp Hobby asked for and got from the Public Relations Office a special subgroup that focused on photographs and stories about women who were making *significant* contributions to the war effort.[60]

Anzio: "All we got was a stranded whale"

When Eisenhower arrived in London on January 15, almost a million Americans were already there. A colleague of *Time* Inc. chief Henry Luce cabled, "There's not a single square inch of London on which an American is not standing, and add to that fact that, if he is standing after dark, he is standing unsteadily." Eisenhower had no time for evening pub crawls; by the next morning he was at his prearranged office, 28 Grosvenor Square.[61] Almost immediately he was in talks with the commander of British ground forces for the invasion, Field Marshal Bernard Montgomery. Both agreed that the three-division initial assault plan that had been advanced by General Sir Frederick Morgan was skimpy. By this time, even Morgan thought so, too. Montgomery made the case that five divisions would broaden the invasion zone to 50 nautical miles, and thus facilitate the taking of a crucial deepwater port at Cherbourg. Although the British had developed remarkably clever artificial harbors called Mulberries that would be adequate for the first few days after the landings, they would not hold up under the heavy transport demands of the invasion follow-on.

Nevertheless, the five-division option created a problem: the ever present shortfall of landing craft. Montgomery had a solution: cancel Anvil, the operation that was to coincide with Overlord and was intended to prevent the German army from massing all of its troops in a single spot, which had been agreed to at Tehran. Canceling it, though, would free up enough landing craft to provide "lift" for a five-division landing in France rather than the previously planned three. With this cancellation option Eisenhower could not agree. As Ed Cray noted, "What once seemed settled was still unsettled."[62]

Despite a debilitating pneumonia that had kept Winston Churchill recuperating in Marrakech, he was vitally interested in the buildup for Overlord and Anvil in London, but he also was troubled by unfinished business on the Italian front, which he saw as integrally connected to those efforts:

> The mounting of "Overlord" was the greatest event and duty in the world. But must we sabotage everything we could have in Italy, where the main strength overseas of our country was involved? Were we to leave it a stagnant pool from which we had drawn every fish we wanted? As I saw it, the campaign in Italy, in which a million or more of our British, British-controlled, and Allied armies were engaged, was the faithful and indispensable comrade and counterpart to the main cross-Channel operation. . . . I was sure that a vigourous campaign in Italy during the first half of 1944 would be the greatest help to the supreme operation of crossing the Channel, on which all minds were set and all engagements made. [63]

Since late fall of 1943, the Allies had been bogged down in a face-off along the Germans' 15-division-strong Gustav Line 40 miles south of Rome, hampered not only by the enemy but also by the freezing cold of an exceptionally bitter winter, muddy impassable roads, and snow-choked mountains.[64] To break the stalemate, and thus march on Rome, Churchill proposed that the Allies make an amphibious landing at the small port of Anzio north of the Gustav Line, hence providing an end run around the machine gun emplacements, barbed wire, and minefields of this seemingly impregnable German defense. The landing was also intended to draw enemy forces toward Anzio, thus weakening the Gustav Line and allowing an Allied breakthrough in the south.

The Allied winter line just south of the
German Gustav position, January 15, 1944
Map prepared by Ryan Jenkins, using File:Italy_template_blank.png

Once that happened, the amphibious operation would link up with the overland force only 30 miles south of their objective, Italy's capital. In a cable to Roosevelt, Churchill argued that this operation would take only three weeks; further, he wanted to keep 56 LSTs slated for Overlord in Italy to "lift" the troops for the Anzio assault.[65] Making his case to Roosevelt in a late December cable, he argued, "What could be more dangerous than to let the Italian battle stagnate and fester on for another three months? We cannot afford to go forward leaving a vast half-finished job behind us." To use these LSTs, Churchill acknowledged, would result in a three-week delay of Overlord, but it would still be within the "sometime in May" timetable established at Tehran. Perhaps to sweeten the message, the prime minister caved at least temporarily on any operation in Rhodes or the Aegean until after the invasion onto the continent.[66]

Marshall, of course, was aware of this proposal, and saw it as another example of the old Mediterranean "suction pump" problem. In a reply drafted by the chief of staff, Roosevelt agreed to release the LSTs, but only with the understanding that Overlord remain "the paramount operation" and that it would be carried out according to the agreements made at Tehran and Cairo. In closing, the president warned, "I cannot agree without Stalin's approval to any use of forces or equipment elsewhere that might delay or hazard the success of 'Overlord' and 'Anvil,'" perhaps a reminder that the Soviet leader would brook no more excuses for the promised second front on the Continent.[67] On December 28, apparently choosing to ignore the last part of the message, the prime minister wrote to Roosevelt, "I thank God for this fine decision."[68]

It was on January 22, 1944, that the VI Corps of Lieutenant General Mark Clark's Fifth Army came ashore at Anzio. After establishing a beachhead, the American and British troops were to have moved quickly toward the heavily fortified Alban Hills that crossed the two major highways to Rome. That would facilitate a breakthrough of the Gustav Line, followed by a link-up with Clark's Winter Line forces for the march on the prize of the Italian boot, Rome. Although this operation, code-named Shingle, was Churchill's "hobby horse," since mostly American troops would be involved in the landing, command fell to U.S. Army Major General John Lucas. His more than 36,000 assault forces landed virtually unopposed because the attention of the Germans was toward the south; further, they did not expect such a deep-winter amphibious attack. The Allied line branched out from the beach, its perimeter seven miles inland at its arc. However, Lucas did not push on to Rome but rather conservatively took a week to regroup, landing reserves that pushed troop strength to 61,000, as he prepared for a possible counterattack. The time delay proved disastrous.

The German commander, Field Marshal Albert Kesselring, quickly moved reserve units protecting Rome, three divisions refitting in the north and two divisions facing the Allied winter line, to seal off the invader's perimeter.[69] The Allies were soon trapped where they had landed, strafed by Luftwaffe pilots and German ground artillery fire. Churchill later lamented, "I had hoped that we were hurling a wildcat onto the shore, but all we had got was a stranded whale."[70] There was a price to be paid for an operation that, in the end, would not bring a quick capture of Rome. Though breakouts were attempted along the edges of the Allied beachhead, they were pushed back by German reinforcements; eventually, the Allies settled into defensive positions, and, as historian Ed Cray noted, "turned tiny Anzio into the fourth busiest port in the world, largely supplied by the LSTs ticketed for Overlord."[71]

"I hope I cleared up that point"

Now, not only was Anvil threatened because of the five-division expansion of Overlord, but the Anzio stalemate added to the problem, especially since Eisenhower didn't have these "in use" landing craft for training and had no assurance that they would be available for a two-pronged assault on the Continent. Eisenhower pushed for a postponement of Overlord until early June—not such a stretch from the "sometime in May" guideline of Tehran. It provided more time to acquire additional LSTs and coincided with favorable tides. Marshall agreed. By February, Churchill was lobbying for a meeting with Marshall and the Combined Chiefs. Realizing that this would be an effort to change aspects of Overlord-Anvil, both the president and Marshall advised against it, as did Admiral King.[72] The landing craft shortage revealed its own little war: King, whose Pacific navy needed LSTs for amphibious island operations, was convinced that the Brits were knowingly underestimating the number of usable landing craft in the British Isles; Eisenhower, though, thought King was "cooking his Pacific books."[73] No matter what was true, this shortage was the primary argument advanced by the British as to why Anvil was impossible. Marshall disagreed and was fighting for it with the Combined Chiefs in Washington.

Eisenhower felt himself caught in the middle. By the end of January, he laid out the differences between American and British positions and alluded to the fact that things were very different in London than in Washington, indicating perhaps the pressure he was under. He made the point that he wanted to be "in complete coordination" with Washington, but pressed his belief that the five-division strengthening had the best chance for success, and then added: "I have earnestly hoped that this could be achieved by the 31st of May without sacrificing a strong Anvil." It was what he added that may have troubled Marshall most: "Some compensation would arise from the fact that as long as the enemy fights in Italy as . . . it is now doing, the action there will in some degree compensate for the absence of an Anvil."[74] Was he in fact taking the British position that Anvil was unnecessary? Marshall told Eisenhower to weigh the situation in Italy against the benefits that could be accrued during Overlord by launching the Anvil attack, seemingly leaving the decision in his hands. But then he added his concern regarding the supreme allied commander's susceptibility to the British: "I will use my influence here to agree with your desires. I merely wish to be certain that localitis is not developing and that the pressures on you have not warped your judgment."[75]

Eisenhower, clearly upset by the implications, fired back a long letter assuring his chief that "no one here has tried to urge me to present any particular view, nor do I believe that I am particularly affected by localitis." Worried about the vehemence of his reply, Eisenhower couldn't sleep that night. In his second cable he noted, "Yesterday I sent you a long telegram in which I think for the first time since I became a Theater Commander I went a bit on the defensive in explaining my views to you. The reason was that there seemed to be an implication in your telegram that I might, merely in the interests of local harmony, surrender my convictions as to operations. I hope I cleared up that point." Marshall didn't respond. It wasn't necessary—the message had been delivered.[76]

"Anvil will probably not be possible"

Eisenhower was determined to stand up to the British in making the case by mid-February that the landing craft needed for Anvil be diverted from the Mediterranean no matter what the current status of the Anzio crisis. A meeting on the 19th with the British chiefs, though, once again eroded his resolve. He cabled Marshall that afternoon that perhaps the "tactical situation" in Italy was going to make Anvil impossible. Keeping his temper barely under control, the chief of staff messaged back: "You were delegated to represent United States Chief of Staff in conference with British . . . on question of Overlord-Anvil. . . . At present we have no clear cut statement of basis of your agreement or disagreement with them and the situation is therefore seriously complicated."[77] Marshall told Eisenhower in so many words to get an agreement or state the disagreements specifically. After the same meeting, the British also wired Marshall that Anvil should be canceled and more resources made available for Italy, so that all efforts could be concentrated on "bleeding and burning German divisions." Given the fact that the Anzio invasion had been a debacle, and efforts from the Allied Winter Line to break through the main front of the German perimeter had not dislodged the tenacious enemy army, Marshall must have concluded, as historian Mark Perry noted, that the only "bleeding and burning" at Anzio had been the Americans and the British. The Germans, tightly concentrated in the bluffs around Monte Cassino, the outer gateway to Rome, were "shooting Allied soldiers as easily as if they were lining them up for execution."[78]

Whatever decision-making Marshall might have left with Eisenhower in January regarding Anvil, by February 21 he took that difficult choice out of the hands of the supreme allied commander. The chief of staff met with Roosevelt, made his case for keeping Anvil, and got his firm approval for the operation. Shortly afterward, Marshall informed Eisenhower that he should apprise the British chiefs that Anvil was not to be canceled. Perhaps the British brass could sway Eisenhower, but they would not go against Roosevelt. Not that they didn't maneuver—asking that a review of the Anvil landings be made on March 20 in the hope that by then the stalemate in Italy would have been broken, or, if not, negotiations might be reopened on the subject of Anvil.[79] Nevertheless, the British agreed that 20 LCTs (Landing Craft, Tank) and 21 LCIs (Landing Ship Infantry transports) would be transferred to Anvil at once.

Although not a micromanager, during these early spring months Marshall was closely involved in this lead-up to Overlord. Eisenhower cabled him nearly every day, sometimes a couple of times a day, outlining in tight detail the complications of juggling Italy with Overlord. Marshall responded and, while correcting Eisenhower only as he thought necessary, carefully monitored the plans for the invasion. Regarding Anvil, the supreme allied commander continued to promote Marshall's views with his British counterparts, but, as he wrote to the chief of staff by the end of March, "We've been over the ground so often that more talk seems completely useless, while I must say that the past two months of argument have not, so far as I can see, changed the convictions of any single individual . . . involved."[80] Marshall must have sympathized, since, in addition to the Anzio-Anvil-Overlord dynamic, he faced other interservice, inter-Allied controversies. In Southeast Asia, General Joseph Stilwell was at loggerheads with the British head of the China-Burma-India Theater, Lord Louis Mountbatten; in the South Pacific, MacArthur continued his critical jabs at the navy.

By early April the Anvil Operation would shift once more, spelled out in a top secret radiogram from Marshall to Eisenhower. It would not be launched simultaneously with Overlord as originally planned—the difficulty of having LSTs (Landing Ship Tanks) and other resources for both offensives proved too daunting—but for now was rescheduled for July 10. And although it might be psychologically beneficial to take Rome, once the Anzio beachhead and forces from the Allied Winter Line broke through the German position at Monte Cassino, "Rome would not be considered a primary effort to the disadvantage of the proposed Anvil."[81] In the end, the July 10 date for the supporting invasion of France would be pushed to August.

"Hamstrung and limited"

Keeping Anvil alive after the endless wrangling with the British had been costly. Landing craft intended for the Pacific would be diverted to the European Theater so as not to decrease the number of these vessels taken from the Italian campaign. Accordingly, General MacArthur and Admiral Nimitz would have to trim offensive operations against the Japanese. Churchill liked the arrangement but was hardly thrilled. He especially found this constant shortage of landing craft "absurd," warning that "how it is that the plans of two great Empires like Britain and the United States should be so much hamstrung and limited by a hundred or two of these particular vessels will never be understood by history."[82] Marshall to some extent must have agreed; after all, it was Admiral King who oversaw naval procurement policy, and shipyards were cranking out vast numbers of freighters and even more large complex vessels. How was it that this linchpin LST shortage persisted?[83] Up to the eve of Overlord, Churchill still fought a "rearguard action" against Anvil. But by making use of their growing ascendancy in the Alliance, according to Mark Stoler, "the Americans virtually bludgeoned the British into Operation Dragoon, the new name for Anvil, and one that aptly summarized Churchill's feelings as to how he had been forced to agree."[84]

"Glaring reports of General Patton's statements"

From the Pentagon on April 26, Marshall let Eisenhower know for "Eyes Only" that Patton was once again making news, and it wasn't good news. Since late January the controversial general had been directing the training of the U.S. Third Army, getting it ready for a post-Normandy invasion, and at the same time commanding a "ghost army"—the First United States Army Group (FUSAG), an operation code-named Quicksilver, part of a broader plan whose purpose was to get the Wehrmacht to divert resources away from the Normandy area. The Quicksilver ruse was to convince the Germans that the famous Patton would lead a major attack not against the beaches of Normandy but the important port of Calais. The military leadership knew that the German High Command feared and respected Patton and had every reason to believe that any important Allied invasion would include him.

The deception was highly structured: dummy tanks, trucks, jeeps, aircraft, and even warships were built of inflatable rubber and put in "camps," or in English ports. With the help of set builders for the British filmmakers, harbors were filled with mock landing craft. Double agents planted false stories and documents with known spies; detailed fake radio reports were transmitted.[85] The situation for Patton's newsworthy comments seemed innocuous enough: he was making "off the cuff and off the record" remarks—he later said he was assured no press was present—to a group of mostly women at the opening of a Welcome Club for soldiers in northwest England at Knutsford near his headquarters. Referring to other welcoming parties in his career, he remarked that his practice had been to "welcome Germans and Italians to the 'infernal regions.'" He made a few other harmless references to "English ladies and American dames," but then came the line that got him into trouble, at least according to the newspapers. Regarding the Anglo-American relationship, he noted that "since it seems to be the evident destiny of the British and Americans to rule the world, the better we know each other the better the job we will do."[86] As Forrest Pogue later wrote: "To some in the United States and Britain who realized how long the Russians had been carrying on the fight . . . while their demands for a second front remained unanswered, Patton's boast seemed untimely." Further, for those who remembered the "slapping incidents" vividly, "this new outburst represented a new high in irresponsibility."[87]

"My first intimation that Patton had broken out again"

Eisenhower responded immediately to Marshall's inquires about this, telling him that the chief of staff's communication had been his first intimation that "Patton had broken out again" and remarking that "apparently he is unable to use reasonably good sense in all those matters where senior commanders must appreciate the effect of their own actions upon public opinion and this arises [*sic*] doubts as to the wisdom of retaining him in high command." The supreme allied commander went on to explain that according to his reports, Patton *had* mentioned the Russians, but Eisenhower also stated that he had "grown so weary of the trouble he constantly causes you and the War Department to say nothing of myself." He ended the "General Marshall's Eyes Only" message by telling the chief of staff that he would defer final action on the matter until he heard from him.[88] Marshall had already informed Eisenhower that the Senate was considering a list of permanent promotions in rank, including one for Patton, and that this whole situation would make that process all the more complex. Eisenhower mentioned that if he thought Patton's behavior would diminish public and government confidence in the War Department, he should be severely disciplined, and asked for a reply "as soon as convenient."

"You carry a burden of responsibility"

In a rather long secret telegram, Marshall quoted an editorial that laid out the problem with Patton: "'We do not mean to be prissy about the matter but we think that Lieutenant generals, even temporary ones, ought to talk with rather more dignity than this. When they do not they run the danger of losing the respect of the men they command. . . . We think that this has happened to General Patton. Whatever his merits as a strategist and tactician he has revealed glaring defects as a leader of men.'" Marshall, though, told Eisenhower that he had been considering the whole matter on "a purely business basis," and reminded him that "Patton is the only available army commander for this present assignment who has had actual experience in fighting Rommel and in extensive landing operations followed by a rapid campaign of exploitation." He continued, "You carry the burden of responsibility as to the success of Overlord; if you feel that that operation can be carried out with the same assurance of success with [General Courtney] Hodges in command . . . all well and good. If you doubt it then between us we can bear the burden of the present unfortunate reaction."[89] With that response from Marshall, Eisenhower elected to keep Patton in command. In his April 29 decision letter, the supreme commander informed Patton, "I want to tell you officially and definitely that if you are again guilty of any indiscretion in speech or action that leads to embarrassment for the War Department, any other part of the Government, or this Headquarters, I will relieve you instantly of command."[90]Although not a part of the initial invasion, which he had so coveted, later that year Patton would be crucial to the Allied advance into Germany, especially during the Battle of the Bulge. Perhaps Marshall and Eisenhower's decisions on "a purely business basis" paid off after all.

Anzio Breakout

The beginning of 1944 in Italy had ushered in a miserable winter stalemate for the Allies. From well-fortified positions in the mountains, the Germans had fired down on their attackers day after day. It was not the kind of modern warfare Marshall had described to his students at Fort Benning. As Ed Cray wrote, "No columns of tanks swept across inviting plains, no artillery-supported divisions punched through enemy lines, then poured into the rear."[91] Indeed, in the winter of 1943–44, there was no war of movement: trucks and tanks proved virtually useless in the mud and snow; supplies were moved by mules, and conditions were remarkably similar to the clumsy and deadly trench warfare of the Great War.[92] By spring, though, the Allies were determined to break the stalemate. In April, the Allied Air Force flew

21,000 sorties against "bridges, railroads, and other German supply lines." The British Eighth Army relieved Clark's Fifth Army at positions along the Gustav Line so that the Americans could move up the coast toward Anzio. On May 11, the big offensive was launched, and the German army began to crumble. On May 18, after enormous loss of life, total destruction of the town, and the Allied bombing to smithereens of its famous 14th-century hilltop monastery, Cassino fell to the Allies.[93] It was May 25, as the Eighth Army continued its push north that elements of the Fifth Army at Anzio under General Truscott, who had replaced Lucas in February, finally broke out, linking up with Clark's II Corps troops. The Anzio perimeter and the Fifth Army's Winter Line were no more.

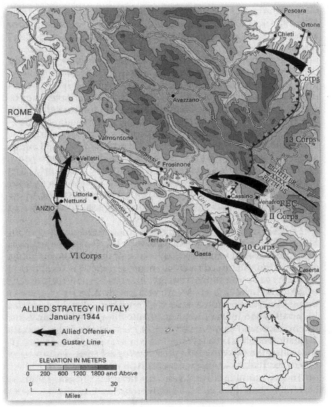

U.S. Army Center for Military History

Meanwhile, elements of Lieutenant General Sir Oliver Leese's British Eighth Army had the German 10th Army on the run, and Truscott's VI Corps was, as ordered, driving northeastward to cut it off. Within a day, they would have stood across the line of Kesselring's 10th Army, which would then have been trapped. Contravening the orders of the British commander,

General Sir Harold Alexander, Clark ordered Truscott to change his line of attack from a position that would have accomplished this, and instead sent him directly toward the prize of Rome. In his memoirs, Truscott later wrote that Clark "was fearful that the British were laying devious plans to be first into Rome," a sentiment somewhat reinforced in Clark's own writings: "Not only did we intend to become the first army in fifteen centuries to seize Rome from the south, but we intended to see that the people back home knew that it was the Fifth Army that did the job and knew the price that had been paid for it."[94] Clark's moment of hubris perhaps revealed in bold relief the difficulty of achieving Marshall's "unity of command" principle, especially in the heat of battle. According to some historians, Alexander had clearly laid down the Army boundaries before the battle, and Rome was allocated to the Fifth Army. Further, the Eighth Army was constantly reminded that their job was to engage the German 10th Army, destroy as much of it as possible, and then bypass Rome to continue the pursuit northward, which they did. Nevertheless, perhaps in part because of the shift in plan, the 10th Army would live to fight again, and just as Marshall had predicted, the "suction pump" of the war north of Rome would do little to advance the overall strategy of victory in Europe.

By June 4, at long last, American forces would finally march into Rome.[95] Clark, arriving in the capital city from the Anzio area in a Piper Cub, called for a rendezvous at 10 a.m. on June 5 with his lieutenants and ordered the II Corps to arrange an escort with clean tanks, trucks, and soldiers. The meeting point was the most sacred of the city's seven hills, where in classical Rome triumphant generals sacrificed a snow-white bull in gratitude for the beneficence of the gods. It was here that Clark met the press. "This is a great day for the Fifth Army," he exclaimed, without mentioning the British Eighth Army at all. A hundred flashbulbs popped as Movietone cameras recorded the scene for posterity.[96] The victorious general had no way of knowing that the Allied landings in France two days later would soon knock the headlines of Rome's liberation from the front pages of newspapers across the world.

The Cost of War

"You have made the American people very happy," the president cabled Clark. Indeed, but the cost of the Anzio breakout and the march on Rome had been high; after all, General Alexander had once remarked, "All roads lead to Rome, but all the roads are mined."[97] From May 11, 1944, there had been 44,000 casualties. Anzio historian Rick Atkinson provided the list: 12,000 British, 9,600 French, 4,000 Poles, and 18,000 Americans, of which 3,000 were killed in action.[98] Marshall was always acutely aware of the

Fifth Army commander General Mark Clark is greeted by celebrating
Italians during a triumphant ride through the city of Rome, June 5, 1944.
U.S. Army Signal Corps, www.liberationtrilogy.com

cost of war, making certain that every few days Roosevelt was apprised
of casualties, with deaths redlined. He later told Forrest Pogue, "I tried to
keep before him all the time the casualty results, because you get hardened
to these things and you have to be very careful to keep them always in the
forefront of your mind."[99] One casualty of this Italian campaign would be
personal.

Allen to Madge—"Now don't get scared."

Second Lieutenant Allen Tupper Brown, Katherine Marshall's youngest son
George C. Marshall Research Library

Marshall certainly knew plenty about the fighting in Italy, as he was daily briefed in his Pentagon offices. He also knew about it through letters the family exchanged with his stepson, Second Lieutenant Allen T. Brown. As a part of the First Armored Division's 13th Armored Regiment, Allen had landed at Salerno that previous September. Early in 1944, before the combined Anzio-Cassino offensives, he complained in letters home of inactivity, but that soon ended. By February 27 he had written to his wife, Madge, that he was involved in the heavy fighting around Monte Cassino, attached to an outfit of New Zealanders, and allowed that "this is not a particularly healthy place to go around making calls, if you get what I mean."[100] To allay her worries, though, he softened his missive a bit: "Now don't get scared. I'm taking good care of myself, and this fighting is right up my alley." By March 6 he reported that he and nine of his comrades were sleeping in a small cottage when "25 shells came in one after another all around this house." There were casualties. Allen ended that letter with a dose of reality: "Don't let anybody ever tell you that they don't get scared under an artillery barrage, because believe me it scares the hell out of you. You get a split second's warning from the whistle of the shell and then she hits. As you can imagine," he concludes, "it is rather an uncomfortable feeling."[101]

A few days later he explained that while he was still at the front, around Cassino—and it was "a little nerve-wracking at times"—he would so much rather be doing something other than "sitting back in the rear just waiting," and he mentioned the comfort he found in looking at the photographs of his wife and their young son, Tupper. As if to hit a light note, Allen described a beautiful day with the "sun in full force," but added that such a scene made it hard to believe that "men are killing or being killed all around me."[102] In a March 19 letter, it's clear that no matter whether he and his men were mired in the mud or the day was Italian bright, danger was constant and close: "I'm very tired and a little bit jangled this morning. We all had a tough night's work last night. Right in the middle of the fight for nine hours straight, completely exposed to constant heavy artillery, heavy mortar and sniper fire."

Despite the crushing demands of the war, Marshall wrote to his stepson every few days, for the most part detailing homey details of family life, without focus on the mega-events that surrounded him. In early March he described how he and Katherine were taking long walks around Fort Myer in the evening; said he hadn't been able to ride his horse along the river because of deep mud; remarked on the progress of his young granddaughter, Kitty, Allen's niece, who walked "pretty well with guidance." He admitted that "I find your mother following news of the Italian Campaign. . . . She doesn't talk about it much but it is constantly on her mind."[103] On March 11, Marshall recorded that in the evening he planned to attend a special occasion "in an attractive setting, with famous oyster dinners." Knowing full well the conditions under which Allen was fighting, he told him, "I wish you could join us and spread yourself in the warmth of a heated room and with the beautiful food that I assume will be at hand." As if to remind himself that Allen was in the heart of the action, and with perhaps a certain amount of wistfulness that he was not, he added, "You are young. I had rather be young and in the mud than at my age and in an office chair, though it seems to me," he conceded, "I spend a great deal of time in the air not to mention slogging over considerable muddy terrain."[104] Although Marshall acknowledged that he couldn't discuss Allen's affairs in a letter, on April 18 he allowed that he probably knew more about them than Allen did. As if to encourage his stepson, he referenced the Pacific war and noted that because of "naval superiority," the "enemy was in a very difficult position." In the same letter, he mentioned Katherine again and the fact that she was handling Allen's predicament well, but he imagined "it was largely a matter of repressing feelings."[105] By May 17, Marshall was well aware that Allen had been sent to the Anzio beachhead, understood with total clarity that his stepson was at the very nexus of a fierce battle. Somehow Katherine thought that Anzio was safer than the Cassino area, and, as Marshall noted, he had "not made any comments about affairs in the beachhead," a clear indication that he intended to protect his wife as long as possible.[106]

On May 21, 1944, South African engineers work to open the road through the decimated town of Cassino.
U.S. Army Signal Corps, www.liberationtrilogy.com

"I am sincerely sorry to report to you"

Just before Memorial Day, on May 30, Katherine had received letters from both of her sons. Allen and Clifton each reported that they had spent three days together after the fighting at Cassino and before Allen left for Anzio. Despite the intense battle that continued, the tone of the letters promised that victory was in sight: "I feel sorry for any Germans in Italy," Allen wrote.

"The horseshoe has held my luck. I shall take it down this Christmas and keep it for the rest of my life." As Katherine recalled, "When George left for his office that morning there was a song in my heart." An hour later, as she stood by the window in her bedroom, her husband entered, closed the door, and told her that Allen was dead. He had given his life the day before in a tank battle on the road to Rome.[107] Marshall surely gave what comfort he could to his grieving wife, and before the day was over had written Madge "the distressing message." The next day, the official word arrived from General Jacob L. Devers, in a packet to be "handled by officer courier only," and labeled "Personal: to be opened by General Marshall": "I am sincerely sorry to report to you that Allen was killed in action on the 29th while leading his platoon in an attack west of Velletri. He was shot by a sniper when he stood up in his turret to observe the front with his field glasses." This was not a usual announcement of a combat death, as the next line revealed, informing the chief of staff that "Clifton was present at his burial today in a cemetery near Anzio. We are forwarding by courier letters from Clifton to you, his mother and Madge."[108]

Clifton's letter, addressed to Mother and Madge, showed handwriting steady and clear, but the message was heartbreaking. "I only wish I could deliver this in person instead of writing. Since I know you will want all of the details, I will take the events of the past 36 hours step by step." He described the 1:00 a.m. phone call informing him that he should be at Fifth Army headquarters at the Anzio beachhead at 8:30 the next morning, May 30. Indeed, he arrived at the appointed hour, filled with dread. The commanding general's aide, Phil Draper, was there and, as Clifton said, "confirmed my worst fears." Draper took Clifton to see General Mark Clark, who was "most kind" and told him he had already informed General Marshall by telegram. The aide and Clifton went to the cemetery where Allen was to be buried. In his letter, Clifton tried to provide comfort to his mother and sister-in-law, saying:

> The captain in charge had Allen . . . in a new uniform, and they brought him out for me to see and he looked very peaceful as if sleeping. Since he was killed by automatic pistol his body was not in the least mutilated. A Chaplain happened to be at the cemetery, so I asked him to say a few prayers. . . . Phil [the aide], Major Langford, and I took Allen's flag draped remains to the grave and there Major Langford said a few prayers and buried him there with some of his comrades in arms. It was a beautiful day and appropriately "Memorial Day."

Clifton stayed for the Memorial Day service and then left to be taken to the army command post where Allen had been killed. Although under fire as his driver took him into that area, he finally made it to headquarters and talked to the men with whom Allen had served. As Clifton pointed out, some were not able to say anything, since they were pretty shaken up from what had been a very hard day. All of the officers had been casualties except one second lieutenant who had taken over command. Clifton again gave comfort to Madge and Katherine by saying, "All of the officers and men were so fond of Allen and they said that his company had done a wonderful job." Before Clifton headed back to his duty, he visited the cemetery once more. He described to Madge and his mom that there were some wild poppies and daisies about, which he picked and placed on Allen's grave. With all the details laid out, Clifton ended his letter: "He loved you both so much and was so courageous and brave in his going. I hope you two can be as brave as he was. That is the way he would want it.[109]

"A blessed numbness"

Katherine would later say of her response to Allen's death, "A blessed numbness comes to one at a time like this." When Marshall had told her the dreadful news, she said, "I could not comprehend his words. I only had one thought—that I must get to Madge, Allen's wife. I do not recall anything of my flight to New York. I kept repeating Allen is dead, Allen is dead—but no realization of what this meant came to me until later." Soon she would resume her duties on a dozen war boards, doing the work that had demanded her time and energy for three years. Only after the launch of the Normandy Invasion, with Marshall in Europe, did Katherine have a chance to go to Fire Island with Clifton. It was during those days at that place, which held so many memories of her lost son's youth, that she faced his death.[110] So it was that Allen, only 28 years old, would become one of the more than 291,000 American battle deaths of that terrible war. With her Shakespearean background, Katherine must have recalled a line from *Macbeth*:

> Your son, my lord, has paid a soldier's debt;
> He only liv'd but till he was a man.

As for Marshall, historian Ed Cray pointed out that he needed no "red lined chart to remind him of the cost of war." Nevertheless, D-Day loomed, and a thousand other thorny issues of managing the theaters of war claimed his time, and perhaps took his mind from the immediacy of his grief.

The Future French Republic

One such complicated issue had to do with the French. With an invasion of Normandy on the horizon, the question arose: What was the best use of French manpower resources? Three groups would be in play: the Free French, the French Resistance, and the Frenchmen who would be available to the Allied command once the beachhead was established and those territories liberated. Then there was the matter of competing leadership between Charles de Gaulle, who since 1940 had commanded the Free French resistance forces, and General Henri Giraud, the leader of all Free French forces released from Vichy control in North Africa after the opening days of Operation Torch in 1942. With about as much enthusiasm as had been exhibited with their handshakes at Casablanca, in 1943 these two forces had fused, creating what came to be known as the French Committee of National Liberation—the C.F.L.N. (Comité Français de la Libération Nationale). DeGaulle continued to make every effort to become both the political and military leader of all Free French forces by edging out this other contender. When the C.F.L.N. was reorganized in April 1944, perhaps by design of the Gaullists, Giraud's role was rendered superfluous. DeGaulle offered a lesser role to Giraud, which he refused, insisting that he remain commander in chief of all French forces. This gave the C.F.L.N. an opportunity to oust Girard from any command position on disciplinary charges, retaining him only as a reserve officer. This led to a shake-up in the leadership of the Free French forces, and soon the very capable Lieutenant General Emile Béhouart was made chief of staff, effectively replacing Giraud. Already Lieutenant General Alphonse Pierre Juin had been what General Jacob Devers described as a "magnificent," smart, and aggressive leader of the French forces attached to the American Fifth Army in the Italian campaign; by that August he would lead all of the Free French forces.[111]

It was all very tricky, though. First of all, by June 2, 1944, the de Gaulle government would have renamed itself the Provisional Government of the French Republic, a foreshadowing of its leader's expectations as to his future role. Nevertheless, since Casablanca, Roosevelt had discussed with Marshall many times that in transactions with de Gaulle it should not be assumed that he represented the entire French population, and he was not to be treated as if he would automatically become the postwar leader of France. In reply to a mid-May communication from Eisenhower to Marshall requesting a meeting with de Gaulle in London prior to the invasion, Roosevelt himself responded: "The French people are naturally shell-shocked from sufferings at the hands of German occupation. . . . As the liberators of France we have no right to color their views or to give any group the sole right to impose on them one side of the case."[112] Roosevelt reminded Eisenhower that he was to discuss only military matters, not political ones. Marshall reiterated the president's message shortly thereafter. Perhaps after the Darlan affair of 1942 it was unlikely that the supreme allied commander would make that mistake again. The political overlay, though, was hard to ignore.

When Eisenhower's aide, Lieutenant General Walter Bedell Smith, replied to Marshall's message, he noted that the allied commander understood that the political future of France was not to be discussed, but he conceded, "When a military commander is operating on foreign soil there is no clear cut line of demarcation between military and civil or political questions."

Second, maintaining French units as effective fighters would be challenging; they were formed from a variety of military formations and needed retraining, re-equipping, and more personnel. Moreover, as they took casualties, it would be doubly difficult for the Americans and British to supply needed replacements. Having been in exile for several years, de Gaulle was anxious to restore the pride and prestige of the French Republic, whose armies were once feared across the continent; further, the Allies were literally entering his homeland, where, as a result, that nation's future would soon be shaped. Indeed, out of political need, de Gaulle wanted plenty of unified French combat units and was rather sensitive about the conditions of their training; he also opposed their being broken apart to shore up other depleted French units.[113] Blending these units under the unified command of Overlord would continue to be one of Eisenhower's worries as D-Day neared.

Operations Aimed at the Heart of Germany

Since February 12, 1944, Eisenhower had in hand official orders from the Combined Chiefs of Staff for the Allied invasion of Normandy: "Task: You will enter the continent of Europe and, in conjunction with the other United Nations, undertake operations aimed at the heart of Germany and the destruction of her armed forces."[114] On May 15 the entire upper stratum of the Allied Command, except for Washington's Joint Chiefs, met in west London for a full briefing on the Normandy landings. Even the king of England was present and offered brief remarks. Regarding the upcoming invasion, Churchill noted in his speech, "Gentlemen, I am hardening towards this enterprise."[115] The word "hardening" perhaps revealed a more frank statement of his views than he intended. Marshall and Eisenhower had battled long and hard to limit Churchill's efforts to expand the peripheral Mediterranean Theater, thus delaying the thrust onto the continent. The prime minister had even told Eisenhower that spring, "When I think of the beaches of Normandy choked with the flowers of American and British youth and when in my mind's eye I see the tides running red with their blood I have my doubts—I have my doubts, Ike—I have my doubts."[116]

Churchill would always defend his strategic view that the assault up Italy's boot, the "back door," and landings at Anzio, as well as continued fighting north of Rome that would last until a year past D-Day, had aided Allied efforts overall: "Any estimate of the value of the campaign must be expressed not in terms of the ground gained, but in terms of its effect on the war as a whole." As Churchill saw it, "Fifty-five German divisions were tied down in the Mediterranean by the [Allied] threat, actual, or potential." He would later write, "The principal task of our armies had been to draw off and contain the great possible numbers of Germans. This had been admirably fulfilled."[117] Further, despite the prime minister's misgivings about Overlord, he had fully supported its preparations in England for several years—the only question, said historian Andrew Roberts, was the date of its launch.[118]

Millions of Everything

The build-up in England for Overlord had in part been accomplished through the awe–inspiring supply capability of the Americans, who had produced such huge quantities of goods that in some cases English docks could not unload them all. Further, that spring the United States was shipping the number of soldiers each month that had composed the entire American army four years previously.[119] But the organizational and administrative efficiency of the British contributed as well, creating a partnership that would amass the largest military effort in world history. As Roberts described it:

> Millions of maps had been printed; thousands of aerial photographs compiled; millions of rounds of ammunition had been stockpiled; hundreds of miles of roads had been built; 6,250 pounds of sweets, 12,500 pounds of biscuits and one hundred thousand packets of chewing gum had been distributed; sixty days' [worth] of poisonous gas was prepared for retaliatory use; 25 square miles of west Devon were evacuated of its civilian population for training; mass rehearsals were conducted with live ammunition; vast encampments were built all over southern England with their own water supplies, field bakeries, post offices and camouflages; immense ingenuity and inventiveness were directed towards making the assault a success, including artificial harbours and underwater petrol pipelines. Although the Americans brought over a great deal in convoys—necessitating forty ships per

armoured division—the British provided a huge amount in terms of logistics too, which Churchill never begrudged.[120]

As Eisenhower worked out the final details of Overlord, Marshall could do little but wait. Although for three years he had carried the banner in support of this cross-channel strategic view, in his role as the chief of staff he was far from the action, handling a range of issues small and large. There had been the Patton "breakout," now settled. He had answered Churchill's complaint that French civilian losses would number 10,000 if the Allies went through with their pre-invasion plan to destroy the French rail system to thwart possible German counterattacks—it would taint the locals' view of the "liberators," the prime minister noted. Marshall was unmoved: "The people of France are being called upon to pay a price for their liberation but this price should not appear too high in the light of the necessity for victory in the coming operation."[121] Uncharacteristically moody and irritable, perhaps masking his grief over Allen's death, he argued with the secretary of war over a petty dispute between the American Red Cross and the Army Emergency Relief Organization. The news of Rome's impending liberation was heartening but was almost certainly a reminder of his personal loss. Meanwhile, at Eisenhower's headquarters at Portsmouth, England, the launch of the long-sought drive into Fortress Europe, scheduled for June 5, boiled down to weather.

"Low clouds, rain and wind, 'channel chop,' high tides"

It was June 3. Already from hundreds of camps throughout southern England, companies of men had been loaded into trucks to join huge convoys headed to the coast. Endless rows of jeeps, stockpiles of artillery and explosives lined their paths. MPs directed traffic, and children were held up for soldiers to kiss as trucks slowed on congested roads. But despite such a stirring array, one element stood in the way: the five-day forecast of Captain J.M. Stagg, weatherman. Late in the day, with troops already at their points of embarkation and tightly berthed in the vessels that would take them to enemy shores, neither the rainy skies nor the sickness-inducing bounce of the transports in the channel surf offered hope. All the commanding officers understood the situation: if storms over the channel delayed the invasion by more than three days, the ratio of rising tide to the time of daybreak would be unfavorable for the landings for another two weeks; if that didn't work, the event could be postponed a month. In addition to changing tide and light conditions, since the assault troops had already been briefed regarding Overlord, they would have to be locked up totally incommunicado. It would be almost impossible to keep a secret known to more than 150,000 men.[122]

In the early morning hours of June 4, after conferences with his commanders, Eisenhower made the excruciating decision. The invasion was on hold for 24 hours. For a good part of the day, the supreme allied commander, the sole arbiter of the invasion's launch, paced outside his headquarters trailer, chain-smoking, drinking coffee. Churchill came by, so did de Gaulle, each weighing in on the pros and cons of the matter. In the late afternoon, Eisenhower had another meeting with senior commanders. This time there was a tiny window of hope. The weather wasn't going to be great by any means, but within a little more than 24 hours—on June 6—Stagg thought it would clear enough for the invasion to proceed. Eisenhower edged toward a go-ahead, despite varied opinions—a yes, a no, a not sure—from his chiefs. During one more meeting the following morning, Stagg delivered a slightly improved report—yes, he thought his forecast for June 6 would hold. It was 4 a.m. June 5. Pacing the room once more, taking the measure of his commanders one last time, Eisenhower finally announced, "Okay, we'll go."[123]

"Halcyon [June 1] plus 5 finally and definitely confirmed"

Sometime in the afternoon of the 5th, Marshall received the coded cable from Eisenhower that the invasion would begin on the next day. A man of habit, the chief of staff kept his schedule: protocol demanded a dress uniform and a trip that evening to the Russian embassy, where he would, with ceremony, receive the Order of Suvarov, the highest decoration the Soviets could award to a foreigner. Afterward, he would leave as soon as politely possible and go home to bed. As historian Mark Perry noted, "Dwight Eisenhower . . . was now leading the most complex and largest invasion in human history. . . . There was nothing Marshall could now do, nothing that he had not prepared. It was out of his hands." As he turned out his light at Quarters 1, assault troops were heading ashore on the Normandy beaches. So it was that on the morning of June 6 the largest amphibious force ever seen hurled itself against Hitler's Atlantic Wall.[124] It didn't take a litany of statistics for the German soldiers in the pillboxes high above the beach to see the magnitude of what was coming as a galaxy of ships emerged from the morning mist, but the numbers were daunting, as historian Mark Perry described:

> The assault would be supported by 6,500 ships forming seventy-five separate convoys. . . . The guns of a flotilla of 1,213 naval combat ships would silence German shore batteries. The air over Normandy would be secured against the Luftwaffe by 11,590 Allied bombers and fighters. Over 156,000 American, British, and Canadian soldiers would be put ashore by 4,126 landing craft.[125]

As Eisenhower would later recall, "The mighty host was tense as a coiled spring, and indeed that is exactly what it was—a great human spring, coiled for the moment when its energy should be released and it would vault the English Channel in the greatest amphibious assault ever attempted."[126] By the time the assembly of ships appeared before the disbelieving eyes of Hitler's defenders, three airborne divisions had dropped behind enemy lines to secure the approaches to the invasion area. Eisenhower had watched their takeoff, tears in his eyes. Tucked into the duffels of most of the pilots and the troops was the supreme commander's typed message: "Soldiers, Sailors and Airmen of the Allied Expeditionary Force! You are about to embark upon the Great Crusade, toward which we have striven these many months. The eyes of the world are upon you. The hopes and prayers of liberty-loving people everywhere march with you." These airborne units had landed, noted Perry, "in the dark, some of them in Normandy's most treacherous terrain, in forests, bogs, swamps, and farm fields, and on the outskirts of Normandy's sleepy rural villages."[127]

General Eisenhower converses with a soldier of the 101st Airborne Division, June 5, 1944, just before it departs for Normandy.

Dwight D. Eisenhower Presidential Library, 65-325-3

"Pride of our nation . . ."

On the morning of June 6, Marshall went to the Pentagon as usual, spending a good portion of the day writing thank-you notes in response to letters of condolences that had arrived after Allen's death. In future interviews he would reveal none of his feelings about this day. As reports of the invasion's progress came in, he relayed them to the White House. Perhaps the president's D-Day prayer, broadcast by national radio feed that evening, was a vivid reminder of the war's personal demands, but Marshall had always respected the sacrifices of individual soldiers from ordinary families all across the nation—his loss was not unique. Still, Roosevelt's words were powerful and moving, and matched Americans' view that the nation would be engaged in a just war:

> Last night, when I spoke with you about the fall of Rome, I knew at that moment that troops of the United States and our Allies were crossing the [English] Channel in another and greater operation. It has come to pass with success thus far. And so, in this poignant hour, I ask you to join with me in prayer:

> Almighty God: Our sons, pride of our nation, this day have set upon a mighty endeavor, a struggle to preserve our Republic, our religion, and our civilization, and to set free a suffering humanity. Lead them straight and true; give strength to their arms, stoutness to their hearts, steadfastness in their faith. They will need Thy blessings. Their road will be long and hard. For the enemy is strong.

> Some will never return. Embrace these, Father, and receive them, Thy heroic servants, into Thy kingdom.[128]

American troops approach Omaha Beach, D-Day, June 6, 1944.

U.S. National Archives, SC 189986

Chapter 12

Omaha Beach to the German West Wall

"Conditions . . . generally favorable"

June–September 1944

The D-Day landings came that June morning. General Omar Bradley would later describe it as "a monstrous jigsaw puzzle that had to be disassembled for ferrying across the channel and then reassembled on the far shore," but success would not be easy. The maps had laid out the plan. Allied troops would make inroads on an area of beach that ran 60 miles all along the jutting French Cotentin Peninsula. The troops would literally emerge from the channel on five sites, code-named Utah, Omaha, Gold, Juno, and Sword. Some aspects of the operation went according to plan: the British army came ashore at Sword and Gold, and with their beaches secure within two hours, the sandy aprons along the shore were soon jammed with British armor. The Canadians at Juno took withering fire, with troops making what one soldier described as the "deadliest runs of their lives," yet, before nightfall 12,000 of them were headed inland. The men of the U.S. Fourth Infantry Division at Utah sustained light casualties that morning and were also off the beaches by the end of the day.[1]

www.dday-overlord.com

319

Nevertheless, the sheer enormity of the operation, with "the vast confusion of invasion," meant that much could go wrong, especially at Omaha beach. One officer would later recall, "We hung on there by our eyelashes for hours. It was god-awful." As historian Stanley Weintraub described it, "Troops too heavily laden, or debarked from LSTs too far offshore, drowned . . . tanks and artillery were swamped in the strong surf. Only five of the first thirty-two amphibious tanks . . . made it ashore."[2] Its approaches formidably defended by experienced German troops delivering lethal fire from cliffs and draws, at Omaha the 1st and 29th Divisions were pinned down for six hours on a strip of beach 10 yards wide. The slaughter was so severe that for a time American troop commander General Omar Bradley considered withdrawing. Finally, a squadron of naval destroyers came in close enough to clear a path to the cliffs above, but it was a costly first day in that sector—1,465 Americans killed, with another 5,000 wounded or missing.[3] Journalist Ernie Pyle described "a museum of carnage . . . abandoned rolls of barbed wire and smashed bulldozers and big stacks of thrown-away life belts and piles of shells still waiting to be moved. In the water floated empty life rafts and soldiers' packs and ration boxes, and mysterious oranges. On the beach lay, expended, sufficient men and mechanism for a small war. They were gone forever now."[4]

Wounded soldiers on Omaha Beach wait for
evacuation to a field hospital, June 6, 1944.

United States Army

Overall, it was a perilous, exhausting, earth-shattering day, but the fact was that at last the Allies were in France. Aided by 13,688 air force sorties to the Germans' 319—Eisenhower had told his men, "If you see aircraft overhead they will be ours"—by evening, 165,000 soldiers had landed on those beaches.[5] American casualties, including 4,570 killed, numbered 9,500; British and Canadian dead and wounded totaled 3,000. While painful, with soldiers' bodies washing ashore for days, the losses did not approach Churchill's dire predictions made to discourage Overlord at virtually every pre-June 6 planning conference.[6]

In the end, Overlord had not been thwarted. The question as to whether or not Marshall's push for the invasion of France could have been made earlier will long be debated. Historian Robert Perry opined that had it come in 1943, the Germans would have been able to concentrate their forces faster before relentless Allied bombing operations had wreaked havoc on their supply lines; the ranks of American troops pouring into England pre-invasion would have been thinned by U-boat campaigns through both '42 and '43. Further, without Torch and Husky the Germans might well have gone on the offensive in the Mediterranean, taking over Malta and retaining their access to the coveted oil fields of the Middle East. Finally, by 1944, hundreds of thousands of Hitler's finest soldiers had been killed by the Soviets on the Eastern Front, which diminished the strength of German divisions that could be brought to bear against the Normandy Invasion.[7]

"The Huns at the top of the toboggan slide"

General Marshall, Army Air Forces General Hap Arnold, and Admiral Ernest King departed Washington on June 8 for London. They justified the trip on the grounds that they needed to be near the scene of the action in case emergency decisions were needed; moreover, now that the invasion was launched, the details of other operations had to be made firm. Perhaps what they didn't say was that having fought so hard and so long for Overlord, they wanted to see it for themselves. Fog made landing in Scotland impossible, so they flew on to Wales, where more terrible weather and train delays held them up again. Finally, they traveled by a mail train express in an unheated car, arriving in London cold and tired to be warmly greeted by the British Chiefs of Staff.[8]

The Combined Chiefs met on June 10 and 11, with strategic subjects such as the long-debated Anvil, operations in North Burma, and questions of the continuing fighting in Italy on the table. However, given the euphoria born of the landings, the initial discussions were amiable. After the second day of meetings, the American Chiefs of Staff joined their British counterparts and Churchill on a private train, enjoying a hospitable meal as they sped overnight toward Portsmouth, where they would embark for Normandy.

Churchill, once convinced that the Normandy Invasion was set in stone, had wanted to cross the channel on D-Day with the invading armies. The British naval commander and Eisenhower had told him a firm no, and in a meeting with Churchill on May 31, King George VI himself weighed in against the idea. Still determined to go, it took a strong letter dated June 2 from the king, outlining the dangers involved and the potential impact to the nation if the prime minister were lost, that kept him from the beaches on June 6. Now, as he chatted exuberantly with the Combined Chiefs, he was primed to get to the battlefront. In fact, for the whole group there was the unmistakable feel of an outing. After all the arguments, strategic loggerheads, and endless troop and supply challenges, the Allies were in France, and those who had planned it for so long wanted a look.[9]

The next morning, a grinning Eisenhower met the group at Portsmouth, which had been the point of debarkation for the troops on June 5–6 and was still an astonishing beehive of activity. The British and American leaders broke into two groups, the U.S. contingent boarding a destroyer for their sector. Forrest Pogue described the scene:

> They moved out of a crowded harbor, jammed with warships and landing craft, under skies filled with roaring planes, marveling at the Allied control of sea and air, which ensured the safety of the Channel. The great charts and loading tables, the tables of organization, the vast build-up of supplies under Operation Bolero—all these suddenly came to life for the Chiefs who had visualized that these miracles could come to pass. For Marshall, who had never let this cross-Channel assault be forgotten, it was a day of fulfillment.[10]

As Marshall and his party approached Omaha Beach they transferred to an amphibious vehicle. Cameramen filmed as the smiling chief of staff, a pistol holstered at his hip, climbed awkwardly onto the sand still littered with the detritus of D-Day's recent ferocious scramble. All heads turned as the top brass of the entire American operation toured the battlefield. Marshall shook hands with privates, captains, and generals, clearly relishing the moment. Lunch was a briefing at Bradley's headquarters in an apple orchard on the cliffs from which, days before, German machine gun nests had delivered their deadly fire. The meal was C-rations, with the officers cleaning up as best they could from one basin filled from a jerrican.[11]

Generals Eisenhower, Marshall, and Arnold leave the amphibious craft on the Normandy beach to tour invasion installations, June 12, 1944.

George C. Marshall Research Library

That evening Marshall returned with King to Portsmouth. They came back to London aboard the PM's special train, General Arnold by light plane. The next day Marshall would have a busy round of meetings with the Combined Chiefs, but on the 14th, he handwrote a top secret update to be radioed to President Roosevelt: "Conditions on the beachhead are generally favorable with but minor difficulties or delays. The Germans appear unable to muster a sizeable counter-attack for some days to come. . . . Morale of all our troops, and particularly . . . commanders, is high. . . . I was very much impressed by the calm competence of . . . Bradley and by the aggressive attitude of his corps commanders. . . . Eisenhower and his Staff are cool and confident, carrying out an affair of incredible magnitude and complication with superlative efficiency." Ending his missive, he was uncharacteristically effusive: "I think we have these Huns at the top of the toboggan slide, and the full crash of the Russian offensive should put the skids under them. There will be hard fighting and the enemy will seize every opportunity for a skillful counter stroke, but I think he faces a grim prospect."[12]

"Vengeance weapons"

Churchill, Marshall, and his colleagues returned to London in the early morning hours of June 13. It was just after the first four of Hitler's newest "vengeance weapons," the pilotless V-1 "buzz bombs," began falling on London. A couple of nights later, during a V-I blitz of 200 such missiles, one dropped within a mile and a half of where the chiefs of staff were sleeping; the concussion knocked Arnold from his bed.[13] Only a few days later, Field Marshall Sir Alan Brooke would be faced with the impact of this new weapon. The Guards' Chapel in London was hit, killing 122 people, among them several of his colleagues as well as his best friend. With this new threat, beleaguered Londoners, many of whom had brought their children back from the safety of the country, had to scramble to return them. Difficult to shoot down, during that June until supplies of the weapon temporarily ran out, 500 of the 700 V-1s launched did their damage, killing more than 2,000 civilians.[14]

"Untrammeled and unforced"

As heartened as the Allied leaders were by their trip to Normandy, one aspect of the return to France continued to complicate: the role of General Charles-Andre-Marie-Joseph de Gaulle, who, as historian Ed Cray put it, "considered himself the de facto president of France."[15] As Roosevelt had declared many times, he did not want outsiders shoving a civil government onto the liberated French—the decision should rest with them. The president insisted to Marshall that he didn't hate de Gaulle, as newspapers articles sometimes claimed; in fact, he was "perfectly willing to have de Gaulle made president, or emperor, or king or anything else so long as the action comes in an untrammeled and unforced way from the French people themselves."[16] When Marshall arrived in London for his post–D-Day visit, he had heard plenty of complaints about the French general. De Gaulle had been offered the opportunity to make a short announcement about the invasion, along with kings and queens and grand duchesses, which would be broadcast to Europe on June 6. He found fault with the order of the messages—not only would he come after kings and queens, but after Eisenhower himself! He complained bitterly that it made him appear subordinate to the American general.[17] He finally made quite an inspirational speech, but while he mentioned Britain, not so the United States and not the authority of Eisenhower. Seemingly in retaliation for what he viewed as slights, de Gaulle allowed only 20 of the 180 bilingual officers who were to go ashore to assist in communication with the French, a hugely important role, to make the trip. When de Gaulle learned just before D-Day that the troops coming into France had been issued specially printed paper francs to use instead of pounds and dollars—this, as Pogue noted, "to avoid the harmful effect on France of the circulation of American and British money"—de Gaulle ordered French officials in the liberated areas to consider it counterfeit.[18]

De Gaulle's attitude brought on one of Marshall's displays of temper, as he admitted later. "I got hold of de Gaulle's staff officer and raised the devil." To another French representative he called the general's actions a "contemptible thing." When British Foreign Secretary Anthony Eden defended some of de Gaulle's actions, it infuriated Marshall, who called the French general's conduct "outrageous," exclaiming that "no Iowa farmers would fight to put up statues of de Gaulle in France." Marshall still had it on his mind years later when he told his biographer, Forrest Pogue, "We had trained French officers for civil affairs, and he [de Gaulle] canceled every damn thing. The first thing Bradley told me in Normandy was that he had messed up their arrangements. They had fixed things up well, and then, by God, de Gaulle had canceled it all."[19]

During one meeting with Churchill and Eden, when the foreign secretary wanted to grant full recognition to the French Committee of National Liberation as the provisional government of France, Marshall, who was not supposed to discuss the political ramifications of the dispute, laid into Eden, telling him that when the American press got hold of the story that de Gaulle had attacked invasion money, and that Frenchmen trained for the very purpose of helping our troops were being withheld, there would be a furor across the country that "would swamp the whole damn British Foreign Office." Eden was so indignant that, red-faced, he left the room.[20]

Despite the anger that Marshall felt toward de Gaulle, he recognized that for the sake of the invasion's continued success, which would include French forces that Eisenhower was counting on, some compromise needed to be struck, even if it included de Gaulle being given special recognition as the representative of Free France. In a conciliatory gesture on the part of Roosevelt in early June, he had invited de Gaulle's to come to Washington for an official visit; further, on June 14 Churchill gave his consent for the French leader, who had been forbidden to go to Normandy earlier for fear of the political ramifications, to cross the channel. In the liberated towns along the invasion zone his countrymen provided a noisy welcome, with tears, cheers, and demonstrations. Slightly tempering his audacious demands, de Gaulle agreed to visit the United States, arriving on July 6. Ironically, it was Marshall himself who during the visit acted as the principal intermediary in the expression of de Gaulle's views. The president, realizing that an accommodation needed to be made, did a flip-flop. He "rolled out the red carpet," recalled his son, Curtis Roosevelt, years later, and "couldn't have been nicer."[21] So it was that Roosevelt informed the press on July 11 that de Gaulle's committee would be "the dominant political authority of France until elections could be held"; nevertheless, added the president, Eisenhower as supreme commander still had the power to maintain peaceful relations within the military zones.

Forrest Pogue compared Marshall's reaction to the compromises struck regarding de Gaulle to how the chief of staff had viewed the so-called Darlan deal of 1942, which was solely in the light of its effect on Eisenhower's operation and American public opinion. As for the long-range political implications—that was for the president to decide.[22]

Anvil—"History will never forgive us if we lost precious time and lives"

While still in England, in meetings with the British chiefs, Marshall once more had to make the case for Anvil. The Tehran Conference decision for an invasion of southern France originally scheduled to coincide with Overlord was now still very much in debate. In the lead-up to D-Day it had been variously abandoned, agreed upon, and finally bounced into the summer for launch. Neither Marshall nor the other U.S. Joint Chiefs had ever given up their preference for this offensive, which they held would draw off Germans from the Normandy invasion sites and open up ports for the delivery of men and matériel to the continental battle. On the other hand, the British continued to argue that those resources should be used in Italy to expand the Italian campaign toward central Europe by pushing through the rugged Alps via Slovenia's Ljubljana Gap, and then northward to Austria. One British officer, Air Marshal Sir John Slessor, spoke of the prize that would derive from having "Anglo-American forces on the Danube before the war came to an end."[23] As they had argued at so many steps along the way, the British chiefs saw it as a logical extension of the hard-fought Italian campaigns using troops already in service there. Such an offensive, they claimed, would keep German troops bogged down in northern Italy and thus unavailable for action in France.

At the heart of the matter were the divergent views of the two Allies as to how the war should be fought, an ongoing vigorous argument that had been in full play since Marshall's first meeting with Churchill and his staff in the December 1941. The British, an island nation whose navy was supreme, continued to favor an opportunistic peripheral approach; that is, intervention through military operations in the smaller beleaguered nations surrounding the threatening power, weakening the enemy rather than facing its full force head-on. Such a strategy drew off the aggressor's resources, both men and matériel, they argued, thus damaging its retaliatory potential. Only after such extensive damage would the British attempt a direct killing thrust. However, the energetic and young Americans, rich in resources and untouched by centuries-old continental struggles for a balance of power, saw the quick and direct destruction of the enemy's army as the best method. As historian Maurice Matloff noted, the reasoning of the United States regarding European hostilities "was to hold off as long as possible, enter only long enough to give the bully who started it a sound thrashing, get the boys home, and then try to remain as uninvolved as before."[24]

Despite the Allied elation over the initial successes of Overlord, this Anvil versus the Italian "push beyond the Po River" controversy continued in spirited debate during the wrap-up of the London meetings. To get the opinions of the military leaders in the Italian Theater regarding this matter, Marshall flew there on June 17. He would meet with the Mediterranean Theater commander, Field Marshal Sir Henry Maitland "Jumbo" Wilson; Field Marshal Sir Harold Alexander, who commanded the Allied forces in Italy; and General Mark Clark, head of the Fifth Army. Soon after Marshall's arrival, Clark gave him a tour of the area. They flew 100 miles northeast of Rome, where the chief of staff observed a division pursuing German troops toward Pisa, sometimes within enemy range. One reporter wrote that "under sporadic Nazi artillery fire," the windshield of Marshall's jeep "was lowered to avoid reflecting the sun, which would have attracted the attention of the enemy."[25] As they toured the sites, Clark tried to convince Marshall that a continued drive from Italy northeast toward the Balkans would be better than Anvil, and he worried about what would happen on this battlefront if the American-British-French team was broken up and sent to southern France. Marshall countered, emphasizing to Clark how badly Eisenhower needed to open up ports in the Toulon-Marseille region to service more troops and supplies in France.

In his meetings with Field Marshal Wilson and his Mediterranean Theater staff, Marshall once again stressed Anvil over an expansion of the Italian thrust northeast. In response to Wilson's misgivings about the southern France operation, Marshall respectfully explained that he had 30 or 40 divisions still in the United States that couldn't be brought to France to aid in the invasion because there were not adequate ports in northwest France (Normandy on the Cotentin Peninsula) to accommodate them. Wilson listened to the American's arguments, especially when Marshall pointed out that the French, who would compose a good bit of the Anvil force, would not have the slightest interest in pushing northeastward from Italy toward the Adriatic, since they very much wanted to get back to the continent to defend their homeland. Wilson later admitted: "Marshall, I must say, impressed me with the way he put his case, and I said, 'Well, General, after what you said, I agree. We will go for the landing on the south of France at the earliest possible date that we can do it.'"[26]

Perhaps Wilson had been swayed by Marshall's arguments, but Field Marshal Alexander was unconvinced. In deference to both Alexander and the view that he knew Churchill held, in his report back to the British chiefs Wilson once more made the argument for a continued offensive in Italy. He pointed out that even if there were an Anvil, it couldn't come until mid-August without compromising the current Allied push against the Italian Pisa-Rimini Line where the Germans held defensive positions.

Back in London, Churchill continued to stubbornly push Alexander's plan for an advance on Vienna. Beneath that highest echelon of power, some of the military chiefs, while continuing to support Churchill, had some nagging misgivings—for example, Field Marshal Sir Alan Brooke. He pointed out to Churchill that at best such an offensive to the east couldn't start until September, and warned that "we would [be] embarking on a campaign through the Alps in winter." Brooke would later say, "It was hard to make him [Churchill] realize that, if we took the season of the year and the topography of the country in legion against us, we should have three enemies instead of one."[27] Brooke and his assistant, Major General Sir John Kennedy, argued that Alexander needed to "finish off Field Marshal Albert Kesselring's forces south of the Alps, after which they would send their surplus forces either to Anvil or around to the Channel coast to reinforce Eisenhower." Churchill, though, continued to support a "drive to Vienna by way of the Julian Alps as a thrust of a dagger 'under the armpit.'" When Marshall sent a directive to Wilson that Anvil be launched by August 1, Churchill drafted a long memorandum once again in favor of the Vienna operation. In response, Kennedy wrote to Brooke, "This last, I think, should be kept to ourselves for the moment." Brooke agreed, telling Kennedy that "we had led the Americans by the nose from Casablanca to Florence, and it would not be easy to put this policy on top of all that."[28]

The American position for Anvil was strengthened when on July 19 a channel storm destroyed one of the two allied artificial harbors—the British Mulberry—at Omaha Beach. Hundreds of vessels were destroyed, and nothing could be landed for four days. Eisenhower pressed again for the launch of Anvil, preferably at least by mid-August. Nevertheless, the British continued to resist, arguing that, after all, as the Normandy invasion advanced, Allied forces would be taking over ports in the north that would serve the needs of landing men and matériel for the continued thrust into the heartland of Europe. After meeting with Churchill, the British chiefs on June 21 drafted a telegram to Marshall, who was by then back in the United States via Italy. They persisted in justifying military action into northern Italy toward the Balkans as a threat to the Germans, who would, they emphasized, need to keep troops there, along with reinforcements, to counter such an offensive. When the British message reached Washington, calling the order for the withdrawal of troops for Anvil from the Italian theater "unacceptable," the reply from Marshall and the joint chiefs was sharp and in kind: "British proposal to abandon Anvil and commit everything to Italy is unacceptable."[29] From his headquarters outside of London, Eisenhower continued to fully back the American chiefs. Gone was the ambivalence the supreme commander had expressed during the first Anvil furor that previous March: "France is the decisive theater," he insisted, adding that "the resources of the United States will not allow us to maintain two major theaters in the European War, each with decisive missions."[30] To reinforce the solidarity of not only Eisenhower but also the Joint Chiefs, Marshall had his staff prepare a memorandum for Roosevelt outlining all of the arguments for Anvil. He wanted the president fully informed.

On June 28, Churchill made one more attempt to scuttle Anvil, attaching a 12-page addition to his cable message to the president in which he outlined the reasons Anvil should be abandoned. Describing the proposed landings in the Toulon-Marseilles area of southern France as "bleak and sterile," and calling the distances from those sites up the Rhone Valley too far from the main effort in the north, he ended by saying, "Let us not wreck one great campaign for the sake of winning another. Both can be won." Roosevelt's 13-paragraph response, drafted by the joint chiefs, urged that the Combined Chiefs of Staff directive authorizing Anvil be issued immediately.[31] Refuting Churchill's arguments one by one, the president concluded, seemingly rather gently: "At Tehran we agreed upon a plan. That plan has done well up till now. . . . History would never forgive us if precious lives and time are lost as a result of indecision and debate. My dear friend, I beg you to let us continue my plan. . . . Finally, in addition to the military, there are political conditions here which must be considered. I would never survive even a minor setback in Normandy if it were known that substantial troops were diverted to the Balkans."[32] Churchill's troubled reply came on July 1. "We are deeply grieved by your telegram," he began:

> If you still press upon us the directive of your Chiefs of Staff to withdraw so many of your forces from the Italian campaign and leave all our hopes there dashed to the ground, His Majesty's Government, on advice of their Chiefs of Staff, must enter a solemn protest. . . . It is with the greatest sorrow that I write to you in this sense. But I am sure that if we could have met, as I so frequently proposed, we should have reached a happy agreement.[33]

Marshall understood the implications of that last sentence perfectly. It was just that circumstance—Churchill's tendency and desire to sway the president when he met with him in person—that had caused the chief of staff to steer Roosevelt away from conferences between December 1943 and September 1944 when these crucial Normandy-Anvil decisions were being so hotly debated. The battle conceded, by July 4 Brooke wrote "cordial greetings for Independence Day" from the British staff, and spoke of the two nations' "complete understanding and mutual trust." Although Churchill was bitter about the outcome of the Anvil debate—"we hope you realize that we have been ill-treated and [are] furious," he would write the Joint Chiefs on the 6th—conciliation was required. By then it seemed clear that Roosevelt and Marshall were in the political and military driving seats.[34] It would remain that way through the end of the war. On July 2 the Combined Chiefs of Staff received the order: Anvil would be launched on

August 15 as a "three-division assault." Delivering extra power to Overlord had carried the day and, as historian Maurice Matloff noted, "sounded the knell for any ambitious plans in south east Europe."[35]

The fear of U.S military planners for attritional-peripheral warfare during this period had everything to do with their worries over the ultimate costs in men, money, and time. This apprehension was heightened by their need to get on with the war against Japan.[36] The Joint Chiefs could not imagine Americans tolerating a long period of maximum mobilization. Nevertheless, while the U.S. military chiefs held fast to their belief in concentration, according to Matloff, it would be inaccurate to think they remained opposed to all Mediterranean operations. After all, the Americans had agreed to the invasion of North Africa; they had supported the Sicily Operation, the push north as far as Rome, and, however reluctantly, the Anzio landings. Matloff noted that "as the debate over the southern France operation shows, a good part of their labors in 1943 and 1944 was actually spent in reconciling Mediterranean operations with the cross-Channel operation."[37] Churchill would always make the case for the value of these Mediterranean efforts to the later success of Overlord: "The principal task of our armies had been to draw off and contain the greatest possible number of Germans. This had been admirably fulfilled."[38]

A Personal Pilgrimage

Although during his trip to Italy, Marshall devoted a great deal of time to the question of Anvil, his trip also included a deeply personal mission. He wanted to visit Allen's grave at the Anzio beachhead. He went through the cemetery where the last of 7,000 interments were being made and located the grave of his stepson not far from the main pathway. Colonel Tristram Brown, Allen's uncle, a public relations officer in that theater, stood quietly with him for a few minutes at the site. As if to punctuate the losses inherent in war, Marshall returned to the beachhead where 20 ambulances of wounded soldiers were lined up. By that time, he had been joined by General "Hap" Arnold, and the two of them went from vehicle to vehicle speaking quietly to the patients.[39]

Marshall wanted to know more about what had happened to Allen, so, as he described in a June 23 letter to Allen's widow, Madge, he "embarked again and flew north, going by Velletri and the ground over which Allen had fought." He noted that the pilot kept the plane at about 300 feet so he could get a good view of the terrain. With the weather threatening, Marshall could go no further over the battle site, so instead he went to General Clark's headquarters. Clark had brought up Lieutenant Druckenmiller, a young man from Nazareth, Pennsylvania, who had commanded one of the platoons in Allen's company, along with Allen's tank driver and gunner. They all gave the bereaved stepfather a detailed account of what had happened. Druckenmiller had Allen's map. Marshall described it to Madge as "a much rumpled paper with the various lines and objectives noted in crayon," which the young man used to recount the action. With clear weather the next morning, Marshall was driven to the Alban Hills and from there boarded a plane to fly over and identify the scene of Allen's last moments. Having shared the details of his trip with Allen's widow, he explained matter-of-factly that he had returned to his starting point that night to meet with "the various commanders, Air, Ground, and Naval," a sure reference to those difficult contentious Anvil meetings. The day before, after the trip to Clark's headquarters, he had been flown back to Rome, where he stayed in the Grand Hotel. He told Madge, "I see by the papers here that I am being criticized because they turned on the hot water in honor of my arrival. Also they apparently moved one of two newspaper men out of their rooms to accommodate our party, which did not please."[40]

Marshall tours the Fifth Army front with
Lieutenant General Mark Clark, June 18, 1944.

U.S. National Archives RG208-UN-110

Moving Inland—Hedgerow Country

By mid-June, with the Normandy beachhead established, U.S. troops began to move out into the French countryside. Three weeks after the landings, they had taken the Cotentin port of Cherbourg, which, though heavily damaged by the Germans to prevent its use, would soon prove important to supplying the troops as they fanned out onto the continent. By late June the furthest point of penetration was 20 miles from the beach. Nevertheless, German forces under Field Marshal Gerd von Rundstedt defended furiously, taking full advantage of the fact that his troops were familiar with how to operate in France's *le bocage,* hedgerow country. Indeed, for many centuries French farmers had built around every pasture a high bank of dirt, now thick with roots, scrubs, and trees, to keep cattle in and to shield crops from the channel's ocean winds. The Germans had established themselves in these fields, turning each into a small citadel.[41] They were adept at establishing defensive positions within these structures, and thus impeded the coordination and momentum of the American's offensive operations. The Allied military, although aware of the area's topography, had focused more on the successful landings and had not given serious enough thought to this terrain. While at a tactical level the U.S. army units found innovative solutions that eventually overcame the difficulties, including outfitting tanks with saw-toothed metal scoops, this barrier slowed their advance inland and upset preordained timetables.[42]

Breakout

Despite the challenges of hedgerows and the Germans' dogged determination, by the end of June almost a million men were on shore in Normandy, as well as 586,000 tons of supplies and 177,000 vehicles.[43] In late July, British and Canadian troops under General Montgomery launched a final all-out assault to capture the historic city of Caen on the western edge of the Allied bridgehead, a goal set but not fully realized in the early days of the landings. Caen was crucial to the Allies since it opened the way for advancement south out of Normandy and into the excellent tank country of the Falaise Plain.[44] Because Caen was an important road and rail center that Hitler also saw as vital, he ordered it defended to the last man. In the brutal fight that followed, the British and Canadian forces suffered heavy casualties, but the city was finally liberated. The fierce air, ground, and tank battles in that region tied down and distracted German units on the western side of the Allied offensive line, allowing General Bradley's troops to position themselves for the execution of Operation Cobra, a plan "to blow a hole in the German line for ground troops to exploit," as historian Rick

Atkinson described it. It would create a breach, he said, that would allow Allied troops to break out of "a narrow bridgehead that was roughly fifty miles by twenty miles deep," and thereby transform "a war of attrition into a war of movement."[45]

The launch of Cobra on July 25 was preceded by one of the most devastating carpet-bombing operations of the war. According to Atkinson, "Some 1,500 B-17s and B-24s dropped more than 3,000 tons of bombs . . . with almost another 1,000 tons of bombs and napalm dropped by medium bombers." It had the effect of unhinging the enemy's defenses. One German panzer commander described it well: "The bomb carpets rolled toward us, most of them passing only a few yards away, bringing a pall of dust, with fountains of earth spewing high in the air."[46] With German command posts in ruins, tanks overturned, communications disrupted, and a thousand enemy soldiers killed, the way was made clear for 100,000 American troops to pour through a debris-littered gap not five miles wide.[47] Despite a slow entry caused by the craters and wreckage left by the intensive bombing, those units were soon turning the Germans' left flank, gaining control of Avranches at the very base of the Cotentin Peninsula, and thereby opening the way to Brittany and its important ports.

Patton in Action Again

Since early January 1944, General George Patton knew that he would lead the Third Army onto the continent. While still maintaining his role as head of the "phantom" army, he also began preparing the Third for what he considered a stunning opportunity to join the fight. On July 6 he crossed the channel into France with the vanguard of Third Army headquarters. Despite the fact that the Allies had been in Normandy for a month, the Germans apparently still believed that Patton's legions would soon launch the primary invasion against the coast of the Pas de Calais, and thus they (the Germans) had kept a large portion of their armored forces in that area, awaiting the "real" attack. To keep that deception alive, Patton arrived in France under the tightest security and in total secrecy.[48]

On August 1, a week after Bradley's First Army had gone into the breach, he was at last in action. With great speed his troops swung southwest toward Brittany, soon surrounding the Germans in the fortified ports of Saint Malo, Lorient, Saint Nazaire, and Brest along the western coast. Facing encirclement, the main force of the German army then withdrew to the east toward the Seine, with the spearheads of Patton's Third Army giving chase. General Bradley then ordered Patton to take his men in a wide encircling maneuver toward the town of Argentan, not far from Falaise. The goal was to link up with Montgomery's Seventh Army, which was attempting to close a 15-mile-wide German pocket and thus hinder that army's exodus. The British and Canadian troops had failed to seal the breach, allowing thousands of the enemy to escape.

Eisenhower would later complain about Montgomery's slowness in reaching the goals set on this eastern edge of the Normandy bridgehead: "He had to get Falaise instantly because the high ground on the South was good for landing grounds. But he couldn't take them. He never really did get them until we had broken out on the western flank and surrounded them."[49] It would be Lieutenant General Courtney Hodges' First Army that would finally close that gap near Falaise, suffering 19,000 casualties in the process.[50] Nevertheless, as General Bradley would later write, "70,000 demoralized Germans were killed or captured in that [the Argentan-Falaise] pocket. . . . The bulk of 19 German divisions had been chewed up within the pocket; only their mobile remnants escaped, and they slipped through in broken pieces." Eisenhower described the carnage: "Forty-eight hours after the closing of the gap I was conducted through it on foot, to encounter scenes that could be described only by Dante. It was literally possible to walk for hundreds of yards at a time, stepping on nothing but dead and decaying flesh."[51] Meanwhile, Bradley split the Third Army in two, with only Patton's VIII Corps remaining in Brittany to tighten port access at Brest and Saint Malo. The rest, with Patton in the lead, continued their quick drive toward the Seine.[52] As Rick Atkinson noted, "The stalemate anxieties of mid-July would soon vanish in a hell-for-leather pursuit of a beaten enemy across France."[53]

Anvil/Dragoon—At Last

On August 1, Operation Anvil, the long-disputed plan for the invasion of the southern French coast, for security reasons, was renamed Dragoon. Churchill considered the change appropriate, since, as he said, "I was dragooned into it."[54] Its launch date, however, remained the same as had finally been agreed upon in early July: August 15. As debarkation day approached, the operation's commander, Lieutenant General Jacob L. Devers, was assembling a task force under Lieutenant General Alexander Patch, along with a contingent of French forces under General Jean de Lattre de Tassigny, at the crowded port of Naples. However, Churchill had by no means given up his fight against the operation. During a British Chiefs of Staff meeting on August 4, there was some dialogue about transferring Dragoon from the south to the Brittany coast, which Churchill said Eisenhower had already endorsed to Marshall. The chiefs quickly telegraphed Washington, backing the plan. The next day, though, on a stop at Eisenhower's headquarters, when the topic came up, Eisenhower squelched it immediately, saying that he had never sent such a message to the chiefs.[55] Remembering Marshall's not so subtle hint of "localitis" when the fight for Anvil had been vociferously debated that previous spring, Eisenhower immediately cabled the chief of staff, reassuring him that "I will not, repeat will not, under any conditions agree at this moment to a cancellation of Dragoon."[56] Still undeterred, on the 7th, Winston Churchill visited General Omar Bradley's headquarters, and while marveling at all that had been accomplished since the landings, he once more raised the possibility that Dragoon could be abandoned. Through a clenched jaw he grumbled, "Why break down the back door when the front door has already been opened by your magnificent Americans?"[57]

On the same day, with Dragoon only a week away, when Churchill tried to convince Eisenhower once more to transfer the operation elsewhere, he got the same response—Dragoon would be launched as planned. Frustrated, the prime minister raged to Eisenhower that the United States was acting like "a big, strong and dominating partner" instead of one that was trying to understand the British viewpoint on the Italian campaign. Sensing defeat, in a histrionic appeal, the prime minister told Eisenhower that he might have to go to the king and "lay down the mantle of high office."[58] In the meanwhile, Churchill had made a last-ditch appeal to the president via a long cable. There was no relation between southern France and the Normandy operations, he argued; besides, the Allies had taken Brittany, why not at least shift the invasion to the region that was already under Allied control? The president, who was on his way to Hawaii to confer with MacArthur and Nimitz, sent his reply, drafted by Marshall. The message once more: the invasion would proceed as planned. Still unsatisfied, Churchill argued to his own staff until finally the Mediterranean commander, General Maitland "Jumbo" Wilson, told him that no changes were possible, since forward units of Dragoon's invasion force had already sailed.[59] Field Marshall Sir Alan Brooke had demonstrated his understanding of the situation in a letter to Wilson that early August: The Americans "now feel that they possess the major forces at sea, on land and in the air," and with "all the vast financial and industrial advantages which they had enjoyed from the start," they were in a far stronger position. "In addition they now look upon themselves no longer as the apprentices at war, but on the contrary as full blown professionals. As a result of all this they are determined to have an ever increasing share in the running of the war in all its aspects."[60]

Rolling Up the Rhone Valley

On that morning of August 15, a fleet of 1,500 ships, including nine aircraft carriers, launched the invasion. It all went much more rapidly than had been predicted, with casualties light. Aided by French guerrillas (Maquis), the American Seventh Army, 77,000 strong, moved up the Rhone Valley northward toward the Seine.[61] By August 28 the sought-after ports of Toulon and Marseilles were under Allied control. Not only did the invasion provide a fast route into the French interior, but as the Allied army moved east toward Germany, these undamaged ports would prove much more accessible for the support of additional supplies and troops than the besieged and badly damaged Brittany harbors to the north. For the next four months Marseilles would unload more tonnage than any other Allied port.[62] Further, the landings brought French troops back onto their native soil and also opened up new air bases for eventual attacks on Germany. After only two weeks, on September 2, Dragoon units, having covered 400 air miles up the Rhone Valley, made contact with Patton's Third Army to the north. With 57,000 German prisoners taken, Operation Dragoon had delivered heavy losses on the Germans' 11-division Army Group B and had hastened the enemy's evacuation of France south of the Loire River.[63]

The Judgment

Only two days before Dragoon launched, Churchill's chief of staff, Lieutenant General Hastings Ismay, warned his colleagues that the prime minister "was just raving last night and absolutely unbalanced. He cannot get over having not had his own way over Anvil [Dragoon]."[64] Nevertheless, with the matter irrevocably settled, on D-Day Churchill was on board a ship watching the landings from afar. Seemingly gracious, he wrote Eisenhower, "All I have seen there makes me admire the perfect precision with which the landing was arranged and [the] intimate collaboration of British-American forces and organizations." Anxious for harmony, and expressing Marshall's views, the supreme commander replied, "I am delighted to note in your last telegram to me that you have personally and legally adopted the Dragoon. I am sure that he will grow fat and prosperous under your watchfulness.[65]

Yet, even after the war Churchill continued to view the invasion of southern France that August as a disastrous mistake. Marshall absolutely disagreed, calling Churchill's proposed strategy to extend the Italian campaign rather than launching the southern France invasion unrealistic. With some vehemence, he told biographer Forrest Pogue in 1956, "I don't agree with the prime minister on the Anvil [Dragoon] question at all. . . . He was intent on one thing and he swayed all his arguments to justify that one thing." Further, he said, "The 'soft underbelly' [of northern Italy] had chrome steel baseboards. Mountainous country. No question in my mind that the west was the place to hit. If we had accepted the Balkan thing, it would have scattered our shots. My idea was that we should defeat the German army. There was the matter of feasibility involved. Longer hauls, more shipping, [The] American public would not favor the Balkans."[66]

"Stripped and mutilated"

Churchill laid out his position in his postwar history of World War II. Referring to General Alexander's forces in Italy as having been "stripped and mutilated" because of Anvil, he bemoaned the lost potential of a thrust north and west toward the Apennines. He argued that the army's landing on the southern coast "at such a painful cost" had arrived too late "to help Eisenhower's main struggle in the north." Speaking of Alexander's troops, he mourned, "Here was this splendid army, equivalent to twenty-five divisions, reduced till it was just not strong enough to produce decisive results against the immense power of the [German] defensive. A very little more, half of what had been taken from us, and we could have broken into the valley of the Po, with all the gleaming possibilities and prizes which lay open toward Vienna. As it was, our forces, about a million strong, could play a mere secondary part in any commanding strategic conception." And then he added, "In these great matters failing to gain one's way is no escape from the responsibility for an inferior solution."[67]

Some have argued that Churchill's passion for the Italian campaign came from his recognition as early as 1943 that the Russians were gaining a foothold in central Europe, and that was his major concern. According to Pogue, while toward the end of the European war the threat of the Soviets to the postwar power arrangement did loom large for the prime minister, the theory that it drove Churchill's anti-Anvil arguments doesn't stand up to the facts. Pogue acknowledged that Churchill was "disquieted as he saw a badly mauled and heavily scarred Red Army recover magnificently for a drive on Budapest and Warsaw and threaten Vienna," and that indeed the prime minister dreaded the coming of the Red Army to the West. Pogue even noted that Lord Moran, Churchill's physician, recorded that one day in the summer of 1944 the prime minister had exclaimed to him, "Good God, can't you see that the Russians are spreading across Europe like a tide; they have invaded Poland, and there is nothing to prevent them marching into Turkey and Greece."[68]

THE EXPANSION OF THE NORMANDY BRIDGEHEAD

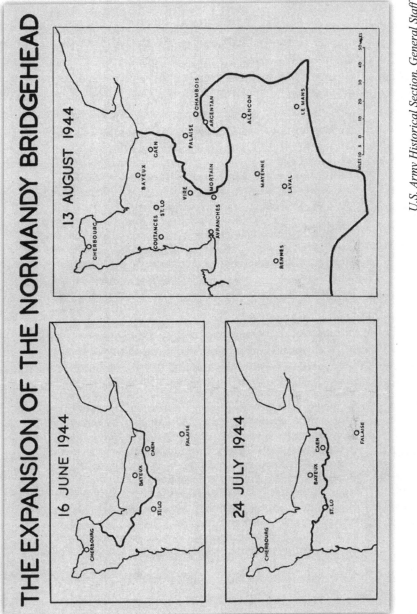

U.S. Army Historical Section, General Staff
www.ibiblio.org/hyperwar

Nevertheless, said Pogue, this was never the argument that Churchill made to Marshall in his objections to Anvil: "His main interest seemed to be ensuring that Alexander had his chance to score a major victory." Pogue also points out that John Ehrman, the official British historian of this period, although seemingly in support of Churchill's strategic point of view, conceded that Churchill did not use fear of the Russians as the rationale for his support of the Italian enlargement over Anvil. Finally, Pogue wrote, given the issues of terrain and weather, there is considerable doubt as to whether a drive to Germany by way of Trieste, the Ljubljana Gap, and Austria would have arrived any sooner than Eisenhower's, achieved by pushing American and British forces to the east out of France to cross the Rhine.[69]

"Tell Ike to get over there"

By mid-August tremendous progress had been made on the continent: the Normandy breakout had been successful, and the Germans were retreating across France in the wake of the Allied effort. Marshall might have taken a good bit of satisfaction over the military operations, but such satisfaction was tamped down by the ongoing disagreements with Churchill, Brooke, and the British staff. Marshall was proud of how Eisenhower had been able to overcome inter-Allied conflicts to forge a system of unified command that he (Marshall) had promoted since the earliest days of the war.[70] Nevertheless, it was bothering him that the British were receiving all the credit for victories won by American generals and their valiant troops, who in the first six weeks of the fighting were dying at more than twice the rate of their British counterparts. Marshall was particularly upset by the headlines he saw in the press regarding Normandy: "Montgomery's Troops Drive on Cherbourg," or "Montgomery's Forces Attack St. Lo." It seemed as if every pronouncement of the war started with the name of this British general. Further, it irked him to read a London newspaper story that sang the praises of Montgomery's brilliance while describing Eisenhower as a distant and uninvolved commander. The article made its way to the *Washington Times Herald*, an anti-Roosevelt paper, which reported: "It is generally recognized in congressional circles and common gossip in military circles that General Eisenhower is merely a figurehead and the actual command of the invasion is in the hands of the British General Staff and the British dominate the American War Department and Army."[71] This story broke at a time when the casualty lists were coming in showing that out of 21,000 dead in the first six weeks of the campaign, 14,000 were American.[72] Further, an accompanying story saying that Bradley would be promoted to equal rank with Montgomery, implying that Bradley's promotion was intended to undermine Montgomery's control over ground forces, added fuel to the flame. While it was true that for months prior to the launch of Overlord it had been decided that once Normandy was secure, Eisenhower would take command of *all* Allied ground troops, Bradley would take charge of American forces, and Montgomery would lead the British and Canadian forces, that had not yet officially happened. To smother a potential firestorm in England, Eisenhower issued a statement confirming that Montgomery would remain ground commander of Allied forces, which for the moment was true. He hoped his account would temper some of the incessant British-American criticism over who controlled what.[73]

Marshall was not happy with Eisenhower's announcement, and told him so in a top secret cable on August 17, his irritation hardly masked: "The recent statement from your headquarters that Montgomery continues in command of all ground forces has produced a severe reaction in the *New York Times* and many other papers and I feel is to be deplored." Not even addressing the "whys" of the confusion about the upcoming change in command, he told Eisenhower, "The Secretary [of War] and I and apparently all Americans are strongly of the opinion that the time has come for you to assume direct exercise of command of the American contingent." He closed the letter with, "The astonishing success of the campaign up to the present moment has evoked emphatic expressions of confidence in you and in Bradley. The late announcement [meaning Eisenhower's] that I have just referred to has cast a damper on the public enthusiasm."[74] President Roosevelt, who had an election coming up, had told Marshall, "Tell Ike to get over there," and that is exactly what Eisenhower did.[75]

General Eisenhower, on August 30, held a press conference in London and announced that he was assuming command of all Allied forces in Europe. He explained that because of Montgomery's experience and seniority, he had initially put Montgomery in tactical control of the Normandy invasion until a successful bridgehead had been established. Now, with the Cotentin Peninsula and Brittany in Allied hands, a change was coming. Despite the fact that both American and some British military leaders had criticized Montgomery for being too cautious, moving too slowly in the taking of Caen, Eisenhower called him one of the great soldiers of "this or any other war," and "a personal friend."[76] Nevertheless, once the word was out in Britain that this command shift was on its way, London newspapers had raised protests about Montgomery's "demotion." Apparently Winston Churchill saw it that way as well. The prime minister announced that effective September 1,

Montgomery, whose name he declared was a "household word" in England, would have the rank of field marshal, making his status higher than all other high-ranking American officers, even Eisenhower and Marshall.

Montgomery was convinced that the whole command adjustment was political, intended to help Roosevelt in the election. Actually, it was the Pentagon that saw the necessity for speeding up what had already been agreed upon. Marshall did have some concerns about Montgomery's fighting spirit, as did Bradley, Patton, and others. Further, now that the U.S. troops battling on the continent outnumbered the British, morale would probably suffer if these American troops continued under British command.[77] Although Eisenhower had pronounced in his London press conference that the public "should not have the slightest impression that any real fears need to be entertained concerning the soundness of the Anglo-American military partnership in Europe," in fact, things had changed. Historian Mark Perry noted that had Marshall been present for the speech, he would have been pleased. The Germans were in retreat, and his great vision had been realized. And despite Montgomery's rank, as Perry opined, "The British, too, had been tamed, if only through the realization that, in any partnership, there must be a senior partner. The Americans now filled that role. Eisenhower was running the war."[78]

Loss: Personal Friends

The war had come close on a personal level for Marshall that summer of 1944, beginning with Allen's death in Italy. Now, within two weeks of each other, two close friends were gone, one from a heart attack, the other by friendly fire. In mid-July he received word that Brigadier General Theodore Roosevelt Jr. had died of a heart attack. Marshall had known and admired him since World War I, when, although severely wounded in the leg, he had refused to leave the battle lines. Roosevelt led the Fourth Division on D-Day at Utah beach, rallying his men, as Marshall told his widow, "with nothing but a walking stick."[79] On July 25, 1944, as General Bradley authorized carpet bombing of the German front in the lead-up to Cobra, the pilots, whose targets came close to the American front, "short-dropped" their payloads, although the lines had been pulled back more than a mile after a misjudged bombing the day before.[80] As a result, 111 soldiers were felled by "friendly fire," among them Lieutenant General Lesley J. McNair. He had been Marshall's trusted and revered ground training chief, and at the time of his death was Patton's replacement as head of the "phantom" U.S. Army Group. McNair was in Normandy to observe the effectiveness of his training methods on front-line troops, and to watch the buildup for the coming breakout attack.[81] Marshall wrote to the widow, telling her: "There is nothing I can say at this time which will be of much comfort to you but I want you to feel that in his death the Army has lost a great leader who will not be forgotten. I pray that you find the faith and courage to bear your sorrow."[82] The death of McNair had been doubly tragic, since just two days after the general's death, the McNairs' young son died fighting the Japanese on Guam.[83] Despite his "desk job" in Washington, the cost of war in human lives was always on Marshall's mind.

Lieutenant General McNair (in foreground) sits
with Major General Omar Bradley during maneuvers in Louisiana, 1942.
U.S. Army Signal Corps, LC-USW33-000421-ZC

Back Home—Mountain Retreats and Global War

During August 1944, Marshall's duties ran the gamut, as suggested by his correspondence. Early in the month, he sought to arbitrate a possible dispute concerning command authority between Generalissimo Chiang Kai-shek and General Joseph Stilwell in the China-Burma-India Theater; on the 15th, he informed Eisenhower that he would be recommending that General Patton receive a promotion, and suggested that the latter be warned not to "smirch a magnificent job by any comments of any kind whatsoever," [and] "to keep out of the camera lens as much as possible." The next day Marshall's memorandum to the president provided a casualty report for the Second Infantry Division, which had landed in Normandy on June 7. Still another *Top Secret* message responded positively to Eisenhower's plan against Calais using airborne support, a move that Marshall believed would destroy launch sites of the V-1 rockets. The war department pouch arrived daily laden with requests demanding his attention. Nevertheless, remarkably, Marshall continued to keep up personal correspondence. On August 17, he answered a letter from his sister, Marie Singer, who was vacationing at a mountain retreat and who had complained of not having the time to write due to golf, country drives, and eating. Marshall was apparently amused at her listing of the activities burdening her time, telling her drily, "Since I write to you and at considerably greater length than you write to me, I take it that Pike Run compares very favorably with the job of global warfare."[84]

"To Paris—yes?"

In late August, as the Allies pressed German forces toward the Rhine, the question of what would happen to Paris was on the minds of the high command. In keeping with Marshall's view, and those of the U.S. Joint Chiefs of Staff, the goal was to destroy the German army. Although sentimentally and politically the liberation of Paris would seem important, for the American planners it was a subsidiary operation and would only serve to draw off supplies and slow the advance toward the German border.[85] The "City of Light" had been occupied since the beginning of the war, and the Allies worried that with liberation would come the burden of feeding 4 million Parisians, a demand that would require an initial 4,000 tons a day and dent the supply demands for armies already stretched thin. General Omar Bradley, in charge of American ground troops, believed that if he could rush on toward the German Siegfried Line with tonnage that might otherwise go to the Parisians, the city would be compensated for its additional weeks of occupation by a shortened war.[86]

Entering that city triumphantly, though, was very tempting to the French Forces of the Interior (F.F.I.) under General Pierre Koenig. The Frenchman had clear orders from Eisenhower that "no armed movements were to go off in Paris or anywhere else" until he gave the command.[87] Nevertheless, without the supreme commander's knowledge, de Gaulle ordered Koenig to seize the capital as soon as he could and told the French armored division commander, Major General Jacque Leclerc, who was also under Eisenhower, to ignore headquarters orders and to enter Paris. When Leclerc's commanding officer,

General Leonard T. Gerow, saw the Frenchman moving his reconnaissance tanks to the east from their position around the town of Argenten, he asked him, "And just where the hell do you think you're going?" "To Paris—yes?" came the reply. Gerow immediately turned him back.[88]

Nevertheless, soon Eisenhower, in discussion with Bradley and Gerow, faced reality. The city's citizens, under occupation for four years, and fully aware that the Allies were virtually at their gates, were ready to explode. Paris police had already gone on strike, and on August 19, 3,000 armed gendarmes had seized police headquarters in the city center. Resistance fighters were emboldened everywhere on the streets. As conditions deteriorated, the German commander, General Dietrich von Choltitz, was ordered by Hitler to destroy the city, including the demolition of its more than 70 bridges. If Paris was to fall into the hands of the enemy, the Fuhrer ordered, it should be "a field of ruins."[89] Although Choltitz did not want to decimate this historic capital, he would not surrender, he said, to an *irregular* army of resistance fighters.

Recognizing the dangers of the city in chaos, Eisenhower permitted Leclerc's Second Armored Division, with the French Tricolor proudly affixed to their Shermans, to enter the city first. The Fourth Infantry Division followed behind.[90] On August 25, Leclerc was at the headquarters of the German commander. He spoke softly to an officer nearby, saying, "Maintenant, ça y est" (Now, here it is), and stepped forward to receive Choltitz's surrender.[91] The city was free. The next day de Gaulle entered his beloved Paris, marching down the Champs-Elysees amid shouts of "Vive le France, Vive de Gaulle!" General Patton was there as well, sending Eisenhower a message at the end of the day to announce that "Today I spat in the Seine."[92]

One day later, on the 26th, both Bradley and Eisenhower were in Paris, gratified to see the French tricolor filling the Arc de Triomphe from its highest point to the street. When they left their car to salute France's unknown soldier, entombed at the site, they were mobbed by the jubilant crowd. Making a run back to the car, as MPs frantically tried to clear a path, Eisenhower was nabbed by a huge Frenchman, who, as Bradley described it, "slathered him on both cheeks." Bradley fared better, getting a lipstick smear of a kiss on his cheek from a "handsome young lady," with others in pursuit.[93] To impress the French people with the strength of the Allied forces, and thus allay their fears of a reoccupation of their city, Eisenhower allowed a division of troops to march through Paris seemingly on parade; in fact, it was also a tactical movement straight through the city and east toward the German border. The realities of the hardships to come put on hold for the moment, celebrations continued for days. There is no doubt that an important psychological victory had been achieved, but it required plenty of fuel and troops, delaying the thrust toward the German defensive West Wall (the Siegfried Line) and the Rhine. General Bradley would later say, "We needed just two more weeks of gasoline [to reach the Rhine]. . . . Those were my thoughts about Paris. I didn't want to lose those two weeks there, and perhaps we did."[94]

At the Arc de Triomphe; from left to right, Generals Omar Bradley, Dwight Eisenhower, and Pierre Koenig stand with British Air Chief Marshal Sir Arthur Tedder.

Dwight D. Eisenhower Archives 68592

A Weekend in Leesburg

These summer days at the Pentagon were grueling for Marshall. Even when the news from Europe and the Pacific was encouraging, the demands of overseeing a global war were never ending. When he could possibly manage it, he joined Katherine at their weekend getaway home, Dodona Manor in Leesburg, a place she would later describe as a great wartime comfort to them. Despite the war, each summer since 1941, Marshall had planted a vegetable garden, and with great pride talked of his home-grown produce—tomatoes, spinach, squash, carrots, beans, and corn, as well as red beets, which no one would eat. In fact, that spring of 1944 Vice President Henry Wallace, who was formerly the secretary of agriculture, had sent Marshall some prized hybrid seed corn, which he had dutifully planted. The crop, an early harvest variety, had done well. One Saturday in August, *Life* magazine came to take photos for a September issue of the popular weekly. The photographer wanted the chief of staff to pose, hoe in hand, near this "Wallace" corn, now reduced to dry stalks. Although Marshall protested, the camera man insisted. When the photo spread came out, featuring Marshall standing in this dead corn, what Katherine described as "the entire crop of corn farmers of the Middle West" wrote to *Life,* the war department, or her husband to comment. "Marshall might know his business as Chief of Staff, but he sure knew nothing about corn," they wrote, or "What kind of corn is this pathetic looking stuff?" and on and on it went. *Life* had to explain in a later issue that it was an early dwarf variety, and that indeed both General Marshall and Vice President Wallace were excellent farmers.[95]

Later that year, Marshall wrote Wallace a letter and explained that a California farmer was going to send him [Marshall] some corn seed that "came across the country in a covered wagon," claiming that it "bore well" and was "disease resistant." Marshall, who noted that he would send that variety along to the vice president, ended the letter by telling Wallace, "I am sorry to have mixed you up in this."[96] Such exchanges no doubt lightened Marshall's mood, just as his time in Leesburg provided a brief respite from Washington. Soon he would be on the road again for yet another conference. This time the destination was Canada.

Back to the Chateau Frontenac—Quebec II

It was Churchill who pushed for another Allied conference in September 1944. Stalin had declined such an invitation, citing too many pressing military decisions, and Roosevelt had returned weary from a trip to the Pacific that July and wasn't ready for another set of long meetings. Still, the prime minister insisted. Back they would go, beginning on September 11, to the Chateau Frontenac, the same beautiful hotel where in the rainy Canadian August of 1943 they had hammered out details of the war, its aims now long delivered. Churchill had questions that only President Roosevelt, face to face, could provide. With hopeful signs of German defeat on the horizon in Europe, what would be Great Britain's role in defeating Japan? Would the Allies provide support to regain the initiative in Burma where the colonial

Indian Army was hanging on by a thread? What would happen to the British army in Italy? Now that Overlord and Anvil were launched, would there be help, or would it be "bled white" by a stalemate?[97]

A Reason for Optimism

So it was that the prime minister, the president, and the Combined Chiefs of Staff gathered once more at this elegant hotel perched atop a cliff overlooking the St. Lawrence for a series of meetings code-named Octagon II. It was the first such conference in nine months. Although Roosevelt was indeed fatigued, he managed a joke, telling an inquiring reporter, "Yes, I *am* tired. So would you be if you had spent the last five years pushing Winston uphill in a wheelbarrow." Churchill himself was coming out of a third episode of pneumonia since that January; indeed, the war had taken its toll on both leaders.[98]

Still, there was a reason for optimism: Allied troops numbered more than 2 million in France; they had broken out of the Cotentin Peninsula, with the hedgerows of Normandy far behind; the port at Cherbourg had been secured; and although badly damaged by the Germans while under siege, Brittany's Saint Malo and Brest were in Allied hands.[99] The Dragoon Operation had gained the southern coastal cities of Toulon and Marseilles, and its units had linked up with the forces of Generals Patton, Hodges, and Montgomery. France was virtually free of the Germans. That July, Soviet forces had crossed their border from the east to begin that promised offensive. By mid-August they were in the Balkans, taking the Romanian capital of Bucharest on the 31st. Finland had agreed to a cease-fire by September 4; Hungary and Czechoslovakia would come next.[100] In Italy the progress had been slower, because of the Dragoon drain, according to Churchill, but perhaps also due to the imposing, unforgiving geography of the region; nevertheless, the Germans were beginning to give ground. In the Pacific, the dual offensives of MacArthur's army and Nimitz's navy were systematically closing in on the Japanese homeland. As Marshall historian Ed Cray noted, "MacArthur looked northward, casting a covetous eye on the Philippines. In the Central Pacific, Saipan, Tinian and Guam had fallen to the Army and Marines after a cave-by-cave battle in mid-August; those islands would provide airfields from which newly operational B-29s were to bomb Japan." Although still powerful—it was estimated that there was still an army of 3.5 million to defend the home islands—the Japanese "imperial war machine," so formidable at Pearl Harbor, was losing steam. While in the wake of some staggering defeats, the warmongering Hideki Tojo resigned his posts as premier, war minister, and army chief of staff, the new government fatalistically declared it would continue the fight.[101]

Warsaw Uprising

The governor-general of Canada hosted the first dinner of the Octagon Conference. Before the meal was finished, though, Generals Marshall and Arnold were called out. That August 1, the Poles in Warsaw, emboldened by the presence of the Russian army virtually at the Vistula River along the outskirts of their city, had risen up against the German occupation forces. With the Soviets poised to strike, the Polish resistance leaders in Warsaw, under the auspices of the Polish government-in-exile, hoped to regain control of the city from retreating German forces, and thus greet the Russians as masters of their well-organized and legitimate non-Communist state.[102] However, instead of continuing their drive toward the capital city, the Soviets deliberately slowed their advance.

The Polish resistance forces were soon in trouble, lacking food or weapons—only one in ten was armed. The Germans had struck back, using tanks, rockets, and air raids, with the city becoming a giant war zone. Even before the call came to Marshall and Arnold at Quebec, the Allies had already attempted to drop supplies, a task made riskier by the Soviets, who refused to let the pilots land on Russian-controlled airfields; further, most of the drops had fallen short of their marks into German hands. Now, the Poles had beseeched the U.S. ambassador to Russia, Averell Harriman, to get another air drop for the beleaguered partisans. This was the plea that came to Marshall and his colleague at the dinner in Quebec.[103] Before the evening was over, Arnold had ordered U.S. air forces to try once more to supply the desperate fighters. The drop was made, but it proved fruitless; most of the city fell into enemy hands. The Russians, whose military aims were superseded by the political one of thwarting potential opponents in Poland, had only reluctantly agreed to this, after having made a half-hearted effort to storm the city shortly beforehand. Hitler had been furious when he heard of Warsaw's audacious and determined rebellion; he ordered the complete destruction of the city and death to its inhabitants. Indeed, at war's end, the historic capital city was rubble. In the 63-day uprising, more than 15,000 insurgents were dead or missing, and civilian deaths numbered over 200,000.[104] The resistance fighters would hold out until early October, when they capitulated once again to the Germans.

What About Vienna? Again

During the first meeting of the Octagon II Conference, General Sir Alan Brooke agreed with the other chiefs that Germany was crumbling, a conversation that opened the way for the umpteenth discussion of an advance through the Ljubljana Gap to Vienna. Although Brooke did not strongly favor the operation—later, he would insist that he actually opposed it, as Forrest Pogue noted—he dutifully made the case for Churchill. Brooke saw "great advantages for a right swing at Trieste and an advance from there to Vienna." It had "not only a military value," he argued, "but also a political value in view of the Russian advances into the Balkans."[105] Brooke conceded that if the forces already in Italy began an operation that fall and the Germans offered fierce resistance, then they could not expect to get through the twisting 2,000-foot-high Ljubljana gap of the Appenines before the harsh winter weather set in. Even so, he insisted, they could at least cross the Adriatic Sea to establish a base on the Istrian Peninsula, occupy Trieste to its north, and thus establish a base for British troops from which they could launch a more ambitious campaign should the Germans seem ready to collapse.

Churchill weighed in, reminding the group that the largest British Empire army in existence was in Italy, and thus General Harold Alexander, who had pitched advances northeast of Italy for months, should not be denied a means to continue. Indeed, Churchill could hardly bear a slow fizzle in that region rather than a significant win; further, by then he was also sincerely alarmed about the Russians. The Americans, who had fought Churchill so hard in the Anvil-versus-Vienna debate that previous spring, were surprisingly amenable.[106] After all, Anvil/Dragoon had finally launched, its mission accomplished. The desperately needed troops and landing craft had been available, so the need to draw off these forces now for the European battles seemed at least momentarily less pressing. After discussion, the Combined Chiefs agreed that they wouldn't pull troops out of Italy until they saw the results of Alexander's current offensive, and that further decisions would come after that, once the Germans withdrew. In other words, they kicked it forward to some future discussion.

Marshall did agree to hold back landing craft for a possible amphibious assault on Istria, this in contrast to his previous close guarding of these precious commodities. Despite Marshall's seeming approval of this line of discussion, the fact is that he and the American chiefs saw the Balkans, as one British general noted, "as a political jungle," and they weren't going to put their troops in there. If the British wanted to get entangled in it, then so be it.[107] Perhaps Marshall was willing to offer landing craft, but beyond that, as he and the American chiefs saw it, the road to Vienna as a means of giving the British a big victory, or even to thwart the arrival of the Russians, wasn't part of the war's grand strategy. At this point in the struggle, there would be no revamping of these hard-fought plans already in place.[108] In the end, it would be the Russians who would liberate the city in April 1945.

Return to the Philippines: Fulfilling a "National Obligation"

Since mid-1942 Marshall and the Joint Chiefs had struggled over command and strategic relationships in the Pacific. With the two service branches arguing over authority, the chiefs, to keep the peace among them and to harness the strengths of each, had divided the Pacific into two theaters, one army and air, one naval. Admiral Chester Nimitz was given the Pacific Ocean area, and MacArthur the Southwest Pacific.[109] By early 1944 a new conflict had erupted. Nimitz wanted to emphasize a naval movement westward, taking Formosa but bypassing the Philippines. He argued that it made a closer and better island stepping-stone to the China coast and the Japanese home islands. From a military rather than a political point of view, Marshall and the Joint Chiefs tended to favor this line of attack.

MacArthur saw this strategy as untenable militarily, politically, and psychologically. Not surprisingly, his plan called for the invasion and liberation of Luzon, the northernmost and largest of the Philippine Islands. Until that happened, he emphasized, it would be difficult to send needed army ground troops to reinforce any battle on Formosa. Further, he argued, not recapturing the Philippines would leave the navy's left flank vulnerable during such an operation. He also pointed out that air bases in China, which supposedly would have provided staging and support for the Formosa attacks, showed little sign of becoming secure: and, besides, the Marianas Islands had been taken that summer, so B-29s could launch attacks on Japan about as well from there as from Formosa.[110] Finally, both psychological and political factors loomed large. A bypass of Luzon, the Philippines, noted historian Mark Stoler wrote, "would relegate MacArthur to a backwater." Further, the general had sworn to return to the Philippines to erase the memory of the piercing defeats that spring of 1942 when the American island defenders became part of what would later be known as the brutal Bataan Death March.[111] "We have a national obligation to discharge," declared MacArthur. "Moreover, if the United States should deliberately bypass the Philippines, leaving our prisoners, nationals and loyal Filipinos in enemy hands without an effort to retrieve them at the earliest moment, we would incur the greatest psychological reaction."[112] Marshall himself acknowledged this aspect when he said to his biographer, Forrest Pogue, "He [MacArthur] had made all of his arguments on the 'I shall return' and all that stuff. Now if we went on by them, he was going to be in for a terrible reaction."[113]

As each theater's forces continued their respective moves toward Japan, Roosevelt had visited the two commanders in Hawaii that past July. At least in part he had wanted to arbitrate this contention over strategic direction. In the end, at those meetings MacArthur made the stronger argument, especially since Nimitz was supporting Admiral Ernest King's view more than his own, and thus was not strong in presenting the case. MacArthur had no such reticence. By the end of the conference, the president grandly assured MacArthur, "We will not bypass the Philippines."[114]

With General MacArthur and Admiral Leahy seated beside him, President Roosevelt listens as Admiral Nimitz with his pointer makes the navy's strategic case, summer 1944.

U.S. National Archives 80-G-46221

Now, at Quebec, September 11, 1944, on the evening of the first session of Octagon, the Philippine timetable would be accelerated, and the change would favor MacArthur. It was in the middle of a formal dinner that the

Joint Chiefs saw radiograms that had been sent and received by Admirals Halsey and Nimitz that very day. Halsey recounted that raids during the past weeks against the Carolines, the Paulus Islands, and the Philippines had reaped little opposition; in fact, in his diary he described the situation as "staggering, the lack of resistance amazing and fantastic." With Japanese aircraft surprisingly few in the area, Halsey recommended in the radiogram exchange that MacArthur skip his planned preliminary assaults on the southern Philippines, including Mindanao, and strike directly at the more northern Leyte archipelago in the heart of the islands.[115] The Central Pacific commander, Nimitz, offered to divert from a planned invasion on the Carolines to MacArthur's command an amphibious fleet embarking from Hawaii. MacArthur's headquarters quickly accepted.[116] With the cables in hand, the chiefs excused themselves from the table and huddled in a nearby room. It didn't take long for a decision: the Carolines invasion was scrapped, along with the planned attack on Mindanao. The result, according to historian Ed Cray, was that "MacArthur was to attack Leyte on October 20, 1944, accelerating the Pacific timetable by two months." Within an hour and a half, the chiefs had redirected the war, and then returned to the beautiful dining room to finish their meal.

Their decision effectively ended the question of whether or not Luzon, with its capital, Manila, would be bypassed. Leyte would provide all of the needed airfields for the big island's capture, MacArthur would "redeem his honor," and it would make unnecessary King's long-desired proposal to invade the more difficult Formosa.[117] Further, bypassing Formosa meant that China would become strategically less important, since air bases along its coast were no longer as needed in support of a Formosa operation. The factors that would influence China policy after that were shaped more by political matters than military realities. This timetable change had important consequences for the continuing war in the two theaters. Now, for the Philippine Operation Nimitz would support MacArthur. But if all went as planned, by January 1945 the emphasis would shift back to the navy, with attacks against the Japanese Bonin Islands. By March these forces would be moving against the enemy's home islands, the Ryukyus, the largest of which was the soon to be infamous Okinawa.[118]

Hail, Britannia

On Winston Churchill's mind early in the conference was what role the British would have in the Pacific war. His motivations were fairly straightforward: "We had to regain on the field of battle our rightful possessions in the Far East, and not have them handed back to us at the peace table." One of the hardest losses of 1942 had been the fall of Singapore, a highly prized British port; the prime minister especially did not want that bypassed. The president, as well as the Joint Chiefs, did not think it necessary to retake Singapore to accomplish the Pacific mission, and all were determined that Allied troops not be drawn into what Marshall called "the colonial thing."[119] In fact, the chief of staff was insistent that American troops not be sacrificed strictly for political purposes and, according to historian Ed Cray, used his "not for attribution" press briefings to prompt public assurances of that policy. Robert Gram Swing, one of the most influential radio commentators of the war years, almost certainly was influenced by one of these briefings when he said in a nationwide broadcast: "We are not going to spend American lives and treasure in freeing imperial possessions from the Japanese and then turn them back. . . . We see it as our assignment to bear the responsibility of defeating Japan."[120]

Nevertheless, Churchill would press Marshall and the other chiefs for a big role in the Pacific. The American military planners mentioned that perhaps British troops could best be used in the Burma-India campaign. No, that wouldn't work, according to the prime minister. He did not have the manpower to sustain a war on the Asian mainland; in fact, he could do little more than provide replacement forces. In the past, Britannia had ruled the waves, so what Churchill offered next must have seemed amazing: Would the United States Navy be willing to use the British fleet under an American commander to defeat Japan? Admiral King, convinced that his navy could win the war through blockade, and thereby gain the glory, had no need to include the British. Perhaps that was King's view, but the president immediately accepted the British offer. One British observer on the scene noted irreverently what he thought should be said in the official minutes of the navy chief's reaction to Roosevelt's announcement: "At this point, Admiral King was carried out."[121] But how would the fleet be used, Churchill wanted to know. Both the president and King equivocated: "My thought is to use it in any way possible," said the former. "The question was being actively studied," replied King. Brooke later recorded in his diary that King had "lost his temper and was opposed by the whole of his own Committee." Churchill, sensing dissension among the American chiefs, questioned the president again about his commitment to using the fleet, and got a "yes." Now, Churchill asked about using the British air force. General Hap Arnold was against it—why share airfields, targets, and, perhaps most of all, credit with the British? Marshall stepped in at this point to mediate: "Would not the British need their air forces in Southeast Asia and Malaya?"[122]

Churchill urged on, this time making the point that for "the sake of good relations," it was of "vital importance" that the British be given "their fair share of the main operation against Japan." Further, because the United States had given such "handsome assistance in the fight against Germany," it should be expected that the British would in return do their part in helping to defeat Japan. Marshall and Arnold equivocated as well, asking that the British provide dates for when their long-range bombers would be available after the German army had been vanquished in Italy.[123] The specifics of how the British navy would be used were not decided. The entire exchange revealed the power shift among these two allied militaries.

Chiang—"The harpoon hit"

While Marshall was still in Quebec, the contentious relationship between General Joseph Stilwell and Generalissimo Chiang Kai-shek in China worsened. The combative American general had attempted since early in the war to get Chinese troops trained and operable, yet Chiang, although constantly demanding ever larger amounts of lend-lease aid in support of his troops, seemed reluctant to use them. Although Marshall had steadfastly backed Stilwell as the best man for the task of handling the thorny Chinese arena, he knew that Stilwell could not abide Chiang and did little to hide it. That July, Marshall had entreated Stilwell to be more diplomatic in his dealings: "I ask you please this time make a continuous effort to avoid wrecking yours and our plans because of inconsequential matters or disregard of conventional courtesies."[124]

Now, by the time of the Quebec conference, Marshall knew that almost certainly Formosa would be bypassed in favor of Luzon, thus rendering the Asian mainland militarily less important. Nevertheless, he also understood that the president still desired to see China as a key postwar member of his nascent United Nations and saw Chiang's government, albeit imperfect, as the best bet for making that happen. A telegram from Stilwell, radioed from Chungking to the Chateau Frontenac mid-conference, described a grimly deteriorating situation. The Japanese had opened a land route from Hanoi in Indochina to Peking and had seized an important air base near Kunming, a crucial supply depot for goods flown over the Himalayan "hump" from India, placing the enemy within range of the Burma Road's northern terminus. Stilwell wrote Marshall that "the jig is up in South China," and the problem was "at the top" due to "lack of proper command."

Indeed, Chiang's forces, rather than turning to fight, seemed to be constantly retreating. Historian Ed Cray, describing the situation, wrote that when the soldiers got out of their own provinces, they tended to plunder peasants rather than taking on the well-ordered Japanese.[125] Further exacerbating the situation, despite a direct cable that July from the president to Chiang to do so, the generalissimo had refused to place Stilwell, with all of his skills, determination, and will to fight, as head of the Chinese forces, keeping that control for himself.

Even General Claire Chennault, who had always taken the generalissimo's side, and who still insisted as he had throughout the war that air power alone was most effective and could retake those bases, was frustrated and calling for more supplies. Despite being so provisioned, though, Chiang had told Stilwell he intended to withdraw, refusing to use his troops in northern Burma to open crucial supply routes. Although Roosevelt had supported Chiang, and had tolerated his failure to deliver services to match the aid he was getting, he was losing patience and moving closer to the Marshall-Stilwell view of Chiang's incompetence. Earlier in the war, Roosevelt, along with much of the American public, had been sympathetic to Chiang, seeing him as a leader who had stood up to the Japanese and whose postwar future boded well for democracy. To the chagrin of both Marshall and Stilwell, in past communications he had often softened the language of his demands. The president had once remonstrated Marshall that the generalissimo had come up the hard way to become the leader of 400 million people, and he reminded the chief of staff that "He [the generalissimo] is the Chief Executive as well as the Commander-in-Chief, and one cannot speak sternly to a man like that or exact commitments from him the way we might do from the Sultan of Morocco."[126] Now, spurred on by Stilwell's message, on September 16 while still in Canada, Marshall crafted a strong and unequivocal letter for the president to send to Chiang.

This time, the president used the forthright language of Marshall's September 16 draft with few changes, telling Chiang, "I have urged time and again in recent months that you take drastic action to resist the disaster which has been moving closer to China and to you. Now, when you have not yet placed General Stilwell in command of all forces in China, we are faced with the loss of a critical area . . . with possible catastrophic consequences." Again, using Marshall's words, the president warned Chiang that the basis for continued aid from the United States to the Chinese army came with the assumption that the generalissimo's forces would fight the Japanese. As if to drive home his point, Roosevelt noted that this huge quantity of assistance had been given despite the fact that "we are fighting two other great campaigns in Europe and the Pacific." The president ended the letter by saying that he had spoken frankly, since it "appears plainly evident to all of us here that all your efforts to save China are to be lost by further delays." Writing in his diary, Stilwell described the scene when Chiang read the letter: "At long last," he wrote, "F.D.R. has finally spoken plain words, and plenty of them, with a firecracker in every sentence. 'Get busy or else.' The harpoon hit . . . right in the solar plexus, and went right through him." Stilwell, though, noted that except for "turning green, and losing the power of speech, he did not bat an eye. He just said to me, 'I understand.' And sat in silence, jiggling his foot."[127]

Stilwell's ecstasy was short-lived. Chiang had no intention of making this general the commander of the Chinese forces, and he was insulted by the tone of the communication. A month later he made it clear to the president that "Your policies will be executed without delay as soon as you relieve Stilwell."[128] Roosevelt still held tight to the political decision that Chiang had to be placated. That mid-October, Marshall, back in Washington from Quebec as well as a trip to the European Theater, defended his friend both in writing and in a meeting with the president, but the fact remained that Stilwell would be relieved of his command. Out of respect for this "fighting general," Marshall gave him due warning. "This flash is to prepare you for what now appears to be inevitable. Make no comment to anyone of this matter until President's decision is finally determined."[129]

Although Roosevelt defended Stilwell in a Marshall-produced statement— "I disagree completely with your statement that General Stilwell lacks the essential qualifications for the command I hoped you would give him. I am most emphatically not in accord with your views on General Stilwell . . . and certainly do not accept the charge that he had any responsibility for the loss of East China"—the reality was that the feisty general was out.[130] In his message to Chiang, the president noted that no replacement would be sent for him. Rather, Lieutenant General Albert C. Wedemeyer, an officer whom Marshall also greatly admired, would act as Chiang's chief of staff. Although Wedemeyer's personality was much less abrasive than Stilwell's, the problem of Chiang's reluctance to make a full commitment to the task at hand remained. General Chennault, always an ally of Chiang, would be in command of U.S. military activities there.[131]

"He never wanted any special notice paid to him"

That summer of 1944, Allen Brown's widow, Madge, had stayed at Fort Myer. When Marshall returned from Quebec, he found that she had already left for her home in New York. There was a letter from her waiting for him, expressing her appreciation for the kindnesses that he and Katherine had shown during this extended visit. She mentioned that she was ambivalent concerning a planned press release and presentation to receive Allen's Bronze Star, awarded for gallantry on May 29, the day of his death. She explained, "As you know, he never wanted any special notice paid him while he was in the Army."[132] Marshall explained to her that Major General Thomas Terry would approach her to arrange a time for this presentation. "That being the case," he said, "a press release would be automatic," and would be written by the Bureau of Public Relations for the War Department. Yes, it would include information linking Allen to the chief of staff. Marshall told Madge that if Allen were alive to receive the medal, then of course he would have been reticent about having such an announcement publicized—the Brown young men always achieved on their own with no hint of undue influence from their famous stepfather. Marshall told Madge that this was a different situation, explaining that:

> He would be gratified to know that what he did and what he suffered was not ignored, in a world which only too quickly forgets the sacrifices people make to bring us comfort and enjoyment. Besides, he has many friends who would be greatly pleased to learn in this manner what a fine job he did, at Cassino, for example, and was doing in the advance on Rome when he met his end. The press release was restrained in tone and merely covered the essential facts.[133]

The press release went forward, and the Bronze Medal was presented to Madge Brown by General Terry on October 23.[134]

"Dying as bitterly"

When Marshall returned from Quebec, it wasn't long before he was on a plane again, this time to Chicago to address the American Legion Convention, September 18, 1944. He had a particular worry on his mind: the supplying of the troops in Europe from the great "arsenal of democracy." There had been some shortages of equipment and ammunition, especially artillery shells, since the D-Day landings. Although there were many reasons for this, including not yet having safe port facilities in France, Marshall believed it also had to do with a slackening of the production effort in the United States. As he told the legionaires, there had been "the feeling that an early victory is assured causes certain people to relax in the war effort and turn to other considerations." His message was clear:

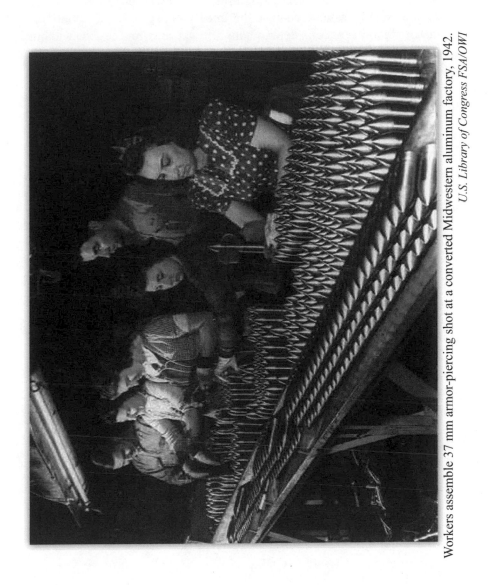

Workers assemble 37 mm armor-piercing shot at a converted Midwestern aluminum factory, 1942.

U.S. Library of Congress FSA/OWI

Before dawn tomorrow . . . hundreds of thousands of American soldiers will move forward from comfortless foxholes and bivouacs, sweating in the tropics, chilled or freezing in the damp European fall, to press an unrelenting assault against the enemy. They will go about this duty with a courageous determination to get on with the job, without hesitation over the question of personal safety. It is our duty to make sure that the flow of reinforcements and of munitions keeps pace with their advances.

The size and fury of the attack must constantly increase. We have a stern duty here at home if our attacks are to surge forward in constantly increasing strength and power during what we all hope are the last hours of the European conflict. We must remember that the individual soldier will place just as much importance on his life in the final week of the victorious advance as he does today. If the protective covering fire of bombs and artillery is curtailed . . . there will be bitter resentment.

I have complete confidence in the success of our military efforts provided we can have steady backing on this side of the oceans until the cessation of hostilities is actually announced.[135]

Perhaps Marshall had complete confidence in the Allies' *eventual* success, but he understood perfectly that the war was far from won. As historian Ed Cray wrote, "The winter would be long and harsh, a season of losses made the more bitter when compared to the succession of Allied victories in the first part of the year."[136] Shortly after D-Day, Marshall had written optimistically to Roosevelt that the United States "had the Hun at the top of the toboggan slide," and the supporting Russian offensive would soon "put the skids" under him. Indeed, the brakes had been applied to the formidable German war machine, but it wasn't yet time to celebrate.[137]

Chapter 13

Brush Fires at Home and Abroad

"Difficult and critical decisions"

Fall 1944–February 1945

A September 11, 1944, issue of *Life* magazine included a three-page spread titled "General Marshall at Home." The subtitle read, "A Great Soldier and Believer in Democracy Dons GI Coveralls to Work in His Garden," and featured a relaxed Marshall on the back stone court of his home in Leesburg. The photographs, some depicting Marshall scuffing among rows of corn with a hoe, or tending his compost heap, suggested a man whose burdens were easing. Yet, ahead lay some of the most frustrating and demanding challenges of the war both at home and abroad.

Pearl Harbor—Again

Although during that summer and fall Marshall's priorities had remained firmly fixed on the current strategic challenges of the war, he also found himself drawn into the political battles of Washington. The undercurrent of unrest regarding the circumstances of the surprise attack of the Japanese on Pearl Harbor had never quite died. True, early on, the two commanders in Hawaii—Admiral Husband E. Kimmel for the navy and General Walter Short of the army, had been unwillingly retired from duty. Both Secretary of War Stimson and Marshall had hoped that was the end of it—water over the dam. However, Roosevelt insisted that the public would want more, and he proposed that both officers have a court-martial hearing, albeit at the end of the war and not before.

Nevertheless, in the summer of 1944, with FDR's reelection bid for a fourth term about to ramp up, a Republican senator from Nebraska, backed by an anti-Roosevelt coalition, managed to get a bill passed that lifted the statute of limitations on court-martial offenses and required the army and navy to investigate the facts of the attack. Although Marshall was assured that nothing of the still secret Magic messages would go on record, he was immediately worried about leaks. A three-member board would conduct the army hearings—Marshall's only requirement as to selection of the members was that none of them be his personal friends. Indeed they weren't—in fact, Marshall had relieved one of them from a command, the second one had been denied the rank of lieutenant general, and the third had not been allowed an overseas command. All had blamed Marshall. He had later said tongue in cheek that these three had been chosen because they were available.[1] During that summer Marshall himself had briefed all of them about Magic, explaining that the code was still in place and that it revealed crucial information about Japanese dispositions. Perhaps because of his briefings, no word of Magic went into the official record.

Marshall testified before the board about his own involvement in the events leading up to Pearl Harbor. He made no effort to defend his actions, except to say that he had given General Short a warning to put his command on alert, and Short had not done so. Always straightforward, if he couldn't remember something Marshall acknowledged that, even if it implied his failings. As the topic of Pearl Harbor remained in the news, it increasingly became a part of pre-election rhetoric. That September, the Republican vice presidential nominee, John Bricker, wondered why "Washington" hadn't been blamed in part for the disaster; why only Kimmel and Short? Perhaps the White House was covering up details, he accused. In fact, it was Marshall and King who were guarding Magic, worried that full-blown investigations into Pearl Harbor would reveal this priceless source.[2]

By the time Marshall was back in Washington from Quebec, he was receiving information that the Republican presidential candidate, New York governor Thomas E. Dewey, knew about the diplomatic code and might, in delivering his accusations, reveal it in a campaign tour throughout the Midwest. The chief of staff understood that it would be smart politically for Dewey to say that the president had known all about what the Japanese were planning and had failed to act, but from a military perspective such a move would be disastrous.[3] Marshall's language in a top secret message to Admiral King on September 25 sounded the alarm: "The whole thing is loaded with dynamite but I feel that something has to be done or the fat will be in the fire to our great loss in the Pacific, and possibly also in Europe."[4]

"Of a highly secret nature"

Marshall felt he had to communicate with Dewey, but he could not go himself without the inevitable press leaks and speculations that would surely make headlines. Instead, he drafted a very unusual letter. It was to be delivered to the candidate on the campaign trail in Tulsa, Oklahoma, by a trusted army intelligence officer, Colonel Carter W. Clarke, dressed in civilian clothes. In the letter, Marshall explained to the governor that he was writing to him

Thomas E. Dewey
U.S. Library of Congress LC-USZ62-106327

without the knowledge of anyone other than himself and navy chief Admiral King; further, Marshall continued, he was about to reveal something of a highly secret nature. Here was the zinger: if Dewey didn't feel he could keep that information to himself, he should read no further, and "return the letter to the bearer."[5] Clarke reported later that Dewey had laid down the letter and told him he "did not want his lips scaled on things that he already knew about Pearl Harbor," and asked if he [Clarke] would discuss it with him. Clarke would not. Dewey handed the letter back, after saying that President Roosevelt knew plenty about codes, if that was what the communication described, and "instead of being reelected ought to be impeached."[6]

When Clarke reported back, Marshall revised the letter, assuring Dewey that he would ask him to keep secret only the portions revealing information that the candidate did not previously know. At the letter's beginning, Marshall stressed that in the lead-up to Pearl Harbor, U.S. cryptographers had cracked *diplomatic* (italics Marshall's) messages, which gave the State Department a good bit of information about Japanese moves in the Pacific but did not make reference to anything whatever regarding its intentions toward Hawaii. Further, he emphasized, because of having broken the diplomatic codes, cryptographers had since cracked other codes as well, all still being used by the enemy and thus extremely valuable. Such breakthroughs had been crucial, he wrote, in the battles for the Coral Sea, Midway, and the attempted Japanese landings in the Alaskan Aleutians. Then he came to the essence of the letter: "You will understand from the foregoing the utterly tragic consequences if the present political debates regarding Pearl Harbor disclose to the enemy, German or Jap, any suspicion of the vital sources of information we possess. I am presenting this matter to you in the hope that you will see your way clear to avoid the tragic results with which we are now threatened in the present political campaign."[7]

After Dewey got the letter, he called Marshall directly to ask that one other person be permitted to read it, thereby to witness exactly what the letter said in case someone wanted to use it against him at some later time. Further, he wouldn't return the copy as requested at the end of the letter since, again, he wanted to protect himself. In the end, Dewey respected the requests made. After all, as historian Ed Cray noted, "If he revealed, if he even hinted the United States had been reading the Japanese codes, he would leave himself open to charges of prolonging the war, of costing the lives of American boys."[8] Perhaps Dewey's decision lost him thousands of votes in what was anticipated as a tight election.

The whole Dewey-Marshall exchange was not revealed until someone on the governor's staff leaked it shortly after the war—an article about it appeared in *Life* magazine's December 17, 1945, issue. Marshall was then pressured to release the letter to the joint congressional committee that was once again investigating Pearl Harbor. By then, Harry S. Truman was president. He suggested that the whole thing be released to the public. Marshall saw this as a bad idea, since some of the information still came to bear on the security of other countries. Finally, the president agreed that the entire correspondence would be given to the committee in executive session, and that ended the matter.[9]

The conclusion of the Pearl Harbor investigation would not go as smoothly as Marshall's resolving of the Dewey issue. The report, issued just after Roosevelt had been reelected to a fourth term, laid the failure "at both ends of the line." It seemed clear to the committee that not only at Pearl Harbor but also in Washington, there had been the erroneous belief that war was "on our doorstep but not on Hawaii's doorstep." Despite Marshall's testimony that the Japanese had "crossed us up" with an attack at Pearl Harbor rather than the Philippines, responsibility lay in Washington and in Hawaii. Specifically, the committee noted that Marshall did not keep General Short at

Pearl Harbor fully informed as to the heightened international situation and the probable outbreak of war at any time.[10] Further, the chief of staff hadn't fully informed his deputies of the secret but critical situation in the Pacific so that they could "act intelligently for him in his absence." Marshall's office learned on the evening of December 6 and the morning of the 7th, the committee reported, regarding the immediacy of a possible attack, and yet the message was not taken to the chief of staff in time for him to act sooner. Finally, Marshall had failed to follow up when he was told as early as November 28 that Short had placed Pearl Harbor on sabotage alert rather than full alert.[11] Marshall, who could usually take criticism from all sources with remarkable stoicism, found this report stinging. For a few days, he was visibly depressed, and told Secretary of War Stimson he was thinking of resigning—after all, he was 64, almost at the usual army retirement age. Stimson waved aside such an action, telling Marshall that he was "the one on whom the fate of the war depended." Stimson wanted the report made public—planning to release it with his own lawyerly vindication of the chief of staff.[12] The president said no, that was not going to happen. When Roosevelt read the report's remarks about Marshall, he quietly shook his head saying, "This is wicked. This is wicked." The press releases from the army and navy talked about "errors in judgment," and not much more, but as historian Ed Cray noted, "The attack on Pearl Harbor was to be a political time bomb ticking under Marshall's reputation through the rest of the war."[13]

Winter's Chill

Marshall's biographer, Forrest Pogue, noted that in the fall and winter of 1944, Marshall, who knew the works of Charles Dickens, must have recalled the opening lines of *A Tale of Two Cities,* "It was the best of times; it was the worst of times."[14] There had been the impressive summer breakout from Normandy, with the Allied armies gaining ground eastward toward Germany and now positioned all along its borders. Nevertheless, the military situation in France was about to get very complicated indeed. It was on the last day of the Octagon Conference, September 17, with Marshall still in Quebec, that the setbacks began. As Ed Cray described it, "General Bernard Montgomery . . . launched a three division air drop in an effort to turn the northern corner of the German lines in the Netherlands. Montgomery's plan, approved by Eisenhower, called for dropping parachute units to seize five bridges over canals and rivers."[15]

The two-pronged plan, code-named Market Garden, would bypass the Siegfried Line—the German "West Wall" system of defenses—thereby opening a path for British armored corps to cross the Rhine. It also had

Waves of Allied paratroopers land in Holland during
Operation Market Garden, September 1944.

U.S National Archives

the potential for gaining control of Germany's Ruhr region, replete with industrial capability. In approving the operation, Eisenhower, who believed that it was better to apply equal pressure all along the Allied line from north to south, might have been influenced by Marshall's belief that highly trained paratroopers could operate as an effective strike force. Further, on the British side, Montgomery chaffed for a significant part of the action and was confident that this was the best way to get into Germany. Perhaps he also wanted headlines for himself such as the ones that Patton had reaped in his race across France the month before.[16]

It would not be victory headlines for Montgomery and his 12th Army Group. Hindered by inadequate, or in some cases ill-heeded, intelligence, which failed to warn of a large number of German defenders—the paratroopers landed near two up-and-ready panzer divisions—the operation was thwarted from the beginning. By September 25, Montgomery knew that the surviving paratroopers on the northern bank of the Rhine at Arnhem—a city just inside Germany that Hitler had ordered defended at all costs—would have to withdraw. The casualties from the operation: 17,000 British, American, and Polish troops, worse than the Allied losses of D-Day.[17]

Patton's Third Army had come to a rather abrupt halt as well, bogged down near the French city of Metz, not far from the German border. The problem:

these fighting units had outrun supply lines, and the weather was worsening daily. Advances were agonizingly slow, especially for a commander such as Patton, with his men going house to house prying out defenders. It wasn't a satisfying run to the West Wall, but rather a stagnant southern front without the matériel support to continue. On Patton's right General Jacob Devers' army, whose charge north from Marseilles after the Anvil launch had been so impressive, was now in a muddy slog into the Vosges Mountains, the formidable geographic barrier to the enemy's boundary. General Courtney Hodges, on Patton's left, was no better off, stopped cold against the West Wall, which ran through the streets of the German border city of Aachen.[18]

For all of these armies, frustrated in the chilling days of autumn, the scarcity of supply was related to the problem of ports. The Allies did not have a usable, undamaged deep water port near the front lines to support their troops. Although Montgomery's army had seized Antwerp, in Belgium, on September 4, its wharves and marshaling yards intact, they did not clear the Germans from the Scheldt Estuary's banks leading to the city, thus rendering the city logistically useless. (The estuary would finally be secured on November 9, but the first shipment of supplies would not be unloaded in Antwerp until the 28th, considerably past the time when fall campaigning weather was best.) The Allies had long since rolled over Brittany, but the Germans tenaciously defended its important port of Brest; others fell into Allied hands after long sieges but had been deliberately badly damaged. It was Cherbourg, 350-400 miles from the action, that handled most of the supply traffic for these armies. Transporting the matériel was problematic as well, since Allied bombing of the railroads prior to D-Day had weakened this means of carrying goods. Eisenhower depended on air transports, as well as truck convoys dubbed the Red Ball Express, which ran 24 hours a day to the front. However, that didn't solve the gasoline situation—the trucks burned 300,000 gallons a day, while Patton's Third Army alone required 275,000 a day when advancing. Patton chaffed at the shortages.[19] To provide support for Montgomery's thrust in the north, Eisenhower had moved Hodges's First Army closer to the British right and, to meet the needs of this shift, was supplying him with more gas. Not surprisingly, Patton was frustrated, and shared his view of it in his diary: "The British have put it over again," he wrote, and to his wife, "I have to battle for every yard but it is not the enemy who is trying to stop me, it is 'They.' . . . If I could only steal some gas, I could win this war."[20]

MP Corporal Charles H. Johnson waves through a "Red Ball Express"
convoy headed toward Alenon, France, September 1944.

U.S. National Archives 531220

"Pretty near blowing off out of turn"

By early October it was time for Marshall to fly to France for an inspection
trip with a view toward solving some of the manpower and supply problems
that were slowing Allied advances toward Germany. Marshall's trip began
on October 5 aboard a new C-54, the *Sacred Cow,* that the president had
made available to him. Marshall's picture graced many newspapers as
commentators reported that after a refueling stop in Newfoundland, the
plane had flown nonstop to Paris, claiming, incorrectly as it turned out,
that it was the first flight to do so since Charles A. Lindbergh's famous
crossing in 1927.[21] After a brief rest from the 19-hour trip, Marshall met
with Eisenhower at his headquarters, now at the "stone-cold" but grand
Trianon Palace Hotel in Versailles. To tackle the problems of supply, the
chief of staff assigned three logistics experts to Eisenhower's command,
each tasked with making the transporting of supplies more efficient. The
problem of supplying fresh troops was just as thorny. There were only

two reserve divisions training in the United States, and that would be it. After that, the army would be training only replacements for casualties.[22] (Marshall had placed a cap on increasing army manpower totals, worried that such a move would draw down too much on civilian workers needed in American factories to provide the matériel of war.) As one way of increasing the troops at the front, under Marshall's guidance Eisenhower would, as historian Mark Perry noted, "cannibalize his army's long administrative tail, arming clerks and cooks with rifles and putting them on the firing line."[23] Marshall also made it clear that back home the case would be clearly made that the United States could not cut back on military production in favor of civilian consumer goods that the public wanted.

On October 7, Marshall met with General Omar Bradley at his headquarters in Verdun after a low-level flight that allowed the chief of staff to take a look at the areas of France that had been the fierce unrelenting battlefields of World War I. Bradley would later recall that in the meetings that followed, even though Eisenhower and the other generals in the field had revised their rosy forecasts of early victory in Europe since the successes of August, Marshall still seemed optimistic about the war, holding to the idea that perhaps the European theater could be secured by the end of the year. Bradley disabused the chief of staff of that notion, telling him that there would be no Christmas gift finish to the struggle.[24] Bradley flew with Marshall to Montgomery's headquarters at Eindhoven, Holland, the next day. Soon the British field commander was requesting a private meeting with the chief of staff. It didn't take long for Montgomery to begin a litany of complaints, mostly about what he considered the poor leadership of Eisenhower. There had been "a lack of grip" ever since Eisenhower had taken over command of troops on the ground, Montgomery nagged. The whole thing had been "ragged and disjointed," and the Allies had gotten themselves "into a real mess," he continued. Although Marshall said little, Montgomery sensed that his remarks were not being well received. Marshall would later tell his biographer, Forrest Pogue, regarding this meeting, "I came pretty near to blowing off out of turn as it was . . . and I was under a terrific urge to whittle him down." The chief of staff kept in control, though, reminding himself that it was Eisenhower's business; besides, as he noted, "there was no logic in what he said, but overwhelming egotism."[25]

"You celebrated all the way up the road"

That was just the beginning of a rather unpleasant day all around. Marshall next visited the French general, Jean de Lattre de Tassigny, who immediately began to bitterly denounce American general Lucien Truscott and his VI

Corps, charging that Truscott's troops had recently done well only because they had gotten most of the supplies, especially gasoline, that was to have been allotted to his French troops. Not only did de Lattre say this within hearing of other American and French officers, but with American and French war correspondents as well, their pencils poised. Marshall felt his temper rise, but instead of letting it flare, as he told Pogue, "I just stopped the thing right there and walked out."[26] Marshall went on to explain that when he saw de Lattre later, in 1948, at a time when he was being considered for a NATO command, the French officer wanted to know if Marshall would oppose his receiving that appointment. Marshall, then attending a UN meeting in Paris as secretary of state, minced no words in his reply, telling de Lattre that what he had done in that fall 1944 meeting had been "outrageous business"; further, his behavior had shown that he had no idea of how Allied forces had to get along. Besides, he continued,

> "You didn't have a leg to stand on. You celebrated all the way up the road [in liberated French towns.]. You were late on every damn thing and there wasn't anything to divide [referring to the gas shortage], and you are critical of Truscott who is a fighter and not a talker. I am not going to oppose you on this at all, because as a matter of fact, that command doesn't amount to much right now. It will, but it doesn't right now. You are no man to command any Allied thing, because you are a politico."[27]

As if realizing that this was something of a rant, he conceded to Pogue, "Actually he was a good fighter. He did a good job out there in Indo-China .... But his performance there [earlier, in France] was terrible."[28]

An Unrelenting Pace

During this journey to France that fall of 1944, it troubled Marshall to see the fissures in the Allied command; nevertheless, he was soon focused on making his way among the troops. He would later describe his trip to a Pentagon deputy, Major General Frank McCoy, telling him in a letter on October 17 that after he left Verdun, he had spent four days, "three of them in a downpour of rain," and had "gone through five Armies, eight Army Corps, sixteen Divisions, and also the commanders and staffs of eight other Divisions."[29] The pace was unrelenting, but he saw his time among these fighting men as absolutely crucial to understanding their needs. As biographer Ed Cray wrote, "Always he had questions of the commanders: How was the winter clothing? What about the condition of their men? How about their morale? Were the new boots any good; why were they experiencing high rates of trench foot?"[30]

Photographs of this trip show Marshall earnestly addressing V Corps soldiers in Holland; at another stop, laughing with a major general over a cup of coffee, and receiving flowers from two French children. As Pogue noted, "In this mosaic we find him reaching out more closely than at any other time in the war to the men who fought and the people who were being aided."[31]

French children present Marshall with
a bouquet of flowers, October 1944.
George C. Marshall Research Library

Marshall promised many officers and men that when he got back home he would contact their families to say they were doing well. To Mrs. Eisenhower he wrote that her husband was "handling his job beautifully." While he acknowledged that Eisenhower was under "a heavy strain," he assuaged her fears by noting that he was bearing up under it "wonderfully." He reassured Beatrice Patton that he had seen her husband and he was "in splendid health and in fine fettle and full of fight."[32]

October 1944 at Patton's headquarters
U. S. Army Signal Corps, www.liberationarmy.com

Madame Jouatte

Marshall had never forgotten the kindness of Madame Jouatte, who had billeted him and other officers in the French town of Gondrecourt during World War I. On this October inspection trip, Marshall had hoped to visit her—the village was not far from Metz, near where Patton and his Third Army were bivouacked. But Marshall's intense focus on seeing as many troops as possible precluded his making a personal visit to see Madame Jouatte. Earlier that fall, he had already written Patton a letter, telling him that when he had nothing else to do "except invade Germany," perhaps he could send one of "your people" to check on her. On one of his inspection trips into that area, Patton had gone to Gondrecourt, as Marshall described it later, "with five thousand armoured troops, two revolvers on," and "a whole truckload of supplies." Apparently the astonishing military array scared the town's mayor, who came out in "fear and trembling" to hear Patton say in rough French, "Where is Madame Jouatte?" She had moved to the south, reported the villagers. Patton turned over the supplies to the rest of her family, enough to last them a long, long time.[33] Nevertheless, before he left, he had gotten her address, and by the time Marshall returned to the United States, Patton had written her a gracious letter inquiring as to her safety and needs. On October 23 Marshall wrote Patton to thank him for his kindness, and the "promptness" with which he "accomplished the mission." Patton had told Marshall that as soon as the military situation permitted, he would make sure someone from his command would find Madame Jouatte and help her as needed. Much later, when he was secretary of state, Marshall would finally visit with the French landlady of his youth.[34]

"Accumulated work"

On Saturday, October 14, 1944, Marshall was back in Washington. In a letter to Eisenhower, thanking him for his "generous hospitality" and remarking on the value of what he had learned on this inspection trip, he mentioned that the flight had been "comfortable" but noted headwinds of 60 miles an hour between Newfoundland and Maine, and a barometer reading the lowest the pilot had ever recorded.[35] There were headwinds of a different kind when he sorted through his desk at the Pentagon on the 15th. As he told a colleague in a letter two days later, "Since my return here I have been buried in accumulated work and difficult and critical decisions." Chief among them was the Stilwell–Chiang Kai-shek imbroglio, soon to be settled by the president. Determined not to risk a breach with Chiang's Nationalist government, Roosevelt had decided to recall the spirited and divisive officer.

By the 18th, Marshall had forewarned Stilwell in a radiogram that he "would be ordered home." As much as he had made the case for the feisty general's value in the China Theater, this time Marshall had to acquiesce to the president's wishes; as Ed Cray noted, "he could no longer stay the executioner's hand."[36] Not wishing to stir up a hornet's nest so close to the presidential election, Marshall instructed Stilwell in the same radio message to make "no comment to anyone of this matter." The warning was too late. Realizing that he was about to be sacked, Stilwell called in *New York Times* reporter Brooks Atkinson and didn't hold back. Atkinson's less than neutral article on the subject splashed across the paper's front pages a few days later, with the writer opining, "The decision to relieve General Stilwell represents the political triumph of a moribund, anti-democratic regime that is more concerned with maintaining its political supremacy than in driving the Japanese out of China."[37] As for Roosevelt, he was still undeterred in his desire that Chiang's government would survive and that China would emerge as a major power in the postwar United Nations organization.[38]

Marshall also had concerns about the shifts in military personnel that would come when the war in Europe ended. Despite the views Bradley and Eisenhower had expressed that the battle on the continent was far from over, Marshall was looking toward the defeat of the German army and a shift to the Pacific. On October 18, he wrote to the head of the war department's personnel division, Major General Stephen G. Henry, about procedures that would be needed for transferring officers from the European to the Pacific theater, and how the reduction in rank of temporary officers would be handled in the subsequent partial demobilization. While most of the regular army officers would automatically head to the Pacific at their current rank, some who had been elevated in command only on a temporary basis might be sent back to the United States, or, if they continued on to the Pacific, would do so at a lower rank. Marshall wondered about the "best scheme" for doing this, one "calculated to avoid hard feelings and possible reflection on a man's career." Marshall recalled what had happened in World War I when "an acute and wholly unnecessary humiliation was caused by actually demoting Generals aboard ship in the harbor on their arrival. They thus returned to their homes for a first visit with lowered rank. Nothing like this must occur again." Clearly wanting to figure this out before the time arrived to act on the "scheme," the chief of staff told Henry that he wanted it done on a "secret basis" to avoid the "usual War Department whispering gallery."[39]

Although Marshall was looking to a European victory, the messages coming in from Eisenhower and Bradley were rather discouraging. The supply difficulties were dire, they emphasized, especially the shortage of ammunition. Marshall had to let both generals know that production was about at its maximum for October and November stateside. He recognized also that the port situation was bad—there were ammunition ships along the French coast that could not be safely unloaded. The estuary to Antwerp would not be taken until early November, and no supplies via that route would be sent out to the battle lines before November 27. Eisenhower had told Marshall that he did not think any great offensive could be launched until Antwerp was secure, so there would be no capitulation of the enemy before the end of January. For all practical purposes, units all along the offensive line were in a static trudge. Even Patton was discouraging, telling his diary, "We roll across France in less time than it takes Monty to say, 'Regroup' and here we are stuck in the mud in Lorraine."[40]

Still, in early December, Marshall wrote Admiral Harold R. Stark, commander of the European Theater's 12th Fleet, "We are engaged in a great many heavy battles, with the great problem of munitions deficiencies here at home to meet the tremendously increased demands. However, I am decidedly optimistic rather than pessimistic about the progress of the war," and described it as "a rosy one in contrast to the desperate plight of the Germans."[41] It didn't seem rosy to Eisenhower, who wrote his wife, Mamie, of American soldiers "squatting in their trenches beneath the cold rain . . . I constantly wonder how civilization can stand war at all." To Marshall he complained, "I am getting exceedingly tired of the weather. Every day we have some report of weather that has broken records existing anywhere from twenty to fifty years."[42]

The Death of a Friend

Perhaps in writing to Stark, Marshall had been more cheerful than he felt. That early November he had lost his friend and colleague Field Marshal Sir John Dill, head of the British Joint Staff Mission. That summer Dill had been so ill from pernicious anemia that Marshall had ordered his aides to keep the contentious Anvil arguments off his colleague's desk. At Quebec, Dill's physical deterioration had been obvious to all. Churchill's doctor, Lord Moran, was shown his medical records and commented, "I saw at a glance that he was not reacting to treatment, and I doubt if he will last long. I wonder if he knows?"[43] Dill's condition continued to worsen. On November 3, Marshall, worried that perhaps he would not see him again, visited Dill at Walter Reed rather than meeting General Stilwell, who would be returning from China to Washington that afternoon. The next day, Dill was dead.

Marshall never thought that Churchill realized the value of Dill's service. Months before, he had made the case to the prime minister that Dill should be kept in Washington at a time when Churchill was thinking of bringing him back to England to serve in another capacity; after all, according to the British, some thought he had "gone native." Marshall, concerned about this possible change, made certain that so much public honor was bestowed upon Dill that Churchill would not dare recall him. The chief of staff "invaded the Ivy League," managing to get special degrees or titles conferred upon Dill at Yale, William and Mary, and Princeton, and making certain that there was plenty of publicity for each ceremony.[44]

Since the beginning of the war, Dill and Marshall had worked together not only as professional colleagues but also as friends. Through Dill, Marshall found that Roosevelt often exchanged cables with Churchill bearing on important strategic decisions without providing that information to his own chief of staff. Marshall later remarked that Roosevelt didn't want things on the record, so there were few written reports.[45] Dill, though, got copies from his British Combined Chiefs, and secretly shared them with Marshall. Sometimes the two prepared strategic responses together, often heading off some of the inter-Allied "sideshows" that sometimes arose from Churchill-Roosevelt meetings.

Although a man who kept his emotions close, there is no doubt that Marshall mourned Dill's loss. Marshall's schedule rarely showed absences for illness, yet entries outlining his schedule for November 6 and 7 noted that he was "out of office, ill with a cold." At Dill's memorial service on the 8th, Marshall read the lesson. One of his cousins who was there said of Marshall's demeanor, "His face was truly stricken."[46] It was virtually unheard of for *this* chief of staff to seek special favors from the Congress. Yet, he managed to get flags flown at half-staff for Dill, the first time a foreign dignitary had been so honored.[47] When Marshall heard that Dill had requested to be buried at Arlington National Cemetery, since the United States was the nation where he felt he had done his most important work, he found a way around the regulation that only Americans would have that honor. Not only was Dill interred at Arlington, but Marshall gained approval, once more against statutory laws, for an impressive equestrian statue at the site.[48]

In a message to Churchill after Dill's death Marshall remarked, "To be very frank and personal, I doubt if you or your Cabinet associates fully realize the loss you have suffered."[49] Only a few weeks after Dill's death, Field Marshal Henry Maitland "Jumbo" Wilson, formerly the supreme commander of the Mediterranean Theater, became Dill's replacement. Although Wilson tried hard, it seemed as if Marshall resented anyone else trying to take Dill's place. Wilson eventually settled into a role that seemed dominated by forwarding and answering messages. According to Marshall biographer Forrest Pogue, "Possibly the sharp tone that appeared at times in Anglo-American correspondence after November might have been moderated had Dill lived. . . . Fortunately, the biggest differences on operations had been settled. There were still sharp issues to be considered but no dangerously divisive matters requiring the close friendship and personal skill that had been supplied by Dill."[50]

"To be able to go in there with my skirts clean"

That fall of 1944 a bill was making its way through Congress to grant eight generals and admirals five-star rank. The purpose was to establish an order of seniority between the highest-ranking members of the two services—army and navy—but perhaps more importantly, as Admiral Ernest King had advocated as far back as 1942, to elevate the status of top U.S. officers to that of their British counterparts. Marshall opposed this from the beginning, and let Secretary of War Stimson know that he would not testify on the bill's behalf before the Congress. Marshall had his reasons, as he later told Pogue: "The chiefs of staff on the British side were already field marshals, so they would be senior to me whatever I was made. I didn't think I needed that rank and I didn't want to be beholden to Congress for any rank or anything of that kind. I wanted to be able to go in there with my skirts clean and with no personal ambitions concerned in it in any way, and I could get all I wanted with the rank I had."[51] There was also another reason: it clearly worried him that the five stars on his shoulders would give him a superior rank to his mentor and father figure, General John J. Pershing, who was ill and in residence at the Walter Reed Hospital. Despite Marshall's reservations, Roosevelt continued to pressure Congress to get this bill passed. Perhaps to assuage the chief of staff's concerns, Stimson visited Pershing at the hospital to get his approval for the move. Although the chief of staff took no part in getting the bill through, he made an important suggestion—that Pershing retain the title "General of the *Armies*," while the new army five-stars would be designated as "Generals of the *Army*." Except for George Washington, who in 1976 posthumously received the "General of the Armies" honor, no other military officer except Pershing has held that exclusive title. On December 15, 1944, the five-star rank was conferred on Marshall, with MacArthur, Eisenhower, and Henry "Hap" Arnold to follow shortly. The navy five-stars—William Leahy, Ernest King, Chester Nimitz, and William "Bull" Halsey—would each hold the title "Admiral of the Fleet."[52] At almost the same time, Congress waived the mandatory retirement age for the chief of staff. Marshall would retain that role until war's end.

Trouble in the Ardennes

At around noon on December 15, 1944, word reached the Pentagon of the new five-star ranks. As Marshall entered his office door that afternoon with General Henry "Hap" Arnold, more than 20 commanders from nearby offices came through the other adjoining entrance. All raised glasses of champagne to toast the new Generals of the Army. It was to be the last pleasantries for a month. That next day, December 16, just as Eisenhower had received word of his promotion, two German panzer armies with their supporting infantry units crashed through the lightly defended Ardennes Forest in Belgium. Although Marshall had maintained his optimism about the chances of ending the war in Europe, while he had been on his inspection trip he had noted the thinly spread 90-mile line along this deeply forested area. Of the three American divisions that were there, two were inexperienced, and the other resting after weeks of being badly mauled in combat. When Marshall mentioned this sparseness to his commanders, they declared that they weren't worried about it—it was a calculated risk. These units had been pulled back to that area because the terrain there wasn't suitable for a German attack, and besides, the Wehrmacht was in a desperate state and couldn't possibly launch an offensive over that ground. Sure, there had been signs of enemy troop movement, but the Germans were expecting an offensive and, in the view of the top Allied officers on the ground, were just getting ready to defend, nothing more.[53]

With the attack in full throttle, Allied commanders were astonished that the Germans would leave their protected positions to begin a major counteroffensive. General Omar Bradley initially called it just a "g—d damn little spoiling attack" to disrupt the Allied build-up.[54] What could they hope to gain from this? The once vaunted and feared German army had literally been pushed to its borders. The fact is that this Ardennes counteroffensive had been Hitler's project from the beginning. He had reasoned that the German army could weaken the Allies in the Ardennes, cutting their forces in two by launching a two-pronged attack toward the Meuse River to threaten Paris and an arc to the north to capture Antwerp. Taking that crucial Allied port, his troops could seize or destroy vital matériel, thus halting or slowing the Allied offensive that was sure to come. Maybe a success would bring a negotiated settlement, something less devastating than an "unconditional surrender"; maybe it would buy time until a "miracle weapon" such as a jet fighter plane, already in development, could be perfected.[55] It was bold and risky, this attack through deep snow in one of the harshest winters on record, but the Fuhrer had little to lose. Everything had been concentrated on achieving the ferocious impact of this attack, including hoarding gasoline, gathering armored units, and calling on "semi-invalids, the old, and the very young" to fill ranks. The Germans finally assembled an array of 250,000 troops to take on the 83,000 Allies that would face them.[56] There were even 2,000 trained special troops, 150 of them English-speaking, who were dressed in American uniforms and driving American jeeps to spread confusion in the rear areas, including cutting telephone lines, misdirecting traffic, and changing road signs. It was when Hitler's weather experts predicted five days of bad weather, enough to keep the feared American bombers on the ground, that his army struck.[57]

Soon known as the Battle of the Bulge for the 55-mile-deep punch the Germans made in the Allied line, it was quickly clear that this attack was no spoiler. The Germans rapidly surrounded a number of infantry regiments; by December 19, almost 8,000 of the U.S. 106th Infantry Division had surrendered to the Germans, the greatest number of prisoners taken in the war thus far, except for Bataan.[58] Nevertheless, Eisenhower responded quickly, soon sending in reinforcements—the 10th Armored Division and the 101st Airborne—to the important crossroads towns of Saint Vith and Bastogne. As the Germans made their way closer to these two villages, defended courageously by the Americans, their advance narrowed and piled up.

U.S. soldiers headed to German POW camps, December 1944
German Federal Archive: Bundesarchiv.Bild. 183-J28589

Shortly after Christmas, the worst was over, although there were plenty of ad hoc vicious skirmishes as Americans continued to slow the German advance.[59] Nevertheless, the seasoned Allied divisions in the Ardennes had dug in, and Eisenhower had successfully shifted units from other fronts, thanks in part to the highly mechanized character of the army. It helped, too, that the weather cleared, making way for formidable Allied air strikes over the combat areas. Two episodes are often recalled from the Battle of the Bulge. One was when General Patton broke off an attack in his own sector, turning elements of his Third Army, close to 100,000 troops, 90 degrees to march 125 snowy, sleety miles in three days to relieve the besieged, brave defenders of Bastogne, thus ensuring that control of that important nexus would hold.[60] The other incident derived from a single word uttered by Brigadier General A.C. McAuliffe, second in command of the 101st Airborne Division at Bastogne during the ferocious fighting there. It was the morning of December 22. Although McAuliffe knew Patton was on his way, the Third Army general and his troops had not arrived; further, the town was short of food and supplies, their field hospital overrun. Two Wehrmacht officers carrying a white flag arrived at the town's perimeter. Taken to the American command headquarters, they presented an ultimatum for surrender. When the regimental commander brought the German message to McAuliffe, he read it and said, "Us, surrender? Aw, nuts." It seemed that the reply needed to be in writing. Asking his staff about the wording, they agreed that his initial terse reply, "Nuts," was hard to beat, so that was the typewritten message delivered to the German officers. The American messenger, realizing that the enemy couriers didn't quite understand, interpreted the meaning of the message as "Go to hell" and returned them to their designated lines.[61]

Don't Bother Him

In Washington, Marshall had watched the incoming battle reports with great concern. Knowing there would be deficits in manpower and supplies, the chief of staff set about to deal with those shortages. In the Office of Operations Division, a colonel looked at Eisenhower's order of battle and, gathering a sheath of recommendations for what should be changed, went to the chief of staff. Marshall told him, "We can't help Eisenhower in any way other than not bothering him. No messages will go from here to the ETO [European Theater of Operations] unless approved by me."[62] Marshall informed Eisenhower that he had given orders: the supreme allied commander was to be left free of interference so he could concentrate on the task at hand. Marshall greatly appreciated Roosevelt's attitude during this crisis. He would later tell Pogue, "Roosevelt didn't send a word to Eisenhower nor ask a question. In great stress Roosevelt was a strong man."[63]

"Go on and give them hell"

During the tumult of battle, just before Patton had begun his bold move north, Eisenhower made a controversial but, in his view, necessary decision. Bradley's First and Ninth Armies were north of the salient established by the Germans in the assault. Setting up communications with Bradley, whose headquarters were to the south of that bulge, was clearly difficult. It made sense to turn over temporary command of these units to Montgomery, whose 21st Army Group was also above the bulge. Eisenhower knew this move would upset Bradley—indeed, Air Marshal Sir Arthur Cunningham

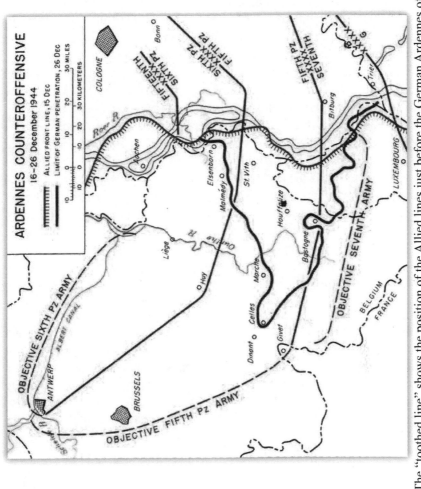

The "toothed line" shows the position of the Allied lines just before the German Ardennes offensive. *United States Army*

remembered that "Brad was absolutely livid. Walked up and down and cursed Monty. Was startling to see Brad like this."[64] It would also give Montgomery a chance to declare that it was his leadership that turned the tide; nevertheless, military logic and not national or personal preference won the day.[65]

By shortly after Christmas the Germans were stopped 18 miles short of their Meuse goal, quite literally out of gas. Marshall was relieved. Although he had interfered not at all in how Eisenhower was handling this extraordinary last thrust of the Germans, by the end of December he would communicate with the supreme allied commander, not because of the battle, which he saw as now well under Eisenhower's control, but because of an escalating Allied political situation involving Montgomery. Since the battle had begun, the British field marshal had been sending gloomy messages back to London about the poor leadership and chaotic performance of the Americans, all the while describing the courageous involvement of his own men. What irked Marshall, though, were the pointed remarks Montgomery made to British reporters along these lines, so much so that newspapers portrayed him as the savior of the battle and opined that in light of Montgomery's superior leadership, he should be made the overall commander of the troops. This infuriated General Omar Bradley as well, since at one point during the battle Montgomery had actually ordered a retreat to "tidy up the lines."[66] As for Marshall, fearing that given the pressure Eisenhower was under, the allied commander might feel the need to make a concession to the British demands, he sent an emphatic radio message on December 30:

> They may or may not have brought to your attention articles in certain London papers proposing a British Deputy Commander for all your ground forces and implying that you have undertaken too much of a task yourself. My feeling is this: Under no circumstances make any concessions of any kind whatsoever. You not only have our complete confidence but there would be a terrific resentment in this country following such action. . . . You are doing a grand job and go on and give them hell.[67]

With Marshall's letter of assurance in his pocket, Eisenhower would bring this internal battle to a head that very afternoon. As it happened, Montgomery's chief of staff, Francis de Guingand, arrived at headquarters to inform Eisenhower that Montgomery on New Year's Day would not attack the bulge, thus beginning the push-back of the Germans, as he had been ordered. Eisenhower's frustration hit its limit. Montgomery had promised the counterattack, and without it, he informed Guingand, the Allies would "fritter away a great opportunity to bag the exhausted Germans."[68] Further, he informed the messenger, Montgomery's ongoing lack of respect for Bradley, as voiced in his statements to the press, would undermine morale among the American general's troops, and that situation would not be tolerated. Eisenhower then showed Guingand a radiogram that he had drafted to Marshall, telling the chief of staff that this continuing struggle was such that something had to be done—one of the Allied commanders would have to go, either him or Montgomery.

Guingand understood immediately the seriousness of this impasse, and entreated Eisenhower to give him 24 hours before he sent the message to Marshall. Flying through the night in heavy weather, he arrived at British headquarters at 4:00 a.m. to warn Montgomery in no uncertain terms regarding the seriousness of the situation. Given the fact that American soldiers outnumbered the British by two to one, if the choice had to be made, without question, Montgomery would be out. Even the stubborn field commander knew he had pushed too far and wrote a placating message to Eisenhower, in which he said, "I'm with you 100 percent. Just tell me what you want and I'll do it," closing with a rather obsequious, "Your very devoted subordinate, Monty."[69]

The next day, Montgomery received new orders from Eisenhower. He was to return Bradley's First Army. The Ninth would remain with the British field marshal, mainly because Eisenhower did not want it to appear that he was punishing Montgomery. Further, the supreme allied commander rejected Montgomery's ongoing strategic design of making a single concentrated thrust into the Ruhr from the British sector, while leaving the Americans in a static defensive position along the broad front. Finally, Eisenhower warned, "You disturb me by predictions of 'failure' unless your exact opinions in the matter of giving your command over to Bradley are met in detail. I assure you that in this matter I can go no further.[70] On the same day, Eisenhower wrote to Marshall, "You need have no fear as to my contemplating the establishment of a ground deputy."[71]

Still, after all of this, on January 7, 1945, Montgomery gave a self-serving press conference, saying, "*I* employed the whole available power of the British Group of Armies," noting that "*I* think possibly one of the most interesting and tricky battles *I* have ever handled, with great issues at stake." Again, the implication was that Montgomery and his British army had rescued the hapless Americans. Again, the American commanders were furious—the British forces had hardly been involved in the Battle of the Bulge at all.

One thing was certain: on the question of an Allied ground commander, Eisenhower now stood firm. Eventually, the British press began to backtrack. It took a political expert to smooth the troubled waters. Speaking before the House of Commons on January 18, Winston Churchill set the record straight:

> I have seen it suggested that the terrific battle which has been proceeding since December 16 on the American front is an Anglo-American battle. In fact, however, the United States troops have done almost all the fighting and have suffered almost all the losses. The Americans have engaged thirty or forty men for every one we have engaged and have lost sixty to eighty men to every one of ours.

> Care must be taken in telling our proud tale not to claim for the British armies undue share of what is undoubtedly the great American battle of the war. I have never hesitated to stand up for our own soldiers when their achievements have been cold-shouldered or neglected . . . but we must not forget that it is to American homes that telegrams of personal loss and anxiety have been coming.

While acknowledging that Montgomery had fallen "unceasingly upon the army in the north," he also spoke of the extraordinary military efficiency from the Metz area by General Patton's army, "who hurled themselves on those intruders from outside of Bastogne."

Finally, Churchill concluded:

> General Omar Bradley was commanding the American forces and so was Field Marshal Montgomery. All these troops fought in magnificent fashion and General Eisenhower, balancing the situation between his two commanders, gave them both the fairest opportunity to realize their full strength and qualities.

> Let no one lend themselves to the shouting of mischief makers when issues of this momentous consequence are being successfully decided by the sword.[72]

It was what had been done to the German army that was of "momentous consequence." Although the German push to the Meuse had been stopped by December 26, it would be Sunday, January 28, 1945, before the last of the Germans were back to their pre-Ardennes defensive lines.[73] They had suffered more than120,000 casualties, of which 36,000 were captives. The Allies had lost a great deal as well—81,000 Americans, including 19,000 who died, most of them infantry. The British casualty numbers stood at 1,400—their fighting had been limited mostly to the tip of the bulge.[74] But despite these heavy Allied losses, it would be the German army that would not recover, especially when it came to the machinery of war. Although both sides had lost more than 800 tanks each, German industry could no longer supply the new ones in sufficient quantity. Further, when the Russians began their mid-January offensive against the Wehrmacht, crossing the Oder River into Germany 100 miles from Berlin on the 22nd, German under-strength divisions, weakened in the Bulge, were not able to stem the Red tide. "Those bottom-of-the-barrel reserves that might have slowed the Russian onslaught," wrote Omar Bradley, "had been squandered instead against us in the Ardennes."[75] There was plenty of ferocious fighting ahead, but the last days of Hitler's proclaimed "thousand-year" Reich had begun.[76]

American soldiers near Bastogne, January 13, 1945,
line up in the snow for "chow."
U.S. Army Signal Corps:liberationtrilogy.com

Tending Fires at Home and Abroad

On December 25, at Fort Myer, General Marshall had enjoyed a traditional Christmas feast with Katherine, his stepdaughter, Molly, and her two young children, Kitty and Jimmy Winn. Katherine had invited the bachelors on Marshall's staff to share the dinner and the day. Marshall had his mind on the soldiers on battlefronts, whether in the icy foxholes of Europe or the stifling hot malarial jungles of the Pacific Islands. Against impossible odds, he had for the second year in a row seen to it that those fighting men enjoyed a hot turkey dinner with all the trimmings, for as he said, "A turkey dinner means home to an American soldier."[77] General Patton, in the midst of the relief of Bastogne on the 25th, visited all of his Third Army divisions that were in contact with the enemy that day, and marveled that virtually every man received turkey for dinner— cold sandwiches for those literally in the fight and a full hot meal for those in the rear. As he later wrote, "No other Army in the world except the American could have done such a thing."[78]

Surely, back home in the warmth of the enclosed sunroom at Ft. Myer, as he watched his grandson play with a collection of painted lead soldiers arrayed in the uniforms and colors of the French and Indian War, Marshall's mind must have wandered to the future of this current brutal war. In the afternoon, he and his wife read the more than 1,000 letters, radios, and telegrams that delivered holiday greetings, including one from General Eisenhower, who wrote, "For my part, I pray that the coming year will see all of your great efforts and plans well on the road to fulfillment."[79] Indeed, those efforts would be rewarded, but there were myriad problems to face before that prayer became reality.

Unhurried and Relaxed

That late December, as 1944 waned, a noted reporter, Frederick Lewis Allen, had visited Marshall in his Pentagon office, and described him as "unhurried, relaxed . . . and unaffected." Allen set the scene of the army chief of staff seated at a large antique mahogany desk, one of six purchased by General Philip Sheridan in the 1880s. Behind him was an impressive oil portrait of General John Pershing; on the opposite side of the room, a dramatic painting of the battle of the Meuse-Argonne. Marshall impressed Allen with his manner: "He spoke quietly, not in any sense speechmaking, not talking down to us," and "the main impression he made on us was one of an absolutely first-class mind, in grasp, range, and judgment."[80]

Despite the pressing needs of the war, on January 1, 1945, Marshall took the time to return Christmas greetings in a letter to Mrs. Robert Nolan, the wife of an old army friend who had been with him on the mapping expedition out of Fort Clark, Texas, in 1905. Remembering Duke, the Nolans' Dalmatian who had provided enjoyment on post those many years ago, Marshall described his family's Dalmatian, Fleet, and explained that his dog had gotten into so much trouble killing chickens and running wild in the neighborhood at the Dodona property in Leesburg that he had been shipped to the K-9 School in Front Royal, Virginia. Marshall enclosed a photo of Fleet and commented that the family pet, alas, had not turned into a particularly valiant army service dog, especially since he "was delighted to see anyone, friend or enemy."[81]

Whatever his outward appearance to visiting reporters, or his cheery missives to old friends, in the year ahead Marshall had thorny issues to face, beginning with the acute post-Bulge need for replacement troops to fill Eisenhower's 73 under-strength Allied divisions in France.

The Replacement Problem

Although it seemed clear that for the long haul Hitler's Ardennes offensive would severely weaken the Germans, the fact was that they had 70 badly mangled but still threatening divisions to throw against these roughed-up Allied armies. Further, although MacArthur's army and Nimitz's naval forces in the Pacific were making progress, planners for both services knew that if the Japanese islands had to be invaded to force capitulation, the needed manpower would be great. If the European war stretched farther into the new year, which in the wake of the Battle of the Bulge seemed inevitable, would those American troops in France and Germany be freed up soon enough for the final thrust against the Japanese home islands?

Since May of 1944, Secretary of War Stimson had argued for an accelerated draft adequate to close anticipated manpower deficits. Marshall was adamantly opposed to this, telling Stimson that it would take almost two years to get such divisions trained and in the field, so they would not be of value to Eisenhower or, in his view, to MacArthur in the Pacific. Not only that, but creating new divisions would interfere with the replacement program that was already in place where new trainees were rotated into under-strength divisions already in action. Finally, and this was crucial, in Marshall's judgment, an accelerated draft would draw down on the civilian population and thus deepen the shortage of workers who could produce the matériel of war, especially since the United States was the top wartime supplier to the Allies as well as the Soviets. When in late 1944, Stimson renewed this argument, the chief of staff was still of the same opinion. Indeed, the secretary of war wrote in his diary on January 4, 1945, "Marshall is very strong against it [the ten divisions]. . . . This is an old difference between us." In fact, Marshall fought it to the point of threatening to resign, informing Stimson that he should relay that message to the president. In that same diary entry, Stimson noted, "This morning I had it out with Marshall in a perfectly friendly but very firm way. I feel a very great responsibility in running any risk of jobbling [*sic*] his elbow, so to speak, when he is under such great strain and we had none of that in our talk and I think that a good deal of good may come out of it. But on the main issue at present of more divisions, he remained firm."[81] In the end, they would hold to the 90-division limit.

Although the president, Stimson, Marshall, and Admiral King supported an early 1945 bill geared to increase the number of inductees into the services, and to stave off a severe shortage in essential wartime industries, it did not pass. The proposed legislation would have allowed draft boards to reexamine men 18–45 who had been classified 4-F (not able to serve due to medical reasons), and to either move them to combat status or see to it that they were in war production jobs. More than 5 million men, one out of every three who went through the draft stations, were rejected because of "physical, emotional, mental, or moral disability."[82] Further, all of the military chiefs had been alarmed at the general letdown on the wartime production front. Despite good pay in these essential factories, many workers anticipated that it wouldn't be long before the war ended, and with it their wartime jobs. Thus, in increasing numbers they were leaving those "defense" jobs, seeking employment in private industry with a view toward permanent work after the defeat of Germany and Japan. This strict bill would have allowed for a compulsory labor draft and would have prevented workers from leaving certain war-essential industries for private manufacturing. In the end, the Senate voted out a weaker version of the bill, its oversight language so vague that it had little impact on the war-industry labor situation. Critics who opposed both measures, including labor and railroad unions as well as the National Association of Manufacturers, complained that it represented dangerous and excessive military control of free markets. These groups insisted that deficits could be made up through eliminating waste, the tightening of wartime manpower regulations already in place, and volunteer commitment. By March and April, with Allied victories mounting, Congress, which throughout the war had supported the military, was much more reluctant to handle such military requests. Improvements would need to be made in other ways.

That January 1945, Marshall, as he had throughout the war, continued to apply pressure at all levels to bump up the numbers of frontline combatants from within the ranks. He ordered a search for men who could go into

Marshall observes a combat demonstration at the Infantry Replacement
Training Center, Fort McClellan, Alabama, December 1944.

George C. Marshall Research Library

combat in Europe from army posts within the United States, the Canal Zone, and Alaska. Further, he directed Eisenhower to comb his own rear echelons to find replacements, including the personnel under Major General John C. Lee, commander of Services of Supply. Although Lee had covered the task of delivering ammunition, petroleum, and other needed goods via long supply lines in the days before the Allies gained control of Antwerp, Marshall questioned whether or not his operation was as lean as needed. Why couldn't he free up more soldiers for frontline combat? As Marshall noted, "It seems absolutely clear to me that little has been done in Lee's command . . . vaguely approximating the drastic measure we have taken back here to obtain Infantry replacements." In referring to Lee's effectiveness, or lack thereof, Marshall noted, "The trouble is, he is involved in both supplying the Front and supplying himself. While the troops on the Front suffer heavily and work with reduced numbers he has continued apparently to operate with plenty of fat meat."[83] Historian Stanley Weintraub wrote that half of Eisenhower's ground army was involved in Lee's support service, and he noted that Lee had taken over 651 hotels in Paris alone.[84]

During this time of post-Bulge replacement shortages, Marshall was particularly irked by what he described as the "racket" of certain public figures being exempted from service because of physical disabilities, something that he had questioned since the war's beginning. In a January 4, 1945, letter to Deputy Chief of Staff Thomas H. Handy, he wrote, "I frequently see soldiers well up in years who, on a superficial basis alone, decidedly lack the stamina necessary to arduous service, yet they are in the Army. At the same time we have athletes engaging in the most violent sport of football and strenuous sport of baseball . . . who have been exempted." He mentioned to Handy that he had sent out instructions to the War Department that celebrities such as radio and motion picture stars would not be exempted without approval from this military agency, not just a doctor's report. Marshall recommended that the same be true of those athletes who had been exempted from military service because of lame excuses such as a punctured eardrum, wetting the bed, or some other "trifling" issue.[85] By January 8, Marshall had made it an official directive: "Professional athletes will not be rejected for military service until each case has been reviewed by the War Department's Personnel Division." Perhaps the overall impact on replacement numbers was small, but it satisfied Marshall's sense of fairness regarding who should be called to fight the nation's wars.

Chapter 14

Victory in Europe

Savored but for a Moment

January – May 1945

The warmth of a family Christmas at Fort Myer soon gave way to a bitterly cold January. Meat, butter, and eggs were rationed, and the citizenry was less inclined to tolerate the required sacrifices. Businessmen had been ordered to turn off neon signs to save power for the war effort, which added to the gloom. Further, Katherine Marshall likened the whole capital city to a huge kennel, since everyone in it appeared to be barking like dogs from winter flus; even the Marshall grandchildren looked pale and run down.[1] As Marshall returned to the Pentagon to begin his complicated, enervating winter work, it was hard to imagine that before the year ended, this whole long ordeal would be over.

Three-Stops—Marseilles, Malta, Yalta

The seasonal weather barely warranted Marshall's concentration. He continued daily to find solutions on the home front to the replacement and supply shortages—his meetings with the joint chiefs and military congressional committees requiring much of his concentration. But his mind was also on Eisenhower and his control of the European Theater of Operations. That early January, certain British newspapers had reported that a new deputy commander might be appointed. On January 10, Eisenhower had written Marshall to outline future operations. He mentioned that he wanted to appoint a "deputy supreme commander" who had infantry experience. It was the last paragraph of the message that gave Marshall pause. Eisenhower mentioned that "because of the great size of the land forces now engaged on this front it would be more convenient for me if my deputy supreme commander were an experienced ground officer rather than air." Explaining the qualities that would be required of such an appointment, he ended by saying, "The only one I could think of myself would be [Field Marshal Harold] Alexander, and manifestly he is not, repeat, not available." Alexander was at that time the supreme commander of all Allied forces in the Mediterranean. "Not available" did not assuage Marshall's concerns. In a radiogram sent the very next day, Marshall told Eisenhower he was thinking of showing Eisenhower's letter to the president because of that last paragraph that may indicate "a weakening on your part under the heavy pressure of the press and British officialdom."[2] Then he outlined what he thought such a move would mean: "First, that the British had won a major point in getting control of the ground operations in which their divisions of necessity will play such a minor part, and for the same reason, we are bound to suffer very heavy casualties; and second, the man being who he is and our experience being what it has been, you would have great difficulty in offsetting the direct influence of the PM [prime minister]." Eisenhower quickly wrote back on the 12th that Alexander was merely the kind of person who would be acceptable, and ended by saying that he would "make no shift in our present arrangements."[3]

Marshall would soon be leaving the United States for two meetings; one with the Combined Chiefs of Staff on the island of Malta, and a second one with Roosevelt, Churchill, and the military chiefs in the Russian Crimea at Yalta. He decided to add another stop. Before he left on January 25 for a flight to Malta by way of Bermuda and the Azores, he had scheduled a face-to-face meeting with Eisenhower. His goal in large measure was to strengthen Eisenhower's resolve in terms of the kind of pressure that the British, especially Brooke of the Imperial General Staff, were likely to apply as strategic decisions for the last thrust into Germany were solidified. On January 17, Marshall had written Eisenhower requesting such a meeting in southern France on January 28. The city of choice was Marseilles; their destination for security purposes code-named Snowball. When they met, Marshall backed Eisenhower's plan for a two-pronged attack to clear the German army from the west bank of the Rhine. With that completed, as historian Ed Cray described, "He [Eisenhower] would launch a left-right combination punch to cross the last barrier into Germany. The major blow, directed by Montgomery, would be aimed at Berlin. That would be supported by a secondary effort under Bradley directed at the Ruhr." Marshall understood full well that this would not suit Montgomery, who had wanted to command a single thrust in the north, with the rest of the divisions left on the defensive. With Marshall's approval of the two-pronged thrust, Montgomery's idea was essentially killed.[4] Further, Marshall promised the supreme commander, "As long as I'm chief of staff I'll never let them saddle you with the burden of an over-all ground commander." Encouraged, Eisenhower wrote, "With General Marshall backing me up there would be no danger of interference with our developing plans." As if to emphasize Marshall's resolve, Eisenhower included a memo for his files, "If this is done, he [Marshall] says, he will not remain as chief of staff."[5]

"The session at Malta was a very hot one"

This day-long meeting with Eisenhower complete, Marshall flew to the Mediterranean island of Malta for the pre-Yalta Combined Chiefs meeting, well prepared for a showdown with the British chiefs on the supreme commander's continuing roles and his strategy for the offensive thrust into Germany. During the first two days, the conference went fairly smoothly. Certain decisions were made. For example, with the help of Field Marshal Sir Alan Brooke, who had come to realize the difficulty of an offensive north of Italy through unforgiving mountainous terrain, the whole Ljubljana Gap concept was finally abandoned—no offensive into Austria would take place. In fact, Brooke agreed that the British in Italy would go on the defensive, and that five of those divisions would be sent to France to fight under Eisenhower. On the third day, though, one session was "a very hot one," as Marshall later described it. Eisenhower's headquarters chief of staff, General Walter Bedell Smith, representing the supreme commander at the meeting, was there to explain and defend the overall strategic plan—the two-pronged thrust across the Rhine, one in the north under Montgomery and another in the south under Bradley. Smith laid it out in some detail for the British chiefs. Brooke didn't like the idea of that second prong, warning that it would have the effect of "weakening the main northern attack."[6] Perhaps it would be okay, though, so long as the second attack was close enough to support Montgomery's main thrust. Marshall would not agree to this, explaining that with all of these forces so concentrated, it would make it easier for the Germans to launch an all-out counterattack. Moreover, such a move also had the effect of bunching many of Bradley's divisions at Montgomery's flank, a move that once again would make it appear that the British were the main force, the only force.

During the meetings, the British chiefs did little to hide their lack of faith in Eisenhower's leadership, with Brooke saying in a tone of voice that grated on Smith that the supreme commander was not "strong enough" for the job. As Ed Cray noted, a deputy commander—British, of course—was the implicit solution. Brooke's comment infuriated Smith, who had heard this British line of thinking in one form or the other for almost four years. He startled Brooke by demanding an explanation. "G—d dammit," he yelled, "Let's have it out here and now." Brooke commented further: the problem was that Eisenhower was too influenced by the field commanders, especially Bradley and Patton, and was seemingly influenced most by the "last man he saw," including General Marshall.[7] Smith defended Eisenhower, saying that he did listen to his generals—that was how he had kept the alliance together.

Further, he told Brooke, if he had that much doubt about Eisenhower, he should formally ask for his relief. That wasn't going to happen, since the British field marshal knew that outcome—it would be nixed immediately by Marshall.

It angered Marshall that in a short period of time he had twice heard this complaint of Eisenhower being influenced by these American generals. He wasn't going to let these comments go unanswered: "Well, Brooke, they [the British high command] are not nearly as much worried as the American chiefs are worried about the immediate pressures and influence of Mr. Churchill on General Eisenhower. The President practically never sees General Eisenhower and never writes to him—that is on my advice— because he is an Allied commander. But we are deeply concerned by the pressures of the prime minister. I think your worries are on the wrong foot."[8]

Things soon got more and more heated. As Marshall would later describe, "At Malta we had a very acid meeting as Smith came on and the British put pressure on him. They were opposing the previously agreed-upon plan and General Eisenhower's procedure and in particular his advance on the Rhine." As the arguments strengthened, Marshall asked for a closed session, and with no official records kept, the words flew. Marshall knew that a lot of the issues with Eisenhower stemmed from Montgomery, and, as Brooke would later report, Marshall expressed his "full dislike and antipathy for Monty." Apparently, Marshall was still talking about the Malta exchange during a meeting with Secretary of War Stimson two weeks later. Stimson recalled that Marshall had "some sharp issues with the British who have been trying to push Montgomery forward in respect to Eisenhower. Marshall who is always very tolerant . . . in dealing with the British was finally quite aroused by this situation and evidently 'lit out' in the conference so vigorously that he carried everything before him."[9] General Smith later wrote to Marshall's deputy that the chief of staff "spoke his mind as only he can do, for about fifteen minutes, and, as a result, the matter was dropped."[10]

Forrest Pogue wrote that if Brooke thought Marshall's harsh words were a vendetta, he had misjudged him. Maybe the chief of staff was influenced by what he described as "this patronizing attitude towards American troops" that he thought was "rather widespread in British circles."[11] Perhaps Marshall was remembering Montgomery's self-serving press conference after the Bulge. Nevertheless, according to Pogue, his anger at Montgomery had to do with his sense that the 21st Army Group commander was not a team player. Marshall later recalled, for example, that Montgomery never came to Eisenhower's headquarters; he made the supreme commander come to him. Said Pogue, "Marshall had always been willing to excuse eccentric and stubborn behavior in commanders; what he could not accept was what he believed to be open contempt of an officer for his superiors."[12] At the heart of it, then, Marshall was always a professional soldier. In the closed meeting that day in Malta, Marshall had said his piece. It was the last tempestuous meeting he would have with the British chiefs. Although during the arguments presented by Smith and augmented by Marshall, Brooke had merely agreed to "take note" of Eisenhower's proposal, he later wrote that "through force of circumstances" he had to agree to the supreme commander's plan, because, as he said, "they [the British] were dealing with a force that was predominantly American, and it was therefore natural that they should wish to have the major share in its handling."[13] Predominantly American, indeed: According to historian Mark Perry, "Three-quarters of all soldiers fighting in Europe in 1945 were American. The United States produced nearly half the world's armaments and two-thirds of its ships. The stark realities of the sacrifices were clear to Marshall. . . . Those who made the greatest sacrifices would retain the most power. . . . The American people would not tolerate a British commander of American troops."[14]

As much as the two-pronged offensive argument seemed to frame the Malta meetings of the Combined Chiefs of Staff, other matters were settled. Although American air force leaders had problems with "morale bombing," Marshall agreed to the British method of "bombing through overcasts" in urban areas, a move that according to the chief of staff would spread confusion beyond the front lines. Further, the U.S. Army Air Forces would be made available to provide aerial support for the Red Army's eastern offensive into Germany.[15] Both Marshall and King outlined strategy in the Pacific. American troops would not be used to free Malaya, a policy that matched Roosevelt's determination not to have the United States involved in reclaiming British colonial possessions in Southeast Asia. The next points of invasion would be Okinawa and the Bonin Islands, moves that would put the Americans within 1,000 miles of Tokyo. Allied airfields on these islands would provide launch sites for the bombing of Japanese industry. That "softening up" would come before the American invasion of the home island of Honshu, scheduled for September 1945.[16]

The president "looked very, very tired"

That February 2, 1945, the day after the "hot" meeting with the Combined Chiefs wrapped up, the heavy cruiser USS *Quincy* slipped into the Malta port of Valletta with the president and Admiral William Leahy on board. By 4:30 p.m., the U.S. Joint Chiefs joined them, and shortly thereafter, so did Churchill and the British chiefs. The prime minister had insisted on this meeting to precede Yalta so he and President Roosevelt could review the recommendations of the Combined Chiefs and get their "ducks in a row" before they saw Stalin. After that meeting, almost all who had been present would comment on Roosevelt's alarming appearance. Marshall was already aware of the Roosevelt's declining health. He had attended the truncated inaugural activities on January 20. He and Katherine later talked about the president's demeanor—the trembling hands, his face pale and drawn, his once resonant voice weak. The president had not gone to the Capitol to be sworn in for a fourth term. The oath was administered in the South Portico of the White House, a venue suitable for a crowd of 5,000, as compared to the audience of 150,000 who had assembled for the 1932 inaugural. Clearly preserving his strength, Roosevelt's speech lasted only about five minutes, emphasizing "engagement, not isolation," as the "road ahead."[17]

Of course, Roosevelt was under a doctor's care; he had been diagnosed with "hypertensive heart failure." Although the physician had recommended that the president lose weight, what the Combined Chiefs noticed was how that loss, actually 35 pounds, made him look gaunt and frail, with his dark woolen cloak hanging loosely from his once powerful shoulders. The British, who had not seen him for a while, were particularly startled, but even Marshall was shocked—later, he would repeat several times that during the Malta-Yalta meetings, the president looked "very, very tired."[18] Usually invigorated by travel by sea, this voyage had done nothing for his energy level. Still, Secretary of State Edward Stettinius, who had replaced Cordell Hull by that time and would provide counsel during Yalta, described the president as alert, equal to the "grueling give and take of the conference table."[19] Charles Bohlen, who served as translator for the American delegation and thus heard virtually all of the exchanges between the key players, recalled that Roosevelt was "lethargic, but when important moments arose, he was mentally sharp."[20] Afterward, the president's level of productivity at these meetings would be hotly debated.

Churchill was also exhausted from the ordeal of a six-year war, his doctor, Lord Moran, describing him as "nearly burnt out." He suffered from a severe cold with fever on the trip to Malta. Nevertheless, in the prime minister's opinion, it was the president who no longer took "intelligent interest" in military matters. Indeed, Roosevelt seemed to rely on Marshall more and more in these affairs, trusting his judgments explicitly; however, the chief of staff would not be of much assistance at upcoming Yalta. The questions to be settled were political, not military: the future of Germany; the cost of the Soviets' entering the war against Japan; the status of eastern European countries.[21]

During this preliminary meeting aboard the *Quincy*, the British chiefs asked for no alterations in the decisions that had been made in the heated debates of the last days, apparently realizing that any such requests would be turned down. Churchill did take issue with the Combined Chiefs' decision to close out the Ljubljana Gap to Vienna concept, saying that "we should occupy as much of Austria as possible, as it was undesirable that more of Western Europe than necessary should be occupied by the Russians." Roosevelt's response was noncommittal, neither positive nor negative. With that tepid reaction, and given that Brooke himself saw the whole idea as unworkable, Churchill seemed to finally accept that the thrust north of Italy toward Austria had died on the vine.[22] Forrest Pogue noted that it had only been a few months since Churchill had talked about how such an offensive would allow the British general Alexander to "have his battle," yet now he emphasized that his motive was to forestall the Soviets. Although some in Churchill's inner circle would later say that the prime minister had made this "threat from the Soviets" argument at an earlier time, this was the first time he made it his major point in support of the push north out of Italy.[23] From that time on, though, he would return to the Soviet threat again and again, and would be viewed by many analysts as having been more prescient about the dangers of communism than his American colleagues.

Other matters were raised in the pre-Yalta meeting—Churchill spoke of the need for food, clothing, and fuel for the people of Italy and France. Communist parties in both countries had been active in the resistance; such hard circumstances would, in the prime minister's view, make the people more vulnerable to these influences during upcoming elections. Marshall demurred on this point, since he was already worried about the supplies needed for Allied troops; he spoke of "the unqualified priority of beating Germany and Japan."[24] Churchill wanted the British to have a role in China if the Americans had to invade the mainland to oust the Japanese. Now Admiral Leahy objected, explaining that the United States wasn't able to fully support the troops already there.[25] When the Allies had taken a major port in China, then those possibilities would be reviewed once more. In the end, the meetings ended inconclusively, with virtually nothing discussed regarding the upcoming conference with the Soviets.[26]

Afterwards, Roosevelt seemed to sense that Churchill was feeling the strain in the Anglo-American partnership. Indeed, the prime minister was very aware that the power grid had strongly shifted to the Americans. Perhaps in a mood of conciliation, the president agreed to make British Field Marshal Harold Alexander Eisenhower's deputy. Marshall surely must have chafed at that offer after all that he had done to warn Eisenhower away from this possibility. Perhaps simply to buy time and to head off any talk of the change being related to Eisenhower's handling of the Bulge, Marshall asked that the appointment be put off for six weeks, and that ended the matter for the moment.[27] After all, things could change, and they would.

A Breakfast of Caviar and Vodka

The next morning, February 3 just after midnight, Marshall and the other chiefs were rousted from their sleep to begin the journey under cover of night from Malta to Yalta. In fact, all of the chief diplomatic and military advisers, as they made their way through a cold rain to the waiting aircraft, were under the tightest security, since they would be flying over airfields still in German hands or only recently evacuated by them. The 25 planes lifted off at 10-minute intervals, maintaining radio silence and, except for those carrying the president and prime minister, without escort. All arrived safely at the Russian air base in Saki, along the Black Sea. Marshall was met by the Red Army's first deputy chief of staff, Aleksei I. Antonov, and taken to a nearby oval tent. There on a table that gleamed with china and crystal, the group saw an array of food fit for an evening banquet—cold cuts of ham, tongue, bologna, along with caviar, curd cake, apples, champagne and hot tea.[28] Marshall simply said, "Let's get going," and left the feast to others. What followed was an 85-mile trip along terrain littered with reminders of the Germans—burned-out buildings and a detritus of wrecked tanks, railroad equipment, and other vehicles. All along the winding journey, male and female officers stood every 50 to 100 yards, offering a salute as each car went by.[29]

The lodging for the Joint Chiefs would be the Livadia Palace, once the summer palace of the last Romanovs. Marshall would be given the czar's bedroom—he would later tease King about residing in the czarina's boudoir en suite. The Germans had previously occupied these regal rooms and had destroyed the furnishings. The Russians, however, had stripped Moscow's grand Metropol Hotel to set up the interiors, if not to their former grandeur, at least to a level of comfort that would suffice. Despite their efforts, the Russians had not managed to get rid of the bedbugs, and the bathroom situation—only one flush toilet for the U.S. military delegation—was challenging.[30] As Marshall's aide, Frank McCarthy, noted, a "time and motion" system had to be put into place.

The exterior of the Livadia Palace as it looked during the Yalta Conference
Franklin D. Roosevelt Library

The Politics of Yalta

On Sunday, February 4, 1945, the president gathered the entire American delegation to review the political position of the United States. Two aspects would influence Marshall in terms of his military responsibilities: American troops could be involved in Indochina so long as they were not used to help France regain prewar colonies. Of particular interest to Marshall, though, was what Soviet ambassador Averell Harriman had to say about the territorial demands the Soviets would make in return for their willingness to declare war on Japan after the defeat of Germany. According to historian Ed Cray, Harriman reported that "The Soviets wanted the southern half of Sakhalin Island and the Kuriles. . . .They also wanted to maintain their dominance of Outer Mongolia, and to obtain control of the railroad serving the port of Darien."[31] (By conference end, Darien would be made an international city, and the railroads providing outlets to that port would be operated jointly by a Chinese-Soviet company.) During this first-day session, Roosevelt let it be known that he agreed to every Russian request but the Mongolian aspect, since he wanted Chiang Kai-shek's approval for that. Nevertheless, the president's approach eased Marshall's mind, confirming the assumption

399

he had held since Tehran: the Allies could count on Russia to enter the war against Japan after victory in Europe. Although Marshall was aware of the "Manhattan Project," which would produce the first atomic bomb—he had signed off on a $100 million request for the undertaking in 1942—it had not been tested, so there were no guarantees that this mega-weapon would work or even that it would be ready soon enough to prevent a full-scale invasion of the Japanese home islands. If the invasion came, Allied casualties alone were projected at 100,000 and up. Without Russia in the war, the cost in lives would be much higher.[32]

That evening the first plenary session began, with Roosevelt presiding. The focus was on the status of military operations. Russian general Aleksei Antonov was first to speak, outlining the progress of the Soviet offensive against the Germans that had begun on January 12. With poor visibility and limited air support, the Soviet army had still managed to wound, kill, or take prisoner 400,000 of the enemy and destroy 45 of their divisions. Antonov pushed for a combined summer offensive to narrow the vise gripping the Germans, perhaps forcing a surrender. Then it was Marshall's turn, offering what Secretary of State Stettinius called "one of the most magnificent presentations I have heard in my life." The chief of staff explained the soon-to-be-launched two-pronged offensive that would allow the Allies to cross the Rhine. Marshall noted that British-American troop strength was on par with the Germans—each side had 80 divisions. (Churchill said, however, that the Allies maintained air superiority, thus giving them the edge.) True, Marshall acknowledged, but that advantage could be offset by bad weather. Further, although the Germans had been pushed back in the Ardennes, the enemy was quite able to pack a punch. Allied supply lines were long, vulnerable to V-bombs; in fact, it was still possible for Antwerp to be taken out. Yet, the attacks against rail lines and oil refineries had gone well, Marshall reported. American and British forces had been able to destroy a couple of Panzer divisions that were headed from the Western Front to the Eastern Front, perhaps a hint that the Allies were in fact helping the Russians.[33]

After that discussion, which ended in time for a dinner banquet, Marshall did not meet with the Stalin-Churchill-Roosevelt triumvirate until the wrap-up meeting at the end of the conference. Admiral William Leahy, as the president's liaison, was present during the intervening sessions. The three leaders were discussing political matters, so it did not involve the American chief of staff. During the days that followed, Marshall did meet with the military commands, both British and Russian. They spoke of coordinating their respective offensives, staying in communication to prevent the

Germans from shifting units back and forth between the two fronts at will. Admiral Leahy suggested that a bombing line be drawn between them. The chiefs covered weather issues that might bear on the launch of the Allied offensives across the Rhine, and asked for and got assurances from the Russians that they could count on support from the Soviet army.

Marshall stands behind Admiral William Leahy and the "Big Three," Churchill, Roosevelt, and Stalin, during the Yalta Conference, February 1945.

George C. Marshall Research Library

Although Marshall played this limited role at Yalta—primarily in discussion only with military leaders—he was later accused, during the Senator Joseph McCarthy "Red Scare" period, of having sat at the elbow of an ailing, faltering president, encouraging him to give away large chunks of Asia to the Russians. This simply was not the case. First of all, as mentioned, the decision for the USSR to come into the war after V-E Day had already been generally agreed to at Tehran and reconfirmed after the Quebec Conference of 1944. Further, as Marshall biographer Forrest Pogue wrote regarding Roosevelt's motivations, "To the President the restoration to Russia of some of the possessions she had held in the Far East prior to the Russo-Japanese War did not mean that he was making the Soviet Union a Pacific Power. Rather, he saw it as shoring up the Soviet Union against Japan's possible recovery of great strength in that area—and a Soviet bulwark there was much to be desired in January 1944."[34] Marshall would later tell Pogue, "I did not talk to the president about the need of making concessions to Russia in order to get help against Japan. Stalin had been very specific as to what he could do if we gave him the time in which to do it. . . . He went into the days required and the character of the attack, as I recall, and actually, he followed out the schedule that we talked over to the day, when the event finally developed in the opening of the war with Japan."[35] Marshall later recalled that he was a bit "amused" when he was described in the McCarthy hearings of being "king of Yalta," since for the final dinner there arranged by the Russians, through an innocent oversight none of the U.S. chiefs of staff were invited, although the British military command was.[36]

Perhaps Marshall didn't mind missing a dinner or two at Yalta. He didn't like fish and, being allergic to all shellfish, would become seriously ill if he touched it. The Soviets sought to be hospitable, providing generous spreads, often replete with caviar, turbot, Black Sea bass, squid, shrimp, and crayfish. Fortunately, Marshall's orderly, Sergeant James Powder, had brought a large supply of chocolate, telling a friend later, "Yalta was the place where he [Marshall] lived on Hershey bars."[37]

A Positive Direction—Or So It Seemed

The political decisions made at Yalta would be debated for years to come. On the face of it, among the three powers assembled there, all seemed optimistic regarding the possibility of postwar harmony. In addition to settlements regarding Russia's entry into the war, Roosevelt, Churchill, and Stalin agreed on many other matters. All three nations would govern Germany at war's end, and they accepted a zone of occupation for the French, albeit one that would be carved from the Anglo-American sectors. All would embrace the United Nations, an organizational manifestation of the idealistic concepts laid down by the Atlantic Charter in Newfoundland in 1941. All committed to attending a conference to discuss its details, scheduled for April 1945. Further, the leaders approved a five-member UN security council that would include China, as Roosevelt had hoped for all along. Many hours were spent debating Poland, which by then had been completely liberated by the Soviets. There would be a Polish provisional government, which would include not only the Soviet-based one already set up in Warsaw, but the noncommunist government-in-exile as well. The Yalta protocol called for "free and unfettered elections" in Poland as soon as possible on "the basis of universal suffrage and secret ballot."[38]

In the end, though, the Soviets came to dominate eastern Europe, and fair elections proved illusory. A remark Stalin had once made proved apt: "Whoever occupies a territory also imposes on it his own social system. Everyone imposes his own system as far as his army can reach. It cannot be otherwise." Roosevelt historian Jon Meacham noted, "Looking back, Averell Harriman [U.S. ambassador to Russia and present at Yalta] thought Roosevelt and Churchill made 'an honest attempt to build an orderly relationship with the Russians and there was a certain amount of give and take on our part in the hope of orderly settlements. The fact that we tried and failed left the main responsibility for the Cold War with Stalin, where it belongs.'"[39] Meacham opined that "whatever compromises the president made at Yalta on issues relating to the postwar world, there is evidence that he would have taken a hard line against Soviet totalitarianism had he lived. 'Yalta was only a step towards the ultimate solution Franklin had in mind,' Eleanor [Roosevelt] recalled." Churchill, too, seemed optimistic upon his return to England, telling the House of Commons, "The impression I brought back from the Crimea . . . is that Marshal Stalin and the Soviet leaders wish to live in honorable friendship and equality with the Western Democracies."[40] Of course, Churchill would live to fight the cold war and communism, albeit with an out-of-office hiatus, but soon Roosevelt would be dead. Whatever his dreams were for the postwar world, they would live or die at the hands of others.

With the Yalta conference over, Marshall decided to fly to the Italian front for an inspection trip of General Mark Clark's Fifth Army. Congresswoman Clare Booth Luce, whose husband was the publisher of *Time,* had made a trip to Italy and called it "the forgotten front." Needless to say, there had been a great deal of publicity on the fighting in France and the gains being made by MacArthur in the Philippines. Still, Marshall wanted to visit this theater to see for himself. He insisted that there be no ceremonies upon his arrival. His aide, Frank McCarthy, had sent a firm message to Clark: "Usual form holds good for the Chief; that is, no aides, no orderlies, no flags, no auto plates, no escort, no fanfare of any kind."[41] Arriving in Florence, Marshall frowned his disapproval as an honor guard was drawn up in front of headquarters. As Ed Cray wrote, "Lined up before him stood a squad of men from each of the thirteen different fighting units," including "the American 34th and the black 92nd Divisions; from the Brazilian Expeditionary Force; from Scottish, Welsh, and Northern Irish regiments; from Punjabi, Newfoundland, Canadian, New Zealand, and South African units; from the Polish Corps; and from both Italian army and Italian partisan units." There were nurses from five countries, the Women's Army Corps, and the Red Cross. Only the French and Japanese Americans were missing, since they had already been sent to France.[42] Marshall's scowl soon turned to a smile—here was the army of the Allies in all its polyglot glory. For three days afterward, he made as many as 15 stops a day, through mud and over mountainous trails, to visit these combat-weary soldiers. Before he left he provided a press release describing the difficult conditions under which these men were fighting, and then saying, "Our U.S. troops and those of the Allies have done a splendid job and made a great contribution to the war. A large German force has been held in Italy and prevented from bolstering the enemy's hard-pressed troops on the Eastern and Western front." Then he mentioned the cooperation of all of these combined forces: "Such a spirit of common purpose, such teamwork, makes certain the destruction of the German military power."[43]

The Bridge at Remagen

By the end of February 1945 all was in readiness for the last thrust into Germany. Seven field armies had penetrated the German West Wall—only the winter-swollen Rhine River stood in the way. The Germans had done everything possible to slow the advance of 53 infantry and 20 armored divisions, but on March 7 soldiers of the U.S. Ninth Armored Division, to their amazement, found a railroad bridge at Remagen intact. Soon a battalion of troops raced across it; by nightfall, three more divisions followed. Within the week, Field Marshal Montgomery began Operation Plunder, the long-planned pincer movement that would trap hundreds of thousands of German soldiers in the Ruhr. Within days, Bradley's 12th Army Group was 10 miles into the Rhineland. As historian Mark Perry noted, "While the Allies faced tough resistance in parts of western Germany, the Wehrmacht's ability to rally its forces for sustained resistance was at an end. The Germans were beaten."[44]

The Rationale

As much as Marshall was gratified by the news coming from Germany, he had plenty of issues to face at home. On February 13, 1945, American and British bombers had virtually destroyed Dresden, a German city rich in artistic and architectural history. The death toll, made worse by the firestorm created by the pattern of bombing, killed between 35,000 and 70,000, most of them civilians. In Britain, the "terror raid" was criticized in the House of Commons; the uproar soon reached the American press as well. Secretary of War Stimson questioned Marshall about it. The chief of staff answered in writing on March 6, calling Dresden "a communication center of major

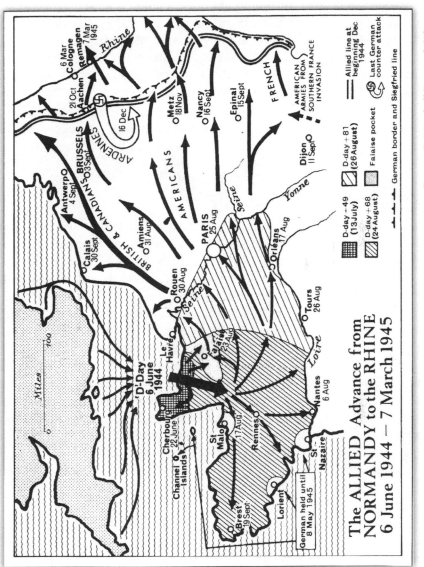

The ALLIED Advance from
NORMANDY to the RHINE
6 June 1944 — 7 March 1945

George C. Marshall Research Library

405

importance, through which [German] reinforcements pass to reach the Russian Front," and defining specific military targets—the marshaling yards and oil installations. He further described the city as "closely related with the German potentialities for launching a counterattack against the southern wing of the great Russian Bulge." Stimson replied, "While the bombing was said to be aimed at military objectives the results were practically unobserved. I think the city should be photographed carefully and the actual facts made known."[45] Perhaps a portion of the damage was directed at military targets, as Marshall claimed, but the fact was that the Joint Chiefs had approved the indiscriminate "overcast bombing" of cities. The Royal Air Force had dropped 1,181.6 tons of incendiary bombs; the U.S. Air Forces 296.5 tons of the same. For whatever purpose, the public saw it as having minimal military significance and a symbol of Allied destruction of both life and property.[46]

"No bed of roses"

That spring of 1945, the chief of staff continued to struggle with the replacement problem. Marshall wrote about it to Eisenhower in a March 6 secret radiogram, describing a speech by Senator Robert Taft railing against the recruitment of 18-year-olds into the armed services and complaining about their lack of training. Specifically, Taft related the story of a friend's 18-year-old son who had been given only 13 weeks of training and then sent to Europe, where he was killed in action shortly thereafter. Marshall had already prepared a press statement for the secretary of war on this issue, stating that all recruits had at least 13 weeks of training, most of them 17, along with further training in staging camps after they arrived in Europe or the Pacific. He noted that "before any man is sent overseas he is submitted to a thorough test to insure that he has assimilated his training and in fact is prepared for combat duty." But then he stated the bottom line: if these young men in a lower age bracket had not been recruited, then it would have delayed the entire campaign in Europe, and probably the Pacific. This, he said, "would mean a tremendous additional loss of life. . . . Such a procedure would be wholly inexcusable."[47] Still, Marshall groused to Eisenhower that at the same time he's hearing this barrage of criticism, General MacArthur was protesting against the shortage in replacements, and other generals behind the lines were complaining about the conversions of their personnel to combat positions. "The combined circumstances could hardly present a more illogical pressure," he said, and concluded that "Making war in a democracy is not a bed of roses."[48] Eisenhower responded that he could certainly relate to Marshall's problems. "Sometimes when I get tired of trying to arrange the blankets smoothly over the several prima donnas in the same bed I think no one person in the world can have so many illogical problems. I read about your struggles concerning the eighteen year old men in combat . . . and went right back to work with a grin.[49]

As the advance into Germany continued, one overriding question remained: Would Eisenhower order Allied forces to take Berlin? The question was answered on March 28, when Eisenhower shifted command of the Ninth Army back to Bradley, giving him the main thrust and precluding Montgomery from having the force necessary in the north to march on Berlin. Field Marshal Sir Alan Brooke called it "unintelligible." This time, though, Churchill faced the facts: "I hope we shall realize that we have only a quarter of the forces invading Germany, and that the situation has thus changed remarkably." He did write a rather mild letter to Roosevelt on April 3 complaining that sending the Ninth Army to Bradley put the emphasis on the American armies in the south and would leave Montgomery's 21th Army Group in a "static position." He talked about the geopolitical aspects as well, suggesting that the Allies should take Berlin. Of the Russians he noted, "If they take Berlin will not their impression that they have been the overwhelming contributor to the common victory be unduly printed in their minds, and may this not lead them into a mood which will raise grave and formidable difficulties in the future?" Historian Robert Andrews noted that Churchill "did not explain what was 'undue' about the impression that the Soviets had been the 'overwhelming contributor,' given that . . . the Russian military dead of at least thirteen million was over twelve times that of the combined British and American."[50]

There were many reasons not to take Berlin, including the fact that at war's end, based on agreements at Yalta as to how Germany would be sectored among the Allies, the city would be 100 miles into the Soviet zone. Further, and most importantly, Marshall, writing the president's reply to Churchill, discounted what he called "psychological and political advantages as would result from the possible capture of Berlin ahead of the Russians." It would take someone in a government position higher than his [Marshall's] to change the strategy of the war. To the chief of staff, the task was to finish the job of defeating the Germans so troops could be deployed to the Far East to finally end the war.[51] Indeed, according to Ed Cray, "The imperative consideration, a reflection of decades of Leavenworth doctrine, was the destruction and dismemberment of the German armed forces."[52] In the end, fighting in Berlin "until the Germans in the last office on the topmost floor of the Reichstag were killed," as Mark Perry described it, would cost the Red Army 352,000 casualties. As Perry noted, "No democracy could afford to expend lives casually for political purposes."[53]

"Pa slept away"

In that spring of 1945 Marshall had assumed greater responsibilities for directing the war. The president was weary, disengaged. Toward the end of March he had left for Warm Springs, Georgia. In 1924, he had established what became the Warm Springs Institute for Rehabilitation to help himself and other polio "patients" enjoy the therapeutic benefits of the site's natural warm springs. In the small cottage he had built within the complex he could relax, in this case with two favorite cousins and an intimate friend, Lucy Mercer Rutherford. Roosevelt had a cold, but he had told a friend before leaving, "All I need is some early spring sun and I will be fine."[54] Marshall and other government advisers carried on in Washington. A packet of official business arrived each day for the president, but the workload was light. Despite the decline in his health, Roosevelt had plenty to look forward to: He planned to attend a huge barbecue organized by the mayor of Warm Springs in the president's honor, set for the evening of Thursday, April 12. After getting that badly needed rest at the Little White House, he was scheduled to be in San Francisco for the founding meeting of the United Nations—an event to which he attached great importance. In June he would travel to England at the invitation of the king and queen. Churchill had said that when the president came, he was going to get "from the British people the greatest reception ever accorded to any human being since Lord Nelson." When a Roosevelt cabinet member worried for his safety in crossing the ocean, warning, "The Germans will get after you," he had confidently replied, "The war in Europe will be over by the end of May." After an arduous investment in this greatest war in history, the president would not live to see its end. That Thursday afternoon, April 12, 1945, as he posed for a watercolor portrait artist, he slumped forward, saying, "I have a terrific pain in the back of my head." By 3:30, Franklin Roosevelt, just 63 years old, was dead.[55]

Eleanor Roosevelt was at a meeting in Washington when the president's aide, Stephen Early, called her to the phone, asking her in a voice unusually subdued and firm to return to the White House. She felt the somber mood immediately, even before he delivered the news. The First Lady kept calm, immediately dictating a short radio message to her four sons, all in uniform: "Darlings: Pa slept away this afternoon. He would expect you to carry on and finish your jobs."[56] The Marshalls were on the porch at Fort Myer that evening when Colonel Frank McCarthy arrived. Mincing no words, he told them, "The president is dead." Within an hour Marshall and Katherine left

The last photograph taken of the president,
April 11, 1945, at Warm Springs

Franklin D. Roosevelt Library

for the White House. Mrs. Roosevelt asked the chief of staff to prepare ceremonies befitting a fallen president. Marshall had already worked on the rituals that would frame a funeral for his mentor, General Pershing, still lingering at Walter Reed Hospital. With those plans as a starting point, the chief of staff harnessed the great machinery of the Pentagon to complete Eleanor Roosevelt's request.[141] Immediately, he dispatched 2,000 soldiers from Fort Benning, Georgia, to Warm Springs to serve in any needed capacity; he identified guards of honor, who would stand at intervals along the tracks as the funeral train made its way slowly toward Washington that Friday.[58]

That same morning, Stimson, King, and Marshall, along with Secretary of the Navy James Forrestal, met with the new president, Harry S. Truman, for the first time. The chief of staff had known Senator Truman when he had chaired the committee on the conduct of the war. Marshall saw him as shrewd and energetic, not a man who suffered fools gladly.[59] During the meeting, King and Marshall provided summaries of the war's progress. The chief of staff reported that the U.S. Ninth Army was only 63 miles from Berlin, near the Elbe River, and would remain there until the Russians arrived in the area for a linkup; the Seventh Army was in southern Germany, Bavaria; intelligence sources estimated that Germany's government, including its military, would cease to be cohesive by May 1. Marshall related that the British had penetrated German defenses in Italy, MacArthur was "mopping up" Japanese units in the Philippines, and American armies were in the Ryukyu Islands, 350 miles from Tokyo. Truman listened, but made only one decision that day: for the time being, he would keep the Roosevelt cabinet.[60] Although Marshall suspected that Truman was a man of toughness and principle, riding back to the Pentagon after the meeting, the chief of staff told Stimson, "We shall not know what he is really like until the pressure really begins to be felt."[61]

By the next morning, April 14, the funeral train arrived at the capital city's Union Station. Honor guards in parade dress accompanied the caisson, pulled by a team of white horses, carrying the president's body. An estimated 500,000 mourners, silent except for an occasional sob, lined the streets all the way to the White House. Marshall and the chiefs, along with their wives, attended the simple ceremony in the East Room that early evening of the 14th. The next day, they flew to West Point and then traveled by car to Hyde Park, New York, where the president would be buried at his ancestral home.

President Roosevelt's funeral procession down
Pennsylvania Avenue, April 14, 1945
U.S. Library of Congress, ID cph.3b14914

There they stood with the rest of the presidential party. They could hear the sound of a dirge-like march as the caisson, escorted by cadets, wound up the hill from the railroad station. The rector from Roosevelt's boyhood Episcopal church delivered the service, followed by the traditional "three volleys" and then "Taps."[62]

When the word of Roosevelt's death reached London, Winston Churchill would later recall that "I felt as if I had been struck a physical blow." Although it was late when the news arrived, the prime minister went immediately to the palace to inform the king. The next day, Churchill addressed the House of Commons. In a voice earnest and hushed, he spoke of the "grievous news which has come to us from across the Atlantic," and of the president "whose friendship for the cause of freedom and for the causes of the weak and of the poor have won him immortal renown." He ended his remarks before the somber assemblage with, "It is not fitting that we should continue our work this day. I feel that the House will wish to render its token of respect to the memory of this great departed statesman and war leader by adjourning immediately."[63]

It's Over!

On the day that Roosevelt was buried, 317,000 German troops surrendered in the Ruhr, more than at any other time in the war. Throughout April there were still pockets of resistance, but the German defensive lines were giving way. As planned, the American troops linked up with the Russians at the Elbe on April 25 in the town of Torgau along the river. Reconnaissance patrols of the U.S. 69th Infantry Division had heard from released American prisoners in the town that some Russians had already reached the east bank of the Elbe. Lieutenant William Robertson decided that it was time to cross the river for the linkup. Realizing that he did not have an American flag so that his men would be recognized as "friendly," he improvised one, using watercolors of red and blue from a nearby shop and a white sheet taken from a civilian. His crude version of the stars and stripes was soon flying from the town's castle tower. With the help of a Russian POW they had just freed, Robertson was able to communicate with the Soviets across the water. Soon he and others from his unit crawled cautiously along the remnants of the Elbe bridge to link up with Soviet Sergeant Nikolai Andreyev, who crept on all fours along the partially destroyed structure to meet him halfway from the other shore. The two hugged without a word—no interpreter required.

The next day was one of celebration, a combination of vodka, Coca-Cola, and chocolate bars. War correspondent and journalist Andy Rooney was there. He remembered later that the Russians had raided a nearby harmonica factory, and from the sounds wafting through the air, it seemed they all knew how to play the handy instrument. Adding to the festive atmosphere was a woman just freed from the German prison who was a singer and who delivered an impromptu concert, with those confiscated harmonicas providing backup. Rooney said it was a scene he would never forget.[64] With troops from both sides assembled before an "East Meets West" sign, the bridge meeting of the day before was reenacted for the sake of the press. This time Lieutenant Alexander Silvashko represented the Soviets; the photo of that scene would appear on page one of the *New York Times* a few days hence.[65]

In this arranged photo, Lieutenant Robertson stands with
Soviet Lieutenant Alexander Sylvashko.

U.S. National Archives 121 (11-sc-205228)

On April 30, 1945, Adolph Hitler committed suicide in the bunker underneath the Reich Chancellery in Berlin, along with his wife of 15 hours, Eva Braun. Five days later, Field Marshal Montgomery took from Admiral von Freideburg the unconditional surrender of all German forces in Holland, north Germany, Schleswig Holstein, and Denmark.[66] All fighting ceased in Italy on May 2, with the surrender of those German troops effective on the 6th; on the same day, the German chief of staff, General Alfred Jodl, arrived at Eisenhower's headquarters in Reims, France, to discuss the surrender of his army. It took another day to work out the details, but a formal ceremony was held just after midnight the next day, with Eisenhower's aide, General Walter Bedell Smith, overseeing the signing. Afterward, Smith escorted Jodl into Eisenhower's office. Did he understand the terms of the surrender, asked the supreme allied commander, and would he agree to implement those? "Ja," said Jodl, and the meeting was over. Almost immediately, Eisenhower sent the official word to the Combined Chiefs of Staff in Washington: "The mission of this Allied Force was fulfilled at 0241, local time, May 7, 1945." All fighting was to end at one minute after midnight on May 8, Victory in Europe Day.[67]

German general Alfred Jodl signs the instrument of surrender.
U.S. National Archives 195337

"The finest soldier"

On May 8, in cities across America, citizens poured into the streets to celebrate. Strangers embraced; champagne flowed; soldiers found it easy to get kisses from pretty girls. Even at the Pentagon, the military chiefs took time to savor the moment. Secretary of War Stimson called Marshall into his office; seated there in a circle was the General Staff. He placed Marshall in the center of the group. The secretary of war had been in public service since 1909 and was 77 years old, yet no one had quite impressed him like General Marshall. Although Stimson's remarks were never recorded, a colonel who was present that same day reconstructed what was said. Acknowledging his "great personal debt" to Marshall, Stimson remarked on the chief of staff's unselfishness in putting "aside such a thing as being the Commanding General of the greatest field army in our history," referring to the chief of staff's refusal to press for command of the Allied invasion of Normandy. Then speaking of his respect and affection for Marshall, he paid the general the ultimate compliment: "I have seen a great many soldiers in my lifetime, but you, sir, are the finest soldier I have ever known." Marshall replied briefly, thanking his colleague for the tribute and for having been a "buttress of integrity and resolute determination" behind him.[68]

That morning, even as Pennsylvania Avenue filled with thousands of celebrants, President Harry S. Truman delivered the official news to the American people from the Radio Room of the White House: "This is a solemn but a glorious hour. I only wish that Franklin D. Roosevelt had lived to witness the day. General Eisenhower informs me that the forces of Germany have surrendered to the United Nations. The flags of freedom fly over Europe." The president emphasized that "the job ahead is no less important, no less urgent, no less difficult than the task which now happily is done. I call upon every American to stick to his post until the last battle is won."[69]

Marshall's radio address of the same day echoed the sentiments of the commander in chief: "Let us celebrate the victory and say our prayers of thanksgiving, and *then* turn with all the power and stern resolution of America to destroy forever and in the shortest possible time every vestige of military power in the Japanese nation."[70] More than three grueling months lay ahead.

Philadelphians focus on the "glorious" part of V-E Day, May 8, 1945.
Special Collections Research Center, Temple University Libraries

Chapter 15

War's End

"These proceedings are now closed"

Summer 1945–December 1945

It was the morning after V-E Day that Marshall sent a congratulatory message to Winston Churchill. With fierce four-year battles over strategy behind them, the sense of completion seemed evident in both the tone and substance of the dispatch: "It has been a long and terrible road for you, Sir, since the fall of France. I can bear personal witness to the grandeur of your leadership since the meeting in Newfoundland in 1941. . . . I can never forget . . . the depth of your vision and your generous attitude in effecting the . . . final crystallization of our combined plans."[1]

Churchill responded with a generous letter to express his thanks for Marshall's leadership, the prime minister's memories of sharp past conflicts fading fast in the face of victory. Although Churchill had once doubted the capability of the American fighting force, ultimately his fears had abated as he witnessed Marshall's skills as a brilliant military organizer. In this letter he acknowledged: "It has not fallen . . . your lot to command the great armies. You have had to create them, organize them, and inspire them. Under your guiding hand the mighty and gallant formations which have swept across France and Germany were brought into being in an amazingly short space of time." Finally, Churchill ended his message with an unabashed statement of admiration for Marshall's "character and massive strength."[2]

Having received this message on May 17, Marshall, not wishing to be cast as superior to his fellow officers, instructed his general staff secretary, Frank McCarthy, to give the following message to the British officer who handled press releases. "General Marshall feels that the release of the Prime Minister's message, while very complimentary to General Marshall, would be embarrassing to him in relation to his Chief of Staff Associates. On the other hand, he has no objection whatever to the Prime Minister releasing his, General Marshall's, message to the Prime Minister."[3]

Marshall had already prepared other messages of congratulations. Shortly before May 8, with the surrender of the German army imminent, he wrote a radiogram to the troops that would be released on V-E Day. He would also use an abridged version as the "voice-over" for a newsreel that would go out to movie theaters within the United States once victory was sure. Marshall

Savoring the victory, Churchill gives his "V for Victory" sign at
Whitehall, the seat of the British government, May 8, 1945.
British Imperial War Museum, H 41849

offered personal thanks "to the leaders and soldiers whose indomitable spirit
and magnificent fight have made this historic victory possible," and deplored
the absence of "the comrades who gave their lives in our behalf." In the third
paragraph, though, he got to the reality of the situation: "Unfortunately, the
conclusion of the European battle does not establish the peace for which
we have been fighting. A bitter struggle is now in progress in the Pacific.
We must continue to do all in our power to terminate the fighting, to end
the sacrifice of lives and the starvation and oppression of peoples all over
the world." Marshall acknowledged the service of "those men now bearing
the burden of the fighting against the Japanese barbarians," and promised
that the destruction of the German Army now made it possible "to deploy
mighty forces in the Pacific to crush the enemy . . . with little delay."[4]

In the final paragraph of his message to the troops, Marshall emphasized
that "the transfer of troops, planes, and supplies to the Pacific will be carried

out with the upmost speed to return the long-term veterans and to secure an early and final victory so that you may return to your homes and enjoy again the blessings of peace and America."[5] The chief of staff had already cautioned Eisenhower to make sure those "long-term veterans" were the first to be brought stateside. In a "restricted" radiogram to the Allied commander that April, he had made his case:

> The matter of selecting and preparing units for redeployment is also of critical importance. Upon the conclusion of World War I, it was too often the case that the most convenient unit was the one shipped back to the United States for demobilization at the expense of a unit which was more deserving. This must not happen again. Furthermore, even though it involves a lot of hard staff work and inconvenience to commanders all the way down the line, those units which are shipped direct to the Pacific theaters must contain to the maximum extent practicable only those people who are least eligible for discharge.[6]

Accrued Points

Marshall fully understood why the redeployment was going to require "hard staff work." The guidelines under which these soldiers were to be brought home was based on an "Adjusted Service Rating," a system of points defined by length of service, overseas duty, the number of battle stars or decorations, and the number of dependent children. The magic number was 85 for men, 44 for women—these personnel would go home first and then be discharged; those with the least would head to the Pacific, perhaps after a brief furlough in the United States; some in the middle range would stay in Europe as an occupation force. Since troops in each of these categories were reorganized into "like" units, it required plenty of reshuffling within the European theater, and perhaps tempted officers to "fudge" a bit on carrying out the strict application of the guidelines.[7] Staging areas near embarkation ports were set up, including at Le Havre, Marseilles, and Antwerp, but the sheer numbers of troops that had to be transferred made the process challenging even to the most diligent organizers. While top priority was given to getting these point-eligible men and women home, it would take months before some would leave.[8] Anticipating inherent morale issues— an "idle soldier becomes a discontented soldier," Marshall had said—he ordered that in "inactive theaters, time be allotted to athletic, recreational, and particularly to educational programs."[9]

Among the first to be sent home under the point system, U.S. Army
veterans head for the harbor at LeHavre, France, May 25, 1945.
U.S. National Archives, 111-SC-207868

"Brass hat hooey"

Once, not long after V-E Day, the Marshalls picked up a soldier who was
hitchhiking, a practice he had started at the beginning of the war. On this
occasion, the chief of staff was in civilian clothes and driving his own
private car; thus, the rider had no idea who the driver was. Soon the soldier
began to talk about his three years of service overseas, including the many
battles in which he had fought, and mentioned that he sure was ready to be
out of the army. Marshall commented that this young man would clearly be
discharged soon. "Not a chance," the man exclaimed. "But you are bound
to have enough points," Marshall had retorted. "Points," said the soldier,
"that's all hooey," complaining that if one didn't have a wife and family,
there was no way to get out.[10] Marshall began to tick off the young man's
points, based on what he had described, and calculated at least 96, way
beyond the required 85. Again, the soldier said that whole thing was "what
the brass hats tell you," just "War Department hooey." Finally, that was as
much as Marshall could take. He told the young man, "Well, I am General
Marshall and you will be out of the Army tomorrow. What is your name

and outfit?" As Mrs. Marshall later recounted, "The man was speechless." Although few servicemen could have the good fortune of this young man, Marshall constantly pressed Eisenhower and the relevant personnel offices to apply a stringent fairness standard.[11]

Even as Marshall turned his attention to the Pacific, also on his mind were anticipated receptions, parades, and publicity for units headed back to the United States, some for good and some for a rest before deployment for the Pacific. On May 7 he had sent two radiograms to Eisenhower, one marked "confidential," that praised the Allied commander: "You have triumphed over inconceivable logistical problems and military obstacles and have played a major role in the complete destruction of German military power."[12] The other message, labeled "secret," tackled this issue of how to handle returning troops. Marshall pointed out that some of the officers would be "natural headliners," while others who had done just as much for the victory would not get as much attention. He noted the resentment that resulted in one group's being given more recognition than the other. Further, he recalled that "when General Pershing returned from France he was mobbed by enthusiastic greeters," but those who returned later were "met by tired reception committees and bored publics."

To counter such situations, Marshall proposed that Eisenhower organize four or five groups of senior commanders with representative delegations from units of different commands, along with small groups of enlisted men and platoon level commanders, "all highly selected for outstanding combat leadership repeat leadership; [and] maybe a sprinkling of Medal of Honor men among enlisted men." Each of these groups would arrive home backed by plenty of advance publicity. The chief of staff cautioned Eisenhower that the timing of his, Eisenhower's, return was important, since it would be anticlimactic for any group to follow the return of the supreme allied commander.[13] By the 11th, Marshall was writing on this subject once more, affirming what he considered an excellent suggestion from Eisenhower— that the men who composed the various groups would be organized according to geographic regions, and the place of the parade or celebration would be within that area of the country. Marshall named the cities, and suggested the names of commanders from each of those regions who might lead a group: for example, Atlanta for General Courtney Hodges, who was born in Georgia, and Chicago for General Mark Clark, who had spent his youth in a suburb of that Illinois city. As for Eisenhower, the supreme allied commander, he would make more than one celebratory stop, including West Point, Washington, D.C., Kansas City, and Abilene, his childhood town.[14]

Beyond the nuts and bolts of getting troops redeployed, there were "a hundred side details," as he described it, to consider. On May 13, he wrote Eisenhower regarding "violent protests" and "bitter editorials" appearing in the newspapers in response to photographs coming from Germany featuring American generals shaking hands with high-level German officials, including arch-Nazi Reich Marshal Hermann Goering, who would later take poison to avoid being put to death for war crimes after the Nuremberg Trials. Marshall referenced "press statements" implying that certain officers had actually lunched or dined with these men. Eisenhower responded to Marshall by telling him that these occurrences were against his express orders, and that he had released a statement stating his disapproval of fraternization, especially between senior officers.[15] A few days later, Marshall wrote Eisenhower that because he (Eisenhower) often was not aware in a timely fashion of the public's reactions in England and the United States regarding postwar issues, an officer should be appointed whose sole task would be to brief him on such matters. As Marshall noted, "I not only see the papers but [also] the telegrams and letters which flood in on me and quickly apprise me of public and political reactions in time for me to take corrective action without appearing to be on the defensive."[16] The fraternization issue would not go away. Soon Eisenhower would struggle with how to handle the widespread tendency on the part of enlisted men, bored as they played a waiting game in the staging camps before redeployment, to develop relationships with German women.

No "optimistic errors"

Despite these "side details," Marshall's primary focus was finishing the war in the Pacific. In any speeches he made during this time, he hammered home the point that the war was not over, not by a long shot. In prepared testimony before the House War Department Subcommittee on May 25, 1945, he acknowledged that the Allies' cumulative momentum was going to bring final victory, but he also cautioned in strong language: "It is of utmost importance that the tremendous power of that momentum be sustained until world peace is actually within our grasp. It would be a costly mistake, a hideous injustice to our men in the Pacific to relax now in optimistic estimates of the situation." There can be no "optimistic errors" or "impatient demands." Marshall spoke of "swift redeployment," and made clear that continuous air strikes would pave the way for the invasion of Japan. "Economy in lives and matériel, as well as the psychology of the American people, demand that we mount a swift, powerful offensive, forcing a victory at the earliest possible date."

To underscore his point, Marshall noted that "we aim to use every man and every weapon practicable," and emphasized again that until victory, a large army had to be maintained. [17] In support of this mission to defeat Japan, he proposed an army strength of close to 7 million, including a reserve force "earmarked for certain eventualities in the Pacific War." In his off-the-cuff remarks after the delivery of the report, he raised the question of "how best to extinguish this Japanese military power," but rejected the notion that a war of attrition centering on blockade and air bombardment alone would work.[18]

As much as the defeat of Japan framed his testimony before the subcommittee, Marshall also spoke on behalf of the half million patients in military hospitals who were suffering from battle injuries and, he said, should receive the best help that "modern surgery and medicine can provide." He noted that during their convalescence these men would need "pleasant surroundings, exercise, and recreation." Once again, Marshall's mind was on the enlisted men waiting to come back to the United States or to be redeployed to the Pacific. The army would continue to help them become more educated. Marshall noted that their educations had been interrupted by war, and thus they deserved help—literacy courses, standard high school curricula, vocational courses, and junior college courses.[19]

"Give us the assurance and backing of a united people"

Marshall wanted to make certain that the American public remained committed to the war effort. On June 4, with joyous V-E Day celebrations still vivid in the minds of the people, *Life* magazine devoted its cover to a letter intended for the "American People" from the Joint Chiefs, headed by Marshall, as well as Eisenhower and Nimitz. The message was clear, buy war bonds to support the continuing war: "Give us not only the needed implements of war, but the assurance and backing of a united people so necessary to hasten the victory and speed the return of your fighting men."[20] Even as this issue hit the newsstands, marine, navy, and army personnel were engaged in the fiercest battle of the Pacific war.

THE PACIFIC—HASTENING THE VICTORY

"I have returned. Rally to me!"

It had been at the second Quebec Conference in the fall of 1944 that, based on information of light resistance to naval raids in the area of the Philippines, Marshall and King had moved up the timetable for the invasion of the island's Leyte archipelago. Once secured, it would provide airfields for the taking of the biggest island, Luzon, and the liberation of its capital, Manila. Rather than a December 1944 launch date, the invasion would begin that October on Leyte Island, the logical stepping-stone toward Luzon. Already MacArthur's army of the Southeast Pacific controlled the coastline of New Guinea, a total of 1,300 miles. With ranger detachments having taken outlying islands in the days before, MacArthur was able to

General MacArthur, in the right foreground, comes ashore at Leyte, the Philippines, October 20, 1944.

U.S. Army Signal Corps, NA-531424

keep his "I shall return" promise" on the exact launch date, October 20. With newsreel cameras rolling, he waded in knee-deep surf from the cruiser *Nashville* via a "whale boat" to seize a truck-mounted microphone already set up on the beach to record the dramatic scene.[21] A radar technician present remembered that an adjutant helped "set the tilt of his cap" and replaced "his dirty leather boots with a fresh pair. He [MacArthur] jutted out his jaw and proclaimed, 'People of the Philippines, I have returned! . . . Rally to me! Let the indomitable spirit of Bataan and Corregidor lead on. As the lines of battle roll forward . . ., rise and strike! . . . The guidance of divine God points the way. Follow in His name to the Holy Grail of righteous victory!'"[22] Shortly after the announcement, MacArthur sent a "freed Philippines" letter to Roosevelt via a Signal Corps courier, supposedly so the president would have the stamp for his extensive collection. The general wrote that he had scribbled it on a pad, since he was "on the combat line." Actually it was only 300 yards from the beach. Roosevelt wrote him back to say, "I know well what this means to you. I know what it cost you to obey my order that you leave Corregidor," a reference to MacArthur being sent to Australia in 1942 after the Japanese overran those islands.[23]

For the next three days, October 23–26, the greatest naval engagement of World War II, the Battle of Leyte Gulf, ensued and would ensure that the Japanese would not thwart the landings of MacArthur's troops. Although the Japanese succeeded in using a decoy force to draw Admiral Halsey's Third Fleet away from the gulf for a time, and despite the fury of the conflict, the Americans prevailed. At the end of the battle, the Japanese had lost four carriers—one large, and three "light," battleships, eight cruisers, and twelve destroyers.[24] Further, more than 10,000 Japanese were killed as compared to the 1,500 deaths for American forces. Losses at Leyte Gulf destroyed for the remainder of the war the potential for the Imperial Navy to launch further large-scale offensive operations and opened the way for the retaking of the Philippine Islands.[25]

Divine Wind

Despite ultimate victory in the Battle of Leyte Gulf, during this time the Americans were introduced to a truly terrifying "human" weapon. It was the first time the Japanese used suicide planes or "kamikazes," which translates to "divine wind," recalling a typhoon that centuries before destroyed a Mongol fleet that was on its way to invade Japan. Each Zero fighter was armed with a 550-pound bomb and a volunteer pilot whose mission was to crash directly onto an American carrier deck.[26] At Leyte Gulf, five kamikazes did damage to escort carriers or were shot down, but a sixth crashed through the flight deck of the USS *St. Lo*, creating an explosive firestorm of bombs and torpedoes that sent the vessel to the bottom of the ocean. Before the war ended, these special attack forces, comprised of pilots all in their early 20s, had sunk 300 ships and inflicted 15,000 casualties.[27]

MacArthur minimized the casualties incurred in retaking Leyte, but in fact the Japanese had pressed hard to deny him his victory. Nevertheless, by December 6–7, 1944, almost exactly three years after the Japanese attack on the Philippines, the Empire of Japan suffered a costly defeat, with the death of 56,263 soldiers as compared to 2,888 Americans. Still, only 389 Japanese surrendered, most of them simply because they were too wounded to do otherwise.[28] With Leyte secure, on December 12, American troops invaded the island of Luzon. It would be February 3, 1945, before elements of MacArthur's forces reached Manila. They would have to battle 20,000 Japanese soldiers, with plenty of the fighting house to house, building to building. Although MacArthur had wanted to advance without much destruction to the city, it took huge amounts of artillery fire as well as air attacks to secure the capital. On February 27 Manila was finally considered safe enough for the Philippine president, Sergio Osmeña, to be reinstated as the head of these islands. Again, as with the fighting on Leyte, the losses were disproportionate. The Japanese suffered 205,535 deaths during the battle for Luzon; the Americans 8,310.[29] The capital city itself was a pile of rubble; only Warsaw, Poland suffered more damage in the war. Even after Manila was freed, the Japanese commander, General Tomoyuki Yamashita, led his troops in a slow fighting withdrawal into three Northern Luzon strongholds where his army held out until its surrender, September 2, 1945.[30]

General MacArthur stands amid the ruins of the Manila Hotel, February 1945.
U.S. National Archives SC 202168

When Marshall wrote his report on World War II to Secretary of War Henry Stimson in October 1945, he referenced a letter written by an unknown Japanese soldier that had been found by the men of the U.S. 32nd Division in the Philippines after the Battle of Leyte. The young man's message hinted at what lay ahead for the Japanese people:

> I am exhausted. We have no food. The enemy is now within 500 meters of us. Mother, my dear wife and son, I am writing this letter to you by dim candle light. Our end is near. What will be the future of Japan if this island should fall into enemy hands? Our air force has not arrived. Hundreds of pale soldiers of Japan are awaiting our glorious end and nothing else. This is a repetition of what occurred in the Solomons, New Georgia, and other islands. How well are the people of Japan prepared to fight the decisive battle with the will to win . . .?[31]

The answer to the young man's question would be swift and terrible. With the Philippines secure, as one historian put it, "Japan lay naked, unprotected by its customary shield of navy power, exposed to assault from almost anywhere."[32]

Iwo Jima

Indeed, Japan's prospects were grim by early 1945, but its people were by no means ready to give up. Their tenacity would be witnessed many times over in the battles for Iwo Jima and Okinawa, both of which would provide important staging grounds for the anticipated attack on the home islands. During the summer of 1944, the Americans had captured the Marianas Islands, including Saipan, Guam, and Tinian, which offered fixed bases for B-29 Superfortress air attacks against Japan. The Japanese had used the island of Iwo Jima as a radar warning station from which they attacked these B-29s en route from the Marianas, thus forcing the pilots to make longer flights to circle the danger. If Americans could control this barren volcanic island of only eight square miles, it would eliminate that danger, and would provide a midpoint between the Marianas and Tokyo, extending the reach of bomber and fighter attacks over Japan. The island had enough flat land to support a large number of these aircraft; further, Iwo Jima could be useful as an emergency landing site for damaged or malfunctioning bombers.[33]

The invasion of Iwo Jima began on February 20, 1945, after 10 weeks of shelling with the big guns of the navy's warships, as well as bombardment from carrier-based planes. The defenders were prepared with extensive minefields, elaborate underground tunnels, caves, and fortified pillboxes with slits positioned menacingly only inches above ground. The primary American invasion force was the legendary Third, Fourth, and Fifth Divisions of the U.S. Marines. Although the casualties during the initial landings were surprisingly light, protected as they were by naval gunfire, moving inland was immediately harrowing, with the men sinking calf-deep in the black volcanic ash as the enemy emerged from its fortified positions.

U.S. marines pour fire into Japanese positions from the north side of Mt. Suribachi, February 21, 1945.
United States Navy Naval History and Heritage Command 204272

From the beach the intrepid American soldiers made their way "inch by bloody inch," literally crawling on their stomachs, sometimes behind tanks as cover. Using flamethrowers, rifles, and grenades, they made their way from bunker to foxhole, finally climbing the island's highest peak, Mt. Suribachi.[34] After three furious days of battle—one historian described it as like "throwing human flesh against reinforced concrete"— the marines raised the Stars and Stripes on that summit. It was an image captured for posterity by Associated Press photographer Joe Rosenthal.[35]

It would be 36 days of brutal combat before the island was fully secured. Of the more than 20,000 Japanese defenders, just 1,083 survived. The price

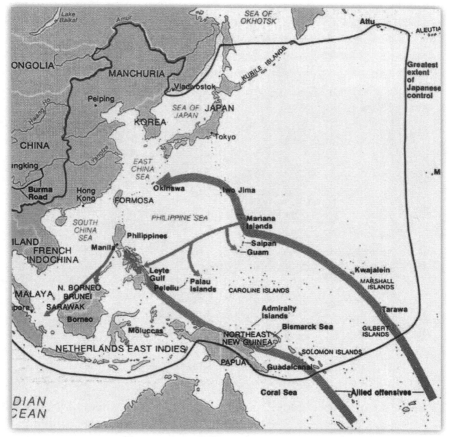

Pacific Theater, 1941-45. The perimeter line
represents the greatest extent of Japanese control.

U.S. National Park Service

was enormous for the Americans—more than 26,000 casualties, including 6,821 dead, the highest the U.S. Marine Corps had faced in its 168-year history.[36] Nevertheless, Iwo Jima proved important. By the end of the war, 2,400 B-29 bombers carrying a total of 27,000 crewmen made unscheduled landings on the island.[37]

Okinawa—A scene "from hell"

If Iwo Jima was the halfway point between the Marianas and Tokyo, the rocky 700-square-mile island of Okinawa was even closer—350 miles— and its strategic value was crucial. With good harbor facilities and room for amassing troops, it was the perfect jumping-off base from which the southernmost home island of Japan, Kyushu, would be walloped into defeat. The battle, which began on Easter Sunday, April 1, 1945, would be one of the longest and costliest of the war. Although the first U.S. units ashore on Okinawa encountered virtually no resistance, that would soon end. Admiral Mitsuru Ushijima had pulled his troops back to the southern end of the island from which they struck the American beachheads and the offshore task forces on April 6 and 7. That assault sank six American ships, but at a cost—135 of the 350 kamikaze planes that had been aimed at task force vessels were destroyed.[38] While the Japanese surely knew at this point that they would not prevail, they continued to fight desperately, motivated to buy time as their fellow citizens at home prepared for what would surely be the invasion of Japan itself.[39] On April 7, Japanese Admiral Seiichi Ito sent the 72,800-ton battleship *Yamato*, and a screening escort, toward shore with no air cover and only enough fuel for a one-way trip; the mission: to beach the ship on Okinawa and fight until defeated. The U.S. Navy sank the vessel in two hours, essentially destroying the last of the Imperial Fleet; in fact, it would be the last action of this once menacing navy for the rest of the war.[40] Still, the kamikazes continued to assail the American fleet. By the time the campaign was over, these suicide planes had killed 4,900 sailors, sunk 26 vessels, and damaged 368 more.[41]

The battle for Okinawa raged on for 82 days. It was a brutal series of pushes by the U.S. 10th Army, as well as the III Marine Amphibious Corps, against what historian Stephen Taaffe described as "three defensive lines honeycombed with hundreds of deep, mutually supporting, and interconnected tunnels."[42] The struggle was made worse that May when monsoon rains sent troops slogging through mud, a nasty brew of garbage, equipment, and the half-buried bodies of the Japanese dead. When the last strongpoint fell, 107,539 enemy soldiers had been killed and another 23,764 sealed in caves or buried by civilian survivors. Okinawa was more populated than other Pacific islands, so U.S. Army figures show a total of 142,058 civilian casualties.[43] Higa Tomiko, a seven-year-old who survived the battle, later described it as "a scene straight out of hell." The Americans—navy, army, and marine—suffered 49,151 casualties, including 12,520 killed.[45] The commanders on both sides died in the battle, American general Simon Bolivar Buckner by artillery fire, and General Ushijima, who, with the island lost, knelt in full-dress uniform and with ceremonial sword committed hara-kiri.[46]

Back Home in Washington

The struggle on Okinawa continued into June. Marshall kept careful watch, scanning casualty reports, alarmed by the daily mortality rates from the Pacific. He had read the stacks of letters coming into his office—anguished relatives who wanted some special recognition for their lost sons or husbands. He knew also that even more than the vicious fighting on Iwo Jima and Okinawa, a battle for the very soil of Japan would be the bloodiest of the war, and it would be the infantry that would bear the brunt. Nevertheless, he believed an invasion would be necessary. Although the Japanese navy and air forces would be powerless, that nation's industry destroyed, and its cities reduced to rubble, he saw no sign that the people would surrender short of defeat on their own land. Reflecting the emphases of their respective services, both Admiral William Leahy and General "Hap" Arnold disagreed with Marshall, arguing that blockade and air power alone would force the issue.[47] The chief of staff opposed this view, judging that such a war of attrition against a desperately determined foe would drag out the struggle through the end of 1946 and maybe even into 1947, much longer than the war-weary and impatient American people would tolerate. Further, as he saw it, despite the hopelessness of the enemy's circumstances, given the "savage resistance" of the Japanese military, still estimated at 5 million-strong in all theaters, only an overpowering force on their home shores would force capitulation.[48] Marshall would later tell his biographer, Forrest Pogue, "We had had the terrific bombing. We had had the hundred thousand people killed in Tokyo in one night [of] bombs and it had seemingly no effect whatsoever. It destroyed the Japanese cities, yes, but their morale was not affected as far as we could tell at all."[49]

As Marshall had outlined during the Combined Chiefs meeting at the Yalta Conference that February, Pentagon planners were developing the details for two attacks on the home islands: a target date of November 1, 1945, was set for the invasion of the outer island of Kyushu (code-named

Olympic), and the spring of 1946 for the main island of Honshu (code-named Coronet).[50] Heavy casualties were to be expected, and certainly those projected numbers were a constant worry to both Marshall and the new president. Since the Russians had pledged to come into the war it was hoped that the Red Army would hold off a significant number of Japanese soldiers along the Manchurian border, and thus reduce Allied casualties at the invasion site.

"We might have called it Hoboken"

While the planning for the assaults of Kyushu and Honshu continued, the possibility of using a new and powerful secret weapon strengthened on the horizon. Secretary of War Henry Stimson and General Marshall had known about the development of this weapon since a few weeks before Pearl Harbor. President Roosevelt had been alerted as early as 1939 by American and European scientists that through experimentation they had discovered the potential for unlocking a powerful source of energy by splitting the atom. They had evidence that German scientists were seeking a way to channel this energy to build a destructive weapon of a magnitude never before imagined. The American scientists wanted Roosevelt's support to pursue their own development of this capability ahead of the Germans. By 1941 Roosevelt had created a "Top Policy Committee" to expedite the research that would eventually lead to the atomic bomb. The committee included Vice President Henry Wallace; Vannevar Bush, the head of the Office of Strategic Research and Development; James B. Conant, head of the National Defense Research Committee; and both Stimson and Marshall. Bush soon suggested that once actual construction of sites for the development of such a weapon began, the army would take over control of the project. From that point on, Stimson would be the president's senior adviser, and Marshall would fulfill that role for the secretary of war.[51]

To get the work started, a headquarters was set up innocuously titled the Manhattan Engineer District—as Marshall would later say, "We might have called it Hoboken, but we called it Manhattan." It was Marshall who selected the man who would lead this effort, Colonel (later lieutenant general) Leslie Groves, best known for having overseen the building of the Pentagon in record time. In the beginning, as Groves submitted reports about matters related to "nuclear fission" and other high-level scientific details, Marshall would head to the *Encyclopedia Britannica* and the dictionary to find out what it all meant. After a while, though, as he said later, "I finally just gave up." What he did do was to make sure he found conduits for funding such a top-secret project. As he related to Forrest Pogue later, "I obtained the first money by taking twenty percent away from an appropriation for a somewhat similar matter—one connected with defense, for example—and this bomb was certainly connected with defense." Having placed trust in Groves, a "brusque, self-assured, push ahead at full steam" kind of guy, he left him to his work.[52] When Marshall needed to step in, he did so; for example, giving full backing in 1943 to efforts by Norwegian guerrillas and Allied bombers to destroy plants in Norway that were making "heavy water," which was needed in the development of the bomb. Marshall also cleared the path for scientists to accompany military personnel as they advanced into Italy, so they could interview Italian scientists in the liberated area who might know something about the Germans' level of atomic development.[53]

"I was going . . . to make him ashamed the rest of his life"

As the Manhattan Project developed, the necessary funding—perhaps a million dollars a month toward the end of 1943—could no longer come from budgets for "expediting production" of defensive weapons. Roosevelt suggested that Marshall and Stimson go up to Capitol Hill, gather the leadership, and make the case for appropriations that would be kept in total secrecy. Regarding the atomic project, Stimson and Marshall quite literally asked the Speaker of the House, plus the majority and minority leaders, to "take our word for it." Amazingly, they did. As Speaker Sam Rayburn said later, "They [Stimson and Marshall] told us it was 'for an important cause; it was something which would help us win the war, but that we couldn't afford to let anything get out about it.'"[54] Others in Congress did not make it easy. Marshall later recounted to Pogue a struggle he had with a member of the Military Appropriations Committee of the House, who, when he heard the project would need $600 million, said it all had to be explained and indicated that he wasn't going to agree to support it unless the details were revealed. The chairman had told Marshall that he couldn't do anything with this congressman. The chief of staff simply insinuated himself into the final markup session of the subcommittee. As he would later say, "I had no right to be present." Nevertheless, Marshall walked in and sat down.

They were all very polite to him, but he took on the man who wouldn't budge and, as he later related, "I said to him that if he forced this thing in the open, if he forced a discussion, which would be a public discussion of something that Mr. Stimson, the honorable secretary of war, and myself had assured these people mustn't be discussed—they must trust us on this as they did the hundreds of thousands of lives of our soldiers—that if he did that, I was going to take the broadcasting radio over and make him ashamed of himself for the rest of his life. Then I got up and left the room, and he shut up and didn't make any more demands." Marshall finished this anecdote by telling Pogue, "We got by that last stumbling block in the effort to get the six hundred million."[55] Nevertheless, such flare-ups with Congress eventually led Groves to suggest that the secrecy be lifted for some members, especially the Military Appropriations Subcommittee. The group was even given a judicious and limited tour of the Oak Ridge, Tennessee, site where uranium was being produced.[56]

Young women at Oak Ridge operate machines used to refine uranium, 1944.
These workers did not know the nature of the project until September 1945.
Ed Westcott, American Museum of Science and Energy

"We couldn't be outstripped"

From the beginning of the Manhattan Project, the goal was to spare no effort in getting the atomic bomb ahead of the nation's enemies. Although at first it all seemed very theoretical, the mission remained the same. When Churchill was meeting with President Roosevelt at Hyde Park in the summer of 1942, they discussed the Manhattan Project—the prime minister had known about the program from the beginning—including the progress being made by the scientists of their respective nations. Recalling their fears, Churchill later wrote, ""We knew what efforts the Germans were making to procure supplies of 'heavy water'—a sinister term, eerie, unnatural, which began to creep into our secret papers. What if the enemy should get an atomic bomb before we did! . . . We could not run the risk of being outstripped in this awful sphere."[57] Marshall and Stimson were similarly motivated. As the secretary of war later wrote: "The entire purpose was the production of a military weapon; on no other grounds could the wartime expenditure of so much time and money have been justified.[58]

By the summer of 1944 the chance that the Germans would develop an atomic bomb lessened, yet the war in Europe was far from over, and Japan showed no signs of quitting. Late in the year, though, the possibility that the United States might soon have the bomb improved. Groves told Marshall that a gun-type bomb, having unheard of destructive potential, could be tested by August 1945, to be followed by the trial of a second even more powerful implosion weapon by that December. During May, with Germany defeated, the key players considered how such a weapon could offset the need for a high-casualty invasion of Japan, considering all aspects related to its use—military, political, and scientific. Late that month, Marshall discussed with Stimson ways of warning the Japanese that the first bomb was launching by identifying ahead of time a specific military target. For a time, he wrestled with the disgrace that would come to the United States from "ill-considered employment of such force."[59]

Stimson had described the Manhattan Project to President Truman shortly after Roosevelt's death. Now, the new president, intent on calling in the experts to consider such a momentous course, organized an innocuously named "Interim Committee" to advise him about "the most terrible weapon known in human history, one bomb of which could destroy a whole city."[60] It met for two long days beginning on May 31, 1945; Stimson, who chaired the committee, and Marshall were both present. A question discussed at length was whether there would be an advance warning to the Japanese. The nuclear physicists on the committee, including Enrico Fermi and J. Robert Oppenheimer, who had led the project, were disturbed by the power of the weapon they had created, and initially advocated a demonstration before representatives of the United Nations on "a barren island," followed by the issuance of an ultimatum to the Japanese.[60] In the end, the committee rejected those possibilities as impractical. One member emphasized that if the Japanese knew the bomb was being "demonstrated," they would "bring our boys who were prisoners of war to that area."[62] There were other risks as well. As Stimson would write in a *Harper's Bazaar* article after the war:

> Even the New Mexico test would not give final proof that any given bomb was certain to explode when dropped from an airplane. Quite apart from the generally unfamiliar nature of atomic explosives, there was the whole problem of exploding a bomb at a predetermined height in the air by a complicated mechanism which could not be tested in the static test of New Mexico. Nothing would have been more damaging to our effort to obtain surrender than a warning or a demonstration followed by a dud—and this was a real possibility. Furthermore, we had no bombs to waste. It was vital that sufficient effect be quickly obtained with the few we had.[63]

In a follow-up report to the president on June 16, 1945, the panel of nuclear physicists reluctantly rejected a "technical demonstration" as likely to bring an end to the war, and concluded that they "could see no acceptable alternative to direct military use."[64]

A Busy Day

No doubt the question of how best to end the war in Japan weighed heavily upon Marshall's mind. Nevertheless, on the morning of June 18, he paused to savor the victorious return of General Eisenhower from Europe to the United States. The chief of staff had already organized the day of celebration in the nation's capital, having outlined the plan in a letter to Eisenhower on June 13: "I will meet you at the airport and ride with you to the Pentagon. . . . The column of cars containing your party will enter the inner court of the Pentagon where the workers in the War Department can see and greet you either from the ground or from the adjacent windows. Your car will stop in front of a balcony where the Secretary of War will greet you."[65] Marshall further outlined the day's events, which included a parade up Pennsylvania Avenue and then on to Congress for a celebratory reception. Indeed, the day went as planned—it turned out to be the largest crowd ever to see a parade in Washington, D.C. Riding in the open limousine with Eisenhower, Marshall told him, "Stand up so they can see you," and then cautioned the chauffeur to "Drive slowly; be careful when you shift gears," so that the hero of the hour would not fall forward.[66] As historian Ed Cray noted, "It was a joyful, tumultuous moment of triumph for the chief of staff and the man he had marked for history's ledger little more than three years before. This was Eisenhower's hour, but satisfying, so satisfying, to the man who made it possible."[67]

Although Eisenhower's wartime mission was finished, Marshall's was not. That late afternoon President Truman held a meeting of the Joint Chiefs of Staff, along with the secretaries of the navy and war and other top-level officials. Soon the president would be leaving for his first wartime conference with Churchill and Stalin at Potsdam, in a suburb of Berlin. He had been thoroughly briefed on the atomic bomb; in fact, Stimson had handed him the written recommendations from the Interim Committee on June 1. Although it had been agreed that if the bomb became available, it would be used, the fact was that the crucial testing had not yet been done. Truman, then, needed to fully understand the implications of the planned invasions of the home islands.

"A strategy of strangulation"

On June 18, as the group gathered at the White House, Marshall did most of the talking, primarily making the case for his plan: "The Kyushu operation is essential to a strategy of strangulation and appears to be the least costly worth-while operation following Okinawa. It is essential, both to tightening our strangle hold of blockade and bombardment on Japan, and to forcing capitulation by invasion of the Tokyo Plain."[68] Truman's key concern was casualties, saying he thought that this proposed assault was "practically creating another Okinawa closer to Japan." Admiral Leahy, who did not favor the invasion approach, pointed out that Allied forces had already suffered 35 percent casualties in that brutal campaign, still ongoing. Further, Truman had read a memorandum from former president Herbert Hoover, who had conducted a study on likely outcomes of the assault on Japan proper and estimated that it would cost half a million to a million American lives, not to mention the death and destruction that would befall the Japanese. During the meeting, Marshall quoted much more optimistic numbers that had been cabled to him by MacArthur, who, it should be pointed out, also supported the invasion concept and hoped to command that operation. His estimate: 50,000 killed or wounded in the first 30 days.[69] It was still a huge concern, especially as Stimson reminded the group that although the Japanese people were as a whole highly intelligent and adaptable, they would "fight tenaciously if attacked on their own ground."[70]

Late in the session, after this lengthy invasion discussion, the president noticed that Assistant Secretary of War John J. McCloy had said nothing, and called upon him for his viewpoint. His input was brief: "Why not use the bomb?" It set off another round of debate. Nevertheless, according to

Marshall, as the meeting ended, the president told the group that he had called them together "to know definitely how far we could afford to go in the Japanese campaign. . . . He was clear on the situation now and was quite sure that the Joint Chiefs of Staff should proceed with the Kyushu operation."[71] Truman closed by saying he would give his "final approval" of the Honshu operation soon. Maybe this allowed time to take into account the impact of the Kyushu campaign and the effect of the Soviet's entry into the war.[72] But perhaps most important of all, that "bomb" option, so close at hand, might soon preclude an invasion, for according to Ed Cray, it was the bomb "that was now driving American policy, or [at least] its manufacture was."[73]

Careless Pilots, Visits, Chemicals, and Illiterate Addresses

Just like the president, Marshall would soon be leaving Washington for the Potsdam Conference. As he prepared for the trip, there were myriad demands on his time, including catching up on correspondence. On June 20, his "secret" letter to Admiral King expressed regret that a careless Army pilot had caused the death of four others because his plane crashed during a series of dangerous and reckless non–battle-related maneuvers. Marshall informed King that subordinate commands were being required to verify that their pilots had been informed of strict safety standards. Further, he told King, the army had tried and dismissed "a number of pilots" who had violated the flying standards, but, in this case, he explained, the pilot had died. Admiral Leahy also received a "top secret" message from the chief of staff, outlining a preliminary plan for Eisenhower to visit Moscow, and later, for the Soviets' most revered and famous Red Army general, Marshal Georgi Zhukov, to visit the United States. Eisenhower would go to the Soviet Union that summer; Zhukov's trip to the United States was delayed because of illness, and by the time he was well, the status of the relationship between the Russians and the Americans had appreciably changed for the worse.[74]

The matter of gas warfare was the subject of another "top secret" message from Marshall, this time to General John E. Hull, the chief of the U.S. Army Operations Division. The question was whether noxious gas production should continue, since the U.S. already had an unused oversupply. That summer the chief of staff had raised the possibility of using disabling gases to drive the Japanese from their bunkers, enough, as he said, "to drench and sicken them so that the fight would be taken out of them." President Roosevelt had said early in the war that the United States would not initiate gas warfare; further, such methods violated the Geneva Convention. Marshall's willingness to push for this option reflected his grave concern about the savage fighting of recent months. Although he knew such an approach would bring public disapproval, he noted that it seemed more humane than "phosphorus and flame throwers," a reference to the method employed by American soldiers to drive the Japanese from their caves and tunnels on Iwo Jima and Okinawa.[75] In answer to Hull's question, Marshall said that the Joint Chiefs would hold off awhile before deciding—in other words, it was still under discussion. In follow-up communications, apparently after the decision not to do this had been made, Marshall made the point that there was no use producing and transporting these chemicals all the way to the Marianas and the Ryukus unless they had some purpose other than on a "retaliatory basis."[76] In the end, the United States would not use chemical warfare.

Marshall also took the time to write to Marjorie L. May, whose husband, Colonel Edwin T. May, had been killed on Okinawa. She had received what she called a "form" condolence card over Marshall's "signature." Apparently, the staff person who had addressed it had done so, Mrs. May complained, as if "he was illiterate." Further, she did not think her husband had received the medals or rank that "lesser men had." Marshall wrote a lengthy reply, telling her that the "suffering experienced by American families as a result of casualties caused by the terrible struggle" was "most distressing to me personally." He explained that almost all medals and decorations were given in the field by theater commanders, and that recommendations for higher rank, such as general, came from those same commanders. He had not received such a request on behalf of the woman's husband. Marshall wrote that he would prefer to send personal sympathies, but simply could not because of "the heavy daily casualty lists," which made it impracticable. Clearly, Mrs. May appreciated the letter, for she wrote him back with an entreaty to "please forgive me for writing you that awful letter." Remarkably Marshall took the time to respond once more, this time thanking her for "writing me so frankly," noting that he had lost his own stepson in the war and explaining the backlog in promotion requests from overseas commanders.[77] By that time, the instruction had already gone out to "have all cards addressed on the typewriter without exception."

"Maybe the dog will get lost"

Tucked among Marshall's somber dispatches of world war were light personal letters to family members. As he continued correspondence on these many serious matters, he responded to a request from his sister, Marie Singer, for an autographed photograph for her doctor, who wanted it in payment for his recent medical services. Marshall asked for more details, including the "fellow's name," and whether or not a particular compliment was desired. He told Marie that Katherine "was down in Leesburg" and was having some domestic issues: "The first cook quit, the dog ran off, and in locating the dog, Molly [his stepdaughter] found another cook who had a reputation for both drinking and stealing." Despite this, she was hired, Marshall explained, but when given a Sunday off, she didn't return until Monday evening, very drunk. She left again the next day and hadn't been heard from since. Apparently it had been the incorrigible Dalmatian, Fleet, who had run away, since Marshall ended the letter by saying, perhaps hopefully, "Maybe the dog will get lost again."[78]

Potsdam

Historian Ed Cray noted that meetings such as the ones that Truman held with the Interim Committee and the Joint Chiefs that early summer of 1945 were "tutorial sessions for a new president with no experience in foreign affairs who found himself about to set off to Germany and his first meeting with Winston Churchill and Joseph Stalin."[79] Indeed, it had been Churchill who had pressed for this meeting, which would be the last of the war. The prime minister's concern had to do with the possibility that British-American power in Europe would, as he said, "melt away." By this time, Churchill had already begun to describe an "iron curtain" that would block any Western influence from the areas that the Red Army had taken over in its march toward Berlin.[80] Even more than the meeting at Yalta, this conference would emphasize political matters, since most crucial military decisions had already been made.

On July 10, Marshall seemed more relaxed than usual as he left Washington with General Arnold—first stop Mingan, Quebec, for a day of salmon fishing. From there they traveled to Frankfurt and on to General Bradley's headquarters. The next day, Bradley joined Marshall and Arnold as they headed to Bavaria, in southern Germany, for more fishing. By July 15, the chief of staff was situated in a house that he would share with Arnold and his aides in the resort location of Babelsberg, across the canal from Potsdam.[81] In that town, only 12 miles from the heart of Berlin, the leaders of the three victor nations would convene at the elegant Cecilienhof Palace, the last one built by Kaiser Wilhelm II. Soon the Soviets would design a "red star" garden on the lawn of a property once owned by the last of the German monarchs.

A Shard of Marble

On the morning of the 16th, the American chiefs met with their British counterparts, an agenda composed mostly of Marshall and Arnold describing Pacific strategy. That afternoon they briefed the president. There should be a single commander for the final campaign against Japan, and that would be MacArthur. Truman agreed. The role of the British would be minimal, and neither they nor the Soviets would be a part of an occupation force after Japan surrendered. That afternoon Marshall and Arnold toured Berlin and got an up-close look at war's destruction: huge heaps of brick and wood, the debris of former shops, homes, and office buildings; the filth and stench of the unburied; trees stripped bare of foliage, stark as winter. Arnold described the "terrible desolation" of the scene, as refugees drifted back on rickety bicycles or pushcarts and began digging among the piles of rubble to begin the agonizingly slow rebuilding process.[82] Marshall, having carried so much of the burden for defeating this formidable enemy, wanted to visit the ruins of the Reich Chancellery and Hitler's office. As Ed Cray wrote, they found among the documents "strewn on the floor . . . thousands of Iron Crosses never awarded." Hitler's marble desk lay in ruins; officers picked up souvenirs; Marshall himself took a small shard of marble.[83]

"Destroyer of worlds"

Even as the Combined Chiefs of the Anglo-British Alliance were meeting that morning, the countdown for detonating "The Gadget," an implosion-type plutonium bomb, began at the test site in the Jornada del Muerto Desert, near Alamogordo Air Base 120 miles south of Santa Fe, New Mexico. It was 5:10 a.m., July 16, 1945. A lively but crackly recording of "The Star Spangled Banner" played in the background. Men lay face down, eyes and ears covered, miles from ground zero. After the blast occurred, they could stand up to watch what one writer described as the "deep growling roar of an explosion" through welder's glasses. The flash and fireball—10,000 times hotter than the surface of the sun—created a shock wave that spread 100 miles from the epicenter, produced a mushroom cloud that rose 7.5 miles into the sky, obliterated every living thing within a mile radius, and turned the desert sand to glass.[84] It prompted J. Robert Oppenheimer, the project's lead physicist, to recall a line from Hindu scripture, the Bhagavad Gita, "I am become Death, the destroyer of worlds."[85]

"The Gadget" as seen at 0.016 after detonation.
Berlyn Brixner, The Los Alamos National Laboratory

"The second coming in wrath"

In Potsdam that evening at 7:30, a cryptic message arrived from Washington for Stimson: "Operated on this morning. Diagnosis is not yet complete but results seem satisfactory and already exceed expectations."[86] The test had been successful. The secretary of war rushed to inform the president and Secretary of State James Byrnes. At noon the next day, July 17, Stimson met with Marshall and Arnold to apprise them of the news. With Assistant Secretary of War McCloy, they discussed a timetable and targets. Stimson already had the names of four cities that would be under consideration: Hiroshima, Kokura, Niigata, and Nagasaki. They agreed that it would be the Air Force commander in the Pacific, Lieutenant General Carl A. Spaatz, who would decide from this list, based on weather conditions and other local factors. The bomb would not be dropped before August 2 and, as was suggested in a memorandum from Stimson on July 2, not before a warning of the impending disaster was sent to the Japanese. In the afternoon Stimson visited Churchill, who later recalled that "Laid before me was a sheet of paper on which was written, 'Babies satisfactorily born.'" Although Churchill had known about the bombs from the beginning, the question was "Were they useless or were they annihilating? Now we knew."[87] As much as he had been kept abreast of the project's progress, the prime minister was nevertheless astonished at the news, telling Stimson excitedly, "What was gunpowder? Trivial. What was electricity? Meaningless. This atomic bomb is the second coming in wrath."[88]

"If the plan . . . did not suit us"

That same afternoon there was another brief meeting of the Combined Chiefs. The Americans agreed that if there was to be an invasion of Japan, the British could participate. Brooke noted that "we wanted a bigger share in the Pacific . . . [but] they are apparently reluctant to provide this share." Indeed, heavy involvement of the British meant a possible "diversion of effort" from the main mission so that former colonies such as Singapore, Hong Kong, and Malaya could be retaken before localized independence movements began.[89] The next afternoon, July 18, Marshall and his colleagues met with their counterparts for the last time. Sir Alan Brooke wrote about the chief of staff's "very nice speech," and how he talked of the need for simplifying control in the Pacific. If the British needed any further evidence of their weakened position in the alliance, it must have come when Marshall noted, as Brooke remembered later, that "if the plan for the invasion of the Tokyo Plain did not suit us we could withhold our forces but they would still carry on."[90]

After such a momentous day, Marshall dined with Churchill alone. In past conferences, the prime minister had often invited the chief of staff for these evening meals, seemingly in an effort to make his strategic case, often at odds with Marshall, one on one. This time they were two warriors, near the end of a struggle whose demands had been staggering beyond comprehension. Churchill had his worries. There had been an election referendum on his government on July 5. The results were being withheld until the soldiers' votes could be counted. All seemed certain that this stalwart of the British cause would remain in office; the stalwart himself vacillated between optimism and depression. It is not recorded what the two men discussed that evening; after all, both had heard about the successful test of the bomb that very day. The fact was that Churchill's work was on the political side of the conference agenda, and fraught with difficulty.

The conference did accomplish certain political goals: it identified four zones of occupation; demilitarized and disarmed Germany; dismantled all war-related industries; repealed discriminatory laws; obliterated the Nazi Party; set up trials for war criminals; and determined that Germany would be recreated politically along democratic lines in a decentralized construct that discouraged the amassing of power under a single party or leader.[91] However, the prime minister's concerns about the postwar status of the

Western powers in the wake of Russia's rise were only validated by the questions raised at Potsdam about Poland. It had been Britain's response to Hitler's invasion of that nation in 1939 that had lit the fuse of world war. Now, at the meeting in Potsdam, Poland's future was on the table. Since Yalta, the Soviets had recognized a pro-communist provisional government in Poland—the Lublin Party. The government of the anticommunist "London Poles" had been, until Yalta, recognized as the legitimate Polish government by both the British and Americans. In exile in England during most of the war, they were thus geographically removed from Warsaw's evolving political landscape. By the end of the conference in the Crimea, though, the status of the "London Poles" had changed: the Big Three had agreed that they would have their chance at shared power through a vaguely worded order for "free and unfettered elections." With no provisions made for external oversight of these elections, it would be a Lublin Party "reorganized on a broader democratic basis" that would be in charge of making it happen. When, as a result of the Potsdam agreement, the Big Three recognized this Soviet-influenced party, now called the Polish Provisional Government of National Unity, as the legitimate government, it effectively abolished the "former government in London."[92]

Border Shifts

The Soviets were already exerting their power in Poland, with the backing of this puppet government, having annexed a big slice of Poland's territory—70,000 square miles—into the Soviet Union, displacing more than a million of its citizens. Further, as a means of extending Soviet influence deep into Europe, the Russians shifted Poland's western border farther into Germany, taking 40,000 square miles of that country, including rich Silesian coal mines and a Baltic Sea coastline.[93] The mass exodus of millions of Germans from that area would be destabilizing, and it placed many of the resources that the Allies would have controlled in the postwar years firmly in the hands of the pro-communist Lublin government. Although the conference protocols confirmed this arrangement, Poland's final boundary would be settled in follow-up sessions of the Council of Foreign Ministers, created at Potsdam to settle these postwar issues, including finalizing treaties. Puppet governments were already in place in Romania, Bulgaria, and Hungary and thus, for all practical purposes, under Russian domination. The reality of the situation was perhaps well articulated by Charles Bohlen, a Soviet expert and Truman's interpreter, as he traveled home from Potsdam: "It seemed obvious to us that wherever the Soviet armies were, the Soviet system, with its highly structured authoritarian control, would be imposed."[94]

443

Hostile Blocs

Since Yalta, the Russians had pressed for heavy reparations from the Germans. Churchill and Truman, as well as the state department officials traveling with the president to Potsdam, were opposed to this. They did not want a repeat of the disastrous 1919 Treaty of Versailles that, with its harsh "war guilt" demands, had led to economic ruin in Germany—a circumstance that had created a perfect brew for the rise of Adolf Hitler. Stalin was unwilling to budge on the Polish border adjustments, and the Western Allies would not agree to the heavy reparations. Although at Yalta there was the hope that a unified Germany would provide a lasting peace, now the decision was made that each sector—British, American, Soviet, and French—would extract its own reparations, although the Russians would receive from the other three sectors percentages of certain industrial products in exchange for its agricultural output. That decision proved crucial to Europe's postwar future. As one historian noted, "It . . . marked the first step toward the division of that country on other related economic issues. . . . Almost inexorably, Europe was being divided into hostile rather than cooperative blocs."[95] Despite directives from the conference that encouraged "the development of a balanced economy which would place Germany on a self-sustaining basis," the Russians would essentially ignore it. They took apart utilities and factories for wholesale shipment east, while demanding food, gasoline, and capital from the Western zones.[96] At Potsdam, Churchill told his personal doctor, Lord Moran, that he felt overpowered by all of these changes being wrought from the war, and complained that he was "weighted down by responsibility and uncertainty."[97]

"I take no responsibility"

Winston Churchill would soon be relieved of this heavy burden, but not in the way he had desired. By July 25, the Potsdam Conference adjourned temporarily so that the prime minister could return to England for the election results. By the next day the answer was in: the wartime coalition government that Churchill had built in 1940 was defeated by the Labor Party; it would be a new prime minister, Clement Attlee, who would return to Potsdam at the end of the break. In the end, it was Churchill's dogged will to win the war that at least in part led to his defeat. That all-consuming passion, overriding legitimate domestic concerns or party politics, had accomplished its goal, but now the British people, ravaged by six years of war, were ready to move on. Churchill would later write that since he thought he would be back to take on all the formidable questions of the conference, he let certain things "stand over." Except for the policies he worked on before he left Potsdam, he would "take no responsibility."[98]

So it was that when the conference reconvened, it would be Joseph Stalin who would be the last of the wartime leaders to see the entire war through to the end. He fully intended for the Soviet Union to stay in America's war until the end, for its own gain.

"Patient progressing rapidly"

Churchill was still very much in the action on July 21, when a courier arrived in Potsdam with a complete report from the New Mexico test site, its message emphasizing the tests' outcome as "beyond expectations." From Washington came an update: "Patient progressing rapidly and will be ready for final operation first good break in August. Complicated preparations for use are proceeding so fast we should know not later July 25 if any change in plans."[99] These messages seemed to make certain the availability of the bomb, and thus made Russia's involvement in the war against Japan much less important. It prompted Truman to inquire of Marshall whether the United States still needed the Russians, or "whether we can get along without them." On the 23rd, Marshall replied that he had thought he had to have the Soviets to counter the Japanese on the Manchurian border, but that purpose had been served because Russian troops were already amassed there. But he also said that even if "we went ahead without the Russians . . . that would not prevent the Russians from marching to Manchuria anyhow . . . to get virtually what they wanted in the surrender terms."[100] The answer seemed less than direct. After all, there was still no assurance that the use of the bomb would force a surrender, and even though intelligence reports revealed that the number of Japanese troops being brought back to the home islands was much greater than had been estimated at the June 18 meeting, there were still plenty of them scattered in China that would have to be brought under control. While Marshall deemed that the United States did not require the Russians to end the war, he clearly believed that their participation would save time and casualties. As if to punctuate that opinion, the final report of the Combined Chiefs, submitted after Potsdam, stated that "the allies should 'encourage Russian entry into the war against Japan.'"[101]

"Glad to hear it"

Both Stimson and Assistant Secretary of War McCloy, along with secretary of state appointee Byrnes, believed that Truman needed to tell Stalin about the bomb before it was used. The Soviets were, after all, allies, presumably on the cusp of declaring war against Japan. Truman agreed, but he did not want to overemphasize the bomb's significance, or give too many details. Even without calling in his own interpreter—that would seem to make the occasion more momentous—he told Stalin the news almost casually after an evening meeting on July 24: The U.S. had developed a "new weapon of unusual destructive force." Stalin's reply could hardly have been blander, remembered Truman: "He was glad to hear it, and hoped we would make good use of it against the Japanese."[102] As one historian put it, "It was not simply the old Bolshevik's stony style that allowed him to seem so complacent. Unbeknownst to the Americans, Klaus Fuchs, the physicist who watched in solitary silence the Alamogordo test, had seven times fed detailed information about the working of the device to Moscow."[103] Marshal Georgi Zhukov would later write in his memoirs that Stalin sent a telegram to Moscow that night telling them to speed up their efforts in the development of the same weapon.[104]

Ultimatum

After the findings of the Interim Committee, and the follow-up military strategy session of June 18, Stimson had written a memorandum to the president regarding the use of the bomb. In the secretary of war's view, it fairly represented the thinking of the American government, including Joseph Grew, the acting secretary of state—Byrnes had not yet been confirmed—as well as the secretary of the navy. Truman approved the main points of the memorandum. It acknowledged that an invasion of the home islands would "cast the die of last ditch resistance" for the Japanese, who were "highly patriotic and certainly susceptible to calls for fanatical resistance to repel an invasion." The alternative was the bomb, but the Japanese should be warned before its use. Although this mega-weapon wouldn't be mentioned explicitly, the warning should be strongly stated so that the "overwhelming character of the force we are about to bring to bear on the islands," and "the completeness of the destruction" that would be inflicted on the people of Japan would be crystal clear. Other elements of the proposed warning were conciliatory—a withdrawal of occupation forces as soon as the economy was "purged of militaristic influence and power; those who misled the country into the war punished, and her territory limited to the home islands."[105] As Stimson would later write, it was important "to emphasize the double character of the suggested warning. It was designed to promise destruction if Japan resisted, and hope if she surrendered." Stimson emphasized that success would depend on the "potency of the warning we give her" and noted her "extremely sensitive national pride" that, when "locked with an enemy," would compel her to "fight to the very death."[106]

At Potsdam, with the timetable for the bomb stepped up, the so-called Potsdam Declaration—which had been shaped and edited for days, becoming a bit less specific with each change—was approved by the president. It would be released on July 26, 1945, under the stewardship of the United States, Great Britain, and China. Churchill's signature on the document was his last official act of the war. One aspect of Stimson's recommendations was conspicuously absent: he had suggested that a sentence be added to let the Japanese know that the surrender would not "exclude a constitutional monarchy under her present dynasty," since "it would substantially add to the chances of acceptance."[107] Such a caveat would have perhaps provided some assurance that the emperor would retain some status in the postwar government, an all-important concern of the Japanese. According to some historians, Truman added nothing about the emperor upon the advice of the Joint Chiefs of Staff in order "not to show a sign of weakness."[108] Perhaps the advice of former secretary of state Cordell Hull had been on Truman's mind as well. As historian Louis Morton later wrote, "Hull's view . . . was that the proposal 'smacked of appeasement' and 'seemed to guarantee continuance not only of the Emperor but also of the feudal privileges of a ruling class.'"[109]

Further, nothing so "crystal clear" or "potent" was included as to alert the Japanese to the exponential military advantage that now belonged to their enemies. Stimson, who had headed the Interim Committee, thought that without any convincing demonstration of the bomb's potential, the Japanese would view any mention of some new and mysterious "atomic force" with contempt.[110] So it was that this new instrument was not mentioned, the specifics shielded by vague references to the capacity of the Allies to end the war in Japan as they had in Europe: "The might that converges on Japan is immeasurably greater than that which, when applied to the resisting Nazis, necessarily laid waste to the . . . whole German people." In listing the terms of surrender, the declaration warned that the representatives of these three nations would "brook no delay," and there was no alternative except "prompt and utter destruction." Offerings of hope were also included, as Stimson's report had recommended: except for war criminals, who would be punished, the military forces, once disarmed, would be returned to their homes; there was no intent to enslave the defeated people, or to destroy their nation. Further, after the Japanese leadership had removed all obstacles to a responsible and democratic government, the occupying forces would withdraw.[111]

On the day before the declaration was issued, Truman informed Marshall that unless the Japanese accepted the ultimatum, or unless he, the commander in chief, gave an order to desist, the atomic bomb would be dropped as soon after August 3 as weather conditions allowed.[112] His decision was official. Marshall forwarded the orders to Lieutenant General Spaatz, who would relay the information to specially trained units already assembled on Tinian Island, in the Marianas chain. Spaatz gave his chief of staff, Major General Curtis E. LeMay, the job of deciding when the weather was right. A copy of the order was to be delivered in person to General MacArthur and Admiral Nimitz. The target date provided one week for a response by the Japanese to the Potsdam Declaration. From that time, as historian Ed Cray wrote, "The clock was ticking."[113]

A Chain of Events

In Japan, the highly militaristic cabinet of Hideki Tojo had been out of power since July 1944, after the Allies were victorious on the island of Saipan in the Marianas. Although there were cabinet members who sided with those who wanted to continue the fight no matter how disastrous, since Tojo's ouster the voices for peace within the government had grown louder. Even as early as September 1944, the Japanese government had approached the Swedish minister in Tokyo in an unofficial attempt to sound out the Allies regarding peace, but that rather weak signal brought no conclusive response. By April 1945, as the battle for Okinawa raged, the more moderate cabinet of Kantaro Suzuki was seated, setting in motion almost continuous efforts to find a way to "honorably" end the war.[114]

Suzuki faced a big problem almost immediately. The Soviets would not, after 1946, renew the neutrality pact that had kept that formidable nation out of the Asian fray throughout the war. Perhaps unbeknownst to the Japanese, the Soviet decision to break that pact coincided with the promise the Soviets had already made, which was to enter the war on the side of the Allies within 90 days of their victory in Europe. With the unspoken backing of the emperor, the Japanese first put out peace feelers, mentioning mediation to the Soviet ambassador in Tokyo in early June 1945 with no real result; by late June, the cabinet approached the Russians through their ambassador to Moscow, Naotake Sato. He was to make arrangements for the emperor's special envoy, Prince Fumimaro Konoye, to meet with the Soviets, who, as mediators with the Allies, would work out the terms for ending the war. The Japanese, quite aware that the Potsdam Conference loomed on the horizon, especially wanted a response before the Russians left for that meeting. The Soviets hedged, almost certainly to delay any action on this matter until after the meeting with the British and Americans.[115] The United States, with its ability to intercept diplomatic messages through "Magic," was reading the almost desperate communications between Sato and the Japanese minister of foreign affairs, Shigenori Togo. Clearly, the biggest obstacle to peace was the "unconditional surrender" terms. The importance of this aspect was revealed in a communication dated July 17, in which Togo reiterated to Ambassador Sato the situation:

> Not only our High Command but also our Government firmly believes that even now our war potential is still sufficient to deal the enemy a severe blow. . . . In such times we continue to maintain our war strength; if only the United States and Great Britain would recognize Japan's honor and existence we would terminate the war and would like to save mankind from the ravages of war, but if the enemy insists on unconditional surrender to the very end, then our country and His Majesty would unanimously resolve to fight a war of resistance to the bitter end. Therefore, inviting the Soviet Union to mediate fairly does not include unconditional surrender; please understand this point in particular.[116]

Sato's reply on July 18 emphasized the problem: that the "so-called" unconditional surrender terms omitted "the problem of protecting the fundamental character of the nation," which was the desire of "70 million citizens as regards our form of government." This without doubt referred to the strong, uncompromising desire of the Japanese people to retain a government system that respected and honored the authority of the emperor.[117]

"We must *mokusatsu* it"

By July 26, Marshall was wrapping up his conference duties by meeting with the Russian military staff. The president would return from the short hiatus brought about by election matters in Britain to hammer out agreements with Stalin and, as it turned out, a new prime minister, Clement Attlee, but for Marshall, his work in Potsdam was complete. He and Admiral King would leave the next morning for some sightseeing in Salzburg, Austria, and on to the beautiful Bavarian town of Berchtesgaden, Hitler's former headquarters near his "Eagle's Nest" mountain retreat. As Marshall would write his sister, Marie, upon his return, "The pleasantest part of my trip was my stay at Berchtesgaden. While Hitler's establishment high up in the mountains had been destroyed the town itself . . . was untouched and exceedingly picturesque." He added that he had stayed in Heinrich Himmler's room at the hotel. Himmler had been the head of the dreaded SS—the Nazi secret police.[118] As the two military men became tourists, the fate of the war was being decided. The Japanese government had received the Potsdam Declaration. As far as the chief of staff was concerned, the planned invasion of the Japanese home islands was still viable; it would be the Japanese response to the proclamation, and the president's judgment afterward, that would decide the matter.

Within the Japanese cabinet there were frenzied meetings to decide what should be done. Although most members were in favor of accepting the declaration, the war minister and two of his chiefs of staff vehemently opposed it, calling it "too dishonorable." The sticking point was that there had been no mention of what would be done about keeping the emperor. The document clearly stated that war criminals would be punished. Would the emperor, who was thought to be a living God, be considered a war criminal? Perhaps he could even be put to death? No one was sure.

As the arguments continued, Prime Minister Suzuki needed to make a public response. During a press conference on July 28, he told the assembled reporters that in regard to the proclamation, "it [the government] does not find any important value in it and there is no other recourse but to [*mokusatsu*] it entirely."[119] In Japanese the word can have several meanings: "to take no notice of; to treat with silent contempt; to ignore by keeping silence; or, to remain in a wise and masterly inactivity."[120] The American translator interpreted the word to mean "ignore." Suzuki later said that what he had actually meant was "no comment," since, with the cabinet still debating, he needed time; and further, before responding, the cabinet wanted to see what would happen when Sato met with the Russians. The Americans took it as a rejection of the proclamation.[121] Stimson would later describe the Japanese as having said it "was unworthy of public notice." As far as the president was concerned, there was the answer. The order that Marshall had sent to the Pacific stood—any time after August 3, weather permitting. It was 2:45 a.m. on August 5, 14 hours earlier than Washington time, when the heavily laden B-29 *Enola Gay,* with her two escort planes following, lifted off from Tinian—destination: Hiroshima, the seventh-largest city in Japan, a military and naval center on the seacoast of Honshu.[122]

Hiroshima

At 8:16 that fateful morning, the crew of the *Enola Gay* dropped its payload onto the city, obliterating more than half of it, almost literally erasing everything in a four-square-mile area. A Japanese journalist described the scene shortly afterward: "Suddenly a glaring whitish-pink light appeared in the sky accompanied by an unnatural tremor that was followed almost immediately by a wave of suffocating heat, and a wind that swept everything in its path." He reported that "thousands of people were scorched by a wave of searing heat. . . . Every living thing was petrified in an attitude of indescribable suffering."[123] Marshall was back in the United States by this time, and throughout the day had awaited word of the mission; uncharacteristically, he called General Groves at his office to see if there were updates. Late that evening Marshall contacted Colonel Frank McCarthy—had any news come into the Pentagon office? The answer was no. A while later, though, Marshall's telephone rang, this time after midnight. Groves had received a message: "Results clear cut, successful in all respects."[124]

Hiroshima near ground zero, August 1945
U.S. Navy Office of Information (CHINFO)

The next morning at the Pentagon, Marshall found an elated General Groves in a celebratory mood. Taking the two-page follow-up report that Groves handed him, he called Stimson on a secure scrambler phone. The secretary of war asked Marshall to inform Truman, who was aboard the *Augusta,* returning home from Potsdam. Groves had prepared a news release. As Marshall read it over, he was somber, noting that despite the implications of this news for ending the war, and soon, it wasn't a time for excessive joy. He cautioned against gloating. After all, he told the general, a lot of civilians had been killed—later estimates would place that total at around 80,000. Groves was quick to retort, "I was not so much thinking about those casualties as I was about the men who had made the Bataan death march."[125]

"The battle of the laboratories"

That same day President Truman issued a statement to the American public explaining for the first time this weapon "two thousand times the blast power . . . of the largest bomb ever used in the history of warfare." In outlining the short history of the Manhattan Project, he told the people that this weapon represented a win in the "the battle of the laboratories." Whether the citizens of the United States could fully grasp the magnitude of what had happened, they understood at least two lines very well: "The Japanese began the war from the air at Pearl Harbor. They have been repaid many fold." As if his message was also directed at the enemy, he ended by saying, "Let there be no mistake; we shall completely destroy Japan's power to make war."[126]

Meanwhile, that nation's heads of government were in a state of panic. By the morning of the 7th, the general staff of the Japanese army had the message: "The whole city of Hiroshima was destroyed instantly by a single bomb."[127] Finally, on the 8th, Ambassador Sato got his meeting with Soviet Foreign Minister Molotov. As Ed Cray described it, "Hopeful of a Soviet offer to mediate between Japan and the United States, Sato instead was brusquely handed a Soviet declaration of war effective the following day."[129] For the Russians, their participation in this war would provide "easy pickings" with minimal effort.[130]

"The hallowed spirits of our imperial ancestors?"

Within the Japanese cabinet, the factions of war and peace argued on, the decision-making at an impasse. Although on August 8 the emperor himself was saying the cabinet had to accept the terms of surrender, still the hard-liners stalled. The next day, the 9th, what Truman had warned would be "a rain of ruin from the air" came down on the city of Nagasaki, a major seaport of Japan, bringing death to more than 60,000.[131] Although the intense bombing raids on Tokyo had killed many more, these deaths were brought by a single bomb. Even so, as nuclear physicist Karl Compton later said, "It was not one atomic bomb, or two, which brought surrender; it was the experience of what an atomic bomb will actually do to a community, *plus the dread of many more, that was effective.*"[132] By the 10th, the Japanese had informed the Americans through the Swiss government that they were ready to accept the declaration with the understanding that it would not "comprise any demand which prejudices the prerogatives of His Majesty the Sovereign Ruler."[133] Long cabinet meetings continued, as the two factions, one for war, one for peace, "raged within." Conventional American bombing continued, and planes dropped thousands and thousands of leaflets describing the terms of surrender to the people. On the 11th, the United States answered that crucial question: "The emperor will be required to authorize and ensure the signature by the Government of Japan . . . of the surrender terms necessary to carry out the provisions of the Potsdam Declaration," and "The ultimate form of government of Japan shall . . . be established by the freely expressed will of the Japanese people."[133]

It was the voice of the emperor, though, that would convince the cabinet and the citizenry that it was time to give up. With the response from the Americans, Suzuki privately asked the emperor to call an Imperial meeting of all 16 cabinet ministers, as well as the chiefs of the bureaus of military and naval affairs, and he did so. Once more, three of the militants argued that they needed a more concrete answer from the United States. Finally, Emperor Hirohito told the holdouts that there was no one who supported their side, and, further, that he "could not bear to see my innocent people suffer any longer."[134] Then, with all the power players in the Japanese government present, he delivered the line that would finally end the arguments: "The American answer seems to me acceptable." That was it! He asked that an Imperial Rescript (edict) be written to stop the war, and said that lest the people doubt the decision, he would himself address them through a radio broadcast.[135]

The emperor's remarks were transmitted to the islands on August 15, the 14th in American time zones. Although he justified his country's motivations, saying that Japan had gone to war to ensure the nation's "self-preservation and the stabilization of East Asia," he acknowledged that "the war had not developed to Japan's advantage," an understatement. Further, he explained, the enemy was using a new and "most cruel" bomb that would obliterate the Japanese nation. "Such being the case, how can we atone ourselves before the hallowed spirits of our ancestors," he asked, except by "acceptance of the provisions of the joint declaration of powers?"[136] Many people, transfixed before their radios as they heard for the first time the voice of their emperor, sobbed as they listened.

A Japanese prisoner on Guam covers his tears as he hears the news of the
emperor's unconditional surrender announcement, August 15, 1945.

U.S. Navy Historical Center 80-G-35453

"Please refrain"

In the days leading up to Japan's anticipated surrender, Marshall was
sending a barrage of messages to handle the many reactions, changes, and
adjustments that bore on that likely possibility. On August 8, the very day
the Japanese ambassador was meeting with Molotov, Marshall sent a brisk
secret radiogram to General Carl Spaatz in the Marianas, telling him that
newspapers were quoting him, Spaatz, as saying that an invasion in the
Pacific wouldn't be necessary, and therefore the army wouldn't be needed
there. Marshall told him in a clipped tone that came through even in the
printed message to refrain from such comments and to see "that those about
you do the same." Apparently, he found such talk careless and premature,
despite what seemed certain to many. On the 10th, as the Japanese minister
to Switzerland approached that government regarding mediating a surrender,
Marshall wrote to the president explaining the importance of seeing to it that
the Japanese government released all Allied prisoners. Further, he explained,
the message should be conveyed to the Japanese that until they did so, naval
and air attacks against the empire would not cease.[137]

One of Eisenhower's tasks in the European theater since V-E Day had included overseeing the process of getting combat troops who had seen the least service, and thus had the fewest "points," to the Pacific for the anticipated invasion. Now on the same day, the 10th, Marshall wrote Eisenhower that as soon as the surrender came in, he should "immediately reverse the priorities for movement . . . of men to the U.S," emphasizing that "we must do everything within our power to release personnel just as rapidly as possible."[138] In other words, the task would now be not to get "low point" young soldiers to the Pacific, but rather to bring them home. "By direction of the President combat operations . . . have been temporarily suspended," wrote Marshall to MacArthur on August 11. Despite the brevity of this top secret message, Marshall must have relished it. In two days that order would stand as permanent. However, in that same message, Marshall noted that for the time being, the navy and the Far East Air Forces would continue the bombing of their tactical targets for the invasion of Kyushu, and, of course, those raids would persist until there were assurances that American prisoners were out of harm's way.[139] On the 13th, Marshall sent out two radiograms to the army air force commander on Okinawa—the first one declaring that a planned 1,000-plane mission should continue against targets in Japan. However, shortly thereafter, even before the bombers had returned, he transmitted a second command: "Suspend air operations until further orders." The next day, the 14th in the United States but already the 15th in the Pacific, Truman received formal word at 6:00 p.m. of Japan's surrender. He announced it via radio at 7:00 p.m. Washington time.

"As if joy had been rationed"

It took virtually no time for the word to spread that the war was over. It seemed as if the entire nation took to the streets to celebrate. A *Life* magazine reporter, writing in the August 27, 1945, issue, described the scene:

> Everyone went on the biggest spree in U.S. History. . . . From New York to San Francisco people were bent on having a glorious holiday and they did. Churches were open and full but so were the bars and nightclubs. . . . It was as if joy had been rationed and saved up for three years, eight months, and seven days since December 7, 1941. The tensions of war exploded in a frenzy of fun. [Around] the clock celebrations in the city went on to a cacophony of church chimes, sirens, honking horns, blaring bands, singing, shrieking, and shouting. Servicemen kissed and were kissed, and ripped shreds from their uniforms and handed them out as souvenirs.

After the party America was due to wake up to a post-war hangover.

Residents of Oak Ridge, Tennessee, gather in the town square to
celebrate the surrender of Japan, August 14, 1945.
With permission from Ed Westcott

President Truman proposed Sunday, August 19, for prayer "to the memory of those who have given their lives . . . and to God that he will support and guide us in the path of peace.[140]

"The long hard pull"

There is no record of how Marshall celebrated the final victory of World War II. On the 15th, the day after the surrender news, he had Winston Churchill on his mind—this formidable wartime prime minister now out of office. The chief of staff sent him a message through channels to be delivered to him personally. "With the termination of hostilities," he wrote, "my thoughts turn to you and the long hard pull up the heights to [the] final triumph of your labors." Otherwise, the correspondence of the day was nuts and bolts: demobilization; occupation forces; maintaining a military in the postwar period; eliminating unnecessary expenditures.[141] With regard to how the war ended, Marshall was unequivocal. He would later tell his biographer, Forrest Pogue, "I regarded the dropping of the bomb as of great importance and felt that it would end the war possibly better than anything else—which it did." In 1951, Pogue asked him if, in retrospect, he had changed his mind, and Marshall replied, "I feel the same way about it. There were hundreds and hundreds of thousands of American lives involved in this thing, as well as hundreds of billions of money. They [the Japanese] had been perfectly ruthless. We had notified them of the bomb. They didn't choose to believe that. And what they needed was shock action, and they got it. I think it was very wise to use it."[142]

Catalytic Agents

Whether or not the bomb was needed to end the war as Marshall thought will be debated for decades to come. World War II historian Louis Morton, who has written extensively on the decision to use this weapon, recognized that indeed by the summer of 1945 Japan was defeated; however, in his view, the military clique was not ready to give up and gave every indication that they intended to defend the homeland. Morton acknowledged that it is "difficult to assert categorically that the atomic bomb alone or Soviet intervention alone was the decisive factor in the bringing the war to an end." However, in his view, "All that can be said on the available evidence is that Japan was defeated in the military sense by August 1945 and that the bombing of Hiroshima, followed by the Soviet Union's declaration of war and the bombing of Nagasaki and the threat of still further bombing, acted as catalytic agents to produce the Japanese decision to surrender. Whether any other set of circumstances [blockade, bombardment, and invasion] would have resolved the crisis and produced the final decision to surrender is a question history cannot yet answer."[143]

Homeward Bound

The formal surrender of the Japanese would wait until all relevant parties could be gathered—September 2, 1945, aboard the battleship *Missouri,* in Tokyo Bay. The ceremony ending the war took less than 30 minutes. All was in readiness by 8:55 a.m. Scaffolding was in place so that the cameramen and news reporters could get a good look; every inch of the ship above, including the gun turrets, was packed with sailors in immaculate white, excited to be a part of such an event. After the invocation and the playing of "The Star-Spangled Banner," MacArthur stood at the microphone near the baize-covered signing table and made brief remarks, including telling those assembled that "I speak for the thousands of silent lips, forever stilled among the jungles and beaches and in the deep waters of the Pacific which marked the way."

Then the signing began, starting with the representatives of the Japanese government, somber in formal cutaways, Foreign Minister Mamoru Shigemitsu, and the chief of Japan's Army General Staff. Next, Admiral Chester Nimitz signed for the United States, and then representatives of China, the United Kingdom, Australia, Canada, France, the Netherlands, and New Zealand. Finally, it was MacArthur's turn. Seated at the table, he took out five pens to affix his name, handing the first to General Jonathan Wainwright, frail and rail thin, after having endured three years of Japanese prison after surrendering his troops in the Philippines in 1942. The second went to the British Lieutenant General Arthur Percival, whose grim duty it had been to concede Singapore to the Japanese in February 1942. One pen was reserved for West Point; another to the Naval Academy. Finally, one would later be given to his wife, Jean, who with their son had escaped the Philippines in a perilous journey to Australia in early 1942.[144]

Rising from his chair, at 9:25 a.m., MacArthur walked to the microphone and announced in a solemn voice, "These proceedings are now closed." Moments later a swarm of B-29s teemed over the sky and, as one witness described it, "made a long sweeping majestic turn as they disappeared toward the mists hiding the sacred mountain of Fugiyama."[145]

Finally, MacArthur spoke of building peace in a time when Western

General MacArthur signs the surrender documents during the final ceremony aboard the USS *Missouri*, September 2, 1945. General Wainwright stands behind him; Lieutenant General Percival is to his left.

U.S. National Archives 520694

scientists had made any other alternative a recipe for Armageddon. His last comment focused on the men who had made the sacrifices of the war and had survived: "And so, my fellow countrymen, today I report to you that your sons and daughters have served you well and faithfully with the calm, deliberate, determined fighting spirit of the American soldier and sailor. . . . Their spiritual strength and power has brought us through to victory. They are homeward bound. Take care of them."[146]

Described as a "Historic Handbook for Every American," General Marshall's Victory Report on the Winning of World War II in Europe and the Pacific, was presented to the Secretary of War on September 1, and released to the American public soon afterwards. Marshall must have felt a moment of pride as he wrote to Secretary Stimson in the publication's introduction. "For the first time since assuming this office six years ago, it is possible for me to report that the security of the United States of American is entirely in our own hands." Although he outlined in some detail the progress of the war in the 123-page booklet, the "mission accomplished" messages regarding the enemies of the United States were straightforward:

> Surrounded on all fronts by chaos and overwhelming defeat, the emissaries of the German government surrendered to the Allies at Reims on 7 May 1945, all land, sea, and air forces of the Reich.

> Japan had been made to pay in full for her treacheries at . . . Pearl Harbor and at Bataan. The enemy situation was hopeless. On 10 August the Japanese Government sued for peace on the general terms enunciated by the Allied powers at the Potsdam Conference.[147]

"We must, if we are to realize the hopes we may dare to have for lasting peace, enforce our will for peace with strength. We must make it clear to the potential gangsters of the world that if they dare break our peace they will do so at their great peril." *Victory Report*, 1945

United States Army

Chapter 16

At the Pleasure of the President

"Terror of the Evildoers!"

November 1945–January 1947

Even before V-J Day, the Marshalls were planning the next phase of their lives. That August, Marshall had given Truman a letter requesting retirement. Katherine pressed her husband almost daily—had the president given a reply? His answer: Truman was too burdened with problems on the home front, a response not particularly satisfying to this wife. Nevertheless, the couple began to imagine a future: first they would go to Leesburg and, after getting things in order, would travel to the genteel golfing community in Pinehurst, North Carolina. Katherine had purchased Liscombe Cottage, nestled along one of the town's secluded shaded streets, in late 1944, anticipating a time when her husband would be free to join her there in that milder clime. Even so, they mulled over options. Maybe they would spend part of the winter in Florida on the Gulf Coast for fishing—it would be a long overdue honeymoon that had been set aside for military duties. As she later wrote, "We worked over maps in the evenings, but they were not maps of the Pacific or the Mediterranean. . . . They charted lovely spots in which to rest and relax."[1]

Marshall was looking forward to it as well, writing a friend on October 9, "I hope to be released from my duties by the end of the month. I had thought I could get out by the first of October but the President would not come across."[2] By November 1, Marshall corresponded with Eisenhower, encouraging him to come to the United States from Europe to receive a Distinguished Service Medal from the American Legion. Knowing that Eisenhower would succeed him as the new chief of staff, Marshall emphasized, in part for his own motives, that he didn't want the supreme commander to be "exhausted by long back and forth trips," explaining that he hoped this proposed visit home would be permanent. "I expect to see the President in the next three or four days to force a decision regarding me. I am waiting now until the strikes and other political programs abate at least by a few hours."[3] "We are counting on moving out of Washington lock, stock and barrel in a very few days," Marshall confidently wrote to his friend and wartime colleague Henry Stimson, already out of Washington and enjoying his Long Island home.[4]

Katherine Marshall was convinced the retirement was coming—she had been busily overseeing the moving of the family's belongings from Quarters #1 to Leesburg. She had advertised for someone to take care of the property, since they planned to be in North Carolina or elsewhere for the winter. Katherine had also resigned from the committees that had kept her so busy during the war—the Red Cross, Army Relief, the Soldiers, Sailors and Marines Club, and various others. She labored to sort and clean out the attic at Fort Myer, which included paintings, plaques, and drawings of General Marshall from many admirers, some of them works of art, but most of them amateurish. One, with the size of her husband's head strangely skewed, came with a note that read, "Painted after six lessons." There were many other tokens of appreciation to the chief of staff: a replica of a famous fort dome, made of bronze and so heavy that it took six men to get it into the storeroom; captured machine guns; swords, sabers, and medals. There was even a canteen with water from Bataan still in it.[5]

"Successive emasculations"

As much as Marshall relished his upcoming retirement, there were still plenty of loose ends. He was deeply concerned about the clamoring of both Congress and the public for almost instant demobilization of the military. Their insistence matched what had happened with every war the United States had ever fought. Marshall had experienced it firsthand when in World War I he saw how woefully thin and unprepared the army was when the nation entered that dreadful fight. He recalled his shock when realizing that young soldiers headed for Europe were being handed a weapon for the first time before they detrained in New York to board their ship, and were getting weapon-firing instructions on the voyage to France. Marshall was Pershing's aide in the aftermath of that war when Congress had put the army through "successive emasculations," as he later described it.[6] Further, as the chief of staff, he had been at the heart of the struggle to mobilize an army before the nation became embroiled in a second world war, and he recalled the relief he felt when Congress renewed his hard-fought 1940 draft by a margin of one vote just two months before Pearl Harbor. While Marshall was no doubt weary from the intensity of these war years, and clung tightly to the dream of retirement ahead, remarkably he had a zealot's energy to vigorously push for Universal Military Training (UMT). This was a concept that he had believed in since his days at Fort Leavenworth, when he became friends with another officer there, John McAuley Palmer, whose views regarding the potential of the citizen soldier influenced him greatly.[7] The idea was that preparedness would *deter* war, not encourage it.

Rose Gets a Lesson

That Marshall was committed to this concept was revealed during a visit with his goddaughter, Rose. In 1937 she had married John Wilson, a tax expert, working for the Sperry Corporation in New York City, where the couple had moved in 1941. While she and Marshall corresponded, albeit infrequently, throughout the war, it was a rare treat for her to see him in person. In the city for a meeting in the spring of 1945, he squeezed in a visit to her apartment, despite his tight schedule. As was the usual process, the general's aide had called ahead to let Rose know that Marshall was coming, but she was out running errands. By the time the aide called back and she was there to answer the phone, Rose had only about 10 minutes' notice before Marshall was to arrive. She scurried around their little home, shoving papers, clothing, and anything else that disturbed the neatness of the place into the bedroom and shut the door. With most of the apartment looking presentable, she greeted Marshall.

He gave her a quick kiss and then said that before they could sit down for a drink and a chat, he needed to make an important phone call. To her horror, she realized that General Marshall was going to walk into her bedroom, which was a shambles. As she said, she "slunk into the living room cursing her luck." When he came out, call finished, he made no comment regarding evidence of poor housekeeping. They sat down to talk. What was on his mind? Universal Military Training. He asked Rose if she knew anything about it. When she said she didn't, he proceeded to give her a crash course in the matter. She later remembered how he said quite earnestly: "I want you to understand, Rose, that a citizen Army is a peacetime Army; its purpose is to avoid war, not to provoke it." After a long explanation, replete with details of how such a program could be delivered, Marshall realized that he had to go. Standing up and exclaiming, "Good Lord," he proceeded to apologize profusely for taking up so much of their visit talking shop.

As he left, though, Marshall couldn't resist a jab regarding the piled-up bedroom. With a mischievous grin, he looked back from the open door, telling her, "By the way, that was a very pretty pink nightgown I stepped on in the middle of the floor!" She followed him to the elevator to breathlessly reveal that she and John were expecting their first baby. With congratulations and a hug, he was gone.[8]

"Against the tragic hour when peace is broken"

That spring of 1945, with the war winding down and Marshall fully aware that Americans felt threatened by large standing armies, subject, as he said, "to the behest of schemers," he set out to describe a concept that he believed would allay this fear.[9] His idea was to create a trained citizens' army that could be called upon in a military emergency but would not be "unduly provocative."[10] Already in his biennial report released that September, he had made the case, beginning with a question: "What then must we do to remain strong and still not bankrupt ourselves on military expenditures to maintain a prohibitively expensive professional army even if one could be recruited?" He then provided his answer:

> Obviously we cannot all put on uniforms and stand ready to repel invasion. The greatest energy in peacetime of any successful nation must be devoted to productive and gainful labor. But all Americans can, in the next generations, prepare themselves to serve their country in maintaining the peace, or against the tragic hour when peace is broken, if such a misfortune again overtakes us. This is what is meant by Universal Military Training. It is not universal military *service* [Marshall's emphasis]—the actual induction of men into the combatant forces. Such forces would be composed during peacetimes of volunteers. The trainees would be in separate organizations maintained for training purposes only. Once trained, young men would be freed from further connection with the Army unless they chose. . . When the Nation is in jeopardy they could be called, just as men are now called.[11]

While some observers believed that the atomic bomb would protect the nation from future wars, Marshall was unconvinced. In his view, these technological advances made the cost of war even more horrible than before and made the issue of deterrence all the more important.[12] Others cast the umbrella of the United Nations over the threat of future war. Marshall demurred. He told an audience during a speech at the *New York Herald Tribune* Forum in October 1945, "I personally am convinced that the organization has not even a remote chance of success unless it is nourished by the strength and fiber of the United States. Obviously, if we have no manifest strength, the nourishment of the United Nations organization will be lean."[13] Then he drove home his major point as he had on various occasions since V-J Day. "We are still strong today but we won't be so a few months hence unless we take very positive and definite measures to give some degree of permanence to the strength for which we have just spent so much of human life and money to develop."[14] Even though he campaigned hard for UMT, and President Truman had formally asked Congress to pass such legislation, support for it was weak. It never passed. As historian Mark Stoler wrote, "Despite his enormous prestige, the chief of staff had to face some personal limits of power in late 1945."[15]

"Dates can only be guesses"

On November 18, 1945, Marshall received a message from the secretary of war, one that he had anticipated for a long time: "By direction of the President, General of the Army George C. Marshall, 01616, Chief of Staff, United States Army, is relieved from detail as a member of the General Staff Corps."[16] On the 20th, during his press conference Truman announced that indeed he had accepted Marshall's resignation, and that Eisenhower would be the acting chief of staff.

Although already well into a Washington winter, it was a crisp sunny day that November 26, warm enough for Marshall's retirement ceremony to be held in the wind-protected central courtyard of the Pentagon. Many dignitaries from the army and navy were there, including his colleague and friend, former secretary of war Henry Stimson. One of his last acts before leaving office had been to suggest that a special congressional medal be struck to honor Marshall's service. In making his case, he delivered high praise: "Show me any war in history which has produced a general with such a surprisingly perfect record as his in this greatest and most difficult of wars in all history." Stimson called him "a generous man who kept in the background so that his subordinates could receive the credit for their deeds well done." Finally, he said, "The destiny of America at the most critical time of its national existence has been in the hands of a great and good citizen. Let no man forget it."[17]

That November morning, in the Pentagon courtyard, President Truman added his accolades, awarding a smiling George Marshall the Oak Leaf Cluster that would embellish his World War I Distinguished Service Medal. A beaming Katherine Marshall stood behind him on the stage. The president's praise was sincere: "He has been a tower of strength as counselor of two Commanders in Chief. His standards of character, conduct, and efficiency inspired the entire Army, the Nation and the world. To him, as much as to any individual, the United States owes its future."[18]

Noting that he was profoundly grateful for the citation, Marshall accepted

This photograph from Stimson to Marshall pictures them between their offices.
Stimson's inscription beneath the photo noted that the door "was never closed."

George Catlett Marshall and Katherine Tupper Marshall Collection,
George C. Marshall Research Library

November 26, 1945, in the courtyard of the Pentagon

U.S. National Archives 198606

it, but described himself simply as "an agent of those who made it possible . . . the soldiers of the great American Army of this war." He then turned his remarks toward those soldiers, speaking of how they "faced death and swallowed fear," and endured the "loneliness and homesickness and starvation for the normal life" they had loved and left behind.[19] The next part of Marshall's remarks stated the realities of the postwar and, although he did not realize it, foreshadowed his future as a statesman:

> Most of you know how different, how fortunate is America compared with the rest of the world. That is something those at home cannot fully appreciate. Today this nation with good faith and sincerity, I am certain, desires to take the lead in the measures necessary to avoid another world catastrophe, such as you have just endured. And the world of suffering people looks to us for such leadership. Their thoughts, however, are not concentrated alone on this problem; they have the more immediate and terribly pressing concerns—where their next mouthful of food will come from, where they will find shelter tonight and where they will find warmth from the cold of winter. Along with the great problem of maintaining the peace we must solve the problem of the pittance of food, of clothing and coal and homes.

Then, directly addressing the men and women of the nation's great "citizen army," he said, "It is to you that we must look for leadership in the critical years ahead."[20]

With the ceremonies complete, the next morning the Marshalls headed to Leesburg and Dodona Manor. Before leaving his office, Marshall wrote a quick note to General Pershing at Walter Reed Hospital, acknowledging a congratulatory note, and telling him, "Katherine and I have been both engaged in moving and also spending most of our time down at Leesburg. We are off again this morning and I soon hope to be able to clear my skirts pretty generally of Washington involvements. Our present plan is to leave for Pinehurst about the 10th; however dates can only be guesses with us at present."[21] That such plans on the calendar were indeed guesses, as well as pipe dreams, was demonstrated later that very day. Once they had arrived at Dodona, Marshall, along with Katherine and his stepdaughter, Molly, spent several hours supervising and unloading the crates of personal belongings that were arriving from Fort Myer. After a late lunch, Katherine went upstairs to take a nap. As she headed toward the second-level bedroom, the phone rang. No matter; others would take the call.

It was Marshall who answered—the president was on the line. Truman skipped the usual polite exchanges of conversation, and got right to the point: Patrick Hurley, the U.S. ambassador to China, had resigned, apparently unhappy with the diplomatic situation there. "General," he said bluntly, "I want you to go to China for me."[22] Marshall's answer was equally brief, even terse: "Yes, Mr. President," he replied, and abruptly hung up the phone. Marshall shared with Molly the president's decision, and the two agreed that it would not be mentioned until at least the next day, since they were looking forward to a "retirement" dinner that evening, just the three of them.

That plan proved illusory. When Katherine awoke from her nap, she was already downstairs just as the three o'clock news came on the radio—the lead story: "Mr. Hurley resigns. President Truman has appointed General of the Army George C. Marshall as his Special Ambassadorial Envoy to China. He will leave immediately." Katherine later recalled her shock, as she stood "rooted to the floor." Seeing her look of disbelief, her husband told her, "I could not bear to tell you until you had had your rest."[23]

Tears welled in Katherine's eyes as she took in this news, yet the three of them—she, her husband, and daughter—finished the dinner with little discussion of this development. Nevertheless, as Katherine would later write, it was a "bitter blow." Marshall fully realized the impact of this change to their anticipated retirement life; as he told the president a few days later, "There was the devil to pay." On many fronts, the month before General Marshall left for China would not be easy. Not only would he be immersed in preparation for the conduct of what would soon be known as "The China Mission," but once more there arose the specter of Pearl Harbor.

Pearl Harbor Investigation—One More Time

This time it was billed "The Joint Committee on the Investigation of the Pearl Harbor Attack" that began its inquiry into this matter on November 15, 1945. As he had at three other hearings during the war, Marshall would be called to testify. With the war over, the army and navy boards had released their findings. As the written follow-up revealed, Marshall had duly taken responsibility for certain failures—including not keeping General Walter Short at Pearl Harbor fully informed about a worsening diplomatic situation, and failing to follow up to be certain that Short had placed the Hawaiian command on full alert. When the reports were released, the news generated a political firestorm. The Republicans, who had been out of office for four terms, once more, as Ed Cray put it, "intended to rattle the skeleton in the

Dodona Manor, Leesburg, Virginia, circa 1945

Virginia Department of Historic Resources

Roosevelt Administration's closet." They would allege that the president had deliberately withheld crucial information from the army and navy officers at Hawaii in order to precipitate a war with Japan and thereby end the nation's isolationist resolve.[24]

This committee was comprised of five senators and five representatives, six of whom were Democrats—holding the majority—and four Republicans. Marshall soon discovered that what he thought was going to be an inquiry about proper military judgment was actually characterized by attacks on the former president. Marshall's behavior, judged in the light of his association with that administration, would soon take on "sinister political implications." He would later tell historian Forrest Pogue, "Remember that the investigation was intended to crucify Roosevelt, not to get me. There was no feeling in the War Department that we had anything to hide."[25] Gordon Prange, the preeminent scholar of these investigations, noted that it was this political atmosphere that took away from the primary question: how were the Japanese able to pull off a surprise attack at Pearl Harbor? "The members of both parties," wrote Prange, "continued to indulge in acrimonious exchanges which wasted time, clouded issues, and derailed valuable trains of thought."[26]

It was December 6, when Marshall first testified before the committee. While other officers arrived with a cadre of aides, the former chief of staff entered alone. As soon as he walked quietly through the doorway, the entire room stood; even the committee stopped the testimony of its current witness to take in the scene.[27] Marshall would testify for what he would later call a "charming" week, as he was grilled for seven grueling days in sessions that ran to four hours or more, on every aspect of the Pearl Harbor lead-up. Asked to recall minute details and reactions to every communication that had come across his desk in those tense prewar weeks, his responses would fill 407 pages of the printed record.[28] Although calm and deferential, these hearings were an ordeal for him. Marshall did not collaborate with other figures who had been involved during the months before Pearl Harbor. As he told Cordell Hull soon after having completed his testimony, he had deliberately avoided doing so in order "that there be no possibility of a claim or assertion being made that I had connived with other leading witnesses to present a story more favorable to me than the facts might justify." Nor did he again go over his own testimony from other investigations, such as the Roberts Board, since, as he said, he "did not wish to be influenced, possibly subconsciously, in what I recalled regarding the occurrences at that time."[29]

General Marshall arrives at the Capitol to testify before
the Pearl Harbor investigating committee, December 10, 1945.

Associated Press

Perhaps, in part as a consequence, Marshall was not the best witness on his own behalf. As Ed Cray wrote, "It was not his nature to defend himself; an officer, after all, took responsibility and suffered the consequences."[30] He did so in these hearings, acknowledging his mistakes. Yes, he had discounted the possibility that Hawaii would be the target—he hadn't thought the Japanese would risk it. Yes, it was true that he could not remember seeing a reply to the War Department alert, but as he agreed, he must have seen it, and while it was his opportunity to intervene—to determine if in fact Short had instituted a full alert—he had not.

On December 12, Marshall was questioned extensively by Republican Congressman Frank Keefe, who, unhappy with his witness's "inability to recall" precise details of policies and the contents of various long-ago meetings, opined that since Marshall had been chief of staff of the entire United States Army, his lack of such information was "problematical."[31] Marshall, who was tired and at a low point in this long process, finally observed:

> You gentlemen are bringing up things to me that have been, to a large extent, rubbed out by 4 years of global war. I have not investigated these things to refresh my memory until the past few days, and so I think it not unduly remarkable that I would not remember the detailed conversations and the frequency of conferences [or] at which one we discussed this, and at which one we discussed that. At the time, of course, I would have had a lively recollection. But there are some rather great events that have intervened. I think I have a fair memory, and I am giving you the best I can under the circumstances.[32]

Republican Senator Homer Ferguson interrogated Marshall for more than nine and a half hours over two days about the Magic intercepts in an effort to show that President Roosevelt had withheld prior knowledge of the attack. Marshall answered the barrage of questions in a courteous and straightforward manner, although such underlying insinuations must have been galling for him.[33] Despite such allegations, when the congressional hearings were over the following May, long after Marshall had left for China, the majority report concluded that no American official, including the president, had deliberately "tricked, provoked, incited, cajoled, or coerced Japan into attacking this Nation in order that a declaration of war might be easily obtained from the Congress."[34] Regarding any complicity on the part of the army and navy chiefs in Washington, Forrest Pogue noted that the strongest defense of any such accusations was the character and public record of both Marshall and his naval counterpart in Washington, Admiral Stark. Both men were at the top of their professions, so no reward could have lured them away from their own convictions. In fact, said Pogue,

> Nothing in their careers suggests that even at executive command would they stifle all the instincts of forty years of service to plot deliberately to allow their forces to be attacked without a chance to defend themselves. On the contrary, the record shows that they made numerous attempts to alert all of their commanders to approaching danger. One can argue that they might have done even more, but it is impossible to say that they did not cry warning.[35]

In addition to dispelling the charges against the president, the committee cleared others in Washington, including the secretaries of state, war, and navy, although they were not without blame. For not realizing that General Short at Pearl Harbor had not put the island on full alert, the War Department was criticized. The War Plans Division was reprimanded as well for failing to give "proper attention" to intercepting messages from Tokyo to Honolulu in September and November asking for information on the Pacific fleet's base, information that might have tipped off the chiefs that Pearl Harbor and not the Philippines would be the attack target. They were also censured for the slowness of their response to the "one o'clock" Magic intercept on December 7, contributing to the fact that the attack was a surprise. Marshall accepted responsibility for these lapses. Finally, the report stated that while the officers in Hawaii failed to properly heed Washington's warnings of the coming attack, these were "errors in judgment and not derelictions of duty."[36] This conclusion did not prevent a minority report that laid the "failure to perform the responsibilities indispensably essential to the defense at Pearl Harbor" at the feet of Roosevelt, Stimson, Stark, and Marshall.[37]

On the last day of his testimony before the committee, December 13, a weary but dignified Marshall left the Senate Caucus Room. As historian Alan Saunders wrote, "The audience, more perceptive than the committee about what the nation owed this man, stood up and applauded him as he exited."[38] For each of those days of testimony, Marshall would spend his lunch break in meetings at the Department of State or the White House to grapple with questions about the China Mission. A man who prepared carefully for any task, the demands placed on him before he left Washington prevented him from immersing himself in the details of the China problem. Still, when he could grab a moment, he studied War Department staff documents and communications, as well as books about China supplied by the Library of

Congress.[39]

China—A Conundrum

Only five days before Christmas 1945, Marshall's C-54 plane landed on an airfield in Shanghai, China, a stop that allowed him to touch base with the commanding general of the China Theater, Lieutenant General Albert C. Wedemeyer. The spitting snow blowing around that city's war-torn streets foretold the gloomy outcome of the work he had been sent to accomplish. For this "special ambassadorial envoy," it would be a hard row to hoe.

Antecedents

The situation in China had been turbulent since the revolution of Sun Yat-sen in 1911 overthrew the imperial government, establishing the Nationalist Party—the Kuomintang. It had been Chiang Kai-shek, the party's right-wing leader who in 1927, two years after Sun's death, used brutal methods to decimate a large element of left-wing opposition in Shanghai, after which he established a government at Nanking, some 150 miles inland from the coast.[40] Another Nationalist leader, Feng Yu-hsiang, known as the "Christian warlord" (missionaries had baptized him), after a year of fighting brought the Manchurian chieftains, albeit reluctantly, into the fold. So it was that by 1928, China was tenuously unified under the Nationalists, with Chiang as its leader. Despite the methods he and others had used to gain that unified government, the United States recognized its legitimacy in 1928.[41]

Chiang still had enemies to subdue. Although at one time the Chinese Communist Party (CCP) had coalesced with the Nationalists to subdue the warlords, by 1928 that relationship had disintegrated. Dissident Communist forces in the south, having formed their own military and government, refused to be a part of the unified government. Soon Chiang launched an anticommunist purge. By the early 1930s, Nationalist forces, some 500,000 strong, pressed hard to strangle these southern elements into submission. Within a year the Nationalist army had severely shrunk the area held by the Communists and had killed 60,000 enemy soldiers. Although the CCP army was almost crushed in the tide of such overwhelming odds, its forces muscled their way out of a Nationalist blockade and began a 6,000-mile retreat to the north, where a second Chinese Communist Party contingent was based. This "Long March," begun in October 1934 with 87,000 soldiers, ended a year later with only 8,000 survivors. While some of the forces had left the march to gain support among the peasants, and others were deserters, most died because of disease, starvation, attacks from both the Nationalists and rural warlords they encountered en route, and challenging geographical conditions.[42] The marchers, poorly supplied and mostly unarmed, crossed a total of 18 mountain ranges—some as high as 16,000 feet—24 rivers, as well as both the barren tracts and marshy grasslands of 11 provinces.[43] During the trek northward, the leadership of Mao Tse-tung was solidified. Mao was cofounder of the CCP, and his doggedness, the methods he employed to evade Chiang's pursuing army, and the wily, sometimes ruthless strategies he applied to weaken factions within the party helped him consolidate support among the survivors. Arriving in Yenan in northwestern Shensi Province after the 368-day march, the remnants of the Communist army, although beleaguered and diminished, had a secure base far away from Nationalist forces.[44] Mao used propaganda to underscore the significance of the march and his role in it. As a result, many of his followers romanticized it to the point of myth, making him a heroic figure among hundreds of thousands rural peasants, especially in the north.

Both Chiang and Mao would soon face an even more formidable adversary. Beginning in 1937 Japan began to rampage over China. The Nationalist and Chinese Communist Party leadership agreed to join forces against this formidable external enemy. As Ed Cray noted, "From 1937 until the end of the war, the two factions became wary partners. They squabbled always, maneuvering for postwar advantage. . . . Anointed at Franklin Roosevelt's insistence as one of the great powers, China had contributed little to the defeat of the Japanese." Chiang had hoarded Lend-Lease supplies, and Mao had spent most of his time garnering political support among the peasants in the north.[45] Still, with the war nearing an end, that spring of 1945 Chiang had made some overtures to Mao, inviting him to attend an assembly to draft a constitution. Mao refused, calling it "a congress of slaves."[46] Coerced by U.S. Ambassador Patrick Hurley, Chiang offered a meeting in Chungking, and Mao agreed to come. That summer, both spent six weeks negotiating internal problems, finally assenting to take part that coming January of 1946 in what would be established as the "Political Consultation Conference." Supposedly it would be open to all parties and would be tasked to establish a constitutionally unified government. Only two months later, though, fighting had broken out again in at least 11 of China's 28 provinces.[47]

Instructions

President Roosevelt had long since insisted and made certain that it would be Chiang Kai-shek and the Nationalist Party and not the Chinese Communists that would help China to emerge as the Asian megapower at the end of the war. General Stilwell had written many a disdainful report outlining how Chiang had left it to the United States to throw the Japanese out of China, describing how Chiang was conserving his troops' strength in that theater for the internal fight to come and constantly reminding Marshall of the corruption and waste among the Nationalist leaders. Nevertheless, it was to be the favored government in these postwar negotiations.[48] That President Truman would continue in that vein was clear in his letter of instructions to Marshall, as well as in the supporting documents that were given to him at a White House meeting on December 14, 1945: "The U.S and the other United Nations have recognized the present National Government of the Republic of China as the only legal government in China. It is the proper instrument to achieve the objectives of a unified China."[49] Granted, that government was to be "broadened to include other political elements in the country," and thus it would be necessary to alter the one-party system established by Sun Yat-sen.[50]

The same letter emphasized the belief of the U.S. government that a strong, unified, and democratic China was important to world peace. Toward that goal, Marshall's mission was to bring China's warring factions together through a cease-fire, integrate the armed forces of the several parties, especially the Nationalists and Communists, and build a viable coalition government. As the editor of the Marshall papers, Dr. Larry Bland, noted, "Implicit in this scenario was the hope that, with an independent China thus pacified, unified, and launched on the road to democratic reforms and economic recovery, the strategic balance of forces in the Far East would be stabilized, the U.S. would not have to confront the Soviets in East Asia, and a major 'threat to peace' would be eliminated."[51]

Perhaps acknowledging that accomplishing this would be difficult, Truman told Marshall, "In your conversations with Chiang Kai-shek and other Chinese leaders you are authorized to speak with the utmost frankness." Further, in connection with the help that China expected to receive—credits, technical and military assistance—Marshall could remind them that "a China disunited and torn by civil strife could not be considered realistically as a proper place for American assistance along the lines enumerated."[52]

"It can't be done"

Maybe a foreshadowing of what was to come could be gleaned by an unusually terse conversation Marshall had with the U.S. commander in

Pictured in the uniform of the Chinese Nationalist Army, Chiang Kai-shek
gave this photograph to Marshall during the China Mission.
George Catlett Marshall and Katherine Tupper Marshall Collection,
George C. Marshall Research Library

China, General Albert Wedemeyer. He, along with the senior U.S. diplomat to China, Walter S. Robertson, had met Marshall when he landed in Shanghai that cold December day. After welcoming ceremonies, the three had been driven to the Cathay Hotel in the heart of the city. Wedemeyer and Marshall lunched alone and spent most of the afternoon together. When Marshall laid out the mission as outlined by Truman, Wedemeyer was incredulous, seeing those goals as being out of touch with reality. Having struggled for 14 months with these contentious groups, he had already warned the State Department of "impending chaos." He told Marshall that he saw no hope of building a successful coalition between the Nationalists and the Communists. "It can't be done," he concluded.

With vehemence, perhaps even a flash of temper, Marshall retorted, "Well, it can be done, and you are going to help me."[53] This response was uncharacteristic of Marshall, who usually appreciated frank assessments. Nevertheless, it was not in his makeup to accept defeat before at least facing the battle—this kind of resignation rankled. Further, although Marshall had honed his skills of negotiation in four years of strategic wrangling with Europe's heads of state, perhaps beneath his disciplined resolve he already saw how complicated this mission would be. Earlier, when at a meeting Truman had handed him his instructions for the mission, Marshall went to the trouble to inquire as to what would happen if "I wasn't able to secure the necessary action by the Generalissimo." Writing up his "Memorandum of Conversation" from that session, Marshall clarified in writing the president's answer to a question he had raised: in the event he wasn't able to get the necessary action from the generalissimo, would it still follow that the U.S. government, through him, would continue to back the Nationalists? That was a "correct summation of his directions," the president had answered.[54] As Ed Cray wrote, "The alternative, support of the Communists, was unthinkable." Indeed, all issues—a reformed multiparty government, military integration, democratization—would have to come under the umbrella of the Nationalists and their leader, Chiang Kai-shek. Thus, said Cray, "Truman was effectively undermining his special envoy. Once the clever Chiang realized Marshall had no power beyond persuasion, there would be no incentive to yield any concessions to the Communists."[55]

"Of short duration"

Of his meeting with Marshall that first day, Wedemeyer would later report, "He was not in good spirits," attributing it to the "grueling work and tremendous strain of the war" that had "exacted a heavy toll both on his

General Wedemeyer sits next to Marshall
at an early 1946 meeting of Chinese leaders.
George Lacks, The LIFE Picture Collection, Getty Images

physical condition and his nerves."[56] It was indeed certain this special envoy was tired. After all, Marshall's longed-for postwar rest had lasted only two days before he was plunged into the blitz of work the month before he left the United States. Late that November he had received a congratulatory letter from General MacArthur wishing him "full contentment in green pastures by still waters." "My retirement was of rather short duration," he replied sardonically, "and the outlook does not indicate still waters."[57] Further, there had been no way for Katherine to join him in China on such short notice, and it weighed on both of them. Not long after her husband left, she had received a bouquet of yellow roses from Colonel Frank McCarthy, who had been Marshall's military secretary, later secretary of the general staff, and now a close family friend. In a letter she thanked him for his thoughtfulness, for, as she said, her "heart was truly sad." She bemoaned the fact that her husband had gotten no rest before he left, and his usual aides—McCarthy, as well as his trusted wartime orderly, Sergeant Powder—would not be joining him. She gave vent to her despair in no uncertain terms:

481

When I saw his plane take off without anyone to be close to him whom he had known and depended on, I felt I could not stand it. . . . I give a sickly smile when people say how the country loves and admires my husband. That last week testifying from nine to five every day, with the luncheon hours spent with the President and Secretary Byrnes, trying to get some idea of what might be done on this mission, then [having it] dumped into his lap to write the whole policy after he got home at night. I shall never forget how this country showed its love and admiration. This sounds bitter. Well, I am bitter. The President should never have asked this of him and in such a way that he could not refuse. This is a long way from yellow roses, but I have kept silent so long I had to get it out to someone and it will be safe with you.[58]

Toasts to "understanding, lasting freedom"

Despite this brittle start, Marshall plunged into the task at hand. Having met with Wedemeyer and Robertson to get their assessments, the next morning, December 21, he flew with the two of them to Nanking. The generalissimo and Madame Chiang met the plane. At a meeting that evening, Marshall made it clear that while the United States "was warmly disposed" toward China, it would not want to interfere in internal struggles or to keep American troops in the country. Marshall emphasized that he was there to listen to all views, and to help.[59] However, he warned, the American public would soon lose sympathy with both the Nationalists and the Communists if it seemed that either was not willing to make some compromises. Although Chiang indicated that he was very anxious for peace, he right away blamed the recent fighting on the Chinese Communists, who, according to him, were thoroughly under the sway of the USSR.[60] The next day, Marshall flew to Chungking, where he would soon set up the mission's headquarters in a Western-style villa made of rough unpolished stone and situated at the confluence of the Kialing and Yangtze Rivers. Marshall surely caught the irony of the villa's name—"Happiness Garden." Inside, warmed with charcoal-burning fireplaces, he would greet all manner of Chinese leaders during those winter months, including six from minority parties that had banded together to form the Democratic League. All came bearing gifts and pleas.[61]

On December 23, only two days after his arrival, Marshall met with Chou En-lai, the vice chairman of the Communist Party's Central Revolutionary Military Council and Mao's chief adviser in this and other upcoming meetings. A man of intellect and political acumen, Chou seemed more

482

flexible and less dogmatic than other party faithfuls. One of the leaders of the Long March, he held Mao's deepest respect and trust.[62] As he had with Chiang, Marshall emphasized that he intended to listen to all sides, but also mentioned, as if a non-negotiable, that it was particularly important to end the existence of two armies, one Nationalist and one Communist. Chou seemed conciliatory. Yes, they understood the wishes of the United States, he assured, even agreeing that Chiang would be the trustee of the new government and that the Nationalists would remain "the senior party." There were toasts to "understanding, lasting freedom, and the mission's success."[63]

Following the key meetings with Wedemeyer, Chiang, and Chou, Marshall determined to acquaint himself with the "whole context" before he developed a mediation plan. By December 29, after having been in China only 10 days, he had written the president, "I have had lengthy interviews with all parties, generally from 9 A.M. until 4 or 5 P.M., including lunch—

Chou En-lai, 1946
Public Domain: Peoples Republic of China

483

Communists, Democratic League, Youth Movement [Chinese Youth Party], T.V. Soong [China's premier, and also Madame Chiang's brother], various Central Government officials, specialists from our Embassy, correspondents, Americans in the employ of the Chinese Government." Although all seemed agreeable with the "high-sounding principles" of a more democratic government, Marshall noted, "the practical procedure to secure these ends . . . are [sic] almost completely lacking." He explained to the president that he had his own ideas about how to counter that. Indeed, early on he instructed his staff to prepare documents with "practical procedures" laid out.[64] By early January there was an organizational structure in place for the discussion of all political and military matters: the Committee of Three—Marshall as chairman; General Chang Chun representing the Nationalists; and Chou, as spokesman for the Chinese Communists.

During the committee's first meeting they struggled over old thorns: the Nationalists were upset that the CCP (Chinese Communist Party) seemed to be taking over the lands north of the Great Wall. When Marshall emphasized that the U.S. wanted Nationalist control over all of China, Chou, at least for the moment, acquiesced. The Nationalists were concerned about two towns controlled by the CCP, abutting Manchuria. According to Chang Chun, the Communists were using those towns as a lookout to keep the Nationalists out while the Soviets looted Manchurian factories.[65] Neither side would yield. Finally, Marshall appealed to Chiang himself to "drop all references in the matter" for the sake of the truce. It simply deferred the matter to another time, when the dispute would be a part of "later political negotiations."[66] Perhaps to make the move toward cease-fire easier, Marshall left the resolution of some of the knottier issues to an "executive headquarters" that would be set up in Peking [Bejing] to arbitrate these matters. From there, the Committee of Three would send out three-man teams to any "hot spots" that threatened peace. By January 10, Marshall had a cease-fire agreement on the table.[67]

"American medicine" and "bully boys"

That same day, the agreed-upon Political Consultation Conference met to begin the process of writing a constitution; each party's central committee had veto power over any proposals. Marshall called his role that of "go-between" rather than an official mediator. He made some suggestions, though, including the idea that "a dose of American medicine"—a Bill of Rights—might be in order.[68] Although Chiang's opening remarks for the conference sounded as conceptually American as could be imagined—freedom of speech; legal status for all parties; free elections; freeing of all political prisoners—in fact, he had his doubts about the concessions that might be required, and about Marshall himself. As Chiang wrote, "More and more he is being taken in by the Communists. The Americans tend to be naive and trusting. This is true even with so experienced a man as Marshall." Further, perhaps Chiang would honor a democratizing mood within China, but the conservatives within his party would not. During the conference, there were reports that Nationalist "bully boys" had broken up meetings of one of the minority parties in attendance—the Democratic League.[69] The agreement to unify the army under the Central Government (actually Chiang's Nationalists) also proved difficult. Chou was waffling on the integration of the two armies. Marshall had a hunch that the Communist's fears were driven by how his somewhat ragtag army compared to Chiang's, trained by Stilwell during the war. Marshall saw a practical solution, offering to establish a training school, with American troops as instructors, for selected Communist officers and men. That seemed to allay Chou's concerns, at least for the moment.[70]

Nationalist Chinese representative Chang Chun is on the left; Chou En-lai is on the right. Marshall looks on as the cease-fire agreement is signed.

George C. Marshall Research Center

The Great Hope of China—Maybe

Despite the numerous complications and point-by-point arguments, after 11 hard days of talks, with Marshall refereeing if not mediating, there was an agreement. Step by step they had overcome the ultraconservative elements in the Nationalist Party and other roadblocks to compromise. The conference attendees had managed to pass a series of resolutions that, according to Mark Stoler, "provided a blueprint for a new coalition government leading to a constitutional democracy; and agreement in principle to integrate the armed forces of the two sides."[71] The two Chinese groups wanted Marshall to sign the formal agreement, but he thought it should have only the signature of those parties—this was an internal matter, and thus not appropriate for an "outsider" to sign. Finally, he agreed to place his signature on the document, but as "adviser," telling them as he wrote, "If we are going to be hung, I will hang with you."[72]

At the ceremony sealing the agreement, Marshall gave a short speech, perhaps reflecting both the hopefulness he felt as well as his nagging fears: "This agreement, I think, represents the great hope of China. I can only trust that its pages will not be soiled by a small group of irreconcilables who for a separate purpose would defeat the Chinese people in their overwhelming desire for peace and prosperity."[73] Although this was the high point of the Marshall Mission to China, as Forrest Pogue wrote, "It wasn't a true peace. On each side were those who believed that an unyielding stance was merely the exercise of one's highest duty. For them the peace and prosperity of China depended on the dominance of their philosophy.[74] A high-ranking U.S. Embassy official, John Melby, who was present at the ceremony, described the message this way: "Marshall is convinced that unless this one works the rest is pure delusion, the cease fire will be meaningless and the PCC [Political Consultation Conference] only a dull debating society. The two-sentence speech that he gave at the signing was a real shock to all present."[75]

Personal Freedom

On January 11, just as the PCC was launching, Marshall took a moment to write to Rose Page Wilson, explaining that he had left the United States hurriedly, and before going, the congressional hearings had taken up most of his days. This was by way of an apology for what he called "god-father" delays. She and John had asked Marshall to fulfill that role for their new baby, John. That Rose's letter was a reminder of how badly he wanted retirement is evident: "I long for personal freedom and my own home and simple pleasures. My shooting trips were all arranged for the winter along with horseback rides on the lovely Pinehurst trails and a month in Florida. . . . But, here I am."[76]

Despite his yearning for "personal freedom," Marshall earnestly and energetically applied himself to the task at hand. The next months, in his opinion, were crucial for the whole of China. He worked ceaselessly to make certain that the cease-fire, and the agreements reached by the Political Consultation Conference, did not unravel. Marshall called on every available resource to bolster the possibility of success, sending memo after memo— soothing, cajoling, or firmly requesting. Were there surplus Quonsett huts that could be used at Executive Headquarters, he asked Washington-based China liaison Colonel James C. David?[77] In a radio message to occupation headquarters in Tokyo, he inquired of General MacArthur on February 22: could he spare "60 young American officers . . . and 60 non-commissioned officers" for temporary duty to help school the guerrilla-trained army of Mao? He arranged and attended a seemingly endless round of meetings, convening, for example, with a group of Chinese editors who were fueling the fires of the more violent protesters with their newspaper/magazine polemics. Marshall was disturbed that reporting had taken on the tone of self-serving political rhetoric. He entreated them in an off-the-record session to show support in their writings for the successful negotiations. "I am not asking you to support me," he told them. "I am nothing in this," Marshall emphasized. "But your PCC [Political Consultation Conference] resolution, your cessation of hostilities and, now next, your reorganization of the army; those are three very great things in the interest of China."[78]

One U.S. magazine writer described Marshall's methods this way: "He talked with the firmness of a Dutch uncle and the adroitness of a donkey driver who knows the value of both stick and carrot."[79] In a letter to a long-time supporter, Congressman Walter G. Andrews, Marshall spoke of his busy, busy schedule and how his work revolved around "a wide variety of people, subjects and certainly of points of view." He spoke of "extremely delicate negotiations regarding the unification of the army, reconstruction and operation of the railroads, and coal mines." In "Communist areas," he said, there were matters of "finance, surplus property transactions, naval and air equipment and organization and, of course, all with a background of political complications." Then at the end, he came back to an underlying theme of his letters home, lamenting to Andrews, "I would like to boil this business all down to the simple proposition of negotiations with Katherine over where we plant the shrubs and flowers, shall it be cabbages or cauliflower, and who gets the car this morning."[80]

First Mao and Then Home

Despite continuously dampening "brush fires" in the weeks after the settlements, Marshall knew he needed to come back to Washington. In a radio to Truman on February 26, he said he wanted to talk with him and the secretary of state about matters "regarding transfer of surplus property and shipping and with regard to loans." Indeed, Marshall understood that without some economic bolstering to stave runaway inflation, and the lack of investment capital, any political successes would soon unravel. Yet, he was guardedly optimistic. Just before he would begin his journey home on March 11, he had completed a 3,500-mile trip to 10 cities in North China, including the Communist capital of Yenan. It was his first meeting with Mao Tse-tung, who promised full cooperation and seemed agreeable to flying to Nanking to confer again with Chiang.[81] Marshall was treated with the respect normally afforded a head of state. He reviewed the Communist Party Honor Guard, was feted at nine-course banquets, and, bundled in winter clothing with a blanket tucked around his legs, watched special performances of drum dancers and folk singers in a cold auditorium. Throughout the trip, Marshall was buoyed by the reception he got, writing Truman on March 6 that the treatment had been "enthusiastic and in cities tumultuous." Indeed, he had been greeted by cheering crowds, some even carrying signs calling him "Terror of the Evildoers" or "Most Fairly [*sic*] Friend of China."[82] It is possible, as Forrest Pogue would later write, that "in common with many a touring leader, Marshall was momentarily blinded by the friendly reception and did not fully see the situation."[83] Although he acknowledged "difficulties," Marshall reported to the president that there was "every indication that affairs would clear up quickly and communications be reopened and normal life for the poor civilians actually gotten under way."[84]

Whereas he would eventually attack Marshall's China policy, General Albert Wedemeyer wrote of Marshall's work as he headed back to Washington after this first go-around, "I doubt seriously whether any other person in the world could have done as much in so short a time," and called the agreements a "stupendous accomplishment."[85] What followed such high praise, however, were Wedemeyer's crushingly prophetic words: "The permanence of his accomplishments however is in my mind contingent upon his physical presence. If he were to be eliminated from the picture for the next several months, I feel that the opposing factions would soon be at each other's throats and the situation that existed last October would again prevail."[86]

General Marshall and Chairman Mao Tse-tung
in discussion at Yenan, March 5, 1946
George C. Marshall Research Library

Whirlwind

The C-47 carrying Marshall back to the United States landed in Washington, D.C., on March 14. In a cover article later in the month, *Time* magazine described the scene:

> A tall man with a weathered, homely face, in which there was a visible touch of greatness, stepped briskly down the ramp of the plane from China. . . . George Catlett Marshall was back in Washington. He had time for a broad, boyish grin and two kisses for his waiting wife, quick handshakes for a cluster of welcoming dignitaries. Then he hurried away, in a long black Packard, to report to the White House on the most significant mission undertaken by a U.S. citizen since the end of World War II.[87]

The next four weeks were a blitz of appointments in and out of various federal agencies, as Marshall sought a comprehensive aid package for China. He managed to secure a new Lend-Lease program. As Ed Cray described, it included "$30 million in cotton credits; a $500 million loan

489

from the Import-Export Bank; additional loans for transportation and communications equipment, . . . and a pledge of $475 million in aid over the next twenty months."[88] In addition, Marshall made a plea that China be given priority status for surplus property from the war, especially ships, trucks, locomotives, and freight cars.[89]As if these responsibilities were not enough, Marshall had to spend another day on Capitol Hill to be grilled one last time by the still active Pearl Harbor investigating committee. As Cray noted, "It was like a half recalled memory of his childhood, so far behind him."[90]

Marshall tried his best to also take care of some personal matters. Knowing how fragile had been the settlements between the Nationalists and the CCP, he felt a strong need to get back to China. The time was short, the activity almost frantic.[91] He and Katherine went to Long Island to see Henry Stimson. On his old friend's beautiful estate, Marshall got a chance to ride horseback along peaceful trails, a badly needed restorative atmosphere. Back in Washington, he paid a visit to General Pershing, 88 years old and in decline at Walter Reed Hospital. His conversations were limited—the once powerful AEF commander was no longer capable of following Marshall's accounts of his complicated work.

To Marshall's delight, it had been decided that when he returned to China, Katherine would be with him. The couple had never been apart for more than five weeks, and he had missed her terribly. For both of them, though, getting her ready for the 12,000-mile trip added to the feverish pace—there were a thousand details involved, including packing clothing suitable for the upcoming sweltering summer climate of Nanking, where Marshall planned to move his headquarters. Chiang would soon be claiming the prewar capital, so it was logical that Marshall should be there as well. There was a small foreign community in that city, so servants would be readily available for a household that included a wife. Marshall hoped it would be comfortable for her, enough so that she could continue work on a memoir she had already begun about her years with her famous husband.[92]

"The situation is so serious"

The *Time* magazine piece of March 25, 1946, whose writer had effused over the miracle of Marshall's successes in the China negotiations, included a photograph of Marshall with Secretary of State James Byrnes—the tag line: "Democracy, after all, is an exportable commodity."[93] Perhaps not. Even before Marshall returned to China, the U.S. chargé d'affaires, Walter

Robertson, had radioed on April 6: "The situation is so serious and is deteriorating so rapidly that your immediate return to China is necessary."[94]

The Marshalls left Washington on April 12. En route to China they were guests of the MacArthurs in Japan, and from there landed in Peking, staying long enough for a tour of the Forbidden City—"indescribable in its magnificence and beauty," wrote Katherine. By the 18th, they were in Chungking, the first stop before their anticipated move to Nanking. The city was suffering from a 100-degree heat wave. If the Forbidden City was beyond description in its beauty, the dust, heat, and stench of this metropolis also defied adjectives. Drapes were drawn against the dirt and humidity, so interior spaces were stifling. Even as Katherine wrote a letter to a friend one late April afternoon, Marshall "poked his head through the door" where she was writing, telling her, "Be glad you were born a girl," as a prelude to outlining the frustrating meetings he had had one after the other with the "Emperor of Indo-China, the Generalissimo [Chiang], and General Mo" [Chou en-lai]. Katherine was unimpressed with the advantages of girlhood, retorting, "Darn good thing you weren't born one or you would be ravingly crazy shut up here."[95]

If Katherine found these conditions depressing, it seemed clear that Marshall also saw little positive about the political situation facing him upon his return. Just as Robertson had warned, the agreements that had held so much promise quickly collapsed when Marshall had gone back to the United States. Manchuria posed a huge problem. Chiang had impeded the travel of the truce teams to tamp down volatile situations in that area. Without oversight it soon became an almost lawless frontier. The Soviets had complicated matters by their slow pullout from Manchuria—apparently they needed more time to complete the looting of anything that could be remotely described as "war booty." As soon as they did get out, the Chinese Communists rushed in, grabbing any materials that had been left behind for their own purposes. Some of the forces of the CCP overran Changchun, the capital of Manchuria, driving out a garrison of Nationalists in clear violation of the agreements. This gave the conservatives within Chiang's party plenty of ammunition: didn't this prove that the Communists weren't about to abide by the terms of the cease-fire?[96]

A Double Policy

When Marshall returned to China, then, he was dismayed to find that the Communists and Nationalists were on the verge of war again. Extremist elements on both sides continued to seek the upper hand in Manchuria, thus filling the vacuum left by the Soviets and fueling the lack of trust between them.[97]As Marshall would tell Truman later in the summer, "Each side takes the same stand with me, that the other is provoking the fighting and cannot be trusted to go through with the agreement."[98] Historian Mark Stoler articulated the problem rather clearly, noting that in reality "each side viewed the other as a mortal enemy and coalition as a threat rather than an opportunity." Further, wrote Stoler, "each had agreed to negotiations primarily for tactical reasons, and were increasingly attracted to advisers who believed all pretense to compromise could be abandoned because total military victory [for each respectively] was obtainable."[99]

One huge problem that contributed to Marshall's frustration when he returned to sort out the unraveling cease-fire was that the U.S. government had insisted that it would be Chiang's Nationalists who should prevail, no matter what. Chiang had figured out that the Americans would help his cause even if he didn't make compromises, and the Communists correctly surmised that the United States was following what Chou En-lai called a hypocritical "double policy" in China, acting under a set of circumstances that made even-handed mediation impossible.[100] Meanwhile, every effort on Marshall's part to listen to legitimate issues raised by the CCP was criticized by Chiang as "appeasing the Communists."[101]

An Unwieldy Stone

By the summer of 1946, conditions had become chaotic. Unwilling to give up, though, Marshall tackled each crisis as it arose. As Undersecretary of State Dean Acheson so aptly put it, with the "tired patience of Sisyphus, General Marshall began rolling his unwieldy stone uphill again."[102] In mid-June, through arduous meetings with both sides, Marshall managed to get a temporary truce. It would soon break down. That July, the Nationalists showed they would not tolerate competing parties, shutting down six opposition newspapers. A pro-Nationalist mob fell upon a peace delegation that had come from Shanghai to Nanking, where Chiang had moved his headquarters, repeatedly beating the delegates, including a 70-year-old woman. When Chiang denied any responsibility, Marshall was furious, telling him, "What you are saying is that your army is completely impotent and I can't swallow that at all." One young foreign service officer, observing these episodes over the summer, wrote in his diary, "Marshall is beginning to get the idea that he is being pushed around, made a fool of, and he doesn't like it at all."[103]

Meanwhile, when the U.S. Marines tried to assist the Nationalists in gaining control of Manchuria, as had been agreed to by the terms of the cease-fire, they were attacked in an area supposedly controlled, if loosely, by the Communists. In late July, a band of guerrillas, possibly Communist but perhaps simply looters, had struck a Marine supply convoy, killing 3 Americans and wounding 12. No matter the source, Marshall, writing to General Wedemeyer, asserted that it was "undoubtedly the result of violent communist propaganda against the so-called military support of the National Government."[104] Further, he condemned the tendency of the Communists to seize upon some incident and then, after exaggerating it "without truth and accuracy," building it to the point of hysteria.[105] Despite these volatile circumstances, throughout August Marshall went back and forth between the competing parties, trying to find a solution, making concessions first to this side and then to the other, but never quite able to get a solid cease-fire.

"George has had a cruel year"

Since the Nationalists' capital had moved to Nanking that May, Katherine and George Marshall were living in a compound that had once served as the home of the German ambassador. Although it was probably one of the best residences in the city, in Katherine's letter to Edmund Coles, the brother of Marshall's first wife, Lily, she described the harsh conditions under which she and her husband had lived since her arrival. "It had been an endurance contest," she wrote, again complaining of the heat—110 degrees, as well as the "dust and filth." She noted that their home had a lawn, but one might as well "go out and sit in a 'Chick Sales' [a slang term for an outhouse] for a pleasant evening as to sit out there." After two months, Katherine continued, she felt "pretty low," explaining that "with the aftermath of eight years of war, inflation, civil war, famine, and epidemics of cholera, it was a pretty grim diet."[106] Apparently, not only the Marshalls but his staff as well lived in the building, and she took her meals at the "regular mess!!" She bemoaned seeing her husband only at breakfast, since he was in conference all day and into the night. That July, Madame Chiang had suggested that she move up to Kuling, where she and the generalissimo maintained a summer estate. Katherine gladly accepted, and relished the privacy of a small stone bungalow "across a gurgling mountain stream" from the Chiangs. Katherine noted that Marshall held many meetings there, since it was the summer capital.[107]

In fact, during that summer and into the fall, Marshall would make nine trips to Kuling. It was quite an ordeal to make the journey some 250 miles from Nanking, as he described in a letter to Frank McCarthy: "2 hours by plane, 3/4 hours by gun boat down the river and across, 1/2 hour by car and 2 hours by chair [powered by eight coolies] up the mountain by a circuitous and fantastic path with frequent stretches of stone steps, one of 937 at about a 40 degree angle."[108] Although in his letter Marshall spares McCarthy the frustrations of the mission, Katherine did not, succinctly outlining to their friend her husband's challenges:

> Three times he has had a stop-fighting order all but signed when new outrages on the side of the Communists or Nationalists have broken out overnight and negotiations come to a standstill again. The hatred is so bitter on both sides that it is hard to get them to see any side but their own. These people [the Chinese], I feel so sorry for them— pawns between two political parties—all they ask for is peace. George has had a cruel year and looked as though he had been put through a wringer in Nanking.[109]

Another Round and Counter-Round

All through the fall, Marshall, along with the new U.S. ambassador, John Stuart, went back and forth between the two sides, along with discussions among leaders of the minority parties, especially the Democratic League—a six-party coalition—still seeking a compromise. Despite Marshall's efforts,

Katherine is seated in the conveyance used to get
the Marshalls to their Kuling retreat.

George C. Marshall Research Library

the Nationalists were determined to clear the northern provinces and Manchuria of Communists, and the CCP was just as determined not to relinquish their gains. Hoping to bring the competing parties together, in early August Marshall used an important trump card against the Nationalists, imposing an embargo on munitions shipments if Chiang did not come to the bargaining table. Chiang was undeterred, since he had hoarded plenty of Lend-Lease stores from World War II for just such a situation.[110] As Marshall would write to Truman, the rank-and-file Communists, being unaware of the instructions that had been placed on ammunition, airplanes, and similar items," were embittered by the fact that they were confronted in the fighting with American munitions. Although Marshall acknowledged that they were being influenced by "vigorous and skillful party propaganda," he understood the natural resentment: "They themselves lack in equipment and ammunition," he wrote, "and they are driven back by American equipment and ammunition."[111] Moreover, even with the embargo, the Nationalists would continue to get more than $900 million in "non-lethal aid," which, of course, prompted the Communists to charge once again that the United States was only on the side of Chiang's government.[112] It did not seem like an evenly balanced scale.

Marshall condemned both sides in early October during a meeting with Chou, stating frankly that each one had manipulated the negotiations, so much so that he could no longer be the middleman. The threat of a Marshall recall prompted Chiang to agree to a 10-day stand-down. Supposedly, a five-man committee, led by Ambassador Stuart, was going to define the terms of Communist participation in the National Assembly. That seemed promising, until Chou En-lai realized that Communist holdings at the gateway to Manchuria would be threatened, as usual. He rejected the temporary truce as insincere, just another means for Chiang to reinforce his own military objectives. Into mid-October, the two sides agreed once more to come to Nanking to talk, while fighting continued. Marshall didn't believe he could endure another round and counter-round, complaining, "I can't go through it again. I am just too old and too tired for that."[113]

On November 7, Marshall, with Ambassador Stuart, had met with Chiang to discuss once again a cease-fire. The generalissimo explained that he had prepared a draft of a statement that would be given out prior to the meeting of the National Assembly scheduled for later that month. The next day, after this meeting, Marshall wrote Truman that the draft was going to complicate the situation, calling it "provocative, lengthy, argumentative and difficult to understand." During the session, when Chiang tried to explain the underlying motives of the draft, Marshall surely must have been alarmed. He heard once again what the generalissimo had said in the November 1 meeting. The Nationalist leader stated that at this point the government was of the unanimous opinion that no further compromise should be made and that the Communists should be *defeated by force*. Further, the delegates who would be legitimate for the upcoming National Assembly, slated to craft the all-important constitution, should be based on those chosen in 1936, and not those who might be allowed to attend as outlined in the guidelines established by the multiparty Political Consultative Committee that previous January.

Apprehensive, Marshall and Ambassador Stuart got permission from Chiang to redraft the statement to at least soften some of the language—to make it less provocative. Returning it to Chiang, its edges blunted but its message similar, Marshall made it clear that he was in complete disagreement with the tone and content of the document.[114] Within the draft that Chiang would release that evening, Marshall could see that trouble loomed. As he explained to the president: although Chiang was saying that government (Nationalist) troops would stop fighting, "the method of stopping the fighting is not conclusive and still holds in effect a threat of renewed battle to force a political decision." And then he got to the bottom line: "The Government approach to the National Assembly is not, in my opinion, in sufficient accord with the PCC [Political Consultative Conference] agreements and means even if all delegates appeared, that a simple majority vote of the overwhelming KMT [Nationalists] numbers could determine the character of the constitution without much consideration of the fundamental guarantees agreed to in the PCC." He ended the top secret message to Truman with the words, "I fear the Assembly will be an ineffective one party proposition."[115]

Foot Jiggling

Despite Marshall's grave concerns about Chiang's cease-fire statement, on the 10th he asked Chou to consider another meeting with the Committee of Three to take a look at the document. Chou told Marshall, "I will make another try." Representing the Nationalists, General Chen Chang presented the proposal on the 11th. Chou said he would take it back to Yenan to be "reanalyzed," although the chances that it would win approval as worded were just about nil. He wanted the National Assembly postponed until a cease-fire acceptable to his interests, especially as it related to government troops in Manchuria, could be worked out. Further, during the meeting he warned the Nationalist representative that if Chiang convened the National

Assembly unilaterally with no Communists present, there would be a split.[116] On November 15 the long-promised National Assembly met. Finding the language of Chiang's statement totally unsatisfactory, the Communists, following up on their threats, boycotted the meeting, as did most of the minority parties. In an official statement on November 16, Chou announced that the door to negotiations had "now been slammed." As if to say good-bye, he told Marshall that despite the failure of negotiations, "I feel that I still have high respect for you personally," and added, "The Chinese problem is too complicated and the changes are tremendous."[117]

Even as late as December 1, 1946, Marshall was trying to emphasize to Chiang that any reasonable proposals for a coalition government were being "neutralized by [his government's] military action." In an earlier meeting, Marshall had already bluntly told Chiang's ministers, "The [Nationalist] army is draining 80 to 90 percent of the budget and if you think the U.S. taxpayer is going to step into the vacuum this creates, you can go to hell."[118] In this important December 1 meeting, Madame Chiang was interpreting. Marshall told her that he was about to say something that might be so harsh that she would not want to translate it for the generalissimo: "You have broken agreements, you have gone counter to plans. People have said you were a modern George Washington, but after these things they will never say it again." "I want him to hear it," said Madame Chiang. Her husband made no response, except for the jiggling of his foot—an action that always accompanied his extreme discomfort, especially after he had been criticized. "His old foot went round and round and almost hit the ceiling," recalled Marshall.[119] In a while, though, Chiang offered his rebuttal—the Communists had never intended to cooperate; they were completely controlled by the Soviet Union. Furthermore, the Nationalists could defeat the CCP armies within 10 months, and, in addition, perhaps the United States should revise its China policy "in light of the present situation" by casting its lot with the Nationalists.[120] Presumably the Communists were not to be a part of a coalition government, they were to be defeated.

Finishing the "never-ending battle"

Even in early fall, Truman had written to his wife, Bess, in Independence, Missouri, "Looks like Marshall will fail in China."[121] Always respectful of Marshall's work, the president had sent word through Marshall's liaison in Washington, Colonel Marshall Carter, that all his envoy needed to do if he thought the mission should be shut down was to contact him. Truman also let Carter know that no one was trying to influence or urge Marshall to withdraw. By December, especially after the revelations of Chiang in the meeting on December 1, at last Marshall was ready to come home. As he had so succinctly described to Eisenhower in a letter that fall, "My battle out here is never ending, with both ends playing against the middle—which is me." He had had enough. Marshall stayed long enough to see the creation of a new constitution, crafted through the National Assembly. It was rejected by Chou as illegitimate. As it came closer to time for Marshall to leave China, he continued to meet with Chiang, encouraging him to make certain the framework of the constitution allowed representation within the government of Communists, liberals, and other minority parties. He emphasized that despite Chiang's dislike for communism and for Mao's leadership, the CCP was a force too large and significant to be ignored and shut out. As he told Chiang, "The best way to defend against Communism is for the existing government of China to accomplish such reforms that it would gain the support of the people."[122]

Although Marshall had hoped that his return from the China Mission would bring him retirement, that early January, as word spread that Marshall was headed home, ostensibly "for consultation on China and other matters," he already knew that it would not be the warmer climes of Pinehurst that would provide the setting for the coming year. Indeed, that May of 1946, U.S. Army Chief of Staff Dwight Eisenhower had flown to Nanking, supposedly to check on the morale of troops still serving in the Far East. In fact, he was on a mission for the president. According to the chief executive, he told Marshall, the current secretary of state, James Byrnes, with whom Truman had clashed, would develop serious "stomach trouble" by midyear and thus would need to resign. Would Marshall consider becoming the secretary of state? Already bogged down in the complexity of the China Mission, Marshall replied, only half in jest, "Great goodness, Eisenhower, I'd take any job in the world to get out of this one."[123]

Farewell

On January 8, 1947, Marshall was ready to leave China. Katherine had already said her good-byes and was waiting for her husband in Honolulu, where they would enjoy a few days of blessed rest. That morning, the C-54 plane sat waiting on the runway, despite the snow, its five stars visible on the tail. As for Marshall, it was time for his farewells. There were final handshakes with Chinese dignitaries huddled in the cold, and with Marshall's trusted colleague and friend, Ambassador Stuart. The Chiangs arrived in their new bulletproof Cadillac to give the returning envoy a send-off.

In an early photograph, Marshall stands with the Chiangs. The
couple would also be present to wish him farewell, January 8, 1947.
George Lacks, The LIFE Picture Collection, Getty Images

Days before, the generalissimo, having realized that Marshall was leaving
China for good, had entreated him to stay as his "supreme adviser," perhaps
to shape the reforms that this American had so vehemently supported.
Marshall demurred. Not only was his course already set, but he understood
perfectly that given the role he had played as mediator/negotiator in the
hyper-attenuated environment of the last year, he would never parlay the
reforms so desperately needed. Now, though, at his time of departure, with
Marshall already on the plane, the Chiangs came on board for a private and
cordial good-bye. Minutes later, the engines revved. George C. Marshall,
the president's special ambassador and China's "Terror of the Evildoers,"
was airborne, headed for the palms and warm breezes of Hawaii.[124] The
announcement to the American press that Marshall would become secretary
of state was released while Marshall was flying to Hawaii. So, too, was his
report on the China Mission.

A "plague on both your houses"

Marshall's "personal statement" regarding his work in China minced
no words, calling the greatest obstacle to peace "the complete almost

overwhelming suspicion with which the Chinese Communist Party and the Kuomintang [Nationalist] regard each other." On the one hand, he noted, Chiang's government hated communism, but on the other, the Communists were committed to building a Marxist government; thus an impasse. He laid blame upon the Communists for the "immensely provocative" propaganda campaigns, delivered without regard for the truth or facts to arouse "bitter hatred" against the Americans and their efforts to bring peace to China. Marshall talked of the unwillingness of the Communists in the recent months to compromise, referring perhaps to their refusal to attend the National Assembly. He castigated extremist elements of both sides, including irreconcilable groups within the Nationalist Party who were simply interested in preserving their own feudal control—a clear jab at ultraconservative reactionaries within Chiang's ranks. Marshall went so far as to say that although he was a soldier, he "deplored the dominating influence of the military within the Nationalist ranks."[125]

One newspaper writer described Marshall's conclusions as a "plague on both your houses," yet even in this harsh message he held out the slightest glimmer of hope, which he said lay with liberal elements and minority groups working under the leadership of Chiang. Marshall deeply respected the minority parties, referring to the "splendid group of men" who had been too few to buck the dominant competing entities. Marshall had also been encouraged by large groups of young men who had become Communists because of their disgust with the corruption of local governments, and who sincerely were willing to put "the interest of the Chinese people above ruthless measures to establish a Communist ideology in the immediate future."[126] In the end, it would be Chiang's government that would or would not allow these reformists into positions of leadership. While Marshall acknowledged that the new constitution was a step in the right direction, he emphasized that change would not come until the Nationalist government was reorganized to include these liberal and minority entities, including the Communists.[127]

"No American solution"

Marshall historian Mark Stoler opined that Americans did not quite understand why China could not be made in their image. In that postwar headiness after defeating the Axis, the citizenry seemed confident that, with American guidance, the Chinese should be able to compromise as easily as the Democrats and Republicans at home and rally around Chiang as their George Washington. As one American senator supposedly said, "With God's help we will lift Shanghai up and up, ever up, until it is just like Kansas City."[128] Stoler conceded that Marshall was much more of a realist, but that he, too, "shared with most other Americans a belief in the universality and exportability of certain American concepts.... Like Stilwell ... Marshall had thought China could be remade in the American image. And like Stilwell, he had discovered that it could not and would not be and that American power in the area had severe limits. . . . As Stilwell's biographer has concluded, 'China was a problem for which there was no American solution.'"[129]

"Ruddy and fit"

The days in Hawaii with Katherine had done wonders for Marshall. The couple had flown to Los Angeles from Honolulu on January 18. After a quick visit with Frank McCarthy, his former secretary of the General Staff and now a motion picture producer in Los Angeles, they traveled to Chicago to get a connecting flight to Washington. The plan was to arrive for a swearing-in ceremony scheduled for the 20th. It was not to be, since icing conditions grounded the plane. They arrived at Union Station on the 21st. Marshall would officially become the secretary of state that afternoon—his nomination had been confirmed without exception by a Republican-controlled Foreign Relations Committee.[130] In Washington that morning, reporters, sheltered in a nearby shed in what was described as a "bitter gale," gathered around Marshall as he detrained with Katherine. They had questions for the new secretary of state, whom one article described as "ruddy and fit." Already there was talk of this prominent military man becoming the nation's chief executive. For someone who followed the army tradition of never voting— career officers considered it a conflict of interest—that idea made him very uncomfortable. Nevertheless, the reporters raised the question: was it possible he would be a candidate for the presidency in 1948? Marshall gave an unequivocal answer: "I think this is as good a time as any to terminate speculation about me in a political way. . . . The popular conception that no matter what a man says he can be drafted as a candidate for some political office would be without any force with regard to me. I cannot be drafted for any political office."[131] That position would never change for Marshall.

Nevertheless, he was about to take on a role that, next to the presidency, was the most powerful in the U.S. government. His leadership during the next two years would be crucial to postwar recovery on the European continent. As a rule, Marshall was not one to look back. He was rested, his energy returned. An hour after he spoke to reporters at Union Station, he was at the White House, greeted by "spontaneous applause" from the staff. Katherine

501

The Marshalls in Honolulu, January 9, 1947
Honolulu Star-Advertiser, George C. Marshall Research Library

stood beside President Truman as the oath was administered.[132] After lunch, the new secretary of state, the first career military officer to hold the office, said good-bye to his wife and immediately headed to the State, War, and Navy Building—the same building where he had reported in 1902, a very young VMI graduate, and where he had served Pershing as an aide in the early 1920s.[133] Whether he noted the full-circle irony of the occasion is not recorded. It was time to go to work.

Marshall is sworn in as Secretary of State, with U.S. Supreme Court
Chief Justice Fred Vinson presiding, January 21, 1947.

U.S. National Archives 199520

Chapter 17

Matters of State

"The whole world hangs in the balance"

January 1947- September 1947

A reporter for the *Christian Science Monitor*, in covering Marshall's statement regarding whether he would consider becoming a candidate for the presidency, used all caps for the ONCE AND FOR ALL part of the new secretary of state's response, seemingly convinced that the man meant what he said. Indeed, James Reston, writing for the *New York Times,* opined that in Marshall's case, normal skepticism about such assertions was being set aside, and that "the statement, therefore, was taken at its face value." By removing himself from the political arena, said Reston, Marshall had "simplified his job as Secretary of State and enhanced his chance of success." The new secretary of state was "not the back-slapping type," Reston continued, noting that Marshall "was a serious man" who "moved not from tactics to action, which is the normal procedure on Capitol Hill, but from principle to action."[1] Not everyone was sanguine about the nomination. Senator Arthur Vandenberg, the chairman of the Senate Foreign Relations Committee and a former isolationist who would eventually forge a strong and productive relationship with Marshall, commented, "I'm not too damned crazy about him." One Texas senator complained that the five-star general's confirmation would create the impression in Europe that "the military is taking over the foreign policy."[2] Despite such concerns, Marshall garnered great respect. Vandenberg put his nomination through the committee without a hearing and won *unanimous* approval from the U.S. Senate on the same day. Marshall would need the advantage of a nonpartisan image as he served in President Truman's cabinet since the year before, during interim elections, the Republicans had gained control of Congress.[3]

As had always been the case throughout his career, Marshall knew the importance of an excellent staff. Lieutenant Colonel Marshall Carter had escorted him over to the White House that first afternoon. Marshall knew Carter's work well, first as a part of the army's Operations Division in Washington during the war, but also as State Department liaison during the China Mission. "Do you know how the State Department operates?"

505

Secretary of State Marshall arrives for work, January 21, 1947.

Harry S. Truman Library

Marshall had asked. He did, came the reply. The new secretary of state then told him, "Well, you'd better sit outside the door then with me and keep me out of trouble until I get my feet on the ground." Informing Carter that he would need to get some civilian clothes, Marshall closed the deal on his personal assistant.[4]

With regard to the rest of the staff, Marshall would not clean house. He asked the chief officers to remain, beginning with Undersecretary of State Dean Acheson. Although anxious to get back to the prestigious and profitable law firm that he had left for government service six years previously, Acheson, flattered by Marshall's request, agreed to stay on for six months. Born of English parents who had immigrated to the United States—his father eventually became the Episcopal bishop of Connecticut—Acheson was elegant and sophisticated, educated at Groton, Yale, and Harvard Law School. He had served as a clerk to Supreme Court Justice Louis Brandeis, and had been under secretary of the treasury in Roosevelt's administration until, due to a policy dispute, he was asked to resign.[5] Marshall informed Acheson that he was to be his chief of staff, and would for all practical purposes run the State Department, coming to him only when he needed help. Acheson would later say that Marshall's look "indicated that it had better not be often." The secretary of state explained that he wanted complete frankness from Acheson, "particularly about myself," he had added, assuring Acheson that "I have no feelings except those I reserve for Mrs. Marshall."[6]

Although it might seem that a career soldier would be uncomfortable in the realm of diplomacy and state-craft, Marshall said, "I found the problems from the viewpoint of geopolitical location and of pressure to be almost identical in many respects to the war years. There was the same problem between East and West; the same limitations as to our capability; there was the same necessity for a very steady and determined stand in regard to these various problems."[7] One such problem was that the State Department needed a more organized structure. Marshall would later point out that his predecessor and, for that matter, most secretaries of state, had been lawyers, and, according to him, "lawyers aren't organizers at all," even naming his wartime friend and colleague, Henry Stimson, in the lot. Marshall saw this lack of order immediately when he began to "learn the ropes" at the State Department. He told Forrest Pogue that he was "horrified" to discover that each department saw itself as a "separate industry," and each reported directly to the secretary, which resulted in his being burdened with an endless barrage of minutiae.[8] The whole operation was characterized by jurisdictional turf wars, lacking cohesive purpose or vision. Marshall's solution was to create a secretariat with a clear chain of command modeled like the one he had organized in the chief of staff's office. Acheson would be the clearing house officer, accepting, as Ed Cray noted, "concise reports with terse recommendations at the conclusion, and small boxes on the page, in which he [Marshall] would initial his approval or rejection."[9]

Acheson appreciated the efficiency of Marshall's reorganization, but he later wrote that sometimes the approach didn't work perfectly. He explained to Marshall at some point along the way that sending up a singular final recommendation for an "accept or reject" left out other alternatives that might be important for the secretary to consider. Acheson made the case that occasionally Marshall needed to go around his own imposed chain of command to sit with groups that were hashing out these thorny issues. The secretary of state agreed to do that from time to time, yet, exasperated with indecision, he was wont to say, "Gentlemen, don't fight the problem, decide it." But as Acheson convinced him, within the State Department sometimes "these problems are not susceptible to an answer, they are susceptible to an action which is less disagreeable than some other action and probably no action is altogether good." Acheson acknowledged that Marshall never liked this tactic but finally "carried it out very strongly."[10]

Although Acheson saw that Marshall's methods were not always perfect for the diplomatic setting, it was clear that he was thrilled to have him as secretary of state. Acheson once told a friend that Marshall had what he called "the rarest gift of the mind to man," the "capacity for decision." At a dinner party that spring, one guest, David Lilienthal, wrote in his diary that Acheson "spent a good deal of time bubbling over with enthusiasm, almost rapture, about General Marshall. To work with him is such a joy that he can hardly talk about anything else," Lilienthal noted. "It has made a new man of Dean and this is a good thing for the country right now."[11]

Knowing that Acheson would be at the State Department for a limited time, Marshall planned ahead, making sure that someone of Acheson's stature would move into that role after the promised "six months." Robert Lovett was a son of privilege out of Texas—his father had been chief counsel and eventually president of the powerful Union Pacific Railroad system. A graduate of Yale, Lovett had become a pilot, eventually commanding a U.S. naval air squadron. Always interested in aeronautics, during the war he served Stimson as special assistant for air affairs and was crucial in the strengthening of the Army Air Forces. It was in this capacity that he had gotten to know Marshall. The two admired each other, perhaps connected by their shared belief in public service. Nevertheless, after the war Lovett had resigned from government service to return to a lucrative Wall Street career. When Marshall called, though, Lovett couldn't turn him down. He became an assistant in the economic affairs division, a "holding" position, but was soon shadowing Acheson's every move as undersecretary of state.

With Acheson in place, Marshall made sure to keep other talented staff within the department. The group included Will Clayton, a square-jawed, handsome six-foot-three Texan, who without formal education had built the largest cotton brokerage firm in the world.[12] A soft-spoken southerner, Clayton was well known for his discipline and self-control. During the war he had worked for the federal government procuring resources needed for the allies, taking no pay for his services. Like Marshall, he was practical, big on efficiency and solutions.[13] As the assistant secretary for economic affairs, he would influence Marshall greatly regarding the need for a program of economic development in Europe that was conceptually stronger than the outright assistance programs characterizing the first postwar year. Another exceptional officer at the State Department, Charles "Chip" Bohlen, a Soviet expert and translator, became Marshall's special assistant and later counselor. A Harvard graduate, he was among the first group of foreign service officers to be trained in Russian, staffing the Moscow embassy when it first opened in 1934. A raconteur, charming and inquisitive, he could also be blunt and honest. Later, he would be crucial in the secretary's dealings with the Russians.[14] As Mark Stoler wrote,

> Marshall had recognized his own limitations in this new environment and surrounded himself with the best and brightest young men available, men who could initiate bold proposals, implement them in his name, and take over once he retired. . . . Although Marshall may not have been the intellectual equal of these men, he was clearly their leader and one of the most respected and extraordinary individuals in their lives. Their memoirs and recollections . . . are unanimous in their praise of him and their awed descriptions of his personality, abilities, and impact.[15]

One aspect of State Department reorganization that Marshall was particularly proud of was the development of the Policy Planning Staff (PPS). He related to Forrest Pogue that when he took office, "there was nothing, no planning agency, at all. You can't plan and operate at the same [time]," he said. "They are two states of mind . . . . One or the other is going to suffer from it."[16] Marshall had learned

William L. Clayton

Charles "Chip" Bohlen

Dean G. Acheson

this lesson as a military man, often complaining that the army spent too much time simply reacting to a crisis. He thought there should be a group within the organization that could, as Pogue described it, "put up their feet and think hard about policy for the future." Marshall had set up such an organization in the War Department, and he wanted one at State. He chose the brilliant George F. Kennan to head the PPS, agreeing to give him time to finish his academic year at the War College, where he lectured as its deputy of foreign affairs. Because of the deepening crisis in Europe, Marshall subsequently changed his mind, and brought Kennan to the State Department that late April, sooner than was originally planned. An excellent writer and an intellectual, Kennan was a Soviet expert. He knew several languages, including Russian, which he understood at a highly sophisticated level, having completed several tours in Moscow.[17] Kennan was perhaps the perfect leader for this new "think tank" concept. As historian Greg Behrman wrote, "No one could have better synthesized all the disparate viewpoints and notions bantered about the department and elsewhere in government."[18] The development of the PPS came slowly—at the end of the first six months Marshall had selected only five or six to compose its staff. "I told Kennan I just didn't want to accumulate any ordinary people," Marshall told Pogue. "They had to be very good or not at all. I'd rather have one good man than five mediocrities."[19] Kennan proved to be a "good man," crucial to what would become the European Recovery Program. A later State Department evaluation described Marshall's Policy Planning Staff, which still exists as an organization today, as the "focus of creative thinking during a vital period."[20]

Learning Curve

In the weeks after becoming secretary of state, it was clear that Marshall was in transition on several levels. Senator Arthur Vandenberg had gotten Marshall's confirmation as secretary of state through the Senate in a day, but very quickly after the swearing in he was asking the new appointee to attend a closed meeting of the Committee on Foreign Relations, perhaps to take the measure of his capabilities. Not surprisingly, Marshall demurred, telling Vandenberg he would be glad to do so but needed some time to gain knowledge of the international situation as well as the people in the State Department. Knowing that his first big challenge as secretary of state would be the upcoming foreign ministers conference in Moscow, he entreated Vandenberg to provide him with suggestions that might be helpful based on his experience as a part of that committee.[21] At the end of January, Marshall told former secretary of state Cordell Hull that he had hoped to come by and see him, but he had been overwhelmed by "orientation work and visitors."[22] Madame Chiang had written her congratulatory letter, and in reply Marshall expressed once more that his "own affairs have been rather overwhelming with a tremendous amount of information to be accumulated in a short time, a large number of people to see, and very pressing problems to meet. It is a little more than an endurance contest," he complained, "with the time factor dominant."[23] Realizing that he still had a tremendous amount to learn, Marshall spoke frankly in his first formal press conference on February 7.

> I want to say that in regard to matters in the European theater, particularly matters of policy and proposals relating to the Moscow meetings that are ahead of us, I am not prepared to answer questions at this time. I have to have more information myself before I can make any public comments so please do not consume time to ask me questions with regard to that which I am not going to answer. . . . I will mention some things myself but I am not at all prepared personally to discuss the details of those matters—later on, yes, but not today.[24]

On the home front, there were also adjustments. The Marshalls had been in China the previous 10 months. That January, he was commuting daily from Leesburg, Virginia, into Washington, about a 70-mile round trip. In the evenings, he quickly donned work clothes to help Katherine get the house and grounds back into shape after such a long absence. To a British colleague, he called his duties at Dodona "the action of the totalitarian government which kept me at work every evening when I returned at 5:30." As he told Madame Chiang in a February 5th letter, "I was employed as common labor . . . doing everything from cleaning out gutters on top of the house to a tremendous amount of pruning and distribution of fertilizer to get the effect of the winter rains and snows."[25]

Katherine was also anxious to get the work wrapped up. She would soon head to their winter home in Pinehurst, North Carolina. Her husband would be in Washington. Not that it wouldn't be a busy time for Katherine. As Marshall delved deeper into his responsibilities as secretary of state, she would be enjoying her new role as author. At the end of 1946, she had completed a memoir of her life with George Marshall titled, *Together: Annals of an Army Wife*. Reflecting later on her years as the partner of a famous general who traveled the world to meet the demands of his job, she commented that perhaps the title should have been *Apart*. The book, which she had completed while they were in China, had Marshall's blessing before it was published. It included charming anecdotal material about the

A promotional poster for Katherine Marshall's memoir used a quote from the
N.Y. Post calling it "a highly literate and deeply moving story."
George Catlett Marshall and Katherine Tupper Marshall Collection
George C. Marshall Research Library

career of this public figure, who rarely offered glimpses into his private life. The book soon made the *New York Times* best seller list, and would remain there for several months. The pages revealed the life of a professional soldier. Whether they had read this pleasant account or not, some writers of newspaper and magazine articles still questioned the wisdom of what they called the "militarizing" of the State Department.

In fact, almost as soon as Marshall took office, he found himself addressing concerns about an army five-star general moving into the highest position within the diplomatic realm. This seemed clear in his response to New York Congressman Walter Andrews' January 22nd request that he appear before an informal, off-the-record, meeting of the House and Senate Committees on Armed Services. He apologetically declined, explaining that since there had been a good bit of doubt expressed about a military man being in his "present position," he didn't think it advisable, and he hoped his response did not "give offense." [26]

"A blue piece of paper"

Marshall had been at his State Department desk for slightly less than a month on Friday, February 21. He was taking time from his preparations for the upcoming Moscow Conference to go by train to New York. There he joined other World War II military leaders, all of whom would receive honorary degrees from Columbia University. Marshall met Katherine in the city, and the two of them continued on to Princeton, New Jersey, the next day where he gave his first official speech at a special convocation celebrating Princeton's 200th anniversary.[27] Back in Washington, State Department staffers were surrounded by a clutter of boxes, since they were still in the process of moving from the old state department structure next to the White House. The shift was needed because they had outgrown the elegant, wainscoted rooms of the older Victorian building, with its formal trappings, including white-gloved messengers in its hallways. The new offices were in a plain sand-colored modern building with little style—a *New York Times* journalist had described it as having "about as much character as a chewing gum factory," but it satisfied the need for more room. The new space had been gradually vacated by the War Department after the Pentagon was built.[28]

Around noon that Friday, Undersecretary Acheson received a call from the British Embassy that the ambassador wished to deliver "a blue piece of paper," jargon in diplomatic circles for an *important* message. The problem: such a message should be received only by the secretary of state, and he was out of town. Knowing that the communication likely signaled a crisis, though, Acheson had a "carbon copy" delivered to him; thus, his staff could attend to the topic of the dispatch and be prepared for Marshall when he returned on Monday. Soon the First Secretary of the British Embassy delivered two documents, both shocking. The British government, in view of its dire situation brought on by the ravages of a six-year war, could no longer grant financial aid to Greece and would pull out of that beleaguered country within the month; the second message said the same for Turkey. It would take a quarter of a billion dollars to shore up Greece against Soviet-backed rebel forces; slightly less for Turkey, with its border abutting a menacing USSR. Without the help of the United States, these countries could not sustain their independence. Would America be willing to assume that burden?[29]

Acheson wasted no time; he assembled the relevant staff, telling them frankly, "We're right up against it now." He let them know their weekends would not be free; in fact, they should get to work immediately to write position papers that he could hand to Marshall on Monday. Only after he had laid out the assignment did he call President Truman and the secretary of state; both agreed with what he had done.[30] Acheson and his cadre of experts worked feverishly outlining the implications and cost of picking up this British burden. By Monday morning, the undersecretary handed Marshall recommendations for providing aid to Greece and Turkey. Marshall made a few comments, asked some questions, and in classic delegation fashion told Acheson to "carry on." When Marshall met with the British ambassador later that morning to formally accept "the blue piece of paper," he had a good idea of the mission. The next day, he got approval of the plan from the president and the secretaries and war and navy.[31] By that Thursday, Marshall and Acheson were meeting with the president at the White House to make the case for aid to Greece and Turkey before an assembled group of key legislators.

Marshall began, explaining that this was a crisis that might greatly extend Soviet domination in Europe and the Middle East, but avoiding anti-communist rhetoric that excited or alarmed. Never very good at reading remarks, Marshall's voice was flat, conveying no emotion. The congressmen listened "sullenly." They were interested in cutting taxes, maybe as much as 20 percent, and certainly were in no mood to assume the burdens of the British Empire.[32] Acheson could see that the presentation was not going well, and whispered to Marshall, "Is this a private fight or can anyone get into it?" With the secretary's consent, Acheson dramatically described the scenario. The United States and the Soviets were divided by "an unbridgeable ideological chasm," the choice was between "democracy . . . and dictatorship."[33] Acheson emphasized that "not since Rome and Carthage had there been such a polarization of power on this earth."[34] Filling in the details of a dismal picture, he warned, "Like apples in a barrel infected by the rotten one, the corruption of Greece would infect Iran and all to the east. It would also carry the infection to Africa through Asia Minor, and to Europe through Italy and France . . . . We and we alone were in a position to break up the play."[35] After a long silence, Senator Vandenberg spoke up: "Mr. President, if you say that to the Congress and to the country, I will support you, and I believe most of the members will do the same." His follow-up statement was more blunt: "The only way you are ever going to get this is to make a speech and scare the hell out of the country." Back at the State Department the next day, Acheson described the meeting, and set his subordinates to work on a presidential message.[36]

Within the next couple of days, the State Department drafters came up with a report that emphasized not a provocative threat to the Soviet Union directly, although the implications were hard to miss, but rather, to governments leaning toward totalitarianism. In the proposed speech was the germ of what would soon be called the Truman Doctrine: "It is the policy of the United States to give support to free peoples who are attempting to resist subjugation from armed minorities or from outside forces."[37] When the draft reached the White House, the president's special counsel and speech writer, Clark Clifford, beefed up that statement by writing, "It *must* be the policy of the United States . . . to give support to free peoples" resisting subjugation.[38] With Truman's resolve to "scare the hell out of the country," Clifford had the president's approval to make other parts of the speech more forceful, framing its message as a contest between forces of darkness and light.

Marshall, working hard to prepare for the Moscow Conference, was not involved in the development of the speech. He was already in Paris on his way to Moscow when he and Chip Bohlen got a copy, which was scheduled for delivery on March 12 to a joint session of Congress. According to Bohlen, the secretary of state saw "a little too much flamboyant anti-communism in it," not to mention the global commitment that the words implied. Further, given that the conference in Russia loomed, this kind of rhetoric could be detrimental to negotiations. Marshall had not yet given up all hope of dealing effectively with the Soviets to finalize post-war matters, although he knew it would be difficult. Marshall cabled Truman, asking that the speech be toned down. The reply: without the rhetoric, Congress would not approve the money.[39] With that response, Marshall let it go. During the simple, forceful speech, which Truman would later say, "had no hedge in it," the president asked for $400 million in aid. Walking back up the aisle afterwards, he was met not with the usual exuberant applause to a presidential address, but with stunned silence. The reaction of many congressmen must have been similar to that of a Chicago commuter quoted in *Time* magazine, "More sand down the rat hole." Perhaps so, but the muscular speech had its impact.[40] By May 8, 1947, the recommended bill had been passed with a substantial vote from both houses of Congress. Marshall was back from the grueling Moscow Conference by then, where the true colors of the Soviet leadership had been revealed.[41]

"Go to the movies and drink Coke"

Assistant Secretary of State Dean Acheson had told an audience in November 1945 that with regard to foreign policy the popular attitude of Americans could be stated in three sentences: "1. Bring the boys home; 2. Don't be a Santa Claus; and 3. Don't be pushed around." The U.S. ambassador to the Soviet Union, Averell Harriman, put it more succinctly than that: Americans just wanted to "go to the movies and drink Coke."[42] Perhaps so, but it wasn't going to be that simple. According to historian Greg Behrman, "the war had created seismic disruptions . . . redistributing power and reshaping the topography of the international political landscape. . . . By 1945, the U.S. accounted for one-half of the world's economic production, two-thirds of the world's gold reserves and three-fourths of its invested capital."[43] Moreover, although Great Britain was still considered a superpower, the war had taken a dreadful toll on that once dominant nation. The other European nations were even more gutted. That left the Soviet Union, the key contributor to Allied victory, which now had the world's second largest economy. It also possessed the greatest military land forces on the planet. What this suggested, wrote Behrman, was an "emergent geopolitical rivalry." [44]

In February 1946, George Kennan was then the chargée d'affaires in Moscow. Having worked among Russians since the 1930s, he believed he had his finger on the pulse of this rising power. Angry and indignant that Americans did not appreciate the danger the Soviets posed, and convinced they didn't understand that nation's underlying motivations, Kennan expressed his concerns in what he would later call "a preposterously long telegram," which outlined what he saw as a primer about the true nature of the Soviet leaders.[45] Just like the czarist rulers of old Russia, the Soviets were insecure to the point of paranoia, he warned. In their view, they lived in a world of antagonistic "capitalist encirclement." According to Kennan, the USSR saw expansion as their only viable defense against the hostility of capitalism, and was "committed fanatically" to the belief that in the long run there would be no "peaceful coexistence" with the United States.[46] As for Marxism, said Kennan, "It is a fig leaf . . . . Without it they would stand before history, at best, as only the last of that long succession of cruel and wasteful Russian rulers who have relentlessly forced the country on to ever newer heights of military power in order to guarantee external security of their internally weak regimes."[47] As if to foreshadow post-war complications, Kennan wrote that the Russians would see international organizations such as the United Nations as opportunities for "diluting or extending Soviet power or of inhibiting or diluting the power of others. . . . They would not see it [the

UN] as . . . a mechanism for a permanent and stable society, but an arena in which aims just mentioned can be favorably pursued."[48]

Kennan did make the point that when confronted with force, and the willingness of a competing power to use it, the Soviet Union would back down. Thus, it would take vigor on the part of the U.S. to act as a counterforce to Soviet actions. Kennan was amazed to discover that in a very short time, what was by then known as "The Long Telegram" was required reading at the State Department and at the Pentagon.[49] Not only was Kennan worried, but more and more it seemed that leading figures in Washington and elsewhere were using sharper language in describing the Soviet threat, including the former leader of the nation's strongest ally, Winston Churchill. That March of 1946 while a guest of the president, Churchill agreed to go with him to Westminster College in Fulton, Missouri to give a speech. He sounded the alarm as well: "From Stettin in the Baltic to Trieste in the Adriatic, an iron curtain has descended across the continent." Further, said Churchill, there was "nothing which they [the Soviets] admire so much as strength, and there is nothing for which they have less respect than for military weakness."[40] At last, it seemed, Kennan was on the same wave length as his leaders.

George F. Kennan

Embassy of the United States, Moscow

Marshall had already received a copy of the Long Telegram while in China. As was his tendency, he wanted to face the Soviets at the Moscow Conference with an open mind, similar to what he had done when he had met the mega-rivals, Mao and Chiang, during the China Mission. The fact that he had already tapped key Soviet expert Kennan for the PPS indicated that he was well aware of the potential Russian threat. The primary goal of the upcoming conference was to finalize a treaty with Germany. Marshall knew that would be hard to get, but he hoped that at the minimum an agreement regarding "the principles that would guide the representatives in drafting such a treaty" might be achieved. Maybe the conference would result at least with an Austrian treaty. The State Department specialists weren't too optimistic, saying it would probably be a five-or six-week ordeal without doing much more than clarifying issues between the major parties.[51]

On March 6, Marshall was in Europe, first stop Paris, where he met with French Premier Paul Ramadier and President Vincent Auriol. The two men wasted no time in expressing to Marshall their fear of a revitalized Germany. They had felt the sting of their neighbor's might in two wars and were anxious that the nation not regain military or economic power. The secretary assured the two leaders that he understood the suffering that their country had endured, not only during the present situation, but in World War I as well. He had spent two years among "artisans, workers and peasants," and was "able to gauge the work of destruction wrought by the Germans and the suffering and courage of the French people."[52] After all, in 1917–18 he had seen the damage first hand. The day after his talks with the French leaders, Marshall laid a wreath at the Arc de Triomphe. He told reporters that the last time he had been there was during a victory parade with Pershing in 1919, and he recalled the joyous cheers of the French citizens.[53] There was little joy in the scenes across France that winter, or the rest of Europe, for that matter.

"The approach of some new peril"

The destruction of Europe was visible as Marshall flew over the continent on his way to Russia. Perhaps he understood General Patton's comment at the end of the war: "You who have not seen it do not know what hell looks like from the top."[54] More than half of the housing in the big cities, and in some cases it went as high as 80 percent, had been turned to piles of debris. A State Department worker stationed in Berlin recalled seeing a German woman through a window with no glass calmly preparing food in a second-story kitchen whose building had only one standing wall. According

to historian Greg Behrman,

> The war had eviscerated Europe. . . . Rubble—an estimated 500 million cubic yards of it in Germany—lay stories high on the sides of cleared thoroughfares. Thousands of bridges and tens of thousands of kilometers of railroad lines had been destroyed. . . . Still worse was the human toll. One historian estimated that 36.5 million people . . . died from 1939 to 1945 from war-related causes. On V-E Day, there were no less than 13 million displaced persons (DPs) in Europe, and the number was growing. . . . According to the United Nations, in the summer of 1946 100 million Europeans were being fed at a level of 1,500 calories per day or less, a level at which health suffers severely. Another 40 million had only a few more hundred calories.[55]

A young girl sits in the rubble left after a V-2 bomb struck
London during the last year of the war.

Library of Congress, cph. 3g04327

In the fall of 1946, before the ground froze, Berliners dug thousands of graves for the deaths from starvation anticipated in the coming winter. On the bombed out Reichstag walls was scrawled, "Blessed are the dead, for their hands do not freeze."[56] Plenty of hands were freezing during that winter of 1947. Around Christmas 1946, a huge high-pressure system began to form near the Arctic Circle, swept through Scandinavia, and then settled over Britain, mocking its normally temperate marine climate. On January 6, 1947, snow fell on London, and within days piled up 20 feet.[57] By the end of the month, the River Thames had frozen. Normal waterway traffic came to a standstill. Coal, so badly needed against the bitter cold as well for any manufacturing, sat in railcars immobilized by drifts of snow. Already crippled from the war, industrial production in Britain during the worst of the storm virtually shut down for three weeks, which one historian noted even the German bombing had never accomplished.

In France, snow fell in St. Tropez on the mild Mediterranean coast where January temperatures averaged 50 degrees Fahrenheit. In the hinterland, the storm destroyed 3.2-3.8 million acres of fall wheat. With goods and services almost nonexistent in the cities, and with no faith in the currency, farmers saw no benefit in taking crops to market, and instead hoarded food to feed their own families.[58] In urban areas, crime rates were high and black markets did a booming business. Winston Churchill, using the King's English in dramatic fashion, wrote, "What is the plight to which Europe has been reduced? Over wide areas a vast quivering mass of tormented, hungry, careworn, and bewildered human beings gape at the ruins of their cities and homes, and scan the dark horizons for the approach of some new peril, tyranny, or terror. Among the visitors there is a babel of jarring voices; among the vanquished there is a sudden silence of despair."[59]

After Paris, Marshall's next stop was Berlin for a briefing with Lieutenant General Lucius Clay, the American military governor for Germany. Once again, Marshall saw war's havoc. Starvation was a real threat in that defeated nation; only $468 million in U.S. and British aid that past year had staunched its dreadful effects. Marshall's meeting with Clay emphasized that Germany was in dire straits, virtually bankrupt. Clay validated the secretary's belief that despite the political and geographical fears of the French and the Russians, Germany had to be rehabilitated. Marshall no doubt would have agreed with a report released by former President Herbert Hoover related to "The President's Economic Mission to Germany and Austria," in which he said, "There is only one path to recovery in Europe. That is production. The whole economy of Europe is interlinked with the German economy . . . . We can keep Germany in these economic chains but it will also keep Europe in rags." Another danger loomed as well, as Lucius Clay warned, "There is no choice between becoming a Communist on 1,500 calories and a believer in democracy on 1,000.[60] Indeed, Communist propaganda was having its

German children play in the rubble, Berlin, 1948.
Bundesarchiv, Bild 183-2005-0803-519

impact in this post-war chaos. In November 1946, that party in France won 29 percent of the vote, the largest of any other party in the election. Communist support was strong in other countries as well, including Italy, where it garnered 40 percent of the vote the same summer, and in Holland and Greece. Some Europeans admired these Communist partisans as young men who had led resistance movements during the war, fighting Nazi occupation forces against all odds. The theme of the Soviet-led international Communist campaign was that capitalism had failed. Witness they said, the world-wide depression of the 30s, which, fueled by capitalist dysfunction, had created the conditions that gave rise to dictators. It was the party of Lenin—the Bolsheviks—they claimed, that offered equality, material stability, and peace. As Greg Behrman wrote, "Each ratchet in desperation . . . was coal fueling Communist momentum."[61]

Stalemate

Marshall arrived at the Moscow airport at 3:30 p.m. on March 9, 1947, and was met by United States ambassador to the Soviet Union, Walter Bedell Smith, a familiar and friendly face. Smith had been secretary to the U.S. Army General Staff during the war, and he greatly revered Marshall. He later wrote that some of the diplomatic staff wondered how Marshall would do with the "tough, Middle Eastern Bazaar traders" that he was about to face. Smith had no doubts: "I had seen General Marshall under all conditions of stress and strain, and I had never before seen him fail eventually to dominate every gathering by sheer force of his integrity, honesty, and dignified simplicity. Moreover, his whole service had been a preparatory course for high-level negotiations."[62] Marshall stayed at the American Embassy residence and settled into a routine that would last for six weeks. In the early morning his assistant, Colonel Carter, brought him messages requiring his immediate attention. He worked through these tasks wearing a full-length quilted robe against the chill of an inadequately heated bedroom. By 10:30 Marshall met in his office with his American advisers to lay out plans for whatever negotiations were scheduled for the sessions in the late afternoon. After lunch he and Carter tried to get some exercise, driving to a beautiful park for a walk. They were followed by a Russian secret police detail, one car in front with six men, one car behind with six more. Once Marshall and Carter began their walk, they soon noticed they had company—six men keeping a discreet distance in front of them, six men behind. By 3:30 they were on their way to the main session with the foreign ministers, with their driver going "like a bat out of hell" along the main thoroughfares, which had been conveniently cleared of all traffic. The main meeting began at 4:00

p.m. and lasted until seven or eight o'clock. Afterward, there was time for a drink, dinner, and then another meeting until midnight or later. The next day, in the morning delegation meetings, Marshall and the advisers tried to reconcile differences related to the discussions from the previous day, problem solving with the ambassador, embassy staff, or via phone calls to Lucius Clay and other key officers in Berlin.[63]

Each day of the conference, Marshall attended the meetings held in the ornate Aviation Industry House, seated around a table that accommodated 24. The other three foreign ministers joined him, along with four each of their delegations. Marshall had worked with Soviet Foreign Minister Molotov both in Washington during the Russian's wartime visit, and at certain high-level conferences. He found him to be doctrinaire, rigid, utterly persistent— virtually never willing to compromise. A loyal party member, Molotov was bureaucratic to the extreme; Lenin had once dubbed him "comrade filing cabinet."[64] Representing Britain was Ernest Bevin, a hard-scrabble Labour Party leader who during the war had mobilized British manpower and industry. Very unlike the Eton-educated, polished political figures that usually characterized such delegations, Bevin was nonetheless a tough negotiator. Marshall and Bevin were most in agreement on the major issues. Then there was Georges Bidault of France. A charming and clever man, he could also be histrionic. Although he had been a highly respected resistance fighter during the war, at the conference he sometimes seemed tentative, unwilling to take a firm stand. Marshall understood why: the Gaullists and Communists within his country were watching his every move. Bidault couldn't afford to be too hard on the Russians, but he also couldn't be too pro-Communist—either position was going to cause him problems at home. As Bidault explained to Marshall, the French had to have time "and avoid a civil war."[65] Although sympathetic, Marshall eventually became impatient and cautioned Bidault by relating his own difficulties in China that had come about in part from trying to please all sides.[66] Since Marshall articulated the American position that Germany was to be unified and reconstructed along democratic lines, he disagreed with Bidault's insistence that the Ruhr industrial region—so crucial to the German economy—be made into a separate four-part zone, a view supported by the Soviets. According to Marshall this wasn't needed; any fears of remilitarization, fed by increased German industrial activity in that region, could be allayed by a simple but strong Four-Power Pact that would specifically and effectively prevent such a move until a formal peace treaty was signed.[67]

The meetings—43 of them—were tedious almost beyond endurance, characterized by long harangues, often from Molotov, and repeated through two long translations. The question of the Ruhr became tangled with the matter of reparations, with Molotov insisting that payment of $10 billion in reparations come out of current production and not later when Germany had a surplus. Marshall expressed the objections of the State Department. This would thwart recovery, and further obligate the Allies to support a country that could not sustain itself because its profits were being drained away—shades of post-World War I Germany. It took no more than a week for negotiations to come to an impasse. Marshall tried to move the group toward German and Austrian treaties, but that bogged down in questions of borders, assigning guilt, and, once again, reparations.[68]

Finally, the delegations moved to the question of what form of government Germany would have. Molotov argued for a strong central government, while Bevin and Marshall opposed that, fearing a top-heavy arrangement would be "peculiarly dangerous in a country like Germany which had no strong traditions regarding the rights of the individual. . . . It could be too readily converted to the domination of a regime similar to the Nazis."[69] Perhaps the biggest fear was that such a government could more easily be captured by a German Communist Party, or through rigged elections as had happened in Poland. As these options were laid out, the secretary reported to Washington that "arguments and counterarguments" ensued. Marshall historian Ed Cray wrote: "Wherever they turned, there was stalemate. . . . On reparations, on peace treaties, on the form of government, on the level of occupation forces in Germany, on the settlement of the German-Polish border, they were unable to move off center."[70]

Red-Inked Wolves

After five weeks of no real progress in negotiations, Marshall finally concluded that Molotov had been deliberately obstructionist, stretching out the arguments as long as possible. As Cray noted, Marshall realized that "delay fostered economic disintegration in Germany, and enhanced the Communists' opportunities in the face of public unrest."[71] Perhaps as was his prerogative—Marshall was the chief diplomat of the United States— it was time for him to make the obligatory courtesy call to the head of state, Joseph Stalin. At Tehran, Yalta, and Potsdam, Marshall had taken Stalin to be "a tough customer, a bank robber for the Soviet cause," but he had worked well with the Soviet leader. In fact, he had found that when Stalin agreed to something, he followed through, and had valued frankness. After all, Marshall had told Eisenhower during the war that the key to dealing

At the conference, Secretary of State Marshall would meet daily these three foreign ministers: Ernest Bevin of Great Britain; Georges Bidault of France; Vyacheslav Molotov of the Soviet Union.

Library of Congress, CPH 3b 17494
www.biography.com/people/georges-bidault-40682
Russian Federation, Law No. 231-FZ

with Stalin was to talk to him in "tough Abilene language." [72] Perhaps if Marshall spoke bluntly with this former ally this time, the logjam of the conference could be broken.

The carefully arranged meeting took place at 10:00 p.m.—Stalin seemed to prefer a late night schedule—on April 15, 1947, deep within the Kremlin. With Chip Bohlen and Walter Bedell Smith by his side, Marshall was shown into a paneled conference room. Stalin appeared old, gray, and worn, his mustard-yellow uniform emphasizing tobacco-yellowed teeth. After pleasantries that recalled the contribution of their respective nations to the victory in World War II, Marshall got down to the business of telling Stalin frankly, as he put it, of his concerns: the fact that the American people, who had respected the Russians so much at the end of the war, were developing a negative attitude, and outlining why he thought the Soviets had contributed to this new distrust. He defined his apprehension about a strong central government and his sense that the Russians were misinterpreting agreements made at Potsdam regarding reparations and borders. Marshall emphasized the importance of helping countries that were suffering from economic deterioration so they would have a chance for survival as strong democracies, and he reiterated that the United States did not want to dominate any country in the world. He had come to Stalin, said Marshall, to "clear away some of the suspicion," and to restore the relationship that had been cooperative during the war.[73] Stalin listened expressionlessly, all the while smoking cigarettes and doodling wolves' heads on a piece of paper with a red pen. He seemed unperturbed, even casual, in response to Marshall's earnest discourse, rationalizing every sincere concern that the secretary had offered—it was because the Russians had suffered so much in the war and thus had other concerns than speed in these negotiations; it was due to sloppiness in American procedures; and on it went.[74] Further, it seemed clear that Stalin didn't find this constant rehashing of issues troublesome. Marshall's report to Truman on the meeting revealed a smug Soviet leader:

> "After all," Stalin said, "these were only the first skirmishes and brushes of reconnaissance forces on the question. Differences had existed before on other questions, and as a rule after people had exhausted themselves in dispute they recognized the necessity of compromise . . . . It was necessary to have patience and not become depressed."[75]

Stalin had told the secretary of state, "We may agree the next time, or if not then, the time after that."[76] Marshall was troubled by Stalin's comments. It wasn't just Molotov's unpleasant personality that was the problem—the policy of argument and delay was coming directly from the Kremlin.

"An imbecile and a scoundrel"

Even so, Marshall went back to the bargaining table, still holding out hope for something that could be salvaged from the talks. It would not be the case. The deadlock continued. Referring to the long and sometimes acrimonious debates, he wrote Katherine on April 17, perhaps as he waited out the interminable translation of the proceedings into both English and French, "Bevin presides now. Molotov this afternoon and I do to-morrow morning. I see the Communist voters are now accusing us of sabotaging the conference. If you believe all you read about it the next two months you will divorce an imbecile and a scoundrel and lose a good houseman and gardener."[77] Days later, the meetings over, Robert Murphy, Lucius Clay's adviser in Berlin, remembered that he and others in the American delegation left with a somber feeling, later writing, "It was the Moscow Conference, I believe, that really rang down the Iron Curtain." Marshall would confirm that, telling Forrest Pogue, "We thought they [the Russians] could be negotiated with . . . . I decided finally at Moscow . . . that they could not be."[78] On the flight home after the meetings, Chip Bohlen realized that "Stalin's indifference had made a deep impression on Marshall." Heading back he kept emphasizing to Bohlen the deteriorating conditions in Europe and talked of finding some initiative to prevent the complete breakdown of Western Europe. [79] From that time on, Marshall would move fast.

Before being plunged into one of the most intense periods of his State Department service, Marshall very much wanted to see his wife. Once back in Washington that Saturday, April 26, Marshall headed straight to Pinehurst. They must have talked through upcoming plans. Soon Katherine would be headed back to Leesburg to open the house for the summer. Even while still in Moscow, Marshall had demonstrated that in regard to their home near Washington, he had both his diplomatic obligations and Katherine's well-being on his mind. In the April 17th letter, he had encouraged her to find a "reliable couple" to help her at Dodona Manor, reminding Katherine that, "We have to expect many tea calls from diplomats, luncheons, etc., as unavoidable." Describing these visits as a part of "diplomatic necessities," he reassured her that "I will of course do as much entertaining as possible officially in Washington, but I cannot run our house as a closed shop or with an 'iron curtain' because some officials will insist on calling on us there and we will have to offer some hospitality in connection with a 70 mile trip." Worried about the strain of these professional realities upon his wife, he told

Katherine's sister, Allene Wilkes, married
Ambassador Sterling Byrd Lacy at Dodona Manor, May 17, 1947.

George Catlett Marshall and Katherine Tupper Marshall Collection
George C. Marshall Research Library

her, "And, above all, I don't want you to be rustling around like a servant, or a lady heading in for a nervous breakdown, nor do I want our precious Anna [their Chinese maid] to blow under the pressure." [80] Although he had little time to think about it, he also knew that Katherine was preparing for a May wedding at Dodona. Her sister, Allene Tupper Wilkes, had tended the house when the Marshalls were away in China. During that time Allene, a divorcée, had met Sterling Byrd Lacy, a businessman who lived in the Leesburg community. By the time the Marshalls returned, a romance had blossomed. To whatever degree these details needed sorting out, it had to be short. That Sunday evening, just 24 hours after arriving at their North Carolina cottage, he was back in Washington, and a whirlwind.

By Monday at 5:00 he had already met with congressional leaders and had his report to the nation on the results of the Moscow Conference ready for an 8:30 p.m. broadcast by national hook-up. Although he didn't call for a direct break with the Soviet Union—that would be up to the president—the address presented a rather gloomy picture. Problems that literally bore on the future of civilization couldn't be solved, Marshall warned, with "general talk or vague formulae—by what Lincoln called 'pernicious distractions.'"

He outlined the issues one by one—the central government debate, the German economy, reparations, boundaries, and treaties. The bottom line, though, came in his closing summary:

> But we cannot ignore the factor of time involved here. The recovery of Europe has been far slower than had been expected. Disintegrating forces are becoming evident. The patient is sinking while the doctors deliberate. So I believe that action cannot await compromise through exhaustion. New issues arise daily. Whatever action is possible to meet these pressing problems must be taken without delay.[81]

"Avoid trivia"

On the Tuesday after his radio address, Marshall called George Kennan to his office and told him that he would need to come over to the State Department "without delay," sooner than the end of the War College's academic year, as had been originally planned. "Europe is a mess," he told Kennan. Something had to be done, and quickly. If the State Department did not take the initiative, others would. There were plenty of ideas being floated in the public arena, from human rights groups, to charities, government agencies, even newspapers. The most influential journalist of the day, with a world-wide readership, Walter Lippmann, had already written columns proposing that European countries get together to develop a common plan for their economies. In the April 5th *Washington Post,* he had opined, "The truth is that political and economic measures on a scale which no responsible statesman has yet ventured to hint at will be needed in the next year or so."[82]

Marshall was a responsible statesman and he was about to hint at a solution. In fact, in his view, it was best for the State Department to go on the offensive, to develop a comprehensive plan, not a piecemeal stopgap. Indeed, such a program needed to be strategic, not tactical. Timing and cohesiveness were important. Certainly requesting another direct aid program, and each time promising it would be the last, would never make it through this Republican-dominated Congress. In fact, realizing the mood of the Congress, which at that very moment was slashing away at a $350 million foreign aid bill, he knew something different was required. Marshall told Kennan to assemble a staff, and to report back to him as to "what you think I ought to do." He would have two weeks. Did the secretary have any more specifics, Kennan wanted to know? "Avoid trivia," was the reply. As Kennan would later write, "with this instruction and the weight of the world on my shoulders," he began.[83]

Kennan had no office and no staff, plus three speaking engagements already on the calendar. Marshall found him a suite of offices right next to his own. Gathering the most experienced minds at State, many of them associated with Will Clayton's economic affairs department, and certainly a group that was familiar with the European crisis, Kennan plunged into the task. He and the staff worked day and night, with Kennan "holding forth" with ideas that had been percolating since his realization of the Soviet danger. For Kennan, it was a period stressful beyond measure, but also utterly exciting, a chance, as he wrote his cousin, "to leave a mark in the conduct of our international business."[84] Once, he startled the Policy Planning Staff during an intense discussion when they saw tears well up in his eyes. Kennan had to excuse himself and, weeping, walked around the building a few times to regain his composure.[85]

No Blank Check

It was three weeks, not two, when Kennan delivered his recommendations, soon to be referred to as PPS1, the first paper of Marshall's new think tank organization. Thirteen pages long, one of its key concepts seemed at variance with Kennan's usual emphases: The PPS didn't see Communist activities as the biggest problem in Western Europe. No, it resulted in "large part from the disruptive effect of the war on the economic, political, and social structure of Europe and from a profound exhaustion of physical plant and of spiritual vigor."[86] The aim of the United States should not be to combat communism, but to provide economic help to the Europeans so they would not be vulnerable to any and all totalitarian movements. Under the category "Long-Term Problem," Kennan wrote that it "would be neither fitting nor efficacious for this Government to undertake to draw up unilaterally . . . a program designed to place Western Europe on its feet economically. This is the business of the Europeans. The formal initiative must come from Europe . . . and the Europeans must bear the basic responsibility for it."[87] The role of the United States should consist of "friendly aid" in drafting the program, and in supporting it at the request of the Europeans. Further, it would need to be a "joint one," agreed to by the several participating European nations.[88] Marshall surely must have liked the section of the paper that made note of the fact that the Truman Doctrine was not a "blank check to give economic and military aid to any area in the world where the communists show signs of being successful." The United States might help, said Kennan, as it planned to in Greece and Turkey, but only when such expenditures of resources and efforts would stand a chance for far-reaching results with a relatively small investment. [88]

Following Marshall's protocol, Kennan handed his report to Acheson on May 26, who took it immediately to the secretary. While Kennan and his staff labored over PPS1, William Clayton, secretary of state for economic affairs, had returned from an inspection trip to Europe. He delivered to Marshall a grim memorandum, which emphasized that the United States had "grossly underestimated the destruction of the European economy by the war." Yes, there was terrible physical destruction, but there were also the "effects of economic dislocation on production," as well as the breakdown in confidence among the population that anything could reverse this dismal situation. Indeed, without further quick and substantive help, wrote Clayton, "economic, social and political disintegration will overwhelm Europe," and something had to be done "to save Europe from starvation and chaos." [89] Clayton mentioned a ballpark figure—six or seven billion dollars in goods over one to three years. It wouldn't be strictly altruistic either—the objective had to be not just a shot in the arm to the suffering people of Europe, but related to the needs and interests of the United States as well. [90] With the Kennan and Clayton report circulating, Marshall assembled the key players, including the two of them plus Acheson and Bohlen, the next day, May 28th. Each man had a chance to say what he thought should be done. It was clear that they needed to act, but was it a good idea, Marshall asked, to include all of Europe? The planners all agreed that Germany had to be stabilized economically, but, asked Marshall, what if the Soviets wanted in? The consensus: better to let the Soviets decide. Otherwise, if a program developed by the State Department omitted the Russians, then the United States would get the blame for dividing Europe. "Play it straight," was Kennan's advice.[91] That said, though, as historian Mark Stoler noted, "They hoped and planned on Communist rejection."[92] Marshall thanked the men for their work, but revealed no decision.

"A few remarks . . . and a little more"

Marshall was now ready to go public. He was going to receive an honorary degree at Amherst College in mid-June; perhaps that would be the occasion to introduce the plan. However, after he absorbed the Clayton-Kennan reports, and the feedback given to him in the meeting, he knew the talk needed to be sooner. In January, Harvard's president, James B. Conant, had written to ask if Marshall would accept an honorary degree at commencement on June 5. The university had offered the distinction before, but during the war Marshall had declined all such offers. He felt it improper to be honored on university campuses when young men were fighting and dying overseas. Without giving that reason—after all, others in positions of military command, both army and navy, had accepted—he would send a polite reply, citing the demands of the war as precluding his attending. This time Marshall had hedged a bit, saying he wasn't sure whether his schedule would permit it. On May 5, Conant wrote again, but still Marshall delayed. Nevertheless, on May 23, General Omar Bradley wrote him to say that he would also receive a degree at Harvard, and, if Marshall also planned to accept the accolade offered, would he and Katherine like to fly with him and his wife to Boston. Marshall agreed. Maybe now the timing was good. This might be just the right setting to introduce the evolving State Department initiative for the rehabilitation of Europe's economy. Indeed, a commencement weekend offered a low-key venue that would receive press coverage, but in the short term might escape conservative political operatives, who would doubtless launch a campaign against it. Marshall later said that he wasn't concerned about "the European connection," since, "I was quite sure they would receive the idea only too willingly." [93] Still minimizing the portent of what this speech would mean, he wrote President Conant on the 28th that he "would be pleased to make a few remarks in appreciation of the honor and perhaps a little more." If academic robes were needed, Marshall added, he did not have his own and would appreciate the university providing those, adding that he was "6 ft. 1 in. tall, weight 200 pounds." [94]

Historians have debated exactly who wrote the so-called "Marshall Plan" speech at Harvard. On May 30, Marshall had asked General Carter (he had been promoted from colonel to brigadier general on April 8) to have someone prepare a less than 10 minute talk, and listed some guidelines for its contents, including the need, in light of the volume of public and political suggestions, "for a very calm and careful consideration of the proper policy to be followed." Apparently Carter chose Bohlen to write the speech, who later reported closeting himself in his office for two long days to complete a draft. However, as evidenced in Forrest Pogue's interview with Marshall in 1953, Kennan got involved in the writing process as well:

> I talked it over with George Kennan in the Plans Section [Policy Planning Staff] and Chip Bohlen, and I told them to each start out wholly independent of the other and give me what they thought. Then I got impatient and right away . . . I dictated something that I thought. And when theirs came in, they were quite apart. . . . And I cut out part of Kennan's speech and part of Bohlen's speech and part of my speech and put the three together, and that was the beginning of the talk. [95]

Marshall also related that he was still making changes in the speech on his way to Boston on the plane. Although his final remarks were drawn more from Bohlen's speech, the fact is that the reports delivered by Kennan and Clayton in the days before June 5 provided the substance and the conceptual framework for the program to come. Once Marshall arrived in Cambridge, he realized he hadn't shown his speech to President Truman. Nevertheless, Truman had been kept informed, especially through meetings not only with Marshall himself, but with Acheson and Clayton as well. In the end, the whole approach was a State Department project, with minimal input from the White House. Having agreed on the overarching goals of the State Department, Truman felt no need to control the process, which was a testament to the respect and confidence he had for Marshall.[96]

On June 5, at Harvard University in Cambridge, only miles from the heart of Boston, all was in readiness for the 286th graduation. The weather cooperated, yielding a glorious early summer day, perfect for the planned outdoor activities. Marshall, wearing a gray three-piece suit, and, as it turned out, without academic robes, led the procession, with other notables following, including General Bradley, the Manhattan Project physicist J. Robert Oppenheimer, and poet T.S. Eliot. Conant presented Marshall's doctor of laws degree and read the citation: "An American to whom Freedom owes an enduring debt of gratitude, a soldier and statesman whose ability and character brook only one comparison [George Washington] in the history of the nation." The graduates stood in an extended ovation.[97] After lunch, a designated group of speakers, partially shaded by old elm trees, gathered in Harvard Yard to address a huge crowd of assembled alumni.

Not a Palliative but a Cure

Marshall stood to speak, fumbling with his glasses, and began by saying that he was "profoundly grateful, touched by the great distinction and honor and great compliment accorded me by the authorities of Harvard this morning. I am overwhelmed, as a matter of fact." Then he shifted to the subject at hand, speaking in calm and measured tones: "I need not tell you that the situation is very serious," he said, and proceeded to outline the complexity of conditions in Europe, not only the physical destruction, but also the "dislocation of the entire fabric of European economy." "Something had to be done to break the vicious cycle," he continued, to "restore the confidence of the European people in the economic future of their own countries and of Europe as a whole." The United States was willing to provide that help, he said, explaining that "Our policy is directed not against any country or doctrine but against hunger, poverty, desperation, and chaos. Its purpose should be the revival of a working economy in the world so as to permit the emergence of political and social conditions in which free institutions could exist." The implication was clear: all countries, whether victor or vanquished, could receive aid, including Germany and the Soviet Union. Using Kennan's words almost verbatim, he cautioned that it "would be neither fitting nor efficacious for our Government to undertake to draw up unilaterally a program designed to place Europe on its feet economically. This is the business of the Europeans. The initiative, I think, must come from Europe." The United States would not simply fill a shopping list of needs from Europe—a piecemeal approach was undesirable. "Any assistance the Government would render must provide a cure rather than a mere palliative," Marshall emphasized, and the effort would be a "joint one," with nations "acting cooperatively" to develop the recovery plan. When they had done so, continued the secretary, the United States would provide "friendly aid."[98]

Anticipating the isolationists who would oppose a plan binding the country to such a European commitment, Marshall warned of the demoralizing effects that disturbances "arising from desperation" would have on the world and noted that "the economic consequences to the U.S. should be apparent to all." Completing his remarks with words that had not been included in the State Department version of the speech released through the public relations office the day before, he told the audience, this time with his voice rising slightly, "We are remote from the scene of these troubles. It is virtually impossible at this distance merely by reading, or listening, or even seeing photographs and motion pictures, to grasp at all the real significance of the situation. And yet the whole world of the future hangs on a proper judgment." He put the onus on the American people to understand the dominant factors involved, and to determine "what was needed; what had to be done; what must be done." The speech, one of the most significant in mid-20th century history, had taken just 12 minutes and 10 seconds.[99]

"A life line"

That early May, Dean Acheson had given a speech to a group of businessmen in Cleveland, Mississippi, that seemed to foreshadow the introduction of the Marshall Plan at Harvard on June 5. Uncharacteristically casual with tie off, sleeves rolled up, Acheson had delivered the talk in a humid school gymnasium. An interviewer asked Marshall later, if this speech had been a "trial balloon" for the Harvard address; Marshall replied with an emphatic,

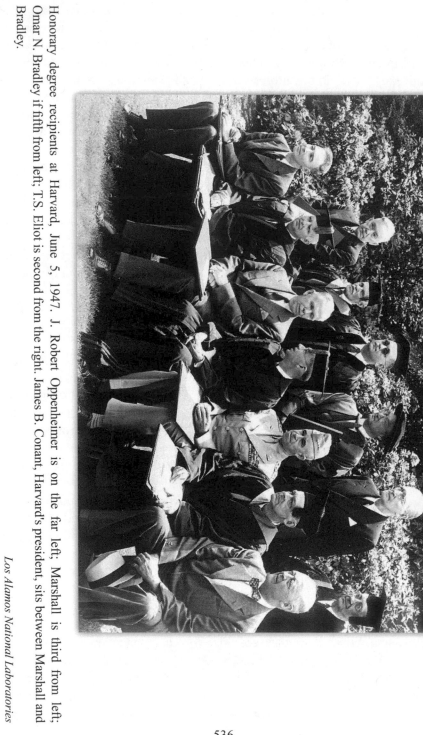

Honorary degree recipients at Harvard, June 5, 1947. J. Robert Oppenheimer is on the far left; Marshall is third from left; Omar N. Bradley if fifth from left; T.S. Eliot is second from the right. James B. Conant, Harvard's president, sits between Marshall and Bradley.

Los Alamos National Laboratories

536

"No."[100] Nevertheless, the language of the undersecretary's remarks reflected the thinking that was gaining momentum within the State Department that something beyond Band-Aid approaches was in the offing. Acheson had told the crowd that "until various countries of the world get on their feet and become self-supporting, there can be no political or economic stability in the world and no lasting peace or prosperity for any of us," and he spoke of grants and loans that would be needed to deliver aid to Europe. As if in warning, Acheson reminded the crowd that "hopeless and hungry people often resort to desperate measures."[101]

A month later, on June 2, BBC correspondent Leonard Miall, along with two other British newspapermen, invited Acheson to lunch. Sensing the undersecretary's importance in the day-to-day workings at the State Department, and rarely privy to the access that other more prominent journalists enjoyed, especially James Reston and Walter Lippmann, they wanted to establish a relationship with Acheson. During the meal he talked a good bit about the Cleveland speech and generally about how the help for Europe might be administered. He emphasized that the initiative for aid would have to come from the Europeans. Although Miall usually delivered straight news coverage, it so happened that he was asked to fill in for a prominent newsman, away on a special assignment, who usually anchored a half-hour weekly program, "American Commentary," scheduled to air the evening of June 5th. By mid-day on the 4th, Miall had already written the script for the episode, much of it based on the luncheon with Acheson. That afternoon at the British embassy, a press officer showed Miall the text of Marshall's Harvard speech, just released, and told him that if he hadn't read it, he should. "It is very interesting stuff," he stressed, as the two parted. Miall picked up his own copy at the State Department press office and, having read it, concluded that he needed to rewrite the entire "American Commentary" text. The pre-taped program would air on BBC London at 10:30 p.m., British time, but as Miall recorded it, he didn't know for certain whether Marshall would have given the speech by the time it aired on British radio. The press office copy did not indicate a time for delivery. Nevertheless, he began by announcing this "exceptionally important speech" which "had propounded a totally new continental approach to the problem of Europe's economic crisis," and then read verbatim portions from its text, including the part that said "the initiative must come from the Europeans."[102]

The British foreign minister, Ernest Bevin, was at home in London that evening, propped up in bed, and it so happened, he was listening to Miall's BBC broadcast on a small radio. He immediately recognized the import of

DEPARTMENT OF STATE

FOR THE PRESS   JUNE 4, 1947
                                                                             No. 455

CONFIDENTIAL RELEASE FOR PUBLICATION WHEN SECRETARY MARSHALL BEGINS TO
        SPEAK. NOT TO BE PREVIOUSLY PUBLISHED, QUOTED FROM OR USED IN
        ANY WAY.

NOTE: It is not known whether Secretary Marshall will speak during the morning, afternoon
        or evening. For explicit information please consult with Harvard News Service at
        the University.

                                                                M. J. MC DERMOTT

                                        - - - - - - - - -

                        REMARKS BY THE HONORABLE GEORGE C.
                        MARSHALL, SECRETARY OF STATE, AT HARVARD-
                        UNIVERSITY ON JUNE 5, 1947

        I need not tell you gentlemen that the world situation is very serious. That must be
apparent to all intelligent people. I think one difficulty is that the problem is one of such
enormous complexity that the very mass of facts presented to the public by press and radio

Copy of Marshall's speech released by the state department
to the press, June 4, 1947, with no specific delivery time noted

The George C. Marshall Research Library

what Marshall had offered. Bevin recalled later that at the time, groggy from being half asleep, he thought he was actually hearing Marshall's voice on the radio. The "initiative must come from the Europeans" line was not lost on him. The next morning, bright and early, he strode into his office asking for a complete version of Marshall's remarks. Since the British Embassy in Washington had not considered the speech that significant—just another "university oration"—they had sent it by surface mail. Sir William Strang, a senior official in the British Foreign Office, told Bevin that since they did not have a copy of the speech, perhaps they should ask "Washington" for clarification. Bevin immediately said no—they were going to trust what Marshall had said. As he would later declare, "It was like a lifeline to a sinking man. It seemed to bring hope where there was none. I grabbed the offer with both hands."[103] With only Miall's BBC words to go by, Bevin told his secretary, "Get me Bidault on the phone." Soon he was discussing Marshall's proposal with the French foreign minister.

"Squeeze maximum political advantage"

On June 17 the two men met in Paris and agreed that they would need to form steering committees that would figure out how to coordinate programs having to do with coal, food, steel and transport.[104] Further, they would invite the Russians to participate, but if they chose not to, they would go ahead at full steam. Before Bevin flew back to England, the two of them agreed to issue an invitation to Molotov. Bidault placed the call to Moscow. By June 27, only 22 days after Marshall's address, the three of them were in Paris. The weather seemed fittingly dramatic. The worst winter in Europe's recent history had given way to drought-like conditions and brutal heat. On the second day of the meetings, the heat wave was briefly broken by wild thunderstorms and dangerous winds preceded by blackened clouds and menacing bolts of sky-to-ground lightning.[105] Although Molotov was in Paris, along with a staff of 89 officials and experts, the Russians had no intention of participating in this offer. As they saw it, it was directed toward the establishment of a Western European bloc . . . aimed at economic and political subjugation of European countries to American capital."[106] Molotov's goals were to subvert the concept of "joint" planning, an idea that would surely yield a mutually beneficial Western bloc that in the Russian view was a threat to their interests. In a manner exactly opposite of the Marshall Plan speech guidelines, Molotov would argue for a country-by-country approach that did not require "group" transparency regarding their needs. Additionally, the Soviet foreign minister had to see to it that the eastern European nations remained in the Soviet orbit; moreover, he was to work against German rehabilitation, making sure the Soviets got reparations and joint control of the Ruhr. In short, Molotov would once again bring out the "old saws" that had bogged down the Moscow Conference that spring. Still, the order from Moscow was that the Russian delegation should be there, appearing to be part of the process, and thus able to "squeeze the maximum political advantage from this."[107]

At the beginning of the conference, the United States had said officially that Germany would be part of this developing program. Molotov asked Bidault directly if he was willing to support the plans of the Americans for German reconstruction. During the Moscow Conference, this question had put them in a shaky alliance of agreement. This time, Bidault didn't take the bait, telling Molotov that German policy would be worked out, but economic relief and recovery could not wait.[108] The feeble French-Soviet partnership that had characterized the Moscow debates was permanently broken. Throughout a week of meetings, Molotov "backed and filled," wrote Ed Cray, refusing "adamantly to list Soviet assets, to state Soviet needs or, most ominously, to allow a central European body to set priorities in distributing the American aid."[109] Another element that the Russians could not tolerate was this: the Eastern bloc countries would be invited to participate and under the "joint planning" umbrella could be lured away with the promise of aid and economic integration. The Soviets had to keep those entities under control—they needed those resources for their own economy. Marshall Plan historian Greg Behrman wrote that:

> At the time, the United States did not fully appreciate the fragility of political conditions in Czechoslovakia, Poland and Hungary . . . . Stalin's grip was tenuous, and as [the Soviet's leading economist] Varga put it, "the Marshall Plan was a dagger pointed at Moscow." Stalin would not permit Soviet participation in the Marshall Plan.[110]

On July 2, Molotov had become scathing, uttering accusations that this requirement of an overall plan threatened the integrity of smaller nations, and was simply an effort by the United States to gain control. Bevin counterargued, finally informing Molotov that he and Bidault would cooperate with any states that "were willing in the restoration of war-shattered Europe." Sometime during that meeting, Molotov was handed a telegram. After he read it, he reiterated a point that had plagued the discussion from the beginning: the Soviet Union would not agree to joint planning. It would not participate in the Marshall Plan.[111] Ironically, it was July 4th, Independence Day back home in the United States, when Molotov and his entourage left Paris. On the same day, Bidault and Bevin issued an invitation for 22 European countries to take part in the Marshall Plan. Even as they met in Paris, the Soviet foreign minister was still in the air, as Behrman noted, "passing over Eastern Europe—and the iron curtain that had fallen behind him." [112]

"Returned a lackey"

Although the withdrawal of the Soviets from the Marshall Plan meetings probably saved the program—the likelihood that the American Congress would approve a proposal that included this communist mega-power was virtually nil—the invitation for the Russians to participate was still proffered. All realized that the Soviets would not walk back through this open door. That part was a relief; nevertheless, the United States sincerely hoped that the Eastern Bloc satellites would participate. If they came to Paris, perhaps they could be persuaded to become a part of the larger Western European community. The Soviet leader knew this did not bode well for him. However, only three days after Molotov got back to Russia, Stalin cabled the Soviet ambassadors in the bloc nations that they should encourage participation in the upcoming meetings, scheduled to begin on July 12. The purpose, however, was not to be a part of the process, but rather to thwart it. The goal would be to show how unacceptable any French-British plan was by not allowing its unanimous adoption. After that they could leave, taking with them as many delegates as possible.[113] Only a couple of days later, though, with hard-liners putting pressure on Stalin, he reversed his directive, discouraging attendance. Only Czechoslovakia, with a fairly balanced coalition government in place, did not immediately withdraw as its neighbors did. Soon Stalin brought the Czech foreign minister, Jan Masaryk, to the Kremlin for a midnight meeting. If Czechoslovakia participated, Stalin told him, "it would show that you want to cooperate in an action aimed at isolating the Soviet Union." As evidence, Stalin even produced newspapers with headlines that read, "Prague Losing Her Ties to Moscow," or "Breach in the Eastern Bloc." The meeting was over in one-half hour, and that ended the matter; the Czechs would not attend. As Masaryk later commented, "I went to Moscow as the foreign minister of an independent sovereign state. I returned as a lackey of the Soviet government."[114]

It was at the Ministry of Foreign and European Affairs in Paris, along the Quai d'Orsay on the left bank of the Seine, that the delegates of the 16 countries met on July 12, 1947.[115] They included Austria, Belgium, Denmark, France, Great Britain, Greece, Iceland, Ireland, Italy, Luxembourg, the Netherlands, Norway, Portugal, Sweden, Switzerland, and Turkey.[116] Bevin was chairman, and under his leadership, the group soon established the Committee of European Economic Cooperation, (CEEC), with each country represented. Bevin tapped Sir Oliver Franks, a distinguished diplomat and Oxford professor who had been a member of Britain's Finance Office in World War II, to head it up. Technical committees were formed as well: Food and Agriculture, Iron and Steel, Fuel and Power, Transport.[117] Although all seemed well-organized, it was going to be a long, hot, and challenging summer. As Greg Behrman noted, "Interests were varied and cross-cutting, and they would be hard to align and reconcile. In the preceding decade, Europe had reverted to economic nationalism, protectionism and autarky. Now those same states were being asked to tear down all safeguards, to subsume their own near-term interest, often against steep internal domestic opinion."[118] Sensing that the longer they waited the harder it would be to get approval of their proposals from the U.S. Congress, they set a September 1 deadline for completing the proposal, which added great pressure to the proceedings. Although Marshall and the policy planning staffers were committed to the concept that the initiative had to come from these nations, Will Clayton, with his strong background in European economics, was on the scene in Paris by mid-July. He moved through the centers of power, almost always in an off-the-record capacity, offering guarded guidance in venues that included dinners, cocktail parties, or late-night conversation over drinks in Parisian bistros. By the end of the month, Clayton was a bit more pointed in his suggestions, holding an official meeting with the executive committee of the CEEC to stress that whatever the Europeans developed, it had to be of limited duration—four years—and salable to the American Congress.

With the Soviets out of the picture, it seemed there would be smooth sailing for developing an "integrated plan" for the rebuilding of Europe. But, in fact, the French became almost a larger obstacle than the Soviets in terms of completing a proposal. Echoing what the president of France had told Marshall in his pre-Moscow trip to Paris, the French feared the rebuilding of Germany, especially if somehow that "enemy" country ended up more rehabilitated than its own. The French people had been invaded by Germany three times in a century, once in 1871, again in 1914, and then in 1940. Now, Germany was supposed to be a part of the Marshall Plan? France wanted very much to keep Germany weak, and one way to do this was to oversee and even retard the recovery of her industrial potential by controlling the great coal and steel-producing region of the Ruhr. They suggested that the Ruhr be made into a four-part zone, with each allied country controlling aspects of production in that region.[119] The problem was that this area was extremely important to the reconstruction of Europe as a whole. As much as this French fear continued to fuel the debates over the summer, many other European nations had enjoyed strong trade ties with Germany in the past. They did not want to see an end to that trade relationship. Delegations from other European nations as well as the United States finally put pressure on the French representatives to change their minds. Germany would be rebuilt as a strong producer nation.

Back in Washington an expected change came to Marshall's staff. He had promised Undersecretary of State Dean Acheson that he would release him from his duties within six months, and he did just that. Robert Lovett, whom Marshall had brought back to learn the role of the undersecretary, had been Acheson's understudy since spring. On July 1, with Acheson headed back to New York and a prestigious law firm, Lovett was plunged into the Marshall Plan challenge. As he had with Acheson, Marshall depended on Lovett to handle the day-to-day workings of the State Department. Meanwhile, virtually every speech Marshall gave emphasized the desperation of the Europeans, and the need on the part of the United States to provide relief within the framework offered in the speech at Harvard. By mid-August, though, Marshall had to shift his focus toward Latin America as he prepared to attend the Pan-American Conference in Rio de Janerio. Lovett was to keep him apprised of developments in Europe via cable.

On August 24, the undersecretary sent a discouraging wire to Marshall in Brazil, telling him that the Europeans so far had come out only with "sixteen shopping lists," and something needed to be done to push the process forward. To add another red flag, Clayton soon broke it to Marshall and Lovett that the CEEC probably would be presenting a proposed budget of $28 billion, which all three knew would never make it through Congress. Soon Marshall agreed that despite wanting to stay out of European planning, Lovett could send Kennan, along with a passel of State Department staffers from the economic side, to Paris to talk with Clayton. Kennan was to assess in what ways the State Department advisers needed to be more aggressive in guiding these countries toward a more cohesive plan. After an intense weekend of meetings with Kennan and his experts, Clayton met with the CEEC's executive committee to describe some "essentials" that needed to be included to ensure passage of the legislation back in the United States.[120] The guidelines were based on Kennan's input. More than a list, their proposal needed to be viable enough that these economies could sustain themselves within four years; dollar amounts during that time needed to gradually diminish; there needed to be some proof of progress or the program could end; the participating nations had to include a plan for stabilizing each country's internal finances and monetary structure and needed to show movement toward liberalizing trade. Further, the nations had to form an organization that could oversee all of these matters.[121] Soon the State Department economic experts were meeting with the technical committees, again offering frank criticism with a view toward a program that was headed to a doubtful Congress back home.

The Baton Had Been Passed Across the Atlantic

They were past their self-imposed September 1 deadline, but by the 22nd the representatives of the participating CEEC countries were gathered for a ceremony marking the completion of the report. After Bevin signed it, he made a short speech. Recognizing the significance of the moment, he told the gathering that the report was not an appeal for charity. Europe was prepared to work, willing to reduce national barriers, and give up a portion of national sovereignty in the interest of a self-sustaining recovery.[122] The report, which included a request now pared down to $17 billion, was just under 700 pages, double bound and tied with a bright pink ribbon. After the signing ceremony, Bevin handed it to his king's royal messenger, Walter Kirkwood, who the next day boarded a flight from Paris to New York and thence to Washington. D.C., to present the proposal to Marshall at the State Department. "It is now for the American people and the American Congress," Bevin had said, "to decide whether this program, undertaken at Secretary Marshall's initiative, should be fulfilled and whether Europe can by this means contribute to the peace and prosperity of the world." Greg Behrman noted, "As Kirkwood arrived in Washington . . . the baton had been passed across the Atlantic. All eyes turned to Congress and to the American people." [123]

Chapter 18

Challenges at Home and Abroad

"In the other direction"

September 1947–December 1948

In a press conference on September 10, 1947, Marshall, home from the Rio Conference, mentioned that during his time away, undersecretary Robert Lovett had kept him fully informed on matters of state. Off the record, he complained to the reporters that it had been his experience the last seven years of his career that he was almost constantly going on trips that involved "all sorts of difficulties and labors," and that when he returned there a "great stack" of issues to be addressed. Marshall admitted that "they had been after me to get a physical examination for several years," which he had not yet done, and he speculated that "they will probably conduct that on the way to the cemetery." He had gone to the dentist, he told them, which had made him very "cheery." Returning to the subject of the "stack," he remarked on the "lengthy conversations" about "the daily grist" that continued to take his time.[1] Surely part of the grist was preparation for the upcoming United Nations meeting—he would address the General Assembly on September 17, just one week hence. His speech would include concerns about the situation in Europe, and the "supreme effort" that would be needed to break the "vicious circles of deepening political and economic crisis."[2] There seems little doubt that his dialogue with Lovett and other colleagues covered this deepening crisis, the "initiative" being taken by the 16 European countries, and the expected report from Paris. In fact, while Marshall was in New York, the heavy document from Bevin had arrived at the State Department. Marshall sent it to President Truman with an official cover letter on the 24th. The secretary flew back to Washington on the 28th, while the UN meeting was still in session, specifically to discuss the requests of the CEEC for $17 billion in aid from the United States.[3]

That Congress would sign on to this European Recovery Program, submitted by Britain's Ernest Bevin on behalf of the participating countries, did not seem promising. Historian Randall B. Woods wrote in *The Marshall Plan: A Fifty Year Perspective* that "despite World War II, and the onset of the cold war, currents of isolationism and economic nationalism still ran strong and deep on Capitol Hill." The 1947 Congress, with its Republican majority, had aligned with conservative southern Democrats to form a powerful coalition, one committed to a *contracted* role for the national government, certainly not an *expanded* one.[4] To some doubters, the very nature of the European Recovery Program forewarned a huge new bureaucracy; after all, who would run these programs? It seemed hard to imagine the U.S. government controlling economic factors in 16 countries. Didn't such oversight smack of socialism? That brought another dark thought: What if one of these nations legitimized a communist government? In France and Italy strong communist groups were making significant inroads. Congress could end up sending aid to "godless communists," a situation legislators would be hard-pressed to defend.

Then there was the money: Fiscal conservatives and moderates within Congress understood all too well that during World War II the national debt had increased by $200 billion. Although they had supported the war against the Axis powers as a righteous cause, they also believed that the United States had done enough. If anything, they wanted to promote a reduction in taxes, not an increase. Who would foot this bill? Other congressmen were concerned about inflation. Many reasoned that if the government was purchasing foodstuffs and raw materials for shipment to Europe, it would further increase demand and hence price hikes. Midwestern senators and congressmen, representing agricultural communities, weighed in: If the plan passed, the supply of machinery and other equipment needed to grow their crops would be in short supply; again, prices would increase and in this backhanded way decrease profits. Indiana Republican congressman Charles Halleck spoke for his voters when he declared, "I've been out on the hustings, and I know, the people don't like it."[5] Constituents from all corners of the country had accused Congress of poor oversight in dispersing earlier postwar aid programs; legislators were not anxious to face such charges again. One Nebraska Republican growled, "Any and all aid that we give them . . . no matter how many billions . . . will in fact become Operation Rathole."[6]

"Hell week"

This, then, was the task before Marshall as secretary of state: developing a bill that Congress would not reject out of hand was one aspect of the upcoming fight. However, part of getting that body to sign on was to convince constituencies all across America that this was a good thing. Marshall understood that for both tasks he had his work cut out for him. It would be primarily State Department staff who would write the piece of legislation that would come before the Congress. Marshall asked Undersecretary Robert Lovett to oversee the process. He tapped a brilliant young economist with a background in investment banking, Paul Nitze, who worked in Will Clayton's Economic Affairs department, to head up the work. From the CEEC a small delegation, led by Sir Oliver Franks, arrived in Washington in early October to work with State Department staff. They joined a score of junior officials, all of whom threw themselves into the task with great dedication. The group labored seven days a week, through meals, and in smoky conference rooms, surrounded by the report, crates full of charts, PPS memos, and tables of statistics. There was endless talk of "dollars, trade gaps, of steel, wheat, and coal."[7]

As the time drew near for President Truman to submit the bill to Congress, the pace intensified. State Department staff worked their way through the plethora of information coming from Europe and recognized that an interim aid bill would be necessary to tide Europe over until the European Recovery Program was in place. Both Kennan and Clayton had recommended it even before the CEEC report arrived. Marshall agreed, outlining the deteriorating situation with Truman. To consider emergency aid to Europe, the president called Congress into special session, with members slated to return on November 17, 1947. Truman was preparing an address that would make the case for that interim assistance, especially for Italy, France, and Austria, all near collapse and vulnerable to communist influence. So it was that State Department staff, in addition to working on the larger overarching legislation, had to prepare material in support of that bill. Lovett called the first days of November "hell week."[8]

Marshall himself was doing his part, meeting with business, labor, and industrial leaders at the White House, speaking about the European crisis at the Herald-Tribune Forum in New York, and giving a major speech in Boston during a CIO (Congress of Industrial Organizations) conference. He testified for three days before both House and Senate Foreign Relations committees, making the case for interim aid.[9] Soon he would be heading to London for the Foreign Ministers Conference, so it was once more Lovett in the hot seat. He testified on Capitol Hill from November 17 through the 30th, and he was often under attack on matters related to relief abuses, reparation disputes, what to do if one of the committed countries went communist, the German currency, and a rash of other concerns related to fears about a European commitment. Lovett, disarmingly friendly and approachable, handled the line of questioning well, although he later admitted that dealing with Congress was "like getting a shave and having your appendix taken out at the same time."[10] Nevertheless, the interim aid legislation, providing $522 million—$80 million less than had been proposed for the three countries—made it through Congress on December 15. Even before the legislation reached Truman's desk, Senator Vandenberg had told Lovett that the bill would pass, but warned, "We're headed for the storm cellar on the Marshall Plan."[11] Perhaps so, but on December 19, 1947, the White House sent the 50,000-word bill, "A Program for the United States in Support of European Recovery," to Congress. It was officially titled the European Recovery Program, soon shortened to "ERP," and then the "Marshall Plan." The president liked that idea, rejecting Clark Clifford's suggestion that it should be called the "Truman Plan." The president had commented realistically, "Can you imagine its chances of passage in an election year in a Republican congress if it is named for Truman and not Marshall? Anything sent up to the Senate and House with my name on it will quiver a couple of times and die."[12]

"The whole show"

Even as Marshall continued to promote a plan for European recovery to varied interest groups, he clearly understood that only Congress could pass the needed legislation. Anticipating the coming storm, he knew that keeping those communication channels open was crucial. Toward that end, he had cultivated a strong relationship with the powerful linchpin of the Senate Foreign Relations Committee, Arthur Vandenberg. Although at the end of World War II, the senator had shifted from his isolationist views, his support for this developing program was initially tepid. Yet it would be through his committee that the bill would eventually reach the floor of the Senate. In the time before he left for the meetings in New York and London, and after he arrived back as well, Marshall met with Vandenberg at least twice a week, sometimes with key members of their respective staffs also present. Avoiding the partisan settings of both the State Department and Capitol Hill, they gathered at the more neutral Blair House, a residence often used as guest quarters for White House visitors. Marshall got the senator's views on virtually every aspect of the process. It was an amazing bipartisan collaboration. Marshall would later tell Forrest Pogue that Vandenberg was "marvelous to work with, and fortunately, he thought I was."[13] This alliance proved a vital ingredient in responding effectively to the opposition arguments presented by the Senate during hearings that fall and in January 1948. "Vandenberg was just the whole show," Marshall acknowledged. Of their relationship, he would say, "We could not have gotten much closer

Senator Arthur M. Vandenberg (R-Michigan) is pictured at work, March 1939.

U.S. Library of Congress LC-H22-D-5976, photograph by Harris and Ewing

unless I sat in Vandenberg's lap or he sat in mine!"[14]

"No progress"

Just before the president addressed the joint session of Congress on November 17, Marshall had met with him to discuss aspects of the proposed interim aid legislation. The next morning he was off to Chicago to give two more speeches related to the European crisis. Returning on the 19th, Marshall had one day to get ready for his flight to London. Twenty-four hours after his arrival in Great Britain, he received an honorary degree at Oxford and, wearing the ceremonial robes of that august institution, delivered remarks to an audience of academics. Two days later the Foreign Minister's Conference began, and it would continue into mid-December. It didn't take long for the delegations of the four nations—the United States, Great Britain, France, and the Soviet Union—to reach an impasse. As the weekday meetings ground on, Marshall was becoming more and more discouraged by what he considered Soviet intransience, which brought to a halt any movement toward a German unification treaty. In a conference report submitted two days after he returned, Marshall provided examples of how impossible it had been to deal with the Russians. He cited Molotov's "categoric [*sic*] refusal" to provide the other three delegations with any information regarding reparations already taken out of the eastern zones. They would not do so, said Molotov, until full agreements had been reached on all of the issues, an impossible chicken/egg deadlock. As Marshall wrote, "We were to tell them what had occurred in the western zones, which we had already done, and they [were to] tell us nothing."[15] No decisions could be made, he emphasized, because no information was available. Eventually, Marshall wrote, he simply suggested that the conference adjourn. As he told Colonel Frank McCarthy in a letter, "It was difficult and unprofitable and rather wearing."[16] These sessions crystallized Marshall's attitude toward the Russians, first realized at the Moscow meetings, heightening his sense that the Soviet leaders would continue throwing up roadblocks to the economic and political reconstruction of Europe.

Not only was Marshall immersed in these difficult meetings, but virtually every moment of his days not taken up with the conference required him to satisfy diplomatic duties. In a letter home to Allen Brown's widow, Madge, he noted that he had not been able to see one of her friends, who had invited him for dinner there in London. Impossible, Marshall noted, since he had had lunch and dinner dates every day that week, from "Queen Mary to nine Labor [Party] leaders yesterday. The Duchess of Kent and the Pilgrims

President Truman gives Secretary Marshall a send-off as he heads for the
Moscow Conference of Foreign Ministers, November 20, 1947.

Harry S. Truman Library

Society tonight."[17] Although he tended to these myriad engagements with a kind of low-key charm and sincerely enjoyed some of the occasions—especially when it included wartime colleagues and friends—it made for days that began at 8:00 a.m. and ended after midnight. Marshall was tired and ready to see Katherine. There was a tinge of disappointment in his letter to her on December 9 from London: "A large envelope coming from Leesburg arrived the day before yesterday and produced no letters from you, only letters to you and to me [from others] and replies. I am looking forward to your first letter from Pinehurst."[18] Marshall was also counting on being in Pinehurst for the Christmas and New Year's holidays. He had been asked to give yet another speech, this time marking Wisconsin's centennial, for just after New Year's, and he did not want that obligation. A State Department appointments secretary, Carlisle Humelsine, wrote Lovett from London that it was "practically an obsession with him [Marshall]" to get that holiday in Pinehurst. Marshall had told Humelsine that he wasn't so much physically tired; he just needed a mental rest. Better to give him his time off, Humelsine wrote Lovett, so he could be rested and ready for the line-up of ERP negotiations with Congress. As much as the Wisconsin event was an opportunity for Marshall to make the European Recovery Program case, he was going to disengage for a while. It would be Chip Bohlen who would make the trip to Madison for the speech.[19]

"No doubt in my mind"

Marshall's image was on the cover of *Time* that January 5, 1947. For the second time in four years, he was "Man of the Year." Describing him as "homely and reassuring," the article noted that congressmen found the secretary of state "a man of stubborn, unswerving honesty—a good man." "His countrymen," continued the writer, "generally knew him as admirable and let it go at that."[20] Well rested and prepared for the ERP battle, Marshall was ready to face both groups during that winter and into the spring, starting in Washington. On January 8, 1948, making his way past reporters and cameramen in the hallway of the Senate Office Building, he entered the marble caucus room on the second floor to testify before the Senate Committee on Foreign Relations. Four days later he went before the House Committee on Foreign Affairs. His arguments were well articulated and reflected the key points that he had laid out at Harvard. It was the business of the Europeans, the assistance had to be adequate, it had to be prompt, and it had to be effectively applied. He noted that some of the best minds in numerous related fields had come together to develop the proposal. In addition, he reminded them, some of the top economic and political brains of

16 European nations had, in an amazingly short time, provided the Congress with their analyses and conclusions. He would work, Marshall emphasized, to make the plan efficient and effective. The program wasn't to be parsed—an inadequate program would be a waste of time and resources. This would not be a "quick-fix" dumping of American money into Europe; indeed, the ERP offered hope of genuine recovery. Reiterating the worsening conditions in Europe, he implored committee members to consider the consequences to the United States if they simply ignored the destabilization of 270 million people. Marshall painted a gloomy picture—ruined coal mines, wiped out steel mills, dead livestock, burnt merchant ships, foreign investment evaporated—laying out an alarming cause-effect scenario:

> As long as hunger, poverty, desperation, and resulting chaos threaten the great concentrations of people in Western Europe ... there will steadily develop social unease and political confusion on every side. Left to their own resources there will be ... no escape from economic distress so intense, social discontents so violent, political confusion so widespread, and hopes of the future so shattered that the historic base of western civilization, of which we are by belief and inheritance an integral part, will take on a new form in the image of the tyranny that we fought to destroy in Germany. The vacuum which the war created in Western Europe will be filled by the forces of which wars are made. Our national security will be threatened. We shall in effect live in an armed camp, regulated and controlled. But if we furnish effective aid to support the now visible reviving hope of Europe, the prospect should speedily change. The foundation of political vitality is economic recovery. Durable peace requires the restoration of west European vitality.[21]

Marshall acknowledged that many had asked the question: "Why must the United States carry so great a load in helping Europe?" The answer, he said, was a simple one: "The United States is the only country in the world today which has the economic power and productivity to furnish the needed assistance." In fact, Marshall explained, special presidential committees had already done studies to determine the economic capability of the United States to support the European Recovery Plan, although sacrifices would be required. Marshall warned senators that should they fail to pass this legislation, it would be Soviet leadership that would exploit Western Europe's economic distress for political motives. At the end of his prepared remarks before the Senate committee, he had intoned, in a voice uncharacteristically emotional, "I would like to close by saying that this

German refugee children shortly after the war. "Do we step aside?"

German Federal Archive: Bundesarchiv, Bild 146-1988-013-34A / CC-BY-SA

is a complex program. It is a difficult program. And you know, far better than I do, the political difficulties involved in this program. But there is no doubt whatever in my mind that if we decide to do this thing we can do it successfully and there is no doubt in my mind that the whole world hangs in the balance."[22] To wrap up his House committee opening remarks, he asked a question: "Do we meet the situation with action or do we step aside and allow other forces to settle the pattern of future European civilization?"[23]

Some were not convinced. One-time Republican congressman Hamilton Fish had warned his colleagues, "There is nothing saintly about [this program] merely because it carries the name of General Marshall. . . . It should be analyzed and broken down in detail just as much as if it carried the name of Joe Zilch."[24] Indeed, by the end of his testimony, Marshall had proven he could do just that. For each question posed by committee members, the secretary of state answered calmly. Now, with this task complete, and the administration's case solidly before Congress, it was time for Marshall to "hit the road." His testimony was just an opener. As Greg Behrman described it, for two months "a cavalcade of government officials—leaders from industry and labor, university professors and editors from leading national publications, women's clubs, church groups, veterans' groups and plain citizens—streamed into the large marble caucus room. What would take place that winter and spring of 1947 was, according to a Vandenberg aide, 'perhaps the most comprehensive public hearing on a foreign policy question every undertaken.'"[25] Behind the scenes, Senator Vandenberg used his influence to broker deals with the naysayers. He worked particularly hard to counter the arguments of conservative senator Robert Taft of Ohio, an equally powerful figure who was dead set against the Marshall Plan, comparing it to past Rooseveltian "giveaway programs."

Hitting the Road

Meanwhile, throughout the winter and spring of 1948, the secretary of state traveled across America, promoting the passage of the ERP. Forrest Pogue wrote of him: "Marshall, who had gained fame and admiration during the war, who had a knack for getting along with the Congress . . . was in a perfect position to take the lead in rallying the troops before a vote on the recovery plan."[26] Although Marshall had always eschewed politics, once wryly noting, "My father was a Democrat, my mother a Republican, and I am an Episcopalian," the secretary of state launched an impressive public relations sweep. Marshall's first stop was Pittsburgh, near his childhood home. The people greeted him warmly as a returning hero, but he found them "wholly unsympathetic." At a huge dinner held there in his honor, he spoke to them in business terms, touting the ERP as a wise long-term investment. In Atlanta he was treated as a celebrity, with newspaper articles describing him as "warm-hearted" and "intensely sincere." The *Atlanta Constitution* even mentioned his attire. "He wore a dark gray suit, a pale green shirt and a blue tie. It all seemed to blend with his iron gray hair and his sunburned complexion." He couldn't have been more serious, though. The secretary's audience was cotton and tobacco farmers, who feared the inflationary effects of farm equipment and fertilizers going to Europe. Marshall made the case for the markets that would open to them if these war-torn countries became prosperous again. Although noting that he no longer smoked, he told the gathering that according to research, the availability of tobacco was an effective stimulus to morale and productivity; thus there was a market for it in Europe as well.[27]

The constant travel wasn't easy. Marshall told his biographer that his effort to deliver a speech to the National Farm Institute in Des Moines, Iowa, almost cost him his life. Flying through a fierce and blinding thunderstorm, his plane had to make an emergency landing in Knoxville, Tennessee. Staff traveling with him managed to find a wire hook-up at the airport, so he delivered his talk via radio.[28] Later, when he went to the Midwest, Marshall provided a perfect opportunity for his conservative nemesis, Bert McCormick, the editor of the *Chicago Tribune*, to deliver a barrage of criticism against the Plan and its "internationalist designs." Marshall grumbled to Vandenberg that he was being pummeled in the Chicago press. The senator was unsympathetic, telling him, "You need to belittle this. I have to sit up here and be called a Benedict Arnold."[29] Writing to his sister in the spring of 1948, Marshall told her that he had finally had time at Dodona to put in some lettuce, radishes, peas, and onion sets, but complained, "It about broke my back [since] I've had no exercise since last September." Speaking of the fight for the ERP years later, he related, "I worked as hard as though I was running for the Senate or the presidency. . . . That's what I'm proud of, that part of it, because I had foreigners, I had tobacco people, cotton people, New York, eastern industrialists . . . and the whole West Coast just going in the other direction."[30] Although Marshall would say, "It was just a struggle from start to finish," in fact, he was persuasive. He dwelt on the importance of European trade to America's prosperity. Hammering away at old isolationist views, he told the assembled crowds: "We are a strong nation. But we cannot live to ourselves and remain strong. . . . The cause of liberty cannot have too many defenders." Pogue noted, "He found audiences reacting to him, and for the first time he caught a campaigner's fire."[31]

Even after his sweep across the country, Marshall was still persuading. He related to Pogue that one day a group of farmers from Ohio showed up unannounced at the State Department to see him. General Carter explained that the visitors wanted to speak with him. As Marshall recalled, they were worried about the short supply of farm machinery, and especially fertilizer, if the ERP got through. Thinking it was a small group, Marshall agreed to meet them. As it turned out, there were 60 farmers, and they had all just had lunch with Senator Taft. The secretary of state sat down at a table across from the men, asking that they outline their concerns. With some pride, Marshall recalled that he spoke with them for 40 minutes, and that they "reversed themselves on Taft."[32] In the end, he said, "We put the thing across." Although Marshall's arguments appealed to American self-interest—the benefits of restored markets, industry, and agriculture, for example—and stoked their fears regarding the communist threat, he also emphasized that accepting this program was the right thing to do, thereby articulating a policy incorporating the nation's ideals.

A Mysterious Death

Meanwhile, other factors helped move Americans toward the passage of the ERP. Even before the congressional debates on the program, congressman and senators traveled to Europe to assess the situation for themselves. Especially notable was a committee headed by Congressman Christian Herter, a Republican internationalist. He put together a group of 19 congressmen, "diverse in their politics, geography, and outlook," and divided them into five subcommittees to investigate conditions in different areas of Europe. It was no boondoggle; indeed, during the no-frills 45-day trip, at least one of the committees visited every country in Europe except Russia, Yugoslavia, and Albania.[33] One member described the process by saying that they had tried "to look at Europe in about the way a banker would look at a bankrupt corporation trying to get a loan." Their findings, based on 17 trunks of data, validated the State Department's grim descriptions. Committee members returned as converts to the aid program, and they did much to soften conservative opposition.[34]

Then, on February 25, 1948, while Marshall was on his campaign swing, Czechoslovakia's non-communist government was replaced with a Soviet-controlled dictatorship. Even more shocking news arrived on March 10. Jan Masaryk, the Czechoslovakian foreign minister, was found dead on the sidewalk three stories below his office. Although communist forces declared it a suicide, others believed he had been murdered. To Americans, Masaryk, a staunch non-communist, was beloved, reflecting the hope that at least this eastern European country might have a chance at democracy. His death had a great impact on the public, accentuating the kinds of dangerous disruptions that would continue to thwart Europe's recovery. At a press conference the next day, Marshall admitted, "The situation is very, very serious."[35]

The Struggle Over

President Truman took advantage of the developing crisis in Czechoslovakia to come before a joint session of Congress on March 17, 1948, where he delivered a "give-'em-hell" speech about the dangers of Soviet aggression. It provided the perfect opportunity to push for rapid support of the European Recovery Program. After a long hard struggle, Vandenberg had already brought the ERP bill to the Senate floor in early March, and it had passed by the 14th in virtually the form that Marshall had advanced. Two days later the House Appropriations Committee reported the bill out with a pass recommendation. Then came the president's scary speech. Perhaps it had an impact, since by the end of the month, the House "shouted the bill through by a voice vote."[36] On April 3, 1948, President Truman signed the Foreign Assistance Act, which embodied the ERP. Ironically, Marshall was not present at the signing ceremony. Tending to his duties as secretary of state, he was at a Conference of the American States in Bogota, Colombia. Despite other leaders who contributed to the passage of the ERP, as well as circumstance and timing factors that moved the citizenry and the Congress to embrace such an unlikely proposal, most historians agree that Marshall was its key mover. The program elements had arisen out of the idea-rarified atmosphere of his Policy Planning Staff, and the concepts generated by these brilliant thinkers were given practical application through Marshall's persuasive leadership. As historian Mark Stoler remarked: "It was he who had pressed for quick action, mobilized subordinates, revised and delivered the pivotal public address . . . implemented the bipartisan approach, and served as the plan's most effective public spokesman."[37]

Only two weeks after Truman signed the legislation into law, the freighter *John H. Quick* sailed out of Galveston, Texas, with 9,000 tons of wheat, headed for Europe.[38] This first cargo represented the initial focus of the Marshall Plan—getting food to the starving Europeans. Soon, however, the emphasis would shift to machinery and other resources that would boost industrial and agricultural production. To administer the programs

President Truman signs the authorizing legislation for the ERP. Also pictured from left to right are Senator Arthur Vandenberg, Secretary of the Treasury John Snyder, Representative Charles Eaton, Senator Tom Connally, Secretary of the Interior Julius Krug, Representative Joseph Martin, Representative Sol Bloom, and Secretary of Agriculture Clinton Anderson.

U.S. Library of Congress, Prints & Photographs Division, photograph by Harris & Ewing

of the Marshall Plan, Congress had established the European Cooperation Administration (ECA), with an American automobile company CEO, Paul Hoffman, as its head in Washington. Averell Harriman, a businessman who had moved into the public arena as ambassador to the Soviet Union and then secretary of commerce, would head the umbrella ECA mission in Paris. In addition, each Marshall Plan country had its own ECA organization. Harriman brought in the top men from the corporate and academic worlds to provide help to the missions. Since the Europeans were to take the initiative and play a large role in their own recovery, they developed the Organization for European Economic Cooperation (OEEC), also based in Paris. That organization, which was staffed by the best economic and financial talent in Europe, worked in tandem with the ECA in Paris to shape the projects of the respective Marshall Plan recipient countries. These two agencies from time to time had vehement differences as they debated priorities; nevertheless the spirit of cooperation remained, along with a dogged determination toward recovery.[39] By the time the European Recovery Program was completed on December 31, 1951, over $13 billion had been distributed to the 16 participating countries, about 1.2 percent of the GNP of the United States. However, dramatic changes came about in large part because of the program. Europe's gross national product rose an overall 32.5 percent over the four years of the program. Industrial production increased 40 percent over what it had been in 1938. Trade between European countries increased by 24 percent, and by 1953 almost 40 percent.[40]

When one considers the impact of the "counterpart funds," a bedrock concept of the Marshall Plan, the results are even more striking. Much of the ERP support came in the form of grants, which did not have to be repaid. Nevertheless, with each country having unique needs and circumstances, the application of the program varied greatly. As a general rule, though, most of the goods sent to Europe were purchased by the U.S. government with taxpayer dollars from American producers and manufacturers. The problem, though, was the "dollar gap." These European countries could not afford to drain their currency reserves with imports from the United States. So that market forces could return to normal as soon as possible, individuals or companies in ERP countries purchased those items at an agreed-upon price in their own currencies.[41] However, the "profit" derived from these sales went into each government's coffers for overarching use within its borders. For example, suppose a shipment of American tractors was headed to France. The tractor company supplying the machinery was paid with *U.S. dollars*, out of funding from the ERP appropriations. The French farmer purchased the tractor in francs. However, the money did not go back to the

President Truman confers with Secretary of State Marshall, and ERP advisors, November 29, 1948. Paul Hoffman is seated next to Marshall, with Averell Harriman on the far right.

Harry S. Truman Library

United States, but rather to the French government as a counterpart fund. It could then be used to support a variety of projects based on need—say, expanding the electric power network, rebuilding destroyed infrastructure, or increasing productivity through technical assistance to industry.[42]

Historians in varying degrees credit the Marshall Plan with thwarting a strong communist movement in Western Europe, restoring and revitalizing economic stability, and paving the way for the development of the European Economic Union. While it had its negative effects—there is no question that it contributed to a Europe characterized by two armed camps—it also played to the most generous humanitarian instincts of the Americans. As has been noted, the program was motivated in part by self-interest, but the impact of the Marshall Plan went far beyond economics and political ideology. Vernon Walters, an assistant to ERP leader Averell Harriman and later U.S. ambassador to the United Nations, once asserted, "The most important achievement of the Marshall Plan was not so much the material aid it gave as the rekindling of hope, the rekindling of energy."[43]

Bogota—Raincoats and Baby Formula

With Marshall in Bogota, Colombia, that spring of 1948, he was getting any news related to the passage of the ERP from Robert Lovett. The State Department delegation at the conference, with Marshall's input, would also keep Washington informed between March 30 and April 30 of the proceedings in this South American capital. There were 24 reports in all. The representatives were working on a multilateral hemispheric defense pact, which by conference end would be chartered as the Organization of American States (OAS). It was a precursor to similar pacts soon to be created in Europe and Asia. The trip went differently than Marshall might have anticipated. With the conference in session, on April 9, the leader of Colombia's Liberal Party was assassinated in the city. A mob caught and killed the assassin, hanging him in front of the presidential palace. Soon armed bands were roving over the city. The conferees had to flee the capitol building, which was, according to Marshall, "completely gutted." The center of the city "was a shambles," Marshall reported, with "fires still burning."[44] He, as well as most other delegates, believed that communists were behind the violence—even if they had not started it, they had capitalized upon it. Thinking more broadly than this local matter, in a speech to the delegates Marshall noted that it resembled the same pattern of strikes and riots as had occurred in Italy and France where communism threatened. Other delegates agreed, since one outcome of the conference was a strong anticommunist resolution.

Despite the violence in the city, Marshall firmly supported continuing the meetings, although Congress and the American press urged the U.S. delegation to return home. The nations could not leave the impression that they had been cowed by these developments and were thus defeated, Marshall emphasized. Indeed, the delegates resumed the meetings three days later at a nearby boys' school, while fires smoldered in the capital. Nevertheless, when the Argentine foreign minister asked the secretary of state for an American airborne division to parachute into Bogota to help quell the bloodshed, he demurred. Sending U.S. troops into another country required careful consideration and could not be crisis-driven: "This was a Colombian problem," he told the minister, "and the Colombians would have to take care of it."[45]

Apparently the protection of the U.S. secretary of state was also a Colombian matter, since a detachment of soldiers was sent to guard the house where Marshall and his staff were staying. Marshall calmly sat reading a Western novel until he noticed that all of the Colombian soldiers were in the front of the house. Perhaps recalling his days of soldiering and lessons of small-unit tactics, he told the young lieutenant in charge how to reposition his troops so that at least some of them were in the back, an area that he recognized as vulnerable to attack. Further, Marshall advised the officer to place others in more mobile positions around the house, thus making them readier to move forward or back as circumstances required.[46] Marshall soon noticed that because of the disruption triggered by the rioters, access to food was very limited. Embassy staff dependents did not have enough for their families, especially milk for infants. The Colombian soldiers, brought unexpectedly into the city because of the crisis, were wet and cold in the torrential rains of the season, and without proper gear. Marshall ordered supplies of food, including baby formula, for the dependent families, and 4,000 raincoats for the troops.[47] Years later, Lovett enjoyed telling the story of how the army totaled up the cost of these supplies and sent the bill to the State Department. Marshall, back at his desk by then, decided the American Red Cross should pay for it. The paperwork was returned to the army and eventually landed with that emergency relief organization. By that time, Marshall had become its president. He took one look and decided the bill should go to the Department of Defense. It wound its way through bureaucratic channels and arrived at Defense just after Marshall had been sworn in as that department's secretary. The papers were so "tattered and worn" that they could not be passed further; at last, the bill was paid.[48]

Marshall was scheduled to arrive back in Washington on April 24, 1948, although the Bogota conference would not wrap up until the 30th. The fundamental goals of the meeting had been laid out; thus he left it to the U.S. delegation to do the rest. With returning home on his mind, Marshall had sent Robert Lovett a letter on April 23. Noting that Truman often came to the airport to meet him when he arrived back from these kinds of meetings, he asked Lovett to discourage the president from doing so. Further, he wrote, "under no circumstances" was Mrs. Marshall to come. Since the conference wasn't officially over, he emphasized, there were to be no press interviews.[49] Indeed, the secretary of state wanted to slip into Washington and quickly head out to Leesburg where he could see his wife and his visiting five-year-old granddaughter, Kitty, and plant a late spring garden. As was usual for him, he always protected Katherine as much as possible from the ceremonial rigors of her role as the wife of a public official. Further, he saw no reason to take up the president's time with such perfunctory gestures. Marshall would soon see him on an issue that loomed large and, as he already knew, would place him in direct conflict with the chief executive. It had to do with the Middle East, specifically Palestine.

A Middle East Refuge

The story of the Jewish people fighting for an independent nation in the Middle East was complex, with beginnings that predated 70 A.D., when the Romans began to drive them from the Judean home where they had lived for a millennium.[50] The thread of history that would come to affect State Department policy on the matter perhaps stemmed from World War I. During that global conflict, the British defeated the Turks, which controlled the area known as Palestine. After the war, the League of Nations gave the British a mandate over the region with the understanding that it would eventually become independent. Both Arabs as well as Jewish immigrants living in that area claimed the land. In 1917, the British foreign secretary, Arthur Balfour, had declared, "His Majesty's Government view with favour the establishment in Palestine of a national home for the Jewish people, and will use their best endeavours to facilitate the achievement of this object." There was a caveat, though, "it being clearly understood that nothing shall be done which may prejudice the civil and religious rights of existing non-Jewish communities in Palestine, or the rights and political status enjoyed by Jews in any other country."[51] With this promise guiding them, Jewish nationalists (Zionists) had expectations of recreating their ancient homeland there. Arab nationalists wanted self-determination within those borders as well. Claiming that Jewish immigration was nothing more than another colonial invasion, they saw themselves as the rightful citizens of the region and demanded that the influx of Jewish immigrants be restricted.[52]

The British were conflicted. In the time after World War I, more and more London-based firms were seeking oil concessions in the Arab nations, which punctuated the importance of maintaining an Arab friendship. The British needed stability in the Middle East to protect the Suez Canal. By 1935, with the rise of Hitler in Germany, a record number of Jewish immigrants were arriving in Palestine. Protecting British interests among the Arab states, the government in London issued a 1939 white paper stating that an independent Arab state would be created within 10 years, and it would be governed jointly by Arabs and Jews. However, it also said that Jewish immigration would be limited for a five-year period, and after that the policy would be decided by the Palestinian government.[53] With the number of Jews allowed in dwindling, and the Arab population increasing, the Zionists saw this as a shut-out.

So it was that at the time Nazis were taking over Germany, the fleeing Jews were not allowed to go to Israel, except illegally, but were also barred from other countries, including the United States. By 1941, Nazi persecution had become genocide, and there was no haven for those who tried to escape. The Allies did virtually nothing to counter Hitler's so-called "Final Solution." However, as concentration camps were liberated by the Allies in 1945, the true horror of what had happened to the Jews of Europe became crystal clear. American soldiers of the Seventh Army were shocked, sickened, and infuriated when in late April of that year they flung open the gates at Dachau, in southern Germany, one of many hellish death camps in Nazi-occupied Europe. As the troops freed more than 30,000 prisoners over a period of three days, they found nearby 30 railroad cars with decomposing bodies, some of the 32,000 prisoners, many of them Jews, who had died. As Ed Cray wrote, "The stark photographs from the camps at Dachau, Buchenwald, and Auschwitz; the 200,000 Jewish survivors wandering between displaced person camps, seeking to emigrate; the unfathomable horror of 6 million dead, all worked to produce an international sympathy for the plight of the Jews."[54]

"No place to go"

Zionist support was particularly strong in the United States, not only among American Jews but overwhelmingly among the general population as well,

Soldiers of the 42nd Infantry Division find bodies in a boxcar outside Dachau, April 28, 1945.

U.S. Army Signal Corps

including Republicans and Democrats. President Truman, whose sympathies always tended to be with the underdog, had an excellent knowledge of history, including the plight of the Jews in ancient times. To him it made sense that Jews be allowed a place in the Middle East, where they had lived so many centuries before. As he told his legal counselor and adviser, Clark Clifford, "Everyone else who's been dragged from his country has someplace to go back to. But the Jews have no place to go."[55]

On the eve of Yom Kippur in 1946, Truman had urged the British to lift the limits for at least 100,000 Jews who wanted to immigrate to Palestine. The plea was to no avail. British leadership was frustrated with its inability to control the fighting breaking out between zealots on both sides of the struggle, and its failure to craft a compromise between the two groups. No longer capable of financing the drain on resources required by such complicated situations, the British government on April 2, 1947, announced that it would withdraw from its mandate the following summer. The Palestine question would be turned over to the United Nations.[56]

After careful study throughout 1947, a UN Special Commission on Palestine recommended that the region be portioned into separate Jewish and Arab states, both of which would become independent after a two-year transition. The authorizing resolution was adopted on November 29, 1947, with both the United States and the Soviet Union voting affirmative.[57] The Pentagon, the State Department, and the intelligence community vehemently opposed partition, saying that such an arrangement would have to be maintained by military force, result in sabotaging Arab-American relations, and quite possibly providing an opportunity for the Soviet Union to, as Ed Cray wrote, "fish in muddied waters." [58] While sympathetic to the plight of the Jewish people, Marshall worried that Israel was not ready to become an independent state. He believed Arab opposition to such a move would be fierce and could result in a bloodbath. Further, if fighting started, American troops could be drawn into the dispute—it would take 100,000 troops, the Joint Chiefs estimated, and the demobilized army could not supply that need. Secretary of Defense James Forrestal had reported to the president that at that time there were no more than 30,000 deployable men, with maybe 25,000 Marines.[59] Even if American troops could be mustered, their presence would anger the Arabs, thus opening the door for increased Russian influence in this vital oil-rich area. Marshall's views reflected those of the State Department's Middle East experts, as well as the top leadership of the newly formed Department of Defense. Although agreeing that eventually there would be an independent Jewish state, both groups favored an undivided Palestine under a UN trusteeship, which would liberalize Jewish immigration to the area and oversee the development over time of both sides into independent entities. In the end, the same goal would be accomplished, but in a more gradual and less provocative fashion. During the spring of 1948, as the violence escalated among the competing Jews and Arabs in Palestine in the wake of the resolution, Marshall and the leadership within the State Department's Near East Division sought ways to alter the partition agreement already made by the UN.

President Truman did not want to reverse the United Nations agreement. His key adviser, Clark Clifford, as well as powerful Zionist leaders, argued that despite the difficulties inherent in partition, to not support the United Nations decision, the first major recommendation of its existence, would undermine its effectiveness as an international peacekeeping body. Besides, given the inaction of the United States during the war, it would simply be morally reprehensible to deny it. Truman was in a close race for the presidency. Failure to back the partition would alienate Jewish and non-Jewish voters who favored that approach. Nevertheless, at a certain point that spring, the president seemed to waffle on the partition option. The State Department was supporting the idea of amending the UN resolution to include intermediate steps—a kind of modified trusteeship—that would buy some time for securing a peace treaty among the warring forces. Such an option would not negate the partitioning decision per se, but would make it more likely that a truce could precede the organizing of the two states. The criticism and pressure that Truman received when rumors swirled that he favored this method were tremendous. Everyone from the Democratic Party faithful, the powerful leader of the World Zionist Organization, Chaim Weizmann, even his former business partner in Kansas City, Ed Jacobson, vociferously criticized the president. Perhaps the angry barrage crystallized Truman's position in favor of an unfettered partitioning agreement, a view that retracked to his initial conviction of what should be done in Palestine. Increasingly, though, the gulf between the thinking of the White House and the State/Defense departments widened. By spring it seemed clear that not only would Truman continue to support partition, but he also planned to recognize the independent Jewish state just as soon as the mandate ended.[60] The British had already set that date—as of May 15, 1948, they would abandon their responsibilities in Palestine, except as it related to participation as a member of the United Nations.[61]

From the outset, Marshall, as secretary of state, saw both of these decisions in terms of foreign policy. It angered him that what he considered sound foreign policy was being linked to a polarizing political debate that might bear on election results. After all, among the strongest critics of any option other than outright partition were highly active Zionist interest groups that would wield influence against Truman's reelection if he failed to support that option. Mark Stoler concedes that Marshall "incorrectly tended to see this as the only issue."[62]

"That is all we need"

As the date for ending the mandate neared, on May 8, Marshall met with Moshe Shertok, a chief leader in the Jewish Agency, a highly organized and powerful Zionist group. Marshall spoke frankly of the dangers he saw in both outright partitioning and especially the declaration of an independent state. He showed Shertok a map of Palestine, telling him as he swept his hand over the Negev Desert, "Here you are surrounded by Arabs. And here in the Galilee, you are surrounded by other Arabs. You have Arab states all around you and your backs are to the sea. . . . Believe me, I am talking about things that I know," he continued. "You are sitting there in the coastal plains of Palestine while the Arabs hold the mountain ridges. . . . They are well trained and they have heavy arms. How can you hope to hold out?[63] There in a nutshell was Marshall's fear. If the Jews could not hold out, the pressure would be on for the United States to get involved, and that he believed would be disastrous. Shertok, a reasonable man but firmly committed to this next step, simply shrugged as if to say that there came a time when a man had to fight.[64] Marshall concluded the meeting by telling the Jewish leader that his agency was taking a gamble, and if it failed, they could not expect military help from the United States. Finally he said, "If it turns out you are right and you will establish the Jewish state, I'll be happy. But you are undertaking a grave responsibility." Shertok took Marshall's warning seriously, telling his Zionist colleagues in a New York meeting that the secretary's words should be given grave thought.[65] Nevertheless, on the same day as the Shertok meeting, Truman already knew without a doubt that the Jews would declare an independent state immediately after the deadline. Clark Clifford urged Truman to issue a preemptive statement saying that the United States would recognize this new nation. Clifford had already drafted the language of the proposed announcement. Truman was ready to do that, but first he wanted to have a meeting with Marshall and his advisers. He had told Clifford he should prepare himself to be a lawyer, since he would be called upon to make the arguments for recognition. "You will be addressing all of us present, of course," Truman said, "but the person I really want you to convince is Marshall."[66]

The meeting was held on May 12 in the afternoon, with the secretary, Lovett, and other White House and State Department advisers present. After a few preliminary remarks, the president turned it over to the State Department representatives. It was Lovett who presented the arguments for the trusteeship option, with Marshall adding his line of reasoning afterward. Both spoke of the risks involved if Arab forces already poised to strike overran the Jewish settlers there; the dangers of the Soviet Union getting involved; the military inadequacies of the United States; the problem of oil to support the resurgent industries of Europe under the Marshall Plan; and the fact that the UN was already trying to broker a truce that would ease the partition process. Then it was Clark Clifford's turn. For the first time in the meeting, he brought up the subject of recognition, arguing that the United States should withdraw from the current truce discussions in favor of the option he was promoting. Speaking in a slow, well-modulated voice, he delivered a carefully crafted 15-minute lecture, making his case: this had been Truman's policy from the beginning. It was an act of humanity, he emphasized, even citing lines from Deuteronomy in support of the Jewish claim on the land.[68]

Lovett countered that to recognize a Jewish state prematurely, before firm boundaries or even the form of government had been decided, would be to buy "a pig-in-a-poke."[69] Besides, argued the undersecretary, it had been the American delegation that had introduced the truce resolution at the UN, and to abandon that effort would damage the position of the United States within that nascent organization.[70] The whole question, thorny though it was, had to stay a UN matter, Lovett emphasized. Finally, he charged, such a move would be seen as a transparent political ploy.[71]

With a harsh blue-eyed stare, the secretary of state had listened to the back and forth between Lovett and Clifford. As historian David McCullough wrote, "On this note, Marshall broke in, speaking gravely with all of the weight of his reputation, his anger just barely in control."[72] Clifford's arguments were wrong, he asserted, and then proceeded to make the point that was driving his anger. Domestic policies shouldn't control foreign policy, he said, and, looking directly at Truman, told him that at stake "was the great office of the President." Then he made an extraordinary statement. If the president followed Clifford's advice, and if he (Marshall) were to vote in November, he would have to vote against him. Clifford later recalled Marshall's "righteous goddamn Baptist tone," which "brought the meeting to a grinding halt." After what Clifford later described as *"awful* total silence," the president just put up his hand, saying he was well aware of the dangers. Telling Marshall that he was inclined to agree with him, he added that perhaps it would be best for all to "sleep on it."[73] The fact is that Truman had already made up his mind. According to Clifford, the president had agreed with Marshall as the meeting broke up in order not to embarrass the secretary, whom Truman held in heroic regard, in front of the others. Afterward, Truman conceded to Clifford that the meeting "was rough as a cob."[74]

That evening Clifford and Lovett talked by phone. Both were deeply worried, since a breach between the White House and the State Department loomed large. Lovett worried that perhaps Marshall would resign over the matter, a move that would be catastrophic for the president in the fall election. The next day, though, after a meeting with the secretary of state, Lovett reported to the president that he thought Marshall had backed away from his opposition to the Jewish State. After all, historian Ed Cray noted, deep within him "ran strains of idealism" that were characteristic of pre–World War I values. Although one of Marshall's greatest strengths was pragmatism, especially a willingness to deal unsentimentally with geopolitical realities, he also wanted that which was for "the general good."[75] Lovett was brilliant in allaying Marshall's concerns about the practical fall-out from recognition: After all, recognition provided more than anything a moral force; it did not necessarily follow that the United States would have to send troops, and neither would it inescapably follow that the Jews would be driven into the sea. The oil issue was not as serious as it might seem on the surface. The worry was for a shortage of oil needed for Marshall Plan programs; there was no reason to think the Arabs would punish the European countries for America's position; besides, argued Lovett, they needed the business. Whether eventually he would have agreed, or not, one thing Marshall understood perfectly. The president intended to grant recognition, and as secretary of state he had only two choices—accept it or resign. He rejected the latter option, explaining, "No, gentlemen, you don't take a post of this sort and then resign when the man who has the constitutional responsibility to make decisions makes one you don't like."[76]

On Friday, May 14, 1948, the new Jewish state was to be declared at 6:00 p.m. Washington time. That afternoon Marshall called the president to tell him that while he couldn't support his position, he would not oppose it publicly. Truman must have felt great relief. "That is all we need," he told Clark Clifford.[77] The new Jewish state was declared on schedule. Eleven minutes later, a White House spokesperson announced that the United

Draft of the recognition of Israel document, May 14, 1948.

Harry S. Truman Library

States was giving de facto recognition to the United States of Israel, as it would be called. There were celebrations in the streets of Brooklyn and the Bronx that night, and synagogues across the country held special services.[63] At the Washington headquarters of the Jewish Agency—its primary mission accomplished—a new flag was unfurled, noted historian David McCullough, "pale blue and white, with a star of David in the center."[79]

Berlin—"A beleaguered garrison"

Although there is no doubt that in the spring of 1948 Marshall's attention had been on the Middle East, he still had to attend to developments in Europe. In fact, the Soviets had been waging their own propaganda war against the United States in the lead-up to the passage of the European Recovery Program, accusing their former ally of creating "the United States of Europe." Since the breakdown of the London foreign ministers conference late in 1947, the tense atmosphere had widened the gulf between the Soviets and their counterparts, the British, French, and Americans. The western zone Allies had seen nothing but obstruction and stagnation in negotiations having to do with the future of Germany. Although the four-power Allied Control Council established by the foreign ministers at the end of the war was supposed to be overseeing the reconstruction of Germany, more and more it became clear that the country was divided into two distinct camps—the eastern sector occupied by the Soviets, and the western zone of the Americans, the British, and the French. In early 1947, the British, beleaguered by deep postwar debt, had already lessened the financial burden of the occupation by merging with the United States.

Now, in the spring of 1948, weary with what they believed to be Soviet intransigence, the three western nations combined their zones into one—some called it Trizonia. In a March meeting in London of the four powers, this new triumvirate announced its plan to create a "German Constitutional Assembly" that would eventually ease those living in the western zones into a new, independent, and unoccupied government.[80] According to the Soviet representatives in London, this action was a violation of the Four Power Accord—the agreement reached at the end of the war for the joint control of Germany. In the wake of such a decision on the part of Trizonia, the Russians declared that the Allied Control Council, which had been the operational arm of the accord, no longer existed, freeing them from the collaborative decisions of the four-power meetings.[81] These moves by Britain, France, and the United States were alarming to Stalin. As Greg Behrman wrote, "He did not want to see a revived Germany, allied with a western capitalist bloc.

. . . Furthermore, a prosperous West German state could attract Germans from the Soviet zone to the East."[82]

Perhaps adding fuel to the flame, in mid-June, the three Allies announced currency reform, something that had eluded the frustrating four-power discussions. In the western zone, the inflationary reichsmark would be replaced with a more stable deutsch mark. The Soviet response came in the city of Berlin, 120 miles into the Russian zone, and resembling, as one writer described it, "four pieces of pie lying on a Red tablecloth."[83] In retaliation, and to force the other three powers out of that city, on June 24, 1948, the Russians shut off all access to Berlin—roads, rail lines, canals, even electrical power that was coming from generators in the Soviet sector. It left 2.5 million Berliners in the western zones of the city with no more than one month's supply of food and coal.[84] It was showdown time.

Marshall had been in Bogota, Colombia, from the end of March until April 23, and throughout the spring the Palestine crisis had been front and center. Both had absorbed his attention and his energy. In late June he was in Walter Reed hospital for extensive physical exams. Under those circumstances, he was not directly involved in the initial decision-making that would lead to an innovative and historic response to the Russians, soon to be known as the Berlin Airlift.[85] Nevertheless, Marshall was kept apprised of the situation by the undersecretary. In Lovett's meetings with the president, it was clear that the United States would not withdraw from Berlin. It had been General Brian Robertson, Lieutenant General Lucius Clay's British counterpart in Germany, who had first suggested using planes to supply the city's western zones. When Truman and Marshall were briefed on the idea, they both agreed. Further, as secretary of state, Marshall prepared a formal statement on the resolve of the United States to remain in Berlin, presenting it formally to the Soviet ambassador on July 6, 1948. Although in diplomatic parlance what Marshall brought to the ambassador's residence was a "note," it was much more than the name implied, laying out in no uncertain terms the position of the United States regarding the blockade. This tactic on the part of the Russians was a clear "violation of existing agreements," he wrote, since Berlin was an "international zone of occupation" to which the United States, Britain, and France had free access. Marshall emphasized that the United States would "not be induced by threats, pressures or other actions to abandon these rights. . . . Furthermore, as an occupying power, the United States had a humanitarian responsibility for the physical well-being and safety of the German population within its territory." The situation was "intolerable," he emphasized, and the United States had to insist that its access rights be fully and immediately restored.[86] While Marshall affirmed that the United States was willing to discuss any question of dispute, it would not do so until the blockade was lifted.

Since the Soviets insisted that they would not back down until the plan for a unified German government in the western zone was withdrawn, the stage was set for a long, dramatic, and astonishing supply mission on the part of the Americans, British, and French. To ensure even minimal survival, the western sectors needed 1,534 tons of food per day. Begun in late June 1948, the flights were dubbed "Operation Vittles" because, as the American general commanding the Wiesbaden, Germany, military post declared, "We're haulin' grub."[87] In addition to food, fuel and coal were absolutely necessary; otherwise, virtually all recovering industries would be shut down. American and British pilots were up to the stupendous task, delivering 2.3 million tons of coal, food, and supplies in 277,569 flights. During the 321 days of the mission, the planes flew around the clock, landing just three minutes apart. The German people helped unload the aircraft from first two and then three airports within the sector. Former Luftwaffe mechanics worked to service the aircraft. Mobile snack bars provided onsite food and weather information. The turnaround time from landing to departing averaged only 25 minutes.[88] For the most part, the flights made it through, even though Soviet fighters buzzed them from time to time. Further, the operation continued through the German winter, a feat that the Russians were sure would encourage the Western powers to quit. Seeing that no benefit was coming from this tactic, on May 12, 1949, the Soviets removed the barriers, and the blockade was history. Instead of the Allies being bullied into accepting this situation, it had simply encouraged them to band together further. West Germany was proclaimed a republic the same month the blockade ended. During the fall of 1948, the Allies stepped up efforts to create a regional defensive alliance in Western Europe, fully supported by Marshall, as a kind of military parallel to the ERP economic blueprint.[89] Soviet moves in Berlin had made this need clear. It would be the next summer, after Marshall had left office, that the U.S. Senate gave its approval to a document creating the North Atlantic Treaty Organization. Nevertheless, Marshall would later tell Forrest Pogue, with uncharacteristic self-satisfaction, "I started NATO from the first jump. I got every living soul, one after the other, to talk to me personally on the thing and to get them stirred up to do this business."[90]

"A six-hour day out in the hot sun"

Early in July 1948 Marshall had held a press conference, and a good deal

A C-54 plane comes in for a landing at Tempelhof Airport, West Berlin, 1948.

United States Air Force

of the Q&A centered upon his health. The secretary of state explained that while he had read that he was "seriously ill or approaching death," it wasn't so. In fact, he told the reporters that his recent stay at Walter Reed Hospital had been about a long-overdue physical, at which time "they examined everything, but my hair." No, he wasn't going to resign, he assured them. As if to prove his healthiness, he explained that just after he had been released from the hospital, he had done "a six-hour day out in the hot sun," in 92-degree temperatures. "I challenge anybody after two hours to do what I was doing," he said, and then described work that involved "pick-ax, shovel, wheelbarrow and I believe, some back-seat driving."[91] Light though the mood was, in reality when doctors examined him they had found a growth on his right kidney, and recommended surgery. Marshall, however, asked that they defer it until after he attended the United Nations Conference in Paris that fall.

By September 20, Marshall was in the "City of Light," this time with Katherine by his side. Back in the United States, Truman's election campaign was in full swing. Marshall knew that no matter the outcome, he would resign before the next inauguration. If Truman lost, he would automatically terminate the post; if the president won, Marshall had made up his mind that he would not accept another four years of intense duty in Washington. A natural time to leave would be just as the new term began—that is, January. Thus, even as Marshall settled into very comfortable quarters at the embassy, there was a sense that in terms of his professional responsibilities, the end was near. Still, there was work to be done. Three days after his arrival, Marshall gave his first address to the United Nations General Assembly at the Paris conference. The tone was moderate and conciliatory, but he laid out the main issues that concerned his government—peace treaties for Germany, Japan, and Austria; an end to the conflict in Palestine; the admission of Trans-Jordan and Israel into the UN; and a system of control for atomic weapons.[92] Perhaps to downplay the more volatile issues, he said nothing about the situation in Berlin; neither did he mention efforts under way to create the mutual defense pact that would eventually become NATO.[93] He did speak of "alleviating tensions," and "not bartering away rights and freedoms of other peoples," but nothing more specific than that. Nevertheless, regarding Berlin, his policy and that of the State Department was clear: the United States would not be forced out of Berlin and would not negotiate under duress. With the aid of neutrals within the United Nations, a means had to be worked out to prevent the Russians from disrespecting the Western powers. Indeed, while the State Department agreed that the best means of resolving the blockade was to submit the issue to the UN Security

Secretary of State Marshall at the United Nations Conference, Paris, fall 1948
Photo by Gerald Waller. Used with Permission. ©1948, 2013 "Stars and Stripes"

Council, and while Marshall acknowledged that any agreement decided upon would be imperfect, the primary positions articulated by the United States had to be safeguarded.[94] In the meantime, the blockade continued into 1949.

Overall, during the Paris conference it was a relaxed Marshall who settled into a daily routine. There were meetings in the morning with the United States delegation, followed by the General Assembly sessions later in the day. A young and impressive John Foster Dulles, formerly a player in the presidential campaign of Thomas E. Dewey and a conservative, headed the delegation. Marshall respected and trusted him to handle issues that arose in the varied policy discussions. Meanwhile, on weekends, or when the conference was in temporary recess, he and Katherine had an opportunity for some travel.[95]

Side Trips to Old Haunts

In early October, the Marshalls toured the battlefields and duty sites of his time in France during World War I, including the Meuse-Argonne. While in the area, he sent an aide to Gondrecourt to see if Madame Jouatte, the woman who had billeted him and other young officers during World War I, was there. Marshall simply wanted to establish that she still lived in the town, but he didn't want Madame Jouatt to be informed that her former resident was coming for a visit. It was to be a surprise. The aide reported back that he had found the residence, located on the center square. Although Marshall had wanted to slip in quietly to see her, it was a Sunday, so many parishioners were coming out of a morning service when his limousine, plus one other, pulled up. Marshall asked Katherine to stay back for a few minutes, so he could greet Madame Jouatte first. Curious about the commotion outside her door as the local citizens gathered to see what might transpire, she came out in a well-worn robe and slippers. As Marshall later told Forrest Pogue of her appearance, "She wasn't a very dressy old lady anyway, and she looked pretty slack in these clothes. But she was unchanged otherwise." Marshall had started toward the entrance to her home when she recognized him, and running toward him, threw her arms around him, kissing him on both cheeks. Soon she was introduced to Katherine, and they all went into the house for a visit, staying for a while for what Marshall described as a "joyous occasion" from which he got "great satisfaction."[96]

Papal Audience and a Return to Anzio

After another week of business at the United Nations Conference, once again the Marshalls enjoyed a long weekend of travel, which included a visit to the country estate of Pope Pius XII on October 19. In his official "Memorandum of Conversation," he mentioned that the pope was pleased that he (Marshall modestly noted that this personal pronoun actually referred to the U.S. government) had been firm in his dealings with the USSR, since, as he opined, this was the only attitude understood by the Soviets.[97] The pope complimented the secretary directly on the European Recovery Plan and how it had helped Italy. They talked about President Truman's burden at being the sole individual in control of the atomic bomb's use, and the complexity within the administration regarding how best to approach Stalin. Marshall called the pope "frank throughout with no evidences of diplomatic circumlocution."[98] His letter to Madge Brown regarding the visit was more personal. Marshall wrote that the pope had spoken to Katherine about Allen's death—he had been killed at the approach to the town in the Alban Hills where the papal estate was located. As Marshall described it, the pope "was very impressive in his attitude and statements to her."[98]

From the papal residence, the Marshalls motored toward Anzio, and on the way saw the exact spot of Allen's last day. Marshall wrote his daughter-in-law that when they arrived in the town itself, which had been the scene of so much fighting, he was delighted to see that it had been "rehabilitated into a lovely sea side resort." In the same letter, he described their visit to the cemetery where Allen was buried. Marshall noted that the whole area was being graded and reconstructed, so the grounds were not as beautifully ordered as was typical of military gravesites. Explaining to Madge that he had anticipated this, Marshall remarked that before they came to Anzio they had visited two other fully finished cemeteries, both pristine and lushly green, so that Katherine could visualize the future beauty of the Anzio burial site.[99] Although Marshall had been over these locations just after Allen's death, Katherine had not. It was clear the visit was very important to her. She would later write:

> As I knelt to place a wreath, two soldiers stood beside me. They laid a blanket of roses over his grave, across which was written, "The United States Army.". . . I felt resigned for the first time that he should remain so far from the land he loved. It seems to me that it was as it should

The Marshalls with Pope Pius XII at his summer
residence at Castel Gandolfo, October 19, 1948
Photographer G. Felici, Fotografia Pontificia

be. I felt that his last resting place should be with his comrades where his life had counted the most, for they had given a country liberty and a people freedom.[100]

That September, before he went to Paris, Marshall had written a friend that the trip to Paris for the United Nations Conference should be his "end run," because, he noted, "my agreement was only to stay to the end of the year." As he had so many times before, he yearned for the freedom of retirement: "It will be a great treat, beyond anything you can imagine, for me to be relieved of responsibility, and be free to pursue my own desires and family life."[101] By mid-November, Marshall thought that the main business of the conference was finished. He was able to leave the rest in the hands of John Foster Dulles and others in the delegation. Marshall could return for the operation to remove the cyst from his diseased right kidney and be out of the hospital by Christmas. Even before he returned from Europe, he had written Madge Brown regarding his immediate future:

> I plan to rest up a few days, see the Army and Navy [football game] and maybe the VMI Thanksgiving game . . . and then have my operation. The last should give me either a permanent "out," or, as I hope, a pleasant period of convalescence until the first part of January. I hope my successor will be appointed in early December."[102]

Despite the fact that he had retirement on his mind, and had already talked with the president about his desire to leave at the end of his term, Marshall had not submitted a formal resignation. While rumors flew, the secretary of state would give no official indication as to his plans. Back in the United States, he held a press conference on November 24. A good portion of the session revolved around issues that had arisen at the UN meeting: the Berlin crisis, the deteriorating situation in China, and the prospects for a European mutual defense pact. However, in the "off the record" portion of the briefing, reporters asked about his tenure in the cabinet. He reiterated what he told the press in Paris: "You brought it up. You discussed it. You have now gotten to the point of absorbing your time in selecting my successor." With perhaps an edge of irritation, he told them, "Question each other; I have never been in it at all." One reporter pressed harder for the answer. "You are shooting up the chimney," Marshall said. "You fellows want me to earn your living."[103]

On December 7, 1948, Marshall underwent the long-needed major surgery at Walter Reed Hospital in Washington, D.C. The operation was a success, but the recuperation slow. Marshall was almost 68 years old. He had been intensely involved in the crises of his country since 1939. By his own admission, he had been off only 19 days since he became army chief of staff. On January 3, 1949, Marshall resigned his State Department post. In the letter to President Truman he expressed his thanks for his "extraordinary consideration and complete support."[104] Reluctantly, Truman accepted, although, as he wrote, "I had hoped that with medical treatment and rest and recuperation you could continue in office. I am, however, unwilling to assume the responsibility of further jeopardizing your health."[105] It would be Dean Acheson who would become the new secretary of state, an appointment that Marshall fully supported.

The official business taken care of, the president made arrangements for Marshall to recover with Katherine on a naval base in Puerto Rico, telling him, "I hope you will spend a lot of time in the sunshine and not worry about things, national or inter-national, until you are fully recovered."[106] On January 29, from his private enclosed officers' quarters in San Juan, Marshall wrote a warm thank-you to the president. Although admitting that he was still experiencing pain "around his abdomen," Marshall also assured Truman that "I have a fine appetite, sleep well and otherwise am in fine shape and getting quite a tan."[107] At least for the moment it seemed that Marshall had wrested retirement from the jaws of public responsibility. It would not last long.

Chapter 19

Final Service

"God bless democracy"

January 1949–October 1951

Marshall was still recovering from his surgery when he and Katherine arrived at their cottage in Pinehurst, North Carolina, by mid-February 1949. He was daily receiving letters of congratulations regarding his retirement, and he dutifully answered them. Each response evoked a man ready to embrace relaxation. In several he mentioned how the trip to Puerto Rico had done wonders, describing it as "a wonderful stay." In early March, he recalled with delight the trip the two of them had made to the home of his former VMI roommate, Leonard Nicholson, who lived in New Orleans and owned the *Times-Picayune* newspaper. Nicholson proudly accompanied them to the grand events of Mardi Gras. With a bit of his own pride, Marshall commented that "Katherine was quite the belle of the Carnival. . . . Got the greatest applause, outdoing the queens. Thoroly [*sic*] enjoyed herself, particularly the luncheon to the Rex queen."[1] He wrote of a not-too-distant time when he was fully recovered and could resume a normal life in Pinehurst and Leesburg. Anticipating being his own driver, he made arrangements to trade in his old automobile for a brand-new 1949 Oldsmobile—the purchase price $2,994.[2] Marshall mentioned his wish to get back to a "long neglected garden" at Dodona, and he wrote of his desire to watch "world developments from a comfortable seat on the sidelines." By the end of February, he was writing his personal secretary, Sally Chamberlain, with his order to the Burpee Seed Company, everything from dahlias and marigolds to lettuce, corn, cabbage, and spinach.[3]

The public was not ready to have Marshall disappear behind the doors of his two retreats. Many of the requests that filled his mailbox daily were solicitations for him to attend certain special events to receive honors or make a speech. There were also lucrative offers to join the boards of directors of prestigious firms. Upon returning in early March from a trip to Miami, where he and Katherine had been guests of Ambassador William D. Pawley, Marshall complained that he had found "a tremendous amount of mail here to plague me. It included eighteen or twenty invitations to go places and make speeches. And the telephone has added several more." He explained to Pawley that the newspapers had covered his visits to Puerto Rico, New Orleans, and other places, so these "inviters" seemed to think he must be up to acknowledging such requests. Marshall was having "a hell of a time loafing," he concluded, and admitted that perhaps the only solution was to "remain in complete seclusion."[4] On March 4, 1949, he had accepted an invitation to the Overseas Press Club of America, which had honored him with an elegant dinner for 2,000 government officials and dignitaries at the Waldorf-Astoria in New York. As a souvenir of their "high regard" for him, the members gave him a gold-plated typewriter. In early March, Marshall wrote to former secretary of state Edward Stettinius, telling him that he could surely see from the number of errors in the letter that he (Marshall) was doing the typing, and then added, "What you can't see is that the murder is being done on a *gold-plated* typewriter that the Overseas Press crowd gave me in New York last Friday as a hint to do my memoirs."[5] Others were pushing him to do just that, including former VMI alumnus Spencer L. Carter. Marshall let Carter know that he had no intention of writing his memoirs, reminding him that he had published a very detailed description of the war just a few weeks after D-Day. The former chief of staff called it an "absolutely accurate history, checked and counter checked," as if to say, "I've already done it."[6]

A Dignified Post

It didn't take long for Truman to broach the subject of Marshall's next service to his country. In mid-January the president had made the trip to Pinehurst for a personal visit with the Marshalls. Upon his return to Washington, Truman wrote a thank-you letter, remarking that he had been "highly pleased at the conversations we had on the various topics we discussed."[7] Perhaps one such topic was whether Marshall would be willing to assume the presidency of the American Red Cross. On March 15, he wrote Truman that he was doing well physically, except for some swelling and tenderness. Marshall mentioned the good time he and Katherine had had in New Orleans, but complained that the trip to New York for the Overseas Writers' dinner had been "a little too tiring." Nevertheless, he told Truman that he had been thinking about the "Red Cross business," and thought he would be able to take on the position after May 1. Indeed, both Marshall and Katherine held that organization in high regard. It seemed like such satisfying work after the tremendous burdens of the war years.[8] In closing his letter to Truman, Marshall expressed appreciation that the president had thought to give him a "dignified post" that would "not be too demanding for my health and peace of mind."[9] Some Truman historians have called this appointment a sinecure for Marshall—as Pogue defined it, "an imposing title with little work." Some even suggested that the president wanted to give Marshall an assured income. Pogue refuted this.[10] Congress in 1946 had passed legislation that made the five-star rank permanent. To avoid having a military officer on active duty while secretary of state, Marshall had voluntarily retired for two years. However, on March 1, 1949, the U.S. Army announced that Marshall had been restored to the active list. Thus, like all of the other World War II five-star generals and admirals, he would receive full salary and benefits, including an office at the Pentagon, a secretary, an orderly, and an aide, as well as the right to fly as needed on U.S. Army planes.[11]

It would be near the end of September 1949 when Marshall took up his duties as president of the American Red Cross. Yet, as he had continued to recuperate, he remained an informal adviser to Truman, which meant that during the spring of 1949 he sometimes had to leave Pinehurst for the capital city. Winston Churchill had visited that March, so Marshall attended a White House dinner and then met with his former colleague at the British Embassy. Still not 100 percent healed from his surgery, Marshall wrote Dean Acheson that "My trip to Washington to see Churchill was an expensive business for me as I was pretty well knocked out for several days."[12]

Nevertheless, he continued to honor his obligations to official Washington. Marshall conferred with John Foster Dulles, who, representing the Republican Party, had expressed strong reservations about the upcoming Foreign Military Assistance Act, which would create NATO. Marshall allayed Dulles's concerns about the dangers of the United States becoming a part of this European defense system. In May, he traveled to New York to address the Foreign Policy Association, again, in support of NATO. Although Marshall prepared for a trip to Washington to testify before the Senate Committee on Foreign Relations on this legislation, he was spared when Secretary of State Dean Acheson told him that he thought there was enough support for the bill, so it wouldn't be necessary. Marshall must have been relieved, since, as he told a friend, what he dreaded most was that "one appearance [before the legislature] will immediately result in calls on ECA [European Cooperation Administration of the Marshall Plan], China, and numerous other questions!"[13]

Although not called upon to testify then, he was asked to do so before the House Committee on Foreign Affairs on August 1, 1949. By that time he was back in northern Virginia and physically stronger. During his testimony, Marshall supported the "desirability" of passing the NATO legislation

Marshall leaving the White House after a
visit with President Truman, on February 8, 1949.
Harris & Ewing photo: George C. Marshall Research Library

"immediately."[14] He warned the committee that ironing out differences among European nations regarding mutual defense might be difficult, and thus rapid action could not be expected or guaranteed. With all of the experience of World War II and the European Recovery Program process still vivid in his memory, he emphasized the complexity of these diverse sovereign nations working out agreements. To underline his point, Marshall related that even in Leesburg, the local citizens were having difficulty agreeing on putting parking meters in the town.[15]

Military matters sometimes required his attention as well. At the Pentagon, Marshall received a draft of the history of the Office of the Chief of Staff in World War II, describing it as a six- to eight-inch volume that he had to go through page by page. The heft of the tome led him to ask U.S. Army Chief of Staff Omar Bradley for a competent officer who could help with the task of review. Later, Marshall provided his recommendations in a detailed report. Attending to other Pentagon concerns, he received as many as 50 letters a day, a good number of them from veterans who needed help. Marshall answered each inquiry, and sometimes intervened personally to resolve problems. Still, the mail poured in, as he told Bradley, "large in volume." Marshall acknowledged that while he was "beset with invitations," and usually declined them all, he understood that not all could be ignored or treated in a perfunctory fashion. Never far from a strong sense of duty, he wrote to Bradley, "Some deserve special consideration and may involve something of help to the Government."[16]

Over the summer, then, interspersed with more relaxing days of gardening, reading, and rest at Leesburg, were any number of meetings with public officials, including trips to the White House, along with a score of public appearances. For many, Marshall was a heroic figure, often covered in the press—both newspapers and magazines. One reporter had asked General Marshall Carter about Marshall's favorite songs. Apparently, Carter told him the old hymn, "Rock of Ages," and the lilting popular tune of the time, "Buttons and Bows." In a letter to his friend and former colleague, Ambassador Lewis Douglas, Marshall wrote with a touch of humor, "Tell Carter his damned selection of 'Rock of Ages' and 'Buttons and Bows' has haunted me in press, magazines, and by orchestras ever since. Wherever I go and there is music, B and B's is introduced with laughter."[17] Most of these obligations where Marshall was called upon to give a formal address bore on topics related either to his past experience as a military leader or as secretary of state, but sometimes the occasion was ceremonial. On September 13, one such event took him to the Jewish Hospital of Brooklyn

The Marshalls are pictured in their front yard at Dodona Manor, June 28, 1949.

George C. Marshall Research Library

for its dedication. Afterward, he autographed two murals in the children's ward, accompanied by the Israeli ambassador. Apparently, Marshall had not forgotten the controversy that had arisen after the press aired his views on the recognition of Israel. In a *New York Times* article the next day, the reporter quoted him as having said, "It is satisfying after all the struggles in public life to have people wish you well after it is over. I've tried to do what I feel is the right thing. Only time will tell whether I was right."[18]

Public Relations Man

On September 22, 1949, Marshall became the president of the American Red Cross, an organization chartered by Congress but financed through private donations. He replaced Basil O'Connor, who was Franklin Roosevelt's former law partner. Although a hard worker, O'Connor had not been able to control the predominantly wealthy and powerful Eastern establishment types who constituted the board of governors and were accustomed to wielding considerable power.[19] No job for Marshall was going to be a sinecure, and it was clear from the outset that he had his work cut out for him. The backbone of the Red Cross was the volunteers, yet the board seemed to be ignoring the decision-making capabilities of these unpaid individuals who worked tirelessly in the field offices across the land. Volunteers were feeling discouraged, especially since postwar interest in the endeavors of the organization was waning. Marshall began to pump new life into the group, speaking publicly on its behalf, while reorganizing it within. He restructured the Red Cross from the top so that regional workers, especially those who offered their services for free, would have a larger voice in the policy making. The number of volunteers increased, and the enthusiasm and zeal of its veteran workers returned.[20]

As unlikely as it seemed, Marshall, in this new role, was becoming something of a public relations man. He had learned the importance of this factor when he visited virtually every corner of the country in late 1947 and early 1948 to sell the European Recovery Program. Now, as president of the American Red Cross, he was doing similar things. Marshall traveled 35,000 miles in one year, visiting local Red Cross chapters in many towns and cities. He spoke to the press, talked on the radio, and posed for photographs in local communities to promote the humanitarian work of the Red Cross. Marshall did a lot of listening. One *New York Times* reporter, Gertrude Samuels, went with him on one of these fact-finding trips, and described his remarkable ability to pay attention: "Arms folded, legs crossed, a deep crease in his left cheek as he leans back to concentrate, immaculately clean from his thinning, silver-gray hair down to his gleaming black shoes, there is something startling about his intensity, as though he were memorizing or separating ideas."[21]

Programs to expand the nation's blood bank and to help the families of servicemen were of special interest to Marshall, who had seen the value of these efforts from personal experience. Through his work in support of the European Recovery Program, he had made important connections with civic groups, farmers, commercial associations, and religious leaders. He tapped these resources to promote the work of the Red Cross. When a group of local businessmen complained that the organization's budget was too high and wanted to know why it wasn't lower since demobilization, Marshall had an answer, informing the group that there were still 110,000 men in veterans' hospitals, and 60 percent of them "are reported to be psychoneurotic . . . . That's not my idea of demobilization," he told them. Not surprisingly, Marshall was still concerned about the troops.[22] The start of the Korean War in June 1950 brought added attention to the work of this organization. It also meant that soon Marshall would be leaving his "not too demanding post" to shoulder a more difficult assignment.

Red Tide Rising

Much had happened the year Marshall was away from the national scene, including the fact that the cold war struggle between the United States and the communist world had gained momentum. It was in early September 1949 that a weather reconnaissance plane, flying from Japan to Alaska, picked up signs of significant radioactivity over the North Pacific. The reality of what David Lilienthal, the chairman of the U.S. Atomic Energy Commission, later called "a whole box of trouble," was confirmed by President Truman to the American people in a news conference on September 23, 1949. "We have evidence," he told reporters crammed into his office, "that within recent weeks an atomic explosion occurred in the U.S.S.R."[23] Although American leaders knew that the Soviets had every intention of developing nuclear capability, the Russians were three to five years ahead of predictions as to when that would occur. As historian David McCullough wrote, "The four-year American monopoly on the atomic bomb was over. And though there was no panic . . . the fears and tensions of the Cold War were greatly amplified. It was a different world now."[24]

The situation in China was disturbing as well. The Nationalist government of Chiang Kai-shek had been so outmaneuvered by the Communist forces of

Mao Tse-tung that even by early 1949 Chiang had already moved his gold reserves to the island of Formosa (Taiwan). An American military adviser, General David Barr, reported that only U.S. troops could save Chiang. In his opinion, it wasn't because the Nationalists lacked ammunition or equipment; rather, the problem was "the world's worst leadership . . . the widespread corruption and dishonesty through the [Nationalist] armed forces."[25] Marshall himself had described the scenario well in his report to Truman on the China Mission when he returned to the United States in 1947. By late in 1949, Chiang was in Formosa with his political allies and the remnants of his army. China's entire mainland came under the control of Mao's communists. The United States would not intervene. As a Joint Chiefs report concluded, "the current disparity between our military strength and our many global obligations makes it inadvisable to undertake the employment of armed force in Formosa." Ed Cray noted that as a national security asset, these military leaders ranked Formosa below Iceland.[26] As if to explain to the public the China situation, Truman had asked the State Department that summer of 1949 to prepare a report on what had happened in terms of United States foreign policy there between 1944 and 1949.

Dean Acheson, Marshall's successor as secretary of state, emphasized in the introduction to the 409-page document that the United States had in fact poured $2 billion into helping Chiang, and it hadn't worked. He cited poor leadership and corruption, a blander description than Truman's, who called the Nationalists "grafters and crooks."[27] The blame lay, said Acheson, with "internal Chinese forces, forces which this country [the United States] tried to influence but could not."[28]Although the report was remarkably thorough, the conclusion, which seemed to be the only part that the press covered, was that the United States could do nothing to help Chiang without making a major military commitment that few wanted.

When the report began to circulate, the Truman administration was almost immediately under fire, especially from the so-called China Lobby, comprised of prominent Republicans, as well as patriotic and religious groups. Despite the ongoing criticisms of the Nationalists, they were sympathetic to the Chiangs as purveyors of democracy, especially when compared to the communist option, and were especially taken in by the rationales of the beautiful, Wellesley-educated Madame Chiang Kai-shek.[29] Beginning with her visit to the Marshalls in late December 1948, she sought economic and advisory help for China via Marshall, even as he lay hospitalized for kidney surgery at Walter Reed. Their friendship notwithstanding, he simply articulated the position of the president and the

State Department. Responding to her entreaties, which she proposed "again and again," Marshall reiterated the limits of the help the United States was prepared to give.[30] Undaunted, Madame Chiang stayed in the country a year, making the case for support and protection to save her husband's crumbling government. If the cabinet-level report was intended to ease concerns about the nation's China policy, it did neither. The China Lobbyists excoriated the president and the State Department. The strident critics claimed that the views of both Truman and the leaders of this powerful cabinet office translated to "abandonment of the Chinese government," appeasement, a surrender of principles, and an alibi for communists and leftists in the State Department.[31]

In the early months of 1950 came more troublesome revelations. In 1933, a brilliant German physicist, Klaus Fuchs, had fled to England when the Nazis came to power, eventually becoming a citizen of the United Kingdom. In 1943, he was among the British scientists sent to the United States to collaborate on the Manhattan Project. He ended up at Los Alamos and was present for the "Trinity" test. On February 3, 1950, under questioning, Fuchs confessed in London that he had passed details of the project to the Soviets through a courier in 1945, as well as information about the development of the hydrogen bomb in 1946 and 1947.[32] Only a few days later, an obscure junior senator from Wisconsin, Joseph McCarthy, gave a speech before a Women's Republican Club in Wheeling, West Virginia. He spoke of America's losing ground against the Soviets, not because of enemies abroad, but because of "traitorous actions of those who have been treated so well by this nation." This was especially true in the State Department, he claimed, "where the bright young men who are born with silver spoons in their mouths are the ones who have been the worst."[33] Waving a piece of paper in the air, he declared that he had in his hand a list of 57 Department of State employees who were communists. In the days that followed, he kept up the attack, again targeting the State Department, which was, according to him, "infested" with "vast numbers of Reds" and "espionage rings." The numbers changed with every speech—first there were 57, but then 205, then 81. He never substantiated a single accusation. The newspapers printed front page articles by the dozens. Denials were given and proven, but that news was tucked into short blurbs buried far to the back.[34] Many readers were not taken in by the polemics, but some wondered: What had happened to the United States of America?

So it was that only four years after the clear-cut victory in World War II, Americans were feeling much less secure. They were becoming suspicious, even paranoid, about the source of these losses, and tended to blame the Truman administration for its failures. Their anxiety was fueled by the Fuchs incident, the situation in China, and the realization that the Soviets had the atomic bomb. It was also given heat by a strong right-wing element in Congress inclined to reject former bipartisan efforts—Secretary of State Dean Acheson, who caught their wrath constantly, called them "the primitives." Such accusations eventually reinforced a trend on the part of the administration to view the cold war in hardline military and global terms. President Truman called for a strong, "get tough" policy toward the Russians. They were the enemy, pure and simple; the United States should prepare to contain them on all fronts. Gains of any size by the Soviets, even in faraway Asia, must be viewed as having a larger goal: expansion and world dominance. In Europe, the Berlin crisis and the formation of NATO reinforced the circumstance that Marshall had seen developing during his time at the State Department. More and more, the world seemed divided into two distinct camps: the United States and its allies versus the Soviet Union and its allies.[35] George Kennan's emphasis on containment as a limited and selective approach, perhaps accomplished primarily through diplomacy, soon gave way to this broader and more military-oriented, bipolar world view.

In light of such growing concerns, Acheson tapped the head of the Policy Planning Staff (PPS), Paul Nitze, to work with the Defense Department to review overall American foreign and defense policy and prepare a comprehensive report. Although the current secretary of defense, Louis Johnson, appointed a deputy of political-military affairs from his department to work with Nitze, that representative was not in good health and thus did not regularly attend the sessions. The product, then, was primarily influenced by the State Department, especially the PPS. Although Truman had committed himself to holding the line on defense spending, and Johnson was also dedicated to defense cuts as a means of balancing the budget, the report was prepared without regard to that consideration. The result, released in April 1950, was NSC-68. Still focusing on Western Europe, the report noted that the Soviet Union's military had 30 elite divisions, as compared to America's 7. In fact, it read, "This Republic and its citizens, in the ascendancy of their strength, stand in their deepest peril."[36] Without conventional forces, if the Russians made a move, the United States would have to use nuclear weapons, which could generate a terrifying atomic war. Given those circumstances, NSC-68 recommended a massive "military shield behind which the free world can work to frustrate the Kremlin design." If necessary, the United States should spend up to 20 percent of its gross national product on rearmament. The paper called for an increase in U.S. conventional forces, as well as further development of more powerful nuclear bombs as a deterrent. In short, defense estimates would run to $35–40 billion a year, much more than Truman's proposed $13 billion budget figure.[37] There is no doubt that Truman fully recognized the dangers of the Soviet Union and, having read the report, agreed with its principles. Yet, because the president had prided himself on seeking a balanced budget, when he considered the costs of the proposed ramping up of the military, he came around grudgingly. What would bring Truman's eventual approval, and by way of legislation the support of Congress, was a new and disturbing circumstance—an undeclared war on an Asian peninsula, Korea.[38]

"I have very serious news"

Korea, once a part of the Japanese empire, came under the control of the Allies at the end of World War II. Although the country was promised its independence, shortly after the Japanese were ousted, American troops occupied the southern part, and Soviet troops the northern regions. A line between the two forces had been established at the 38th parallel of latitude, a rather arbitrary division that was considered temporary until elections could be held. However, as Mark Stoler explained, "The Soviets rejected U.S.-sponsored resolutions in the U.N. calling for elections to unify the peninsula, and by 1949 each side had established a Korean government friendly to itself."[39] A communist government, headed by Kim Il-Sung, was set up in North Korea. In South Korea, a U.N.-supervised election established an anticommunist government headed by President Syngman Rhee. As the two Allied powers began to remove their occupation troops, each Korean government threatened to combine the country by force.

By Saturday afternoon, June 24, 1950, President Truman was in his hometown of Independence, Missouri—his first time back since Christmas—for a weekend with his wife, Bess, and daughter, Margaret. In the evening, the three were enjoying quiet conversation outdoors on the cooler front porch when a call came from Secretary of State Acheson: "Mr. President," he said, "I have very serious news. The North Koreans have invaded South Korea." Truman was ready to leave immediately for Washington. No need to alarm the country, Acheson told him. The president could wait until the next day.[40] On Sunday, even as Truman flew home aboard his plane, the *Independence,* the UN Security Council, already informed by the State Department, had met and adopted an American-proposed resolution: There was to be an immediate end to hostilities, it read, and North Korean forces were to withdraw back across the 38th parallel. Although the Security Council required a unanimous vote of its five permanent members—the United States, France, Britain, China, and the Soviet Union—the Russians weren't there with what surely would have been a "nyet" vote. They were boycotting the UN, a protest against the refusal of that body to oust the Nationalist Chinese and seat the government of Mao Tse-tung as the legitimate "China."[41]

The Truman administration interpreted North Korea's aggressive action not in local terms but as a Soviet-directed cold war move. It reminded the president of Hitler's occupation of the so-called demilitarized Rhineland in 1936. To ignore Korea was to raise the specter of appeasement. He was determined to meet aggression with aggression. In two war cabinet meetings on Sunday and Monday, which included Dean Acheson, Johnson, and the Joint Chiefs, quick decisions were made to provide air and naval backing to the South Koreans and to press for immediate United Nations military assistance. On Tuesday, the 27th, 40 congressional leaders gathered with the president in the West Wing, giving him their full support, so much so that these key legislators did not see the need for a war resolution and told Truman he could proceed to take the needed action using his executive powers alone.[42] By that same evening, UN support was forthcoming. With the Soviets still absent, that international peace-keeping organization agreed for the first time in its short history to commit collective armed forces to stop aggression. Truman seemed to have the nation's backing as well. Cards, letters, telegrams, phone calls—all seemed to have one message: Continue on your "bold course." One Republican from Illinois wrote that although the president might be a "whiskey guzzling poker playing old buzzard," at last "the United States has a grass roots American in the White House."[43]

"One arm behind my back"

By the time Truman arrived back in Washington from Independence, the military picture in Korea had been conveyed to the Joint Chiefs at the Pentagon. Led by Soviet tanks, six columns of North Korean regulars and two amphibious units had cut a deep swath into the south. The Republic of Korea soldiers (ROKs) were no match for the well-trained northern troops. The commander of the Japanese occupation forces, General Douglas MacArthur, had initially dismissed the attack as a border skirmish, declaring that "if Washington will not hobble me, I can handle it with one arm tied behind my back."[44] He was soon proven wrong. Even as MacArthur ordered occupation troops from Japan, they were of little help. Poorly trained and out of shape from light duty in the postwar period, they rapidly became

South Korean refugees flee advancing North Korean troops, summer 1950.
U.S. Defense Department

part of a mass retreat. It was soon a depressing pattern of fighting to fall back, under atrocious conditions. July was monsoon season, so the troops struggled in torrential rain and 100-degree heat. Incredibly thirsty, and often with no fresh supply of water, they drank from rice field drainage ditches, soon adding acute dysentery to the challenge. They were also hindered by thousands of fleeing refugees on slippery, mud-clogged dirt roads.[45] By mid-July, MacArthur, now in command of all UN forces, was hustling for men and supplies. American troops, alongside the ROKs, continued the fight to staunch the North Korean landslide. Finally, on the 29th, the American ground commander, General Walton Harris Walker, issued a "stand-or-die" order at the southeastern port of Pusan, almost to the tip of South Korea, and the line finally held.[46]

"A most interesting morning"

The president had emphasized to reporters gathered on June 29, 1950, for his first press conference since the North Korean attack, "We are not at war." Probing, a reporter inquired if it could be called a police action under the United Nations. Seizing upon that language, Truman replied, "Yes, that's exactly what it is, a police action."[47] No matter what label might be applied to this new and alarming circumstance, for all practical purposes, it was a war. For the president two huge problems loomed. First, deep defense spending cuts had led to the reduction of virtually every aspect of the military. Indeed, the army was woefully thin and unprepared for a battle in far-off Asia. Second, as the challenges of the Defense Department mounted, Truman was finding the actions of his current secretary of defense, Louis Johnson, more and more troublesome. Johnson had created deep dissension between his department and the rest of the cabinet. Indeed, as the crisis gained momentum, this could not be tolerated. Truman knew that at some point in the future he would need to fire the secretary of defense.

Louis Johnson, a West Virginia Democrat, did massive fund-raising for Truman in the 1948 election campaign, and perhaps in part as a reward, the president had appointed him to a cabinet post. Early on, the secretary of defense managed to alienate the entire Department of the Navy by "red-lining" monies appropriated for a well-designed new super carrier in favor of an untested air force bomber.[48] Moreover, Johnson offended everyone in the cabinet. As Truman wrote, "He played no favorites; all of them were included." The president described how by 1950 Johnson had "begun to show an inordinate egotistical desire to run the whole government." Furthermore, said Truman, "he tried to use the White House press men for

Two U.S. Army soldiers dug in along the Pusan Perimeter, September 4, 1950

U.S. Army Signal Corps Photo 8A/FEC-50-7815

blowing himself up and everyone else down, particularly the secretary of state."[49] That July, with the fight going so badly in Korea, wasn't the time to fire Johnson. After all, maybe some of the military deficits that were causing such problems in the face of this mounting military crisis were because Johnson had vigorously promoted the president's cost-cutting efforts at the Pentagon.[50] For the time being, Truman would keep the secretary of defense, but perhaps it was time to call upon a trusted friend.

It was July 4, appropriately marked on the president's calendar as a "Holiday" with no appointments listed. Truman got into his automobile, and with his daughter, Margaret, took a country drive to see Marshall at Dodona Manor in Leesburg. Supposedly it was just for a pleasant visit, but there's little doubt that Truman wanted to see how physically well the general was, and how much he was attuned to what was happening in Korea. Of his time in Leesburg, the president wrote cryptically in his diary that he had enjoyed "a most interesting morning."[51]

That July, General Douglas MacArthur, as commander of U.S., UN, and ROK troops, had a straightforward and immediate military goal. Drive the North Koreans back up the peninsula. Yet, by the first week in August, there was still no letup in the fierce fighting around the "stand-or-die" perimeter. The retreat had ended and so had the monsoons, but now the troops struggled with dry heat and dust so thick that vehicle headlights had to be left on at midday.[52] Nevertheless, the North Korean advance to Pusan had cost the enemy heavily, with high casualties and greatly overextended supply lines. Further, by now MacArthur was pouring fresh troops, tanks, and artillery into the region in rapid order, and UN forces controlled both the sea and air. Even Omar Bradley, in a meeting with the president on August 12, called the situation "fluid but improving."[53]

A Country Store Phone Call

Although the phone call seemed unexpected, perhaps it wasn't. There had been that "interesting morning" on July 4. Almost certainly Marshall had already been asked to consider returning to public service as the secretary of defense. Perhaps in the light of Truman's July visit, Marshall had begun to pay more attention to the news coming from Korea. Nevertheless, by that late August, he and Katherine had escaped the heat of Northern Virginia, enjoying a fishing vacation in the beautiful Huron Mountains of Michigan's Upper Peninsula. Although the Marshalls' location was remote, White House operators soon found them. A messenger arrived at the resort where they were staying to say that Marshall needed to come down the road to a small country store—a phone call awaited. While the store's local cronies listened in, all the time showing no outward interest, Marshall talked briefly with Truman. "Yes, Mr. President," they heard him say. He had agreed to "drop in and see him" upon his return to Washington.[54] In the September 6 meeting that followed at Blair House, where the president had taken up residence during a much-needed White House renovation, Truman got right to the point. Johnson had to resign. Would Marshall act as secretary of defense until the crisis passed? Marshall agreed to serve for six months, and definitely no more than a year. Bent as he was on retirement, Marshall felt he had to accept the challenge. As he later told his goddaughter, Rose Page Wilson, "When the President comes down and sits under our oaks and tells me of his difficulties, he has me at a disadvantage."[55]

"I do not believe I know the man"

Marshall's confirmation by the U.S. Senate was not automatic. The National Security Act of 1947 had reorganized and strengthened the military. Its provisions included merging the Departments of Navy and War into a national military establishment headed by a secretary of defense. It recognized the U.S Air Force as an independent service branch and formalized the Joint Chiefs of Staff. Also tucked within the legislation was the proviso that a military officer who had been on active duty within the past 10 years was not eligible to become the secretary of defense, supporting a time-honored American belief in strong civilian control over the military.[56]

Allowing an exception in Marshall's case required an amendment to the act. Although most of the opposition on both sides of the aisle was motivated by sincere reservations about a military man being chosen, the debate also opened the door to vicious attacks from the ultra-conservatives. Paranoia and suspicion had reached Congress. The worst assault came from Republican Senator William Jenner of Indiana. In a long diatribe he lumped together Roosevelt, Truman, Acheson, and Marshall—they were responsible for Pearl Harbor, were sellouts to Russia, betrayed China, and on and on it went. Jenner called the nominee "an errand boy, a front man, a stooge or co-conspirator for this administration's crazy assortment of collectivist cutthroats, and Communist fellow-traveling appeasers." Marshall, according to Jenner, was a "living lie." The Senate was used to some tough charges and dramatic rhetoric, but as Pogue wrote, "this had gone beyond the pale."[57] In a time of casting blame and seeking scapegoats, Marshall would not be spared the slings and arrows of these attackers. As for Jenner, though, even the

Republicans disassociated themselves from his poisonous volleys. Marshall was unperturbed. During the hearings, he answered Jenner's outrageous questions with a combination of "dignity, honesty, and contempt."[57] Later, when asked about Jenner's attacks, Marshall replied sardonically, "Jenner, Jenner? I do not believe I know the man."[59] The National Security Act was duly amended, and a few days later on September 21, 1950, Marshall was confirmed as secretary of defense by a vote of 57–11.

The hearings behind him, Marshall got to work, settling into the Pentagon E-ring, taking the office of his old friend, Henry Stimson. The new secretary of defense brought no entourage. Only General Marshall Carter continued with him. Marshall, though, also wanted Robert Lovett, his former undersecretary of state, to be his second man. As Pogue wrote, "Marshall prized Lovett's brilliance, his tendency to go straight to the heart of matters, his great sense of humor, his aversion to the limelight, and his ability to work well with a wide collection of military, political, and business leaders."[60] Knowing that Lovett had only recently returned to a profitable law practice after years of public service, Marshall hesitated to ask him to come back, but one morning at 7:30, he put in the call. Reluctantly, Lovett agreed, although he had already turned down repeated efforts from Dean Acheson to get him to accept an ambassadorship. As Lovett later ruefully admitted, "There are two persons to whom I cannot say no; my wife and General Marshall."[61]

Woman Power and Manpower

Marshall had one more appointment that he saw as extremely important. He wanted Anna M. Rosenberg to become the assistant secretary of defense for manpower. She had a background in industrial and labor relations, and she had worked for both Roosevelt and Truman to study the army's manpower programs. Her work during the war had been so impressive that Generals Eisenhower and Walter Bedell Smith helped to get her the Medal of Freedom and the Medal of Merit.[62] A huge plus in Marshall's view was that Rosenberg always backed the concept that he had pushed so vigorously in the past, Universal Military Training.

Nevertheless, as Ed Cray wrote, getting her confirmed by the Senate Armed Services Committee was "one of the uglier little episodes of the McCarthy era."[63] Not only was she a woman and Jewish, but Rosenberg was a liberal, an unabashed New Dealer. The critics decried that she had even supported a movement for national health care. Small, stylish, and feminine, with high heels and jangling bracelets, she was an unusual sight among the starched uniforms of the Pentagon. She was also a torrent of productive energy. Rosenberg had proven herself an excellent public relations manager as well as an effective mediator and problem solver. She faced a barrage from the ultra-conservatives. In addition to equating her New Deal zeal as proof of her communist leanings, they had also confused her with another Anna Rosenberg that the committee had investigated. She had to face anti-Semites, who spoke of the great fight to keep this "Zionist Jew" from becoming the "dictator of the Pentagon."[64] Others insisted that despite her impressive work in World War II, this wasn't a job a woman could perform. Marshall was unfazed. He asked Eisenhower and Bedell Smith to write letters of recommendation. He also called on his old friends, Bernard Baruch and James Byrnes, both southerners, to speak on her behalf to Richard Russell, the powerful Georgia senator who chaired the committee. She was confirmed.[65] When the news was announced, Marshall and the Joint Chiefs were at the Pentagon, their coats on, ready to leave for a meeting at the White House. Rosenberg burst in to share the outcome. "That's good," said Marshall, obviously pleased. Apparently the whole confirmation process had been quite nerve-racking. It prompted Marshall to make a totally uncharacteristic comment about her appearance: "Go home and get a facial; you look like hell." The Joint Chiefs seemed shocked not only by his statement but also by the fact that Marshall knew anything about facials.[66]

A Respectable Military Force—UMT

One of Marshall's biggest tasks in this new role was to mobilize an army. He later commented, "I was getting rather hardened to coming in when everything had gone to pot and there was nothing you could get your hands on, and darned if I didn't find the same thing when I came into the Korean War." Unlike prior to World War II, when he had fought hard for a draft that would at least build a minimal army for the approaching conflict, in 1950 there was a draft law in place. That made Marshall's challenge somewhat easier. Mark Stoler wrote that "by April 1951 he had doubled the army's strength, with more men obtained in the preceding ten months than in the entire 18-month period from August 1940 to February 1942."[67]

As the United States scrambled to build a military whose capabilities had been slashed in the demobilization, once again Marshall made the case for Universal Military Training (UMT). Since the '20s he had promoted this concept as vital to American security. He understood the public's aversion to a heavy military presence, but he was also dismayed that when war came, the country was utterly unprepared to meet its demands. His idea was

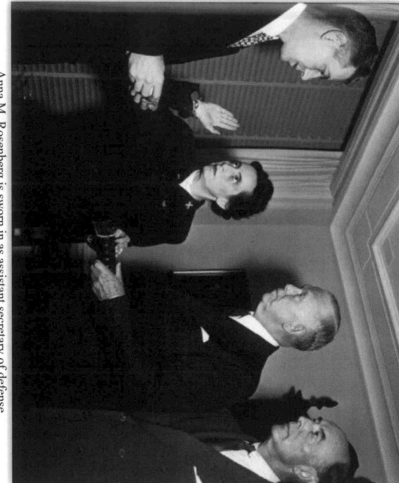

Anna M. Rosenberg is sworn in as assistant secretary of defense, November 15, 1950. Robert Lovett stands to Marshall's left.

Harry S. Truman Library

to give every able-bodied young man in America six months of rigorous military training, using the very best officers and equipment the army had to offer. After six months, these young soldiers would go back into the civilian population. But if an emergency arose, the United States would have a substantial reserve of trained "citizen soldiers" and officers who could be called into active service with a minimum loss of time.[68] Marshall touted it as an excellent compromise for integrating global military needs in a democratic society. In fact, Marshall later insisted that it was the only way to "create a respectable military force, in a sense, without having the fellows constantly in uniform." He complained that in rebuilding this army for Korea, it took "months and months to get divisions ready . . . and then their training wasn't complete. I just sent them ahead anyway," he told his biographer.[69]

Marshall's efforts to gain congressional approval for UMT failed; critics saw it as too expensive, unpopular with constituencies, and an unnecessary kind of government control.[69] Still, drawing on his past experience, his organizational skills, and the efforts of Lovett and Rosenberg, Marshall once again built the army into a fighting force. In June 1951, Congress passed legislation extending the draft for four years, lowered the draft age to 18½, and increased the period of active duty to two years. Finally, it tacked on a six-year term in the inactive reserve.[70] This legislation was as close as Marshall would get to accomplishing his goal of maintaining a prepared force.

State Outranks Defense

With troop strength building, Marshall had an internal problem to solve— restoring harmony between the Department of Defense and the State Department. This was where past relationships paid off. Almost all of the key figures in these two cabinet posts were people with whom Marshall had previously worked. Dean Acheson, now secretary of state, had been the undersecretary at the beginning of Marshall's State Department tenure— the two had formed a highly effective team and friendship. General Omar Bradley was chairman of the Joint Chiefs of Staff. He had been a part of the "Benning Revolution" and gained Marshall's high esteem as the commander of American ground troops during the Normandy invasion. All of these players knew and respected Marshall's views on international relations and national defense. Moreover, as Forrest Pogue wrote, the basis of this respect came from "his character, his known distaste for intrigue, his demand for simplicity of plans and organization, his fierce insistence on clear channels of command, his belief in responsibility and loyalty up and down."[71] Soon Marshall was able to smooth ruffled feathers and bring unusual accord between these important cabinet-level teams. Marshall had always respected the separation between the civilian government and the military. During his first meeting with the combined staffs of the departments, Marshall made certain he sat on the civilian side of the table, across from the admirals and generals. Since the State Department outranked the newly formed Defense Department in the cabinet hierarchy, Marshall insisted that Acheson enter a room in front of him. Feeling thoroughly uncomfortable with such an arrangement, Acheson later wrote that "To be treated so by a revered and beloved former chief was a harrowing experience."[72] He tried at first to simply refuse. That didn't work. Marshall seized Acheson's arm and virtually pushed him ahead. Though these inter-cabinet skirmishes had been put to rest under Marshall's leadership, all knew full well that the real war was in Korea, not in walnut-paneled offices along the Potomac.

"The wildest idea"

When Marshall became secretary of defense, strategy and policy for fighting the war in Korea had already been determined, and he had little to do with it. In the beginning, the North Koreans had pushed the South Koreans almost to the southern tip of the peninsula. Over that summer, as Marshall wrapped up vacation outings along with professional commitments, word began to circulate within the Pentagon of a bold MacArthur strategy. He intended to hit the North Koreans from behind—to outflank them. The Joint Chiefs were skeptical, but when Truman sent his special assistant, Averell Harriman, and General Matthew Ridgway, the deputy chief of staff, to Tokyo to assess the Korean situation, they came back "believers" in MacArthur's idea. The daring plan called for an amphibious landing on the western side of Korea at the port of Inchon, 200 miles north of Pusan. This would be difficult, since the tides were rough, 30 feet, and there were no beaches, only sea walls.[73] For the plan to succeed, troops would have to strike at high tide, which would land them at the edge of a fair-sized city, with all of its potential for defense. To land at low tide was out of the question, since the landing craft would sink immediately into the muck of sandless mudflats.[74] Back in Washington, U.S. Army Chief of Staff Omar Bradley called the strategy of "the wildest kind," and the Joint Chiefs expressed "the gravest misgivings about it," but Truman eventually came around, giving his approval for the operation.

On September 15, 1950, the invasion force struck, taking the lightly defended city completely by surprise. Inchon surrendered in a day. Eleven days later, Seoul was back in the hands of the South Koreans and UN forces. It was a spectacular success. Meantime, according to plan, General Walker's Eighth Army broke out of the Pusan Perimeter and headed north. By the end of the month, North Korean troops were trapped in a huge vise between Inchon and Pusan. It was a change in fortune that seemed almost miraculous.[75] The combined effect resulted in the North Koreans' being pushed back north of the 38th parallel. In fact, this action accomplished the UN's goal of halting aggression by defeating the North Korean invasion. However, MacArthur's progress had been so impressive, so dramatic, that many officials sought to return to the earlier postwar aim regarding Korea—unifying the whole peninsula under one government. Marshall, who had just come on board as this policy was being shaped, approved the approach.

Indeed, by now, MacArthur's victory seemed a counterforce to any notion of status quo antebellum. Very few on the Washington scene wanted to stop at the 38th parallel; even Acheson declared that "troops could not be expected . . . to march up to a surveyor's line and stop. . . . As a boundary it had no political value."[76] Most at the State Department agreed, even though Soviet experts Chip Bohlen and George Kennan, along with PPS head Paul Nitze, spoke out regarding the risk of a land war in Asia if the ROKs and the UN forces got too close to China. Few listened. As Averell Harriman later wrote, "It would have taken a superhuman effort to say no. Psychologically, it was almost impossible not to go ahead and complete the job."[77]

Marshall, barely ensconced in his Pentagon offices, sent an EYES ONLY message to MacArthur that seemed to reflect the groundswell of opinion: "We want you to feel unhampered tactically and strategically to proceed north of the 38th parallel." Marshall later explained that he was simply giving MacArthur permission to cross the 38th parallel—General Walker's Eighth Army was poised there awaiting orders—and that it didn't have the broader implications as interpreted by MacArthur. Perhaps so, but the UN commander saw that comment as carte blanche permission to press far to the north, wiring back, "I regard all of Korea open for military operations."[78] In fact, MacArthur had been authorized to destroy North Korean forces north of the 38th parallel, but there were clear caveats. For example, if the fighting got anywhere close to the Yalu River, North Korea's border with China, only South Korean (ROKs), not American or UN troops, were to participate. Under no circumstances was MacArthur to allow any troops to cross the Yalu, and any air or naval operations against Chinese or Soviet territories were strictly banned. Finally, if there was any threat that major Communist Chinese or

General MacArthur aboard the USS Mount McKinley
during the Inchon Landings, September 15, 1950
U.S. Army Signal Corps Collection, U.S. National Archives

Soviet forces would cross the Korean border from the north, MacArthur was to go on the defensive, act passively, and notify Washington.[79] Without question he was to do nothing to precipitate "a general war with Communist China."[80] As Forrest Pogue wrote, "Washington officials could have gone no further to ensure against a chance clash with the Chinese communists or the Soviet Union. . . . But these conditions seemed timid strictures to a commander flushed with victory."[81]

"Very little chance"

By mid-October 1950, MacArthur's forces were moving deep into North Korea and were almost at the gates of the capital, Pyongyang. Nothing seemed in the way of an advance to the Yalu River on the Chinese border. The Joint Chiefs once more warned MacArthur that he was not to go into China and to keep in mind that this was a United Nations operation. Already India's ambassador to Peking had relayed to the State Department Chinese foreign minister Chou En-lai's warning that "the Chinese did not intend to sit back with folded hands and let the Americans come up to their border." MacArthur called it a bluff, but did admit that the Chinese were moving troops to an area north of the Yalu. Bluff or not, Marshall and the Joint Chiefs amended MacArthur's instructions for operations north of the 38th parallel to say that if his troops came into contact with major Chinese units, they could fight back as long as they had a chance of success. However, if that happened, MacArthur was to get specific authorization for any further military action.[82] Perhaps it was these warnings from China, or worry concerning MacArthur's fast-paced entry into North Korea, that beckoned Truman to schedule a meeting with the supreme commander.

To accommodate MacArthur's wish of not being too far from his base in Tokyo, Truman traveled 14,425 miles to Wake Island, a tiny speck of land in the vast Pacific. As David McCullough wrote, "To many the whole affair looked like a political grandstand play to capitalize on the sudden, unexpected success of the war and share in MacArthur's Inchon glory on the eve of the off-year elections in November."[83] Although most likely this element was at work, the fact was that Truman had never met this iconic figure of World War II who had not been in the United States for 14 years. Perhaps the president wanted to take the measure of this strong, almost mythical man whose leadership bore so significantly on the war. Whatever his motivations, the president's three-plane entourage landed at 6:30 a.m. on Sunday, October 15, 1950. General MacArthur had arrived the night before and was at the airstrip one-half hour early to greet Truman when his plane landed. Although he wore an open-collar shirt and failed to salute his commander-in-chief, MacArthur shook the president's hand while at the same time grasping his arm, gestures that the onlookers recognized as "the number one treatment."[84] Bradley, as chairman of the Joint Chiefs of Staff, was there, too, along with the secretary of the army and the assistant secretary of state, Dean Rusk. Since the trip had been rather impromptu, with no detailed preparations made, Marshall and Acheson stayed in Washington in case of an emergency.[85]

At the Wake Island meeting, MacArthur was in an optimistic mood. Any opposition from the North Koreans should be over by Thanksgiving, he assured the president, and mentioned twice that he would have the Eighth Army back in Japan by Christmas. Moreover, MacArthur confidently reported that most likely the UN could begin organizing elections for a unified Korea by January. With that possibility ahead, a lot of the discussion centered on the reconstruction of Korea when victory was complete. Still, with that circumstance not yet a reality, Truman was concerned about keeping to a limited war. He wanted to know, "What are the chances of Chinese or Soviet interference?" "Very little," came the reply. "They are thoroughly whipped. The winter will destroy those we don't."[86] Although MacArthur conceded that the Chinese had large forces on the China side of the Yalu, perhaps as many as 125,000, the UN commander didn't think they would cross the border because they lacked air power. If they tried that, he told the president and Bradley, "there would be the greatest slaughter."[87] "It goes against my grain to destroy them," he added, since "they are only fighting to save face."[88] These were reassuring words for the commander-in-chief.

The conference lasted only a few hours. At some point in the morning, MacArthur, looking at his watch, let it be known that he had pressing war matters in Tokyo. A planned luncheon with the president was duly canceled; service crews hustled to get their respective aircraft ready. MacArthur remained on the airstrip, not boarding until the door of Truman's aircraft was closed.[89] Although more sinister interpretations were later placed on the Wake Island meeting, the fact is that both Truman and MacArthur came away pleased with the results, their previous prejudices about one another softened by the exchange. As McCullough wrote, "The whole spirit of Wake Island was one of relief and exhilaration."[90]

General MacArthur greets President Truman on the tarmac at Wake Island, October 15, 1950.

U.S. Department of Defense 1111-SC-353136

Interlude

Although Marshall's schedule that fall was crowded with meetings related to the Korean War, on November 1, 1950, he had a special mission at Arlington National Cemetery: to attend the dedication of the equestrian statue sculpted in memory of his wartime colleague and friend, Sir John Dill. After Dill's death in 1944, Marshall had worked around regulations regarding burial of foreign soldiers at Arlington National Cemetery. He also found his way around other prohibitions to get this statue erected in Dill's honor. Countering fierce opposition from American Legion leadership, Marshall pushed the project, even taking a leading role in fund-raising.[91] That early November afternoon Truman was scheduled to unveil the statue. When the president arrived at the cemetery, he greeted Marshall and other dignitaries, looking calm but also grim. Ten minutes later, the assembled audience of more than 100 knew why. A White House photographer whispered the news, and it crackled quickly through the crowd: Just an hour and a half before, two radical Puerto Rican nationalists looking to publicize their cause had attempted to assassinate Truman at Blair House. The attack had left one guard dead and another in the hospital severely wounded. Standing beside the bronze statue that honored the memory of the man Marshall had described as a fine soldier, "a noble character," Truman, in firm voice, delivered his prepared remarks as if nothing had happened.[92]

Warnings

Despite MacArthur's optimistic view of a quick wrap-up to the war, in late October U.S. troops and their allies were making intermittent but fierce contact with the Communist Chinese on the North Korean side. On November 2, Chairman Mao blandly announced that they were simply "volunteers" helping the North Korean Army protect an important hydroelectric power plant that spanned both sides of the Yalu.[93] MacArthur wanted to bomb the bridges that brought these Chinese soldiers across the river. Lovett, who got word of this plan first, enlisted the support of Acheson and Marshall to forbid the bombings. It was too dangerous an enterprise, since it risked a war with China, and perhaps the Soviet Union. Besides, the Yalu was shallow enough that it would soon freeze, and thus the Chinese troops could easily get across anyway. MacArthur was outraged at Washington's interference, and he warned that it could result in "a calamity of major proportions."[94] This was from someone who had called these incursions "not alarming." As it turned out, after a meeting on November 6, the Joint Chiefs, Marshall, and Lovett grudgingly granted permission for the bombing runs. They were

President Truman and Marshall at the ceremony for the unveiling of a statue honoring Sir John Dill, November 1, 1950

Harry S. Truman Library

reluctant to second-guess the judgment of the ground commander, operating in winter conditions with multinational forces in a faraway mountainous land.[95]

Yet, Marshall was uneasy. It bothered him that MacArthur had split his army into two forces. The Eighth Army and the X Corps were on different sides of a long north-south mountain range. It was difficult for the separated columns to communicate and almost impossible for one side to provide relief for the other. Further, into November 1950, the Washington leadership didn't know the extent of the encounters between the UN troops and Mao's "volunteers" because MacArthur was short on specific information. Nevertheless, Acheson would later admit, "We had the clearest idea among ourselves of the utter madness and folly of what MacArthur was doing up north. . . . We sat around like paralyzed rabbits while MacArthur carried out this nightmare."[96] Acheson wondered about what he called Marshall's "curious quiescence." He once asked him why, if he was so dissatisfied with MacArthur's strategy, he didn't order him to pursue a different one, or recommend that he be relieved. Perhaps his reply was not that surprising. Marshall told Acheson that, after all, he was no longer the chief of staff. It was important for him to bend over backward to present "a civilian attitude." Further, just as Marshall had always believed and practiced, once a commander was in the field, it was critical to let him operate without interference. Finally, Marshall surely realized that recommending the relief of MacArthur, such a heroic figure in the public eye, would set off a congressional firestorm and maybe a constitutional crisis.[97] This was perhaps one time when Marshall's scrupulous belief in civilian-military separation, and noninterference with military operations, did not well serve him, the president, or the country.

"An entirely new war"

It was November 24, 1950, when MacArthur launched what he described as the operation that would "close the vise" around the enemy. He assured the press at his headquarters that if this attack succeeded, the boys would begin returning home by Christmas."[98] That fantasy was about to evaporate. For weeks, during what seemed to the UN forces like a strange lull in the fighting, thousands more Chinese soldiers began to cross the icy, wind-swept Yalu. Masses of Mao's well-disciplined Chinese "volunteers" and supply porters, operating without radios or light, slipped into Korea undetected. Everything was done to achieve what would be an element of total surprise. Even the food the soldiers ate was cooked under tarpaulins before five a.m. to avoid the possibility of visible smoke.[99] Just before dawn each day,

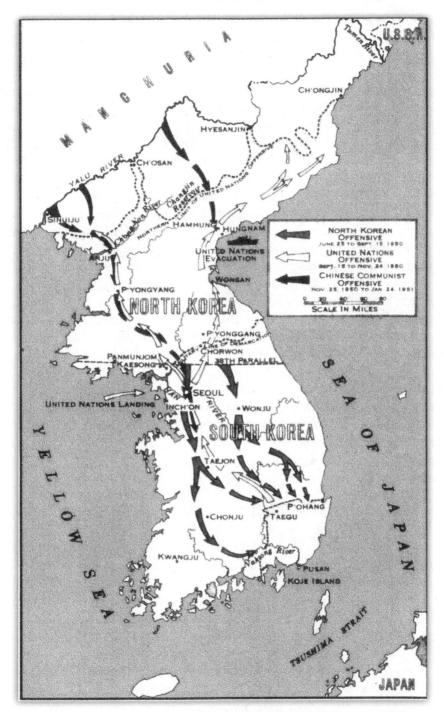

George C. Marshall Research Library

coerced villagers or farmers went out onto the ice to sweep away the tracks of these resolute forces. Hiding in ravines and mountain gorges, wearing light quilted uniforms and sneakers, they hunkered down.[100]

Then on the night of November 25, 300,000 Chinese came screaming from their hidden encampments, surrounding General Walker's thinly scattered Eighth Army and the separated X Corps. Historians Walter Isaacson and Evan Thomas described the scene: The Chinese soldiers advanced with "eerie cymbals, bells, whistles, shrieks, and cries of 'Son of a bitch marine we kill! Son of a bitch marine, you die!'"[101] The two-pronged offensive that had taken U.S. troops almost to the Chinese border was stopped cold. "Within days," wrote Cray, "entire divisions were cut off, battalions and regiments hacked from the main body one by one, then decimated as they turned southward to fight their way to safety."[102] It was a disaster. On November 29, a shaken MacArthur radioed the Joint Chiefs of Staff, "We face an entirely new war." With MacArthur's army in panicked retreat, total defeat seemed likely.[103] One of MacArthur's two "prongs" had to be rescued by sea, and the other retreated below the 38th parallel. By early December, the Eighth Army had fallen back nearly 300 miles from its positions along the Yalu. On December 24, its commander, General Walton Walker, was killed in a jeep accident. His replacement, General Matthew Ridgway, was in Korea by Christmas Day. By early 1951, under Ridgway's excellent leadership, the badly mauled Eighth Army, now combined with the X Corps, escaped the Chinese trap. Soon troops were once more on the offensive and by March approached once more the 38th parallel.[104]

Asia-Firster

That spring of 1951, with the disasters of November and December eased, the military situation somewhat stabilized, it was time once more to reexamine the mission of the Americans in that war. The United States could not risk a war with China. Expanding the war in Asia would not advance the nation's foreign policy objectives, which were to focus on strengthening the European countries through NATO. Furthermore, war with China would certainly create a global crisis. If the United States used its nuclear capability in a full-scale war against Communist China, the Soviet Union would most likely use its nuclear wherewithal. The president, as well as his secretaries of state and defense, believed that this could precipitate another world war, a risk they were not willing to take. Further, although China seemed to be the main player in this Korean War, military and civilian leaders in Washington, including Marshall, didn't discount the motivations of the Russians. The

Washington leadership suspected that the Soviets, while holding the line in Europe against an increasingly powerful Western Alliance, were glad to see the Chinese take the brunt as guardians of communist interests in Asia. Indeed, the Russians were still very much players. An expanded war in China would weaken the nascent NATO, keeping troops tied down and bled white while far from Western Europe.[105] Responding to pressure from UN allies, the Truman administration began weighing the possibility of halting any counteroffensive at the 38th parallel, thus abandoning the "unified Korea" objective and returning to the status-quo antebellum plan. Toward that end, on March 21, 1951, Truman submitted the draft of a presidential statement recommending a cease-fire order to the other 17 UN nations whose troops were fighting in Korea.[106]

General MacArthur, always an "Asia-firster," disagreed with these limited objectives. He had suffered a humiliating defeat at the hands of the Red Chinese and, with his immense ego and reputation as a military genius, he very much wanted to launch a major counteroffensive. Within the military hierarchy, MacArthur certainly had the right and was encouraged to offer alternative approaches for fighting the war. Yet, he was duty-bound to obey any directives his superiors gave him, even if they did not choose his methods. Moreover, MacArthur had already been warned about carrying into the public arena his disagreements with policies shaped by the president and his cabinet. That previous December, the UN commander had made several statements to the press that placed blame for the military debacle on others. As Ed Cray wrote, "He charged that European governments— and, by extension, Washington—had a short-sighted preoccupation with NATO."[107] He also complained to a *U.S. News and World Report* writer that the restrictions preventing his air forces from chasing Chinese jets into Manchuria were "an enormous handicap without precedent in military history." Truman would later say of this incident that he should have relieved MacArthur then and there. Instead, he took a less severe course, issuing an order that any public statements having to do with foreign or military policy had to be cleared by Washington before their release.[108]

On March 20, the Chiefs of Staff informed MacArthur of the cease-fire initiative, a drop-dead indication that there would be no war with Red China. General Bradley would later say MacArthur's realization that a war with China was not going to happen "snapped his brilliant but brittle mind."[109] Despite orders to the contrary, MacArthur continued to act as if unification of Korea was the goal of the United States. On March 24, 1951, in Korea (the 23rd in Washington), he issued a public proclamation of his own. MacArthur insulted the Red Chinese, calling them industrially and militarily weak, and criticized their poor showing in Korea against UN troops operating under "inhibitions." He implied that if the United Nations departed only slightly from its "tolerant effort to contain the war to the area of Korea," Communist China "would be doomed to collapse." Furthermore, he was ready to meet at any time with the Chinese commander to discuss terms. MacArthur's statements assured that Chairman Mao would not be amenable to negotiating a cease-fire. The Soviets weighed in, calling MacArthur a "maniac, the principal culprit, and the evil genius" of the war.[110]

The president was furious, saying in later years, still with more than a hint of anger, that he "was ready to kick him into the North China Sea. . . . MacArthur thought he was the proconsul for the government of the United States and could do as he damned pleased."[111] MacArthur's words, Truman fumed, had been "in open defiance of my orders as president and commander-in-chief. This was a challenge to the authority of the president under the Constitution."[112] Truman was ready to fire him, yet he knew he would need the approval of Marshall and Acheson. In a meeting to discuss the situation, with Lovett acting in this instance on Marshall's behalf, they told Truman of their concerns about the public fallout if MacArthur was relieved of command. After long conversations with the two of them, the president made his decision, surprisingly benign. He would not fire MacArthur this time, but would send him a reprimand with a reminder that all public statements were to be cleared with the White House. Further, if the enemy came forward to discuss an armistice, MacArthur was to refer the matter directly to the Chiefs of Staff.[113]

"Old soldiers never die"

In fact, even as MacArthur was issued this stringent "gag order," he had already sealed his fate. Some days earlier, he had responded to a letter written by the conservative Republican leader of the House, Joe Martin. Martin had asked MacArthur to comment on a speech he had recently given in which he proposed that Chiang Kai-shek be released to open a "second front" against the Chinese mainland. In his remarks, Martin had said, "What are we in Korea for—to win or lose? . . . . If we are not in Korea to win, then this administration should be indicted for the murder of American boys."[114] MacArthur had agreed with the essence of Martin's remarks, and complained about the UN's emphasis on Europe instead of Asia, writing, "The real war is here in Asia, not in Europe." Finally, he concurred with a particular line in Martin's speech that "there was no substitute for victory."[115]

On Thursday, April 5, Martin, who had not been restricted by MacArthur on the grounds of confidentiality, decided that he was "duty-bound" to read the entire response on the floor of the House.

By Friday, April 6, the official limos of the key players—Acheson, Marshall, Bradley, and the president's special assistant, Averell Harriman—lined the White House driveway. Truman was determined by then to relieve MacArthur, but not without consultation with his key advisers. Marshall urged caution. Huge military appropriation requests were before Congress—it could affect its willingness to meet the hefty defense budget as recommended. MacArthur was a heroic figure—there would be brutal criticism of the president and his administration. It might also affect the morale of the troops fighting in Korea if their fearless, revered commander was sacked. Both Marshall and Bradley wanted more time. In the afternoon, all four of them were gathered again, this time at Marshall's Pentagon office. He offered an alternative. Why not bring MacArthur home for consultation, to sort out the issues of authority as a means of preventing a more drastic final step. Acheson was against this, pointing out that such a move might backfire, giving MacArthur an opportunity to make a dramatic grandstand appeal to Congress and the country.[116] Over the weekend Marshall reviewed all of the documents, statements, and press releases related to MacArthur's case. Finally, on Sunday, April 8, at 4:00, the Joint Chiefs met in Marshall's office. He polled them one by one. All recommended MacArthur's relief. They agreed that he had shown a severe lack of sympathy for the president's efforts to limit the war in Korea—a commander needed to be more in tune with the civilian leader. His actions had thwarted the president's efforts to open negotiations with the Chinese, and, finally, MacArthur had not fully respected that the military must be controlled by civilian authority, as mandated by the Constitution.[117]

On Monday morning, April 9, 1951, at Blair House, President Truman met with the big four again—Marshall, Acheson, Harriman, Bradley. This time they concurred as well. MacArthur should be relieved. Bradley was to draw up the orders. That afternoon all four came to the Oval Office, bringing the drafted letter. Truman affixed his name. It was important that MacArthur receive these orders in person; the message was not to be conveyed through regular army communications. Via the American ambassador in Korea, they were to be given to Secretary of the Army Pace, already on the ground there, who would hand them to MacArthur. All of that soon fell apart. The *Chicago Tribune* leaked the news in an article that indicated a "major resignation" in Tokyo. The implication was that perhaps MacArthur had heard of the decision and was going to preempt the president by resigning. Truman decided he had to take the offensive, announcing a press conference at 1:00 a.m. on Wednesday morning, April 11. At the State Department, Dean Rusk, the assistant secretary of state for Far Eastern affairs, spent the night placing phone calls to the ambassadors of all of the countries that had troops in Korea. Meanwhile, due to a transmission glitch, the president's orders for MacArthur's relief did not arrive for General Pace to make his delivery. When Truman realized this, he was afraid that MacArthur would get the word ahead of time and resign. He then directed that the orders be sent through regular communication channels. As Truman wrote in his diary, "He's not going to be allowed to quit on me. . . . He's going to be fired." MacArthur got the word at lunch, when his wife, Jean, handed him the brown Signal Corps envelope.[118]

As Marshall had predicted, the storm came fast and furious. The telegrams piled up in the White House, 125,000 in all. For the most part the sentiments were similar: The president was an imbecile, a Judas, nothing but a little "ward politician;" almost all used the word "impeachment." In the first 48 hours after the word of MacArthur's relief was out, Republicans in Congress received 44,358 telegrams—all but 334 taking the side of the sacked commander, and, as with the White House messages, most of them called for Truman's impeachment.[119] Some Americans in towns and cities all across the country expressed their displeasure by flying flags upside down or at half-staff. A man in Denver started a Punch Harry in the Nose Club.[120] MacArthur returned home and was back in Washington on April 19. Marshall was there to greet him when his plane, *Bataan*, landed. A smiling MacArthur greeted Marshall with "Hello, George," and a handshake. An unsmiling but respectful Marshall responded, "Hello, General." After brief exchanges with MacArthur, it took 15 minutes to get the officials into their respective limos as the waiting multitudes swarmed around their returning hero.[121]

That afternoon prolonged cheers greeted MacArthur as he arrived in the House chamber to address a joint session of Congress. MacArthur was now free to say what he firmly believed. "Once war is forced upon us," he told the senators, representatives, and packed gallery, "there is no other alternative than to apply every available means to bring it to a swift end. War's very object is victory—not prolonged indecision."[122] He ended his speech with a sentimental line from a barracks ballad, that "'old soldiers never die, they just fade away.'. . . I now close my military career, an old soldier who tried to do his duty as God gave him the light to see that duty. Goodbye."[123]

Congress gave him a standing ovation and thunderous applause. The next day, confetti rained from the windows of New York offices as MacArthur starred in the biggest ticker tape parade in that city's history.[124]

In the congressional hearings relating to the relief of MacArthur that followed, he asserted that Marshall and the Joint Chiefs had backed every one of his strategic concepts for Korea, and he argued that politicians shouldn't be allowed to intervene in military affairs. However, when Marshall and the Joint Chiefs testified, they effectively refuted MacArthur's claims, making the case that the U.S. commander in the Pacific had overstepped his orders. As Bradley said on the first day of the testimony, "Frankly, in the opinion of the Joint Chiefs of Staff, this strategy [MacArthur's] would involve us in the wrong war, at the wrong place, at the wrong time, and with the wrong enemy."[125] The testimony of the Joint Chiefs and Marshall tamped down the criticism that had flowed against Truman. It seemed clear that the president had acted within his constitutional authority and that his policy had been appropriate. According to Marshall, MacArthur had grown so out of sympathy with the policy that there was grave doubt as to whether he could be trusted to make decisions based on its key concepts. That was his sworn duty, and when he could not do it, the only choice was to relieve him. Moreover, Marshall explained and defended the president's position of limited engagement in Korea, telling the committee that national policy had been, and still was, to defeat the aggression from the north without provoking a third world war.[126] In the end, hysteria about MacArthur died down. As Ed Cray wrote, "Marshall the accomplished soldier-diplomat had methodically buried MacArthur as a global strategist. Bradley's subsequent testimony threw dirt on the grave."[127]

Although the MacArthur crisis had simmered down by summer, the vicious attacks by the Republican right wing continued; Marshall was once more a target. The worst was a 60,000-word attack that Senator Joseph McCarthy read on the Senate floor on June 14, 1951. In effect, this 169-page "book," written by a Washington newspaperman, accused Marshall of treason, calling him a man "guilty of an immense conspiracy" and a leader who had made "common cause with Stalin."[128] McCarthy continued reading even as the crowd in the Senate gallery began to thin, telling his smaller audience that Marshall "created the China policy that destroyed China," and on and on he went. As it got closer to the dinner hour, he was still reading, yet skipping many pages of his text as even he wore out. By the time he gasped to the end of the long screed, most of the gallery audience had left, and only two senators remained to listen. Still, he insisted that every word of it

General MacArthur with his son Arthur and wife Jean leave the
U.S. Capitol on April 19, shortly after he addressed the Congress.

National Archives SC 361736

be placed in the *Congressional Record*. Dozens of senators, congressmen, journalists, and military men came to Marshall's defense, even those who had disagreed with his policies. When Marshall was besieged by reporters wanting to know what he thought, he refused to respond. A noted newspaper columnist, Clayton Fritchey, gathered materials to help Marshall rebut Senator McCarthy's accusations, to prove him wrong. Marshall declined the offer, saying, "I do appreciate that, but if I have to explain at this point that I am not a traitor to the United States, I hardly think it's worth it."[129]

Tired to the Bone

During the war years, Marshall, in frustration while melding military needs with political considerations, had written, "God bless democracy, I approve of it highly, but suffer from it greatly."[130] Although Marshall seemed unaffected by the slander against his name, perhaps the viciousness of McCarthy's attacks had increased his resolve to retire. After all, he was worn out. At almost 71, he was weary with the intense schedule he kept; moreover, it bothered him that his hearing wasn't good, a failing that he found serious for a public official. Marshall believed that a person in his position needed to have the vigor for its obligations. In June, as if to demonstrate that he could meet the demands of the job, Marshall even made an inspection trip to Korea, visiting battle sites in a light plane with General Ridgway. When squalls, wind, and rain violently buffeted the plane, Marshall asked Ridgway, "If you were alone, would you turn back?" Ridgway's answer: "No." The pilots shuddered to hear Marshall say, okay, then, they would continue the flight to the next planned troop stop.[131]

Nevertheless, Marshall had told Truman he would stay six months at the Department of Defense, and that late summer it had been almost a year. Finally, he could see his way clear to resign. As Mark Stoler wrote,

> The war was under control, the armed forces mobilized, and interservice and interdepartmental coordination restored. A powerful field commander's rebellion had been effectively stopped and established strategy and policy successfully reasserted. That was an enviable record for one year of service.[132]

Robert Lovett, the undersecretary, had known since he came on board with Marshall in September 1950 that he would become the next secretary of defense. Already, he was doing much of Marshall's work. On September 17, 1951, he turned it over to Lovett with his sincere congratulations. After 49 years of service to his country, Marshall was ready to go home to Leesburg, this time for good.

Marshall watches as Robert A. Lovett is sworn in as secretary of defense, September 17, 1951.

Harry S. Truman Library

Chapter 20

At Ease

Congratulations and Farewell

September 1951– October 1959

In the fall, the Marshalls settled into a comfortable routine at Dodona Manor. As the days became cooler, it was a wonderful season to be out of doors. Marshall spent his time harvesting the last of the summer vegetables; Katherine weeded the flower beds, and added bulbs for the following spring. At lunch, still in their work clothes, they ate a simple meal with iced tea on the shaded stone patio that they had added to the house shortly after moving in. One *Washington Star* writer, who had visited Dodona, noted the general's love of being outdoors, and the article included pictures of him pruning trees in the back yard. The reporter mentioned Marshall's membership in the Catoctin Farmers Club, a local organization. As Marshall explained, "These are serious men. It is surprising how thoroughly they discuss agricultural problems. I get a great deal from the meetings." Marshall enjoyed experimenting with the best soil for growing his vegetables, including working a rich compost heap. Someone told him that a corn or tomato crop would yield better if a fish head was placed in the hole at planting time, a method that the Native Americans had used in olden days. Marshall's aide brought him a bucket of fish heads from the wharf of the Potomac River in Washington, and they were duly planted under both crops. Marshall had to leave for a few days, and when he returned, Katherine gave him the news that there had been a convention of cats in the backyard, and few fish heads remained. Apparently, the tomatoes escaped, since they were planted deeper in the soil, but not the corn. Marshall enjoyed telling this story, as well as other facts related to this relaxed side of his life. He had a young fruit orchard, and with some pride related to the visiting writer that some of them were descendants of a tree from George Washington's Mount Vernon farm.[1]

When rainy days drove the Marshalls inside, they had the luxuries of naps, and in the evening reading in a cozy study, Marshall in a well-worn red leather chair, Katherine on a buttercup-yellow slipcovered sofa. One wall was lined with books, and although the shelves had plenty of novels, especially paperback Westerns, more and more of the volumes were gifts from famous friends or authors, autographed and inscribed. Marshall corresponded often with Winston Churchill, who was writing a history of World War II. Each new installment arrived signed shortly after its publication. Marshall devoured them, telling Churchill after the first one came, "The weeds in my garden at Leesburg will rejoice in the knowledge that between them and their fate stand over 600 pages of your unexcelled prose."[2]

During Marshall's professional life, especially after 1939, he had spacious, even elegant, offices. In retirement he kept a small desk in a tiny room off the study at Dodona. Once a week his aide, Master Sergeant (later lieutenant colonel) C. J. George, brought him letters that had arrived at his Pentagon office. He read all the correspondence, and although he usually directed that secretaries, specialized officers, or other staff handle these matters, he often answered the requests of former soldiers himself. Mostly, though, at Dodona his letters, frequently hand-written, were for family. He kept in touch with his stepdaughter, Molly; his sister, Marie Singer; Allen's widow, now remarried, Madge Brown Pendleton; Rose Page Wilson, his goddaughter; and a number of former colleagues.

In 1948, the Marshalls moved the gate to their 3.88-acre property to the less traveled side of the residence, no doubt to provide the privacy that they both so treasured. Most of the time, Leesburg residents treated the Marshalls as regular town folk, offering a friendly greeting, conversing for a few minutes about the weather or some other local matter, and moving on. Sometimes, though, there would be a knock at the door, and a stranger would be there, hoping to meet the famous World War II general. One day Marshall was on a ladder cutting a dead limb from a tree when a navy officer came up the gravel drive. Apparently, the young man and his companion did not immediately notice Marshall perched above. He saw them, and got down to ask them what they wanted. Embarrassed, the curious couple drove away in a hurry.[3]

Since late 1948, after his five-star status was reactivated, Marshall had an orderly, Sergeant William Heffner, who lived at Dodona or Pinehurst for eleven years. He ran errands, got the "general" packed for trips, and, although Marshall sometimes drove himself, also acted as an impromptu chauffeur. In 1949 the Willys-Overland Company, perhaps in appreciation for Marshall's introduction of their general service Jeep into production in World War II, gave him a civilian station wagon version of the famous vehicle. While the family Oldsmobile, and later a Buick, was available, Heffner often drove the Jeep for everyday duties, including picking up groceries. On many Sundays, Heffner took the Marshalls to St. James Episcopal Church in town,

Marshall sits outside to read his mail shortly after his retirement
as secretary of defense, September 12, 1951.

George C. Marshall Research Library, Harris and Ewing

and sometimes joined them at lunch for the colonial-style cuisine of the Laurel Brigade Inn. Occasionally Heffner's duties took him out of Leesburg. Marshall was deeply interested in the battles of the Civil War. At least a couple of times a year, the sergeant would chauffeur him and a couple of his friends to the scenes of battles, especially Gettysburg, or Antietam, where they would tour the battlefield and discuss what Heffner called, "the whys and the wherefores."[4]

In the late fall, the Marshalls flew to Pinehurst for the winter. Heffner went ahead of them, loading the vehicle with luggage and supplies so that all was in readiness when they arrived. It was a charming place, its resort town centerpiece the famous Carolina Hotel, with awning-shaded windows and sweeping verandas. When friends visited, the Marshalls booked rooms for them in this fine establishment. The beautiful dining room, with its traditional Southern cuisine, provided a pleasing atmosphere for them to entertain. When Greece's Queen Frederika came for a brief stay, she created quite a stir as she entered the restaurant with the Marshalls. As he had in Leesburg, throughout the winter Marshall attended Rotary in Pinehurst. One professor of military history at Duke University was disconcerted when he arrived as a guest speaker at the club to lecture about World War II strategy. To his consternation, sitting directly in front of him was none other than General Marshall. Afterward, he was relieved as Marshall congratulated him warmly for his excellent talk.[5] While Marshall was not a golfer, he enjoyed spectating and was the most recognized figure steering a cart on the course. The Marshalls never headed back to Leesburg each year until after the North and South Golf Amateur Tournaments, one for men and one for women, held in late March and mid-April. Often Marshall was called upon to hand out the trophies.[6]

Despite Marshall's efforts to stay home and tend his garden, or to fish and hunt, he took plenty of trips away from both Leesburg and Pinehurst. Still very much a a sought-out public figure, in the fall of 1951 and throughout 1952, Marshall left home to give speeches—at the Governor's Association in Gatlinburg, Tennessee; in Washington for the dedication of the American Red Cross Building; before the Council of World Affairs in Cleveland, Ohio; for the commencement address at Woodberry Forest School, Virginia, where both Allen and Clifton had graduated.[7] Sometimes Marshall agreed to give speeches in places that didn't require travel; for example, to offer a few remarks on Leesburg's courthouse lawn on Memorial Day, or at the dedication of the town's war memorial. Whether in small or grand venues, managing the calendar in the face of dozens of requests dueled constantly

Marshall speaks at the ceremony commemorating the installation of a war memorial at the courthouse in Leesburg, Virginia, May 30, 1956. *The Winslow Williams Photograph Collection, Thomas Balch Library, Leesburg, Virginia*

with Marshall's need to enjoy a time of leisure.

Shadows

In the fall of 1951, a dark shadow fell upon their untroubled days. Katherine's oldest son, Clifton Brown, was suffering from lung cancer. A lieutenant colonel in the U.S. Army during the war, he afterward had become a businessman in New York and then Washington. Clifton was divorced from Em Bowles Locker, with whom he had a daughter, Carter Boardman Brown. At the time of his illness, he was engaged to be married to Mary Lee, a descendant of Robert E. Lee. In late January 1952, the Marshalls came to Washington from Pinehurst, staying at Clifton's apartment near Walter Reed Hospital to be near him as he underwent lung surgery that the family hoped would eradicate his disease.[8] Kathcrine's letters from Pinehurst to him that winter reflected her worries about his health. At any sign of improvement that winter and into the spring, she expressed hope that Clifton would feel well enough to come for a long and relaxed visit to Pinehurst. That was not to be. While receiving further treatment at Walter Reed, he died on May 11, 1952, at the age of only 38. The funeral was at Fort Myer Chapel, the burial at Arlington National Cemetery.[9] The loss was crushing. Within nine years, two of Katherine's three children had died. To comfort her mother, Molly came to Dodona with her son, Jimmy, and daughters, Kitty and Ellene, staying as long as possible. In early June, President Truman and Margaret visited for the day. Mary Lee and her mother, Helen, were there as well, and stood with the Marshalls for a group photo on the front porch. The laughter of grandchildren and the attention of good friends greatly cheered them, but the reality of deep loss hovered close.

Early the previous year, Marshall had agreed to be the chairman of the American Battle Monuments Commission. The first to lead the organization, which had been established in 1923, was John J. Pershing. By taking on the position shortly after Pershing's death in 1948, Marshall honored his long-time mentor and father figure. It wasn't a taxing role and it seemed appropriate, since it allowed him to show the greatest respect possible by overseeing the burial sites of courageous fallen soldiers. As Pershing had said, this commission was important so that time would not "dim the glory of their deeds."[10] In the fall of 1952, the Marshalls took a trip to Europe so he could inspect American cemeteries on the continent. Mary Lee went too—perhaps the trip would be an important change of scene for all of them. On September 13, 1952, Marshall dedicated the World War II memorial at the Suresnes American Cemetery, five miles from Paris. In his brief remarks,

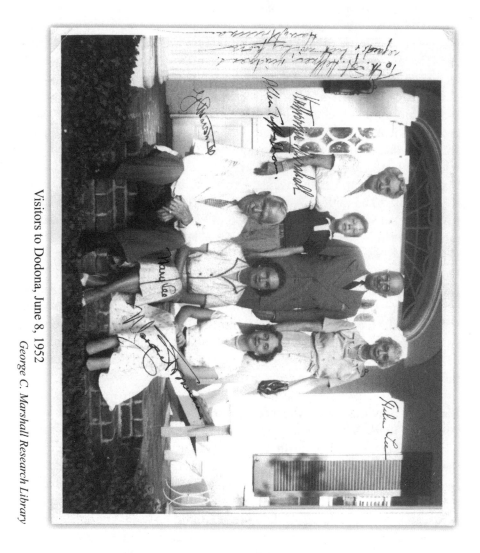

Visitors to Dodona, June 8, 1952

George C. Marshall Research Library

he emphasized his hope that the sacrifice of these men "will finally lead to genuine bonds of good will and good faith on this earth."[11] The personal cost of war was not far from their minds, since once more they visited Allen's grave at Anzio, placing a bouquet of red roses at the site.

An Omission in Milwaukee

Though Marshall wasn't as busy as before, he stayed informed of current news by reading several newspapers and, when he and Katherine weren't traveling, listening to the radio in his small study at Dodona. His wartime colleague, Dwight D. Eisenhower, was the Republican candidate for the presidency that summer and fall of 1952. During the campaign season, Marshall became aware once more that the ugly influence of Senator Joseph McCarthy was still around. In August, General Eisenhower had distanced himself from any candidate whom he said used "un-American methods" for fighting communism, a veiled reference to McCarthy without calling his name. On a campaign swing in Denver, Eisenhower specifically praised Marshall, and, as if to refute the vitriol of McCarthy, Jenner, and others, declared that "there was nothing of disloyalty in General Marshall's soul . . . if he was not a perfect example of patriotism, I never saw one."[12]

Later in September, when it seemed that a moderate Republican who was running for governor in Wisconsin was in a tight race, and control of the Senate was also in question, party officials pressed Eisenhower to campaign in that state. After all, Truman had won there in 1948. The Democrats must not win Wisconsin again. Although Eisenhower agreed to a stop in Milwaukee, where McCarthy would also be present, he told his speech writer that he wanted a big portion of his talk to be a defense of Marshall. No one knows how McCarthy found out about this plan, but he went to the trouble of flying to Peoria, Illinois, where Eisenhower was campaigning, to discuss it with him personally.[13] Although McCarthy would later speak about the "very, very pleasant conversation" that they had, a campaign speech writer, Kevin McCann, who was stationed outside the door of the hotel suite where the meeting was held, told a different story. He recalled that Eisenhower lit into McCarthy, condemning his "thuggish tactics and his attack on Marshall." Eisenhower was so angry," remembered McCann, that "he turned the air blue. I never heard the General so cold-bloodedly skin a man."[14]

On the way to Milwaukee, though, Eisenhower's resolve to defend Marshall came unhinged. The Republican campaign manager, Sherman Adams, and others warned that such a tribute would be seen as a direct attack on

McCarthy and might lose them the state. Reluctantly, Eisenhower agreed to leave out the "praise of Marshall" portion of his remarks. Unfortunately for him, the complete text of his speech was in the hands of the *New York Times*. The next day, its publisher, Arthur Hays Sulzberger, wired Adams, "Do I need to tell you that I am sick at heart?"[15] The omission was the most newsworthy aspect of the Milwaukee trip for the candidate. Headlines screamed that McCarthy had bullied Eisenhower into submission. Truman said that he couldn't believe Eisenhower could "stoop so low," and spoke of him having "betrayed his principles" and "deserted his friends."[16] The fact is that this incident soured his relationship with Eisenhower almost until the end of his days.

Marshall, however, didn't let the situation destroy his association with Eisenhower. He made no public statements about it, but Marshall told his goddaughter, Rose Page Wilson, who was furious and let him know it, that "Eisenhower was forced into a compromise, that's all it was."[17] Later when reporters came to Dodona and asked Marshall what he thought of the incident, he replied: "I am not going to talk about that. You know what he said—I don't need to comment on it. Now, can someone tell me how to keep the blackbirds out of my marigolds?" When the reporters printed Marshall's remarks, he got many letters offering helpful advice on his gardening problems. Though Eisenhower may have shown a moment's weakness regarding his old friend, he worked hard to display his respect throughout the years. Katherine Marshall, when interviewed years later, said of the Milwaukee omission, "Don't attack President Eisenhower about the McCarthy thing; he did everything in the world to make it up to George and me."[18]

Arches and Abbeys

Despite the ongoing controversies regarding Marshall among conservative Republicans, most Americans highly valued his service to the country, perhaps none more than the faculty at his alma mater, the Virginia Military Institute in Lexington, Virginia. In 1949 VMI had added a new barracks to the existing buildings.[19] The entrance to the new cadet quarters was via an archway similar to two others along the parade grounds named in honor of George Washington and Thomas "Stonewall" Jackson, who had been on the faculty before becoming a Civil War general. On May 15, 1951, exactly 50 years after Marshall graduated from the Virginia Military Institute, it celebrated "Marshall Day," proudly naming the third arch for one of its most famous graduates. Marshall relished the events of that splendid sunny day,

George C. Marshall Research Library

At VMI on "Marshall Day," May 15, 1951

which included cadets on parade, remarks by the governor, and attendance by old friends from his class of 1901 as well as wartime colleagues. Moved by the tribute that had been paid him, the next day Marshall told a former classmate that the dedication "was a big day in my life, for V.M.I. paid me a great honor. . . . The day was perfect in all respects."[20]

In March 1953, Marshall was asked to represent the United States at the coronation of Queen Elizabeth II of England. It was President Eisenhower who made the appointment, even though his political advisers stressed that McCarthy was still accusing Marshall of losing "a hundred million persons a year to international communism." The Marshalls were treated like royalty themselves, arriving in London for days of celebration, but also to visit old friends from the war years. Before he left, Truman had asked Marshall to write him and describe the ceremonies. He provided the former president with a remarkably detailed account of the events. As an official delegate, Marshall was invited to attend the coronation itself at Westminster Abbey, but not Katherine. Nevertheless, military aides made certain that she and other special guests were in a location where they could see the procession into the abbey and afterward were taken to a prime spot for the parade that followed. Inside, at a place near the altar, Marshall had a unique life experience—witnessing the coronation of the queen. Winston Churchill was once again prime minister, having won back that position in 1951. Dressed in the Robes of the Realm, Churchill spotted his old ally, already seated. As Marshall told Truman, "He dignified me in the Abbey by turning out of the procession to shake hands with me after he reached the dais."[21] What he didn't mention, but was related by General Bradley later, was that Sirs Alan Brooke and Bernard Montgomery did the same. Marshall also did not include another touching incident. As Marshall and General Omar Bradley entered the abbey, everyone stood up. General Marshall looked around and asked, "Why are they standing?" Bradley provided the answer: "They're standing for you."[22]

Marshall was a man who had met plenty of royalty in his time—in fact, he and Katherine had dined with then Princess Elizabeth and the Duke of Edinburgh at the Canadian Embassy in Washington as recently as November 1951. Yet Marshall seemed almost boyishly pleased in telling Truman about the coronation events:

> The banquet at Buckingham Palace was the most brilliant gathering I had ever seen. The Queen's party of about thirty was seated at an oval table in the center of the hall, surrounded by tables of twelve.

I was included at her table . . . and was, I think, the only commoner so honored. I sat between the Princess [Alice, great-grandmother of Prince Phillip] and the Queen Mother, and two chairs removed from the Queen. [23]

Although Marshall had gone head-to-head with Churchill over strategic issues during the war, with the battle won they now delighted in each other's company. The Marshalls sat with Churchill in the Steward's box at the Derby and enjoyed a private luncheon that he arranged. Marshall must have felt relief that he had set aside the burdens of public life when he observed the pressure Churchill now faced. He commented to Truman that "The strain he underwent during the Coronation bears [beggars] description, because all of the colonials were meeting with him on service matters, and all of the visiting royalties and prime ministers were seeking interviews with him on a variety of subjects."[24]

Several days after the Marshalls returned home from England, a gift arrived from Winston Churchill, an oil painting. For many years, the prime minister had been an amateur artist, a hobby he took up during times in his career when he had been turned out of office and sought solace in that medium. In a letter dated June 10 that accompanied the painting, Churchill explained that the scene depicted was a village called Tinerhir, in Morocco, set against the Atlas Mountains.[25] Perhaps while they were together in England, Churchill and Marshall had talked about the time in Morocco when they were key players at the Casablanca Conference during the war. In any case, Morocco had been a favorite place for Churchill to paint, and this work had been finished on a holiday trip he had taken there in early 1951, just before he once more became prime minister. On June 28, 1953, Katherine wrote a thank-you letter to Churchill, telling him, "Yesterday was a gala day for me for we hung your painting. It has added so much to the beauty of our living room and has the place of honor." She also mentioned with a light note of sarcasm that "on the opposite side of the room is a 'modern' called 'evening' given to George by Mr. Molotov when we were 'dear Allies.' So you are in rare company." Marshall had been given that painting by the prickly and difficult Soviet foreign minister after the Moscow Conference in the spring of 1947.[26]

A Trip to Oslo

An even greater distinction would come to General Marshall later that year. In late October 1953, he learned he would receive the Nobel Peace Prize for his work in the development of the European Recovery Program. It had been President Truman who proposed that he receive it. Marshall had not been well that fall—he was suffering from a particularly serious case of influenza. He rose from his sick bed and, in a silk dressing robe, greeted reporters in his Pinehurst home. Characteristically, he credited others, telling the assembled press that it was a tribute "to the American people" and praising the work of the late Senator Vandenberg. Soon afterward, when President Eisenhower received word that he and Katherine would not be able to attend a state dinner at the White House for Queen Frederika and King Paul of Greece because of illness, he sent his congratulations and let Marshall know that he would send a plane to Pinehurst that would fly him to Washington for treatment at Walter Reed Hospital.[27] It was there that Marshall received the official announcement from the Nobel Committee. He wrote Katherine about it, telling her that according to the information, the ceremonies would be held in Oslo, Norway, rather than Sweden, where the Nobelists in other categories would be honored. As the days passed, he kept Katherine updated on the progress of his recovery, noting on the 11th that the doctor had told him his chest was clear and expressing the hope that he could get back to Pinehurst that weekend. As always, he conveyed his deep affection for his wife. "Dearest, I am so anxious to see you and so impatient to get back. I love you very much and miss you hourly."[28]

As Marshall was confined to his hospital bed, he had a delightful surprise. Since he was too ill to attend the state dinner, Queen Frederika paid him a visit at Walter Reed. Madame Chiang Kai-shek had written him her congratulations on the award, and in reply he told her about the queen's visit. "She is a very beautiful and most interesting woman and you might consider her 'working' royalty, as she certainly devotes all of her time and energy to her people."[29] Marshall reminded Madame Chiang that she had visited him in the same hospital after his kidney surgery, and commented, apparently referring to both visits, that "whenever I receive women of this stature, I am a patient in the hospital."[30]

Since the announcement of his Nobel Peace Prize, Marshall had known that Winston Churchill had also received the Nobel honor, his for literature. The prime minister had sent him a congratulatory telegram. Marshall wrote Churchill that he was embarrassed that he had not sent *his* compliments, but had wanted to wait until he was up to writing a "very personal long-hand note." He conceded to Churchill that "I still am on the flat of my back but hope to be able to go to Oslo."[31]

Marshall was still in the hospital as the date of the Oslo presentation drew nearer. Katherine did not want him to make the trip, fearful for his health. She had already decided that she was not physically strong enough for the journey. After 16 days at Walter Reed, Marshall returned to Pinehurst somewhat better but by no means 100 percent. Still, he decided he could make it, opting for an eight-day voyage on the Italian liner *Andrea Doria* via a southern route that would go into the port of Naples, Italy. He hoped to regain some of his strength along the way. That wasn't what happened. Marshall wrote Katherine from sea on December 3. There was weariness in his tone as he told her that while he was in New York he had a "pretty strenuous interview" in front of "8 large T.V. cameras" and supposed that he would "have another ordeal at Naples." As for his main task, that wasn't going well either. Marshall confessed to Katherine that he was "having a terribly hard time getting down to the business of writing my lecture. I can't seem to concentrate." He tried to lighten the mood by relating a shipboard anecdote. "During the movie yesterday a heavy sea ran all the chairs down to one side of the room partially piling them up there. The racket was terrific. The 'grown ups' were frightened and the youngest children delighted." Still, he was lonely. "I send you a great deal of love, dearest. I miss you in my cabin, at meals, and on deck." Her health never far from Marshall's mind, he closed by saying, "I do hope you are well and not concealing some ailment."[32]

From Naples, Marshall flew to Paris, where he was a guest at the home of General Alfred Gruenther, the commander of SHAPE (Supreme Headquarters Allied Powers Europe). Once again he wrote Katherine regarding how he was handling the trip. Apparently, the Gruenthers had made him comfortable in a rather private suite, where he "remained in bed all day," he said, "except for dinner at 7." Having written "not a line" of his speech, the first morning there he had a stenographer come in. He told Katherine, "I gritted my teeth and plunged into the lecture." Marshall wasn't satisfied with the results. At his request, Gruenther and some of his officers offered suggestions, and finally the commander sent in "his brilliant young speechwriter" (Colonel Andrew Goodpaster, a future general, and commander of NATO) to collaborate with him. Goodpaster got down on the floor in Marshall's suite to put the various typed ideas together into one piece. When retyped and edited a bit more, Marshall was ready, telling his wife of the final product, "I did this over and closed the deal. So I don't have to worry any longer."[33]

On November 10, 1953, in Oslo University's Festival Hall, Marshall received the Nobel Prize for his work in the cause of peace. Just as the general stood to walk to the platform, three men in the balcony began yelling and throwing leaflets over the railing. Among other things, the pamphlets accused Marshall of the deaths of "100,000 people in Hiroshima and Nagasaki."[34] Marshall wrote Rose Page Wilson,

> The Commy business was more press than fact. . . . The shouter only got off four words—"I thought this was" when the Agricultural Attaché of the American Embassy slapped his mouth shut and jerked his head back, and my pilot administered a one-two punch which terminated matters. [35]

What Marshall doesn't mention is that Norway's King Haakon VII immediately stood to applaud him; moments later, the entire audience was on its feet and the enthusiastic applause drowned out the commotion on the second floor.[36]

When presented with the award, Marshall once again made clear that he did not credit himself:

> I accept this honor with profound gratitude as it has been conferred upon me by the Nobel Committee. And I do it not merely for myself, more specially for the American people who, alone, made possible the authority and possible the funds which made the European recovery program a reality.[37]

At the white tie dinner that evening, Marshall gave his lecture, addressing the fact that he was the first professional soldier to receive this honor:

> There has been considerable comment over the awarding of the Nobel Peace Prize to a soldier. I am afraid this does not seem as remarkable to me as it quite evidently appears to others. I know a great deal of the horrors and tragedies of war. . . . The cost of war in human lives is constantly spread before me, written neatly in many ledgers whose columns are gravestones. I am deeply moved to find some means or method of avoiding another calamity of war. Almost daily I hear from the wives, or mothers, or families of the fallen. The tragedy of the aftermath is almost constantly before me.[38]

Marshall did not feel that his Nobel lecture was his best, and yet certain lines embodied the key concept that he had articulated at war's end. It was this idea that ultimately provided the philosophical basis for the European Recovery Program for which he was being honored:

> Tyranny inevitably must retire before the tremendous moral strength of the gospel of freedom and self-respect for the individual, but we have to recognize that these democratic principles do not flourish on empty stomachs and that people turn to false promises of dictators because they are hopeless and anything promises something better than the miserable existence that they endure.[39]

Like an Old Man

Back in Pinehurst for Christmas of 1953, Marshall wrote to Allen's widow, Madge. They exchanged letters often, and in the secretary of state years when Marshall came to Washington during the winter months, after Dodona was closed for the season, he would stay at her home in Washington. She had remarried in late 1949, and the groom was John Pendleton. Marshall remarked to a friend that "Strange to say his father and mother were close friends of Lily's and mine in Lexington."[40] He and Katherine had been thrilled when in September 1950 Madge gave birth to a baby girl. His letter of December 26 thanked her for holiday gifts. Marshall noted that he and Katherine had "a very pleasant Christmas." The grandkids—Molly's children—had come for dinner and stayed until dark, watching TV "without developing any riots." He mentioned that while he had been in Europe, he had stayed in bed every day "except in Oslo," saying nothing of what had taken him to that city. The rest of the letter chronicled his efforts to recover from the flu—"I go along cautiously," he told her. Marshall's "P.S." was revealing: "The letter reads like that of an old man only concerned with his state of health," he wrote. "I'll do better in the future."[41]

An Effort to Downsize

In 1954 Marshall stayed reasonably healthy, but he was never as vigorous as in earlier years. He had a spate of illnesses, some of which sent him back to Walter Reed for brief stays—colds, bronchitis, a rash. His hearing worsened, as did his balance. Often, it felt more secure to walk with a cane. Katherine had health issues as well, including painful bouts of shingles. The Marshalls experienced more family losses beginning in December 1954, when Katherine's brother, Tristam Tupper, died. It had been his publishing business, Tupper and Love, Inc., that had issued her book, *Together: Annals of an Army Wife*. In the spring of 1955, Sterling Lacy, Katherine's brother-

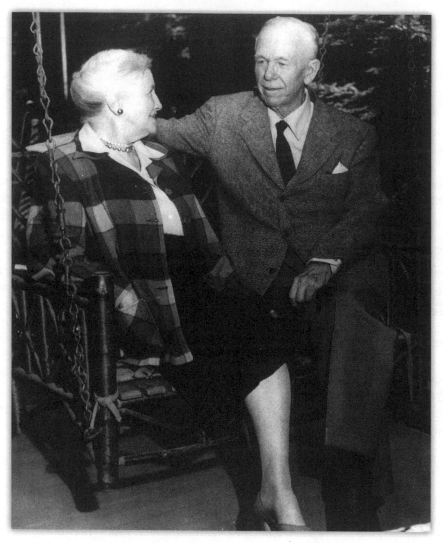

The Marshalls relax at Eagles Mere, August 1955

George C. Marshall Research Library

in-law, died, and less than a month later, her sister Allene suffered a severe stroke. It seemed difficult to realize that this could have happened so soon to the beautiful couple who had wed at Dodona in May of 1947.

Summer came. Marshall had difficulty recognizing his right to simply accept retirement and slow down. He complained to Madge in a letter that July, "I continue lazy and good for nothing." He also lamented that the rabbits had devoured most of his garden—"beans, beets, cucumbers, most of our marigolds, many of our zinnias." It had been severely hot that month, so he told her that despite the depleted garden, he would "not trouble to replant." That August the Marshalls fled the heat of Leesburg for a cottage at Eagles Mere, a rustic, woodsy resort area in Pennsylvania. Colonel George had been involved in making the arrangements for the month-long stay. Marshall reported to him a couple of days into their visit that the cottage was large and comfortable, and that George's friend who worked at the hotel on the property had "fought off reporters and photographers to delay them a few days."[42] Still very much a public figure, Marshall yearned for privacy. He and Katherine did enjoy solitude and quiet that month in the cooler mountains, but soon responsibility called. That October, Marshall wrote his goddaughter, Rose Page Wilson, that the time at Eagles Mere had been wonderful, but they had hurried back to take care of Allene, whose condition had not improved. The Marshalls left for Pinehurst earlier than usual to get her into a convalescent home there.

In a November 1955 letter, Marshall shared with a wartime colleague, General Charles D. Herron, his regret that he had not been able to attend the funeral of General John McAuley Palmer, who had been a very influential figure in his young military life. He told Herron that it "is mandatory to preserve my health, which is seemingly good at the moment. . . . Long trips are arduous and it takes me several days to recuperate."[43] It seems clear in the letter that he had already told Herron of a plan to sell Dodona Manor, their primary summer home. Marshall acknowledged that "the decision to sell the Leesburg place wasn't an easy one to make, but it became evident that it was too much house for just the two of us, and the domestic situation made the program more acute." He explained that he and Katherine would spend most of the year at Pinehurst and long summers at Eagles Mere. In fact, a notice of the Marshalls' intention to sell Dodona had already appeared in the *Washington Post*—the selling price: $75,000.[44]

Once the word was out that the Marshalls intended to buy a cottage at Eagles Mere, they got several offers to help them find property there. Marshall wrote one friend that in terms of a move, "the one dark cloud . . . has been the serious illness of Katherine's sister." Apparently, she had suffered another stroke and was, as Marshall wrote, "steadily sinking." By April 1956, Colonel George had written a real estate agent in Eagles Mere that because "of Mrs. Marshall's sister's illness . . . and confinement in a nursing home in Pinehurst and the possible sale of their home at Leesburg," they would not be able to make firm arrangements for either a rental or a sale in the upcoming season. Whether the Marshalls concluded that Pennsylvania was too far away from Allene, or simply did not get a suitable offer for the sale of the Leesburg property, they seemed to have abandoned that idea by the time they returned to Pinehurst in the fall. Allene never recovered, but lingered until January 1958.[45]

Service Not for Sale

A reporter from the *Chicago American* newspaper had interviewed Marshall that spring of 1955 and remarked to him that "military figures" from World War II had "tumbled over each other racing into print with modern memoirs. Would he like to break his silence?" Marshall's answer was not surprising: "If I were to write my memoirs," he said, "I'd want them to be completely honest, historical and factual. To meet those qualifications, I would have to step on the toes of too many people. It's better to write nothing under these circumstances."[46] Already in 1952, others were interested in preserving his work. President Truman had talked to the VMI superintendent about building a Marshall Library on campus. Before leaving office, he issued an order for government departments to make available to the organizers of such a library all pertinent papers related to Marshall. Although magazines and publishing houses had offered to pay him handsomely to tell his life story, Marshall continued to refuse. He didn't want to profit from a book, he told them, as his service to the country was not for sale. Nevertheless, Frank McCarthy, C. J. George, and Marshall Carter convinced him that he should allow a potential biographer to interview him; otherwise, they argued, a great deal of important history would be lost. Finally, Marshall agreed, but under certain conditions. He would not choose the biographer, neither he nor his family would profit from the book, and he would not answer any questions that could easily be found by reading his military papers. Meanwhile, John D. Rockefeller Jr., who had long admired General Marshall, in 1956 wrote a personal check for $150,000 to provide funding for the George C. Marshall Foundation, the organizing agency that would set up a research library at VMI.[47] It was the foundation that selected Forrest C. Pogue, a military historian, as Marshall's biographer.

From the fall of 1956 until the spring of 1957, Marshall spent many days answering questions, which the writer recorded on audiotape. But that spring, he complained of not being able to recall certain details. The interview sessions were shortened. So that Marshall would not need to go up and down the steps more than once, Pogue came in the afternoons when Marshall made his way from his second floor bedroom to stay until after dinner. No doubt about it—he was slowing down. In August 1958, he had a cyst removed from his eye at Walter Reed Hospital. When it seemed he was about ready to go home, he broke a rib in a fall, and had to stay longer.[48] Although Marshall insisted that he was perfectly fine "from the neck up," he told Pogue wryly that he heard Mrs. Marshall saying that she had to take him for a walk in the garden, as if she thought he were an invalid.

Memories and Farewell

When Marshall returned to Pinehurst that fall, the Walter Reed doctors had arranged that a medical corpsman from nearby Fort Bragg be outside his room at all times. When Rose Page Wilson called Katherine to check on Marshall's condition that November, she revealed that he was not well. When she inquired if it was the flu again, Katherine told her, no, it was "just about everything." Rose, who lived with her husband and children in Durham, North Carolina, only about 85 miles away, asked if she could come to see Marshall. She was there the next afternoon. Over the next months her visits, about every 10 days, with her godfather were a delight to her. Almost from the start, though, Rose understood with total clarity that Marshall was in decline and would not recover. Nevertheless, although he was gaunt, his hair thinned and snow white, his mind was sharp. Relaxed, he talked nothing of his public life, but often regaled her with memories of his childhood. Marshall vividly recalled snowy winters in Uniontown, tobogganing down a steep hill—the invigorating joy of it. It prompted Rose to remark that she was sorry his father hadn't lived long enough to see what a great son he had reared. "He would have been very proud of you," she told him. "Do you really think so?" he asked. Startled by his reply, she couldn't help but laugh at his "silly" question. He had been thinking of his father a lot, he told her, and then, almost wistfully, added, "I'd like to believe he would have approved of me."[49] Throughout the rest of the year until the following March, Rose's visits continued in a well-developed pattern. She sat by his bed holding his hand and talked with him of simple things—her children and husband, the weather, and memories of her childhood at the Washington residential apartments where she had first met Lily and "Colonel" Marshall.

Rose's times with Marshall were a gift to Katherine, too, who for a few hours could rest or get away without worry.[50]

Although he was dressed and seemingly chipper as he enjoyed a cake to celebrate his 78th birthday, not long afterward, in late January 1959, Marshall suffered a stroke. A month or so later, he suffered another, this one more severe. By March he had been transferred from a hospital at Fort Bragg, and from there to Walter Reed. For a time he seemed to be a bit better. He could sit up in a wheelchair and visit with old friends who dropped by. Some days he recognized them and greeted them in a low whisper. Other days he seemed stronger and exchanged with army friends the slightly embellished stories of old soldiers. Eventually his condition worsened, and he lay in a near coma. Still, past comrades came to pay their respects: Eisenhower, Truman, even Winston Churchill, who stood at the doorway to his room with tears in his eyes. To be with him daily, Katherine stayed in a guest cottage nearby. At any time she was away from Marshall's side, Sargeant Heffner kept a vigil in a straight-backed chair by his bed. He was there when, on the evening of October 16th, Marshall peacefully died.

Taps

Despite the ceremonial aspects of his many professional roles, in every way possible Marshall had avoided pretension. So it would be at his death. He had told his aide quite emphatically that he wanted no state funeral. He remembered having planned Pershing's in 1948. It had been a brutally hot day punctuated by a heavy downpour. Twenty generals, including Eisenhower and Bradley, had marched behind the casket from the U.S. Capitol to Arlington National Cemetery, a distance of more than two miles. No, Marshall had no need for such rituals. In 1956 he put it in writing. He named his pallbearers—two orderlies, Sergeant Powder and Sergeant Heffner, along with his postwar aide, Colonel George. Frank McCarthy and Robert Lovett were included, as well as Bedell Smith, but only if "it was convenient and he wasn't out of town."[51] Marshall insisted that there would be no eulogy, no long list of public officials, and no lying in state at National Cathedral. Katherine altered that request a bit, allowing his closed casket to rest overnight in a small chapel there. Crowds lined up to pay their respects. On the 20th, a spectacularly crisp and sunny day in Arlington, the short service was held at Fort Myer Chapel. Presidents Truman and Eisenhower were there, seated beside each other, and for the moment united in their shared grief. The service was short and simple. Only once did the Episcopal minister refer to Marshall when during the prayer he entreated God to "take thy Servant George."[52]

From the chapel the family, pallbearers, and small group of invited guests followed the flag-draped caisson the short distance into Arlington National Cemetery to a spot not far from the Tomb of the Unknown Soldier. There Marshall was laid to rest, a final posting for a good soldier. Off in the distance lay the capital city where for so long he had served his country. The crack of gunfire from the honor guard rifles and the mournful sound of "Taps" caught the air and for a few brief moments muted the low hum of workaday Washington.

Copyright by Bill Mauldin (1950). Courtesy of Bill Mauldin Estate LLC

Wartime Conferences Attended by General George C. Marshall

Conference Name	Code Name	Location	Dates	Primary Participants*
Atlantic	RIVIERA	Argentia, Newfoundland	8/9 – 12/41	Roosevelt, Churchill
1st Washington	ARCADIA	Washington, DC	12/22/41 – 1/14/42	Roosevelt, Churchill
London	MODICUM	London, England	4/4 – 13/42	Churchill, British General Staff
2nd Washington		Washington, DC	6/20 – 25/42	Roosevelt, Churchill
Casablanca	SYMBOL	Casablanca, Morocco	1/14 – 24/43	Roosevelt, Churchill, De Gaulle, Giraud
3rd Washington	TRIDENT	Washington, DC	5/12 – 27/43	Roosevelt, Churchill
Quebec	QUADRANT	Quebec City, CN	8/17 – 24/43	Roosevelt, Churchill
Cairo	SEXTANT	Cairo, Egypt	11/23 – 26/43	Roosevelt, Churchill, Chiang kai-Shek
Tehran	EUREKA	Tehran, Iran	11/28 – 12/1/43	Roosevelt, Churchill, Stalin
2nd Cairo	SEXTANT	Cairo, Egypt	12/4 – 6/43	Roosevelt, Churchill, Inonu
2nd Quebec	OCTAGON	Quebec City, CN	9/12 – 16/44	Roosevelt, Churchill
Malta	ARGONAUT & CRICKET	Valleta, Malta	1/30 – 2/2/45	Combined Chiefs, Roosevelt, Churchill
Yalta	ARGONAUT & MAGNETO	Yalta, USSR	2/4 – 11/45	Roosevelt, Churchill, Stalin
Potsdam	TERMINAL	Potsdam, Germany	7/17 – 8/2/45	Truman, Churchill, Stalin, Atlee

Heads of state were accompanied by key military advisors and staff.

650

World War II Operations, Code Names

Code Name	Objective	Actual Date	Comments
ALAMO	Invasion of New Britain (Papua, New Guinea)	December 1943	
ANAKIM	Recapture of Burma	N/A	Canceled
ANVIL	Invasion of south coast of France	N/A	Replaced by DRAGOON
BOLERO	Build-up of forces and supplies for cross-channel invasion of France	June 1944	
BUCCANEER	Invasion of the Andaman Islands (Bay of Bengal)	N/A	Canceled
CATAPULT	Accost and neutralize French Naval vessels	July 1940	
COBRA	Allied break-out from Cotertin Peninsula (northwest France)	July 1944	
CORONET	Invasion of Honshu Island, Japan	N/A	Canceled (Japan surrendered)
DRAGOON	Invasion of south coast of France	August 1944	
GYMNAST	Invasion of French North Africa	N/A	Replaced by TORCH
HUSKY	Invasion of Sicily (southern coast)	July 1943	
MARKET GARDEN	Airborne assault into Netherlands to bypass Seigfreid Line	September 1944	
OLYMPIC	Invasion of Kyushu Island, Japan	N/A	Canceled (Japan surrendered)
OVERLORD	Cross-channel invasion of France	June 1944	
PLUNDER	Pincer operation to trap German forces in the Ruhr	March 1945	
PRICELESS	Proposal for post-HUSKY operations	N/A	Never implemented
QUICKSILVER	Formation of the fictitious First US Army Group FUSAG)	January 1944	
ROUNDUP	Cross-channel invasion of France (Normandy coast)	N/A	Replaced by OVERLORD
SHINGLE	Invasion of Anzio, Italy	January 1944	
SLEDGEHAMMER	Cross-channel invasion of France (Limited scope contingency)	N/A	Replaced by OVERLORD
TORCH	Invasion of French North Africa	October 1942	

Acknowledgments

Undertaking and completing a book of this scope requires the assistance and support of many individuals and institutions. My sincere appreciation must begin with the George C. Marshall International Center, whose president and CEO, Patricia Magee Daly, has been committed to this effort from the beginning. While she gave me the freedom to tell the story of Marshall as I saw fit, she made certain that funding was available for the resources needed to produce the book and trusted me implicitly to finish this project. I cannot thank the board members, docents, and other volunteers at the center enough for their enthusiastic endorsement of this work, and for never doubting me when once more I told them, "No, the book isn't quite finished yet, but it will be." Certain board members along with many docent readers who have considerable knowledge of Marshall and his world scoured early versions of the text, without benefit of photos, providing valuable editing suggestions. With my appreciation, they include Bill and Diane Babics, Diane Hinckley, Bonita Metz, Warren Reufer, and Keith Wauchope. Special thanks also go to Bill Brooks, Jack Partlow, Frederick Morefield, and Anne Thomas, who read later drafts of the text through the China Mission chapter.

I am deeply indebted to Pamela Banks, Tom Bowers, and Michelle Thrush, who not only read the earlier versions but also spent many hours painstakingly checking all 20 chapters, providing invaluable feedback. Their input was crucial in both finding pesky "gremlin" errors and shaping the narrative flow of the book. A thank-you is also in order to Don Eager, who assisted me in contacting museum sites, newspapers, and magazines to find copyright information about photos that I wished to include. Don also developed the conference and code name charts that appear at the back of the book. My gratitude goes to Tom Flynn, who was on the list of early readers, and in addition carefully reviewed the finished product.

In the development of various Marshall-related projects culminating in the writing of this biography, I enjoyed the vigorous support of two past board presidents, Stephen C. Price and Frederick L. Morefield. I am also indebted to my friend and colleague, Alisa Soderquist, who, as the Center's exchange coordinator, was important in providing a European perspective, especially as it related to the post–World War II sections of the book.

For the initial set up and formatting of the text, I am grateful to Janet R.

van der Vaart, currently the Director of Grants at the Center. I must also acknowledge four impressive people who were crucial in the design and production of the book, beginning with the copy editor, Susan Burke, who contributed immensely to a clean and professional text. My sincere thanks also to Barbara Boughton, who typed hundreds of endnotes and bibliography entries with great care, meticulously cross-checking every four-line-long web address or book title. Graphic designer Ryan Jenkins placed the book into its publishable form and was a wonder in converting Word files and photographs into a proper print format. He never wavered when I requested one more change in a chapter title or asked him to move an image from this page to that. Finally, I appreciate the detailed and careful way that Estalita Slivosky indexed the book—no proper noun could escape her careful eye. From start to finish, this support team made my life easier, since in addition to being consummate professionals, they also happen to be kind, considerate, and affirming individuals.

This book would not have been possible without the George C. Marshall Museum and Library in Lexington, Virginia. My introduction to this remarkable institution came in 1998 when Anne H. Horstman, who at that time was the director of the Center's Education Programs and would later become its executive director, selected me to develop a curriculum package suitable for high school students about the leadership and legacy of George C. Marshall. Like Patricia Daly, she valued my judgment as an educator and encouraged me at every step along the way. With her support, I soon traveled to the Lexington site, where I enthusiastically delved into the rich materials available there. Through the staff at the museum and library I met Mary Scott Scutt, with whom I partnered to write a short biography of Marshall for inclusion in these education materials. Mary introduced me to Dr. Larry I. Bland, who for almost 30 years was the editor of the *Papers of George Catlett Marshall*. From that first meeting Larry was unstinting in offering his perspective, skills, and prodigious knowledge every time I asked one more question about George Marshall. I have missed his generous assistance since his untimely death in 2007. In producing this book, other staff members there have been especially helpful. Jeffrey S. Kozak, the archivist and assistant librarian, patiently aided me in identifying the photographs that would enhance the book and provided valuable input regarding copyright issues. Mame Warren, assistant editor of volumes six and seven of the *Papers*, generously took time to provide copies of documents not yet published that she knew would be of particular value to me. Joanne D. Hartog, assistant editor of *Papers*, provided both tangible assistance in identifying documents and moral support as I undertook this ambitious effort.

Not only was the staff at the Marshall Museum and Library gracious and helpful, but also the resources available there were absolutely essential to writing this book. The mother lode was the superbly annotated *Papers of George Catlett Marshall*, now edited by Mark A. Stoler. The availability of these thick tan treasures meant that I could study Marshall from the comfort of my office; otherwise, I would have spent many months in Lexington searching for the original documents on my own. In writing about Marshall's professional life, I first began with these pages, telling his story as often as possible by using his exact words from the letters, reports, or speeches found therein. Following close on the heels of *Papers* as a fine resource was *George C. Marshall, Interviews and Reminiscences for Forrest C. Pogue*, edited by Larry and Joellen Bland, which included marvelous anecdotal material straight from Marshall's recollections.

The next tier of rich material was the four-volume definitive biography of Marshall by Forrest C. Pogue. Especially when the writing covered Marshall's military career, they were the "go-to" source, although Larry Weintraub's *15 Stars* and Robert Andrews' *Masters and Commanders* were also very helpful. Other exceptionally valuable published works included Ed Cray's comprehensive and engaging biography, *George C. Marshall, Soldier and Statesman*, as well as Mark Stoler's scholarly and succinct *George C. Marshall: Soldier-Statesman of the American Century*. For background on the European Recovery Program, Greg Behrman's *The Most Noble Adventure* was excellent, particularly in following the narrative thread of the program's complex development. For material related to post–World War II topics, Walter Isaacson and Evan Thomas's *The Wise Men*, as well as David McCullough's *Truman*, were highly beneficial. Finally, I would be remiss if I didn't mention the value of the Eisenhower, Roosevelt, and Truman Presidential Libraries. Their websites were a treasure trove of original documents, and, miracle of miracles, if I still had a question, the human voice of a research archivist was only a phone call away five days a week.

For three years I worked on this book. Throughout the process, my family has been such an important touchstone, always bringing me back to that which I treasure above all else—their love and support. My husband, Ken, could not have done more to help me during these many months. He has forgone travel, taken on added household tasks normally in my bailiwick, and never failed to gently ask me at the end of a long workday, "How did it go? Do you think you made progress?" In many ways, Ken reminds me of George Marshall: principled, disciplined, utterly without artifice, and solid as a rock.

Index

659

speech at Westminster College, 518
support of Soviets by, 129–130
at Trident Conference, 217–222
on Vienna, 328–331, 350–351
visit with Bradley, 336
visit with Marshall, 586
in Washington, 215
at the White House, 165
CIGS (Chief of the Imperial General Staff), 159–160, 177
CIO (Congress of Industrial Organizations), 547
Citadel, 233
Clark, Greenville, 126
Clark, Mark, 187, 199, 251, 296, 303–304, 309, 311, 327–328, 331–332, 403
Clarke, Carter W., 362
Clay, Lucius, 521
Clayton, William, 509, 531–532, 541–543, 547
Clemençeau, Georges, 68
Clifford, Clark, 516, 548, 567–571
Cline, Ray S., 254
Coal Lick Run, 6
Cobra operation, 333–334, 650
Coles, Edmund, 493
Collins, J. Lawton, 285
Colombia, 562–564
Combined Bomber Offensive, 233
Combined Chiefs of Staff, 166, 235, 259, 268–269, 297, 321–322, 324, 392–393, 395–396, 413, 440, 442, 445
Committee of Three, 484
Committee on Foreign Relations, 511
Communist Party Honor Guard, 488
Communist Party, 482–483
Company C (10th Pennsylvania regiment), 26
Compton, Karl, 452
Conant, James B., 431–432, 532, 533, 532–533
Congress, 50, 377, 388, 432, 433, 435, 463, 466, 473
Conner, Fox, 63, 65, 165
Cooper, James Fenimore
The Last of the Mohicans, 8

Coral Sea, Battle of the, 180
Coronet Operation, 430–431, 650
Corregidor, 170
COSSAC (chief of staff to the supreme allied commander), 250–251
Cotentin Peninsula, 319–320, 333, 341, 348
Council of Foreign Ministers, 443
Council of World Affairs, 629
Craig, Malin, 33, 116, 117
Cray, Ed
on Algiers press conference, 223
on the Allies, 230, 360
on Americans under European command, 56
on Anzio, 297, 302
on Arab-American relations, 567
on atomic bomb, 437
on Barbarossa operation, 128–129
on Berlin, 407
on bringing Chiang to Cairo, 256
on Casablanca, 204–205
on Communists, 480
on concentration camps, 565
on cost of war, 310
on Craig, 116–117
on de Gaulle, 324–325
on distribution of manpower, 290
on Eisenhower, 392–393
on end of war in Japan, 435
on honor guard for Marshall, 403
on inadequacies, 59
on Japan/China relationship, 477
on Joint Chiefs meetings, 279
on Korean War, 616
on Lend-Lease program, 489–490
on MacArthur, 348, 353–356, 617, 621
on Marshall, 40–41, 85, 111, 164, 201, 276–277, 364–365, 370, 373, 571
on mediation between Soviets and Japan, 452
on Moscow Conference, 539
on Overlord operation, 294
on Pearl Harbor investigation, 470, 472–473
on Potsdam, 439–440, 448

at funeral of Marshall, 646
headquarters in Reims, France, 412–413
Husky operation, 221–223, 228
on invasion, 196
on Italian invasion, 287–290
in Italy, 263
on Japan, 172
in London, 189, 293
on Market-Garden plan, 365–367
Marshall Memorandum, 175
Marshall on, 324–325, 340–345, 371
meetings with Marshall, 283–285, 368–369, 392
in Moscow, 437
in Nanking, 498
negotiation with Giraud, 198
Normandy invasion, 312, 322
Overlord operation, 274–275, 314–316
in Paris, 345–346
plan to end French resistance, 200–202
presidential candidacy of, 633, 634
return from Europe by, 435–436
role in European Theater, 455
on Rosenberg, 603
Strout on, 249
Tunisia, 212–215
'unity of command' concept, 193, 232
on war in Europe, 374
Eisenhower, Mamie, 284, 371
Eisenhower Doctrine, 175–176
El Alamein, 193–202
Elbe River, 409–410, 411
Eliot, T.S., 534
Elizabeth II, Queen of England, 636, 637
Emmanuel Episcopal Church, 90
Enabling Act of March 1933, 108
Encyclopedia Britannica, 431–432
English Channel, 316
Enola Gay, 450, 451–452
Enterprise (carrier), 181, 203
ERP (European Recovery Program), 545–546, 556–557, 560, 562, 573–574, 580, 637–638
Ethiopia, invasion of, 107

ETO (European Theater of Operations), 187, 300, 380, 391, 455
Eureka Operation, 253, 266, 649
Europe. See also specific topics
deteriorating situation in, 115
victory in, 391–415
Europe First Strategy, 181, 242
European to Pacific Theater, 374
Executive Headquarters, 487
Executive Order 9319, 292

F

Falaise, France, 335
Far East Air Forces, 455
Farrell, Leo, 117
Fascist Party, 107
Federal Emergency Relief Administration, 115
Feng Yu-hsiang, 476
Ferdinand, Francis, 44
Ferguson, Homer, 473
Fermi, Enrico, 434
FF.I. (French Forces of the Interior), 344
Field Day, 30
Fifteenth Infantry Regiment, U.S., 75
Fifth Army, U.S., 296, 311, 327, 403
Fifth Infantry Brigade, of 3rd Division, U.S., 99–105
Fifth Panzer Army, German, 202
Fifth U.S. Marine Division, 427
Fiji, 279
Finland, 348
Fire Island, New York, 89, 90, 105, 310
"Fireside Chats," 120
First Armored Division, U.S., 228–229, 306–308
First Army, U.S., 290, 335, 367, 380, 383
First Division, U.S., 59, 61, 70, 84, 288, 320
First Infantry Division, 55
First United States Army Group, 334
First Washington Conference, 649
Fish, Hamilton, 555
five-star rank, 376–377

Manhattan Engineer District, 431–432

Manhattan Project, 400, 431–435, 452, 593

"manifest destiny," 26

Manila, Philippines, 27, 32, 41–42, 168, 170, 423

Mao Tse-tung, 110, 237, 477, 482–483, 487, 488, 498, 591–592, 612, 618

March, Peyton, 71

Marianas Islands, 351, 426, 438, 448, 454

Market-Garden two-pronged plan, 365–366, 650

Marseilles, France, 337, 392

Marshall (Lubetkin), 55

Marshall, Elizabeth Carter Coles "Lily" (first wife),

deteriorating health and death of, 82–83

at Fort Leavenworth, 36

initial relationship with, 20

in Japan, 43

in New York, 77

relationship with Rose, 74–75

returned to Philippines with, 44

R&R with, 33, 70–71

social life of, 79–80

U.S. victory tour with, 72–73

wedding to, 22, 24

Marshall, George Catlett, Jr.

addressing American Legion Convention, 358, 360

in Africa, 205

at Allen's grave, 331–332

ancestry of, 9

applied pressure to bump up numbers of front line combatants, 388, 390

appointed Rosenberg, 603

Army commission granted, 22, 24

arrived in Quebec, 234

asked to act as secretary of defense, 600, 601, 602

asked to lecture at War College, Washington, D.C., 81

asked to represent U.S. at coronation, 636

assigned to 33rd Division of Illinois National Guard in Chicago, 96–97

as assistant chief of staff of War Plans Division, 104, 106

in Berlin, 521, 523

on Berlin Airlift, 574

in Bogota, Colombia, 562–564

as brigadier general, 99

business ventures of, 5–7

in Casablanca, 206–207

on CCC, 104

celebrated final victory of World War II, 456

as chairman of American Battle Monuments Commission, 631

as Chief of Staff of Operations, 53

childhood in Uniontown, Pennsylvania (1880-1897), 1–11

in China, 470, 491, 499–500

college years at Virginia Military Institute (VMI) (1897-1901), 13–24

commanding battalion of 8th Infantry, 92

commuting from Leesburg to Washington, 512

confirmation by U.S. Senate, 601

constant travel of, 556

on coronation of Queen Elizabeth II, 636–637

correspondence of, 101, 173–174, 179, 362–365, 582, 626–627, 640, 643

courtship with Katherine, 88–89

death of, 646

death of Lily's mother, 87

as deputy chief of staff, 115

on draft bill, 126

as executive officer of Fifteenth Infantry, 77–81

on fierce competition between services, 162–163

on finishing war in Pacific, 421–422

at Fort Leavenworth, 36

in France, 368–373, 370–371

funeral of, 646

health of, 575, 577, 583, 638, 641, 646

on his future, 582

603, 605
updated methods of military tactics at Infantry School, 84–85
as U.S. Army chief of staff, 117
at Vancouver Barracks, Washington, 99–105
on Vandenberg, 548, 550
visit with Churchill, 586
visit with Pope Pius XII, 580–583
visit with Truman, 600
visits with Rose Page Wilson, 645
wartime conferences attended by, 649
wedding to Katherine, 90
wedding to Lily, 22, 24
on welfare of ordinary soldiers, 282
winter in Pinehurst after retirement, 631
on worsening conditions in Europe, 553
wrote formal request to be relieved of staff position for troop duty, 62
as a young lieutenant (1902-1916), 26–46
Marshall, George Catlett, Sr. (father)
active in Masons, 5
death of, 40
influence of on Marshall, Jr., 8–11
wrote regarding Army entrance, 20, 22
Marshall, Hero of Our Times (Mosely), 94
Marshall, John, 9, 14
Marshall, Katherine Boyce Tupper Brown (second wife),
about, 87–105
as an author, 512–513
at Anzio, 580
on Anzio, 308
in China, 481, 490, 491, 498–499
Christmas 1944, 385–386
courtship of, 88–89
on death of Allen, 308–309, 310
on dental health, 103–104
Fort Myer, 307
health of, 641
home life of, 132–134
on Marshall after Pearl Harbor, 174

on Marshall having to go to China after retirement, 470
during Marshall's retirement, 626–627
in Miami, 283–285, 290
on Milwaukee, 634
in Paris, 579–583
planning sisters' wedding, 529
during post-surgery recovery of Marshall, 584–585
preparing for Christmas in 1943, 280
preparing for Marshall's retirement, 462, 463
preparing to leave Fort Myer, 252–253
provided birthday cake for Dill, 161
received oil painting from Churchill, 637
on Roosevelt's declining health, 396
R&R of, 82, 346–347, 439
surprised Marshall with Dodona Manor, 179–180
thank you letter to Churchill, 637
Together: Annals of an Army Wife, 87, 132, 512–513, 641
upon Marshall receiving Oak Leaf Cluster, 466
upon Roosevelt's death, 408–409
visited Stimson on Long Island, 490
on Washington D.C., 391
at Washington Redskins game with Marshall, 190–191
wedding to Marshall, 90
Marshall, Laura Emily Bradford (mother), 1, 10
Marshall, Marie Louise (sister), 1, 33
Marshall, Stuart (brother), 1, 10, 13, 33, 42–43
"Marshall Day," 634
Marshall Island, 209
Marshall Library, 644
Marshall Memorandum, 175–176
Marshall Plan, 533, 558, 559–561
The Marshall Plan: A Fifty Year Perspective (Woods), 545–546
Martin, Joe, 618
Masaryk, Jan, 541, 557–558
Massachusetts National Guard, 40

British leaders on, 299
at Chateau Frontenac, 347, 348
on Chennault, 240
on Chiang Kai-shek, 477–478
on China, 256
communication with staff, 162–164
conference with Churchill, 207
on conference with Stalin, 260
correspondence about Marshall, 98
on cost of war, 304–305
on Darlan, 200
D-Day prayer from, 317
on de Gaulle, 311–312, 324–325
death of, 408–410
declining health of, 395–398
discussion with Churchill, 156
"Fireside Chat," 120
freezing of Japanese assets by, 142–143, 149
funding request to, 122–123
funeral of, 410–411
on gas warfare, 437
on going to sea on a Friday, 253–254
on Malaya, 395
on Manhattan Project, 432–433
Marshall on, 380
meeting with Churchill, 134–137, 210–211
on Munich Agreement, 113–114
New Deal principles, 131
on Pearl Harbor, 361, 365
on planes, 125
presiding over first plenary session, 400
pressuring Congress, 377
proposed Lend-Lease bill, 128
received globe from U.S. Army, 203
on Roundup operation, 218–219
running for reelection, 190
seeking to avert hostilities, 148
serving second term, 111
Sledgehammer Operation, 176, 181–186, 188
on Sommervell issue, 248
State of the Union Address, 115–116
on Stilwell, 373–374
support of Chiang, 356–357

"Ten Points," 144–145
visit with Morgan, 251
Yalta meetings, 399
Roosevelt, Theodore, Jr., 58, 342
Root, Elihu, 34–35
Rosenberg, Anna M., 226, 602–603
Rosenthal, Joe, 427
Rotary Club, 629
Roundup Operation, 178, 188, 189, 273, 650
Royal Air Force, 127, 406
Rusk, Dean, 610, 620
Russia, 128–129, 523–528. See also Soviet Union
Russian Crimea, 392
Russo-Japanese War (1905), 41, 43
Rutherford, Lucy Mercer, 408
Ryukyus, 353, 410, 438

S

SA (storm troopers), 108
Sacred Cow, (plane), 368
St. Georges Hotel, 223, 225, 274
St. Lawrence River, 233
St. Malo, France, 334, 348
St. Mihiel, France, 63–69, 77
St. Nazaire, France, 334
St. Vith, Belgium, 379
Saipan, 348, 426, 448
Saki, (Soviet air base), 398
Salzburg, Austria, 449–450
Samuels, Gertrude, 590
Santa Fe, New Mexico, 440–441
Sarajevo, Bosnia, 44
Sardinia, 206, 221
Sato, Naotake, 448, 449, 452
Saunders, Alan, 62, 474
George C. Marshall, General for Peace, 69
Savannah, Georgia, 92
Scottish regiment, 403–404
Sea Lion Operation, 127
SEAC (Southeast Asia Command), 240
Second Battle of the Marne, 63
Second Front, 183
Second Armored Division, U.S., 345

correspondence with Marshall, 374–375

on Japanese embargo, 142–143

meeting at sea, 134

meeting with Marshall, 151

as member of war cabinet, 152

transferred to London, 163

State Department, U.S., 474, 480, 507–508

Stayer, Morrison, 85, 87

Stettinius, Edward, 396, 400, 585

Stilwell, Joseph

on Chiang, 478

in China, 237–240

as commander of China Theater, 85

disagreement with Mountbatten, 299

dispute with Chiang, 343–344, 355–357

forewarned by Marshall of his impending sacking, 373

Marshall on, 238

plenary meetings, 256, 258

Stimson, Henry

Arcadia Conference, 165–166

argued for an accelerated draft, 387–388

ASTP, 292

on atomic bomb, 431–432, 434–435, 445–447

correspondence with Marshall, 462–463

on crises, 172

on Hiroshima, 451

made Hobby director of WAAC, 226

on Manhattan Project, 434

on Marshall, 413–414, 466

Marshall and Katherine's visit to, 490

Marshall on, 507

meeting with Marshall, 394

meeting with Truman, 409–410

as member of war cabinet, 152

at National Guard maneuver, 40

Potsdam, 441

questioned Marshall on Dresden, 404

on Railway Brotherhoods, 281

on Russian Bulge, 406

on Sommervell's reorganization plan, 245

support of early 1945 draft bill by, 388

threatened to resign, 161

visit with Churchill, 441

in White House, 231–232

Stoler, Mark, 18, 31–32, 44, 48, 61–64, 111, 117–118, 162, 175, 178, 226, 238, 273, 300, 351, 466, 486, 492, 500–501, 509, 558, 595, 603, 623

Strang, William, 538

Strout, Richard, 249

Stuart, John, 494, 495–496, 498

Stumme, Georg von, 195

Sudetenland, 112

Suez Canal, 185, 194

suicide planes, 424, 429

Sulzberger, Arthur Hays, 634

Summerall, Charles, 83

Summersby, Kay, 284

Sun Yat-sen, 78, 476, 478

Supreme Military Command, 148

Suresnes American Cemetery, 631

surgical thyroidectomy, 99, 101

Suzuki, Kantaro, 448

Swing, Robert Gram, 354

Sword of Stalingrad, 266–267

Sword operation, 319–320

Symbol Conference, 649

T

Taaffe, Stephen, 429

Taft, Robert, 53, 406, 407

A Tale of Two Cities (Dickens), 365

Tehran, 262, 272, 273, 282, 296

Tehran Conference, 326, 649

"Ten Points" program, 144–145, 148, 149, 151–152

Tenadores (boat), 54

Tennessee (battleship), 152

10th Armored Division, U.S., 379

10th Army, German, 303, 304

10th Army, U.S., 429

10th Panzers, German, 286

10th Pennsylvania Regiment, U.S., 26

Terminal conference, 649

Rehabilitation, 408
Warsaw, Poland, 349, 425, 443
Washington, George, 8, 377, 497
Washington and Lee University, 14
Washington Barracks, 82
Washington Times Herald, 340
Wasp (carrier), 203
Wavell, Sir Achibald, 170
Webster, Donovan, 238, 239
Wedemeyer, Albert C., 357, 476, 480–481, 482, 483, 488
Wehrmacht, 118, 120, 123, 378, 385, 404
Weimar Republic, 107, 108
Weintraub, Stanley, 244, 320, 390
Welsh regiment, 403–404
West Point, 17–18, 284, 458
West Virginia (battleship), 152
West Wall (Siegfried Line), 344, 346, 365–366, 404
Westminster Abbey, 636
Wheeler, Burton, 155
"White Force," 41–42
White House, 22, 70, 231, 408–409, 414, 474, 478
White Sulphur Springs, West Virginia, 284
White Swan Tavern, 3
Wilhelm, Kaiser, 50, 439
Williamsburg, Virginia, 219
Willys-Overland Company, 627
Wilson, Henry Maitland "Jumbo," 327, 328, 329, 336, 376
Wilson, John, 464, 486
Wilson, Rose Page, 464, 486, 634, 640, 643, 646
General Marshall Remembered, 73
Wilson, Woodrow, 47, 48, 49, 50, 56, 67–68
Winant, John, 156
Winn, James, Jr. (son-in-law), 134, 225, 228–229
Winn, Jimmy (stepgrandson), 228–229, 280, 385–386
Winn, Kitty (stepgranddaughter), 228–229, 280, 307, 385–386

Winn, Molly Brown (stepdaughter)
about, 87–91
Christmas 1944, 385–386
correspondence with Marshall, 133
home life of, 98–99, 105, 228–229, 469
marriage to Captain James Winn, Jr., 134
preparing for Christmas in 1943, 280
Women's Republican Club, 593
Woodberry Forest School, 629
Woodring, Harry, 111
Woods, Randall B.
The Marshall Plan: A Fifty Year Perspective, 545–546
Works Progress Administration, 115
World War I Distinguished Service Medal, 466
World War II, 42, 84, 85, 650

X
X Corps, 614, 616

Y
Yalta, 392, 399–402, 649
Yamamoto, Isoroku, 145, 148, 180–181
Yangtze River, 482
"Yellow Peril," 41
Yenan, 477
Yorktown (carrier), 181
Youth Movement, 484

Z
Zhukov, Georgi, 202, 437, 445–446
Zilch, Joe, 555
Zimmermann, Arthur, 50
Zionist support, 565–566

Endnotes

Chapter 1
1. Bland and Bland, *Interviews and Reminiscences*, 20.
2. Bland, "The Lexington Connection," 508.
3. Bland, *Papers*, vol. 1, *The Soldierly Spirit*, 6.
4. Bland and Bland, *Interviews and Reminiscences*, 37.
5. Frye, *Marshall, Citizen Soldier*, 32.

Chapter 2
1. Bland and Bland, *Interviews and Reminiscences*, 40.
2. Bland, *Fully the Equal of the Best*, 3.
3. Bland, "The Lexington Connection," 510.
4. Stoler, *George C. Marshall*, 9.
5. Frye, *Marshall, Citizen Soldier*, 55.
6. Bland, *Fully the Equal of the Best*, 9.
7. Ibid., 5.
8. Bland and Bland, *Interviews and Reminiscences*, 118.
9. Stoler, *George C. Marshall*, 10.
10. Bland, *Fully the Equal of the Best*, 10.
11. Frye, *Marshall, Citizen Soldier*, 55.
12. Bland, "The Lexington Connection," 513.
13. Bland and Bland, *Interviews and Reminiscences*, 91.
14. Cray, *General of the Army*, 29.
15. Bland and Bland, *Interviews and Reminiscences*, 86.

Chapter 3
1. Bland, *Papers*, vol. 1, *The Soldierly Spirit*, 9.
2. Bailey and Kennedy, *American Pageant*, 576.
3. Bland and Bland, *Interviews and Reminiscences*, 122.
4. Ibid.
5. Ibid., 125.
6. Frye, *Marshall, Citizen Soldier*, 75.
7. Pogue, *Marshall*, vol. 1, *Education of a General*, 78.
8. Ibid.
9. Stoler, *George C. Marshall*, 17.
10. Pogue, *Marshall*, vol. 1, *Education of a General*, 84.
11. Ibid., 89.
12. Bland, *Papers*, vol. 1, *The Soldierly Spirit*, 36.
13. Stoler, *George C. Marshall*, 21.
14. Frye, *Marshall, Citizen Soldier*, 87.
15. Bland and Bland, *Interviews and Reminiscences*, 160.
16. Stoler, *George C. Marshall*, 22.
17. Bland, *Papers*, vol. 1, *The Soldierly Spirit*, 39–41.
18. Cray, *General of the Army*, 41.
19. Pogue, *Marshall*, vol. 1, *Education* of a General, 120.
20. Cray, *General of the Army*, 44.
21. Ibid.
22. Frye, *Marshall, Citizen Soldier*, 110.
23. Bland, *Papers*, vol. 1, *The Soldierly Spirit*, 83–84.
24. Stoler, *George C. Marshall*, 27.
25. Ibid., 29.
26. Bland, *Papers*, vol. 1, *The Soldierly Spirit*, 96.
27. Pogue, *Marshall*, vol. 1, *Education of a General*, 130.

Chapter 4
1. Bailey and Kennedy, *American Pageant*, 654.
2. Stoler, *George C. Marshall*, 33.
3. Ibid., 34.
4. Pogue, *Marshall*, vol. 1, *Education of a General*, 136.
5. Ibid., 138.
6. Frye, *Marshall, Citizen Soldier*, 120.
7. Bailey and Kennedy, *American Pageant*, 652.
8. Ibid.
9. Ibid., 653.
10. Bland, *Papers*, vol. 1, *The Soldierly Spirit*, 100.
11. Bland and Bland, *Interviews and Reminiscences*, 186.
12. Bland, *Papers*, vol. 1, *The Soldierly Spirit*, 100.
13. Ibid.

14. Ibid., 104.
15. Bland and Bland, *Interviews and Reminiscences*, 189.
16. Marshall, G.C., *Memoirs of My Services*, 9.
17. Bland, *Papers*, vol. 1, *The Soldierly Spirit*, 646.
18. Lubetkin, *Marshall*, 38.
19. Pogue, *Marshall*, vol. 1, *Education of a General*, 147.
20. Stoler, *George C. Marshall*, 35.
21. Cray, *General of the Army*, 55.
22. Marshall, G.C., *Memoirs of My Services*, 26.
23. Pogue, *Marshall*, vol. 1, *Education of a General*, 150.
24. Bland and Bland, *Interviews and Reminiscences*, 197.
25. Cray, *General of the Army*, 57.
26. Bland and Bland, *Interviews and Reminiscences*, 198.
27. Frye, *Marshall, Citizen Soldier*, 136–37.
28. Bland, *Papers*, vol. 1, *The Soldierly Spirit*, 129.
29. Stoler, *George C. Marshall*, 38.
30. Saunders, *General for Peace*, 32.
31. Cray, *General of the Army*, 63.
32. Stoler, *George C. Marshall*, 38.
33. Ibid., 39.
34. Cray, *General of the Army*, 69.
35. Ibid.
36. Marshall, G.C., *Memoirs of My Services*, 138.
37. Stoler, *George C. Marshall*, 40.
38. Frye, *Marshall, Citizen Soldier*, 159.
39. Marshall, G.C., *Memoirs of My Services*, 139.
40. Stoler, *George C. Marshall*, 41.
41. Current et al., *American History*, 664.
42. Bailey and Kennedy, *American Pageant*, 707.
43. Marshall, G.C., *Memoirs of My Services*, 218.
44. Saunders, *General for Peace*, 34.
45. Marshall, G.C., *Memoirs of My Services*, 167.
46. Wilson, *General Marshall*, 58–59.
47. Ibid., 64
48. Ibid., 11.
49. Ibid., 144.

Chapter 5
1. Bland, *Papers*, vol. 1, *The Soldierly Spirit*, 265.
2. Stoler, *George C. Marshall*, 52.
3. Pogue, *Marshall*, vol. 1, *Education of a General*, 232–33.
4. Cray, *General of the Army*, 98.
5. Bland, *Papers*, vol. 1, *Soldierly Spirit*, 277.
6. Ibid., 286.
7. Ibid., 295.
8. Ibid., 293–94.
9. Pogue, *Marshall*, vol. 1, *Education of a General*, 246.
10. Frye, *Marshall, Citizen Soldier*, 201.
11. Bland, *Papers*, vol. 1, *The Soldierly Spirit*, 315.
12. Pogue, *Marshall*, vol. 1, *Education of a General*, 247.
13. Bland, *Papers*, vol. 1, *The Soldierly Spirit*, 383.
14. Cray, *General of the Army*, 105.
15. Stoler, *George C. Marshall*, 56.
16 Cray, *General of the Army*, 104.
17. Stoler, *George C. Marshall*, 56.
18. Wilson, *General Marshall Remembered*, 185.
19. Marshall, K.T., *Together*, 2–3.
20. Pogue, *Marshall*, vol. 1, *Education of a General*, 266–67.
21. Marshall, K.T., *Together*, 6.
22. Pogue, *Marshall*, vol. 1, *Education of a General*, 269.
23. Ibid., 278.
24. Cray, *General of the Army*, 113.
25. McEntee, "CCC and National Defense," 1.
26 Bland, *Papers*, vol. 1, *The Soldierly Spirit*, 392.
27. Ibid., 392–96.
28. Mosley, *Hero of Our Times*, 105.
29. Marshall, K.T., *Together*, 17.
30. Ibid.
31. Cray, *General of the Army*, 116–17.
32. Pogue, *Marshall*, vol. 1, *Education of a General*, 282–83.

33. Ibid., 285–86.
34. Ibid., 290–91.
35. Cray, *General of the Army*, 119.
36. Frye, *Marshall, Citizen Soldier*, 235.
37. Marshall, K.T., *Together*, 22–24.
38. Mosley, *Hero of Our Times*, 115.
39. Frye, *Marshall, Citizen Soldier*, 237.
40. Marshall, K.T., *Together*, 25–27.
41. Ibid., 28.
42. Frye, *Marshall, Citizen Soldier*, 238–39.
43. Pogue, *Marshall, vol. 1, Education of a General*, 311.
44. Marshall, K.T., *Together*, 30.
45. Pogue, *Marshall*, vol. 1, *Education of a General*, 308.
46. Bland, *Papers*, vol. 1, *The Soldierly Spirit*, 598.
47. Stoler, *George C. Marshall*, 62.
48. Pogue, *Marshall*, vol. 1, *Education of a General*, 316.

Chapter 6
1. Pollard, "Problems and Failures," 30.
2. "Benito Mussolini (1883–1945)."-
3. Mussolini, "What Is Fascism.*"*
4. Pollard, "Problems and Failures," 28.
5. Current et al., *American History*, 762.
6. Meier, "Adolf Hitler's Rise to Power,*"* 5–6.
7. "Adolf Hitler Biography,*"* 2.
8. "World War II in Europe."
9. Pogue, *Marshall*, vol. 1, *Education of a General*, 313.
10. Zich, *The Rising Sun*, 19.
11. Ibid., 22.
12. Ibid., 23.
13. Ibid.
14. Cray, *General of the Army*, 126.
15. Stoler, *George C. Marshall*, 63.
16. Ibid.
17. Ibid., 64.
18. "1938: Peace for Our Time."
19. Ibid.
20. "Munich Agreement. House of Commons, October 5, 1938."
21. Cray, *General of the Army*, 129.
22. Stoler, *George C. Marshall*, 64–65.
23. Pogue, *Marshall*, vol. 1, *Education of a General*, 322.
24. Cray, *General of the Army*, 131.
25. Stoler, *George C. Marshall*, 64.
26. Roberts, *Masters and Commanders*, 26.
27. Bland, *Papers*, vol. 1, *The Soldierly Spirit*, 651.
28. Ibid.
29. Pogue, *Marshall*, vol. 1, *Education of a General*, 326.
30. Cray, *General of the Army*, 135.
31. Ibid., 136.
32. Ibid., 137.
33. Ibid., 138.
34. Bland, *Papers*, vol. 1, *The Soldierly Spirit*, 641–42.
35. Cray, *General of the Army*, 139.
36. Stoler, *George C. Marshall*, 66.
37. Saunders, *General for Peace*, 51.
38. Bland, *Papers*, vol. 2, *We Cannot Delay*, 47
39. Stoler, *George C. Marshall*, 69.
40. Cray, *General of the Army*, 151.
41. Ibid., 152.
42. Pogue, *Marshall*, vol. 2, *Ordeal and Hope*, 28–29.
43. Ibid., 29.
44. Ibid., 30–31.
45. Cray, *General of the Army*, 154–55.
46. Ibid.
47. Mosley, *World War II*, 19.
48. Churchill, "Their Finest Hour."
49. Pogue, *Marshall*, vol. 2, *Ordeal and Hope*, 51–52.
50. Cray, *General of the Army*, 167.
51. Stoler, *George C. Marshall*, 76.
52. Cray, *General of the Army*, 171.

53. Stoler, *George C. Marshall*, 77.
54. Churchill, *Memoirs*, 376.
55. "Lend Lease: Franklin Roosevelt's Press Conference," 3.
56. Bland, *Papers*, vol. 2, *We Cannot Delay*, 400–401.
57. Cray, *General of the Army*, 197–98.
58. Churchill, *Second World War*, vol. 3, *Grand Alliance*, 331–32.
59. Bland, *Papers*, vol. 2, *We Cannot Delay*, 553.
60. Cray, *General of the Army*, 203.
61. Bland and Bland, *Interviews and Reminiscences*, 303.
62. Ibid.
63. Cray, *General of the Army*, 209.
64. Stoler, *George C. Marshall*, 83.
65. Bland and Bland, *Interviews and Reminiscences*, 303.
66. Marshall, K.T., *Together*, 83–84.
67. Stoler, *George C. Marshall*, 76.
68. Marshall, K.T., *Together*, 67–68.
69. Pogue, *Marshall*, vol. 2, *Ordeal and Hope*, 35.
70. Bland, *Papers*, vol. 2, *We Cannot Delay*, 285.
71. Meacham, *Franklin and Winston*, 105.
72. Bland and Bland, *Interviews and Reminiscences*, 285.
73. Ibid., 286.
74. Meacham, *Franklin and Winston*, 115.
75. Parrish, *Roosevelt and Marshall*, 191.
76. Ibid., 192.
77. Current et al., *American History*, 770.
78. Parrish, *Roosevelt and Marshall*, 195.

Chapter 7
1. Bland, *Papers*, vol. 2, *We Cannot Delay*, 627.
2. Stoler, *George C. Marshall*, 85.
3. Bland, *Papers*, vol. 2, *We Cannot Delay*, 496.
4. Bland and Bland, *Interviews and Reminiscences*, 534.
5. Cray, *General of the Army*, 175.
6. Pogue, *Marshall*, vol. 2, *Ordeal and Hope*, 97.
7. Bland and Bland, *Interviews and Reminiscences*, 476.
8. Current et al., *American History*, 771.
9. Pogue, *Marshall*, vol. 2, *Ordeal and Hope*, 177.
10. Ibid.
11. "A New Order in Asia," 1.
12. Matsuoka, "Address," 2.
13. Cray, *General of the Army*, 226.
14. Ibid., 227.
15. Pogue, *Marshall*, vol. 2, *Ordeal and Hope*, 182.
16. Cray, *General of the Army*, 229.
17. Pogue, *Marshall*, vol. 2, *Ordeal and Hope*, 170.
18. Bland, *Papers*, vol. 2, *We Cannot Delay*, 441.
19. Zich, *The Rising Sun*, 25–26.
20. Pogue, *Marshall*, vol. 2, *Ordeal and Hope*, 194.
21. "Japanese Proposal (Plan B)," 1.
22. Pogue, *Marshall*, vol. 2, *Ordeal and Hope*, 204.
23. "American Counter-Proposal to Japanese Plan B," 1.
24. Zich, *The Rising Sun*, 27.
25. Parrish, *Roosevelt and Marshall*, 205.
26. Cray, *General of the Army*, 241.
27. Pogue, *Marshall*, vol. 2, *Ordeal and Hope*, 209.
28. Prange et al., *At Dawn We Slept*, 402.
29. Ibid., 406.
30. Parrish, *Roosevelt and Marshall*, 204.
31. Prange et al., *At Dawn We Slept*, 403.
32. Pogue, *Marshall*, vol. 2, *Ordeal and Hope*, 211.
33. Ibid., 212.
34. Cray, *General of the Army*, 245.
35. Ibid., 246.
36. Pogue, *Marshall*, vol. 2, *Ordeal and Hope*, 220.
37. Prange et al., *At Dawn We Slept*, 211.
38. Roosevelt, "To Emperor Hirohito of Japan,"
39. Cray, *General of the Army*, 251.
40. Pogue, *Marshall*, vol. 2, *Ordeal and Hope*, 221.
41. "Pearl Harbor Attack Documents."
42. Prange et al., *At Dawn We Slept*, 475.

43. Ibid., 476.
44. Cray, *General of the Army*, 253–54.
45. Ibid., 254.
46. Prange et al., *At Dawn We Slept*, 493.
47. Ibid., 494.
48. Pogue, *Marshall*, vol. 2, *Ordeal and Hope*, 230–31.
49. Prange et al., *At Dawn We Slept*, 554.
50. Ibid.
51. Cray, *General of the Army*, 259–60.
52. Ibid., 261.
53. Zich, *The Rising Sun*, 57.
54. Marshall, K.T., *Together*, 99.
55. "FDR's 'Day of Infamy' Speech."
56. Roosevelt, "Joint Address to Congress Leading to a Declaration of War."
57. Isserman, *World War II*, 29.

Chapter 8
1. Churchill, *Memoirs of the Second World War*, 505.
2. Churchill, *Second World War*, vol. 2, *The Grand Alliance*, 539–40.
3. Cray, *General of the Army*, 267.
4. Churchill, *Memoirs of the Second World War*, 510.
5. Ibid.
6. Churchill, *Second World War*, vol. 2, *The Grand Alliance*, 541.
7. Ibid., 568.
8. Morton, "Germany First," 37–38.
9. Roberts, *Masters and Commanders*, 69.
10. Pogue, *Marshall*, vol. 2, *Ordeal and Hope*, 265.
11. Ibid., 262.
12. Roberts, *Masters and Commanders*, 66.
13. Pogue, *Marshall*, vol. 2, *Ordeal and Hope*, 265.
14. Ibid., 265–66.
15. Bland and Bland, *Interviews and Reminiscences*, 413.
16. Ibid.
17. Stoler, *George C. Marshall*, 90.
18. Bland and Bland, *Interviews and Reminiscences*, 431.
19. Cray, *General of the Army*, 272.
20. Pogue, *Marshall*, vol. 2, *Ordeal and Hope*, 277.
21. Ibid., 278–79.
22. Roberts, *Masters and Commanders*, 80–81.
23. Pogue, *Marshall*, vol.2, *Ordeal and Hope*, 236.
24. Faber, *Soldier and Statesman*, 122,
25. Cray, *General of the Army*, 284.
26. Parrish, *Partners in Command*, 83.
27. Cray, *General of the Army*, 284.
28. Bland, *Papers*, vol. 3, *The Right Man for the Job*, 148.
29. Zich, *The Rising Sun*, 96–97.
30. Ibid., 100.
31. Current et al., *American History*, 774.
32. Ibid.
33. Pogue, *Marshall*, vol. 2, *Ordeal and Hope*, 304.
34. Ibid., 289.
35. Perry, *Partners in Command*, 72.
36. Pogue, *Marshall*, vol. 2, *Ordeal and Hope*, 295.
37. Bland, *Papers*, vol. 3, *The Right Man for the Job*, 112.
38. Marshall, *Together*, 109–10.
39. Bland, *Papers*, vol. 3, *The Right Man for the Job*, 145.
40. Stoler, *George C. Marshall*, 93.
41. Ibid., 97.
42. Pogue, *Marshall*, vol. 2, *Ordeal and Hope*, 305.
43. Ibid., 307.
44. Ibid.
45. Parrish, *Roosevelt and Marshall*, 266.
46. Ibid., 272.
47. Roberts, *Masters and Commanders*, 137–39.
48. Bland and Bland, *Interviews and Reminiscences*, 580.
49. Pogue, *Marshall*, vol. 2, *Ordeal and Hope*, 320.
50. Roberts, *Masters and Commanders*, 138.
51. Marshall, K.T., *Together*, 118–19.
52. "Battle of Midway June 4–7, 1942," 1.
53. Pogue, *Marshall*, vol. 2, *Ordeal and Hope*, 325.

54. Roberts, *Masters and Commanders*, 173–74.
55. Parrish, *Roosevelt and Marshall*, 276–77.
56. Cray, *General of the Army*, 284.
57. Roberts, *Masters and Commanders*, 176.
58. Pogue, *Marshall*, vol. 2, *Ordeal and Hope*, 328.
59. Meacham, *Franklin and Winston*, 181–82.
60. Pogue, *Marshall*, vol. 2, *Ordeal and Hope*, 329–30.
61. Parrish, *Roosevelt and Marshall*, 285.
62. Churchill, *Second World War*, vol. 2, *The Grand Alliance*, 584.
63. Parrish, *Roosevelt and Marshall*, 286–87.
64. Cray, *General of the Army*, 324.
65. Roberts, *Masters and Commanders*, 204.
66. Cray, *General of the Army*, 325.
67. Parrish, *Roosevelt and Marshall*, 289.
68. Pogue, *Marshall*, vol. 2, *Ordeal and Hope*, 340–41.
69. Parrish, *Roosevelt and Marshall*, 291–92.
70. Pogue, *Marshall*, vol. 2, *Ordeal and Hope*, 346.
71. Parrish, *Roosevelt and Marshall*, 296.
72. Pogue, *Marshall*, vol. 2, *Ordeal and Hope*, 349.
73. Marshall, K.T., *Together*, 128–30.

Chapter 9
1. Cray, *General of the Army*, 337.
2. Perry, *Partners in Command*, 128.
3. McCullough, *American Heritage Picture History*, 235.
4. Ibid., 218.
5. Churchill, *Memoirs of the Second World War*, 615.
6. McCullough, *American Heritage Picture*, 219.
7. Ibid.
8. Ibid.
9. Bland, *Papers*, vol. 3, *The Right Man for the Job*, 428.
10. Churchill, "The End of the Beginning."
11. McCullough, *American Heritage Picture History*, 220.
12. Perry, *Partners in Command*, 127.
13. Cray, *Solder and Statesman*, 349.
14. McCullough, *American Heritage Picture History*, 220.
15. Bland, *Papers*, vol. 3, *The Right Man for the Job*, 291.
16. Pogue, *Marshall*, vol. 2, *Ordeal and Hope*, 417.
17. "Operation Catapult," 1.
18. Pogue, *Marshall*, vol. 2, *Ordeal and Hope*, 420.
19. McCullough, *American Heritage Picture History*, 243.
20. Perry, *Partners in Command*, 139.
21. Sherwood, *Roosevelt and Hopkins*, 654.
22. Perry, *Partners in Command*, 140.
23. Weintraub, *15 Stars*, 151.
24. Bland, *Papers*, vol. 3, *The Right Man for the Job*, 446.
25. Ibid., 445.
26. Ibid., 447.
27. Churchill, *Memoirs of the Second World War*, 662.
28. Cray, *General of the Army*, 352.
29. Perry, *Partners in Command*, 143.
30. Ibid., 145.
31. McCullough, *American Heritage Picture History*, 253.
32. Ibid., 344.
33. Pogue, *Marshall*, vol. 2, *Ordeal and Hope*, 425.
34. Robinson, "The President's Globe," 1.
35. Cray, *General of the Army*, 354.
36. Sherwood, *Roosevelt and Hopkins*, 664.
37. Matloff, *Strategic Planning*, chap. 1, "Casablanca," 18.
38. Cray, *General of the Army*, 355.
39. Pogue, *Marshall*, vol. 3, *Organizer of Victory*, 15.
40. Cray, *General of the Army*, 355.
41. Pogue, *Marshall*, vol. 3, *Organizer of Victory*, 18.
42. Ibid.
43. Cray, *General of the Army*, 358.
44. Sherwood, *Roosevelt and Hopkins*, 674.
45. Matloff, *Strategic Planning*, "Casablanca," 21–23.
46. Pogue, *Marshall*, vol. 3, *Organizer of Victory*, 22.
47. Bland, *Papers*, vol. 3, *The Right Man for the Job*, 515–16.
48. Matloff, *Strategic Planning*, "Casablanca," 35–36.

49. Churchill, *Memoirs of the Second World War*, 669.
50. Berthon, *Allies at War*, 245.
51. Ibid., 246.
52. Pogue, *Marshall*, vol. 3, *Organizer of Victory*, 33–34.
53. Ibid., 31.
54. Stoler, *George C. Marshall*, 101.
55. Matloff, *Strategic Planning*, "Casablanca," 29–30.
56. Perry, *Partners in Command*, 154.
57. Pogue, *Marshall*, vol. 3, *Organizer of Victory*, 179.
58. Perry, *Partners in Command*, 180.
59. Ibid., 175.
60. Cray, *General of the Army*, 381.
61. Pogue, *Marshall*, vol. 3, *Organizer of Victory*, 187.
62. Bland, *Papers*, vol. 3, *The Right Man for the Job*, 568–70.
63. Cray, *General of the Army*, 383–84.
64. Marshall, K.T., *Together*, 141.
65. Pogue, *Marshall*, vol. 3, *Organizer of Victory*, 176.
66. Churchill, *Memoirs of the Second World War*, 688–89.
67. "The TRIDENT Conference," 1.
68. Parrish, *Roosevelt and Marshall*, 350.
69. Pogue, *Marshall*, vol. 3, *Organizer of Victory*, 198.
70. Parrish, *Roosevelt and Marshall*, 347.
71. Ibid.
72. Pogue, *Marshall*, vol. 3, *Organizer of Victory*, 201.
73. Cray, *General of the Army*, 388.
74. Bland, *Papers*, vol. 3, *"The Right Man for the Job,"* 698.
75. Roberts, *Masters and Commanders*, 365–66.
76. Bland, *Papers*, vol. 3, *The Right Man for the Job*, 697.
77. Roberts, *Masters and Commanders*, 367.
78. Matloff, *Strategic Planning*, chap. 7, "From Husky to Avalanche," 146–47.
79. Roberts, *Masters and Commanders*, 372.
80. Cray, *General of the Army*, 398.
81. Ibid., 399.
82. Bland and Bland, *Interviews and Reminiscences*, 553.
83. Cray, *General of the Army*, 400.
84. Pogue, *Marshall*, vol. 3, *Organizer of Victory*, 220.
85. Cray, *General of the Army*, 401.
86. Parrish, *Roosevelt and Marshall*, 355.
87. Bland, *Papers*, vol. 4, *Aggressive and Determined Leadership*, 9.
88. Bellafaire, "The Women's Army Corps," 2.
89. Bland, *Papers*, vol. 4, *Aggressive and Determined Leadership*, 27.
90. Ibid.
91. Stoler, *George C. Marshall*, 123.
92. Bland, *Papers*, vol. 4, *Aggressive and Determined Leadership*, 31.
93. Marshall, K.T., *Together*, 152–53.
94. Cray, *General of the Army*, 405.
95. Matloff, *Strategic Planning*, chap. 10, "Quadrant," 211–12.
96. Bland, *Papers*, vol. 4, *Aggressive and Determined Leadership*, 85–86.
97. Ibid.
98. Roberts, *Masters and Commanders*, 394.
99. Ibid.
100. Matloff, *Strategic Planning*, "Quadrant," 213–14.
101. Ibid.
102. Ibid.
103. Matloff, *Strategic Planning*, "Quadrant," 215–16.
104. Parrish, *Roosevelt and Marshall*, 363.
105. Weintraub, *15 Stars*, 190.
106. Roberts, *Masters and Commanders*, 395.
107. Churchill, *Memoirs of the Second World War*, 722.
108. Roberts, *Masters and Commanders*, 396.
109. Matloff, *Strategic Planning*, "Quadrant," 215–16.

Chapter 10
1. Roberts, *Masters and Commanders*, 392.
2. Ibid., 393.
3. Bland, *Papers*, vol. 4, *Aggressive and Determined Leadership*, 91.
4. Ibid.
5. Cray, *General of the Army*, 412.
6. Bland, *Papers*, vol. 4, *Aggressive and Determined Leadership*, 91.
7. Ibid., 92.

8. Cray, *General of the Army*, 406.
9. Ibid., 410.
10. Stoler, *George C. Marshall*, 132.
11. Webster, *The Burma Road*, 14.
12. Ibid., 16.
13. Ibid., 57.
14. Stoler, *George C. Marshall*, 133.
15. Ibid., 134.
16. Cray, *General of the Army*, 393.
17. Webster, *The Burma Road*, 61.
18. Stoler, *George C. Marshall*, 134.
19. Roberts, *Masters and Commanders*, 404.
20. Bland, *Papers*, vol. 4, *Aggressive and Determined Leadership*, 95.
21. Ibid., 96–97.
22. Cray, *General of the Army*, 411.
23. Perry, *Partners in Command*, 216.
24. Bland, *Papers*, vol. 4, *Aggressive and Determined Leadership*, 95.
25. Ibid.
26. Weintraub, *15 Stars*, 193.
27. Bland, *Papers*, vol. 4, *Aggressive and Determined Leadership*, 94.
28. Pogue, *Marshall*, vol. 3, *Organizer of Victory*, 264.
29. Sherwood, *Roosevelt and Hopkins*, 759.
30. Weintraub, *15 Stars*, 103.
31. Cray, *General of the Army*, 414.
32. Bland, *Papers*, vol. 4, "Aggressive and Determined Leadership," 129.
33. Ibid.
34. Bland, *Papers*, vol. 4, *Aggressive and Determined Leadership*, 116.
35. Parrish, *Roosevelt and Marshall*, 365.
36. Sherwood, *Roosevelt and Hopkins*, 760.
37. Pogue, *Marshall*, vol. 3, *Organizer of Victory*, 271.
38. Cray, *General of the Army*, 416.
39. Pogue, *Marshall*, vol. 3, *Organizer of Victory*, 270.
40. Cray, *General of the Army*, 416.
41. Bland, *Papers*, vol. 4, *Aggressive and Determined Leadership*, 128.
42. Pogue, *Marshall*, vol. 3, *Organizer of Victory*, 270.
43. Sherwood, *Roosevelt and Hopkins*, 76144.   Marshall, K.T., *Together*, 163.
45. Bland, *Papers*, vol. 4, *Aggressive and Determined Leadership*, 130–31.
46. Sherwood, *Roosevelt and Hopkins*, 764.
47. Pogue, *Marshall*, vol. 3, *Organizer of Victory*, 269.
48. Cray, *General of the Army*, 416.
49. Ibid.
50. Sherwood, *Roosevelt and Hopkins*, 762.
51. Ibid., 765.
52. Perry, *Partners in Command*, 251.
53. Cray, *General of the Army*, 417.
54. Pogue, *Marshall*, vol. 3, *Organizer of Victory*, 276.
55. Weintraub, *15 Stars*, 217.
56. Pogue, *Marshall*, vol. 3, *Organizer of Victory*, 277.
57. Weintraub, *15 Stars*, 197–98.
58. Bland, *Papers*, vol. 4, *Aggressive and Determined Leadership*, 185.
59. Ibid., 165.
60. Marshall, K.T., *Together*, 159–64.
61. Parrish, *Roosevelt and Marshall*, 377–80.
62. Bland, *Papers*, vol. 4, *Aggressive and Determined Leadership*, 188.
63. Parrish, *Roosevelt and Marshall*, 382–83.
64. Pogue, *Marshall*, vol. 3, *Organizer of Victory*, 305.
65. Cray, *General of the Army*, 423.
66. Pogue, *Marshall*, vol. 3, *Organizer of Victory*, 304.
67. Roberts, *Masters and Commanders*, 436.
68. Cray, *General of the Army*, 424.
69. Pogue, *Marshall*, vol. 3, *Organizer of Victory*, 308.
70. Bland and Bland, *Interviews and Reminiscences*, 622.
71. Cray, *General of the Army*, 424.
72. Bland and Bland, *Interviews and Reminiscences*, 622.
73. Leighton, *Command Decisions*, 11.
74. Cray, *General of the Army*, 425–26.
75. Matloff, *Strategic Planning*, chap. 16, "Cairo-Tehran," 4.
76. Parrish, *Roosevelt and Marshall*, 392.
77. Matloff, *Strategic Planning*, "Cairo-Tehran," 4.
78. Chen, "Invasion of Sicily."

79. Matloff, *Strategic Planning*, "Cairo-Tehran," 4.
80. Churchill, *Memoirs of the Second World War*, 757.
81. Leighton, *Command Decisions*, 5.
82. Cray, *General of the Army*, 426.
83. Parrish, *Roosevelt and Marshall*, 397.
84. Matloff, *Strategic Planning*, "Cairo-Tehran," 6.
85. Ibid., 8.
86. *Meacham, Franklin and Winston*, 249–50.
87. Ibid.
88. Ibid.
89. Matloff, "*Strategic Planning*, "Cairo-Tehran," 8.
90. Ibid., 9.
91. *Meacham, Franklin and Winston*, 252.
92. Cray, *General of the Army*, 430.
93. Meacham, *Franklin and Winston*, 252.
94. Sherwood, *Roosevelt and Hopkins*, 786.
95. Meacham, *Franklin and Winston*, 256.
96. Cray, *General of the Army*, 431.
97. Ibid.
98. Parrish, *Roosevelt and Marshall*, 405.
99. Ibid.
100. Meacham, *Franklin and Winston*, 258.
101. Ibid.
102. Sherwood, *Roosevelt and Hopkins*, 789.
103. Pogue, *Marshall*, vol. 3, *Organizer of Victory*, 313.
104. Cray, *General of the Army*, 434.
105. Ibid., 434–35
106. Meacham, *Franklin and Winston*, 261.
107. Churchill, *Memoirs of the Second World War*, 768.
108. Meacham, *Franklin and Winston*, 263–64.
109. Stoler, *George C. Marshall*, 107.
110. Matloff, *Strategic Planning*, "Cairo-Tehran," 21.
111. Ibid., 116.
112. Pogue, *Marshall*, vol. 3, *Organizer of Victory*, 320.
113. Sherwood, *Roosevelt and Hopkins*, 803.
114. Bland and Bland, *Interviews and Reminiscences*, 344.
115. Parrish, *Roosevelt and Marshall*, 416.
116. Sherwood, *Roosevelt and Hopkins*, 803.

Chapter 11
1. Cray, *General of the Army*, 438.
2. Pogue, *Marshall*, vol. 3, *Organizer of Victory*, 323.
3. Bland, *Papers*, vol. 4, *Aggressive and Determined Leadership*, 199.
4. Cray, *General of the Army*, 438.
5. Bland, *Papers*, vol. 4, *Aggressive and Determined Leadership*, 199.
6. Weintraub, *15 Stars*, 21213.
7. Cray, *General of the Army*, 440.
8. Bland, *Papers*, vol. 4, *Aggressive and Determined Leadership*, 199.
9. Bland and Bland, *Interviews and Reminiscences*, 365.
10. Cray, *General of the Army*, 440.
11. Ibid.
12. Ibid.
13. Weintraub, *15 Stars*, 214.
14. Cray, *General of the Army*, 440.
15. Weintraub, *15 Stars*, 215.
16. Ibid., 216.
17. Marshall, K.T., *Together*, 173.
18. "U.S. at War: The General," 17.
19. Parrish, *Roosevelt and Marshall*, 420.
20. Pogue, *Marshall*, vol. 3, *Organizer of Victory*, 349.
21. Bland, *Papers*, vol. 4, *Aggressive and Determined Leadership*, 234.
22. Parrish, *Roosevelt and Marshall*, 421–22.
23. Pogue, *Marshall*, vol. 3, *Organizer of Victory*, 351.
24. Ibid., 350.
25. Ibid., 351.
26. Bland, *Papers*, vol. 4, *Aggressive and Determined Leadership*, 233.
27. Ibid., 237.
28. Pogue, *Marshall*, vol. 3, *Organizer of Victory*, 326–27.
29. Weintraub, *15 Stars*, 145.
30. Bland, *Papers*, vol. 4, *Aggressive and Determined Leadership*, 215.

31. Ibid., 232.
32. Pogue, *Marshall*, vol. 3, *Organizer of Victory*, 371.
33. Cray, *General of the Army*, 444.
34. Bradley, *A Soldier's Story*, 43–44.
35. Jones, "General George S. Patton," 1.
36. Bland and Bland, *Interviews and Reminiscences*, 460.
37. Perry, *Partners in Command*, 178.
38. Weintraub, *15 Stars*, 161.
39. Cray, *General of the Army*, 408.
40. Perry, *Partners in Command*, 208.
41. Ibid., 209.
42. Ibid.
43. Ibid., 209–10.
44. Ibid., 211.
45. Pogue, *Marshall*, vol. 3, *Organizer of Victory*, 372.
46. Ibid.
47. George C. Marshall Papers.
48. Perry, *Partners in Command*, 212.
49. Cray, *General of the Army*, 444.
50. Bland, *Papers*, vol. 4, *Aggressive and Determined Leadership*, 239.
51. "What Was General Patton Doing on D-Day?"
52. Cray, *General of the Army*, 441.
53. Weintraub, *15 Stars*, 234.
54. Bland, *Papers*, vol. 4, *Aggressive and Determined Leadership*, 190.
55. Ibid., 221–24.
56. Ibid., 263.
57. Ibid., 262.
58. Ambrose, *Citizen Soldiers*, 274.
59. Ibid., 275.
60. Bland, *Papers*, vol. 4, *Aggressive and Determined Leadership*, 246–47.
61. Weintraub, *15 Stars*, 226.
62. Cray, *General of the Army*, 444.
63. Churchill, *Second World War*, vol. 5, *Closing the Ring*, 441.
64. McCullough, *American Heritage Picture History*, 375.
65. Cray, *General of the Army*, 445.
66. Churchill, *Memoirs of the Second World War*, 783.
67. Churchill, *Second World War*, vol. 5, *Closing the Ring*, 441.
68. Ibid.
69. Perry, *Partners in Command*, 273.
70. Churchill, *Second World War*, vol. 5, *Closing the Ring*, 488.
71. Cray, *General of the Army*, 445–46.
72. Ibid., 446.
73. Ibid.
74. Roberts, *Masters and Commanders*, 461–62.
75. Perry, *Partners in Command*, 266.
76. Ibid.
77. Ibid., 278–79.
78. Ibid.
79. Ibid.
80. Ibid., 282.
81. Bland, *Papers*, vol. 4, *Aggressive and Determined Leadership*, 374.
82. Weintraub, *15 Stars*, 238.
83. Ibid.
84. Stoler, *George C. Marshall*, 114.
85. "What Was General Patton Doing on D-Day?"
86. Pogue, *Marshall*, vol. 3, *Organizer of Victory*, 383.
87. Ibid., 384.
88. "Eyes Only."
89. "Outgoing."
90. "Secret" Letter.
91. Cray, *General of the Army*, 448.
92. McCullough, *American Heritage Picture History*, 391.
93. Ibid., 392.
94. Atkinson, *The Day of Battle*, 549.
95. Ibid., 570.
96. Ibid., 574.
97. Ibid., 253.
98. Ibid., 572–73.
99. Bland and Bland, *Interviews and Reminiscences*, 416.
100. A. Allen Brown to Madge Brown, Feb. 27, 1944.

101. Ibid., March 6, 1944.
102. Ibid., March 7, 1944.
103. Bland, *Papers*, vol. 4, *Aggressive and Determined Leadership*, 320.
104. Ibid., 335.
105. Ibid., 423.
106. Ibid., 460.
107. Marshall, K.T., *Together*, 195.
108. War Department: Lt. General Devers to George C. Marshall, May 31, 1944.
109. Brown, C. Clifton S. Brown Jr. to Katherine T. Marshall and Madge Brown, A., to Madge Brown, May 31, 1944.
110. Marshall, K.T., *Together*, 202.
111. Bland, *Papers*, vol. 4, *Aggressive and Determined Leadership*, 451–52.
112. Ibid., 452–53.
113. Ibid., 453.
114. "D-Day: État des Lieux."
115. Roberts, *Masters and Commanders*, 482.
116. Perry, *Partners in Command*, 283.
117. Atkinson, *The Day of Battle*, 582.
118. Roberts, *Masters and Commanders*, 482.
119. Cray, *General of the Army*, 453.
120. Roberts, *Masters and Commanders*, 482.
121. Cray, *General of the Army*, 453.
122. Bradley, *A Soldier's Story*, 259–60.
123. Perry, *Partners in Command*, 296–97.
124. McCullough, *American Heritage Picture History*, 483.
125. Perry, *Partners in Command*, 285–86.
126. McCullough, *American Heritage Picture History*, 482.
127. Perry, *Partners in Command*, 285–86.
128. Eisenhower, "Document for June 6th."

Chapter 12
1. Perry, *Partners in Command*, 301-3.
2. Weintraub, *15 Stars*, 247.
3. Cray, *General of the Army*, 455.
4. McCullough, *American Heritage Picture History*, 503.
5. Roberts, *Masters and Commanders*, 489.
6. Weintraub, *15 Stars*, 248.
7. Roberts, *Masters and Commanders*, 489.
8. Pogue, *Marshall*, vol. 3, *Organizer of Victory*, 390–92.
9. Ibid.
10. Ibid., 394.
11. Cray, *General of the Army*, 460.
12. Bland, *Papers*, vol. 4, *Aggressive and Determined Leadership*, 479–80.
13. Cray, *General of the Army*, 462.
14. Weintraub, *15 Stars*, 250–51.
15. Cray, *General of the Army*, 462.
16. Ibid.
17. Ibid., 463.
18. Pogue, *Marshall*, vol. 3, *Organizer of Victory*, 400.
19. Ibid.
20. Ibid., 403.
21. Berthon, *Allies at War*, 318.
22. Pogue, *Marshall*, vol. 3, *Organizer of Victory*, 403.
23. Cray, *General of the Army*, 464.
24. Matloff, "The ANVIL Decision," 384–85.
25. Pogue, *Marshall*, vol. 3, *Organizer of Victory*, 403.
26. Ibid., 406.
27. Ibid., 409.
28. Ibid., 409–10.
29. Ibid., 410.
30. Roberts, *Masters and Commanders*, 495.
31. Ibid., 498.
32. Pogue, *Marshall*, vol. 3, *Organizer of Victory*, 412.
33. Roberts, *Masters and Commanders*, 499.
34. Ibid., 500.
35. Matloff, "The ANVIL Decision," 384–85.
36. Ibid., 397.
37. Ibid.
38. Atkinson, *The Day of Battle*, 582.
39. Pogue, *Marshall*, vol. 3, *Organizer of Victory*, 404.

40. Marshall, *George C. Marshall to Madge Brown.*
41. Matloff, Maurice, *World War II*, 100-101.
42. Doubler, "Busting the Bocage.
43. Matloff, *World War II*, 101.
44. *Drive on Caen.*
45. *Operation Cobra and the Breakout at Normandy*, 1.
46. Ibid., 2.
47. Ibid.
48. Bradley, *A Soldier's Story*, 355.
49. Mosley, *Hero of Our Times*, 287.
50. Ibid., 379–80.
51. Perry, *Partners in Command*, 321.
52. Decker, "Logistics and Patton's Third Army."
53. "Operation Cobra and the Breakout at Normandy," 1.
54. McCullough, *American Heritage Picture History*, 484.
55. Roberts, *Masters and Commanders*, 506.
56. Weintraub, *15 Stars*, 261.
57. Bradley, *A Soldier's Story*, 369.
58. Pogue, *Marshall*, vol. 3, *Organizer of Victory*, 414.
59. Ibid.
60. Roberts, *Masters and Commanders*, 505.
61. McCullough, *American Heritage Picture History*, 484.
62. Weintraub, *15 Stars*, 261.
63. "Campaign in Southern France," 1.
64. Roberts, *Masters and Commanders*, 507.
65. Pogue, *Marshall*, vol. 3, *Organizer of Victory*, 414.
66. Bland, *Papers*, vol. 4, *Aggressive and Determined Leadership*, 556, 612.
67. Churchill, *Memoirs of the Second World War*, 834–35.
68. Pogue, *Marshall*, vol. 3, *Organizer of Victory*, 417–18.
69. Ibid.
70. Perry, *Partners in Command*, 324.
71. Ibid.
72. Mosley, *Hero of Our Times*, 284–85.
73. Perry, *Partners in Command*, 324.
74. Bland, *Papers*, vol. 4, *Aggressive and Determined Leadership*, 550–51.
75. Mosley, *Hero of Our Times*, 285.
76. Perry, *Partners in Command*, 326.
77. Pogue, *Marshall*, vol. 3, *Organizer of Victory*, 426.
78. Perry, *Partners in Command*, 326.
79. *Bland, Papers, vol. 4, Aggressive and Determined Leadership*, 522.
80. Weintraub, *15 Stars*, 257.
81. Perry, *Partners in Command*, 316.
82. Bland, *Papers*, vol. 4, *Aggressive and Determined Leadership*, 534.
83. Pogue, *Marshall*, vol. 3, *Organizer of Victory*, 427.
84. Bland, *Papers*, vol. 4, *Aggressive and Determined Leadership*, 544–51.
85. McCullough, *American Heritage Picture History*, 484.
86. Bradley, *A Soldier's Story*, 386–87.
87. McCullough, *American Heritage Picture History*, 484.
88. Bradley, *A Soldier's Story*, 392.
89. "WW2 Letters of Private Melvin W. Johnson," 1.
90. Bradley, *A Soldier's Story*, 390-93.
91. Churchill, *Memoirs of the Second World War*, 826.
92. McCullough, *American Heritage Picture History*, 485.
93. Bradley, *A Soldier's Story*, 395.
94. McCullough, *American Heritage Picture History*, 485.
95. Marshall, K.T., *Together*, 205–6.
96. Marshall, *GC Marshall to Mr. Wallace.*
97. Cray, *General of the Army*, 468.
98. Ibid., 471.
99. "The Battle for Brittany," 1–2.
100. "World War II Timeline," 4.
101. Cray, *General of the Army*, 468–69.
102. Radzilowski, "Warsaw Uprising," 1–2.
103. Pogue, *Marshall*, vol. 3, *Organizer of Victory*, 433.
104. Radzilowski, "Warsaw Uprising," 3.
105. Roberts, *Masters and Commanders*, 515.
106. Pogue, *Marshall*, vol. 3, *Organizer of Victory*, 436.
107. Roberts, *Masters and Commanders*, 517.
108. Pogue, *Marshall*, vol. 3, *Organizer of Victory*, 437.
109. Stoler, *George C. Marshall*, 119.

110. Matloff, Maurice, *World War II*, 131.
111. Stoler, *George C. Marshall*, 119.
112. Pogue, *Marshall*, vol. 3, *Organizer of Victory*, 443.
113. Bland, *Papers*, vol. 4, *Aggressive and Determined Leadership*, 569.
114. Cray, *General of the Army*, 470.
115. Ibid., 475.
116. Pogue, *Marshall*, vol. 3, *Organizer of Victory*, 453.
117. Cray, *General of the Army*, 475.
118. Pogue, *Marshall*, vol. 3, *Organizer of Victory*, 454.
119. Bland, *Papers*, vol. 4, *Aggressive and Determined Leadership*, 567.
120. Cray, *General of the Army*, 473.
121. Pogue, *Marshall*, vol. 3, *Organizer of Victory*, 453.
122. Cray, *General of the Army*, 472.
123. Ibid.
124. Bland, *Papers*, vol. 4, *Aggressive and Determined Leadership*, 509.
125. Cray, *General of the Army*, 476.
126. Shephard, "Warriors and Politics.".
127. Bland, *Papers*, vol. 4, *Aggressive and Determined Leadership*, 509–10.
128. Cray, *General of the Army*, 487.
129. Bland, *Papers*, vol. 4, *Aggressive and Determined Leadership*, 631.
130. Ibid., 627.
131. Ibid.
132. Bland, *Papers*, vol. 4, *Aggressive and Determined Leadership*, 614.
133. Marshall, *George C. Marshall to Madge Brown*.
134. Bland, *Papers*, vol. 4, *Aggressive and Determined Leadership*, 614.
135. Ibid., 589–93.
136. Cray, *General of the Army*, 482.
137. Bland, *Papers*, vol. 4, *Aggressive and Determined Leadership*, 480.

Chapter 13
1. Cray, *General of the Army*, 478.
2. Ibid., 479.
3. Pogue, *Marshall*, vol. 3, *Organizer of Victory*, 471.
4. Bland, *Papers*, vol. 4, *Aggressive and Determined Leadership*, 604.
5. Ibid., 605.
6. Cray, *General of the Army*, 480.
7. Mosley, *Hero of Our Times*, 304–6.
8. Cray, *General of the Army*, 480.
9. Pogue, *Marshall*, vol. 3, *Organizer of Victory*, 473.
10. "Pearl Harbor Attack."
11. Ibid.
12. Cray, *General of the Army*, 481.
13. Ibid.
14. Pogue, *Marshall*, vol. 3, *Organizer of Victory*, 470.
15. Cray, *General of the Army*, 482.
16. Ibid.
17. Ibid.
18. Ibid., 483.
19. Taaffe, *Marshall and His Generals*, 237.
20. Irving, *The War Between the Generals*, 269.
21. Bland, *Papers*, vol. 4, *Aggressive and Determined Leadership*, 621.
22. Cray, *General of the Army*, 483.
23. Perry, *Partners in Command*, 333.
24. Cray, *General of the Army*, 483.
25. Bland and Bland, *Interviews and Reminiscences*, 345.
26. Pogue, *Marshall*, vol. 3, *Organizer of Victory*, 475–76.
27. Bland and Bland, *Interviews and Reminiscences*, 333–34.
28. Ibid.
29. Bland, *Papers*, vol. 4, *Aggressive and Determined Leadership*, 629.
30. Cray, *General of the Army*, 485.
31. Pogue, *Marshall*, vol. 3, *Organizer of Victory*, 477.
32. Bland, *Papers*, vol. 4, *Aggressive and Determined Leadership*, 636.
33. Ibid., 589.
34. Bland and Bland, *Interviews and Reminiscences*, 217–18.
35. Bland, *Papers*, vol. 4, *Aggressive and Determined Leadership*, 626.
36. Cray, *General of the Army*, 487.
37. Ibid., 488.
38. Ibid., 487–88.
39. Bland, *Papers*, vol. 4, *Aggressive and Determined Leadership*, 630.
40. Perry, *Partners in Command*, 339.

41. Bland, *Papers*, vol. 4, *Aggressive and Determined Leadership*, 685–86.
42. Perry, *Partners in Command*, 339.
43. Pogue, *Marshall*, vol. 3, *Organizer of Victory*, 481.
44. Parrish, *Roosevelt and Marshall*, 469.
45. Bland and Bland, *Interviews and Reminiscences*, 623.
46. Roberts, *Masters and Commanders*, 529.
47. Parrish, *Roosevelt and Marshall*, 469.
48. Roberts, *Masters and Commanders*, 529.
49. Bland, *Papers*, vol. 4, *Aggressive and Determined Leadership*, 654.
50. Pogue, *Marshall*, vol. 3, *Organizer of Victory*, 483.
51. Bland and Bland, *Interviews and Reminiscences*, 456.
52. Cray, *General of the Army*, 491.
53. Pogue, *Marshall*, vol. 3, *Organizer of Victory*, 484–85.
54. Weintraub, *15 Stars*, 285.
55. Weintraub, "General George S. Patton and the Battle of the Bulge."
56. Perry, *Partners in Command*, 339–40.
57. Pogue, *Marshall*, vol. 3, *Organizer of Victory*, 485.
58. McCullough, *American Heritage Picture History*, 525.
59. Taaffe, *Marshall and His Generals*, 269.
60. Weintraub, "General George S. Patton and the Battle of the Bulge." 5.
61. "'Nuts!' Revisited."
62. Perry, *Partners in Command*, 341.
63. Pogue, *Marshall*, vol. 3, *Organizer of Victory*, 486.
64. Roberts, *Masters and Commanders*, 534.
65. Taaffe, *Marshall and His Generals*, 266.
66. Cray, *General of the Army*, 493.
67. Bland, *Papers*, vol. 4, *Aggressive and Determined Leadership*, 721.
68. Cray, *General of the Army*, 494.
69. Mosley, *Hero of Our Times*, 289.
70. Cray, *General of the Army*, 495.
71. Bland, *Papers*, vol. 4, *Aggressive and Determined Leadership*, 721.
72. Bradley, *A Soldier's Story*, 488–89.
73. Roberts, *Masters and Commanders*, 535.
74. Ibid., 535.
75. McCullough, *American Heritage Picture History*, 526.
76. Ibid.
77. Marshall, K.T., *Together*, 225.
78. "Battle of the Bulge."
79. Marshall, K.T., *Together*, 226.
80. Pogue, *Marshall*, vol. 3, *Organizer of Victory*, 505–6.
81. Bland, Papers, vol. 5, *The Finest Soldier*, 9.
82. Weintraub, *15 Stars*, 308.
83. Pogue, *Marshall*, vol. 3, *Organizer of Victory*, 497–98.
84. Weintraub, *15 Stars*, 308.
85. Bland, *Papers*, vol. 5, *The Finest Soldier*, 6.

Chapter 14
1. Marshall, K.T., *Together*, 229.
2. Bland, *Papers*, vol. 5, *The Finest Soldier*, 27.
3. Ibid., 28.
4. Cray, *General of the Army*, 500.
5. Ibid., 500–501.
6. Ibid., 502.
7. Ibid., 503.
8. Bland and Bland, *Interviews and Reminiscences*, 541.
9. Pogue, *Marshall*, vol. 3, *Organizer of Victory*, 515.
10. Roberts, *Masters and Commanders*, 543.
11. Ibid.
12. Pogue, *Marshall*, vol. 3, *Organizer of Victory*, 517.
13. Roberts, *Masters and Commanders*, 542.
14. Perry, *Partners in Command*, 352.
15. Cray, *General of the Army*, 503.
16. Ibid., 504.
17. Meacham, *Franklin and Winston*, 314.
18. Bland and Bland, *Interviews and Reminiscences*, 402.
19. Cray, *General of the Army*, 505.
20. Meacham, *Franklin and Winston*, 319.
21. Ibid., 317.
22. Roberts, *Masters and Commanders*, 544–45.
23. Pogue, *Marshall*, vol. 3, *Organizer of Victory*, 517.

24. Cray, *General of the Army*, 505.
25. Ibid., 506.
26. Roberts, *Masters and Commanders*, 545.
27. Cray, *General of the Army*, 506.
28. Pogue, *Marshall*, vol. 3, *Organizer of Victory*, 519.
29. Roberts, *Masters and Commanders*, 545.
30. Ibid., 546.
31. Cray, *General of the Army*, 507.
32. Pogue, *Marshall*, vol. 3, *Organizer of Victory*, 533.
33. Cray, *General of the Army*, 508–9.
34. Pogue, *Marshall*, vol. 3, *Organizer of Victory*, 526.
35. Bland and Bland, *Interviews and Reminiscences*, 404–5.
36. Ibid., 403.
37. Mosley, *Hero of Our Times*, 316.
38. "The Yalta Conference, Feb. 1945."
39. Meacham, *Franklin and Winston*, 319.
40. Ibid., 322–24.
41. Weintraub, *15 Stars*, 319.
42. Cray, *General of the Army*, 514.
43. Bland, *Papers*, vol. 5, *The Finest Soldier*, 51.
44. Perry, *Partners in Command*, 354.
45. Bland, *Papers*, vol. 5, *The Finest Soldier*, 80.
46. Pogue, *Marshall*, vol. 3, *Organizer of Victory*, 546.
47. Bland, *Papers*, vol. 5, *The Finest Soldier*, 64.
48. Ibid., 77.
49. Perry, *Partners in Command*, 354.
50. Roberts, *Masters and Commanders*, 565.
51. Pogue, *Marshall*, vol. 3, *Organizer of Victory*, 575.
52. Cray, *General of the Army*, 522.
53. Perry, *Partners in Command*, 355.
54. Meacham, *Franklin and Winston*, 337.
55. Ibid., 343.
56. Cray, *General of the Army*, 523.
57. Ibid., 524.
58. Pogue, *Marshall*, vol. 3, *Organizer of Victory*, 558.
59. Mosley, *Hero of Our Times*, 320.
60. Cray, *General of the Army*, 525.
61. Mosley, *Hero of Our Times*, 320.
62. Pogue, *Marshall*, vol. 3, *Organizer of Victory*, 559–60.
63. Meacham, *Franklin and Winston*, 349.
64. Rooney, "Just Like the Russians."
65. Herzog, "Treat Them Nicely."
66. Roberts, *Masters and Commanders*, 150.
67. Cray, *General of the Army*, 530–31.
68. Bland, *Papers*, vol. 5, *The Finest Soldier*, 171.
69. "Broadcast to the American People.".
70. Bland, *Papers*, vol. 5, *The Finest Soldier*, 172.

Chapter 15
1. Churchill, *George C. Marshall to Brigadier Cornwall-Jones*.
2. Churchill, *Winston Churchill to George C. Marshall*.
3. McCarthy, *Frank McCarthy to Brigadier Cornwall-Jones*.
4. Bland, *Papers*, vol. 5, *The Finest Soldier*, 173.
5. Ibid.
6. Ibid., 143.
7. "Occupation Troops."
8. Ibid.
9. Bland, *Papers*, vol. 5, *The Finest Soldier*, 20310.   Marshall, K.T., *Together*, 280.
11. Ibid.
12. Bland, *Papers*, vol. 5, *The Finest Soldier*, 168.
13. Ibid., 169–70.
14. Ibid., 177–78.
15. Ibid., 185–86
16. Ibid., 189.
17. Bland, *Papers*, vol. 5, *The Finest Soldier*, 200–1.
18. Ibid., 204.
19. Ibid., 203.
20. Marshall et al., "To the American People."
21. Weintraub, *15 Stars*, 273.
22. Ibid., 273.

23. Ibid.
24. Hickman, "World War II: Battle of Okinawa."
25. Ibid.
26. McCullough, *American Heritage Picture History*, 532.
27. Ibid.
28. Ibid., 533.
29. "Iwo Jima Operation."
30. Ibid., 2.
31. McCullough, *American Heritage Picture History*, 533.
32. Ibid.
33. "Iwo Jima Operation."
34. McCullough, *American Heritage Picture History*, 35.
35. "Battle for Iwo Jima, 1945."
36. Ibid.
37. Ibid.
38. McCullough, *American Heritage Picture History*, 588.
39. Taaffe, *Marshall and His Generals*, 301.
40. McCullough, *American Heritage Picture History*, 588.
41. Taaffe, *Marshall and His Generals*, 301.
42. Ibid., 301–2.
43. "Battle of Okinawa," 1.
44. Prados, "Battle of Okinawa," 1.
45. "World War II: Battle of Okinawa," 1.
46. McCullough, *American Heritage Picture History*, 589.
47. Cray, *General of the Army*, 540.
48. Parrish, *Roosevelt and Marshall*, 489.
49. Bland and Bland, *Interviews and Reminiscences*, 423.
50. Pogue, *Marshall*, vol. 4, *Statesman*, 8.
51. Ibid., 10.
52. Ibid., 11.
53. Ibid., 12.
54. Ibid., 13.
55. Bland and Bland, *Interviews and Reminiscences*
56. Pogue, *Marshall*, vol. 4, *Statesman*, 15.
57. Churchill, *Memoirs of the Second World War*, 582.
58. Stimson, "The Decision to Use the Atomic Bomb," 1.
59. Pogue, *Marshall*, vol. 4, *Statesman*, 17.
60. Cray, *General of the Army*, 538.
61. Morton, "The Decision to Use the Atomic Bomb," 6.
62. Ibid., 7.
63. Stimson, *"The Decision,"* 4.
64. Oppenheimer et al., "Recommendations on the Immediate Use of Nuclear Weapons," 1.
65. Bland, *Papers*, vol. 5, *The Finest Soldier*, 227.
66. Perry, *Partners in Command*, 365.
67. Cray, *General of the Army*, 540.
68. Bland, Papers, vol. 5, *The Finest Soldier*, 232.
69. Weintraub, *15 Stars*, 347.
70. Stimson, *"The Decision,"* 7.
71. Bland, *Papers*, vol. 5, *The Finest Soldier*, 234.
72. MacEachin, *Final Months of the War with Japan.*
73. Cray, *General of the Army*, 541.
74. Bland, *Papers*, vol. 5, *The Finest Soldier*, 234–35.
75. Cray, *General of the Army*, 534–35.
76. Bland, *Papers*, vol. 5, *The Finest Soldier*, 238.
77. Ibid., 240.
78. Ibid., 234–35.
79. Cray, *General of the Army*, 543.
80. Bland, Papers, vol. 5, *The Finest Soldier*, 243.
81. Weintraub, *15 Stars*, 349.
82. Cray, *General of the Army*, 543.
83. Ibid.
84. Sullivan, "Detonation of the First Atomic Bomb," 1.
85. Ibid.
86. Isaacson and Thomas, *The Wise Men.*
87. Churchill, *Memoirs of the Second World War*, 980.
88. Cray, *General of the Army*, 546.
89. Ibid., 544.
90. Bland, *Papers*, vol. 5, *The Finest Soldier*, 245.
91. "The Potsdam Conference."
92. "The Berlin (Potsdam) Conference," 1.

93. "Poland in 1945."
94. Isaacson and Thomas, *The Wise Men*, 308.
95. Ibid., 307.
96. McCullough, *American Heritage Picture History*, 42–43.
97. Cray, *General of the Army*, 544.
98. Churchill, *Memoirs of the Second World War*, 987–8.
99. Isaacson and Thomas, *The Wise Men*, 302.
100. Pogue, *Marshall*, vol. 4, *Statesman*, 21.
101. Bland, *Papers*, vol. 5, *The Finest Soldier*, 349.
102. Isaacson and Thomas, *The Wise Men*, 305.
103. Ibid., 305.
104. Ibid.
105. Stimson, "The Decision," 7.
106. Ibid.
107. Ibid.
108. Isaacson and Thomas, *The Wise Men*, 310.
109. Morton, *Command Decisions*, 21.
110. Isaacson and Thomas, *The Wise Men*, 310–11.
111. Butow, *Japan's Decision to Surrender*, 1.
112. Cray, *General of the Army*, 547.
113. Ibid.
114. Morton, *Command Decisions*, 13.
115. Ibid., 13–14.
116. "Japanese Peace Feelers in the Soviet Union," 6.
117. Ibid., 6.
118. Bland, *Papers*, vol. 5, *The Finest Soldier*, 253.
119. Kitchens, "1945: Japanese Response," 1.
120. "mokusatsu, One Word, Two Lessons," 1.
121. Correll, "The Decision that Launched the Enola Gay," 3.
122. Ibid.
123. McCullough, *American Heritage Picture History*, 612, 616.
124. Cray, *General of the Army*, 548.
125. Weintraub, *15 Stars*, 359.
126. Truman, "Statement by the President of the United States."
127. Cray, *General of the Army*, 548.
128. Ibid., 549.
129. Correll, "The Decision that Launched the Enola Gay," 3.
130. Stimson, "The Decision," 9.
131. "Counting the Dead."
132. Stimson, "The Decision," 10.
133. "Japan's Surrender," 9.
134. McCullough, *American Heritage Picture History*, 591.
135. "United States Strategic Bombing Survey."
136. "Emperor Hirohito," 1.
137. Bland, *Papers*, vol. 5, *The Finest Soldier*, 263.
138. Ibid., 264.
139. Ibid., 269.
140. "Victory Celebrations."
141. Bland, *Papers*, vol. 5, *The Finest Soldier*, 278.
142. Bland and Bland, *Interviews and Reminiscences*, 425.
143. Morton, *Command Decisions*, 26.
144. Manchester, *American Caesar*, 530.
145. Ibid.
146. Ibid., 531.
147. *General Marshall's Victory Report.*

Chapter 16
1. Marshall, K.T., *Together*, 260.
2. Bland, Papers, vol. 5, *The Finest Soldier*, 326.
3. Ibid., 347.
4. Ibid., 355.
5. Marshall, K.T., *Together*, 263.
6. Bland, *Papers*, vol. 5, *The Finest Soldier*, 305.
7. Cray, *General of the Army*, 645.
8. Wilson, *General Marshall Remembered*, 296.
9. Stoler, *George C. Marshall*, 143.
10. Ibid., 645.
11. *General Marshall's Victory Report*, 118–19.
12. Stoler, *George C. Marshall*, 143.
13. Bland, *Papers*, vol. 5, *The Finest Soldier*, 338.

14. Ibid.
15. Stoler, *George C. Marshall*, 144.
16. Bland, *Papers*, vol. 5, *The Finest Soldier*, 363.
17. Ibid., 304.
18. Bland, *Papers*, vol. 5, *The Finest Soldier*, 365.
19. Ibid., 366.
20. Ibid., 367.
21. Ibid.
22. Ibid., 372.
23. Marshall, K.T., *Together*, 282.
24. Cray, *General of the Army*, 557.
25. Pogue, *Marshall*, vol. 2, *Ordeal and Hope*, 431.
26. Prange et al., *At Dawn We Slept*, 685.
27. Cray, *General of the Army*, 558.
28. Weintraub, *15 Stars*, 385.
29. Bland, *Papers*, vol. 5, *The Finest Soldier*, 392.
30. Cray, *General of the Army*, 558.
31. Bland, *Papers*, vol. 5, *The Finest Soldier*, 387.
32. Ibid.
33. Cray, *General of the Army*, 558.
34. Pogue, *Marshall*, vol. 2, *Ordeal and Hope*, 434–35.
35. Ibid., 434.
36. Ibid.
37. Cray, *General of the Army*, 559.
38. Saunders, *General for Peace*, 68.
39. Bland, *Papers*, vol. 5, *The Finest Soldier*, 396.
40. Cray, *General of the Army*, 560.
41. Ibid.
42. "Long March," Encyclopedia Britannica.
43. "The Long March," China and East Asia Chronology.
44. Ibid.
45. Cray, *General of the Army*, 560.
46. Ibid.
47. Ibid., 561.
48. Ibid., 560.
49. Byrnes, "State Department Statement of U.S. Policy.".
50. Ibid.
51. Bland, *Papers*, vol. 5, *The Finest Soldier*, 394.
52. Ibid.
53. Wedemeyer, *Wedemeyer Reports*, 363.
54. Bland, *Papers*, vol. 5, *The Finest Soldier*, 393.
55. Cray, *General of the Army*, 562.
56. Wedemeyer, *Wedemeyer Reports*, 363.
57. Bland, *Papers*, vol. 5, *The Finest Soldier*, 372.
58. Pogue, *Marshall*, vol. 4, *Statesman*, 29–30.
59. Bland, Papers, vol. 5, *The Finest Soldier*, 400.
60. Cray, *General of the Army*, 564.
61. "Policies and Principles," 29.
62. Cray, *General of the Army*, 565.
63. Bland, *Papers*, vol. 5, *The Finest Soldier*, 402.
64. Ibid., 405–6.
65. Cray, *General of the Army*, 565.
66. Bland, *Papers*, vol. 5, *The Finest Soldier*, 416.
67. Cray, *General of the Army*, 566.
68. Ibid.
69. Ibid.
70. Ibid., 567.
71. Stoler, *George C. Marshall*, 148.
72. Pogue, *Marshall*, vol. 4, *Statesman*, 95.
73. Ibid.
74. Ibid., 96.
75. Ibid.
76. Bland, *Papers*, vol. 5, *The Finest Soldier*, 418.
77. Ibid., 476.
78. Ibid., 474.
79. "Policies and Principles," 30.
80. Bland, *Papers*, vol. 5, *The Finest Soldier*, 453, 455.
81. Cray, *General of the Army*, 569.
82. Ibid.
83. Pogue, *Marshall*, vol. 4, *Statesman*, 102.

84. Bland, Papers, vol. 5, *The Finest Soldier*, 490.
85. Pogue, *Marshall*, vol. 4, *Statesman*, 106.
86. Ibid.
87. "Policies and Principles," 28.
88. Cray, *General of the Army*, 570.
89. "Policies and Principles," 31.
90. Cray, *General of the Army*, 570.
91. Ibid., 571.
92. Ibid.
93. "Policies and Principles," 28.
94. Bland, *Papers*, vol. 5, *The Finest Soldier*, 525.
95. Marshall, Katherine T. *Katherine T. Marshall to Sally G. Chamberlin.*
96. Cray, *General of the Army*, 571.
97. Stoler, *George C. Marshall*, 148.
98. Bland, *Papers*, vol. 5, *The Finest Soldier*, 666.
99. Stoler, *George C. Marshall*, 149.
100. Ibid.
101. Cray, *General of the Army*, 572.
102. Ibid., 573.
103. Ibid., 577.
104. Bland, *Papers*, vol. 5, *The Finest Soldier*, 639.
105. Cray, *General of the Army*, 577.
106. Bland, *Papers*, vol. 5, *The Finest Soldier*, 668.
107. Ibid., 696.
108. Bland, *Papers*, vol. 5, *The Finest Soldier*, 696.
109. Ibid., 668–69.
110. Cray, *General of the Army*, 578.
111. Bland, *Papers*, vol. 5, *The Finest Soldier*, 722.
112. Cray, *General of the Army*, 578.
113. Ibid., 580–81.
114. Bland, *Papers*, vol. 5, *The Finest Soldier*, 740–41.
115. Ibid.
116. Pogue, *Marshall*, vol. 4, *Statesman*, 131.
117. Ibid., 132.
118. Ibid.
119. Cray, *General of the Army*, 582.
120. Ibid., 583.
121. Ibid., 578.
122. Ibid., 583.
123. Ibid., 574.
124. Ibid., 584.
125. Bland, *Papers*, vol. 5, *The Finest Soldier*, 772–76.
126. Cray, *General of the Army*, 584.
127. Pogue, *Marshall*, vol. 4, *Statesman*, 142.
128. Stoler, *George C. Marshall*, 150.
129. Ibid., 151.
130. Pogue, *Marshall*, vol. 4, *Statesman*, 144.
131. Ibid., 145.
132. Cray, *General of the Army*, 588.
133. Pogue, *Marshall*, vol. 4, *Statesman*, 146.

Chapter 17
1. Bland and Stoler, *Papers of George Catlett Marshall*, 8.
2. Ibid., 7.
3. Stoler, *George C. Marshall*, 154.
4. Cray, *General of the Army*, 587.
5. Pogue, *Marshall*, vol. 4, *Statesman*, 146.
6. Cray, *General of the Army*, 588.
7. Stoler, *George C. Marshall*, 155.
8. Bland and Bland, *Interviews and Reminiscences*, 561.
9. Cray, *General of the Army*, 590.
10. Pogue, *Marshall*, vol. 4, *Statesman*, 148.
11. Isaacson and Thomas, *The Wise Men*, 391.
12. Chace, *Acheson*, 101.
13. Behrman, *Most Noble Adventure*, 49.
14. Isaacson and Thomas, *The Wise Men*, 430–31.
15. Stoler, *George C. Marshall*, 156–57.
16. Bland and Bland, *Interviews and Reminiscences*, 562.
17. Pogue, *Marshall*, vol. 4, *Statesman*, 150.
18. Behrman, *Most Noble Adventure*, 61.

19. Bland and Bland, *Interviews and Reminiscences*, 563.
20. Pogue, *Marshall*, vol. 4, *Statesman*, 151.
21. Bland and Stoler, *Papers*, 9.
22. Ibid., 12.
23. Ibid., 17.
24. Ibid., 23.
25. Bland and Stoler, *Papers*, 16–17.
26. Ibid., 9.
27. Pogue, *Marshall*, vol. 4, *Statesman*, 161.
28. Isaacson and Thomas, *The Wise Men*, 387.
29. Pogue, *Marshall*, vol. 4, *Statesman*, 163.
30. Isaacson and Thomas, *The Wise Men*, 389.
31. Cray, *General of the Army*, 594.
32. Isaacson and Thomas, *The Wise Men*, 394.
33. Ibid., 395.
34. Stoler, *George C. Marshall*, 160.
35. Cray, *General of the Army*, 595-96.
36. Isaacson and Thomas, *The Wise Men*, 395.
37. Ibid.
38. Cray, *General of the Army*, 596.
39. Isaacson and Thomas, *The Wise Men*, 397.
40. Ibid., 398.
41. Pogue, *Marshall*, vol. 4, *Statesman*, 167.
42. Behrman, *Most Noble Adventure*, 15.
43. Ibid.
44. Ibid., 16.
45. Cray, *General of the Army*, 592.
46. Kennan, *George Kennan to James Byrnes*, 1.
47. Ibid., 6.
48. Ibid., 9.
49. Cray, *General of the Army*, 592.
50. McCullough, *Truman*, 489.
51. Pogue, *Marshall*, vol. 4, *Statesman*, 172.
52. Bland and Stoler, *Papers*, 65.
53. Cray, *General of the Army*, 599.
54. Behrman, *Most Noble Adventure*, 23.
55. Ibid., 21.
56. Isaacson and Thomas, *The Wise Men*, 386.
57. Behrman, *Most Noble Adventure*, 24.
58. Ibid., 25.
59. Ibid., 24.
60. Ibid., 29.
61. Ibid., 28–29.
62. Pogue, *Marshall*, vol. 4, *Statesman*, 172.
63. Ibid., 173.
64. Behrman, *Most Noble Adventure*, 34.
65. Pogue, *Marshall*, vol. 4, *Statesman*, 194.
66. Cray, *General of the Army*, 601.
67. Bland and Stoler, *Papers*, 66.
68. Cray, *General of the Army*, 603.
69. Bland and Stoler, *Papers*, 115.
70. Cray, *General of the Army*, 603.
71. Ibid., 604.
72. Pogue, *Marshall*, vol. 4, *Statesman*, 188.
73. Bland and Stoler, *Papers*, 100.
74. Pogue, *Marshall*, vol. 4, *Statesman*, 189.
75. Ibid., 190–91.
76. Cray, *General of the Army*, 605.
77. Marshall, *George C. Marshall to Kathryn Marshall*.
78. Pogue, *Marshall*, vol. 4, *Statesman*, 195–96.
79. Ibid., 196.
80. Marshall, *George C. Marshall to Kathryn Marshall*.
81. Bland and Stoler, *Papers*, 121.
82. Behrman, *Most Noble Adventure*, 60.
83. Gaddis, *George F. Kennan*, 265.
84. Ibid., 266.
85. Isaacson and Thomas, *The Wise Men*, 405.
86. Kennan, *Director of the Policy Planning Staff*, 223–30.
87. Ibid., 226.
88. Ibid., 229–30.

89. Chace, *Acheson*, 177.
90. Cray, *General of the Army*, 611.
91. Ibid.
92. Stoler, *George C. Marshall*, 163.
93. Bland and Bland, *Interviews and Reminiscences*, 558.
94. Bland and Stoler, *Papers*, 141.
95. Bland and Bland, *Interviews and Reminiscences*, 559–60.
96. Behrman, *Most Noble Adventure*, 67.
97. Pogue, *Marshall*, vol. 4, *Statesman*, 212.
98. Bland and Stoler, *Papers*, 147–49.
99. Ibid., 150.
100. Price and Foulke, "Interview IV," 3.
101. Cray, *General of the Army*, 609.
102. Vandegrift, "BBC Correspondent Leonard Miall," 4.
103. Behrman, *Most Noble Adventure*, 71.
104. Ibid., 80.
105. Ibid., 85.
106. Ibid., 93.
107. Ibid., 84.
108. Ibid., 86.
109. Cray, *General of the Army*, 615.
110. Behrman, *Most Noble Adventure*, 87.
111. Cray, *General of the Army*, 615.
112. Behrman, *Most Noble Adventure*, 90.
113. Ibid., 92.
114. Ibid., 94–95.
115. Ibid., 96.
116. Bland and Stoler, *Papers*, 175.
117. Behrman, *Most Noble Adventure*, 97.
118. Ibid.
119. Woods, *The Marshall Plan*, 16–17.
120. Behrman, *Most Noble Adventure*, 107–9.
121. Woods, *The Marshall Plan: A Fifty Year Perspective*, 17.
122. Behrman, *Most Noble Adventure*, 112.
123. Ibid., 113.

Chapter 18
1. Bland and Stoler, *Papers*, 206.
2. Ibid., 212.
3. Ibid., xxvi.
4. Woods, *The Marshall Plan*, 19.
5. Isaacson and Thomas, *The Wise Men*, 424.
6. "Seeing the Victory Through."
7. Behrman, *Most Noble Adventure*, 126.
8. Ibid., 128.
9. Bland and Stoler, *Papers*, xxvii.
10. Isaacson and Thomas, *The Wise Men*, 425.
11. Ibid., 428.
12. McCullough, *Truman*, 564.
13. Bland and Bland, *Interviews and Reminiscences*, 527.
14. Isaacson and Thomas, *The Wise Men*, 424.
15. Bland and Stoler, *Papers*, 301.
16. Ibid., 296.
17. Marshall, George C. Marshall to Mrs. Allen Brown ("Madge").
18. Bland and Stoler, *Papers*, 285.
19. Ibid., 293–94.
20. Pogue, *Marshall*, vol. 4, *Statesman*, 237.
21. Bland and Stoler, *Papers*, 310.
22. Ibid., 293–94.
23. Ibid., 326.
24. Cray, *General of the Army*, 621.
25. Behrman, *Most Noble Adventure*, 146.
26. Pogue, *Marshall*, vol. 4, *Statesman*, 244.
27. "State Secretary with Big Grin."
28. Bland and Bland, *Interviews and Reminiscences*, 557.
29. Behrman, *Most Noble Adventure*, 151.
30. Bland and Bland, *Interviews and Reminiscences*, 557.
31. Pogue, *Marshall*, vol. 4, *Statesman*, 246.
32. Bland and Bland, *Interviews and Reminiscences*, 556–57.
33. Behrman, *Most Noble Adventure*, 115.

34. Ibid., 116.
35. Ibid., 157.
36. Cray, *General of the Army*, 625–26.
37. Stoler, *George C. Marshall*, 167.
38. Cray, *General of the Army*, 626.
39. Hug, "The Marshall Plan: Investment in Peace," 10.
40. Woods, *The Marshall Plan: A Fifty Year Perspective*, 27.
41. Behrman, *Most Noble Adventure*, 179.
42. Ibid.
43. Machado, *In Search of a Usable Past*, 32.
44. Bland and Stoler, *Papers*, 436.
45. Cray, *General of the Army*, 653.
46. Ibid., 652–53.
47. Ibid.
48. Pogue, *Marshall*, vol. 4, *Statesman*, 392.
49. Bland and Stoler, *Papers*, 438.
50. Hooker, "The Diaspora," 1.
51. "Balfour Declaration," 1.
53. "British White Paper of 1939," 1–4.
54. Cray, *General of the Army*, 656.
55. McCullough, *Truman*, 597.
56. Pogue, *Marshall*, vol. 4, *Statesman*, 339.
57. "Milestones: 1945–1952, Creation of Israel, 1948," 1-2.
58. Cray, *General of the Army*, 657.
59. McCullough, *Truman*, 603.
60. Stoler, *George C. Marshall*, 172–73.
61. Cray, *General of the Army*, 657.
62. Stoler, *George C. Marshall*, 173.
63. Cray, *General of the Army*, 658.
64. Ibid.
65. Pogue, *Marshall*, vol. 4, *Statesman*, 371.
66. McCullough, *Truman*, 614.
67. Cray, *General of the Army*, 659.
68. McCullough, *Truman*, 615.
69. Ibid., 616.
70. Pogue, *Marshall*, vol. 4, *Statesman*, 371.
71. McCullough, *Truman*, 616.
72. Ibid.
73. Ibid.
74. Ibid., 617.
75. Cray, *General of the Army*, 660.
76. Ibid., 661.
77. McCullough, *Truman*, 618.
78. Ibid., 618.
79. Ibid.
80. Behrman, *Most Noble Adventure*, 202.
81. Bland and Stoler, *Papers*, 489.
82. Behrman, *Most Noble Adventure*, 202–3.
83. Ibid., 203.
84. Ibid.
85. Bland and Stoler, *Papers*, 489.
86. Ibid., 494.
87. "The Berlin Airlift."
88. Ibid., 3.
89. Cray, *General of the Army*, 663.
90. Bland and Bland, *Interviews and Reminiscences*, 561.
91. Bland and Stoler, *Papers*, 491.
92. Cray, *General of the Army*, 663.
93. Ibid.
94. Pogue, *Marshall*, vol. 4, *Statesman*, 411.
95. Ibid., 410.
96. Bland and Bland, *Interviews and Reminiscences*, 218.
97. Bland and Stoler, *Papers*, 597.
98. Marshall, George C. Marshall to Mrs. Allen T. Brown ("Madge"), October 12, 1948.
99. Ibid.
100. Marshall, Katherine T., *Gilman Country School Memorial Scholarship Presentation*, 6.
101. Bland and Stoler, *Papers*, 539.
102. Marshall, George C. Marshall to Mrs. Allen T. Brown ("Madge"), November 17, 1948.
103. Bland and Stoler, *Papers*, 629.
104. Ibid., 645.

105.   Ibid., 648.
106.   Ibid., 656.
107.   Ibid.

Chapter 19
1.   Bland and Stoler, *Papers*, 667.
2.   Ibid., 660.
3.   Ibid., 664–66.
4.   Ibid., 675.
5.   Ibid., 672.
6.   Ibid., 663.
7.   Ibid., 656.
8.   Cray, *General of the Army*, 672.
9.   Bland and Stoler, *Papers*, 673.
10.   Pogue, *Marshall*, vol. 4, *Statesman*, 415.
11.   Cray, *General of the Army*, 669.
12.   Bland and Stoler, *Papers*, 681.
13.   Ibid., 682.
14.   Ibid., 742.
15.   Ibid., 743.
16.   Ibid., 677.
17.   Ibid., 684.
18.   Ibid., 747.
19.   Pogue, *Marshall*, vol. 4, *Statesman*, 415–16.
20.   Cray, *General of the Army*, 673.
21.   Ibid.
22.   Ibid.
23.   McCullough, *Truman*, 747–49.
24.   Ibid.
25.   Ibid., 743.
26.   Cray, *General of the Army*, 674.
27.   Ibid., 668,
28.   McCullough, *Truman*, 743.
29.   Ibid., 744.
30.   Bland and Stoler, *Papers*, 634.
31.   Cray, *General of the Army*, 674.
32.   "Klaus Fuchs."33.   Chace, *Acheson*, 236.
34.   Isaacson and Thomas, *The Wise Men*, 493.
35.   Stoler, *George C. Marshall*, 179.
36.   McCullough, *Truman*, 772.
37.   Cray, *General of the Army*, 690.
38.   Stoler, *George C. Marshall*, 181.
39.   Ibid.
40.   McCullough, *Truman*, 775.
41.   Ibid., 777.
42.   Ibid., 780.
43.   Ibid., 781.
44.   Weintraub, *15 Stars*, 430.
45.   McCullough, *Truman*, 787.
46.   Ibid., 788.
47.   Ibid., 782.
48.   Cray, *General of the Army*, 683.
49.   Pogue, *Marshall*, vol. 4, *Statesman*, 421.
50.   McCullough, *Truman*, 793.
51.   Pogue, *Marshall*, vol. 4, *Statesman*, 420.
52.   McCullough, *Truman*, 794.
53.   Ibid.
54.   Pogue, *Marshall*, vol. 4, *Statesman*, 422.
55.   Cray, *General of the Army*, 684.
56.   Pogue, *Marshall*, vol. 4, *Statesman*, 424.
57.   Ibid.
58.   Stoler, *George C. Marshall*, 182.
59.   Cray, *General of the Army*, 686.
60.   Pogue, *Marshall*, vol. 4, *Statesman*, 436.
61.   Cray, *General of the Army*, 687.
62.   Pogue, *Marshall*, vol. 4, *Statesman*, 431.
63.   Cray, *General of the Army*, 688.
64.   Pogue, *Marshall*, vol. 4, *Statesman*, 433.
65.   Cray, *General of the Army*, 688.
66.   Pogue, *Marshall*, vol. 4, *Statesman*, 436.

67. Stoler, *George C. Marshall*, 183.
68. Wilson, *General Marshall Remembered*, 295.
69. Bland and Bland, *Interviews and Reminiscences*, 442.
70. Cray, *General of the Army*, 725.
71. Pogue, *Marshall*, vol. 4, *Statesman*, 436.
72. Isaacson and Thomas, *The Wise Men*, 539.
73. McCullough, *Truman*, 795.
74. Cray, *General of the Army*, 691.
75. McCullough, *Truman*, 798–99.
76. Ibid., 799.
77. Cray, *General of the Army*, 692.
78. Isaacson and Thomas, *The Wise Men*, 533.
79. Pogue, *Marshall*, vol. 4, *Statesman*, 456.
80. Cray, *General of the Army*, 693.
81. Pogue, *Marshall*, vol. 4, *Statesman*, 457.
82. Cray, *General of the Army*, 695–96.
83. McCullough, *Truman*, 800.
84. Ibid., 802.
85. Pogue, *Marshall*, vol. 4, *Statesman*, 458.
86. Weintraub, *15 Stars*, 440.
87. McCullough, *Truman*, 804.
88. Cray, *General of the Army*, 696.
89. Weintraub, *15 Stars*, 441.
90. McCullough, *Truman*, 807.
91. Pogue, *Marshall,* vol. 3, *Organizer of Victory*, 482.
92. McCullough, *Truman*, 811.
93. Isaacson and Thomas, *The Wise Men*, 535.
94. Ibid., 536.
95. Cray, *General of the Army*, 700.
96. Isaacson and Thomas, *The Wise Men*, 537.
97. Ibid., 538.
98. Weintraub, *15 Stars*, 446.
99. Weintraub, *MacArthur's War*, 225.
100. Weintraub, *15 Stars*, 446–47.
101. Isaacson and Thomas, *The Wise Men*, 541.
102. Cray, *General of the Army*, 701.
103. Weintraub, *15 Stars*, 447.
104. McCullough, *Truman*, 835.
105. Stoler, *George C. Marshall*, 185.
106. McCullough, *Truman*, 835.
107. Cray, *General of the Army*, 703.
108. Ibid.
109. McCullough, *Truman*, 836.
110. Isaacson and Thomas, *The Wise Men*, 549.
111. McCullough, *Truman*, 836.
112. Cray, *General of the Army*, 708.
113. Pogue, *Marshall*, vol. 4, *Statesman*, 480.
114. McCullough, *Truman*, 838.
115. Pogue, *Marshall*, vol. 4, *Statesman*, 481.
116. Ibid., 482.
117. Cray, *General of the Army*, 711.
118. McCullough, *Truman*, 843.
119. Ibid., 845.
120. Isaacson and Thomas, *The Wise Men*, 550.
121. Cray, *General of the Army*, 712.
122. MacArthur, "Farewell Address to Congress."
123. Ibid., 5.
124. Cray, *General of the Army*, 713–14.
125. Stoler, *George C. Marshall*, 188–89.
126. Ibid., 189.
127. Cray, *General of the Army*, 721.
128. Ibid.
129. Ibid., 723.
130. Stoler, *George C. Marshall*, 189.
131. Pogue, *Marshall*, vol. 4, *Statesman*, 488.
132. Stoler, *George C. Marshall*, 190.

Chapter 20
1. "General Marshall at Home," 8.
2. Marshall, George C. Marshall to Winston S. Churchill, July 9, 1948.

3. "General Marshall at Home," 9.
4. Heffner, Interview with Larry I. Bland and Joellen Bland.
5. Pogue, *Marshall*, vol. 4, *Statesman*, 493.
6. George C. Marshall to Mrs. Claude M. Adams.
7. *The Papers of George Catlett Marshall*, Chronology, June 7, 1952.
8. Ibid., January 30–February 1, 1952."
9. "Folks Here Attend Rites for Brown."
10. Suresnes American Cemetery and Memorial, 1.
11. Marshall, "Remarks at the Dedication of the Memorial
12. Gibbs and Duffy, *The President's Club*, 82.
13. Ibid., 83.
14. Ibid.
15. McCullough, *Truman*, 911.
16. Ibid., 912.
17. Cray, *General of the Army*, 728.
18. Pogue, *Marshall*, vol. 4, *Statesman*, 497.
19. "A Brief History of the VMI Barracks Timeline and Online Exhibits," 2.
20. Bland, *Fully the Equal of the Best,* 36.
21. Pogue, *Marshall*, vol. 4, *Statesman*, 502.
22. Ibid.
23. Ibid.
24. Ibid., 503.
25. Churchill, Winston S. Churchill to George C. Marshall, June 10, 1953.
26. Marshall, K.T., Katherine T. Marshall to Winston Churchill, June, 28, 1953.
27. Pogue, *Marshall*, vol. 4, *Statesman*, 504.
28. Marshall, George C. Marshall to Katherine T. Marshall, November 11, 1953.
29. Pogue, *Marshall*, vol. 4, *Statesman*, 505.
30. Ibid.
31. Marshall, George C. Marshall to Winston S. Churchill, November 12, 1953.
32. Marshall, George C. Marshall to Katherine T. Marshall, December 3, 1953.
33. Ibid.
34. Cray, *General of the Army*, 703.
35. Wilson, *General Marshall Remembered*, 368.
36. Cray, *General of the Army*, 731.
37. Marshall, Nobel Acceptance Speech.
38. Marshall, "Essentials to Peace."
39. Cray, *General of the Army*, 731.
40. Bland and Stoler, *Papers*, 698.
41. Marshall, George C. Marshall to Madge Pendleton, December 26, 1953.
42. Marshall, George C. Marshall to Lieutenant Colonel G. J. George, August 2, 1955.
43. Marshall, George C. Marshall to General Charles D. Herron, November 7, 1955.
44. Ibid., annotation.
45. *Papers of George Catlett Marshall*, Chronology.
46. Madigan, "A Glimpse into Marshall's Mind."
47. Pogue, *Marshall*, vol. 4, *Statesman*, 508.
48. Cray, *General of the Army*, 733.
49. Wilson, *General Marshall Remembered*, 388.
50. Ibid., 388.
51. Pogue, *Marshall*, vol. 4, *Statesman*, 512.
52. Ibid., 513.

Bibliography

"38 Excerpts from the Press Conference on D-Day, June 6, 1944." Franklin D. Roosevelt Presidential Library and Museum. http://docs.fdrlibrary.marist.edu/04DD009.html. Accessed July 2012.

"1938: 'Peace for Our Time'—Chamberlain." *On This Day*, BBC News, 2007. http://news.bbc.co.uk/onthisday/hi/dates/stories/september/30/default.stm.

Adolf Hitler Biography. *Encyclopedia of World Biography.* www.notablebiographies.com/He-Ho/Hitler-Adolf.html. Accessed December 2011.

Ambrose, Stephen E. *Citizen Soldiers: The U.S. Army from the Normandy Beaches to the Bulge to the Surrender of Germany.* New York: Touchstone, an imprint of Simon and Schuster, 1997.

"American Counter-Proposal to Japanese Plan B—November 26, 1941." *ibiblio, The Public's Library and Digital Archive.* www.ibiblio.org/hyperwar/PTO/Dip/PlanB.html.

Atkinson, Rick. *The Day of Battle.* New York: Henry Holt, 2007.

Atlantic Charter. In *Public Papers and Addresses of Franklin D. Roosevelt,* vol. 10 *(1938–1950),* ed. Samuel Rosenman, 314. New York: Random House, 1950.

Bailey, Thomas A., and David M. Kennedy. *The American Pageant: A History of the Republic.* Lexington, MA: D.C. Heath, 1979.

"Balfour Declaration." *Jewish Virtual Library.* www.jewishvirtuallibrary.org/jsource/History/balfour.html. Accessed January 4, 2014.

"Battle of Anzio." *Olive-drab.com.* http://olive-drab.com/od_history_ww2_ops_battles_1944anzio.php. Accessed October 12, 2011.

"The Battle for Brittany." *History Learning Site.* www.historylearningsite.co.uk/battle_for_brittany.htm.

"Battle of the Bulge." *Time on Target: 945th Field Artillery Battalion in World War II,* chap. 10. www.timeontarget.us/book-chapter10.html.

"Battle for Iwo Jima, 1945." *Navy Department Library.* www.history.navy.mil/library/online/battleiwojima.htm. Accessed September 2013.

"The Battle of Midway June 4–7, 1942." www.willamette.edu/~rloftus/midwaypage.html. Accessed April 2012.

"Battle of Okinawa." *GlobalSecurity.org.*www.globalsecurity.org/military/facility/okinawa-battle.htm. Accessed September 2013.

Behrman, Greg. *The Most Noble Adventure: The Marshall Plan and How America Helped Rebuild Europe*. New York: Free Press, 2007.

Bellafaire, Judith A. "The Women's Army Corps: A Commemoration of World War II Service." CMH Publication 72-15. www.history.army.mil/brochures/wac/wac.htm. Accessed March 2012.

"Benito Mussolini (1883–1945)." *BBC History,* 2011.www.bbc.co.uk/history/historic_figures/mussolini_benito.shtml.

"The Berlin Airlift." Berlin Airlift Historical Foundation. www.spiritoffreedom.org/airlift.html. Accessed January 4, 2014.

"The Berlin (Potsdam) Conference, July 17–August 2, 1945." Yale Law School, Lillian Goldman Law Library: *The Avalon Project*. http://avalon.law.yale.edu/20th_century/decade17.asp. Accessed January 4, 2014.

Berthon, Simon. *Allies at War*. New York: Carroll & Graf, 2001.

Best, Geoffrey. *Churchill: A Study in Greatness*. New York: Oxford University Press, 2003.

Bischof, Gunter, Anton Pelinka, and Dieter Stiefel, eds. *The Marshall Plan in Austria,* vol. 8, *Contemporary Austrian Studies*. New Brunswick, NJ: Transaction Publishers, 2000.

Bland, Larry I. 1990. "George C. Marshall: The Lexington Connection." In *Proceedings, Rockbridge Historical Society*, vol. 10 (1980–89). Lexington, VA, 1990.

———. *Fully the Equal of the Best: George C. Marshall and the Virginia Military Institute*. Lexington, VA: George C. Marshall Foundation, 1996.

Bland, Larry I., ed. *George C. Marshall's Mediation Mission to China: December 1945–January 1947*. Lexington, VA: George C. Marshall Foundation, 1998.

———. *The Papers of George Catlett Marshall*. 5 vols. Baltimore: Johns Hopkins University Press, 1981.

Vol. 1: *The Soldierly Spirit,* December 1880–June 1939.

Vol. 2: *We Cannot Delay,* July 1, 1939–December 6, 1941.

Vol. 3: *The Right Man for the Job,* December 7, 1941–May 31, 1943.

Vol. 4: *Aggressive and Determined Leadership,* June 1, 1943–December 31, 1944.

Vol. 5: *The Finest Soldier,* January 1, 1945–January 7, 1947.

Bland, Larry I., and Joellen K. Bland, eds. *George C. Marshall Interviews and Reminiscences for Forrest C. Pogue*. 3rd ed. Lexington, VA: George C. Marshall Foundation, 1996.

Bland, Larry I., and Mark A. Stoler, eds. *The Papers of George Catlett Marshall: The Whole World Hangs in the Balance*, vol. 6. Baltimore: Johns Hopkins University Press, 2013.

Bradley, Omar N. *A Soldier's Story*. New York: Rand McNally, 1951.

"A Brief History of the VMI Barracks Timeline and Online Exhibits."
www.vmi.edu/Content.aspx?id=18237&libID=17875, 2.

"British White Paper of 1939." Yale Law School, Lillian Goldman Law Library:
The Avalon Project. http://avalon.law.yale.edu/20th_century/brwh1939.asp.
Accessed January 4, 2014.

"Broadcast to the American People Announcing the Surrender of Germany."
Harry S. Truman Library and Museum. www.trumanlibrary.org/calendar/
viewpapers.php?pid=34. Accessed April 2013.

Brown, Allen. Allen Brown to Madge Brown, Feb. 27, 1944; March 6, 1944;
March 7, 1944. Tupper Brown Collection. George C. Marshall International
Center, on loan to George C. Marshall Research Library, Lexington, VA.

Brown, Clifton S., Jr. Clifton Brown to Katherine T. Marshall and Madge
Brown, via War Department, May 31, 1944, Tupper Brown Collection,
George C. Marshall International Center, on permanent loan to the George C.
Marshall Research Library, Lexington, VA.

Bruyns, Ruud. "The Battle for the Seaports." *MilitaryHistoryOnline.com*.
www.militaryhistoryonline.com/wwii/articles/battleforseaports.aspx.

Butow, Robert J.C. *Japan's Decision to Surrender*. Palo Alto, CA: Stanford
University Press, 1954.

Byrnes, James. "State Department Statement of U.S. Policy Toward China."
Washington, DC: Operations Division Records, Record Group 319 [U.S.
Army Staff], National Archives and Records Administration.

"The Campaign in Southern France." In *U.S. Army in World War II: European
Theater of Operations: The Supreme Command*. ibiblio, *The Public's Library
and Digital Archive*. www.ibiblio.org/hyperwar/USA/USA-E-Supreme/USA-
E-Supreme-12.html, 1.

Chace, James. *Acheson: The Secretary of State Who Created the American World*.
New York: Simon & Schuster, 1998.

Chen, C. Peter. "Invasion of Sicily and Italy's Surrender." *World War II Database*.
http://ww2db.com/battle_spec.php?battle_id=53. Accessed August 26, 2007.

———. "Philippines Campaign, Phase 2." *World War II Database*.
http://ww2db.com/battle_spec.php?battle_id=27%20WW2DB:%20
Reclaiming%20the%20Philippines. Accessed September 11, 2013.

———. "Trident Conference." *World War II Database*.
http://ww2db.com/battle_spec.php?battle_id=66. Accessed February 5, 2006.

"Churchill and the Great Republic." Library of Congress.
www.loc.gov/exhibits/churchill/wc-unity.html. Accessed 2004.

Churchill, Winston. "The End of the Beginning." The Lord Mayor's Luncheon,
Mansion House. The Churchill Society, London, 10 November 1942. www.
churchill-society-http://www.london.org.uk/EndoBegn.html.

——. *The Second World War.* New York: Houghton Mifflin, 1953.

    Vol. 3: *The Grand Alliance.* Boston: Houghton Mifflin, 1950.

    Vol. 5: *Closing the Ring.* Boston: Houghton Mifflin, 1951.

——. *Memoirs of the Second World War.* Abridgment by Denis Kelly of the six volumes of *The Second World War.* Boston: Houghton Mifflin, 1959.

——. "Their Finest Hour." *Modern History Sourcebook*, Fordham University, 1940/1998. www.fordham.edu/halsall/mod/1940churchill-finest.html.

——. Papers. *George C. Marshall to Brigadier Cornwall-Jones*, May 9, 1945. Memo. George C. Marshall Research Library, Lexington, VA.

——. Papers. *Winston Churchill to General Marshall*, May 17, 1945. Memo. George C. Marshall Research Library, Lexington, VA.

——. *Winston S. Churchill to George C. Marshall,* June 10, 1953. Letter. Churchill Archives Centre, Cambridge, England.

Correll, John T., ed. "The Decision That Launched the Enola Gay." *Air Force Magazine: Online Journal of the Air Force Association*, April, 1994. www.airforcemag.com/MagazineArchive/Pages/1994/April%201994/0494decision.aspx.

"Counting the Dead." *AtomicBombMuseum.org.* http://atomicbombmuseum.org/3_health.shtml. Accessed September 2013.

Cray, Ed. *General of the Army, George C. Marshall, Soldier and Statesman.* New York: First Cooper Square Press edition, 2000.

Current, Richard N., Harry T. Williams, Frank Freidel, and Alan Brinkley. *American History Survey*, 7th ed. New York: Alfred A. Knopf, 1987.

Daugherty, Leo J., III. "Supplying War: Interservice and Interallied Cooperation in China-Burma-India." *Joint Electronic Library,* Summer 1996. www.dtic.mil/doctrine/jel/jfq_pubs/1712.pdf.

"D-Day: Etat des Lieux." www.6juin1944.com.

Decker, Major Jeffrey W. "Logistics and Patton's Third Army Lessons for Today's Logisticians." www.airpower.au.af.mil/airchronicles/cc/decker.html.

Doubler, Michael D. "Busting the Bocage: American Combined Arms Operations in France, 6 June–31 July 1944." *Combined Arms Research Library Digital Library.* http://cgsc.cdmhost.com/cdm/ref/collection/p4013coll8/id/2707.

The Drive on Caen, Northern France, 7 June–9 July 1944. In "Second World War Commemorative Booklets." *Gov.UK.* www.gov.uk/government/uploads/system/uploads/attachment_data/file/30055/ww2_caen.pdf. Accessed December 10, 2012.

"Drive Up to the Gustav Line." In *Fifth Army at the Winter Line (November 15, 1943–January 15, 1944).* U.S. Army Center of Military History, July 20, 2001. www.history.army.mil/books/wwii/winterline/winter-drive.htm.

Eisenhower, Dwight D. "Document for June 6th: D-Day Statement to Soldiers, Sailors, and Airmen of the Allied Expeditionary Force, 6/44." National Archives and Records Administration. College Park, MD: NARA. www.archives.gov/historical-docs/todays-doc/index.html?dod-date=606.

"Emperor Hirohito, Accepting the Potsdam Declaration, 14 August 1945." Radio broadcast. *mtholyoke.edu.* www.mtholyoke.edu/acad/intrel/hirohito.htm. Accessed September 2013.

"Eyes Only." Classified Message: Eisenhower to General Marshall, April 29, 1944. George C. Marshall Research Library, Lexington, VA.

Faber, Harold. *Soldier and Statesman: George C. Marshall.* New York: Ariel Books, 1964.

"FDR's 'Day of Infamy' Speech: Crafting a Call to Arms." National Archives and Records Administration. College Park, MD: NARA, 2005. www.archives.gov/publications/prologue/2001/winter/crafting-day-of-infamy-speech.html.

"Folks Here Attend Rites for Brown at Fort Myer." *Loudoun Times Mirror.* May 14, 1952.

Ford, Ken. *Cassino 1944: Breaking the Gustav Line.* Oxford: Osprey, 2004.

Frye, William. *Marshall, Citizen Soldier.* Indianapolis and New York: Bobbs-Merrill, 1947.

Gaddis, John Lewis. *George F. Kennan: An American Life.* New York: Penguin Press, 2011.

Gawne, Jonathan. *Spearheading D-Day: American Special Units of the Normandy Invasion.* Ligugé, France: Histoire & Collections, 1998.

"General Marshall at Home." *Washington Star Pictorial Magazine,* July 30, 1950: 8.

General Marshall's Victory Report: Biennial Report of the Chief of Staff of the United States Army, 1943 to 1945, to the Secretary of War. Leesburg, VA: American Legion Post no. 34, 1945.

Gibbs, Nancy, and Michael Duffy. *The President's Club.* New York: Simon & Schuster, 2012.

Gordon, Bill. "Greater East Asia Co-Prospoerity Sphere." http://gordon.web.wesleyan.edu/papers/coprospr.htm. Accessed December 2011

Harding, Andrew S. "Two Generals Apart: Patton and Eisenhower." *Militaryhistoryonline.com.* 2004. www.Militaryhistoryonline.com/wwii/articles/twogeneral.aspx.

Heffner, William. Interview with Larry I. Bland and Joellen Bland. June 30, 1995. George C. Marshall Research Library, Lexington, VA.

Herzog, Martin. "Treat Them Nicely." *Atlantic Times* 5 (April 2005). www.atlantic-times.com/archive_detail.php?recordID=185.

Hickman, Kennedy. "World War II: Battle of Leyte Gulf." *About.com Military History.* http://militaryhistory.about.com/od/worldwari1/p/leytegulf.htm. Accessed September 2013.

———. "World War II: Battle of Okinawa." *About.com Military History.* http://militaryhistory.about.com/od/worldwarii/p/battle-of-okinawa.htm. Accessed September 2013.

Hogan, Michael J. *The Marshall Plan: America, Britain, and the Reconstruction of Western Europe, 1947–1952.* New York: Cambridge University Press, 2002.

Hooker, Richard. "The Diaspora." *Jewish Virtual Library.* www.jewishvirtuallibrary.org/jsource/History/Diaspora.html. Accessed January 4, 2014.

Hug, Kathleen E., ed. "The Marshall Plan: Investment in Peace: 50th Anniversary." Booklet, United States Information Agency, 1997.

Irving, David. *The War Between the Generals: Inside the Allied High Command.* New York: Congdon and Weed, 1981.

Isaacson, Walter, and Evan Thomas. *The Wise Men: Six Friends and the World They Made.* New York: Touchstone, an imprint of Simon and Schuster, 1986.

Isserman, Maurice. *World War II: America at War.* New York: Facts on File, 1991.

"Iwo Jima Operation, February–March 1945, Maps and Wide-Area Aerial Views of Iwo Jima." *Naval History & Heritage.* www.history.navy.mil/photos//events/wwii-pac/iwojima/iwojima.htm. Accessed September 2013.

"Japanese Peace Feelers in the Soviet Union." *NUCLEARFiles.org.* www.nuclearfiles.org/menu/library/correspondence/togo-sato/corr_togo-sato.htm. Accessed September 2013.

"Japanese Proposal (Plan B) of 20 November 1941." *ibiblio, The Public's Library and Digital Archive.* www.ibiblio.org/hyperwar/PTO/Dip/PlanB.html. Accessed January 2012.

"Japan's Surrender: Continued Pressure on Japan." *Reports of General MacArthur*, vol. 1, *The Campaigns of MacArthur in the Pacific.* U.S. Army Center of Military History. www.history.army.mil/books/wwii/MacArthur%20Reports/MacArthur%20V1/ch14.htm. Accessed September 2013.

Jones, Taylor. "General George S. Patton." *General George Patton website.* www.generalgeorgepatton.us/ww2.html.

Kennan, George F. *The Director of the Policy Planning Staff (Kennan) to the Under Secretary of State (Acheson)*, May 23, 1947. Letter. *Foreign Relations, 1947,* vol. 3. George C. Marshall Research Library, Lexington, VA.

————. *George Kennan to James Byrnes*, February 22, 1946. Telegram. Harry S. Truman Library & Museum. www.trumanlibrary.org/whistlestop/study_collections/coldwar/documents/index.php?documentdate=1946-02-22&documentid=6-6&pagenumber=1. Accessed January 4, 2014.

Kershaw, Alex. *The Bedford Boys*. Cambridge, MA: Da Capo Press, 2003.

Kiernan, Denise. *The Girls of Atomic City: The Untold Story of the Women Who Helped Win World War II*. New York: Simon & Schuster, 2013.

Kitchens, Susan. "1945: Japanese Response: Backgrounder." July 28, 2005. www.2020hindsight.org/2005/07/28/1945-japanese-response-backgrounder. Accessed September 2013.

"Klaus Fuchs (1911–1988)." atomicarchive.com. www.atomicarchive.com/Bios/Fuchs.shtml. Accessed January 14, 2014.

Laurie, Clayton D. "Anzio 1944." U.S. Army Center of Military History. www.history.army.mil/brochures/anzio/72-19.htm. Accessed January 21, 2010.

————. "Rome-Arno 1944." U.S. Army Center of Military History. www.history.army.mil/brochures/romar/72-20.html. Accessed October 3, 2003.

Leighton, Richard M. *Command Decisions: OVERLORD Versus the Mediterranean at the Cairo-Tehran Conferences*. U.S. Army Center of Military History. www.history.army.mil/books/70-7_10.htm.

"Lend Lease: Franklin Roosevelt's Press Conference, December 17, 1940." Our Documents. *FDR Library*. http://docs.fdrlibrary.marist.edu/odllpc2.html. Accessed October 2011.

"Long March." Encyclopedia Britannica. www.britannica.com/EBchecked/topic/347303/Long-March. Accessed August 2013.

"The Long March." China and East Asia Chronology. *The Web Chronology Project*. www.thenagain.info/webchron/china/LongMarch.html. Accessed August 2013.

Lord Moran (Dr. Charles McMoran Wilson). "The Struggle for Survival." In *Churchill: Taken from the Diaries of Lord Moran*. Boston: Houghton Mifflin, 1966.

Lubetkin, Wendy. *Marshall*. New York: Chelsea House, 1989.

MacArthur, General Douglas. "Farewell Address to Congress." Speech presented April 10, 1951. *American Rhetoric: Top 100 Speeches*. Accessed January 14, 2014. www.americanrhetoric.com/speeches/douglasmacarthurfarewelladdress.htm

MacEachin, Douglas J. *The Final Months of the War with Japan*. Monograph. *Central Intelligence Agency Library*. https://www.cia.gov/library/center-for-the-study-of-intelligence/csi-publications/books-and-monographs/the-final-months-of-the-war-with-japan-signals-intelligence-u-s-invasion-planning-and-the-a-bomb-decision/csi9810001.html. Accessed September 2013.

Machado, Barry. *In Search of a Usable Past: The Marshall Plan and Postwar Reconstruction Today*. Lexington, VA: The George C. Marshall Foundation, 2007.

Madigan, John. "A Glimpse into Marshall's Mind." *Chicago American*, October 29, 1959. Retirement file. George C. Marshall Research Library, Lexington, VA.

Manchester, William. *The Glory and the Dream: A Narrative History of America, 1932–1972*. New York: Bantam Books, 1990.

———. *American Caesar: Douglas MacArthur 1880–1964*. New York: A Laurel Book, an imprint of Dell Publishing, 1978.

Marshall, George C. Nobel Acceptance Speech, December 10, 1953. *nobelprize.org*. Accessed February 23, 2014. www.nobelprize.org/nobel_prizes/peace/laureates/1953/marshall-acceptance.html.

———. "Essentials to Peace." Nobel Lecture. December 11, 1953. *nobelprize.org*. www.nobelprize.org/nobel_prizes/peace/laureates/1953/marshall-lecture.html. Accessed February 23, 2014.

———. *George C. Marshall to General Charles D. Herron*, November 7, 1955. Letter. Retirement file. George C. Marshall Research Library, Lexington, VA.

———. *George C. Marshall to Katherine Marshall,* April 17, 1947. Letter. George Catlett Marshall and Katherine Tupper Marshall Collection, George C. Marshall Research Library, Lexington, VA.

———. *George C. Marshall to Katherine T. Marshall,* November 11, 1953. Letter. George Catlett Marshall and Katherine Tupper Marshall Collection. George C. Marshall Research Library, Lexington, VA.

———. *George C. Marshall to Katherine T. Marshall,* December 3, 1953. Letter. George Catlett Marshall and Katherine Tupper Marshall Collection. George C. Marshall Research Library, Lexington, VA.

———. *George C. Marshall to Lieutenant Colonel G. J. George,* August 2, 1955. Letter. Retirement file. George C. Marshall Research Library, Lexington, VA.

———. *George C. Marshall to Madge Pendleton,* December 26, 1953. Letter. Allen Tupper Brown Collection. George C. Marshall Research Library, Lexington, VA.

———. *George C. Marshall to Mrs. Claude M. Adams,* April 1, 1955. Letter. George C. Marshall Research Library, Lexington, VA.

————. *George C. Marshall to Madge Brown,* June 23, 1944.
Letter. The Tupper Brown Collection. George C. Marshall International
Center, Leesburg, VA.

————. *George C. Marshall to Mrs. Allen Brown ("Madge"),* December 12,
1947. Letter. Allen Tupper Brown Collection. George C. Marshall Research
Library, Lexington, VA.

————. *GC Marshall to Mr. Wallace,* December 31, 1944.
Letter. Henry A. Wallace file. George C. Marshall Research Library,
Lexington, VA.

————. *George C. Marshall to Winston S. Churchill,* July 9, 1948.
Letter. Churchill Archives Centre, Cambridge, England.

————. *George C. Marshall to Winston S. Churchill,* November 12, 1953.
Letter. Churchill Archives Centre, Cambridge, England.

————. *Memoirs of My Services in the World War 1917–1918.*
Boston: Houghton Mifflin, 1976.

————. *The Papers of George Catlett Marshall.* vol. 7. Draft. Chronology,
June 7, 1952. George C. Marshall Research Library, Lexington, VA.

————. "Remarks at the Dedication of the Memorial in the Suresnes Cemetery,
September 13, 1952." George C. Marshall Research Library, Lexington, VA.

Marshall, George C., et al. "To the American People." *Life.* June 4, 1945.

Marshall, Katherine T. *Gilman Country School Memorial Scholarship
Presentation.* Booklet. The George C. Marshall International Center
Collection, Leesburg, VA.

————. *Katherine T. Marshall to Sally G. Chamberlin,* April 24, 1946.
Letter. Katherine T. Marshall Correspondence, the China Letters file. George
C. Marshall Research Library, Lexington, VA.

————. *Katherine T. Marshall to Winston Churchill,* June 28, 1953.
Letter. Churchill Archives Centre, Cambridge, England.

————. *Together: Annals of an Army Wife.* New York: Tupper and Love, 1946.

Matloff, Maurice. "The ANVIL Decision: Crossroads of Strategy." In *Command
Decisions,* ed. Kent Roberts Greenfield, 384. Washington, DC: United States
Army Center of Military History, 1987

————. *Strategic Planning for Coalition Warfare 1943–1944.* Washington, DC:
U.S. Government Printing Office, 1959.
www.history.army.mil/books/wwii/sp1943-44/index.htm#Contents.

Chapter 1: "Casablanca-—Beginning of an Era: January 1943."

Chapter 7: "From Husky to Avalanche: May–mid-August 1943."

Chapter 10: "Quadrant—Shaping the Patterns: August 1943."

Chapter 13: "British-American Plans and Soviet Expectations: August-
November 1943."

Chapter 16: "Cairo–Tehran—A Goal Is Reached: November–December 1943."

Chapter 18: "Concentration for the Big Blow: January–May 1944."

Matloff, Maurice, ed. *World War II: A Concise Military History of America's All-Out, Two-Front War.* Adapted from *American Military History,* Office of the Chief of Military History, United States Army. New York: Galahad Books, 1982.

Matsuoka, Yosuke. "Address by Foreign Minister of Japan." Speech delivered at the 76th session of the Imperial Diet, Tokyo, Japan, January 21, 1941. *ibiblio, The Public's Library and Digital Archive.* www.ibiblio.org/pha/timeline/410121bwp.html. Accessed February 2012.

McCarthy, Frank. Papers. *Frank McCarthy to Brigadier Cornwall-Jones,* May 17, 1945. Memo. George C. Marshall Research Library, Lexington, VA.

McCarthy, Senator Joe. *The Story of General George C. Marshall.* Washington DC: Self-published, 1952.

McCullough, David. *Truman.* New York: Simon & Schuster, 1992.

McCullough, David G., ed. *The American Heritage Picture History of World War II.* New York: American Heritage Publishing, 1966.

McEntee, James J. "The CCC and National Defense." *American Forests.* July 1940. http://newdeal.feri.org/forests/af740.htm.

Meacham, Jon. *Franklin and Winston: An Intimate Portrait of an Epic Friendship.* New York: Random House, 2004.

Meier, David A. "Adolf Hitler's Rise to Power.*"* 2000. www2.dsu.nodak.edu/users/dmeier/Holocaust/hitler.html.

"Milestones: 1945–1952, Creation of Israel, 1948." U.S. Department of State, Office of the Historian. http://history.state.gov/milestones/1945-1952/creation-israel. Accessed January 4, 2014.

"mokusatsu, One Word, Two Lessons." Baidu. http://wenku.baidu.com/view/a4e89f6427d3240c8447ef9a.html. Accessed September 2013.

Morton, Louis. "Germany First: The Basic Concept of Allied Strategy in World War II." *Command Decisions.* www.history.army.mil/books/70-7_01.htm.

———. "The Decision to Use the Atomic Bomb." *Command Decisions.* www.history.army.mil/books/70-7_23.htm.

Mosley, Leonard. *Marshall, Hero of Our Times.* New York: Hearst Books, 1982.

———. *World War II.* Alexandria, VA: Time-Life Books, 1977.

"Munich Agreement. House of Commons, October 5, 1938." Churchill Centre and Museum at the Churchill War Rooms, London. www.winstonchurchill.org.

Mussolini, Benito. "What Is Fascism, 1932." *Modern History Sourcebook.*
Fordham University, 1932/1997. www.fordham.edu/halsall/mod/mussolini-fascism.html.

"A New Order in Asia." Torrey Pines High School Social Science Department.
http://teachers.sduhsd.k12.ca.us/tpsocialsciences/world_history/totalitarianism_ww2/asia.htm. Accessed January 2012.

"'Nuts!' Revisited." *Drop Zone Virtual Museum.*
www.thedropzone.org/europe/bulge/kinnard.html.

"The Occupation Troops." In *The U.S. Army in the Occupation of Germany: 1944–1946.* U.S. Army Center of Military History, July 20, 2001. www.history.army.mil/books/wwii/Occ-GY/ch18.htm.

"Operation Catapult." *Historynet.com.* August 31, 2006.
www.historynet.com/operation-catapult-naval-destruction-at-mers-el-kebir.htm.

Oppenheimer, J.R., et al. "Recommendations on the Immediate Use of Nuclear Weapons, June 16, 1945." Memorandum. www.atomicarchive.com/Docs/ManhattanProject/Interim.shtml. Accessed September 2013.

"Outgoing" Classified Message: General George C. Marshall to General George S. Patton, April 29, 1944. George C. Marshall Research Library, Lexington, VA.

Pakula, Hannah. *The Last Empress: Madame Chiang Kai-shek and the Birth of Modern* China. New York: Simon & Schuster, 2009.

Parrish, Thomas. *Roosevelt and Marshall: Partners in Politics and War.*
New York: William Morrow, 1989.

Patton Papers. Dwight D. Eisenhower to George C. Marshall, April 29, 1944.
Telegram. George C. Marshall Research Library, Lexington, VA.

———. Dwight D. Eisenhower to George C. Marshall, April 29, 1944.
Radio transmission. George C. Marshall Research Library, Lexington, VA.

———. George C. Marshall to Dwight D. Eisenhower, April 29, 1944.
Telegram. George C. Marshall Research Library, Lexington, VA.

"Pearl Harbor Attack." *ibiblio, The Public's Library and Digital Archive.*
www.ibiblio.org/pha/pha/invest.html.

"Pearl Harbor Attack Documents, 1941." *Modern History Sourcebook.*
Fordham University, 1932/1997. www.fordham.edu/halsall/mod/1941PEARL.html.

Perry, Mark. *Partners in Command: George Marshall and Dwight Eisenhower in War and Peace.* New York: Penguin Press, 2008.

Pogue, Forrest C. *George C. Marshall.* 4 vols.
New York: Penguin Books (1963–1991).

Vol. 1: *Education of a General, 1880–1939.*

Vol. 2: *Ordeal and Hope, 1939–1942.*

Vol. 3: *Organizer of Victory, 1943–1945.*

Vol. 4: *Statesman 1945–1959.*

———. "The Campaign in Southern France." In *U.S. Army in World War II: European Theater of Operations: The Supreme Command. ibiblio, The Public's Library and Digital Archive.* www.ibiblio.org/hyperwar/USA/USA-E-Supreme/USA-E-Supreme-12.html.

———. "SHAEF Revises Plans for the Attack." In *U.S. Army in World War II: European Theater of Operations: The Supreme Command. ibiblio, The Public's Library and Digital Archive.* www.ibiblio.org/hyperwar/USA/USA-E-Supreme/USA-E-Supreme-6.html.

"Poland in 1945." *United States Holocaust Memorial Museum: Holocaust Encyclopedia,* May 11, 2012. www.ushmm.org/wlc/en/article. php?ModuleId=10005599.

"Policies and Principles." *Time,* March 25, 1946, International section, 29.

Pollard, John. "The Many Problems and Failures of Liberal Italy." *New Perspective—For History Students* 9, no. 3 (March 2004). www.history-ontheweb.co.uk/new_pers/pdf_93_mussorise.pdf.

"The Potsdam Conference." *U.S. Department of State Office of the Historian.* http://history.state.gov/milestones/1937–1945/PotsdamConf. Accessed September 2013.

Prados, John. "Battle of Okinawa." In *The Reader's Companion to Military History*, ed. Robert Cowley and Geoffrey Parker. New York: Houghton Mifflin Harcourt, 1996. www.history.com/topics/battle-of-okinawa.

Prange, Gordon W., with Donald M. Goldstein and Katherine V. Dillon. *At Dawn We Slept: The Untold Story of Pearl Harbor.* New York: Penguin, 1981.

Price, Harry B., and Roy E. Foulke. "Interview IV." George C. Marshall Foundation. http://marshallfoundation.org/library/documents/Price_and_Foulke_1_000. pdf. Accessed January 11, 2014.

Pugsley, Christopher. "Sextant: The Watershed." In *Second World War: 60th Anniversary: The Battles for Monte Cassino Central Italy 12 January–5 June 1944.* www.mod.uk/NR/rdonlyres/BD4E5087-F367-4D5D-82A8-B8784EDFB34E/0/ww2_montecass.pdf.

Puryear, Edgar F., Jr. *American Generalship: Character Is Everything: The Art of Command.* Novato: Presidio Press, 2000.

Radzilowski, John. "Warsaw Uprising 1 Aug 1944–2 Oct 1944." *World War II Database.* http://ww2db.com/battle_spec.php?battle_id=150.

Richter, Hannes. *Images of the Marshall Plan in Europe.* Innsbruck: Studienverlag, 2009.

Roberts, Andrew. *Masters and Commanders: How Four Titans Won the War in the West, 1941–1945.* New York: Harper Collins, 2009.

Robinson, Arthur H. "The President's Globe." *Imago Mundi* 49 (1997): 143–52.
JSTOR. www.jstor.org/stable/1151340.

Romanus, Charles F., and Riley Sunderland. *U.S. Army in World War II: The China, Burma, India Theater: Stillwell's Command Problems. ibiblio, The Public's Library and Digital Archive.* www.ibiblio.org/hyperwar/USA/USA-CBI-Command/index.html. Accessed March 2012.

Rooney, Andy. "Just Like the Russians." *CBS News,* February 11, 2009.
www.cbsnews.com/8301-18561_162-527831.html. Accessed September 2013.

Roosevelt, Franklin D. "Joint Address to Congress Leading to a Declaration of War Against Japan." Speech, December 8, 1941, Washington, DC. America's Historical Documents. National Archives and Records Administration. Washington, DC: NARA. www.ourdocuments.gov/doc.php?doc=73&page=transcript.

———. "The President's D-Day Prayer." Library of Congress leaflet. Washington DC, 1945. http://memory.loc.gov/cgi-bin/query/h?ammem/rbpebib:@field%28NUMBER+@band%28rbpe+24204200%29%29.

———. "President Roosevelt to Emperor Hirohito of Japan [94], 6 December 1941." Pentagon Papers. National Archives and Records Administration. College Park, MD: NARA, 2005.
http://research.archives.gov/description/5890518.

———. "Radio Address Delivered by President Roosevelt from Washington, December 29, 1940." *FDR Library.*
www.mtholyoke.edu/acad/intrel/WorldWar2/arsenal.htm.

_____. "Statement by the President of the United States." *Truman Library.*
www.trumanlibrary.org/whistlestop/study_collections/bomb/large/documents/index.php?documentdate=1945-08-06&documentid=59&studycollectionid=abomb&pagenumber=1. Accessed September 2013.

Saunders, Alan. *George C. Marshall: A General for Peace.*
New York: Facts on File, 1996.

"Secret" letter: General Dwight D. Eisenhower to Lt. General George S. Patton, April 29, 1944. George C. Marshall Research Library, Lexington, VA.

"Seeing the Victory Through: The 50th Anniversary of the Marshall Plan." Video transcript. USAID. http://blog.usaid.gov/2010/12/seeing-the-victory-through-the-50th-anniversary-of-the-marshall-plan/. Accessed January 10, 2014.

Shephard, John E., Jr. "Warriors and Politics: The Bitter Lesson of Stilwell in China." *DTIC Online.* www.dtic.mil/dtic/tr/fulltext/u2/a517708.pdf.

Sherwood, Robert E. *Roosevelt and Hopkins: An Intimate History.*
New York: Harper & Brothers, 1948.

Sorel, Eliot, and Pier Carlo Padoan, eds. *The Marshall Plan: Lessons Learned for the 21st Century.* Lexington, VA: The George C. Marshall Foundation, 2007.

"State Secretary with Big Grin." *Atlanta Constitution*, January 23, 1948. From *The Marshall Immersion Workshop Notebook*. Leesburg, VAGeorge C. Marshall International Center, Leesburg, VA.

Stimson, Henry L. "The Decision to Use the Atomic Bomb." *Harper's Magazine*, February 1947, 1.

Stoler, Mark A. *George C. Marshall: Soldier-Statesman of the American Century*. New York: Twayne, 1989.

Sullivan, Michael Ann. "Detonation of the First Atomic Bomb at the Trinity Site, 1945." *New Mexico Office of the State Historian*. www.newmexicohistory.org/filedetails.php?fileID=452. Accessed September 2013.

Suresnes American Cemetery and Memorial. Visitors brochure. www.abmc.gov/cemeteries/cemeteries/su.php, 1.

Taaffe, Stephen R. *Marshall and His Generals: U.S. Army Commanders in World War II*. Lawrence: University Press of Kansas 2011.

"The TRIDENT Conference—New Patterns: May 1943." U.S. Army Center of Military History, 1990. www.history.army.mil/books/wwii/sp1943-44/chapter6.htm. Accessed June 2012.

Truman, Harry. "Statement by the President of the United States," *Truman Library*. www.trumanlibrary.org/whistlestop/study_collections/bomb/large/documents/index.php?documentdate=1945-08-06&documentid=59&studycollectionid=abomb&pagenumber=1. Accessed September 2013.

Tupper Brown Collection. Collection of the George C. Marshall International Center, on permanent loan to the George C. Marshall Research Library, Lexington, VA.

"United States Strategic Bombing Survey: Japan's Struggle to End the War." Truman Library. www.trumanlibrary.org/whistlestop/study_collections/bomb/large/documents/fulltext.php?fulltextid=29. Accessed September 2013.

"U.S. at War: The General." *Time* 43, no. 1(1944): 17.

Vandegrift, Barbara. "BBC Correspondent Leonard Miall and the Marshall Plan Speech: An Interview." September 19, 1977. George C. Marshall Foundation. http://marshallfoundation.org/library/oral_histories_miall_interview.html. Accessed January 10, 2014.

"Victory Celebrations." *Life*, August 27, 1945.

War Department. Classified message: Lt. General Devers to George C. Marshall, May 31, 1944. Tupper Brown Collection, George C. Marshall International Center, on loan to George C. Marshall Research Library, Lexington, VA.

Webster, Donovan. *The Burma Road*. New York: Perennial, an imprint of Harper Collins, 2004.

Wedemeyer, General Albert C. *Wedemeyer Reports!*
New York: Henry Holt & Company, 1958.

Weintraub, Stanley. *15 Stars: Eisenhower, MacArthur, Marshall: Three Generals Who Saved the American Century.* New York: Free Press, 2007.

———. "General George S. Patton and the Battle of the Bulge." Historynet.com, May 17, 2007. www.historynet.com/battle-of-the-bulge.

———. *MacArthur's War: Korea and the Undoing of the American Hero.*
New York: Simon and Schuster, 2001.

"What Was General Patton Doing on D-Day?" General George Patton Museum of Leadership, Fort Knox, Kentucky, 2012. www.generalpatton.org/D-Day/Patton_Dday.htm.

Wilson, Rose Page. *General Marshall Remembered.*
Englewood Cliffs, NJ: Prentice-Hall, 1968.

Wilson, Woodrow. "Joint Address to Congress." Speech, U.S. Congress, Washington, DC, April 2, 1917. America's Historical Documents. National Archives and Records Administration. College Park, MD: NARA, 2005. www.ourdocuments.gov/doc.php?flash=true.&doc=61.

Woods, Randall B. *The Marshall Plan: A Fifty Year Perspective.* Washington, DC: German Marshall Fund of the United States, 1987. Reprinted. Lexington, VA: George C. Marshall Foundation, 1997.

"World War II: Battle of Okinawa." *About.com Military History.*
http://militaryhistory.about.com/od/worldwarii/p/battle-of-okinawa.htm.

"World War II in Europe: The Night of the Long Knives." History Place, 1996. www.historyplace.com/worldwar2/timeline/roehm.htm.

"World War II: General George S. Patton's Race to Capture Messina." Historynet.com, June 12, 2006.www.historynet.com/?s=race+to+capture+messina.

World War II: Operation Cobra—Breakout from Normandy.
http://militaryhistory.about.com/od/worldwarii/p/World-War-Ii-Operation-Cobra-Breakout-From-Normandy.htm.

"World War II Timeline." *GuidetoRussia.com.*
www.guidetorussia.com/world-war-2.asp.

"The WW2 Letters of Private Melvin W. Johnson."
www.privateletters.net/featured_2ndArmoredFrench.html.

"The Yalta Conference, Feb. 1945." *Modern History Sourcebook.*
Fordham University, August 1997. www.fordham.edu/halsall/mod/1945YALTA.html.

Zich, Arthur, and the editors of Time-Life Books. *The Rising Sun* (World War II Series). Alexandria, VA: Time-Life Books, 1977.